Progress and Challenges of Nonfinancial Defined Contribution Pension Schemes

VOLUME 2

Progress and Challenges of Nonfinancial Defined Contribution Pension Schemes

VOLUME 2
ADDRESSING GENDER, ADMINISTRATION, AND COMMUNICATION

Robert Holzmann, Edward Palmer,
Robert Palacios, and Stefano Sacchi

WORLD BANK GROUP

Contents

Boxes

Figures

Map

Tables

Preface

For many years, Italy was not as effective as Sweden and other countries in promoting abroad its pension reforms, in particular its nonfinancial defined contribution (NDC) scheme, introduced in 1995. Therefore, it was important that—following the two early NDC conferences held in Sweden in 2003 and 2009—the third conference took place in Rome in 2017.

Italy's 1995 pension reform introducing the NDC approach followed the 1992 parametric reform, which was a turning point in Italian policies. The issue of pension reform had been extensively discussed since the late 1970s, but no major action was taken until the early 1990s when changes became extremely urgent. Italy's pension system had three main problems: high and rising expenditure, inadequate labor market incentives, and chaotic distributional effects.

Pension expenditure, which had increased from 5 percent of gross domestic product (GDP) in 1960 to about 15 percent in 1992, was expected to increase further and get close to 25 percent of GDP by 2030. The contribution rate needed to cover private sector employees' benefits was set to increase from 44 percent in 1995 to 60 percent in 2025. The pension formula, the eligibility conditions, and the indexation rules granted rates of return that were considerably higher than the rate of growth of the social security tax base.

The lack of any link between the size of the pension benefit and the age of retirement was an incentive for the earliest possible retirement. In other words, there was a high implicit tax on continuing to work. This situation contributed to the low employment rates of older men and women. In addition, the segmentation of the pension system into several separate pension schemes, each one operating with its own rules, hampered the mobility of workers both between and within the public and private sectors.

There were also equity reasons for the reforms. The rate of return on contributions was extremely uneven across different groups of workers. It was usually higher for individuals with earnings rising toward the end of their careers. Inflation affected the relative value of retirement benefits.

The 1992 reform primarily addressed the sustainability issue. It deleted overnight about a quarter of existing public pension liabilities. The retirement age for old-age benefits was raised (over a 10-year period) from 55 to 60 for women and from 60 to 65 for men in private employment. The reference period for calculating pensionable earnings was lengthened from 5 to 10 years; for younger workers it was extended to the whole working life. The minimum number of contributing years for entitlement to an old-age pension was raised from 15 to 20. The reference index for the indexation of pension benefits was changed from wages to prices. The minimum number of years of contributions required for public sector employees to be entitled to a seniority pension was gradually raised to 35, a threshold previously applied only to private sector workers. By breaking the deadlock of Italian pension policy and immediately restraining expenditure increases, the parametric reform of 1992 set the conditions for better planned and more systematic changes.

The 1995 reform focused on incentives and distribution. Its design was a big step forward in both areas. The reform determined a shift from a defined benefit to a defined contribution system in which the notional accumulated contributions on individual accounts are transformed into an annuity at retirement. Italy moved toward homogeneous retirement rules and uniform rates of return. Although expenditure forecasts and the high level of contribution rates that would be needed to finance spending pointed to the need for further expenditure restraint, this was not the primary objective of the reform.

In contrast with other countries, in Italy the introduction of an NDC system came without an extensive debate about its merits and usefulness. Relatively little preparatory work was done, no major report was released to the public, and the pension formula was not immediately published. Maybe also because of that, the reform had some weak points:

- It envisaged a long and complex transitory arrangement: only those who started working after 1995 were fully under the new regime.
- It postponed the first revision of conversion coefficients until 2005.
- It envisaged a relatively low minimum retirement age (57 years).
- Self-equilibrating mechanisms were not fully adequate.

The reform represented a major step forward, but it was also somewhat incomplete, shifting some political tensions into the future. Moreover, little effort was made to explain the new pension rules to the public. This obviously reflected the lengthy transition. It is likely that the fact that the new rules were not well communicated or well understood reduced the positive impact on labor market incentives. It is possible that notional funding was also little understood by policy makers.

Some of these problems were tackled in the following years, when several changes were introduced, mostly to modify the eligibility requirements and other aspects applying to workers not fully under the new NDC regime. In 2011 the NDC rules for benefit computation were extended pro rata to all workers, starting from 2012. The statutory pension age was raised to 66 for all workers beginning in 2012. From 2013 onward, the statutory pension age was automatically indexed to increases in life expectancy. The fast tightening of eligibility criteria for retirement in a difficult macroeconomic context created some tensions. In recent years, some measures have been taken to allow disadvantaged groups of workers to retire earlier. Furthermore, more significant measures are now under discussion.

Two corrective mechanisms (the revision of retirement age and of the coefficients converting contributions into pensions) now work in parallel to offset the impact of increasing life expectancy.

Labor market trends are in line with reforms increasing retirement age. The employment rate among people ages 50–64 increased from about 41 percent in 2004 to 59 percent in 2017, and this rate is still gradually rising.

It would have been preferable to implement from the very outset a full NDC regime for all groups of workers and cohorts, but—in the end—Italy now has a sustainable and homogeneous pension system providing appropriate economic incentives. The longer you work and pay contributions, the better your pension will be.

In many ways, the challenges facing the Italian NDC system are similar to those of other countries with NDC systems.

The first issue is flexibility. The degree of flexibility in retirement is obviously a primary issue: What is the ideal age bracket for old-age pensions? One should also consider whether there should be flexibility in contribution rates (both up and down) and in the choice of the risks covered by the NDC scheme (for example, survivors' benefits). Obviously, solutions are now constrained by the need to limit expenditure growth in the short term.

Another issue is that of equity. Life expectancy at retirement is affected by education, income, occupation, and gender. Identical transformation coefficients for everyone induces a systematic redistribution of lifetime resources among different categories. If a correlation exists between longevity and lifetime income, the poorer groups of the population subsidize the richer groups. This is not exclusive to NDC systems, but in NDC systems the issue is more transparent, other redistributive mechanisms having been removed. Group-specific transformation coefficients might be a solution, but one should be careful about introducing new forms of fragmentation into the system.

Again on the equity side, one should consider the coordination of the NDC regime with welfare schemes. One has to avoid situations in which low-income earners do not get any return on their contributions. However, NDC schemes cannot be expected to prevent poverty in old age for the entire population. In Italy the issue was addressed with two main tools: supplementing the defined benefit pensions up to the so-called minimum level, and providing welfare pensions (*pensione sociale*) to the elderly poor. Only in recent years did Italy move toward a universal welfare scheme. By providing a framework for transparent distributional policy, the NDC scheme can easily be combined with a universal welfare scheme.

Another issue that may require policy attention is that of individuals with less than full careers. Younger cohorts entering late into the regular labor market may end up with insufficient contributions and relatively poorer pensions. Although this problem applies to any form of earnings-related pension scheme, it is highly visible in NDC pension schemes.

One should also evaluate whether the pace of adjustment to demographic changes and to economic shocks is adequate. If automatic adjustments are too slow, the rules will need to be changed, which might affect the credibility of the link between contributions and benefits.

In evaluating any change of the current rules, one should keep in mind that after the many reforms introduced since 1992, a certain stability in legislation may be necessary. People should perceive that the returns on their contributions are predictable and certain.

Finally, communication to the public is still an open issue. In recent years the efforts to inform the public have increased significantly, but further progress is warranted.

It has been heartening to see that the 2017 conference and the ensuing anthology address many of these issues at the conceptual, empirical, and policy level, thus offering food for thought for Italy and other countries.

Daniele Franco
State Accountant General, Ministry of the Economy, Italy

In June 1994, the Swedish government presented a bill to Parliament—prepared by the Working Group on Pensions—proposing a public nonfinancial defined contribution (NDC) pension scheme. This was to be accompanied by a public financial defined contribution (FDC) scheme and a minimum guarantee benefit at retirement. Both the NDC and FDC schemes are personal saving schemes in the sense that individuals forgo current personal consumption through their payment of contributions noted on personal accounts. And in both, the benefit received is based on the individual's account balance and life expectancy at the time of retirement. The 1994 reform provided universal longevity insurance to the whole of the Swedish population, placing the individual's role in saving for future retirement in the forefront.

The "simple" idea of an NDC scheme—although novel at the time—has numerous positive features. If carefully designed and introduced, it is a public pension scheme that delivers affordability and long-term financial sustainability that through its design manages the economic and demographic risks confronting all public pension schemes. The indexation (rate of return) of accounts and of pension benefits steers the scheme in the direction of economic balance and results in the sharing of ups and downs in economic growth between workers and pensioners. And the interaction of the benefit calculation with life expectancy constitutes a vital adjustment mechanism in addressing the financial pressures of a constantly aging population.

Sweden is still unique in going "all the way" in its NDC scheme design through two additional mechanisms. One is the maintenance of a reserve fund, within the pay-as-you-go-based NDC scheme, that distributes funded contributions over time between larger and smaller ("cyclical") generations, for example, those associated with baby boom or migration cycles. The second is the use of the solvency ratio, with a "balancing index" that adjusts liabilities to assets when the solvency ratio falls below unity. This is based on the sum of the explicit accounts of workers and the implicit accounts of pensioners, which are the liabilities of the provider—in the NDC case, the Swedish Pensions Agency—to participants. The assets in the context of the solvency ratio are the estimated value of future contributions and the market value of the reserve fund. From a macroeconomic standpoint, the Swedish NDC design strives to create autonomy from the state budget for the country's publicly provided universal longevity insurance scheme.

Sweden's NDC scheme is supported by a broad span of the political spectrum. When the original legislation was passed in 1994, it was supported by more than three-quarters of the members of Parliament. The NDC scheme today still has the active support of three-quarters of Parliament members, as represented by a contemporary cross-party working group on pensions that meets regularly to discuss Sweden's pension system. Of course, some fine-tuning has occurred, not the least in the technical application of the income index and balancing mechanism following the global recession of 2008–09.

Sweden sponsored the first conference on NDCs, which resulted in 2006 in the first of what has become a series of NDC anthologies published by the World Bank. The overriding aim of that first conference was to gather international experts to discuss the conceptual strength of the new NDC paradigm. The second two-volume NDC anthology (published in 2012–13) had a strong focus on maintaining financial stability and sustainability, including the Swedish accounting structure that underlies the calculation of the solvency (balance) ratio and the triggering of the balancing mechanism. It also added a focus on gender-specific issues.

This third anthology arose out of an October 2017 conference held in Rome in a joint effort with Italy. It moves the perspective toward a host of issues at the forefront of the current discussion in Sweden and, I believe, in many other countries. What are these issues, then? They include the importance of labor market policy that accommodates the dynamics of the labor market accompanying increasing globalization; the possible roles for pension policy in preempting and bridging the gender pension gap; the technical challenges of creating fair and sustainable annuities and how to deal with issues arising from socioeconomic differences in life expectancy; communication with participants; and much more.

Today's issues for countries' pension systems are a reflection of the larger dynamics of the socioeconomic foundations of modern societies and economies—education and skills attainment, spouses' time sharing, and formal labor market participation. They also give rise to consideration of strategies at the individual and societal level for recognizing and addressing changing technologies in all segments of the labor market. The challenges have always been great and will continue to be so. The current issues reflect an ongoing evolution. Hence, to do what we do within the area of pensions best, we need to bring together the worlds of policy and academia and to familiarize ourselves with, understand, and weigh how new knowledge gained from the experience of others and developments in research can help move our own and other countries forward. This was the overriding theme of the Rome conference and is the overriding theme of this third NDC anthology. We are pleased to have had the opportunity to share the responsibility for this undertaking with our Italian cosponsor and are grateful for the buy-in of the World Bank in this project.

In closing, I wish to thank the many academic scholars and experts from international organizations from around the world who participated in the creation of this publication. It is my belief that efforts of this nature are important for spreading knowledge and learning from the experience of others. This particular effort is an important contribution for countries that share the goal of providing affordable, financially sustainable, and adequate national pension schemes that cover the entire population.

Daniel Barr
Director General, Swedish Pensions Agency

Over the past decades, nonfinancial defined contributions (NDCs) emerged as a key tenet in global thinking about pensions. The inspiring and diverse perspectives of many thinkers have contributed enormously in enriching and advancing NDC policy and research.

This new anthology, alongside two preceding anthologies edited by Robert Holzmann and Edward Palmer, represents the most important intellectual effort for bringing together evidence on NDCs and pension reforms more broadly. Whereas previous anthologies were mostly concerned with the design and sustainability of NDC schemes, this new endeavor provides a stronger focus on the sufficiency of pensions under NDCs. Importantly, it also offers precious insights into the political economy of successful and failed NDC reforms. The richness of experiences presented in the ensuing pages will benefit both policy makers and the international agencies supporting them, including the World Bank and other actors.

The contributions enshrined in this anthology cover a wide and comprehensive array of topics from a theoretical, practical, and policy perspective. The studies' authors are well-known academics, policy makers, and practitioners, often combining more than one role at different times of their careers. Interestingly, the studies provide a variety of approaches to pension design and implementation that will be valuable for analysts and decision makers.

The completion of this comprehensive study on NDC pension schemes could not be more timely: the nature of work is changing and labor markets are evolving, leading to a profound rethinking of traditional Bismarckian social insurance arrangements.

Defined contribution systems (both financial and nonfinancial) have challenged the conventional wisdom on pension system design. Yet they have predominantly been perceived as alternatives to contributory pension schemes for wage employment. The challenge today is to develop more suitable systems to respond to the needs of workers in the new digital and gig economy, with labor markets increasingly expanding toward different forms of self-employment and more flexible jobs.

The pension systems of future generations will undoubtedly look different from those of the past. It is still a matter of debate whether this will expand or narrow the space for defined contribution schemes. The World Bank's vision and my own is one in which social insurance is extended to all workers independently of how they engage in the labor market. From this standpoint, governments have a key role to play in providing a basic level of pension to prevent large groups of the population from falling into poverty in old age. This, in turn, will leave a broad second level to individually financed social insurance covering primarily middle- and higher-income earners. Although this does not imply any preference for a specific financing model, the best fit will be the one that most closely links contributions with benefits. NDCs are potentially the best solution, as this anthology correctly argues, although not the only possible solution. In the years to come, we will probably witness a revival of the discussion about the comparative strengths of each approach to providing the best combination of low risk and high income replacement in old age.

Now more than ever we need the best available evidence to manage complex, diverse, and diversifying labor markets. This anthology not only lives up to such challenges but will provide a linchpin for a renewed debate on alternative approaches to pension policy making.

Michal Rutkowski
Senior Director, Social Protection and Jobs Global Practice, World Bank

Acknowledgments

This is the third anthology devoted to issues and challenges for universal public nonfinancial defined contribution (NDC) pension schemes. The anthology exists because of the contributions and incredible dedication of more than 70 academic scholars and institutional experts from all corners of the globe in seeing the project through to the end. Their generously provided time made this publication possible.

The project could have never been undertaken without the two key financial sponsors of the enterprise.

The first was the Italian sponsor of the conference in Rome in October 2017, the Istituto Nazionale per l'Analisi delle Politiche Pubbliche (INAPP), led by coeditor and colleague Stefano Sacchi, where the authors of the first drafts were gathered to present and receive feedback on papers—and interacted over the course of two days. INAPP's Massimiliano Deidda organized the event perfectly.

The second was the Swedish financial sponsor of the publication (that is, language and copy editing, layout, and typesetting and printing)—the Swedish Pensions Agency. To this end, we are especially grateful for the support of the agency's chief economist, Ole Settergren, also a third-time contributor.

In addition, we are grateful to the World Bank and its formal publishing program for enabling the publication of this NDC anthology. Its support provides an important gateway, enabling the two-volume work to reach scholars, institutional pension experts, and policy makers in both developed and emerging market economies. Robert Palacios, an experienced pension economist with a long legacy of work in emerging market economies and also a coauthor and coeditor, took the lead for the World Bank.

The quality of the project was enhanced by the generous efforts of 21 external international reviewers, and we are thankful to Tabea Bucher-Koenen, Elisa Chuliá, Erland Ekheden, Csaba Feher, Georg Fischer, Steven Haberman, Krzysztof Hagemejer, Alain Jousten, Jukka Lassila, Annamaria Lusardi, Andrew Mason, Alicia H. Munnell, Heikki Oksanen, Mike Orszag, Carmen Pagés, Joakim Palme, Eduard Ponds, Mauricio Soto, Viktor Steiner, Olle Sundberg, and Xinmei Wang. These external reviewers, together with the internal reviewers (that is, other authors) and the editors, were a critical part of the enterprise. The review process generated comments and suggestions for revision that substantially improved the quality of all chapters of the anthology.

Finally, we want to thank Amy Gautam for her skillful copy editing of the draft chapters and her experienced and superb management in putting the volumes together; Roberta Gatti, who reviewed the outcome of the project and gave the sign-off as Chief Economist for the Human Development Practice Group at the World Bank; and colleagues in the World Bank's publishing program—Jewel McFadden, Susan Mandel, and Yaneisy Martinez—for all their work and support in the many and very important steps of the final production of this publication.

About the Authors

Susanne Alm is an Associate Professor of Sociology at the Swedish Institute for Social Research (SOFI), Stockholm University. Her main research concerns the relationship between childhood living conditions and different aspects of social problems and social exclusion in adulthood, predominantly criminal offending, drug abuse, and housing eviction, but also poverty and long-term unemployment.

Jennifer Alonso-García has been an Assistant Professor at the University of Groningen in the Netherlands since July 2018. Previously she worked at CEPAR; University of New South Wales, Sydney; and Université Catholique de Louvain. Her research combines the areas of actuarial science and household, pension, and quantitative finance to study the design, risk sharing, and financing of funded and pay-as-you-go retirement income schemes. She is an expert on the fiscal sustainability and adequacy of nonfinancial defined contribution public pension schemes.

Nicholas Barr is a Professor of Public Economics at the London School of Economics and the author of numerous books and articles, including *The Economics of the Welfare State* (Oxford University Press, 5th edition, 2012), *Financing Higher Education: Answers from the UK* (with Iain Crawford; Routledge, 2005), and *Reforming Pensions: Principles and Policy Choices* (with Peter Diamond; Oxford University Press, 2008).

Mirko Bevilacqua is a researcher at Inarcassa (Pension Scheme of the Liberal Professions for Italian Engineers and Architects) and an Adjunct Professor of Economics and Statistics at University of Cassino and Southern Lazio, where he earned a PhD in economics in 2009. He formerly worked in the Research Department of the Swedish Social Insurance Agency.

María del Carmen Boado-Penas is a Senior Lecturer in Actuarial Mathematics at the University of Liverpool, U.K. She holds a PhD in actuarial science (Doctor Europeus) from the University of Valencia, Spain, and an MSc in quantitative finance. She has cooperated on pension projects at the Swedish Social Insurance Agency and at the Spanish Ministry of Labour and Immigration.

Tito Boeri is a Professor at Bocconi University. From March 2015 to February 2019 he was President of the Italian social security administration (INPS). He has been Scientific Director of the Fondazione Rodolfo Debenedetti since its inception and is Centennial Professor at the London School of Economics. He is the founder of the economic policy watchdog website, lavoce.info; on the editorial board of VOX Europe; and the Scientific Director of the Festival of Economics in Trento.

Boele Bonthuis has been an Economist at the Directorate for Employment, Labour and Social Affairs of the Organisation for Economic Co-operation and Development (OECD) since December 2016. Previously he worked at the Research Centre of the Deutsche Bundesbank (2013–16) and the Economics Directorate of the European Central Bank (2011–13). He holds a PhD in economics from the University of Amsterdam (2016) in the area of labor markets and pensions.

Sonia Buchholtz is an assistant in the Economics Department 1, Warsaw School of Economics, and a member of the Polish Pension Group. Her research interests include the economic and social activity of aging populations, pension economics, and economic policy.

Marcelo Abi-Ramia Caetano has a PhD in economics from Universidade Castelo Branco and a bachelor's degree in economics from Federal University of Rio de Janeiro. He was an IPEA Planning and Research Technician and Secretary for Social Security at the Ministry of Finance in Brazil. In 2019, he became General Secretary of the International Social Security Association in Geneva.

Agnieszka Chłoń-Domińczak is a Professor at the Warsaw School of Economics and Director of the Institute of Statistics and Demography. Her main research interests are generational economics and consequences of population aging, pension systems, labor markets, and life-course developments.

Rogério Nagamine Costanzi has a master's degree in economics from Universidad de São Paulo. He is a specialist in public policies and government management for the Brazilian government. He was Special Adviser to the Minister of Pension and Director of the Department of General Pension Regime.

Maria Cozzolino has been the Head of the Social Security Analysis Office in the INPS Research Department since 2015. Previously she was a Senior Economist at the Italian Ministry of Treasury (2013–15) and at several public Italian research institutes (ISAE and Istat from 1998 to 2012). Her research interests and main publications focus on welfare economics, pension systems, public finance, and microsimulation models.

Gustavo Demarco is the Pensions Global Lead at the World Bank. As a Lead Economist, he has led the World Bank's operations and policy dialogue on Pensions, Social Protection, and Labor across the Middle East and North Africa region for more than 10 years. He was a Program Leader for Human Development for the Arab Republic of Egypt, the Republic of Yemen, and Djibouti. He also led the pension capacity-building program at the World Bank Institute, including four editions of the World Bank's Pension Core Course and several regional events. Before joining the World Bank, he served at the Pension Supervision Authority of Argentina as Director of Operations and Planning. He was a core member of the Argentine pension reform team in the 1990s. Earlier in his career, he was Professor of Economics at the Universities of Córdoba, La Rioja, and Buenos Aires. He is the main author of or a contributor to seven books on economics and pensions. He has published several articles in specialized journals and contributed to World Bank publications on pensions, social safety nets, and social protection systems. He earned an economics degree from the University of Córdoba in Argentina. He did his doctoral studies at the same university and his postgraduate studies on development economics and planning at ECLAC (Economic Commission for Latin America and the Caribbean) in Chile.

Edoardo Di Porto is an Associate Professor at University of Naples Federico II. Currently on leave, he is working as a public manager at INPS–Direzione Centrale Studi e Ricerche. He is a CSEF Fellow (University of Naples Federico II) and an affiliated researcher at Uppsala University. His research focuses on public economics, urban economics, and applied econometrics.

Mark Dorfman is a Senior Economist with the Pensions and Social Insurance Global Solutions Group in the Social Protection and Jobs Global Practice of the World Bank. During his more than 30 years with the World Bank, he has worked on different areas of pensions, social security, aging, and financial markets in the South Asia, East Asia and Pacific, Sub-Saharan Africa, and Latin America and the Caribbean regions, respectively. He has directed the World Bank's Pensions Core Course since 2008.

Per Eckefeldt is currently Head of Sector in the Sustainability of Public Finances Unit in the Fiscal Policy and Policy Mix Directorate of the Directorate-General for Economic and Financial Affairs (DG ECFIN) at the European Commission in Brussels. Recent work includes carrying out long-term economic and budgetary projections for the European Union member states (*Ageing Report* and *Fiscal Sustainability Report*).

Erland Ekheden holds a PhD in insurance mathematics from Stockholm University. Since 2017 he has been the Chief Actuary at Pensionsmyndigheten (the Swedish Pensions Agency). He also worked as an actuarial consultant in life and pension from 2014 to 2017.

Eduardo Fajnzylber is a Professor of Economics and Public Policy at the School of Government of the Adolfo Ibáñez University in Chile. Until February 2009, he headed the Research Department at the Chilean Pension Fund and Unemployment Insurance Supervisory Agency, in charge of conducting theoretical and applied studies relating to the Chilean pension system and the individual accounts unemployment insurance program. His current research involves applications of econometric techniques to evaluate the impact of interventions on social security programs.

Elsa Fornero held the chair of Economics at the University of Turin, Italy (retired since November 2018). She served as Minister of Labor, Social Policies and Equal Opportunities in Italy's "technocratic" government (November 2011 to April 2013), and in this capacity conceived of and drafted the pension and labor market reforms. She is Scientific Coordinator of the Center for Research on Pensions and Welfare Policies (CeRP) and vice president of SHARE-ERIC (Survey of Health, Ageing and Retirement in Europe–European Research Infrastructure Consortium). Her research focuses on public and private pension systems and reforms, labor markets, population aging, household saving, retirement choices, life insurance, and economic-financial education.

Dennis Fredriksen earned a master's degree in national economics in 1988 and has been employed at the Research Department of Statistics Norway ever since. He has played a key role in the development, maintenance, and application of the dynamic microsimulation model MOSART.

Róbert Ivan Gál is a Senior Researcher at the Hungarian Demographic Research Institute, a Senior Extern at TARKI Social Research Centre, a Senior Fellow at the Social Futuring Centre, and an Affiliated Professor at Corvinus University, all in Budapest.

Bernd Genser was a Professor of Economics at the University of Konstanz in Germany, from which he retired in 2013. He holds an honorary doctorate from the University of Freiburg, Germany. From 2001 to 2005 he was Chairman of the Public Economics Committee of the German Economic Association and from 2002 to 2010 editor of FinanzArchiv/Public Finance Analysis. His main fields of research are theory of taxation, income and business taxation, international taxation, and tax harmonization.

Marek Góra is a Professor at the Warsaw School of Economics and Chair of Economics Department 1; a visiting Professor at the College of Europe; an IZA Research Fellow; the codesigner of the current Polish pension system; and the founder of the Polish Pension Group. He has publications in labor economics, pension economics, and social policy.

Sandro Gronchi is a Professor of Economics at Sapienza University of Rome, where he also taught Economics of Social Security for the master's program in Public Economics. In 2002, at the request of the Italian Ministry of Economy and Finance, he was appointed Temporary Lecturer at the ministry's newly founded School of Economics and Finance, and then consultant on social security issues to the President of the National Council for Economics and Labour. In the early 1990s he proposed an NDC reform program for the Italian pension system, and in 1995, he was appointed consultant to the government with the task of developing a bill for such a reform.

Igor Guardiancich is a Researcher in the Institute of Law, Politics and Development (DIRPOLIS) of the Sant'Anna School of Advanced Studies in Pisa and recently worked as a Senior Technical Officer on Social Dialogue in the Governance and Tripartism Department at the International Labour Organization. His main research interests are European social policy, welfare states in Central and Eastern Europe, and the political economy of transition and integration.

Erik Hernæs earned a master's degree in economics (Candidatus Oeconomices) in 1972. He was employed in the Research Department of Statistics Norway from 1972 until 1988 and has been employed at the Frisch Centre and its predecessors since. Since 2005 he has been project manager for analyzing the labor market effects of the Norwegian pension reform, mainly by econometric research based on administrative register data.

Erling Holmøy has an MSc in economics. He has worked in the Research Department of Statistics Norway since 1984, mainly with model-based analyses of supply-side policies, such as taxation and industry policy, and economic growth, including fiscal effects of population aging and migration.

Robert Holzmann is Governor of the Austrian National Bank and Member of the Governing Council of the European Central Bank (since September 2019) and Full Member of the Austrian Academy of Sciences (since 2016). He has held academic positions in Austria, Australia, Germany, and Malaysia; senior economist positions at the Organisation for Economic Co-operation and Development and the International Monetary Fund; and senior management positions at the World Bank, where he led the worldwide pension work. He has published 39 books and more than 200 articles on financial, fiscal, and social policy issues.

Anna Klerby is a PhD student at Örebro University and Dalarna University, Sweden. Her PhD work focuses on understanding gender inequality in terms of market failure in the context of cultural norms and values and identifying structural policy measures aimed at addressing these failures. For several years Anna has been consulting with local and regional governments in Sweden on how to perform gender analyses of their resource allocation, based on the gender budgeting method.

Bo Könberg was Swedish Minister of Social Insurance and Health from 1991 to 1994 and Chairman of the Swedish Working Group on Pensions, responsible for the Swedish 1994 pension reform. He was the Principal Investigator for the establishment of the Swedish Pensions Agency in 2010 and Chairman of the Board of the Pensions Agency from 2010 to 2015.

Irena E. Kotowska is a Professor of Demography, Warsaw School of Economics; Chair of the Committee on Demographic Studies and member of the Committee on Labour and Social Policy, both at the Polish Academy of Sciences; and a member of the Scientific Council on Statistics of the Central Statistical Office. Her main fields of research are population and economy; fertility, family, gender, and labor markets; population aging; demographic projections; population-related policy; and social policy.

Héloïse Labit-Hardy commenced work as a Senior Research Associate in the ARC Centre of Excellence in Population Ageing Research at University of New South Wales in September 2016. She completed her PhD at the University of Lausanne in the Department of Actuarial Science and graduated from the French Institut de Science Financière et d'Assurances. She works on mortality modeling, more specifically on longevity risk management, heterogeneity in mortality, cause-of-death mortality modeling, and morbidity.

Bo Larsson is a Swedish economist with expertise in public finance and financial economics.

Ronald Lee has an MA in demography from the University of California, Berkeley, and a PhD in economics from Harvard University. He has worked at Berkeley in demography and economics since 1979, after working eight years at the University of Michigan.

He works on macroeconomic consequences of population aging, intergenerational transfers, demographic forecasting, and evolutionary biodemography.

Vincent Leyaro is currently a Senior Lecturer in the Department of Economics of the University of Dar es Salaam in Tanzania. He was previously an Associate Economics Affairs Officer at the United Nations Economic Commission for Africa in Addis Ababa. He is also an External Research Fellow at the Centre for Research in Economic Development and International Trade at the University of Nottingham, U.K. He completed a PhD in economics at the University of Nottingham in 2010.

Maciej Lis is an Economist on the Ageing and Pensions Team in the Directorate for Employment, Labour and Social Affairs at the OECD. His work is focused on the cross-country comparison of pension systems using microsimulation tools. He contributed to the OECD's *Pensions at a Glance* and *Pensions Outlook* publications as well as to country-specific reviews of pensions. Before joining the OECD, he published papers on labor and health economics. He holds a PhD from the Warsaw School of Economics.

Bei Lu is a CEPAR Research Fellow located at the University of New South Wales Business School and a Research Fellow with Tsinghua University and Zhejiang University, China. Her research focuses on demographics, health, pensions, and population aging–related social welfare and economic issues. She has published in various journals.

Iga Magda is an Assistant Professor at the Warsaw School of Economics and Vice President of the Institute for Structural Research in Warsaw. Her work is centered on labor economics, in particular gender gaps, collective bargaining, wage and income inequalities, and family policies.

Poontavika Naka is a Lecturer in the Department of Statistics, Chulalongkorn Business School in Thailand. She holds a PhD in mathematical sciences, with a concentration in actuarial mathematics, from the University of Liverpool. Her research interests are focused on nonfinancial defined contribution pension schemes, health care financing, and mortality modeling.

Milton Nektarios is a Professor at the University of Piraeus, Greece, and former Governor of the Social Insurance Organization (1999–2004).

Kenneth Nelson is a Professor of Sociology at the Swedish Institute for Social Research (SOFI), Stockholm University. His specialty is research on the causes and consequences of welfare states and social policy. His most recent book is on generational welfare contracts, published by Edward Elgar.

Rense Nieuwenhuis is an Associate Professor of Sociology at the Swedish Institute for Social Research (SOFI), Stockholm University. He examines how family diversity and social policy affect poverty and economic inequality. His recent focus is on single-parent families, how women's earnings affect inequality between households, and family policy outcomes.

Sergio Nisticò is a Professor of Economics at the University of Cassino in Italy, where he is also Scientific Director of the Economic Research Center on Creativity and Motivations. He is the author of numerous publications.

Noemi Oggero is a PhD student at the University of Turin in Italy. She collaborates with the Center for Research on Pensions and Welfare Policies at the Collegio Carlo Alberto and has been a research associate at the Global Financial Literacy Excellence Center at George Washington University.

Robert Palacios is Global Lead for the Pensions and Social Insurance Group in the Social Protection and Labor Practice of the World Bank. From 1992 to 1994 he was a member of the research department team that produced the World Bank's influential volume on international pension systems, *Averting the Old Age Crisis*. He has worked in more than 30 countries across the world and has published on old-age poverty, health insurance, and a wide range of pension policy issues.

Edward Palmer is Senior Fellow at the University of Uppsala Center for Labor Studies in Sweden. He held professorships, first at Gothenburg University and then Uppsala University, while serving as Head of Research and Evaluation at the Swedish Social Insurance Agency, and in later years as Senior Advisor. He has worked extensively with governments of numerous countries as a consultant on pension reform.

John Piggott is Director of CEPAR, a major research center focused on population aging based at University of New South Wales, Australia, where he is Scientia Professor of Economics. He has published widely in the areas of pensions, retirement, and aging. He has worked extensively on the pension system in China and a range of other nations in the Asian region and has undertaken contract work for a range of international organizations, including the Organisation for Economic Co-operation and Development, the Asia-Pacific Economic Cooperation, the World Bank, the Asian Development Bank, and UNESCAP.

William Price is CEO of D3P Global Pension Consulting, a Program Leader and Advisory Board member of the Insurance and Pensions Program of the Toronto Centre for Global Leadership in Financial Supervision, and an Ambassador for the Transparency Taskforce. He has worked for the World Bank, U.K. Treasury, and U.K. Pensions Regulator and in collaboration with the Organisation for Economic Co-operation and Development and International Organization of Pension Supervisors. He has a master's degree in economics from University College London.

Riccardo Puglisi is an Associate Professor of Economics at the University of Pavia in Italy. His research interests are mainly in the fields of political economy and public economics, with a specific focus on the political and economic role of mass media.

Monika Queisser is Head of Social Policy at the Organisation for Economic Co-operation and Development in Paris.

Márta Radó is a Junior Researcher at the Hungarian Academy of Sciences CSS RECENS, a Junior Fellow at the Social Futuring Centre, and a doctoral candidate at Corvinus University of Budapest.

Ranila Ravi-Burslem leads customer strategy and proposition development for the small and medium enterprise (SME) market as Director of SME Solutions for Aviva in the United Kingdom. Previously she was Director of Marketing for the National Employment Savings Trust (NEST), where she was responsible for customer propositions and digital and customer insight.

David Robalino is a Senior Advisor for McKinsey and Professor of Public Finance at the American University of Beirut. He was the Manager and Lead Economist of the Jobs Group at the World Bank and Co-Director of the Labor and Development Program at IZA. His policy work and research focus on issues related to jobs, social insurance, and fiscal policies. He has worked in more than 60 countries around the world, providing advice to governments and international organizations.

Michal Rutkowski is a Senior Director for the Social Protection and Jobs Global Practice in the World Bank. In his World Bank career he has worked on issues of pensions, labor markets, social security, and social assistance. In the late 1990s he was Director of the Office of the Government Plenipotentiary for Pension Reform in Poland and coauthor of the pension reform package that shifted the system to defined contribution principles.

Anna Ruzik-Sierdzińska, PhD, is an Assistant Professor at the Warsaw School of Economics. Her areas of expertise include labor markets, pension systems, health economics, and social policy.

Stefano Sacchi is an Associate Professor of Political Science at LUISS University in Rome (on leave from the University of Milan). He is also President of the Italian National Institute for Public Policy Analysis in Rome.

Miguel Sánchez-Romero obtained his PhD in economics from Universidad Autónoma de Madrid. He was a Fulbright postdoctoral researcher under the supervision of Professor Ronald Lee at the Center on Economics and Demography of Ageing at the University of California, Berkeley (2008–10). He has worked as a researcher at the Max Planck Institute for Demographic Research in Rostock, Germany (2010–14). Since 2014 he has been a Senior Research Scientist for the Wittgenstein Centre for Demography and Global Human Capital; in 2018 he joined the Vienna University of Technology. He works on labor and demographic economics, intergenerational transfers, and computable general equilibrium models.

Will Sandbrook is Executive Director of NEST Insight, the in-house think tank of the National Employment Savings Trust (NEST) pension scheme. He has worked within the United Kingdom's pension reform agenda since 2004, including in policy and marketing roles within the U.K. government and, beginning in 2008, as Strategy Director of NEST Insight at NEST and now as Executive Director.

Ole Settergren is Director of the Research Department at the Swedish Pensions Agency. As an insurance expert at the Ministry of Health and Social Affairs (1995–2000), he proposed the automatic balance method of securing the financial stability of the new Swedish pension system. He also developed the accounting principles that have been used since 2001 in the *Annual Report of the Swedish Pension System* and was its editor from 2001 to 2007.

Otávio José Guerci Sidone has a master's degree in economics from University of São Paulo. He is a Federal Auditor of Finance and Control of Brazil's Ministry of Finance and General Coordinator of Technical Studies and Conjunctural Analysis of the Secretariat of Social Security in the Ministry of Finance.

Sandra Stabina has been the Director of the Social Insurance Department of Latvia's Ministry of Welfare since 2016. In 1996 she started work on the Latvian pension system and was part of the modeling team for long-term projections. She is a member of the European Union (EU) Economic Policy Committee Working Group on Ageing Populations and Sustainability, was involved in an EU-financed twinning project in Azerbaijan, and took part in the European Commission–organized technical mission in Tajikistan.

Nils Martin Stølen earned a PhD in national economics in 1993 and has been employed in the Research Department of Statistics Norway since 1982. Since 2005 he has been project manager for analyzing the effects of the Norwegian pension reform, mainly by using the dynamic microsimulation model MOSART.

Paweł Strzelecki, PhD, is an Assistant Professor at the Warsaw School of Economics and an economic expert at the National Bank of Poland. He is also a national expert in the Working Group on Ageing (European Commission). His work focuses on the demographic dimension of labor economics and on population projections.

Platon Tinios is an Assistant Professor at the University of Piraeus, Greece.

Andrés Villegas is a Lecturer at the School of Risk and Actuarial Studies and an Associate Investigator at the Centre of Excellence in Population Ageing Research, where he was previously a Research Fellow. He completed his doctoral studies at Cass Business School in London, focusing on the modeling and projection of mortality. His research interests include mortality modeling, longevity risk management, and the design of retirement income products.

Kent Weaver is a Professor of Public Policy and Government at Georgetown University and a Senior Fellow in the Governance Studies Program at the Brookings Institution. He has written extensively on both the politics of pension reform and the impact of pension system design features such as automatic balancing mechanisms, centrally administered defined contribution systems, and collective investment funds. He received his MA and PhD in political science from Harvard University.

Hernan Winkler is a Senior Economist in the Jobs Group at the World Bank. He is a labor economist, with a focus on technological change and the sources and consequences of poverty and inequality. His research has been published in peer-reviewed economics journals, including the *Review of Economics and Statistics* and the *Journal of Development Economics*. He holds a PhD in economics from the University of California at Los Angeles.

Yuwei Zhao de Gosson de Varennes is currently an Economist in the Analysis Division of the Swedish Tax Agency. Her research interest is in public economics. She holds a PhD from the University of Uppsala.

Bingwen Zheng is Director-General of the Center for International Social Security Studies at the Chinese Academy of Social Sciences, Beijing. He is a member of China's National Social Insurance Consultation Commission of the Ministry of Human Resources and Social Security and a member of the Advisory Committee of Major Decision-Making Experts of the China Banking and Insurance Regulatory Commission.

Abbreviations

ABM	automatic balancing mechanism
AI	artificial intelligence
APS	Pension Solidarity Component, Chile
ARR	average replacement rate
ASM	automatic stabilizing mechanism
ATP	Allmän tilläggspension, general supplementary pension
AWG	Ageing Working Group
BA	bilateral arrangement
BPU	basic pension unit
CEE8	Central and Eastern European 8 (Czech Republic, Estonia, Hungary, Latvia, Lithuania, Poland, Slovenia, Slovak Republic)
CPI	consumer price index
CR	contribution rate
DB	defined benefit
DC	defined contribution
DeSUS	Democratic Party of Pensioners of Slovenia
DTA	double taxation agreement
DWP	Department for Work and Pensions
EAP	East Asia and Pacific
EC	European Commission
ECA	Europe and Central Asia
ECB	European Central Bank
EC-EPC (AWG)	European Commission Economic Policy Committee Working Group on Ageing Populations and Sustainability
EU	European Union
EU-SILC	European Union Survey of Income and Living Conditions
FAZ	Frankfurter Allgemeine Zeitung
FDB	financial defined benefit
FDC	financial defined contribution
FUS	Fundusz Ubezpieczeń Społecznych, Polish Social Insurance Fund
GDP	gross domestic product
GPG	gender pay gap
GUS	Central Statistical Office, Poland
HFP	hypothetical future pension
HR	human resources

HRS	Health and Retirement Survey
ILFS	Integrated Labour Force Survey
ILO	International Labour Organization
IMF	International Monetary Fund
IPD	implicit pension debt
IT	information technology
IV	instrumental variable
KPST	Kosovo Pension Saving Trust
LAC	Latin America and the Caribbean
LC	Lee-Carter model
LCGLIG	life course gender labor income gap
LFPR	labor force participation rate
LFS	Labor Force Survey
LI	labor income
LO	Landsorganisationen
M&E	monitoring and evaluation
MA	multilateral arrangements
MOF	Ministry of Finance
MOHRSS	Ministry of Human Resources and Social Security
MPG	Minimum Pension Guarantee
MSOA	middle layer super output areas
NASEM	National Academy of Sciences, Engineering and Medicine
NDB	nonfinancial defined benefit
NDC	nonfinancial defined contribution
NEST	National Employment Savings Trust
NIS	National Insurance System
NKr	Norwegian kroner
NPS	National Pensions System
NRA	normal retirement age
NSP	New Solidarity Pillar
NTA	National Transfer Accounts
OA	old-age
OASDI	old-age, survivors', and disability
OECD	Organisation for Economic Co-operation and Development
ONS	Office for National Statistics
PAD	Palmer-Alho-Zhao de Gosson
PASIS	Assistance Pension, Chile
PAYG	pay-as-you-go
PB	pension base
PBS	Basic Solidarity Pension, Chile
PP	pension payments
PQA	pension qualifying amount
PQAC	Pension Qualifying Amount for Children, Sweden
PSL	Polish Peasants Party
RURPS	Rural and Urban Residents Pension Scheme
SES	socioeconomic status

SHARE	Survey of Health, Ageing and Retirement in Europe
SKr	Swedish kronor
SLD	Democratic Left Alliance, Poland
SME	small and medium-size enterprises
SPA	standard pensionable age
SSA	Sub-Saharan Africa
TATSI	total absolute tax subsidy indicator
TRR	theoretical replacement rate
UEPS	Urban Employee Pension Scheme
UN	United Nations
UPPS	universal public pension scheme
USAID	United States Agency for International Development
VAT	value-added tax
VSS	Vietnam Social Security
Zl	Polish zlotys
ZUS	Zakład Ubezpieczeń Społecznych, Polish Social Insurance Institution

Family and Gender

CHAPTER 17

Gender and Family: Conceptual Overview

Nicholas Barr

Introduction

Social policy aims to increase individual well-being along multiple dimensions:

- Income security, through earning opportunities, insurance, consumption smoothing, and poverty relief
- The maintenance and improvement of physical and emotional health
- Education and training for labor market activity and personal development

Family policy aims to promote the achievement of those objectives for all family members, and in a way that promotes gender equity.

This chapter considers how pensions can contribute to these aims. Specifically, it considers how pension design can contribute to policies about gender and family.[1] To frame the issues it is helpful to go back to fundamentals, in particular, labor market experience and pension design.

LABOR MARKET EXPERIENCE

In a contributory system, a person's pension entitlement is generally determined by the following:

- Total contributions by that individual each year, which depends on his or her hourly wage, w, and the number of hours in covered work, L
- The individual's contribution density, that is, the number of years of paid work, N

Internationally, the empirical facts are that women fare less well than men on all these dimensions. On average, they have the following:

- Lower wages than men (w lower)
- A greater likelihood of part-time work (L lower)
- Shorter careers because of, among other things, more career breaks (N lower)[2]

The author is grateful to Waltraud Schelkle for helpful comments. This chapter draws on Barr and Diamond (2008, 2010) and Barr (2012, 2013).

PENSION DESIGN

The effect of the gender pay gap (a snapshot at a point in time) is compounded by women's less-complete history of paid work and may be further exacerbated by the way pensions are designed; for example,

- Minimum pension age for women may be lower than for men.
- Annuities may be priced using separate life tables for men and women.
- The fraction of a couple's pension that continues after the death of one spouse may not be sufficient to maintain the living standard of the other. Because women are more likely to survive their husbands than vice versa, the problem affects women disproportionately.
- Indexation of pensions in payment that fails to protect replacement rates affects women more strongly given their longer life expectancy on average.

Thus, for reasons with roots in both labor markets and pension design, it is no accident that elderly poverty is greater among women than among men.

The system of fully funded individual accounts in Chile illustrates the problems of design that, in different combinations, arise in different pension plans. The system presents women with a quadruple whammy:

- Lower pay on average
- More gaps in employment; note that in a defined contribution (DC) plan, missing contribution years are particularly costly when younger (that is, when women are having children)
- An earlier pension age[3]
- The fact that it is legal for annuities to be priced using separate life tables for men and women

The first two result in women having smaller accumulations on average than men; the last two mean that for a given accumulation a woman receives a lower pension than a man.

OVERVIEW OF INCOME POVERTY

In every country shown in table 17.1, women experience a higher rate of elderly poverty; and in every country except Poland, older pensioners (disproportionately women) are at higher risk of elderly poverty than pensioners ages 65–75.

The question this chapter addresses is, What policies help reduce the number of (mainly) women experiencing income poverty in old age?[4] After some framing discussion in "Framing the Issues," the rest of the chapter is organized around three strategic policy directions:

- Increasing the size and duration of earnings
- Redirecting resources within the pension system, including for survivors and after divorce
- Adding resources from outside the pension system

TABLE 17.1 **Income poverty rates by age, sex, and household type, selected countries, 2014**
percentage with incomes less than 50 percent of median household disposable income

| | Older people (older than age 65) | | | | | |
| | By age | | | By gender | | |
	All 65 and older	66–75	76 and older	Men	Women	Whole population
Australia	25.7	23.4	29.2	23.6	27.5	12.8
Canada	9.0	8.5	9.9	6.7	11.0	12.6
Chile	16.3	16.2	16.4	16.1	16.4	16.1
Denmark	3.2	2.1	4.9	2.3	4.0	5.5
Finland	5.2	2.9	8.5	3.2	6.8	6.3
France	3.6	2.8	4.5	2.7	4.2	8.2
Germany	9.5	8.4	10.3	6.8	11.5	9.5
Greece	8.2	7.1	9.5	6.9	9.3	14.8
Italy	9.3	8.9	9.7	6.7	11.2	13.7
Japan	19.0	17.0	21.3	15.1	22.1	16.1
Netherlands	3.7	2.5	5.5	3.4	3.9	7.9
New Zealand	10.6	7.7	15.2	6.6	14.0	10.9
Norway	4.3	2.2	7.3	1.9	6.3	8.1
Poland	7.6	8.3	6.7	4.6	9.3	10.4
Portugal	9.7	8.5	11.2	7.1	11.6	13.5
Slovak Republic	3.8	3.3	4.8	1.9	4.9	8.7
Spain	5.4	4.7	6.2	3.7	6.7	15.3
Sweden	10.0	6.6	15.2	6.4	13.1	9.0
Switzerland	19.4	16.3	23.8	16.6	21.8	9.9
United Kingdom	13.8	10.4	18.5	11.1	16.0	10.9
United States	20.9	17.6	25.7	17.2	23.9	16.8
OECD	12.5	10.7	13.9	8.7	13.6	11.5

SOURCE: OECD (2017c), table 6.3.

NOTE: OECD = Organisation for Economic Co-operation and Development.

Framing the Issues

POLICY ISSUES

In thinking about pension design it is mistaken to base analysis entirely on a typical case.
It is important to take account of diversity of living arrangements and of individual and
family behavior.

Living arrangements are diverse and do not remain static

Some adults are single and live alone, others are single and share housing and other consumption, and others are married or in other recognized partnerships. Married couples differ in the extent to which they share resources. Some stay married until one of them dies, other marriages end in divorce after varying lengths of time, and many people remarry after a divorce or the death of a spouse.

Tax and benefit rules can affect men and women differently

Taxes and benefits affect the behavior of family members. That conclusion is inescapable—it is not possible to have a policy that does not affect incentives. Examples include the following:

- *Marriage*. Policy design can encourage or discourage marriage. Taxes may be higher or lower on two people if they remain single than if they marry. Similar issues arise with pensions, particularly for people considering marriage in middle age or later.
- *Consumption patterns*. Consumption can differ depending on whether benefits are paid to the husband or the wife. Evidence suggests that if child benefits are paid to the mother, a greater fraction will be spent on children (Goode, Callender, and Lister 1996). Other evidence (for example, Case and Deaton 1998) suggests that the noncontributory old-age pension in South Africa provides family poverty relief via grandmothers.
- *Labor supply of men and women*. Gender-neutral taxes have different effects on average because men and women have different labor supply elasticities.
- *Labor supply of mothers of young children*. Policy design can encourage or discourage paid work, depending on the design of child-care subsidies or income tax, the length of school hours, and the employment rules applicable to people with young children. Also relevant is the subsidized provision of pension credits for those caring for young children.

Resulting questions

These different impacts suggest a series of questions with both positive and normative aspects, the answers to many of which are outside the scope of this chapter:

- How should consumption be shared within the family?
- Should the earnings of husband and wife be taxed on an individual or family basis?
- Are labor supply and caring decisions made on the individual or household level?
- Should taxes and benefits encourage mothers with young children to accept paid work or discourage them from doing so?
- If policy is intended to encourage mothers with caring responsibilities to take paid work, should policy subsidize a carer at the time of child rearing or in retirement?
- Should taxes and benefits be designed to encourage marriage? If other policy goals can be met only by rules that discourage marriage (for example, if some benefits are lost upon marriage), how much weight should be given to that disincentive when designing such policies?
- How should pensions be organized for survivors or upon divorce?

The reason for posing these questions is to make it clear that none has an unambiguous answer. The conclusion is that there is not—and cannot be—a single optimal policy that applies universally. Discussion instead considers policy options that make sense in different contexts, with no pretense at setting out definitive answers.

ANALYTICAL APPROACH

The analysis in the chapter has four centers of gravity.

Multiple objectives

Pension systems have multiple objectives that cannot all be fully achieved at the same time. In analytical terms, the task is to optimize across different objectives concerning marriage, labor supply during working years, and the distribution of consumption within the household and over time, including old-age economic security. The optimum will depend on the relative weights given to the various objectives; and since those weights reflect differences in individual tastes and in social values (for example, between paid work and care activities), views about policy are likely to differ widely. Complicating matters is that it is often not clear whether a particular outcome, for example, a woman forgoing paid work to care for young children, is the result of choice or constraint.

Holistic

As the previous paragraph suggests, it is necessary to evaluate a pension plan in the context of the pension system as a whole. To illustrate, an exclusive focus on consumption smoothing (for example, a pure nonfinancial defined contribution [NDC] plan) suggests an arrangement in which benefits bear a fairly exact relationship to a worker's accumulated contributions; but such a system would fail to relieve old-age poverty for low-paid workers and would not offer insurance against adverse labor market outcomes, both problems with a substantial gender element.

In what follows, some of the discussion is specific to the NDC design and some is also relevant to other designs and to other parts of the pension system.

Second best

Analysis should be couched in what economists call "second-best" terms, that is, assuming a world with imperfect information, incomplete markets, and distorting taxation. For example, the goal of minimizing (as opposed to optimizing) labor supply disincentives is mistaken because any pension system that includes poverty relief inescapably creates distortions. Thus, minimizing distortions would imply little or no poverty relief—the cure would be worse than the disease. Pension systems can have substantial effects on behavior, including labor supply, saving, and the division of resources within a household. But these effects are not necessarily adverse; furthermore, even if they are, the system will still raise welfare if the welfare gain from improved old-age security outweighs the costs of adverse incentives. In short, policy has to seek the best balance among poverty relief, insurance, and containing distortions, which again will depend on the weights given to the different objectives.

Distribution matters

Many people (particularly non-economists) think that economics is only or mainly about efficiency. That view is deeply mistaken: economics has always been about equity as well as efficiency—indeed, one of the major thrusts of the optimal taxation literature (Diamond and Mirrlees 1971a, 1971b) was to integrate the two concerns.

Strengthening Earnings Records

Approaches to strengthening earnings records include general labor market policies to assist paid work, policies that support paid work alongside caring activities, and policies that facilitate longer working life. These approaches help reduce the gender gap in pensions, whether DC, NDC, or defined benefit (DB).

LABOR MARKET POLICIES TO ASSIST PAID WORK

Four types of labor market policies assist paid work:

- *Equal pay for equal work.* Though hugely important, this aspect of economic and social policy lies outside the scope of a chapter on pension design. The policy direction is firmly noted but not discussed further.

- *Active labor market policies.* These can help (usually) mothers return to the labor force after a period of unpaid work.

- *Labor market legislation.* Labor codes can be more or less helpful in providing flexibility, notably in supporting part-time work.

- *Tax policy to encourage paid work by second earners.* The design of personal income tax affects labor supply by different family members. A family base taxes the income of a second earner at the family's marginal tax rate. With individual taxation, the marginal tax rate a person faces is independent of marital status; the mother of young children faces lower tax rates than with family taxation and hence, at least via the substitution effect, is more likely to take paid work.

POLICIES TO FACILITATE PAID WORK ALONGSIDE CARING ACTIVITIES

Three sets of policies facilitate paid work alongside caring activities:

- *Sharing care-related tasks.* One way to assist paid work is to share tasks more equally within a household (OECD 2017a). This aspect relates more to social change than to specific policies. In addition, a range of policies, notably those connected with child care, facilitate paid work in younger years.

- *The quantity and quality of child care.* Prenursery-school children need care throughout the day, and school children need care outside school hours. Women are more likely to take paid work if child care is readily available (that is, the facility has space for the child) and is available locally. Different elements in the solution include the following:
  - Enough child care facilities with good geographical coverage
  - Closer alignment of the length of the school day with the work day, for example, breakfast clubs and after-school clubs
  - Facilities that combine child care with office space (*Financial Times* 2017).

- *The cost of child care.* Child care has to be affordable as well as available. Thus, the extent to which child care is subsidized, either through transfers to the parent or through tax-financed facilities, is directly relevant.

FACILITATING LONGER WORKING LIFE

Three further policies address longer working life.

Setting minimum pension age

Though less frequent today, it remains the case that in some countries, the minimum pension age for women is lower than for men (OECD 2017b, table 2.4). A lower mandatory retirement age unambiguously disadvantages women, in terms of both earnings opportunities and pension benefits, if the latter would be higher with longer work. A lower actual retirement age for women than men, either because retirement is mandatory or as a consequence of social attitudes, will reduce benefits for women in many pension arrangements. Also relevant is whether other rules, such as eligibility for disability benefits and the opportunity to contribute to tax-favored retirement accounts, are based on the minimum pension age. In such respects also, a lower retirement age can place some women at a disadvantage.

A good design will have three features: minimum pension age will be the same for men and women; retirement at that age is not mandatory; and minimum pension age will be related to life expectancy. Box 17.1 discusses the importance of the last feature using arrangements in Sweden.

BOX 17.1 **Sweden: Faulty adjustment to increasing life expectancy**

Adjusting pensions to rising life expectancy requires reducing benefits at each age of withdrawal from the labor force. In principle this can be done by focusing on one or both of the following:

- The *level* of the pension, by reducing monthly benefits at the minimum pension age
- The *age* at which the pension is first paid, by gradually increasing the minimum pension age, with no compensating increase (or a less-than-actuarial increase) in pension

The minimum pension age in the nonfinancial defined contribution pension in Sweden is 61 years. The benefit a person receives at that age is based on (a) the size of his or her accumulation, and (b) the remaining life expectancy of his or her birth cohort. Thus, monthly benefits go down as life expectancy rises. A rational response would be to work longer. However, lessons from behavioral economics call into question uncritical adherence to the assumption of rationality (Thaler and Benartzi 2004). Considerable evidence shows that many people retire as soon as they are allowed to do so, whether or not that is in their own long-run best interests or those of their dependents.

These arguments suggest that a pension system should adjust to rising life expectancy in two ways, by doing the following:

- Adjusting the level of the pension for longer life expectancy assists the financial sustainability of the pension system.
- Increasing the minimum pension age broadly in line with life expectancy assists adequacy of benefits in cases in which behavior deviates from simple economic rationality.

The gender relevance of the last point is that a later start to pension, by increasing the benefit, is important to preserve living standards not only at the time of retirement, but into older ages reached disproportionately by women. Adjusting the minimum pension age to reflect rising life expectancy is possible (and desirable) in any pension design.

Adjusting pension benefits for earlier or later retirement

Whether a person retires at minimum pension age or delays taking benefits will depend partly on how a person's pension is affected by a delayed start. It is desirable if someone with a short contribution record has the option to fill some of the gaps caused by a late start or career interruptions by delaying the commencement of benefits. Central to this element are the incentives to retire later built into the pension design.

Incentives to continue work past the minimum pension age can vary between men and women depending on the structure of the benefit formula and differences in the earnings histories of men and women. If, for example, a large jump in benefits occurs when crossing a threshold number of contribution years, and if more women than men are just below the threshold when reaching minimum pension age, the incentive to work longer will be stronger for women than for men.

Good design suggests two elements to address the relationship between pension benefits and the age at which pension is first received:

- The pension should be larger for a worker who is older when benefits begin, so as to preserve incentives to work until a suitable age for stopping work.
- Benefits should either start at a given age without requiring an end to work or should increase significantly for a delayed start.

Both elements are inherent in a DC design, whether NDC or funded DC. They can (and should) be incorporated into other designs.

Flexible retirement

The argument for later retirement as part of the response to rising life expectancy is well understood. There is less understanding of the gains from more flexible retirement. Even if there were no concerns about sustainability, such choice is good policy for two sets of reasons:

- Individuals vary widely in their preferences. Though many people retire as soon as they are allowed, others do not, because of the extra earnings, because postponing retirement raises their pension, or because they continue to enjoy working in their current job or another one.
- Individuals face different constraints. In the present context a particular gain is the possibility of improving incomplete contribution records.

Pension design should seek to accommodate differences across individuals by offering choice over how a person moves from full-time work to full retirement (box 17.2 illustrates how this is done well in the system in Sweden); and labor market policy should facilitate institutions that allow people to move from full-time work toward full retirement along a time path of their choosing.

Redirecting Resources within the Pension System

The previous section discusses ways of improving the earnings records—and hence contribution records—of people with caring responsibilities. In a strictly individual design a person accumulates pension saving that he or she draws down in retirement. Any other design requires an element of pooling with the pension wealth of others (addressed in this

---

BOX 17.2 Sweden: The good news: Partial pensions

Sweden is an outlier internationally—and an example for other countries to follow—in allowing workers initially to draw only part of their pension. As in most countries, on reaching minimum pension age, workers can choose to draw all of their pension or none of it. In Sweden, workers also have the option to draw 25 percent, 50 percent, or 75 percent of their pension.[a] The deferred element continues to grow; and if individuals carry on working, they will pay additional contributions, further increasing their eventual pension.

This arrangement is possible with DC, NDC, and DB pensions, and should become a standard feature. The particular advantage for women is the options it offers to improve on any earlier gaps in contributions or years of low pay.[b]

a. Norway offers a similar set of options.

b. The effects of flexible retirement are not simple. Börsch-Supan et al. (2017) find that flexible retirement increased the labor force participation of older workers but decreased total hours worked.

---

section) or finance from outside the pension system (addressed in the "Adding Resources from Outside the Pension System" section later in this chapter).

The term "redirecting" is used because it covers the pure cases of risk sharing (for example, actuarially priced individual annuities) and of redistribution (for instance, counting years spent on caring activities as contribution years in a DB plan), and intermediate cases. The examples are presented in terms of redirecting resources within the pension system, though in some instances they could, as an alternative, be financed from outside the pension system.

The following categories, though not mutually exclusive, help clarify the discussion. Different designs provide the following:

- Pooling among individuals to cover the longevity risk
- Pooling within the family
- Pooling among pensioners
- Pooling among workers and pensioners

POOLING AMONG INDIVIDUALS: IMPROVING ANNUITIES

A simple annuity pays a pension benefit for life: it can cover an individual or a couple, and it can be indexed in different ways or not indexed at all. Key aspects concern actions on the demand and supply sides of the market.

What requirement to annuitize?

Annuitization insures the individual against longevity risk. A strong case exists against simple voluntarism. Reliance on drawdown forgoes the welfare gains of insurance, both for the individual and for other family members. Behavioral economics gives insights into why a voluntary system leads to people not annuitizing, or not annuitizing enough.

The resulting potential ill effects are twofold: pensioners may spend too much too soon; or they may spend too little, either for fear of running out of money or to avoid "spending the children's inheritance." Such tendencies do not imply that mandatory full annuitization is optimal. Uncertainty about future expenditures and bequest motives both imply that not all wealth should be annuitized (Davidoff, Brown, and Diamond 2005). Some countries have a requirement to annuitize, but also an option for workers to take part of their accumulation as a lump sum when first drawing a pension.[5]

The supply of annuities

Insurance can cope with risk (when the probability is known) but not with uncertainty (when it is not). In principle, annuities are priced on the basis of the expected remaining lifetime of the annuitant, which is treated as a risk. That model may have been appropriate when the gap between typical retirement age and life expectancy was small (for example, five years). Today, however, many people retire in their early sixties and may live for another 30 years. Retirements are typically much longer than in the past; as a result, the "funnel of doubt" about remaining life expectancy at the time a person retires is large. It can therefore be argued that life expectancy is not a simple risk but has a significant element of uncertainty.

Various ways exist to address the supply-side problem, including variable annuities (in which the annuity adjusts from year to year reflecting changes in life expectancy of the cohort of annuitants, and perhaps also financial market outcomes). That approach shares risks among annuitants. Other approaches, of which two stand out, share risk more widely. Governments, unlike private insurers, can raise income from sources other than insurance premiums; in addition, governments can change contractual arrangements (for example, raising the state pension age) in ways that have democratic legitimacy—forms of adjustment that are not available to private insurers. One way to address uncertainty is for the government to be the annuity provider. This is the approach in Sweden.

A private sector solution would be through longevity bonds. Suppose that official figures underestimate increases in life expectancy, leading to losses by annuity providers who therefore either leave the market or price future annuities conservatively. One way to address the problem is for government to sell longevity bonds. In this arrangement, in, say, 2020, an insurance company would sell an annuity to, say, a 70-year-old, priced on official estimates of the remaining life expectancy for a 70-year-old in 2020. If the cohort of annuitants lives longer than the 2020 projection the taxpayer finances the resulting extra cost. Thus, the insurance company takes on the risk, the taxpayer the uncertainty. This is a sensible division of labor. The role of government is to fill the missing market.[6]

What role for deferred annuities?

Persons without an annuity must draw down their pension savings, with the risk of spending too much too soon or too little too late. One approach is a rule-of-thumb for drawdown. In the United States, for example, there are tax penalties for drawing down too little and too much.[7]

In principle, a useful approach is to combine drawdown with a deferred annuity— that is, an annuity bought at (say) age 65 that pays an annual benefit for life from age 85. That arrangement could be voluntary, or there could be a nudge or mandate. In practice, the market for deferred annuities is thin. But such an instrument would be useful both to allow drawdown over a known period (that is, from retirement until the start date of the deferred annuity) and to protect against old-age poverty. If such an annuity is joint-life (discussed next), it also protects elderly survivors, disproportionately widows.

POOLING WITHIN THE FAMILY

As noted earlier, personal income tax poses the question of whether to think of the individual or the family as the economic unit for policy design. The same is true for pension systems. Should a person in a rich family with low earnings or low pension benefits be eligible for the same redistribution as someone with similar earnings or benefits in a poor family, or on their own? Many people would say no, but a complicating factor is that family structures have become more fluid: more than in the past, family at the time when a pension starts may be different from family at the time when its members worked and made pension contributions. And divorce settlements may or may not have taken into account future pension benefits.

Organizing pensions on an individual rather than a family basis, with women having pensions only in their own right, is argued by some to be a better fit for societies with such fluidity. On the other hand, as with income tax, family structure affects available resources and the demands on those resources.

Pooling within the family has at least three aspects: sharing pension pots during working life, survivors' pensions, and accommodating divorce.

Sharing pension pots year by year during working life

Consider a couple in which the husband has a record of continuous high-earning employment, and the wife one of low earnings and low contribution density. The husband has a large pension and the wife a small one. If the couple (a) stays married throughout working life and retirement, (b) does not differ greatly in age, and (c) shares income amicably, this arrangement might be a useful rule of thumb. However, a case can be made for giving couples some flexibility over the division of pension capital. The issue is particularly relevant if a couple divorces during working life.

A minimal approach is to allow pension entitlements to be shared on a voluntary basis. A more radical option (Barr 2001, 150) is to require that one-half of a husband's contribution goes into his wife's accumulation and vice versa. The argument for doing so is that caring for children (or elderly dependents) has costs, and those costs have to fall somewhere. Pooling pension pots means that the costs of child rearing in terms of forgone pensions is shared between parents. These accounts belong to the individual and would be carried through a divorce. Against these advantages, however, is the problem that arises when the ages of husband and wife significantly differ, and they have had very different earnings, and the higher earner is older. In such a case, dividing pension assets undercuts their ability to finance the couple's retirement if they remain married. This is clearest in the case of a one-earner couple. When the worker reaches retirement age, only half of the benefit is available until the younger spouse has reached retirement age.

Survivors' pensions

The specific question is whether pension design should allow, encourage, or mandate joint-life annuitization. The main argument for joint-life annuitization of at least a part of a worker's pension is to prevent poverty for the surviving spouse, most often the wife. The root of such poverty is twofold:

- Economies of scale arise in household formation. A single survivor of a couple typically needs about 65–70 percent of the couple's income to maintain a broadly constant standard of living. If spouses are the same age and have identical earnings histories and identical pension benefits, the death of one may lower the living standard of the other. This is part of the reason why poverty is more frequent among widows than among married elderly women.[8]
- In addition, as discussed, compared with men, women on average have lower earnings, a lower contribution density, or both.

While social policy can help address the second reason, the first is inherent.

For both reasons, survivors' pensions are important for preserving the living standards of the elderly. Several ways of organizing such benefits are available. A worker's accumulation could be used to buy a joint-life annuity with a suitable fraction (50 percent is common) for the survivor, based on the actuarial conversion of a single-life annuity into the relevant joint-life annuity. In a two-earner couple this could be done by both partners.

Mandatory joint-life annuitization can create winners and losers because of the following:

- Life expectancy at a given age is generally lower among lower earners than higher earners (OECD 2017c); thus standard annuity pricing—whether single- or joint-life—redistributes from poorer to richer people.
- In some systems, survivors' benefits do not adjust for the age difference between spouses, redistributing from couples of similar age to ones with a large difference.

If joint-life annuitization is voluntary, the potential issue is adverse selection: couples who think that, even having adjusted for the age difference between spouses, one will live considerably longer than the other are more likely to purchase such annuities.

A DB system could offer a similar set of options, based on the actuarial conversion of a single-life annuity into the relevant joint-life annuity. Alternatively, survivors' benefits could be provided out of the revenues of the pension system as a whole.

Different designs give different degrees of "nudge." Joint-life annuitization could be voluntary, or could be the default, or could be a stronger default by requiring both partners to agree in writing that the default should be replaced by a single-life annuity for the worker. Alternatively, joint-life annuitization could be mandatory. Sweden is an outlier internationally in ruling out joint-life annuitization in the NDC pension, an arrangement assessed in box 17.3.

The main conclusion is that there are powerful arguments against organizing pension benefits—whether NDC or other designs—on a strictly individual basis.

Divorce

Divorce is common and, if there is no adjustment, divorce after many years of marriage can result in very low benefits for a person with a limited earnings history. Poverty rates for elderly divorced women who do not remarry are high in the United States.[9]

There are rules, often involving the courts, about the division of accumulated assets (sometimes including human capital) of a couple upon divorce, with particular focus on accumulations during the marriage.

BOX 17.3 **Survivors' pensions in Sweden**

Unusually, the NDC pension in Sweden:

- Does not allow transfers of notional capital between spouses and registered partners, either during a marriage or upon divorce; and

- Has no option for joint-life annuities. When (as is more usually the case) the husband dies, his NDC pension dies with him.[a]

The argument in Sweden for this design is that either arrangement would violate gender equity if it discouraged married women's labor supply—the more generous the survivors' benefits, the more powerful the disincentive. The issue is important because the gender pay gap persists, and gender equality is elusive even in Sweden (OECD 2018).

However, several counterarguments follow:

- In efficiency terms, the design places heavy emphasis on first-best rationality, that is, that the prospect of a low pension in the future will increase a woman's labor supply in the present.

- It implies that the costs of parenting should fall on women in old age to the extent that a woman earns less than her husband. Many would dispute this value judgment, both directly, and particularly if the reason she earns less is forgone career opportunities because of caring activities.

- It ignores the reality, noted above, that a couple is not in all respects the same thing as two single individuals.

- It takes insufficient account of changes in family structure, in particular that divorce is more common than in the past.

The Swedish design is not an inherent part of the NDC design; joint-life annuities are possible in NDC plans, as in funded DC plans and DB plans.

a. The fully funded premium pension in Sweden allows joint-life annuities, but with no requirement or nudge.

Different strategies are used to provide benefits after a divorce, implemented through decisions at the time of retirement or at the time of divorce. One strategy is to provide benefits when a divorced person reaches retirement age. This can be done as a transfer of benefits between spouses. For example, when a worker starts to draw a pension, benefits are adjusted to provide some benefits not only to a current spouse, but also to previous spouses, using a formula relating to the lengths and timing of the marriages. Future availability of such benefits could be factored into a divorce agreement. Alternatively, benefits for a divorced spouse could be financed from the resources of the pension system generally, without reducing the benefit of the worker entitled to the pension, as in the United States.

A second strategic approach is to transfer pension wealth between spouses at the time of a divorce, based on their earnings records during the marriage. With a funded DC plan the actual assets are divided; in an NDC plan the notional capital is divided. Such transfers are also possible in a DB plan. For example, in Canada, when a marriage or common-law partnership ends, the entitlements to the Canada Pension Plan built up by the couple during the time they lived together may be divided equally between them as part of a divorce settlement.

A third approach, discussed earlier, is to divide earnings records on an annual basis during the marriage, for example, with individual accounts, so that each year the earnings of husband and wife are divided between them.

POOLING AMONG PENSIONERS

Resources can be pooled more widely than only within families. Two main approaches are discussed.

Gender-specific or joint mortality tables

Governments can provide annuities based on a single mortality table for men and women in a given birth cohort or require that private providers do so. As a result, a man and a woman with the same accumulation and retiring at the same age receive the same monthly pension. However, with a single mortality table, men on average receive less in present value terms per dollar of accumulation than women because of their lower average life expectancy.

Alternatively, governments may allow pension providers to base annuities on gender-specific mortality tables. Given different life expectancies, a man and woman with the same accumulation and retiring at the same age would receive differ-ent monthly pensions, the man receiving a larger one. This practice is outlawed in employer-organized systems in the United States and the European Union, and many countries require joint mortality tables not only for the mandatory system but also for voluntary pensions.

Joint mortality tables, however, are not the end of the story. Because higher earn-ers tend to live longer than lower earners of the same gender, uniform pricing tends to benefit them; additionally, market pricing will reflect administrative costs, so that people with higher benefits may get better pricing. Given that men on average have higher earnings, such outcomes have a gender effect even in a system that mandates joint mortality tables.

Indexing pensions in payment

Once a pension is awarded it can be increased each year in line with prices, wages, or a combination, raising another set of issues (Barr and Diamond 2008).

For a given initial pension, the more rapidly benefits grow, the more expensive the system; the less rapidly they grow, the further pensioners fall behind average liv-ing standards over time. Price indexation places greater emphasis on containing costs and preserving purchasing power, and wage indexation greater emphasis on the rela-tive adequacy of benefits. Pension design needs to strike a balance between these two aspects.

At a given long-run cost, a tradeoff arises between the initial level of pensions and the subsequent rate of growth of benefits: the more rapidly benefits grow, the lower the initial benefit needs to be set. This is the way that initial benefits are determined in a system with annuities in funded DC systems and in the calculation of initial benefits in the NDC system in Sweden.

Because workers differ in life expectancy, different combinations of initial benefit levels and growth rates of benefit with the same aggregate long-run cost will affect different workers differently:

- A worker with a shorter expected life will prefer higher initial benefits with slower subsequent growth.
- Both men and women with higher earnings tend to live longer; thus, the choice of growth rate of benefits has important ex ante distributional effects.
- On average women live longer than men, so there is also a gender issue.

To illustrate, at a given long-run cost, price indexation generates a higher initial pension, benefiting people with shorter lives, but exposing elderly pensioners (typically widows) to being left further and further behind. With wage indexation, the reverse occurs.

POOLING AMONG WORKERS AND PENSIONERS

Pooling among workers and pensioners can take place in four ways.

Less stringent contribution requirements

A DB plan can cover gaps in the contributions of some workers from the contributions of other workers. Some countries give no benefit unless a person has contributed for at least a minimum number of years, while others provide benefits after any contribution. Because women on average contribute for fewer years than men, the latter approach tends to provide at least some pension for more women. For the same reason, a smaller number of years of contributions necessary to qualify for a full benefit tends to help second earners.

Pension credits are a particular example of this approach. In a DB plan, years spent in caring activities could be included as contribution years, with caring-related gaps financed from the contributions of other workers. As discussed shortly, in a DC plan, tax-financed contributions could be paid on behalf of the carer. In an NDC plan, such contributions could be notional (that is, financed from within the NDC plan) or real (that is, involving outside finance) (Chłoń-Domińczak, Franco, and Palmer 2012).

Three other forms of pooling, though with no specific gender aspects, benefit women by assisting the adequacy and sustainability of the pension system.

Minimum pension age

Earlier discussion points to several conclusions: that minimum pension age should be the same for men and women, and that retirement at that age should not be mandatory. A third issue is how minimum pension age adjusts to rising life expectancy.

In a DC or an NDC plan, pension benefits decline automatically as life expectancy rises. In such a plan the purpose of raising the minimum pension age is to protect the adequacy of benefits rather than the economic sustainability of the plan. In a DB plan with a given pension age, rising life expectancy leads to increasing costs and hence problems of sustainability. Raising the minimum pension age with no compensating increase in monthly pension benefits is a way of pooling the longevity risk between workers and pensioners, given the tradeoff between higher contributions and a higher minimum pension age.

Pooling across workers and pensioners: Collective DC pensions

The Netherlands has funded industry pension plans. The system is evolving but in broad terms offers workers a career-average benefit, but (a) contingent on fund performance, and (b) with a cap on the employer contribution rate. The combination of a career-average design with solvency-contingent indexing of liabilities results in a plan that is a hybrid of DB and DC.

A collective arrangement of this sort has advantages. Collective risk pooling offers wider risk sharing than an individual plan. As an example,

> [I]f a cohort lives longer than expected, the resulting lower funding rate harms the indexation of the deferred annuities offered to younger cohorts. Moreover, by linking pension benefits to the wages of workers, pension funds allow retirees to share in the wage risks of workers. (Bovenberg and Gradus 2014, 6)

Pooling across workers and pensioners: Accrual in an NDC plan

Suppose that the stock market crashes. The annuity that a worker invested in the stock market will buy will fall correspondingly (if the value of an accumulation falls from 100 to 75, so will the resulting annuity). An NDC plan can spread that risk more widely because accrual works differently.

In an NDC plan a person's pension wealth is crystallized year by year. As box 17.4 explains, an economic crisis late in a person's career has a smaller effect than with fully funded individual accounts.

BOX 17.4 Accrual in an NDC plan shares risk

In contrast with a fully funded DC system, a person's pension wealth in an NDC plan is crystallized year by year. More specifically, in my first year in the labor force, my contribution, $C_1 = tY_1$, where t is the contribution rate and Y_1 my earnings in year 1. C_1 then earns a notional return, r_1; and C_1 $(1+r_1)$ earns a notional return r_2 in year 2, and so on. In a good year, r will be higher and vice versa. Thus in year 1, I earn a "slice" of my pension. Ditto in year 2, and so on, so that when I retire, my pension is the sum of those "slices," not unlike a career-average DB plan. If a major crisis strikes in year n, the effect is mainly via the accrual rate on the flow of new contributions and the indexation of benefits in payment rather than on the value of the stock of notional assets.

The NDC design gives pensioners more protection than fully funded individual accounts by sharing risk more widely. Adjustment to protect previously accumulated "slices" does not fall entirely on pensioners (as in a pure DC plan) but is shared between pensioners and workers. The calculation of the "slice" each year is on a DC basis, but its preservation is more like a DB system.

Adding Resources from Outside the Pension System

Old-age security is affected by institutions outside the pension system in many ways. This section outlines four: supporting contribution records during working life; subsidizing pensions in payment; noncontributory pensions; and the role of insurance, particularly to cover age-related risks.

SUPPORTING CONTRIBUTION RECORDS DURING WORKING LIFE

In a DC plan, the contributions of someone not in paid work because of caring activities can be paid year by year on (more usually) her behalf by taxpayers. The pension contributions of low earners could similarly be supplemented (the DC plan in Mexico incorporates a taxpayer subsidy that declines as earnings rise and fully tapers away for high earners [OECD 2015, 306]). An NDC plan has analogous options.

SUBSIDIZING PENSIONS IN PAYMENT

Pensions in payment can also be subsidized by the taxpayer, for example, paying a full benefit on the basis of a combination of contributions and pension credits. That arrangement is possible with DC plans (for example, cover for maternity in Chile), in NDC arrangements (for instance, a minimum pension guarantee), and in DB plans.

NONCONTRIBUTORY BENEFITS

A noncontributory pension is awarded on the basis of a test of age and residence, but without a contributions test. The benefit can be awarded on the basis only of age and residence, as in the Netherlands and New Zealand, or could be subject also to an income or assets test.

Because women on average have lower contribution densities and often smaller contributions, a noncontributory pension has a particular benefit for them. A reinforcing design would provide a higher basic pension for a single person than for a member of a couple, helping preserve the replacement rate of the surviving partner.

The existence or otherwise of benefits financed from outside the pension system has a fundamental bearing on gender equity. To illustrate with an extreme example, if there was a Europe-wide noncontributory pension of €1 million per year for each elderly person irrespective of marital status, this chapter would be much less salient.

GOOD INSURANCE

The more comprehensive a country's insurance for covering the costs of medical care and long-term care, the less the need for precautionary saving, hence the greater the fraction of pension wealth that can be converted into an annuity. The general point is that greater support from noncontributory sources and better insurance against risks faced disproportionately by older people are a powerful separate source of gender equity in old age, illustrating the point made early in the chapter of the importance of thinking about pension systems holistically.

Conclusion

BALANCING MULTIPLE OBJECTIVES

This section returns to some of the questions listed earlier.

Who should bear the costs of child-rearing, and when?

Should society assist with the costs of child-rearing and, if so, should it do so at the time of caring or in retirement? Different ways of recognizing care activities have different distributional and incentive effects. One approach is to credit a person's pension record with a fixed amount for each year that he or she provides care, as in the NDC plans in Sweden and Poland. Sweden also credits a caregiver's individual funded account. Thus, her pension is larger because of additional deposits into her account, paid out of general revenue.

In some countries pensions are based on career-average earnings, typically incorporating people's highest earning years. In this case a uniform level of credit per year of child care raises the pension of someone with a short career or sufficiently low earnings, while offering less (or no) help to someone with a long career and high earnings.

In other countries, years spent in caregiving may be dropped from the calculation, reducing the number of years used in calculating career-average earnings. With an earnings-related pension, this approach implicitly credits a higher-earning woman with a larger amount than a lower-earning woman.[10]

These different approaches also have different implications for finance: with a fully funded or NDC plan, the cost of a pension credit has to be met at the time that the credit is earned; in a DB plan, the cost can be left until the pension is paid.

A broader question is whether offering pension credits for caregiving is good policy. The credit is a blunt instrument that does not distinguish between cases in which labor supply is affected by the credit and cases in which labor supply is not affected. A parent in a well-off household may have no paid work, and hence be eligible for a credit, but also employ a full-time nanny. That is, a pension credit does not distinguish between those who look after the children themselves and those who do not.

The underlying question is whether support for child-rearing should be back-loaded by supporting the carer's future pension or front-loaded with support at the time of caring. The latter type of support can include child benefit or subsidies for child care. The choice of balance between support at different stages in the life cycle is to a considerable extent a matter of social values and politics, and hence a matter for each country to decide.

To what extent should paid work be encouraged?

Decisions about old-age security need to be considered alongside policy preferences about the balance between paid work and caring for children. The fact that some designs encourage paid work does not mean that paid work should necessarily be maximized. A central policy question is the balance between encouraging paid work on the one hand and encouraging caring in the home on the other. The issue is controversial because answers depend both on social values and on hard-to-measure empirical magnitudes, such as the benefits of parenting and whether a stay-at-home carer does so out of choice or constraint.

Incentives to take paid work are stronger when subsidies for child care are conditioned on the caregiver having paid work, and taxation of secondary earners[11] is lower. Incentives to take paid work are weaker when caregiving is recognized through a pension credit. In contrast, a child benefit paid independent of work (as is typical) has an income effect on labor supply but no substitution effect.[12]

The relative sizes of these elements determine the balance of incentives between paid work and caregiving. For example,

- The incentive to stay at home to care for children can be strengthened by making child benefits or pension credits, or both, available only to people with no (or little) earnings.

- To strengthen the incentive to take paid work, a subsidy for child care could be conditioned on working at least a minimum number of hours. Such a subsidy encourages (a) the use of paid child care by those who earn income, and therefore (b) the willingness to accept work.

- It is possible to separate the incentive to work from the incentive to use paid child care by changing the balance between (a) the child care subsidy, and (b) lower taxes or higher pension credits for those working. Design can make part-time work more or less attractive relative to full-time work.

What should be the relative treatment of different types of families?

The balance between different instruments has distributional effects that are diverse and complex. A greater emphasis on pension credits or child benefits assists families with children relative to those without. A greater emphasis on lower taxation of secondary earnings benefits couples with children relative to single parents. Unless the lower taxation of secondary earnings is available only to those with small children, it does not match a pension credit. And a pension credit does not perfectly match a child care subsidy, because use of child care is not universal among those who work.

Potential distributional effects also arise between better- and worse-off families. For example, if pension credits go primarily to members of high-earning families (perhaps because they are the most likely to be able to afford to have someone not in paid work), the situation is very different from one in which the credit goes primarily to low-income single parents, who would otherwise have very small pensions. The case for a pension credit needs to be evaluated with a focus on who receives it and on the extent to which that fits policy makers' distributional objectives.

CENTRAL CONCLUSIONS

This chapter puts forward three sets of arguments about gender and family issues in pension design:

- No unambiguously best design exists, but some designs are unambiguously bad.

- Policy should not focus only on the design of the pension system but should recognize the impact on eventual pension benefits of other policies, for example, the taxation of earnings, subsidies for child care, all-day schools, and regulations about flexibility of work for parents of young children.

- The argument is not that women ought to work or ought to care for children; rather it is that tax and pension systems (and other policies) inevitably create incentives that affect decisions about paid work, care activities, and leisure and therefore should be chosen to reflect social values and individual preferences and constraints, all of which will differ within and across countries.

More concretely, pension design needs to be sensitive to the differing impacts on men and women. To that end it should do the following:

- Consider what recognition is appropriate, and in what form, of years spent in socially valued activities such as caring for children, disabled people, and elderly dependents, balancing such recognition with incentives to participate in paid work
- Set common rules for pension eligibility and determination
- Require the use of joint life tables if the system includes mandatory annuitization
- Ensure that satisfactory pension arrangements are in place for surviving spouses and after a divorce

Notes

1. For a parallel study, see Chłoń-Domińczak (2017).

2. For a wide-ranging study of the gender wage gap, see Blau and Kahn (2017), and on Latin America, Amarante, Colacce, and Manzi (2017).

3. Note that many of the countries in Central and Eastern Europe have already equalized pension age or are on a path to do so.

4. The examples in this chapter are frequently presented in terms of husband and wife, with the woman as the primary carer, but recognizing throughout that other types of partnerships flourish and that the man may be the primary carer. Examples also often assume that the woman has the lower earnings in a couple, again recognizing that this is far from always the case.

5. In the United Kingdom, workers used to be required to convert at least 75 percent of their accumulation into an annuity, so could take up to 25 percent as a tax-free lump sum. The rules were recently relaxed.

6. For a fuller discussion, see Thomsen and Verner Andersen (2007) and Blake, Boardman, and Cairns (2010).

7. Individuals are required to withdraw the Required Minimum Distribution (RMD) from age 70½. Failure to do so incurs a tax penalty of 50 percent of the shortfall, that is, if the RMD is US$50,000 someone who withdraws only US$30,000 faces a tax penalty of US$10,000. See https://www.irs .gov/retirement-plans/retirement-plans-faqs-regarding-required-minimum-distributions#8.

8. Although the chapter discusses surviving spouses, a well-designed system also has benefits for young survivors, notably young children.

9. In 2014, the poverty rate in the United States was 4.9 percent for married women older than age 65. The comparable figures for widows and divorced women were 16.3 percent and 18.4 percent, respectively—see https://www.ssa.gov/retirementpolicy/fact-sheets/marital-status -poverty.html.

10. To see this, suppose a pension is normally based on a person's 40 highest earnings years. For someone who has 30 years of earnings and spent 10 years caring for children, the average will be based on those 30 years of highest earnings, with the next-highest 10 years of earnings dropping out of the calculation. Those 10 years are credited with the average of the highest-earning 30 years rather than zero. This is worth more to a woman with higher earnings in those 30 years than to one with lower earnings. For women with more than 30 years of positive earnings, the gain depends on earnings in the highest-earning 30 years relative to earnings in lower years.

11. The secondary earner is the spouse with the lower earnings.

12. By increasing parental income, the child benefit reduces the incentive to take paid work; however, the benefit has no effect on the net return to additional work, and thus creates no disincentive via the substitution effect.

References

Amarante, Verónica, Maira Colacce, and Pilar Manzi. 2017. "The Gender Gap in Pensions in Latin America." *International Social Security Review* 70 (2): 57–85.

Barr, Nicholas. 2001. *The Welfare State as Piggy Bank: Information, Risk, Uncertainty and the Role of the State*. Oxford and New York: Oxford University Press.

———. 2012. *The Economics of the Welfare State*. 5th ed. Oxford and New York: Oxford University Press (also in Polish and Chinese).

———. 2013. *The Pension System in Sweden*. Report to the Expert Group on Public Economics (ESO). Stockholm: Ministry of Finance. http://eso.expertgrupp.se/wp-content /uploads/2013/08/Till-webben-ESO-2013-7.pdf.

Barr, Nicholas, and Peter Diamond. 2008. *Reform in Pensions: Principles and Policy Choices*. New York and Oxford: Oxford University Press.

———. 2010. *Pension Reform: A Short Guide*. New York and Oxford: Oxford University Press (also in Spanish, Polish, and Chinese).

Blake, David, Tom Boardman, and Andrew Cairns. 2010. "The Case for Longevity Bonds." Center for Retirement Research at Boston College, Issue Brief 10-10, Boston College, Boston. http:// crr.bc.edu/wp-content/uploads/2010/06/IB_10-10-508.pdf.

Blau, Francine D., and Lawrence M. Kahn. 2017. "The Gender Wage Gap: Extent, Trends, and Explanations." *Journal of Economic Literature* 55 (3): 789–865.

Börsch-Supan, Axel, Tabea Bucher-Koenen, Vesile Kutlu-Koc, and Nicolas Goll. 2017. "Dangerous Flexibility—Retirement Reforms Reconsidered." *Economic Policy* 33 (94): 315–55.

Bovenberg, Lans, and Raymond Gradus. 2014. "Reforming Dutch Occupational Pension Schemes." Netspar Discussion Paper. 05/2014-017, Netspar, Tilburg, the Netherlands. https:// d2vry01uvf8h31.cloudfront.net/Organisaties/WI/2014__Bovenberg__Gradus__Reforming _Dutch_occupational_pension_schemes.pdf.

Case, Anne, and Angus Deaton. 1998. "Large Cash Transfers to the Elderly in South Africa." *Economic Journal* 108 (September): 1330–61.

Chłoń-Domińczak, Agnieszka. 2017. "Gender Gap in Pensions: Looking Ahead." European Parliament, Brussels. http://www.europarl.europa.eu/thinktank/en/document .html?reference=IPOL_STU(2017)583150.

Chłoń-Domińczak, Agnieszka, Daniele Franco, and Edward Palmer. 2012. "The First Wave of NDC Reforms: The Experiences of Italy, Latvia, Poland, and Sweden." In *Nonfinancial Defined Contribution Pension Schemes in a Changing Pension World: Volume 1 Progress, Lessons, and Implementation*, edited by Robert Holzmann, Edward Palmer, and David Robalino, 31–84. Washington, DC: World Bank.

Davidoff, Thomas, Jeffrey R. Brown, and Peter A. Diamond. 2005. "Annuities and Welfare." *American Economic Review* 95 (5): 1573–90.

Diamond, Peter A., and James A. Mirrlees. 1971a. "Optimal Taxation and Public Production I: Production Efficiency." *American Economic Review* 61 (1): 8–27.

———. 1971b. "Optimal Taxation and Public Production II: Tax Rules." *American Economic Review* 61 (3): 261–78.

Financial Times. 2017. "Bringing Up Baby in the Office: Workplace Hybrids Ease the Transition from Home for Parents and Children." June 6. https://www.ft.com /content/00d51272-3ee2-11e7-82b6-896b95f30f58.

Goode, Jackie, Claire Callender, and Ruth Lister. 1996. *Purse or Wallet? Gender Inequalities and the Income Distribution within Families on Benefit*. London: Policy Studies Institute.

OECD (Organisation for Economic Co-operation and Development). 2015. *Pensions at a Glance 2015*. Paris: OECD Publishing.

———. 2017a. *Dare to Share: Germany's Experience Promoting Equal Partnership in Families*. Paris: OECD Publishing. https://read.oecd-ilibrary.org/social-issues-migration-health/dare -to-share-germany-s-experience-promoting-equal-partnership-in-families_9789264259157 -en#page1.

———. 2017b. *Pensions at a Glance 2017*. Paris: OECD Publishing.

———. 2017c. *Preventing Ageing Unequally*. Paris: OECD Publishing. https://read.oecd-ilibrary .org/employment/preventing-ageing-unequally_9789264279087-en#page1.

———. 2018. *Is the Last Mile the Longest? Economic Gains from Gender Equality in Nordic Countries*. Paris: OECD Publishing. https://read.oecd-ilibrary.org/social-issues-migration-health/is-the-last -mile-the-longest-economic-gains-from-gender-equality-in-nordic-countries_9789264300040 -en#page1.

Thaler, Richard H., and Shlomo Benartzi. 2004. "Save More Tomorrow: Using Behavioral Economics to Increase Employee Saving." *Journal of Political Economy* 112 (1, part 2): 164–87.

Thomsen, Jens, and Jens Verner Andersen. 2007. "Longevity Bonds—A Financial Market Instrument to Manage Longevity Risk." *Monetary Review*—4th Quarter: 29–44. http://www .oecd.org/finance/private-pensions/41668679.pdf.

CHAPTER 18

Drivers of the Gender Gap in Pensions: Evidence from EU-SILC and the OECD Pension Models

Maciej Lis and Boele Bonthuis[1]

Introduction

Women's pensions are significantly lower than those of men in the European Union (EU). On average, women's pensions were 27 percent lower across EU countries in 2013–14, according to the European Union Survey of Income and Living Conditions (EU-SILC).[2] Although this gender gap in pensions (GGP), observed in all EU countries, is narrowing in some countries, few signs indicate that it is doing so across the board.

The GGP is an important indicator of pension systems for at least three reasons. First, gender equality is an integral part of social policy (OECD 2012, 2016), and the GGP is an important indicator of gender equality in old age. Second, the GGP reveals the impact of broader labor market inequalities on pensions, given that women have lower employment rates, higher rates of part-time work, and lower wages in many countries. Finally, deconstructing the GGP into its various drivers can indicate future policy avenues for reducing gender inequality.

This chapter explores recent trends and drivers behind the GGP in Europe, focusing on countries with nonfinancial defined contribution (NDC) schemes: Italy, Latvia, Norway, Poland, and Sweden. Based on current gender gaps in the labor market, it relates the progressivity of pension systems, the coverage of child care–related periods, and other elements of pension systems to the GGP.

With an increasingly tight link between labor income and pensions in many pension systems, it is likely that the GGP will remain persistently high if the labor market position of women does not significantly improve. This should be especially evident in NDC schemes in which—at least theoretically—risk sharing among individuals is limited, compared with defined benefit (DB) schemes. Low or absent labor income should lead to low pensions, especially in the absence of survivors' pensions. The unfunded nature of NDC systems is irrelevant in that respect.

However, the chapter shows that countries with NDC schemes do not perform significantly worse as a group than other European countries in terms of pension outcomes for women. Nevertheless, countries with NDC schemes differ significantly from one another. Even when NDC sustainability rules are followed strictly, the choices of indexation of pensions in payment and survivors' pension options have a strong impact on gender inequalities that are mainly driven by the labor market.

Current pensions are affected by NDC rules to varying degrees. Latvia was the first country to fully implement an NDC scheme in 1996, and all people who retired after that year have had their pensions determined based on the NDC formula. Poland introduced an NDC scheme in 1999, but only cohorts born after 1949 are affected. Sweden's NDC scheme was also introduced in 1999, affecting fully only cohorts born from 1954 onward. Italy introduced an NDC scheme in 1996, but all past entitlements were honored; its NDC scheme started to partially affect new pensions as of 2011 and will only be fully effective after 2040. Norway's NDC scheme was introduced in 2011 and started to gradually affect new pensions as of 2016.

With regard to links between lifetime earnings and pension calculation, NDC rules are similar to those of point systems: higher earnings mean higher pensions, and past earnings are valorized with the average wage (with some sustainability factors in some countries); however, life expectancy does not directly affect the pension amount (unless indirectly affecting the sustainability factor). Such systems have been implemented since the 1990s in, among others, Croatia, Estonia, Germany, Lithuania, Romania, and the Slovak Republic.

The GGP captures the difference in monthly pension income, which is crucial for both poverty prevention and consumption smoothing. It misses the cumulative life-cycle dimension that could be captured by pension wealth or the rate of return to individual pension contributions. This is important, because women tend to live five years longer than men, on average, across the Organisation for Economic Co-operation and Development (OECD) countries (OECD 2017a). Longer lifespans of women, and therefore, potentially, longer periods of their claiming pensions make the GGP substantially higher than the gender gap in pension wealth. Although a full wealth analysis is beyond the scope of this chapter, the impact of gender longevity differences is discussed in the "Longevity Differences and the GGP" section.

Recent reports confirm the existence of a significant GGP in European countries (Bettio, Tinios, and Betti 2013; Burkevica et al. 2015; Flory 2012; Gardiner, Robinson, and Fakhfakh 2015; Grabka et al. 2017; Hänisch and Klos 2014; Lodovici et al. 2016; OECD 2012). Among them, three focus specifically on the pension gap in the EU. Bettio, Tinios, and Betti (2013) carried out a statistical analysis with the 2009 EU-SILC that showed that the EU-27 (excluding Croatia) weighted-average GGP is 39 percent. They also pointed out that short careers, which many women have, were associated with lower pensions. However, that relationship is not linear. The gender structure of employment matters; the lowest gender gaps were in the public sector, and the largest gaps were for the self-employed. Marital status also matters: the GGP was smaller for single women and widest for married women, with divorced women in the middle.

Burkevica et al. (2015) observed GGPs in 2012 similar to those found by Bettio, Tinios, and Betti (2013). Gaps in lifetime earnings were found to be among the main drivers behind the GGP. They also found that child care and other care activities could exacerbate the pension gap, particularly where child care was too expensive, of insufficient quality, not suitable, or not available.

Lodovici et al. (2016) found a weighted average EU-28 GGP of 40 percent in 2013 for the 65–74 age group. This gap is much higher than the average EU gender pay gap and the gender gap in annual earnings. The GGP has remained stable in the EU as a whole since the 2008–09 financial crisis; it was 40 percent in 2008. They also pointed out that the shift toward multipillar pension systems with a closer link between lifetime contributions and benefits means that pension entitlements are strongly related to career length. Accordingly, GGPs mirror gender gaps in employment, working years, part-time jobs, and pay.

Chłoń-Domińczak (2017) proposed a forward-looking indicator for the GGP. It includes three dimensions—career length, work intensity, and pension system features—in mitigating the effect of labor market differences. When the future indicator of the GGP is calculated, these three dimensions are weighted according to expert assessment of the risk that the selected indicators pose to the future gender pension gap. For example, the gender gap in employment is given a weight twice that of the gender pay gap or work intensity gap in all countries.

This chapter provides evidence of how each dimension of the gender gap in the labor market (hourly earnings, number of hours worked, and career length) and elements of the pension system (progressivity and coverage of child care, survivors' pensions, and indexation of pensions) affect the GGP separately and in interaction with each other. Because the GGP is simulated using labor market outcomes for various years, the direction of future changes in the GGP is also shown.

"Gender Gaps in Pensions—Current Values and Recent Trends" provides insights into the GGP distribution across European countries; "Labor Market Drivers of the GGP" explores the employment-related drivers behind the GGP and how they interact with pension systems, especially NDC designs. "Longevity Differences and the GGP" shows how gender longevity differences affect the GGP, particularly given the existing indexation of pensions and survivors' benefits.

Gender Gaps in Pensions—Current Values and Recent Trends

In the EU-28 in 2013–14, the GGP was 27 percent (see box 18.1 for the definition of the GGP; this is an unweighted average, which will be the case from here on unless specified otherwise). When the size of the population age 65 and older is taken into account, the weighted average increases to 34 percent. However, considerable heterogeneity arises at the country level. In 2014, the GGP stood at more than 40 percent in Cyprus, Germany, and the Netherlands; it was less than 10 percent in Denmark, Estonia, and the Slovak Republic (figure 18.1).

The reported value of the average GGP across the EU is significantly lower than that reported by other recent studies, which show an EU average of about 40 percent (Burkevica et al. 2015; Lodovici et al. 2016). However, the country-level estimates in these reports are very similar to the ones presented in this chapter. Country-level estimates from Burkevica et al. (2015) enable calculation of an average for the EU-28 when giving all countries equal weights, which stands at 27 percent. The value of

BOX 18.1 Measuring the GGP

The established definition of the gender gap in pensions (GGP) is used (Betti et al. 2013; Eurofound 2016):

$$GGP = 1 - \frac{women's\ average\ pension}{men's\ average\ pension}$$

The GGP is calculated with European Union Survey of Income and Living Conditions data. Four variables are added to calculate total individual pensions: public pensions (PY100G), private pensions (PY080G), survivors' benefits (PY110G), and disability benefits (PY130G). The GGP is calculated only for people age 65 and older who obtain at least one of the listed benefits. Excluding those without pensions follows the definition of the gender pay gap, which is calculated only among those working. Survivors' benefits are included in the pension gap, because they are an integral part of the pension system. Excluding survivors' pensions would ignore an important (individual) source of income, especially for older women, while other intrahousehold transfers are outside of the pension system.

The definition has two important features:

- First, only individual benefits are included, so first-tier pensions granted at the household level are not accounted for. In some countries basic pensions might also be excluded. Therefore, and given the lower employment rates among women, in some countries the computed GGP might be lower only because people who have not met the eligibility conditions for contributory pensions and receive safety net benefits are excluded from the calculation.

- Second, in contrast to other studies, disability pensions are added to pension income. This is done to ensure better cross-country comparability. In some countries, disability benefits are directly transformed into old-age benefits when reaching retirement age, whereas in others they are not.

The GGP can be measured across various parts of the pension distribution using positional statistics such as, for example, the median or quantiles. Thus, the GGP at quantile X is defined as follows:

$$GGP_{Dx} = 1 - \frac{X\ quantile\ of\ pension\ distribution\ among\ women}{X\ quantile\ of\ pension\ distribution\ among\ men}$$

40 percent for the EU-28 is obtained when the GGP is calculated from microdata the same way for the EU as a whole as for each country separately (Burkevica et al. 2015). Calculating it this way means that the richest and the most populous countries—such as France, Germany, and the United Kingdom, which incidentally also have the highest GGPs—boost the average. Moreover, the relative balance between men and women across countries matters for the final GGP. Such an average should not be

FIGURE 18.1 **Gender gap in pensions in European countries, 2003, 2007, and 2013**

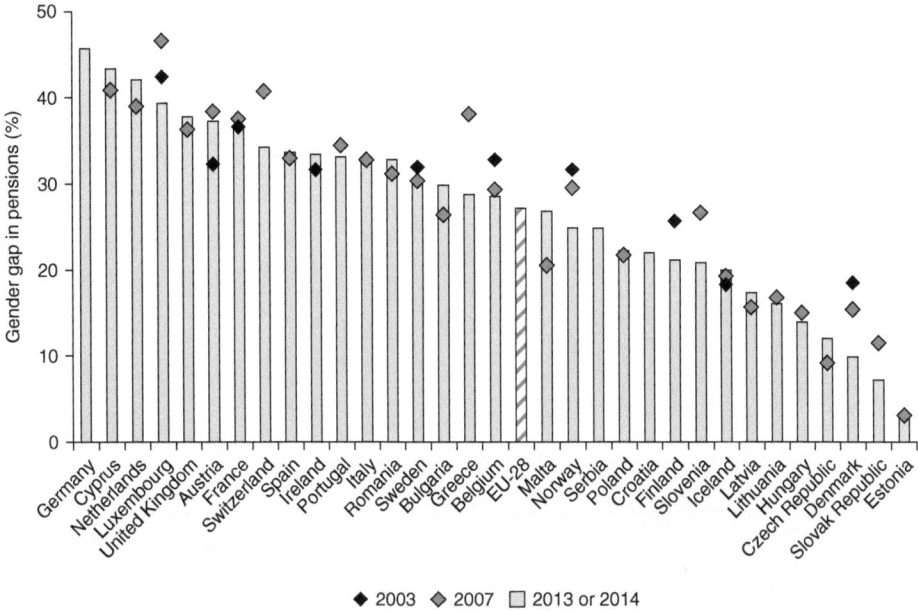

◆ 2003 ◆ 2007 ☐ 2013 or 2014

SOURCE: EU-SILC.

NOTE: The gender gap in pensions is calculated for persons age 65 and older. It includes persons who obtain an old-age benefit (public or private), a survivors' pension, or a disability benefit. Differences are expressed in percentage points (see box 18.1).

compared with the average estimates of gender wage gaps and gender pay gaps when they are weighted differently.

The GGP decreased only slightly in recent years across EU countries. On average, for the 26 EU countries for which data were available in 2007 (this excludes Croatia and Germany), the GGP decreased from 27.2 percent in 2007 to 26.6 percent in 2014. Recent reports also show a relatively stable GGP in the EU (Burkevica et al. 2015; Lodovici et al. 2016). Moreover, on average for the eight EU countries for which data were available in 2003, the pension gap decreased from 30.2 percent in 2003 to 28.2 percent in 2014.[3]

The GGP does not account for people who do not obtain any individual pension (box 18.1). In countries with noncontributory universal pension schemes, the whole population would receive a pension at old age, and no coverage gap would exist. By contrast, in countries where first-tier pensions include only means-tested social assistance granted at the household level, given their more limited attachment to the labor market, many women would not receive individual pensions, even though the safety net benefits might be generous. Survivors' pensions—in combination with the means-tested first-tier pensions—result in rising coverage with age, given that only after the death of a spouse would some people, mainly women, receive individual pensions. In 10 of 28 EU countries, the gap in incidence of obtaining no individual pension was larger than

FIGURE 18.2 **Gender gap in incidence of obtaining individual old-age pension in European countries, 2003, 2007, and 2013**

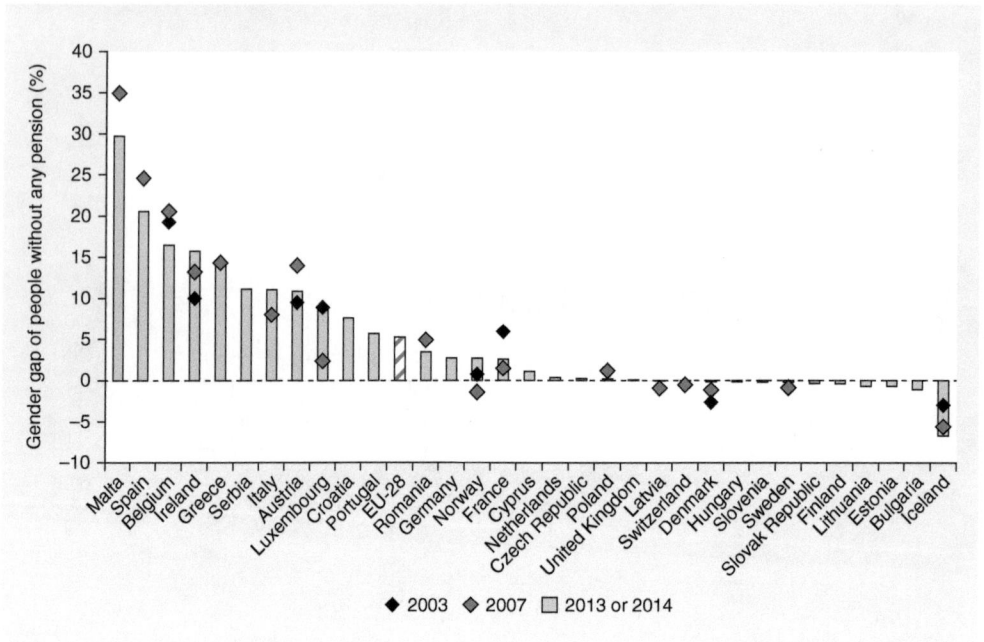

SOURCE: EU-SILC.

NOTE: The gender gap in incidence of obtaining individual pensions is calculated as the difference in shares of women and men not obtaining individual pensions.

5 percentage points, with Malta and Spain standing out at 30 and 21 percentage points, respectively (figure 18.2).

Labor Market Drivers of the GGP

Gender differences in the labor market have a profound effect on the GGP. Women are less likely to be employed than men; when they are employed, they earn less, work fewer hours, and have shorter careers, on average. These differences are mirrored in the GGP (Lodovici et al. 2016). The reform trend to pension systems with a stronger link between earnings and pensions has exacerbated the already weak pension position of many women (OECD 2015; Queisser, Whitehouse, and Whiteford 2007). However, rising women's participation rates have improved the pension prospects for many women.

EMPLOYMENT (INTENSIVE AND EXTENSIVE MARGINS)

The duration of working life is a crucial variable affecting the GGP. In Europe, women have shorter working lives than men, usually because of unpaid care activities (Lodovici et al. 2016).

The method of calculating the duration of employment and nonemployment spells is presented in box 18.2. The method is based on cross-sectional monthly data on main

BOX 18.2 **Duration of employment and nonemployment spells**

To calculate the gender gap in duration of specific spells, Eurostat's concept of duration of working life is used. The duration of working life is a theoretical measure and is based on the activity rate by age and mortality rates by age. Eurostat uses Labor Force Survey (LFS) data to calculate duration of working life. Here the method is modified to use more detailed European Union Survey of Income and Living Conditions variables on labor market status in each month of the year before the survey.

Similar to Eurostat, the average duration of a specific spell (*DS*) is based on the following concept:

$$DS = \sum_{i=15}^{70} ds_i \times S_i$$

in which ds_i is number of months spent in the specific state divided by 12 at age i and S_i is an age-specific survival function. All age profiles for ds_i were estimated with a nonparametric smoother. Based on the age- and gender-specific mortality (m_j), the survival function can be calculated:

$$S_i = \prod_{j=15}^{i} \left(1 - m_j\right).$$

All the statistics can be calculated for each gender separately. The SILC data on main activity in each month allow more accurate duration calculation than the one based on LFS data. Only data on main labor market status are available, so separate statuses are mutually exclusive.

economic status from EU-SILC. Following cross-sectional patterns from 2013, on average in EU countries, a woman at age 15 can expect to work 4.2 years less during her career compared with her male counterparts. In almost one-half of the countries, the gap is larger than three years. In Italy, the career length gap is about seven years (figure 18.2). By contrast, Latvia managed to entirely eliminate the gender gap in career length.

Men not only work more often but also work full-time more frequently. The gap in career length in full-time employment is, on average, almost one year longer than in total employment, reaching 4.9 years, on average, in EU countries. It exceeds 15 years in the Netherlands and Switzerland (figure 18.3). In many countries, women's increasing labor market participation mainly leads to more part-time employment rather than full-time employment.[4] The gender gap in part-time employment is negative in all EU countries. The more positive the gap in full-time employment, the more negative it is in part-time employment, with a linear correlation coefficient between the two of –0.85. The gap in the prevalence of self-employment adds to the total employment gap. In all countries, men are more likely to be self-employed, with an average gap of almost three years. Self-employment has a lower impact on the GGP than full-time employment, because in many countries, the self-employed contribute less to the pension system.

FIGURE 18.3 **Gender gap in average duration of employment spells for lifespans of 15–70 years in European countries, 2013**

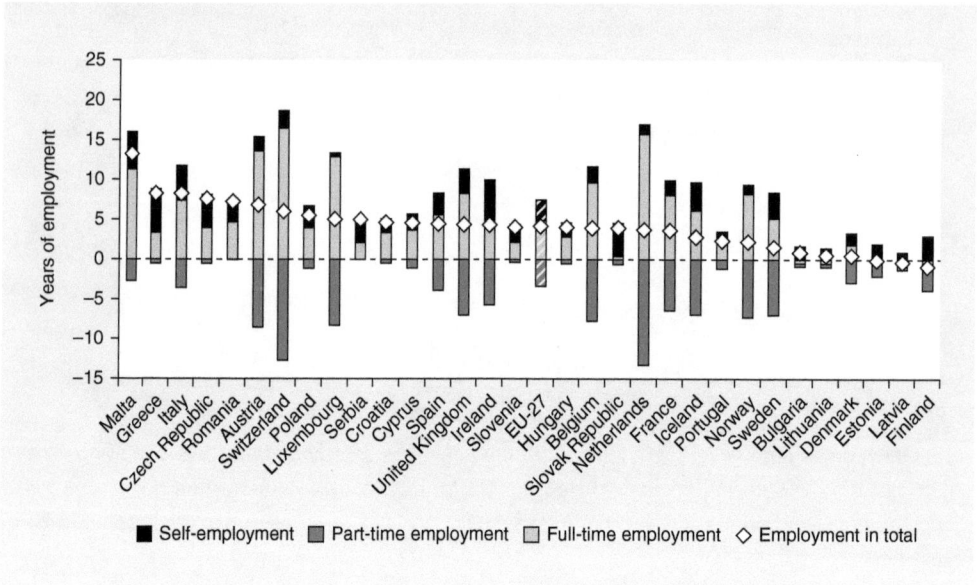

SOURCE: EU-SILC 2013.

NOTE: The gender gap in average duration of spells is calculated as the difference between men and women in the number of years expected to be spent in selected spells in their whole careers (box 18.2). Germany is excluded due to lack of data availability.

Periods of part-time employment in a person's career have a significant impact on the level of income in old age because these periods strongly influence career advancement and, more generally, lifetime earnings. Part-time work is often a consequence of family duties and inadequate child-care services (Lodovici et al. 2016). Women still perform the bulk of care activities, which leads to a much higher incidence of part-time work compared with men (OECD 2017c). In 2012, personal and family responsibilities were the reason for part-time employment of 44 percent of women across the EU-27, whereas only 11 percent of men listed these responsibilities as a reason (Burkevica et al. 2015).

Current data on main monthly economic activity imply that women at age 15 in EU countries can expect to spend, on average, 6.2 years more in nonemployment compared with men until they reach age 70 (figure 18.4). Almost the entire difference (5.1 years) comes from their engagement in domestic tasks and care activities. Retirement by age 70 is expected to last six months longer among women than men. Remaining nonemployment spells (unemployment, disability, and other inactivity) have together almost no impact on the gender differences, on average, in the EU. This lack of effect is because the average shorter duration of unemployment among women equals the longer duration of other inactivity spells. In their total careers, women are expected to spend 11 months less unemployed, on average, in EU countries.

FIGURE 18.4 **Gender gap in average duration of nonemployment spells for ages 15–70 in European countries, 2013**

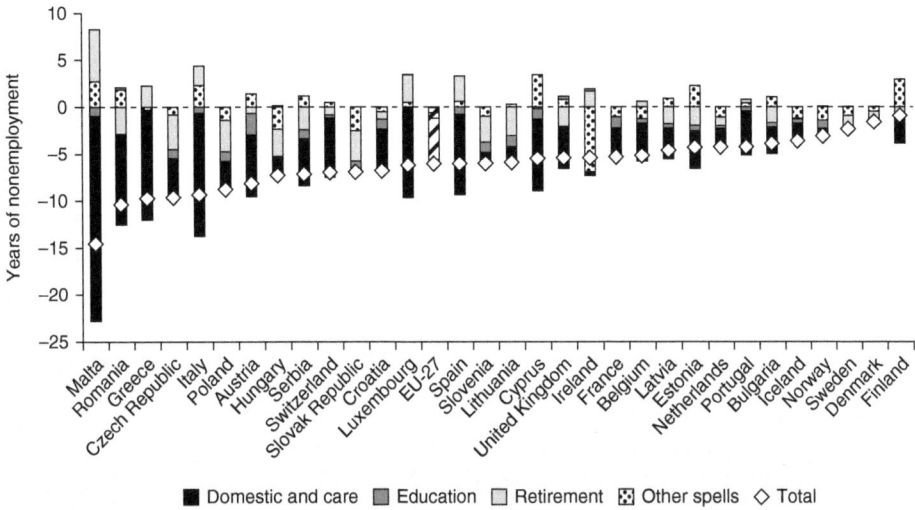

SOURCE: EU-SILC 2013.

NOTE: The gender gap in average duration of spells is calculated as the difference between men and women in the number of years expected to be spent in selected spells in the whole career (box 18.2). Germany is excluded due to data availability.

EARNINGS GAPS

A second key determinant of the GGP is the gender pay gap, that is, the difference in average hourly wages between men and women divided by the average hourly wage for men. The gender pay gap is 14 percent on average across EU countries; it varies from less than 10 percent in Belgium, Croatia, Italy, Luxembourg, Poland, Romania, and Slovenia, to more than 20 percent in Austria, the Czech Republic, Estonia, Germany, and the United Kingdom (figure 18.5).

The gender pay gap is generally much lower for new labor market entrants and tends to widen with age (OECD 2012). However, these differences among age groups can have different patterns across countries. The gender pay gap might increase with age as a result of the career interruptions that women experience. This is particularly the case for older women, who have benefited less from more recent policies promoting gender equality in the labor market (OECD 2012). Wages in the public sector, which are more compressed, generally lower the gender pay gap in all EU countries.

Women earn less because they are paid less for the same job but also because of sorting mechanisms. The latter include educational choices and later on occupational and sectoral choices. Women tend to work more often in education, human health, and social work activities (OECD 2017c). The concentration of women in specific

FIGURE 18.5 **Gender pay gap (unadjusted) in European countries, 2016 or latest available**

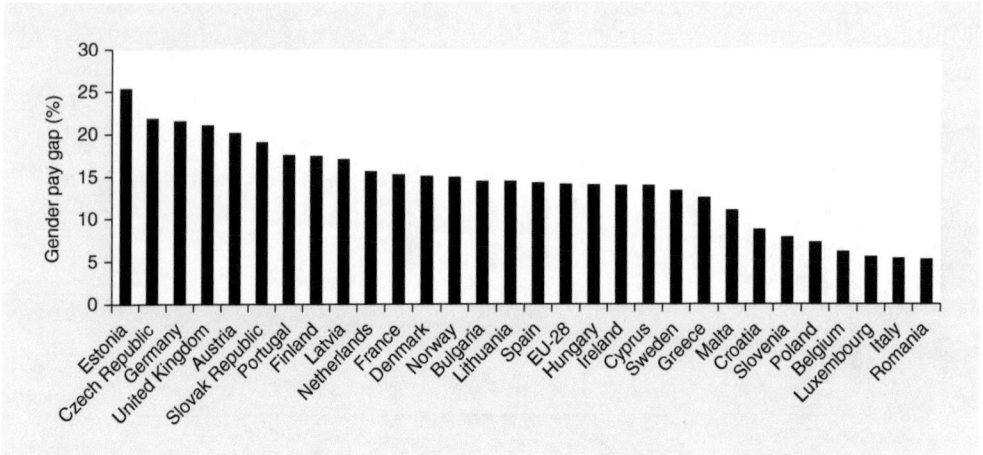

SOURCE: Eurostat.

NOTE: Eurostat defines the unadjusted gender pay gap as the difference in men's and women's average hourly wages divided by men's average hourly wage. The adjusted gap is calculated with regressions that account for observable individual characteristics such as age, education, and occupation and firm characteristics such as company size and economic sector.

sectors increased from 2008 to 2014 (Eurofound 2016), resulting in almost 30 percent of women working in female-dominated sectors in 2014, compared with only 8 percent of men working in these sectors. Wages in sectors dominated by women are typically lower than in other sectors. This sectoral gender gap partially explains the GGP (Grabka et al. 2017).

The gender gap in annual labor market earnings (which excludes people with no earnings) is wider than the gender pay gap. The pay gap measure only reflects differences in hourly wages, whereas annual earnings account for part-time employment, breaks in employment, and all types of labor contracts, including self-employment. The average gender gap in annual labor income in EU countries is 25 percent, compared with a 27 percent GGP. The gender gap in annual labor income varies from more than 40 percent in Austria and the Netherlands to less than 15 percent in Croatia, Romania, and Slovenia (figure 18.6).

The average gender gap in total labor earnings including individuals with zero earnings across EU countries is significantly higher, at 40 percent, than the average GGP of 27 percent in EU countries (excluding Germany, figure 18.7). Sweden has a substantially higher GGP than the gap in total labor earnings, whereas in Norway the GGP corresponds closely to the labor market gap. Current GGPs remain relatively low in Central and Eastern European countries partly because of labor market conditions that prevailed before the transition of these economies. In addition, redistributive elements in pension systems such as minimum, basic, and survivors' pensions; contribution ceilings; and recent increases in women's employment rates mitigate the labor market inequalities in later life.

FIGURE 18.6 **Gender gap in annual labor earnings in European countries, 2013 or 2014**

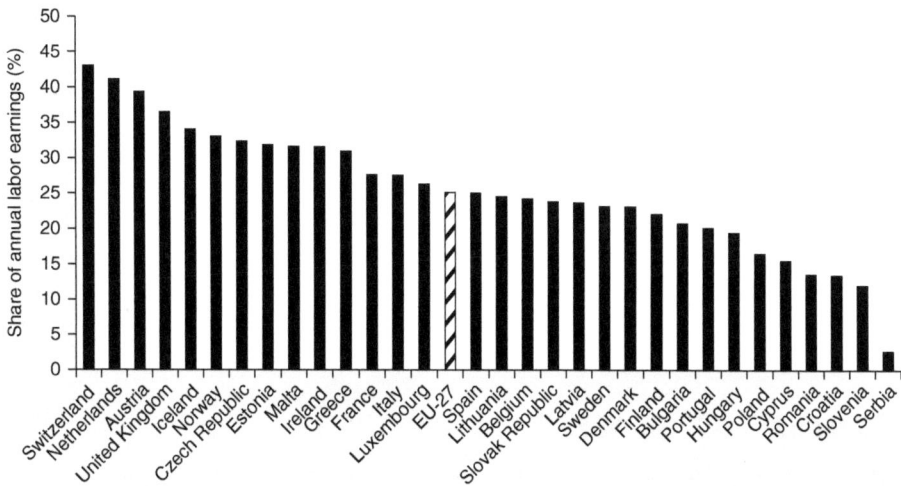

SOURCE: EU-SILC 2013, 2014.

NOTE: The gender gap in gross annual labor earnings is calculated for all labor income (dependent and self-employed). Persons with no labor income are excluded. Germany is excluded due to data availability.

FIGURE 18.7 **Gender gap in total labor earnings (including no earnings) and gender gap in pensions in European countries, 2013 or 2014**

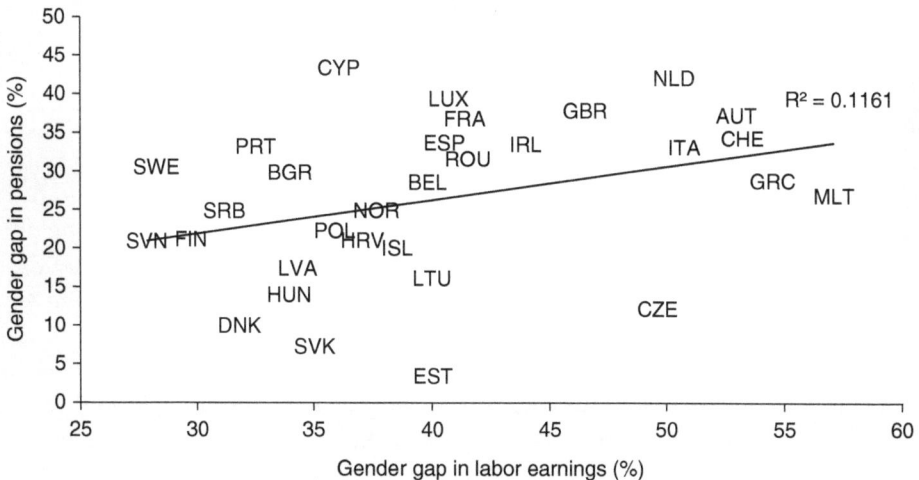

SOURCE: EU-SILC 2013, 2014.

NOTE: The gender gap in gross annual labor earnings is calculated for all labor income (dependent and self-employed). Persons with no labor income are included with zero earnings. Germany is excluded due to data availability.

The current gender gaps in total yearly labor earnings account for only 12 percent of the variation of the current GGP across countries (figure 18.7) for many reasons. First, inequalities in yearly earnings can only partially proxy cumulative lifetime earnings inequalities. Second, the labor market situation has changed across cohorts; currently, much higher employment rates of women are observed. Moreover, pension systems have changed substantially; for instance, links between labor market income and pensions have been strengthened, and retirement ages between men and women have been equalized. Additionally, the differences between pension systems are very significant. Countries differ with respect to redistributive elements of pension systems and the coverage of nonemployment spells related to care activities, mitigating the gender difference in labor market earnings. In countries such as Austria, Italy, and the Netherlands, high labor market inequalities coincide with high GGPs. Denmark, Estonia, the Czech Republic, and the Slovak Republic manage to achieve low levels of the GGP, even though gender gaps in total labor earnings remain high (figure 18.7).

LABOR MARKET DIFFERENCES IN NDC COUNTRIES

Judging purely from the overall GGP in countries, it is difficult to pinpoint the influence of the pension system on the outcome. Even though the Netherlands has a DB system, it has one of the highest GGPs. The Slovak Republic also has a DB scheme but a very low GGP. Like the Netherlands, Denmark has a funded system but a relatively low GGP. For the countries with NDC schemes, the GGP ranges from greater than 30 percent in Italy and Sweden to 20 percent and less in Latvia and Poland. Norway has a GGP in the middle at 25 percent. Since 2007, the GGP decreased in Norway; it remained stable in Italy and Sweden; and it increased in Poland and Latvia.

Therefore, the difference in design of the pension system between defined contribution (DC) and DB systems might have less of an influence on the GGP than labor market differences in combination with the strength of the link between pensions and labor earnings.

A closer look at these labor market differences for NDC countries shows that countries with NDC schemes differ in terms of drivers of employment gaps. Sweden and Norway managed to eliminate gender gaps in employment, in particular, those related to child care. Italy stands out as a country with very long breaks due to domestic and child-care tasks. In Poland, nonemployment is driven equally by domestic care and early retirement of women. In Latvia, the gap in average duration of nonemployment spells is five years less than the one for employment spells, partly because the life expectancy difference between Latvian men and women is one of the highest (more than five years).

Norway, Poland, and Sweden show important gaps in full-time employment and in self-employment. In Sweden and Norway, these gaps are almost fully offset by women working more often part-time. However, in Poland, part-time employment among women can only slightly decrease the total employment gap. Latvia has hardly any gap in either full- or part-time employment duration. Therefore, NDC schemes are represented along the full spectrum of employment gaps.

The (unadjusted; see note at figure 18.8) gender pay gaps in Latvia, Norway, and Sweden are around the EU average, at 17 percent, 15 percent, and 13 percent, respectively. Countries with NDC schemes still show various levels of gender gaps in annual labor

FIGURE 18.8 **Progressivity of mandatory and voluntary pension schemes in European countries**

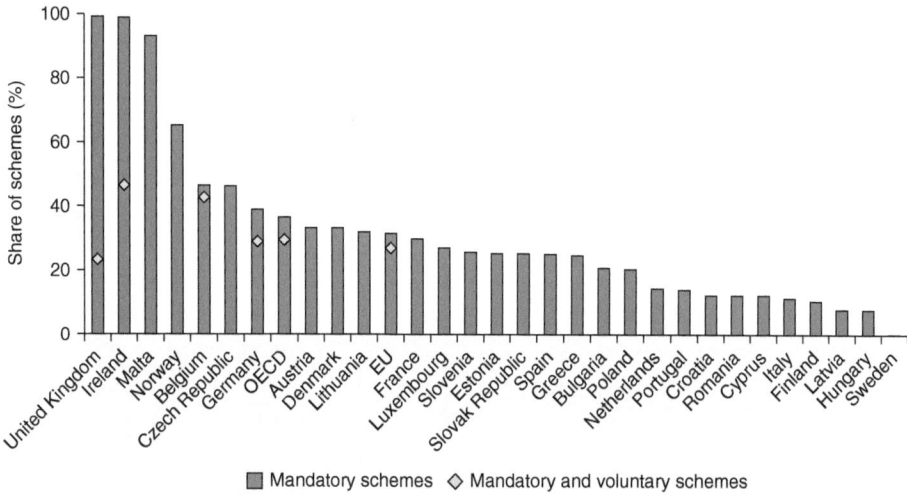

SOURCE: Calculations based on OECD 2017a, figure 4.15.

NOTE: The progressivity index is calculated as 1 minus the Gini coefficient of projected pension entitlements divided by the Gini coefficient of wages. The wage distribution is assumed constant across countries. It is first assumed that the distribution comprises people with zero, low (50 percent of average wage), average (100 percent), and high (200 percent) earnings over the entire working lifetime. It is further assumed that 15 percent of people have zero earnings and that the total earnings distribution generates a score of 0.35 on the Gini index. It follows that the shares of low earners, average earners, and high earners are 16.5 percent, 45.3 percent, and 23.3 percent, respectively. The index was recalculated based on the model results from OECD (2017b). Voluntary schemes are included for the countries where they are widespread: Belgium, Germany, Ireland, and the United Kingdom (OECD 2017a).

earnings, however, from 33 percent in Norway, 27 percent in Italy, 24 in Latvia, and 23 percent in Sweden, to 16 percent in Poland. This variety of labor market gaps among NDC countries leads to a variety of GGPs.

DECOMPOSITION OF THE LABOR MARKET DRIVERS OF THE GGP (THE PROGRESSIVITY OF REPLACEMENT RATES)

Labor market differences between men and women can be mitigated by a redistributive pension scheme. Although pure NDC schemes do not contain any redistributive elements, they interact with first-tier pensions (minimum and basic pensions or general safety nets). Additionally, NDC schemes often provide a contribution ceiling, resulting in lower replacement rates for high earners. On top of the progressivity of the pension system, earlier labor market exit of women, the coverage of nonemployment spells (for instance, child care), the indexation of pensions, and the generosity of survivors' pensions can all have a significant impact on the GGP.

Cumulative lifetime earnings inequalities are—to different degrees—mitigated by mandatory pension systems. All EU countries provide lower bounds of income for older people within the pension system (minimum and basic pensions) or outside the pension system (safety nets). Noncontributory old-age benefits (residency-based basic pensions and safety nets) vary from less than 15 percent of average earnings in Bulgaria, Croatia, the Czech Republic, Estonia, Hungary, Latvia, and Lithuania to greater than 25 percent in Austria, Belgium, Denmark, France, Greece, Ireland, Luxembourg, Malta, and the Netherlands. Minimum pensions or contribution-based basic pensions provide higher benefits. Countries with NDC schemes provide different solutions to first-tier pensions. Norway and Sweden provide basic pensions at 33 percent and 22 percent of average earnings, respectively. Poland and Latvia set full minimum pensions at 22 percent and 14 percent of average earnings, respectively, while Italy has a safety net benefit at 19 percent of average earnings.[5] On the other end of the spectrum, some countries provide upper bounds of benefits through ceilings on pensions or contributions in mandatory schemes. Belgium and France place a ceiling for public pensions on pensionable earnings slightly greater than average earnings; the ceiling is low in Norway at 115 percent of average earnings, and substantially higher in Poland at 250 percent; in Italy, Hungary, Latvia, and the Slovak Republic, the ceiling exceeds three times average earnings (OECD 2017a). The ceiling is low in Sweden at 105 percent of average earnings, but the increasing contributions to occupational DC plans make this ceiling less important for overall pension inequalities. Among NDC countries, the Norwegian system is therefore the most progressive, having high minimum benefits and a low effective ceiling on pensions from the public scheme; the Latvian system is the least progressive, with a very low level of first-tier benefits and a very high ceiling on mandatory contributions. Given the difference in labor market outcomes between men and women, these redistributive elements in the pension system also affect the GGP.

A progressivity index of pension schemes measures the transmission of the cumulative lifetime inequalities into pensions (OECD 2017b, 158). The index shows how a given level of inequalities of lifetime earnings affects pension inequalities, both measured by the Gini coefficient (see the note to figure 18.8). A value of 0 percent means that lifetime earnings are fully carried through to pensions on a one-to-one basis. Conversely, a value of 100 percent means that the pension scheme provides a flat benefit; therefore, earnings inequalities are not carried through to benefits at all. The progressivity index shows how lifetime earnings inequalities translate into pensions for earnings between zero (hence, relying fully on safety nets and basic pensions) and 200 percent of average earnings. However, it does not account for the impact of career breaks, for example, those related to child care.

Figure 18.8 shows that, on average, mandatory pensions systems reduce lifetime earnings inequalities by 37 percent in the OECD and by 32 percent in the EU. Although a generic NDC scheme would provide almost full transmission of labor income inequalities into pensions, the actually implemented ones appear at all parts of the distribution compared with the EU countries. Norway mitigates inequalities to a great extent, while Sweden does not at all (but this is rather due to the quasi-mandatory occupational plans than its NDC scheme per se). Italy, Latvia, and Poland show rather low levels of progressivity: their pension systems reduce earnings inequalities by less than 20 percent, partly because only a small fraction of the population shows earnings twice as high as average earnings, and the progressivity index is not affected by ceilings on pensionable earnings being twice as high as average earnings.

The progressivity of pension systems affects the transmission of lifelong cumulative gender earnings inequalities into pensions. Merging the future OECD pension model with actual cross-sectional data on average earnings by age and gender approximates the GGP stemming from current labor market gaps in combination with the pension rules for someone starting a career in 2016. In particular, it allows simulating the NDC rules. Box 18.3 discusses technical details of the procedure, whereas figure 18.9 presents the simulated GGP compared with the actually observed ones. If a country is below the 45-degree line, it means that the simulated GGP is lower than the actual one and vice versa.

BOX 18.3 **Simulating and decomposing the GGP**

Gender gaps in pensions (GGPs) are simulated for persons who start their careers in 2016 at age 20 and retire at the normal retirement age, based on average earnings by age and gender at a given year using European Union Survey of Income and Living Conditions microdata. Average earnings account for earnings for dependent employment and self-employment, as well as employment probabilities, that is, people not working are included with zero earnings when the average is calculated. The average age-earnings profiles from 2013 are shown in figure B18.3.1. The profiles are calculated in a given year and should not be interpreted as a projection for any cohort but rather as an average for the cohorts. On top of age effects (earnings profiles), real earnings are projected to increase at 1.25 percent a year (OECD 2017a).

Based on these earnings profiles, the first pension received at the normal retirement age is then calculated for each gender separately. This simplified approach does not account fully for the impact of shorter careers of women, the impact on eligibility conditions, child-care credits,

FIGURE B18.3.1 **Average total annual earnings profile relative to average earnings for men and women**

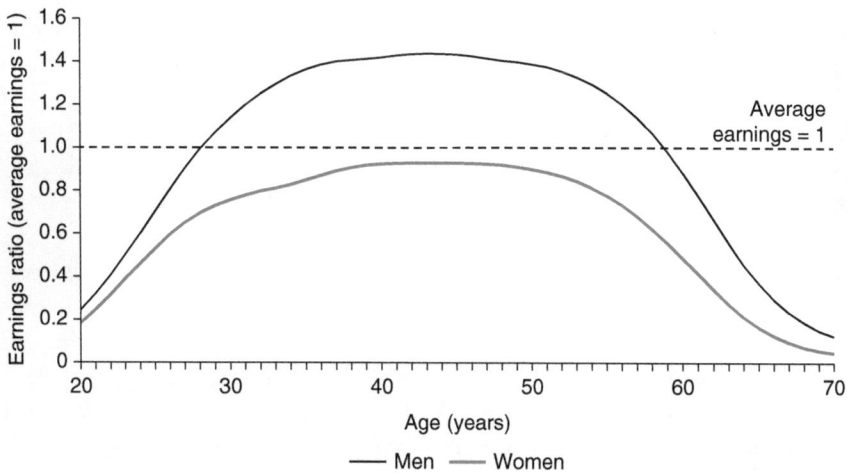

SOURCE: EU-SILC 2014.

(continues next page)

BOX 18.3 **Simulating and decomposing the GGP (continued)**

indexation of pensions, and survivors' pensions, but it provides important insights into the role of the labor market–related determinants of the GGP; it also makes it possible to check how current labor market developments would transmit to the GGP in the future. The voluntary schemes are used only in the countries where they are widespread (OECD 2017a); it is assumed that both men and women participate in the schemes.

The decomposition of the simulated GGP shows how the gender gaps in hourly wages, numbers of hours worked, and employment probabilities affect the simulated GGP separately in each country. The average yearly earnings E at a given age a for each gender g are a product of hourly earnings w, number of hours worked per worker h, and employment probabilities e at year t:

$$E_{a,g}^t = w_{a,g}^t \times h_{a,g}^t \times e_{a,g}^t$$

The role of each contribution factor (hourly earnings, hours worked, and employment probability) in the simulated GGP is quantified in the following way. First, the pension of a woman is calculated using the gender-specific earnings, hours, and employment profiles. Then, one by one, each factor is substituted for by the values for men. The reduction in the GGP indicates the contribution of that factor to the overall simulated gap. Because only one factor is substituted at a time, the interaction between them is not accounted for.

The simulated GGPs differ from the currently observed ones but the correlation between the two at 32 percent is substantially higher than the 12 percent correlation between lifetime earnings and pensions. This shows that despite the limitations of approximation (including lack of cohort effects), the simulated GGPs reasonably mirror the cross-country variation. Also, the average level of the simulated GGPs at 30 percent across the EU-27 comes close to the observed 26 percent GGP.

The discrepancies between the two are meaningful because they show the impact of elements of the systems not included in the simulations, as well as the role of recent developments in the labor market (cohort effects) and in the pension system. First, many countries provide pension credits based on factors other than earnings (child care, unemployment, residency, derived pension rights) that lower the GGP. Second, in the Czech Republic, Estonia, Hungary, Latvia, Poland, and the Slovak Republic, the simulated GGPs are higher than the actual ones. In the past, benefits were less tightly linked to lifetime earnings, while women's labor participation was higher in some Central and Eastern European countries. In particular, the NDC schemes introduced in Latvia in 1996 and Poland in 1999 are examples of such policies. As a consequence, some countries with low current GGPs (less than 20 percent) might expect strong increases in the future.

The looser relationship between benefits and lifetime earnings in the past would also explain the higher simulated GGPs in Austria, Italy, and Spain, even though women's labor market participation has been increasing in these countries. Italy is gradually

FIGURE 18.9 **Simulated gender gaps in pensions and actually observed ones in European countries**

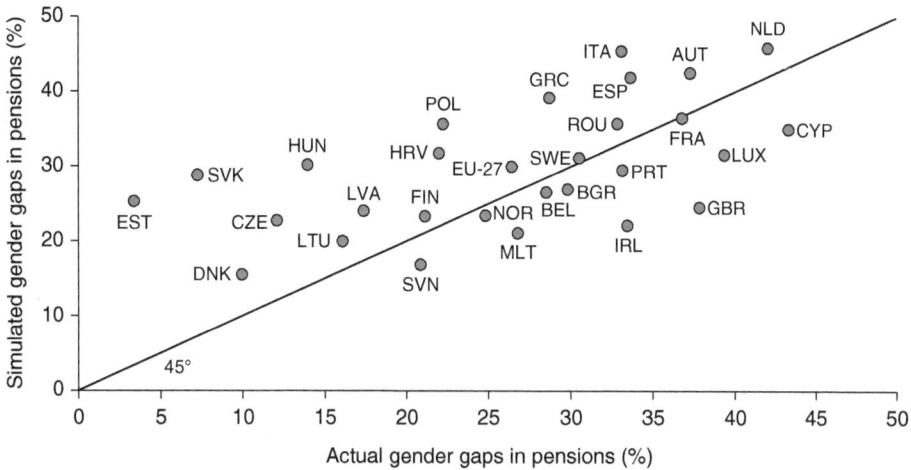

SOURCE: OECD pension model.

moving from a pay-as-you-go DB pension system to an NDC system; in Spain and Austria, the benefit calculation takes into account a larger share of the career than in the past. In contrast, the simulated GGP is lower in, among others, Ireland and the United Kingdom, where the public pension is mainly a flat benefit. Before 2016 in the United Kingdom, mandatory pensions included an earnings-related component (SSA 2002–16; Bozio, Crawford, and Tetlow 2010). Leaving high redistributive elements in the Norwegian NDC means that moving to an NDC scheme is not expected to affect the GGP substantially. By contrast, introduction of an NDC scheme in Italy is expected to substantially increase its GGP.

The simulated GGP allows the impact of labor market developments on GGPs to be isolated because the pension rules remain fixed for all simulations. Because of data availability, labor market developments can be tracked back to 2007 for most countries and to 2003 for a few of them. The simulated GGP, which does not account for cohort differences but only for the changes in employment and earnings by age and gender, declined almost everywhere between 2007 and 2013, by 5 percentage points on average for 23 EU countries (figure 18.10, panel a). The decrease was substantial in Italy, Latvia, and Sweden but much less in countries in which labor markets were less affected by the financial crisis, namely, Norway and Poland. This decline is related not only to increasing employment among women, but also to a decrease of employment rates among men following the financial crisis. In Spain, the employment rate among men decreased from 77 percent in 2007 to 60 percent in 2013; for women, it only decreased from 55 percent to 52 percent, which led to a decrease in the simulated GGP of 15 percentage points. These changes were strongly linked to the cyclical movement of the labor market; the long-run trends are expected to be slower. Before the global financial crisis, between 2003 and 2007 employment rates were rising in many countries, but the simulated GGP hardly

FIGURE 18.10 **Dynamics of simulated gender gaps in pensions in European countries, 2003–13**

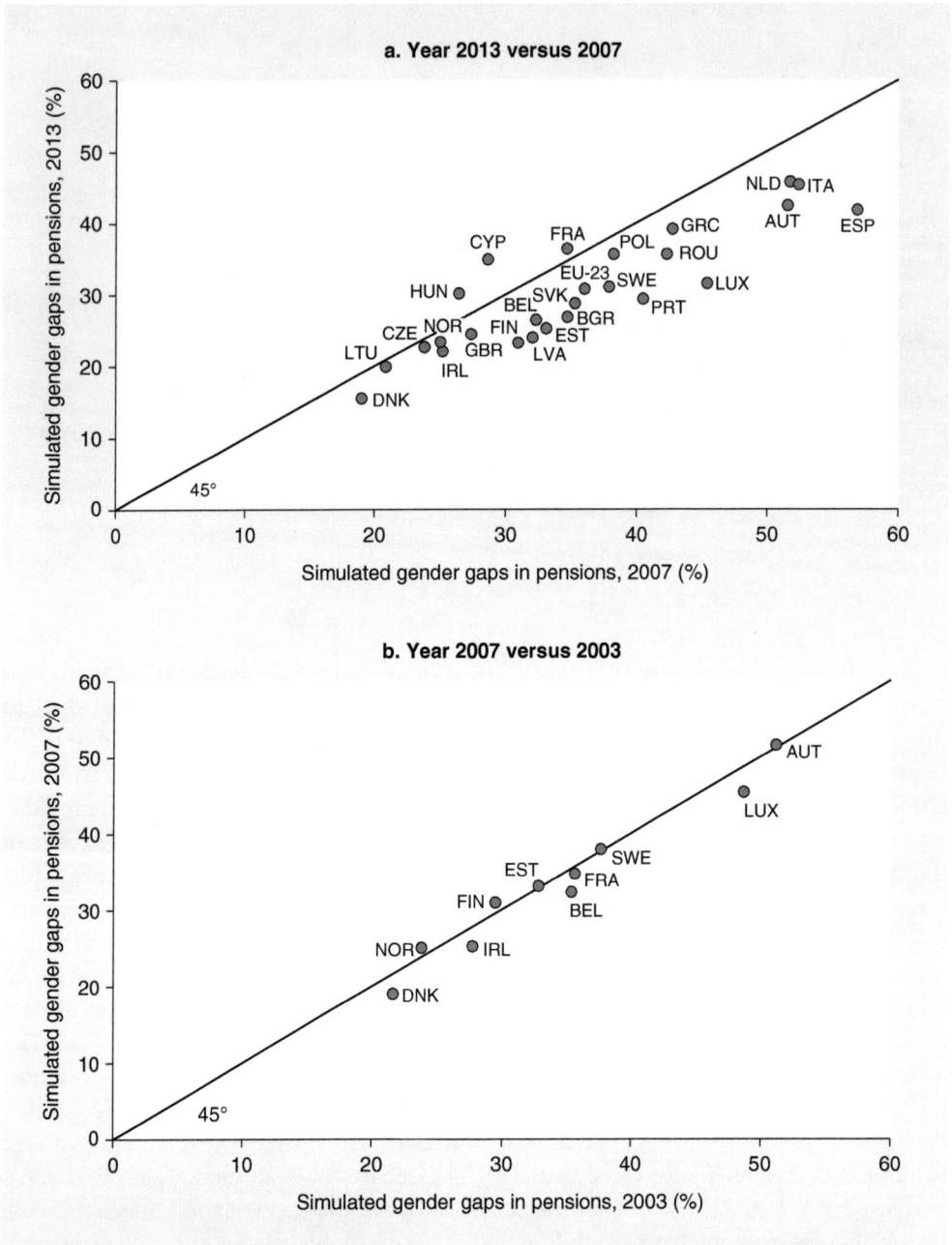

a. Year 2013 versus 2007

b. Year 2007 versus 2003

SOURCES: OECD pension model; and EU-SILC.

changed (figure 18.10, panel b). Therefore, the reduction in the GGP might not be as fast as implied by labor market developments during the crisis.

The separate effects of different drivers in lifetime earnings on the GGP—wage gaps, hours worked, and employment rates—can be quantified using the simulations (box 18.3). First, eliminating the gender gap in hourly wages alone would reduce the GGP

FIGURE 18.11 **Decomposition of the simulated gender gap in pensions in European countries**

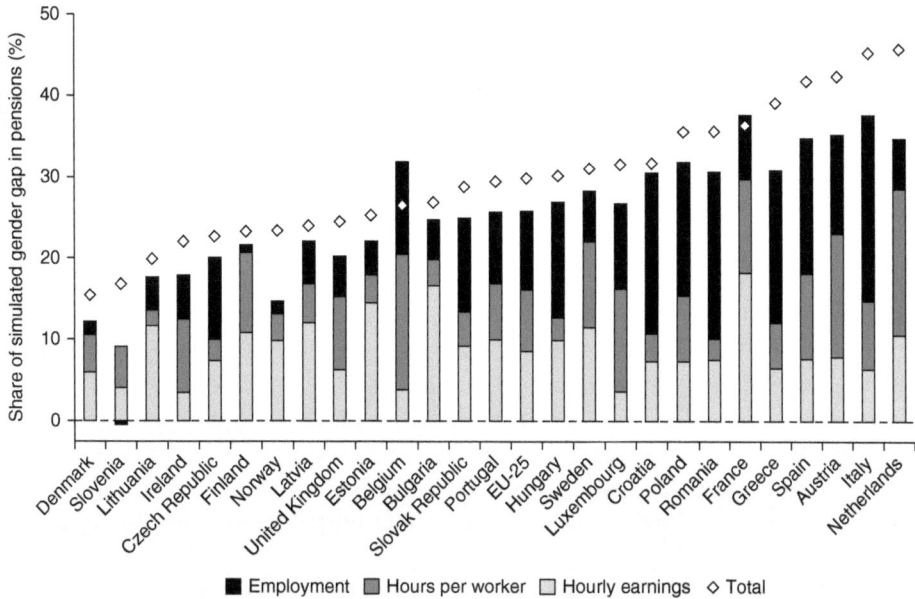

SOURCES: OECD pension model, and EU-SILC 2014.

by 9 percentage points, on average, and by more than 10 percentage points in Bulgaria, Estonia, France, Latvia, Lithuania, and Sweden (figure 18.11). Coudin, Mailard, and Tô (2018) find that the high gender gap in hourly wages in France stems from a strong segregation of women to firms with low earnings. Second, in turn, eliminating the gap in working hours would lead to an average reduction of 7 percentage points and more than 10 percentage points in Austria, Belgium, France, the Netherlands, Spain, and Sweden. Third, eliminating the gap in employment rates would decrease the GGP by 10 percentage points, on average, and by more than that in Austria, Belgium, Croatia, the Czech Republic, Greece, Hungary, Italy, Luxembourg, Poland, Romania, the Slovak Republic, and Spain. The countries with NDC schemes differ significantly in terms of the drivers of earnings gender inequalities: they are mainly employment in Italy and Poland, mainly hourly wages in Norway and Latvia, and mainly hourly earnings and number of hours worked in Sweden.

The three factors—hourly wages, hours worked, and employment rates—can be strongly related; hence, closing the gender gap in one dimension might help close it in others as well. In many occupations, such as lawyers, longer working hours result in higher hourly wages, while working part-time is often linked with a penalty in terms of hourly wages. Work experience results in pay increases from the accumulation of firm-specific human capital or tenure-based pay policies. As a result, groups with lower employment rates are likely to face lower hourly wages. Finally, part-time workers are often the first to be dismissed, and shorter working hours lower employment probabilities.

A substantial part of the simulated GGP is not explained by the three contributing factors because pension systems are not linear, and the interaction between the factors is not accounted for. In countries with large basic pension components or with progressive replacement rates—such as Greece, Luxembourg, the Netherlands, Norway, and Slovenia—closing all labor market gaps brings stronger results than adding the effects of closing them separately. In contrast, the contribution factors explain more than the full gap in Belgium and France, where low ceilings for pensionable income lower average pensions of men and make it possible to equalize pensions without fully equalizing earnings.

ROLE OF CHILD-CARE CREDITS

Child care and time spent fulfilling domestic tasks are the main reasons for lower employment rates among women in many EU countries (figure 18.4). On average for the EU-27, women spend 5.2 years during their lifetimes on child care and domestic tasks, which is 4.9 years more than men. The average duration of child care as the main activity varies among countries: it is less than 1 year in Denmark, Ireland, the Slovak Republic, and Sweden but more than 10 years in Greece, Italy, Luxembourg, and Malta. Countries with NDC schemes are therefore represented at both tails of the duration of child care–related career breaks.

All EU countries provide some pension entitlements for such periods. In France, Germany, Italy, and Spain, pension bonuses are granted for having a child and are independent of the actual length of the child-care break. In France and Germany, these bonuses are equivalent to two and three years of individual annual earnings for each child, respectively. Italy lowers the actuarial factor for mothers and increases the final pension by about 3 percent, whereas Spain grants a direct bonus that increases with the number of children: 5 percent, 10 percent, and 15 percent for having two, three, and four or more children, respectively. The bonuses in these countries outbalance the effect of lost earnings from short career breaks. For a one-year break, the pensions are even higher than in the case of having no break and not having children (figure 18.12). Moreover, in countries with DB schemes in which shorter periods than the full career are used to calculate the final pension, short and early career breaks might not affect pension entitlements at all if careers are long enough at the time of retirement. As a result, having two children and not working for five years increases pension amounts in France and Spain even compared with someone working full time.

In countries with high residence-based basic pensions (for example, Ireland, the Netherlands, Norway, and the United Kingdom), career breaks have no impact on this component of benefits. Still, private pensions in these countries widen the GGP. A break of five years results in a decrease of about 6–7 percent in pensions in these countries.

Some countries, including those with NDC schemes, grant pension credits in the form of paid pension contributions related to individual earnings, economy-wide minimum earnings, or economy-wide average earnings during maternity, paternity, and parental leave (Latvia, Norway, Poland, and Sweden). The duration of coverage varies among countries. For example, Norway and Sweden provide coverage until children reach ages six and four, respectively. Poland also provides coverage until children reach the age four,

FIGURE 18.12 **Child care–related career breaks of 1, 5, and 10 years and pension amounts in European countries**

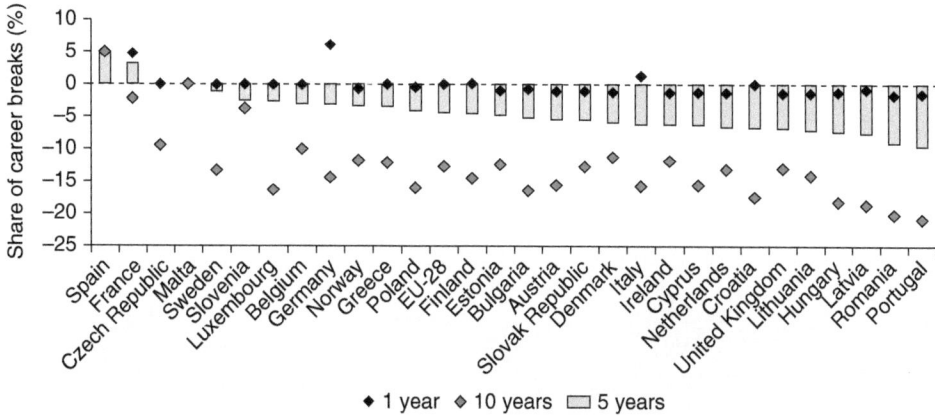

SOURCE: OECD pension model.

NOTE: Pensions for full and incomplete careers are calculated for a woman earning 90 percent of average earnings, starting a career at age 20, and retiring at the future normal retirement age. In the incomplete career case, a woman gives birth at age 30 and 32, and the career break starts at age 30 and takes 1, 5, or 10 years.

but after one year the contribution declines to 60 percent of previous earnings with a ceiling of less than the economy-wide average wage. In Latvia, only one-and-a-half years of child care are covered by pension credits. As a result, a five-year career break for child care results in a pension decrease of 1 percent in Sweden, 3 percent in Norway, 4 percent in Poland, and 8 percent in Latvia.

The actual impact of child care career breaks on the GGP depends on both the pension coverage of these spells and on their actual length. Figure 18.13 shows how the simulated GGP (figure 18.10) changes when pension credits for child care are accounted for and what the simulated GGP would be if women did not experience career breaks related to child care or domestic tasks.

Child-care credits lower the GGP substantially in a few countries (figure 18.13). When these credits are included, the simulated GGP drops from 30 percent to 27 percent on average across 25 EU countries. It is almost exactly the actual GGP observed in the data at the EU level (figure 18.1). Pension credits reduce the simulated GGP by more than 4 percentage points in Austria, Bulgaria, the Czech Republic, Estonia, and France. By contrast, the credits do not change the simulated GGP in the Netherlands and the United Kingdom, where basic pensions are independent of child-care periods. Average career breaks of less than two years in Denmark, Hungary, Ireland, Norway, the Slovak Republic, Slovenia, and Sweden result in the limited role of existing pension credits: they lower the simulated GGP by less than 2 percentage points.

Child-care credits cover the employment gap only partially. If all career breaks resulted in the same pension entitlements as employment at average earnings for women, the simulated GGP would drop further from 27 percent to 20 percent. In particular, it would drop by more than 20 percentage points in Italy, Romania, and Spain. By contrast,

FIGURE 18.13 **Pension credits for child care and the simulated gender gap in pensions**

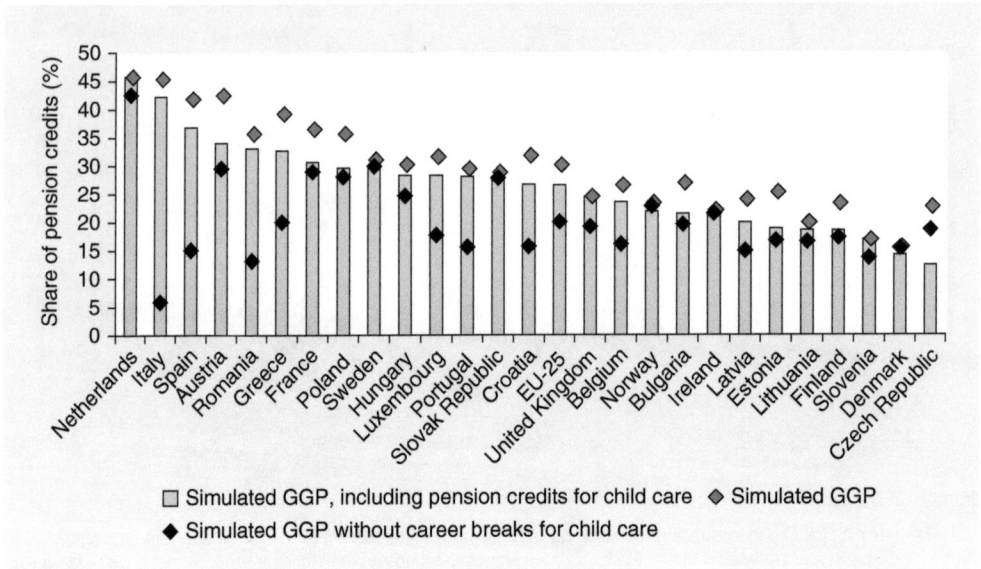

SOURCES: OECD pension model; and EU-SILC 2014.

NOTE: The simulated GGP without career breaks is calculated as if women worked and earned their average wage instead of child-care spells. The impact of child-care spells is modeled as a pension reduction to the full career case due to child-care break of length equal to the average duration of child-care spell. Germany, Cyprus, and Malta are excluded due to data availability. GGP = gender gap in pensions.

the gap would increase in France because of the lost bonuses for having children. Short breaks of less than two years and wide coverage in countries like Denmark, Ireland, Norway, the Slovak Republic, and Sweden leave hardly any pension gap resulting from child care, whereas in the Czech Republic the average actual career break for child care of five years is fully covered by pension credits.

After having children, women's employment and earnings diminish permanently; therefore, child care–related breaks have long-lasting consequences for lifetime earnings that go way beyond the lost earnings and contributions from child care itself. Kleven, Landais, and Søgaard (2018) show that earnings and employment rates are similar for men and women until a child is born, but they start to diverge afterward, and the gap increases with time. Indeed, employment and earnings of women without children are much higher than those of mothers. Therefore, while child-care credits can compensate for even a few years of career break, they do not compensate for lower earnings and employment possibilities after the break.

The coverage of other spells such as unemployment would have a much smaller impact on the simulated GGP. On average among 27 EU countries, other spells than those related to child care and domestic tasks add only one year to the nonemployment difference between men and women (figure 18.4). Moreover, because of lower labor market participation, the total duration of unemployment spells over the life cycle is even lower for women than for men.

FIGURE 18.14 **Gender differences in life expectancy at age 65 in European countries, 2016**

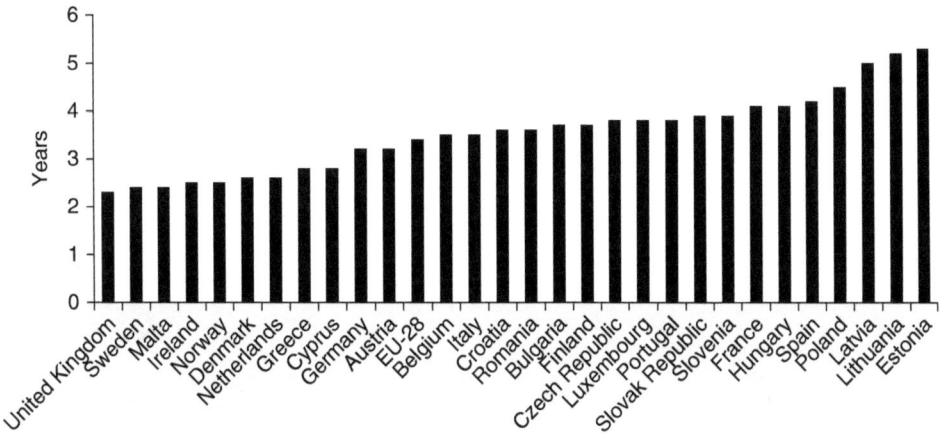

SOURCE: Eurostat.

NOTE: Women have higher life expectancy than men.

Longevity Differences and the GGP

LONGEVITY DIFFERENCES

Life-expectancy differences have a significant influence on the GGP. Women live 3.4 years longer than men after age 65, on average, among EU countries. In Italy, the difference is close to the EU average; it varies from more than 4.5 years in Estonia, Latvia, Lithuania, and Poland to less than 2.5 years in Ireland, Norway, Malta, Sweden, and the United Kingdom (figure 18.14). The indexation of pensions, the use of unisex life expectancy for benefit calculations, and the prevalence of survivors' pensions have an effect on the GGP through differences in life expectancy.

The differences in life expectancy result in higher shares of women at older age groups. In all EU countries, the share of women among those younger than age 65 is about 50 percent; on average, this share increases to 58 percent among those age 65 and older and to 69 percent among those age 85 and older. Women constitute more than 75 percent in the oldest age group in Estonia, Latvia, and Lithuania but less than 65 percent in Cyprus, Greece, and the United Kingdom (figure 18.15). Poland's ratio is higher than the EU average, Italy's is about the average, and Sweden's and Norway's ratios are substantially less than the average.

INDEXATION AND SURVIVORS' PENSIONS

In many countries, pensions are indexed to prices (Italy among the NDC countries) or a combination of prices and wages, wage bill, or GDP growth (Poland and Latvia). In both Norway and Sweden, pensions are indexed to wages, but a fixed percentage is deducted in exchange for a more favorable initial pension amount. Because wages and GDP typically

FIGURE 18.15 **Share of women in the total population, by age, in European countries, 2017**

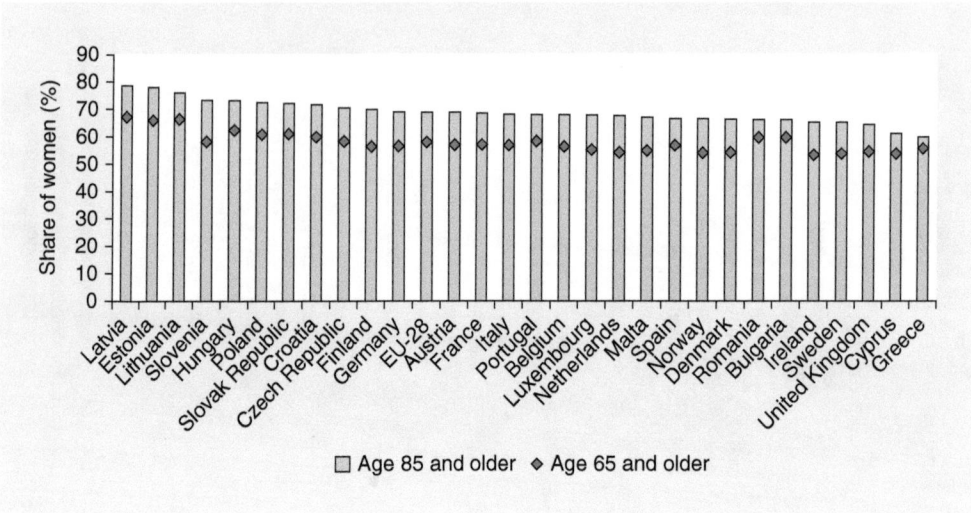

□ Age 85 and older   ◆ Age 65 and older

SOURCE: Eurostat.

grow faster than prices, the older people get, the lower their pensions will be, compared with the average wage but also compared with the pensions of younger cohorts. A larger part of these older pensioners is women; as a result, more front-loaded indexation of pensions exacerbates the GGP.

Similar to private DC annuities, when an NDC annuity is calculated, the initial pension level depends on how the benefits are indexed when being paid. In the base case, the nonfinancial capital is divided by the unisex life expectancy, and pensions in payment are indexed to the internal rate of return, which, according to the NDC design, should be changes in the wage bill. However, Italy, Norway, and Sweden choose to grant a higher pension in the beginning but index the pensions less favorably. Norway and Sweden decrease the indexation of pensions by 0.75 and 1.60 percentage points, respectively, and increase the initial pension level accordingly. Italy, by contrast, indexes pensions only to prices, while increasing initial pensions by including a discount factor of 1.5 percent in the calculation. By contrast, Latvia and Poland calculate initial pensions as if they were indexed with the wage bill, but then they index pensions less favorably. These countries therefore exacerbate the GGP.

In contrast, in some European countries, unisex life expectancy is used to calculate initial pensions, and life expectancy does not affect the pension level at all (as in most DB schemes). Not accounting for gender-specific life expectancy lowers the GGP.

Marital status has a large impact on the GGP. The pensions of married women are lower, on average, than those who are divorced, separated, or widowed. Compared with the average pension of men age 65 and older, the GGP is highest for married women, at 36 percent, whereas it is lower for divorced and separated women at 26 percent (figure 18.16). The GGP is even lower for widows at 20 percent and the lowest for never-married women at 15 percent.[6] Among the countries with NDC schemes, Italy shows the highest gap for married women, which is, however, reduced

FIGURE 18.16 **Gender gap in pensions by marital status in European countries, 2013**

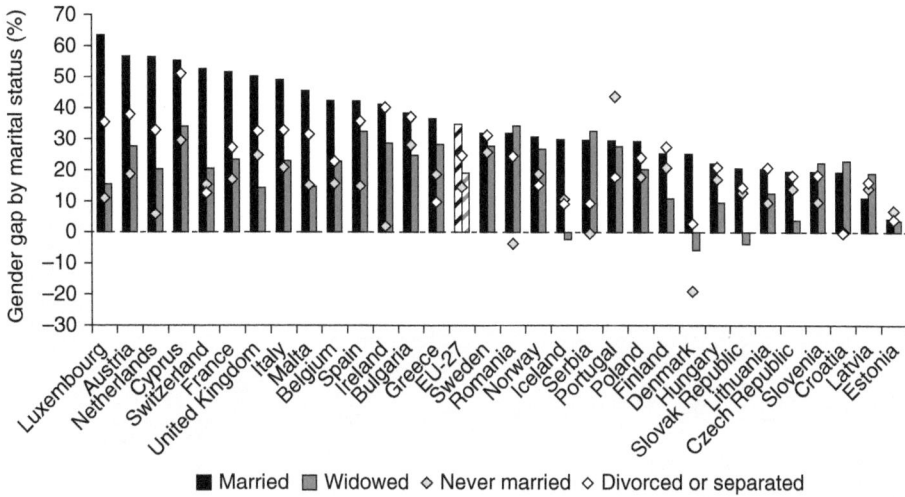

SOURCE: EU SILC.

NOTE: Women's pension by marital status is compared to the average pension of all men. Germany is excluded due to data availability.

substantially for widows. In Norway, Poland, and Sweden, widows' pensions are substantially higher than those of married women but are lower in Latvia, where no survivors' pensions are available.

Many opposing forces influence the link between marital status and the GGP. On the one hand, never-married women are typically more attached to the labor market. On the other hand, they are not granted any survivors' pensions. Marital status is also an important determinant for the probability of working full-time versus part-time; not being married is associated with a higher probability of working full-time (OECD 2016). Married women are less attached to the labor market, in part because of care activities; in some countries, however, they are granted pension credits for child care. Moreover, widows are granted survivors' pensions in most countries.

Married female pensioners may be entitled to a proportion of their partners' pensions in the event of their deaths. Survivors' benefits play an important role in averting poverty among widows and widowers and are likely to lower the GGP.

Most beneficiaries of survivors' allowances are women, given their longer life expectancy and the fact that they are generally the younger partner in couples. Large differences arise in the prevalence of survivors' benefits in general. In the United Kingdom, for instance, only 1 percent of female pensioners receive survivors' benefits (figure 18.17). In Estonia, Latvia, and the Netherlands, fewer than 5 percent of women receive survivors' pensions.[7] In Luxembourg and Spain, however, more than one-half of female pensioners receive a survivors' benefit; in Cyprus, Hungary, and Italy almost one-half of them do. On average, 30 percent of female pensioners receive survivors' benefits, compared with only 6 percent of men.

FIGURE 18.17 **Share of European pensioners receiving survivors' benefits, by gender, 2015**

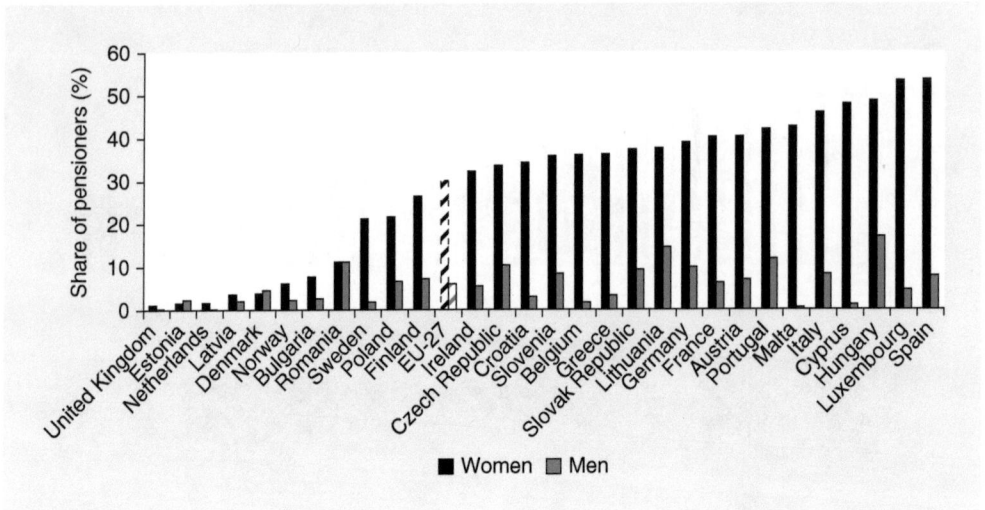

SOURCE: Eurostat.

As with the other elements of pension systems in European countries, no consistent approach exists to the rules governing allowances for survivors. In most countries, they are built into DB pension systems, which, whether funded or pay-as-you-go, constitute an element of transferal following a spouse's death. They supplement the individual pension that the surviving spouse already receives. In DB schemes, survivors commonly receive a proportion of their deceased spouse's entitlement. In both Estonia and Finland, for example, that proportion is 50 percent of the earnings-related component; in Belgium, it is 80 percent.

However, benefits are often capped, with payment dependent on the survivor's own earnings-related pension or reduced over time (James 2009). Moreover, in many DB schemes, neither contributions nor benefits depend on whether a survivors' pension might have to be paid. Survivors' pensions often redistribute from singles to couples (especially single-earner couples), from working women to nonworking women, from couples with slight age differences to couples with wide age differences, from divorcees to nondivorcees, and from low- to high-income families (James 2009).

Some NDC countries also provide survivors' benefits. In Italy, survivors' pensions are built into the NDC framework and are accounted for when the annuity factors are calculated. In Latvia, Norway, and Sweden, survivors' pensions for spouses are excluded from the NDC scheme. In Norway and Sweden, they are still granted as a previously acquired entitlement. In Poland, survivors' benefits function as in a DB scheme without affecting the actuarial factor in the pension formula.

Apart from the survivors' benefit option, many DC schemes offer the option to take out retirement savings as a lump sum. Orlova, Rutledge, and Wu (2015) find that taking out a cash lump sum heightens the risk of falling into poverty. Similarly, not opting for a joint-and-survivor annuity considerably increases the surviving spouse's risk of poverty. The recent switch to DC pension systems with a greater choice of survivors' pension options has thus increased the potential risk of old-age poverty among widows and widowers in DC schemes.[8]

Conclusions

Pensions of women are substantially lower than those of men, by 27 percent, on average, across the EU but by more than 40 percent in a few European countries. This average gap is higher than the one for hourly earnings at 14 percent, but it is substantially lower than the one for total yearly labor earnings at 40 percent. In none of the countries with NDC schemes were all current pensions granted according to the NDC rules; in all, a transition is taking place. Latvia, Poland, and Sweden are more advanced, while only Italy and Norway are partially affected by the NDC. These countries show various levels of the GGP: 33 percent in Italy, 31 percent in Sweden, 25 percent in Norway, 20 percent in Poland, and 17 percent in Latvia.

The main driver of the GGP stems from gender differences in the labor market. Current gender labor statistics by age suggest that women work 4.9 years less than men in full-time jobs, on average across EU countries, and 2.6 years less in self-employment. However, they work 3.3 years more in part-time employment. Women work less because they spend 5.1 years more on care activities between ages 15 and 70, but also 0.6 of a year more in education and 0.5 of a year more in retirement. Moreover, women more often work in lower-paid jobs; even when they work in similar positions as men, they face lower wages and fewer promotion opportunities. As a result, they earn on average 15 percent less per hour than men across the EU. These three factors—employment, hours worked, and wages—contribute at similar magnitudes to the GGP at the EU level, but their relative role varies substantially among countries. In terms of labor market characteristics, countries are more similar to regional peers than to other countries with NDC schemes: Latvia and Poland show features similar to those of other Central and Eastern European countries, Italy to the Southern European countries and to Spain in particular, and Sweden and Norway to other Northern European countries.

Gender gaps in hourly pay and part-time employment remained stable over the recent decade, while employment gaps decreased in many countries. These changes have been affecting pensions slowly. However, in some Central and Eastern European countries with very low GGPs, labor market gaps increased in the past 30 years, and so the GGP might increase in these countries in the future. Moreover, the financial crisis affected the employment of men more than that of women. The subsequent economic recovery is expected to at least partially restore gender inequalities in labor earnings in many countries.

Pension systems manage to reduce cumulative labor earnings inequalities to a different extent in EU countries, but the current labor market gaps are still expected to create substantial GGPs. First-tier pensions, progressivity of pension replacement rates, child-care pension credits, and survivors' pensions mitigate labor market gender gaps, but they are not sufficient to eliminate them. Pension systems cannot simply solve the gender gaps resulting from cumulative labor market inequalities. In particular, some countries manage to almost entirely eliminate the impact of employment breaks due to child care; however, the long-lasting effects of career breaks, such as shorter working hours and wage gaps, are not eliminated with compensation measures in the pension systems. Moreover, because women live longer, their average pensions are affected more heavily by less favorable indexation. There are two women for every man among those age 85 and older in EU countries, on average. Finally, survivors' pensions substantially improve the income of widows in some countries and therefore reduce the GGP.

NDC pension formulas by themselves do not reduce earnings inequalities, in particular, gender gaps in employment or wages. However, minimum and basic pensions, as well as contribution ceilings and child-care credits, can substantially reduce the GGP, even more strongly than DB schemes can, as is the case for Norway. Some features in existing NDC schemes worsen gender gaps, however, because women live longer on average, namely, the lack of joint annuities as a mandatory, default, or even available option; and the higher initial amount of pensions instead of more favorable indexation of benefits. Survivors' pensions for spouses are included in the NDC scheme only in Italy; in other countries they are either being abolished (Latvia, Norway, and Sweden) or they exist outside of the NDC design (Poland). This is unnecessary because survivors' benefits can be sustainably embedded within NDC schemes.

Notes

1. The opinions and arguments expressed herein are those of the authors and do not necessarily reflect the official views of the OECD or its member countries. This document was produced with the financial assistance of the European Union. The views expressed herein can in no way be taken to reflect the official opinion of the European Union. The authors are grateful to Hervé Boulhol, Monika Queisser, two referees, and the editors for comments and suggestions.

2. This is an unweighted average. Similarly, all averages calculated for EU countries are unweighted.

3. Austria, Belgium, Denmark, Finland, France, Ireland, Luxembourg, and Sweden.

4. The overall significant gap in the share of part-time employment between women and men at 16 percentage points in 2017, on average, across EU countries is one of the main drivers of gender gaps in lifetime earnings and thus also of the GGP.

5. Italy also has a minimum pension, but it will not apply to pensions granted purely from the NDC scheme.

6. Bettio, Tinios, and Betti (2013) confirm the smaller gender gap for single women compared with married women, with divorced women somewhere in the middle. However, even for single women the gap remains wide.

7. The low share of survivors' benefits in Latvia stems from the absence of survivors' benefits for spouses (it exists for children). In Sweden, survivors' pensions in the public scheme are being abolished.

8. Whether women are more likely to take their pension as a lump sum is not entirely clear. On the one hand, women are typically more risk averse than men (Borghans et al. 2009), which would lead to a lower prevalence of lump-sum taking among women. On the other hand, retirement savings are often lower for women than for men and smaller amounts of retirement savings are more often taken as lump sum. Which effect dominates is not entirely clear.

References

Bettio, Francesca, Platon Tinios, and Gianni Betti. 2013. "The Gender Gap in Pensions in the EU." European Institute for Gender Equality, Rome, Italy.

Borghans, Lex, Bart Golsteyn, James Joseph Heckman, and Huub Meijers. 2009. "Gender Differences in Risk Aversion and Ambiguity Aversion." *Journal of the European Economic Association* 7 (2–3): 649–58.

Bozio, Antoine, Rowena Crawford, and Gemma Tetlow. 2010. "The History of State Pensions in the UK: 1948 to 2010." Institute for Fiscal Studies, London.

Burkevica, Ilze, Anne Laure Humbert, Nicole Oetke, and Merle Paats. 2015. "Gender Gap in Pensions in the EU." European Institute for Gender Equality Research Note to the Latvian Presidency, Vilnius, Lithuania.

Chłoń-Domińczak, Agnieszka. 2017. "Gender Gap in Pensions: Looking Ahead." European Parliament, Brussels.

Coudin, Elise, Sophie Maillard, and Maxime Tô. 2018. "Family, Firms and the Gender Wage Gap in France." Working Paper18/01, Institute for Fiscal Studies, London.

Eurofound. 2016. "The Gender Employment Gap: Challenges and Solutions." Publications Office of the European Union, Luxembourg.

Flory, Judith. 2012. "The Gender Pension Gap: Developing an Indicator Measuring Fair Income Opportunities for Women and Men." Study, Federal Ministry for Family Affairs, Senior Citizens, Women and Youth, Berlin.

Gardiner, Jean, Andrew Robinson, and Fathi Fakhfakh. 2015. "Exploring the Private Pension Gender Gap and Occupation in Later Working Life." *Work, Employment and Society* 30 (4): 687–707.

Grabka, Markus, Björn Jotzo, Anika Rasner, and Christian Westermeier. 2017. "Der Gender Pension Gap verstärkt die Einkommensungleichheit von Männern und Frauen im Rentenalter." Report Volume 5, DIW, Berlin.

Hänisch, Carsten, and Jonas Klos. 2014. "A Decomposition Analysis of the German Gender Pension Gap." Discussion Paper 2014–04, Wilfried-Guth-Stiftungsprofessur für Ordnungs- und Wettbewerbspolitik, Universität Freiburg, Freiburg.

James, Estelle. 2009. "Rethinking Survivor Benefits." Social Protection and Labor Discussion Paper 928, World Bank, Washington, DC.

Kleven, Henrik, Camille Landais, and Jakob Egholt Søgaard. 2018. "Children and Gender Inequality: Evidence from Denmark." Working Paper 24219, National Bureau of Economic Research, Cambridge, MA.

Lodovici, Manuela Samek, Serena Drufuca, Monica Patrizio, and Flavia Pesce. 2016. "The Gender Pension Gap: Differences between Mothers and Women without Children." European Parliament Study for the FEMM Committee, Luxembourg.

OECD (Organisation for Economic Co-operation and Development). 2012. *Closing the Gender Gap—Act Now.* Paris: OECD Publishing.

———. 2015. *Pensions at Glance 2015.* Paris: OECD Publishing.

———. 2016. *Dare to Share: Germany's Experience Promoting Equal Partnership in Families.* Paris: OECD Publishing.

———. 2017a. *Pensions at a Glance.* Paris: OECD Publishing.

———. 2017b. *Preventing Ageing Unequally.* Paris: OECD Publishing.

———. 2017c. *Report on the Implementation of the OECD Gender Recommendations—Some Progress on Gender Equality but Much Left to Do.* Paris: OECD Publishing.

———. 2018. *OECD Reviews of Pension Systems: Latvia.* Paris: OECD Publishing.

Orlova, Natalia, Matthew Rutledge, and April Yanyuan Wu. 2015. "The Transition from Defined Benefit to Defined Contribution Pensions: Does It Influence Elderly Poverty?" Working Paper 17, Center for Retirement Research at Boston College, Boston, MA.

Queisser, Monika, Edward Whitehouse, and Peter Whiteford. 2007. "The Public-Private Pension Mix in OECD Countries." *Industrial Relations Journal* 38 (6): 542–68.

SSA (Social Security Administration). 2002–2016. "Social Security Programs throughout the World." SSA, Washington, DC. https://www.ssa.gov/policy/docs/progdesc/ssptw/.

CHAPTER 19

The Impact of Lifetime Events on Pensions: Nonfinancial Defined Contribution Schemes in Poland, Italy, and Sweden, and the Point Scheme in Germany

Agnieszka Chłoń-Domińczak, Marek Góra, Irena E. Kotowska,
Iga Magda, Anna Ruzik-Sierdzińska, and Paweł Strzelecki

Introduction

The pension system and the labor market are two sides of the same coin. In prepaid pension systems, contributions paid by workers matter for their future pensions.[1] In the case of nonfinancial and financial defined contribution (NDC and FDC) systems, the link between contributions and benefits is close. In other types of pension systems, such as nonfinancial and financial defined benefit (NDB and FDB) schemes, the link to contributions is partial and depends on the benefit formula design and the insureds' perceptions of contributions as quasi-taxes.[2] In tax-financed, typically flat-rate pensions, such as social pensions, no link exists between contributions and pension benefits at the individual level. The lack of a direct individual link between contributions and pensions can lead to efficiency losses, weaker incentives to prolong working life, and increased exposure of the pension system to political pressure. If the link is individualized, lifetime developments have a direct impact on future pension levels.

Pension wealth losses caused by interrupted or broken careers lead to lower expected benefits in all types of pension systems. For example, according to OECD (2015) estimates, women from Organisation for Economic Co-operation and Development (OECD) countries who earn the average wage and interrupt their career for five years to care for two young children would lose, on average, 4 percent of their pension income. In two of the analyzed countries, this difference is much higher: Germany stands out, with the steepest decline in pension entitlements at 11 percent; in Italy, it amounts to 10 percent (OECD 2015). There is a need for flexible interventions in the labor market to reduce risks from leaving jobs for extended periods. Such policy measures are highly relevant in pension systems that have a close link between contributions and benefits, such as NDC schemes.

The authors acknowledge the research support from the statutory research of the SGH Warsaw School of Economics. Iga Magda also acknowledges the support of the Polish National Science Centre (Grant No. 2013/10 / E / HS4 / 00445). The authors represent the Polish Pension Group (SGH-PPG) and are grateful to reviewers for comments and suggestions.

This chapter investigates how different employment patterns over a life course affect expected pension levels. It analyzes three countries that have implemented NDC systems—Italy, Poland, and Sweden—as well as Germany, which has a point system that also provides a direct link between lifetime wages and pension levels.

The four countries differ with respect to the design of their pension systems,[3] but more importantly, their labor market characteristics differ. They have different employment rates and wage levels in general and for specific groups of workers. In particular, employment rates and wages between men and women differ substantially between the four countries. In all countries, men usually work longer than women and have higher wages. However, the majority of the comparative studies to date have focused on the expected outcomes of pension systems, simulated using similar assumptions about working careers (such as *Pensions at a Glance* reports [OECD 2015] or *Pension Adequacy Reports* [European Commission 2018]).

This chapter analyzes how different developments in the working lives of men and women in the four countries affect their potential pension incomes. In particular, it answers two sets of questions. The first set focuses on labor market characteristics and covers the following questions:

- How do employment rates, wages, and labor incomes differ for men and women of different ages?
- What are the differences and similarities in the working histories of workers in the four countries?
- What are the patterns of full and interrupted careers for men and women in the four countries?

The second set refers to pension system outcomes:

- How do different patterns of working histories affect expected levels of pensions under NDC and point systems?
- Can people with similar life course developments expect similar outcomes in terms of pensions in different countries?
- How do pension levels differ among countries as a result of pension system design, life expectancy, or labor market characteristics?
- Do interrupted careers lead to a higher risk of old-age poverty? How does this relationship differ across countries?

The first section of this chapter provides evidence of current labor market developments, with a particular focus on the differences between men and women by age. It looks at the gender gap in pay and employment and their changes after 2000, making use of data from the Labor Force Survey (LFS) and European Structure of Earnings Survey. The stylized life course labor incomes of men and women are compared using the National Transfer Accounts (NTA) profiles for European countries (Istenic and Sambt 2016). Then, the employment histories collected in the Survey of Health, Ageing and Retirement in Europe (SHARE) are used to identify groups of workers with "interrupted" and "full" careers.

The second section applies the stylized labor market profiles to simulate hypothetical future pensions (HFPs) in the four countries, based on the identified sex-specific employment patterns; this assesses the level of pensions considering the country- and gender-specific profiles of employment over the life courses of individuals. To separate the impact of differences in the labor market and differences in the pension system on hypothetical pensions, country-specific employment profiles and the Swedish pension system are used to calculate hypothetical pensions.

The final section concludes with recommendations on integrated policies, focusing on policies supporting both a high level and a high quality of employment over the life courses of individuals as key to ensuring adequate pensions in the NDC framework.

Labor Market Differences: What Can Be Learned from Recent Developments?

Many factors contribute to differences in labor market participation and wages between men and women. These include, most importantly, choices of nonstandard employment, including part-time employment or self-employment. Women choose these forms more frequently than men to reconcile their work and family lives, which can be more difficult in some countries than in others. These choices have implications for pension levels once the women retire. This section discusses the evidence related to the gender gap in the labor market and its accumulated impact on life course labor income. Accordingly, the focus is on both employment and wage gaps, as well as their impact on the difference in life course earnings by men and women. Typical profiles of full and interrupted labor market careers of men and women in the four countries are identified; these profiles reflect the differences observed at the macro level, using labor market histories of individuals gathered in the SHARELIFE survey.

LABOR MARKET PARTICIPATION

Labor market participation, which is crucial for future old-age pension entitlement in defined contribution (DC) systems, differs significantly among the four countries. Sweden experienced the highest increases in the labor force participation rate (LFPR) for both men and women in past decades. Participation rates have steadily increased since 2000, reaching 89 percent for men and 84 percent for women in the 20–64 age group in 2016. The German labor market is characterized by an equally high and stable LFPR for men (86.5 percent), but a much lower rate for women (77 percent in 2016). Yet women's labor market participation also increased—between 2000 and 2016, it rose by 11 percentage points.

In Italy and Poland, the LFPR of 20–64-year-old men slowly increased, reaching about 80 percent in 2016 in both countries. Labor market participation is lower for women (59 percent in Italy and 66 percent in Poland). As a result, the gap between the LFPR of men and women is highest in these two countries, particularly in Italy (figure 19.1). The difference in the LFPR of men and women has declined in Italy since 2000, which may indicate gradually changing patterns of economic activity. The German labor market reveals a similar development. In Poland, the gender gap in employment remains stable.

The employment rate in age groups 50 and older increased between 2002, 2010, and 2016 in all studied countries, particularly in Germany, Italy, and Sweden (figure 19.2). In Italy, the employment rate declined for those in the prime age group. Older workers survived the last economic crisis relatively well; in some aspects, they were in a better situation in 2016 compared with the years before 2007.

The Italian labor market has nearly come back to its precrisis employment level, which is still relatively low, especially for women. However, it struggles with a high share

FIGURE 19.1 **The gap between men's and women's labor force participation rates, ages 20–64, 2002–16**

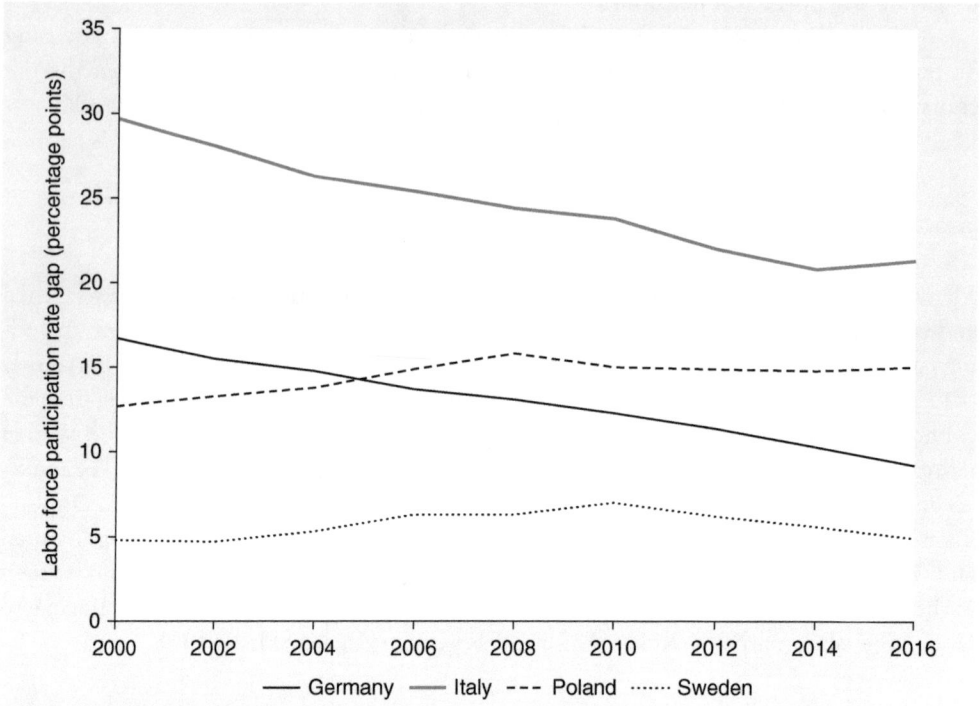

SOURCE: Eurostat database.

of nonstandard contracts, such as "employer coordinated freelance work" (*Contratto di Collaborazione Coordinata e Continuativa, co.co.co*), "project work" (*Contratto di Collaborazione a Progetto, co.co.pro*), and self-employment, which can also lead to lower levels of access to social protection (Spasova et al. 2017). Swedish employment rates for both sexes stabilized at a high level. Employment rates in Germany are at a high level as well. Despite an increase in employment of people older than age 50, the women's employment rate in Poland is the lowest among all four countries. With the exception of Italy, where women work on average less than men at any age, employment rates between sexes differ mainly at older age groups.

The level of education influences employment as well as the gender gap in employment. The highest difference between men's and women's employment rates is among those with the lowest level of formal education. It is particularly high but declining in Italy. In Poland, a rising employment gap is observed between men and women with less than tertiary education. In Germany, the gender gap in employment by educational attainment is declining. In Sweden, virtually no differences exist in employment rates of men and women with tertiary education. With the rising share of highly educated women in the population, the total gender gap in employment is expected to decline in all countries (figure 19.3).

The high employment rates of women in Germany and Sweden are partly due to higher part-time work shares (figure 19.4). Part-time employment in Italy has been rising for more than a decade. Marginal part-time work (less than 20 hours a week) is relatively

FIGURE 19.2 **Employment rates, by age group, gender, and country, 2002, 2010, and 2016**

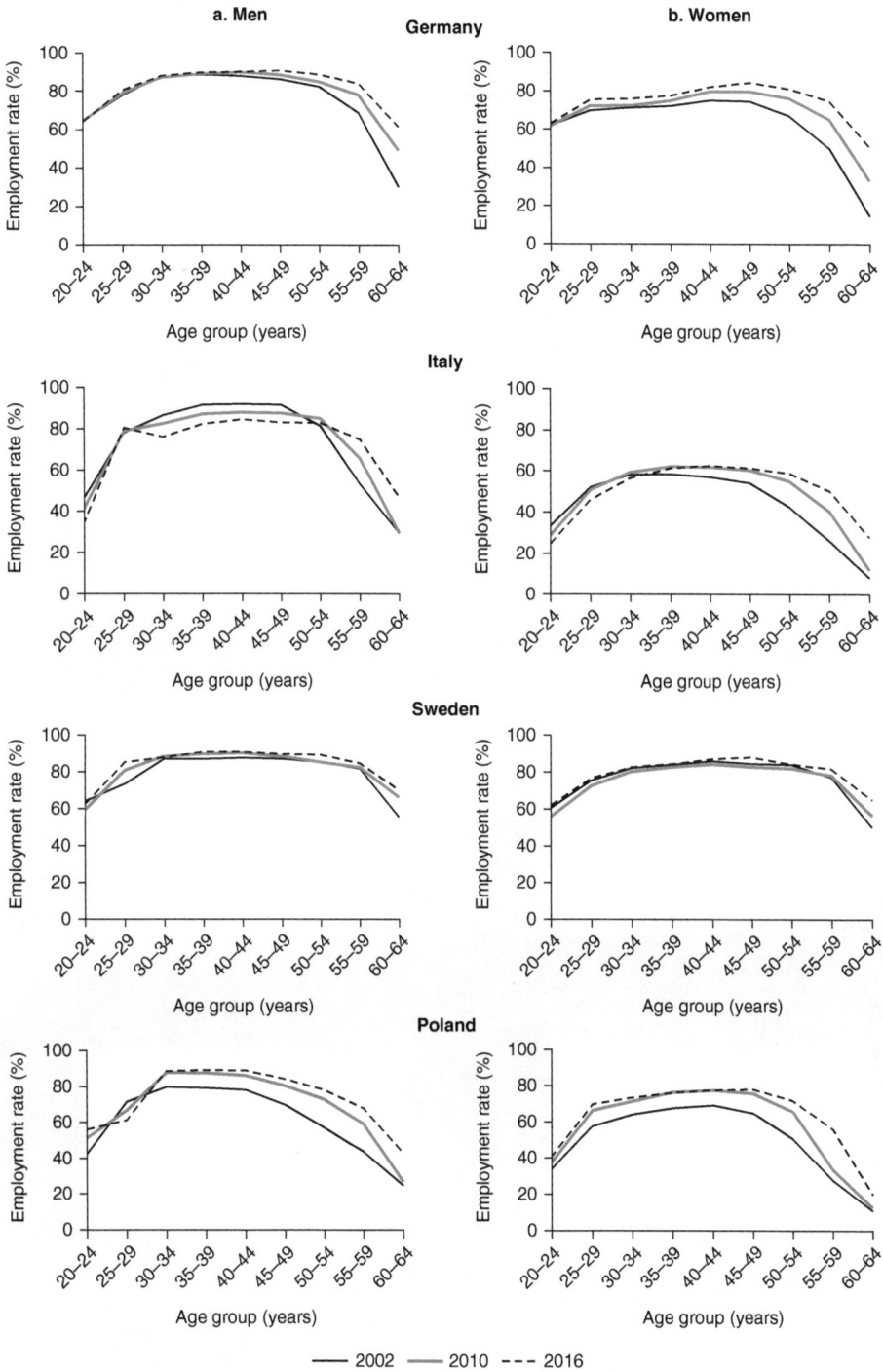

SOURCE: Eurostat Labor Force Survey database.

FIGURE 19.3 **Differences between men's and women's employment rates by education, 2002–16**

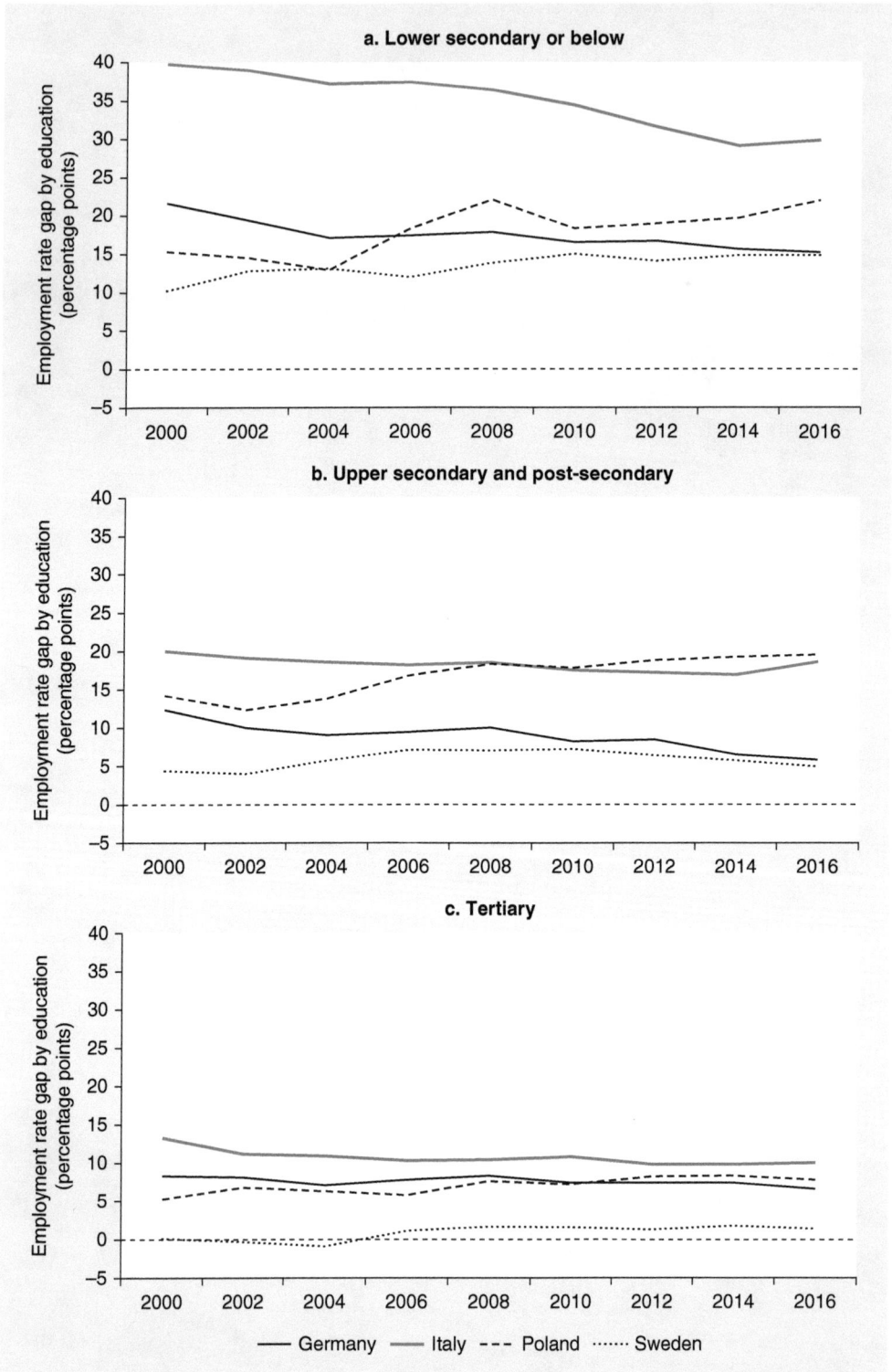

SOURCE: Eurostat Labor Force Survey database.

NOTE: ISCED = International Standard Classification of Education.

FIGURE 19.4 **Part-time employment as a share of total employment ages 20–64, 2000–16**

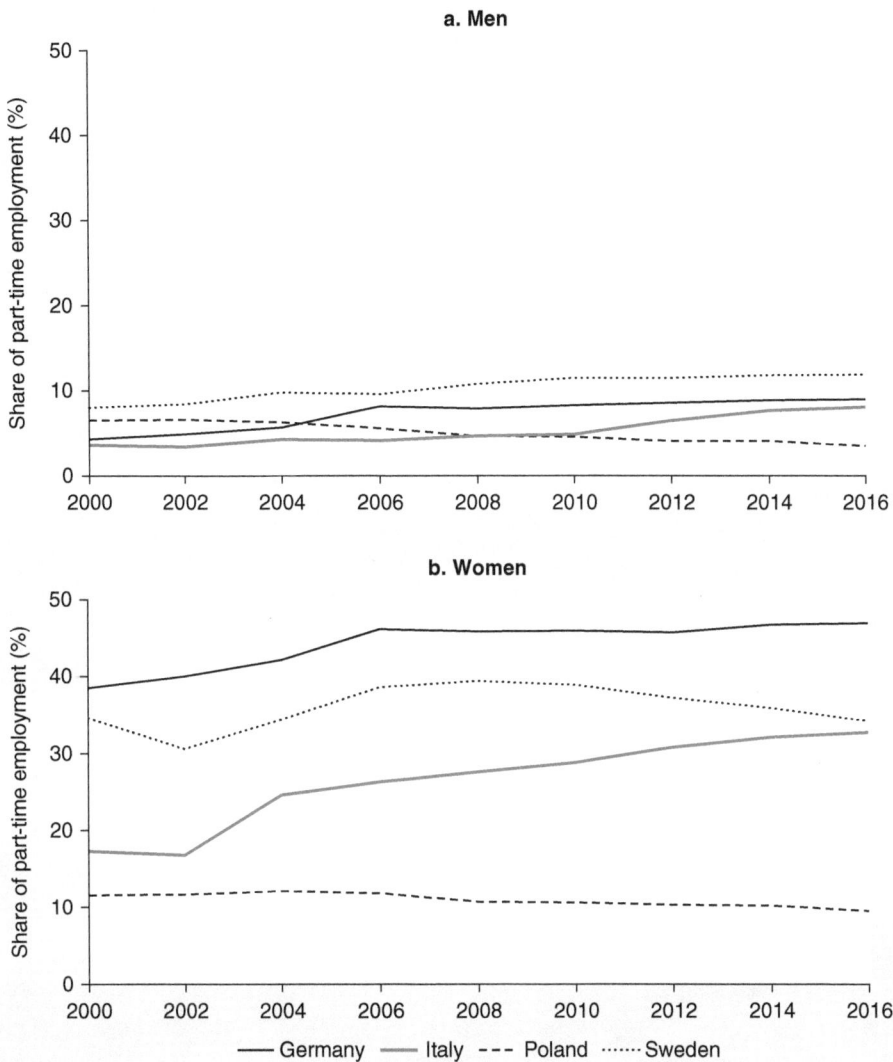

a. Men

b. Women

——— Germany ——— Italy - - - Poland ······· Sweden

SOURCE: Eurostat Labor Force Survey database.

high in Germany (15 percent in 2014), partly due to popular "Minijob" regulations. It is about 8 percent in Sweden and Italy, and it is low and stable in Poland at 3 percent. The incidence of part-time employment is four times higher for women than for men in Germany and three times as high in Sweden. This means that the interrupted career profiles in these two countries are through part-time employment rather than a withdrawal from the labor market, which is discussed later in the chapter. An increasing share of part-timers accompanies the increasing women's employment rate in Italy. Moreover, because of the economic downturn, involuntary part-time work has increased significantly in Italy to 63 percent in 2014, from an already high level. To compare, 31 percent of part-timers involuntarily work less than full time in Poland, 13 percent in Germany, and 23 percent in Sweden (European Parliament 2016, 81).

A higher incidence of interrupted careers among women results mainly from the need to reconcile work and family obligations, especially those related to children (Hofäcker and König 2013; Matysiak and Węziak-Białowolska 2016; Rostgaard 2014). Consequently, employment rates of women with small children are much lower in Germany, Poland, and Italy, in comparison with childless women of the same age (table 19.1).

The largest gaps in employment caused by the presence of children is seen in Germany and Poland. Interestingly, in 2016, employment rates of Swedish women with children were higher, compared with childless women; in general, the employment rates of Swedish women were the highest of all countries, the result of the developed and affordable institutional care for small children in this country. In Italy, even childless women demonstrate lower employment rates than those observed in the other countries.

The presence of children contributes not only to the lower labor force participation of mothers but also to a reduction in the number of hours worked. The strongest reduction of working time among mothers with young children is observed in Germany and Sweden.

TABLE 19.1 **Employment rates of men and women ages 20–49 with at least one child younger than age 6, by number of children and country**

		Men (%)			Women (%)		
		2005	2010	2016	2005	2010	2016
Germany	No children	79.0	83.4	83.6	79.7	83.9	84.4
	1 child	87.7	91.8	92.6	51.6	62.2	69.3
	2 children	89.8	92.1	92.8	47.4	53.2	63.1
	3 or more children	81.9	84.9	83.8	32.8	38.8	43.6
Italy	No children	81.0	76.5	70.7	66.9	65.2	62.0
	1 child	93.8	90.8	87.7	58.4	58.4	59.1
	2 children	93.3	90.8	88.1	49.5	51.5	51.9
	3 or more children	90.5	84.8	80.8	35.7	34.5	39.1
Poland	No children	67.4	75.4	79.2	67.2	74.5	78.8
	1 child	87.0	90.3	93.5	56.8	64.1	69.1
	2 children	85.4	91.1	94.5	52.8	60.3	66.0
	3 or more children	77.0	86.7	88.7	45.7	54.3	49.2
Sweden	No children	—	78.6	77.6	—	74.4	74.5
	1 child	—	90.0	95.1	—	69.3	85.1
	2 children	—	95.0	94.2	—	80.4	80.8
	3 or more children	—	87.4	92.1	—	74.9	79.5

SOURCE: Eurostat Labor Force Survey database.

NOTE: — = not available.

Summing up, the gender gap in employment exists in all four countries, despite the increasing labor force participation of women. It is higher in Italy and Poland, compared with Germany and Sweden. Lower educational attainment and a larger number of children increase the gender gap. In Sweden, the gender gap in employment is low; it is non-existent between men and women with tertiary education. Employment rates of women ages 55 and older drop quickly in Italy and Poland; they remain stable around 60 percent in Germany and Sweden.[4] This positive development is, to a certain extent, offset by a large share of women working part time, particularly in Germany and Sweden. A major increase is also observed in the share of women's part-time employment in Italy. Only in Poland do workers most often work full time.

GENDER PAY GAP

Differences in wages earned by men and women are another important determinant of the gender pay gap (GPG), particularly in DC pension systems (Chłoń-Domińczak 2017). This section looks at GPGs in the four selected countries to determine their level and cross-country differences, as well as age and cohort patterns.[5]

The following discussion refers to raw GPGs, which reflect the difference in average wages earned by men and women. Adjusted pay gaps (accounting for different compositions of male and female workers with respect to their age, education, or other job-related factors) are a better indicator of gender wage inequality; yet from the perspective of the pension system and gender pension gaps, raw GPGs reflect the labor market characteristics that contribute to future pension inequality. Thus, most of the analysis is based on the raw differences in wages earned by men and women.

Considerable differences arise in average hourly wages of men and women in all four countries studied (figure 19.5). In 2014, the average hourly wage of women in Poland was 11 percent lower than the average hourly wage of men; in Germany, this gap exceeded 18 percent; it reached almost 33 percent in Italy.

Differences in the hourly wages of men and women fail to show the entire impact of the GPG on gender pension gaps. Since women work shorter hours in part-time employment, they accumulate less pension wealth. To account for this, raw GPGs are presented in terms of hourly and monthly earnings (figure 19.5). Gender differences in average monthly earnings are higher than gender differences in hourly earnings in each of the four countries. Thus, the overall gender pay gap in earnings—which are the base for pension contributions—amounts to about 20 percent in Poland and Sweden, but it exceeds 30 percent in Germany and 40 percent in Italy. The difference between hourly and monthly pay gaps is particularly striking for Germany, where a large share of women work part time (Matysiak and Steinmetz 2008). Although part-time employment makes combining work and family life easier, at the same time it constitutes a significant pension disadvantage.

The size of the GPG varies by age, although the age patterns are strongly country specific. The differences are highest in Germany, where young women (ages 20–29) earn wages approximately 15 percent lower than those of men (figure 19.6). This gap is almost double that for those ages 30–39, and it exceeds 40 percent for men and women ages 40–49 (slightly decreasing after age 49). In Poland and Sweden, GPGs also increase with age and show a similar pattern, but the differences are much lower. In Italy, young men and women display substantial differences in average wages; these gaps increased substantially

FIGURE 19.5 **Raw hourly and monthly gender pay gaps, 2014**

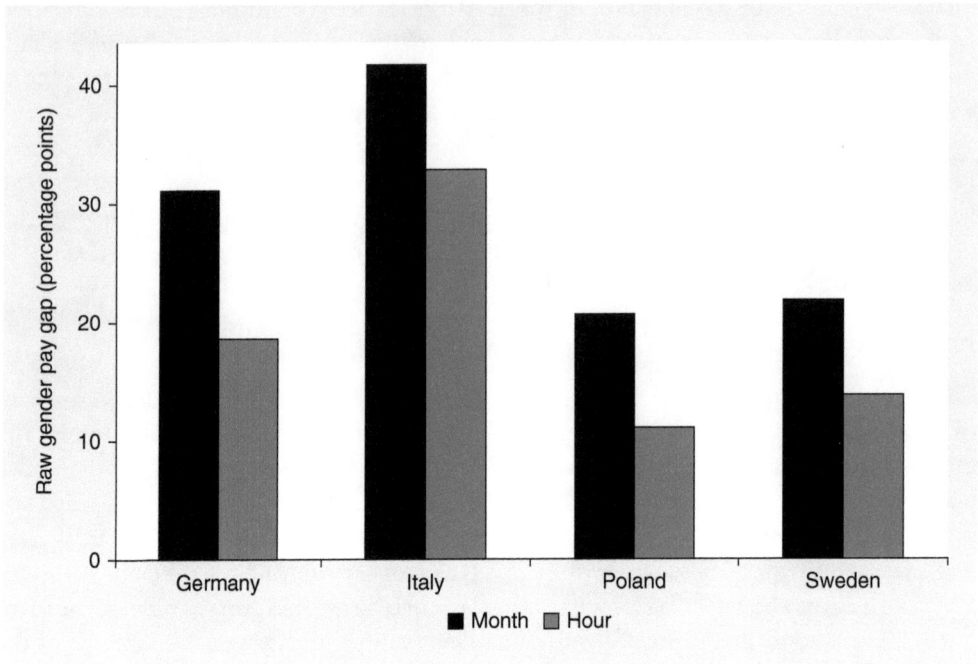

SOURCE: Original analysis of the European Structure of Earnings Survey 2014.

in 2014. This finding may relate to the decline in the employment gap among low-skilled men and women—the increased share of low-paid women translated to a higher pay gap. For older Italian workers, the differences are similar across age groups.

Finally, the dynamics of the GPG over time are investigated from a cohort perspective. The question asked is whether, for example, today's young women are less disadvantaged in terms of pay, compared with young women in the early 2000s; this finding would be expected, given the implementation and promotion of antidiscriminatory legislation and equal pay policies in most European countries. To this end, raw GPGs, in average wages by age groups are examined at four points in time (2002, 2006, 2010, and 2014[6]) in all four countries.

The expected drop in the GPG over time for subsequent cohorts is not found in any country except Sweden (figure 19.7, panels a–d). In Germany, Italy, and Poland, GPGs for the respective age groups in 2014 are higher than in 2002–06. In Germany, the GPG increased, particularly between 2006 and 2010. In Poland, the GPG decreased during this time, but it subsequently increased by 2014. Italy experienced no change in GPG between 2002 and 2010, and it had a substantial increase after that time. Finally, Sweden had a substantial increase in GPG in 2006—and a strong fall afterward. Overall, although the patterns of increasing or decreasing GPGs vary among countries, no trend of more equal wages can be observed, at least in the medium term captured by these data.

What could explain the differences in GPG by age? It seems that the institutional setting is likely to play a major role (Baran et al. 2014). For instance, the fact that the GPG

FIGURE 19.6 **Age patterns of gender pay gap differences, 2014**
monthly earnings

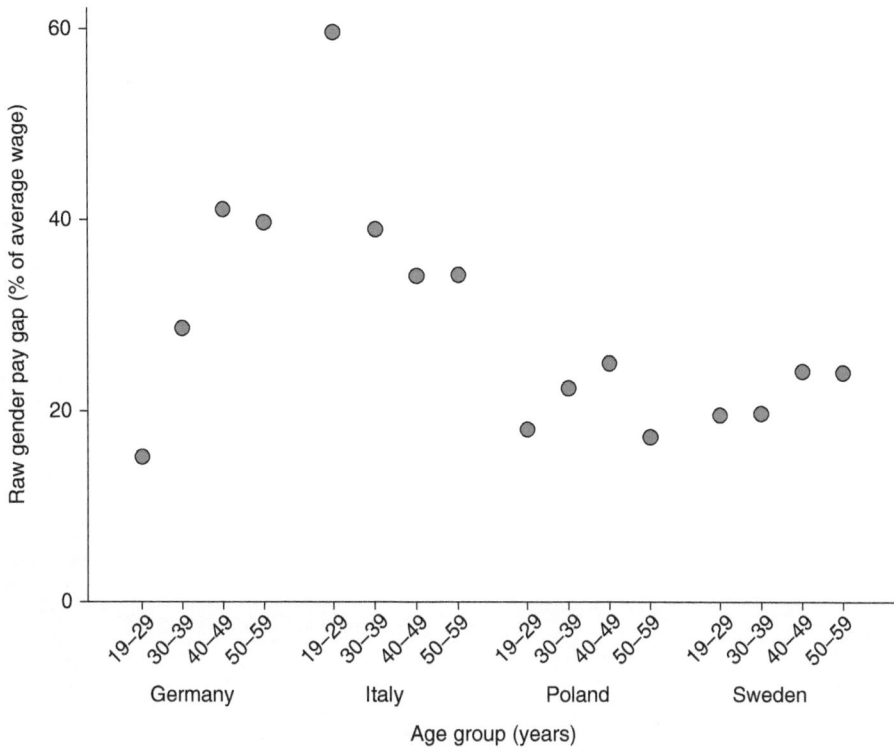

SOURCE: Original analysis of the European Structure of Earnings Survey 2014.

decreased for the oldest age group (49–59) in Poland (and Germany to a lesser extent) is likely explained by self-selection of better-earning women, reflecting large flows of women to inactivity in that age group, explained by the availability of early retirement schemes. The fact that older women are much more disadvantaged in terms of pay than younger women—in virtually all of the countries studied—points to the importance of cumulated job experience, which is lower for women, and the different job careers of men, which are rarely interrupted for family reasons. The strong age disadvantage observed in Germany likely reflects its family policy setting, which included several incentives for women to withdraw from the labor market, with low support for equal partnership policies (OECD 2017).

EMPLOYMENT AND WAGES COMBINED: THE GENDER GAP IN THE LABOR MARKET

The combination of average wages and employment rates by age and sex indicates the overall labor market gap. This gap is estimated based on the data structure of the European Structure of Earnings Survey, as well the results of the NTA (Istenic and Sambt 2016), which use the European Union Statistics on Income and Living Conditions (EU-SILC) to estimate the age profiles of labor income.

FIGURE 19.7 **Gender pay gaps by cohort, 2002–14**

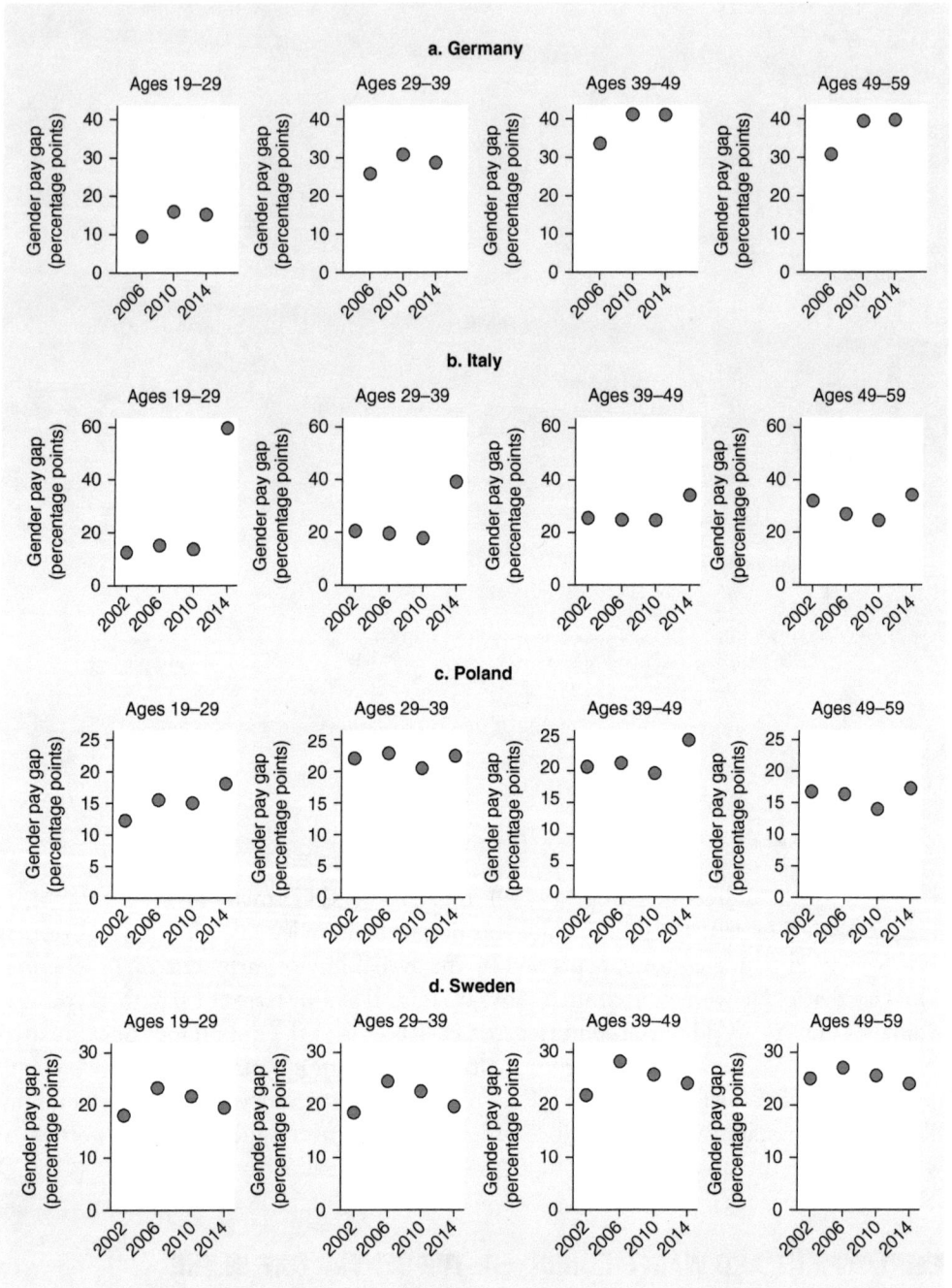

SOURCE: Original analysis of the European Structure of Earnings Survey 2002, 2006, 2010, and 2014.

Stylized profiles of labor income of men and women are shown in figure 19.8. Combining the two dimensions shows that the gender gap in labor income is higher, compared with the wage gap. Germany tends to have the highest income gap, and Sweden has the lowest.

The gender gaps at different ages lead to a higher cumulative gender gap in the life course. Summing the stylized life course income for men and women, the accumulated life course gender labor income gap (LCGLIG) is substantial. To measure the LCGLIG, the following equation is proposed:

$$LCGLIG = 1 - \frac{\sum_{i=20}^{65} w_i^f \times e_i^f}{\sum_{i=20}^{65} w_i^m \times e_i^m} \text{, in which}$$

w_i^m—average wage of men at age i measured in relation to the average wage in the country

e_i^m—employment rate of men at age i

w_i^f—average wage of women at age i measured in relation to the average wage in the country

e_i^f—employment rate of women at age i.

FIGURE 19.8 **Stylized age profiles of labor income estimated using Labor Force Survey and European Structure of Earnings Survey data, 2014**

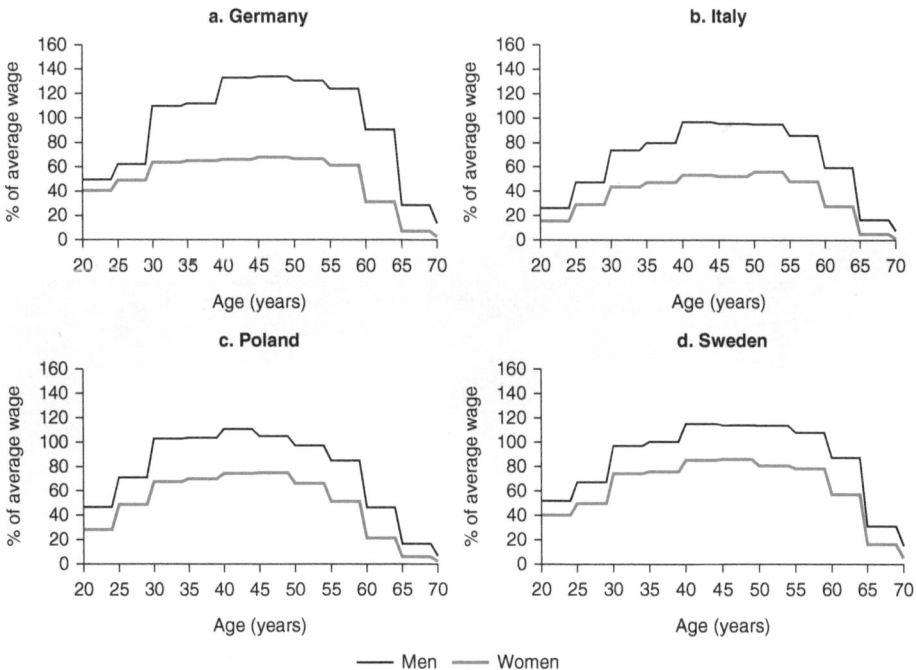

SOURCE: Original calculations.

NOTE: Age profiles are calculated by multiplying average wages in 10-year age groups and employment rates in four age groups.

Based on Eurostat data, the estimated value of LCGLIG is highest in Germany, at 46.8 percent. In Italy the value is 44.3 percent, in Poland it is 35.4 percent, and in Sweden it is 27.3 percent. This finding shows that even relatively low differences at given ages can lead to large differences in lifetime income, which translates directly into similar differences in the level of pensions.

The impact of both lower labor market participation and wage gaps on labor income at various ages is confirmed by the shape of the age profiles of labor income estimated using the NTA methodology (Lee and Mason 2011; Mason et al. 2009).

As shown in figure 19.9, the labor income of women in all countries is less than that of men, which is consistent with the stylized profiles shown in figure 19.7. The NTA estimates are based on actual reported incomes, which are complemented by analysis of the reasons for the existing gaps in labor income related to employment gaps and wage gaps, as presented in figure 19.8. Both estimates show that the gender differences are already visible for women younger than age 30, particularly in Germany and Sweden, which can be a result of career breaks caused by childbearing periods.

Women's income at their prime age is also below that of men. The largest differences refer to persons at prime age. Only in Sweden does the labor income of men and women converge at later stages of the life course.

FIGURE 19.9 **Age profiles of labor income in four countries, National Transfer Accounts estimates, 2010**

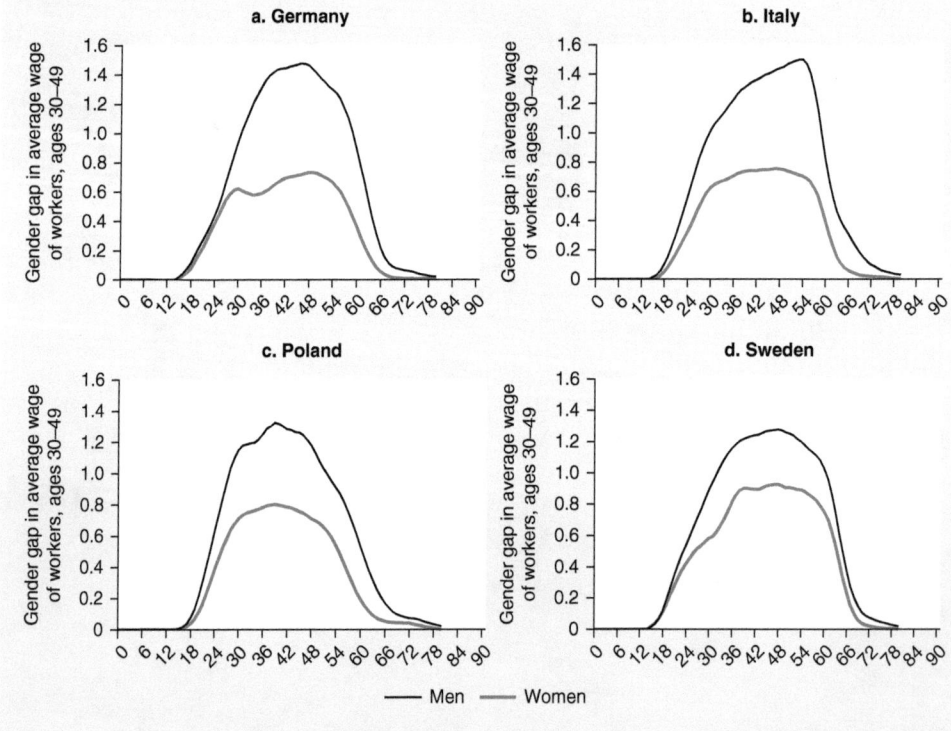

Both estimates confirm that a combination of three factors—the GPG, gender differences in employment rates, and lower work intensity caused by the higher share of women working part time—leads to a significant gap in per capita incomes that will undoubtedly translate into a gender pensions gap. The estimates of the LCGLIG on the gender-specific NTA labor income profiles indicate higher differences between men and women, compared with the profiles derived from the LFS and European Structure of Earnings data. In Germany, the LCGLIG reaches 49.2 percent, in Italy 48.3 percent, in Poland 42.1 percent, and in Sweden 30.5 percent.

EMPLOYMENT PATHS: DO DISTINCT EMPLOYMENT PATTERNS EXIST IN THE COUNTRIES?

Interruptions in work careers are usually not randomly distributed in the population but cumulated for specific persons. They are omitted in the analysis of the aggregate average age profiles. The following section addresses that problem by comparing individual work careers from the retrospective survey to find typical patterns of full and interrupted careers characteristic of the analyzed countries and gender. The average differences in labor market participation of men and women result from a combination of different individual life course developments that lead to interrupted employment careers, particularly for women. However, unstable and interrupted work careers are not only assigned to women. Many explanations arise for different patterns of work careers. One explanation is the family situation. As discussed, employment rates are lower in families with children, particularly for women. As a result, persons can have limited or no work experience. There are also persons who decide to reconcile work and family life by taking more frequent career breaks or by working part time. This heterogeneity of decisions can be explained by psychological factors that lead to more child-care-oriented behavior (Hakim 2003; Vitali et al. 2007). However, such choices frequently reflect the limitations of institutional child care. The differences in labor market choices of persons with different numbers of children have an impact on individual pension levels (Kotowska, Stachura, and Strzelecki 2008; Vitali et al. 2007;).

Another determinant of the divergence in patterns of the stability of work experiences is the heterogeneity of health and disabilities in the population (Adeline and Delattre 2017). The process of collecting human capital during a life course can also lead to heterogeneity in patterns of more and less educated persons. Persons with tertiary education usually enter the labor market later but are more attached to employment in later ages. The significant share of unstable work careers can be an indicator of a dual labor market, with relatively better opportunities for persons without interrupted careers, and fewer stable jobs for persons with career interruptions (Elger 2015; Reich, Gordon, and Edwards 1973).

To address the problem of the heterogeneity in employment biographies, retrospective data from the SHARE database Waves 1, 2, 3 (SHARELIFE), 4, 5, and 6[7] are used (see Börsch-Supan et al. [2013] for methodological details). This section uses data from the generated Job Episodes Panel[8] (see Antonova et al. [2014] and Brugiavini et al. [2013] for methodological details). The Job Episodes Panel release 6.0.0 is based on SHARE Waves 1, 2, and 3 (SHARELIFE).[9]

The SHARE data set contains retrospective data about past employment based on the answers of persons ages 50 and older. This analysis uses data about episodes of work in each year of a career for all four countries. The limitation of this approach is the fact that employment histories are typical of people from already retired generations; younger generations most likely experience different patterns. Nevertheless, the country differences illustrate the divergent labor market developments that are still likely to affect different pension outcomes for people by country.

To analyze the typical patterns of work careers based on retrospective data, a sequence analysis technique is applied that allows definition of the measure of similarity between different life paths (Brzinsky-Fay, Kohler, and Luniak 2006). For each year of the analysis, three possible states are distinguished: full-time employment, part-time employment, and inactivity or unemployment. In the calculations of the distances between work careers, it is assumed that part-time employment is halfway between full-time employment and not working. The concept of the sequence analysis is illustrated in figure 19.10.

The result of the sequence analysis is a matrix of distances among persons, reflecting the similarity of their work careers. Then the matrix defined at the micro level is used in a cluster analysis with the Ward metric to identify the two most distinct clusters. In the majority of countries, the difference is rather clear. For example, for women in Poland, sequences that describe working life can be divided into two clusters (figure 19.11). In the second cluster, sequences are similar mainly because they consist of elements of full-time careers. Episodes of not working usually appear at the end of working life and are rather short in comparison with periods of work. In contrast, the first cluster groups the sequences that contain mainly episodes of not working or part-time work. The episodes of full-time work are relatively short. Clearly such a procedure leads to identification of the two groups. The first cluster represents similar interrupted careers, and the second cluster can be interpreted as a normal "full-time" career pattern specific to Polish women.

For other countries and sex groups, two similar distinct clusters are identified (see all results in annex 19A). The first one is always constituted by people with interrupted careers, characterized by periods of inactivity or part-time work. The second one includes people with usually uninterrupted full-time work careers. The division of population in the two clusters makes it possible to calculate age-specific employment rates, with

FIGURE 19.10 **Conceptual diagram of a sequence of labor market episodes**

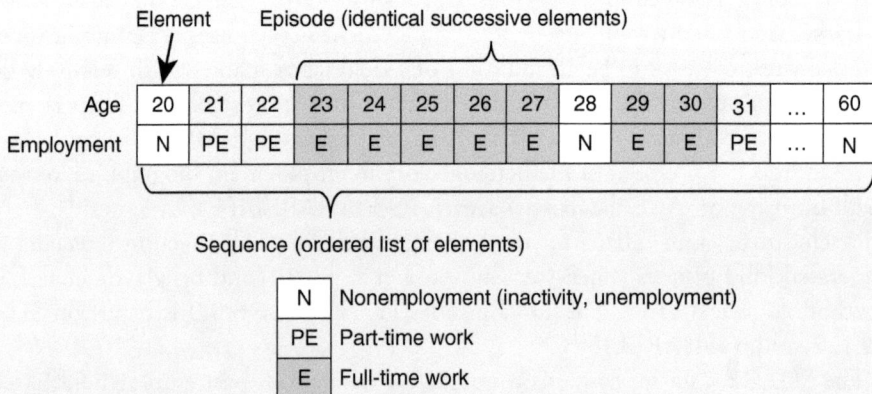

SOURCE: Based on Brzinsky-Fay, Kohler, and Luniak 2006.

FIGURE 19.11 **Labor market sequences of individual persons' job episodes in two clusters for women in Poland**

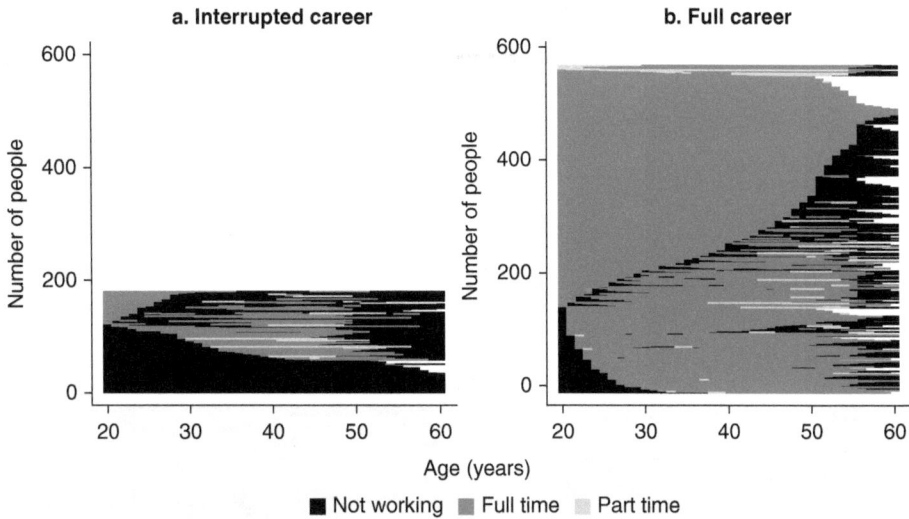

SOURCE: Original estimates based on SHARE Job Episodes Panel data.

additional distinction of full-time and part-time jobs. The first cluster with lower employment rates in full-time jobs appears more frequently among women, but it is also observed to some extent among men (figures 19.12 and 19.13).

The meaning of the interrupted work pattern also differs among countries and between sexes. In Germany, Italy, and Poland, the main difference between full and interrupted careers among men was employment at ages 50 and older (figure 19.12). In general, shorter labor market careers were considered as interrupted. The interrupted careers of men in these countries accounted for 21–36 percent of all careers. In Sweden, the typical interrupted career of men described a group of persons with maximum employment rates during the whole working life of about 40 percent and relatively frequent part-time work. However, this group accounted for about 4 percent of men (figure 19.12). The remaining 96 percent of men had very stable and high employment rates up to age 60.

The meaning of interrupted career is even more diverse for women (figure 19.13). In Italy, women's labor force participation is generally low, the result of the nearly complete lack of labor market participation of almost one-half of women. It seems to be the extreme case of this type of interrupted career. In Poland, women with full-time careers have relatively high employment rates. Interrupted careers seem to have been a result of initial withdrawal from employment in childbearing and childrearing periods, as well as limited returns to the labor market at later stages of their life course. Part-time employment is hardly used. At the same time, part-time employment seems to be very frequent among women with interrupted patterns of work careers in Germany and Sweden. These outcomes are consistent with the earlier findings on the employment characteristics of men and women in the four countries.

FIGURE 19.12 **Average employment rates of men in full-time and part-time age profiles in two clusters: Interrupted career and full career**

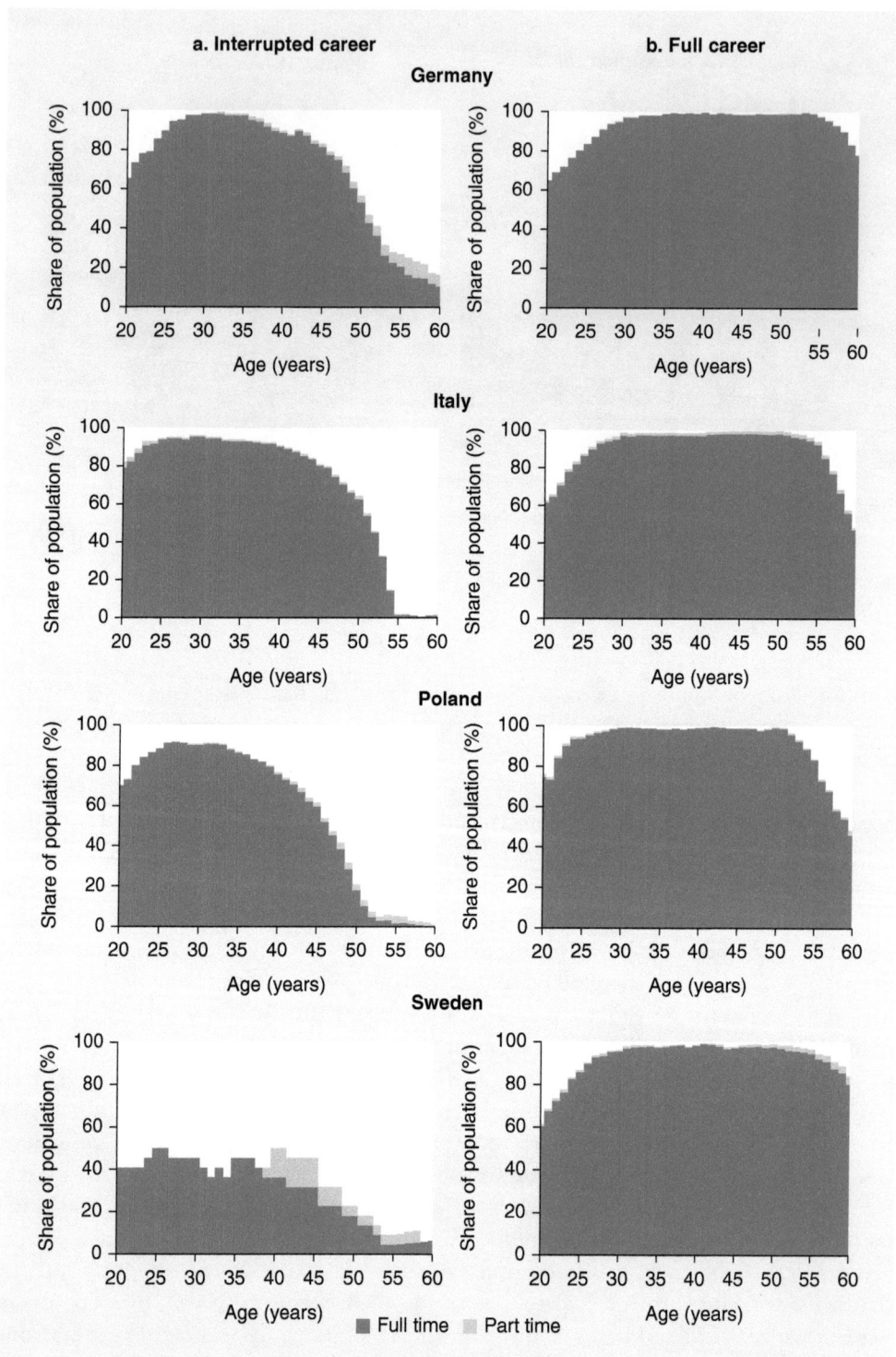

SOURCE: Original estimates based on SHARE Job Episodes Panel data.

FIGURE 19.13 **Average employment rates for women in full-time and part-time age profiles in two clusters: Interrupted career and full career**

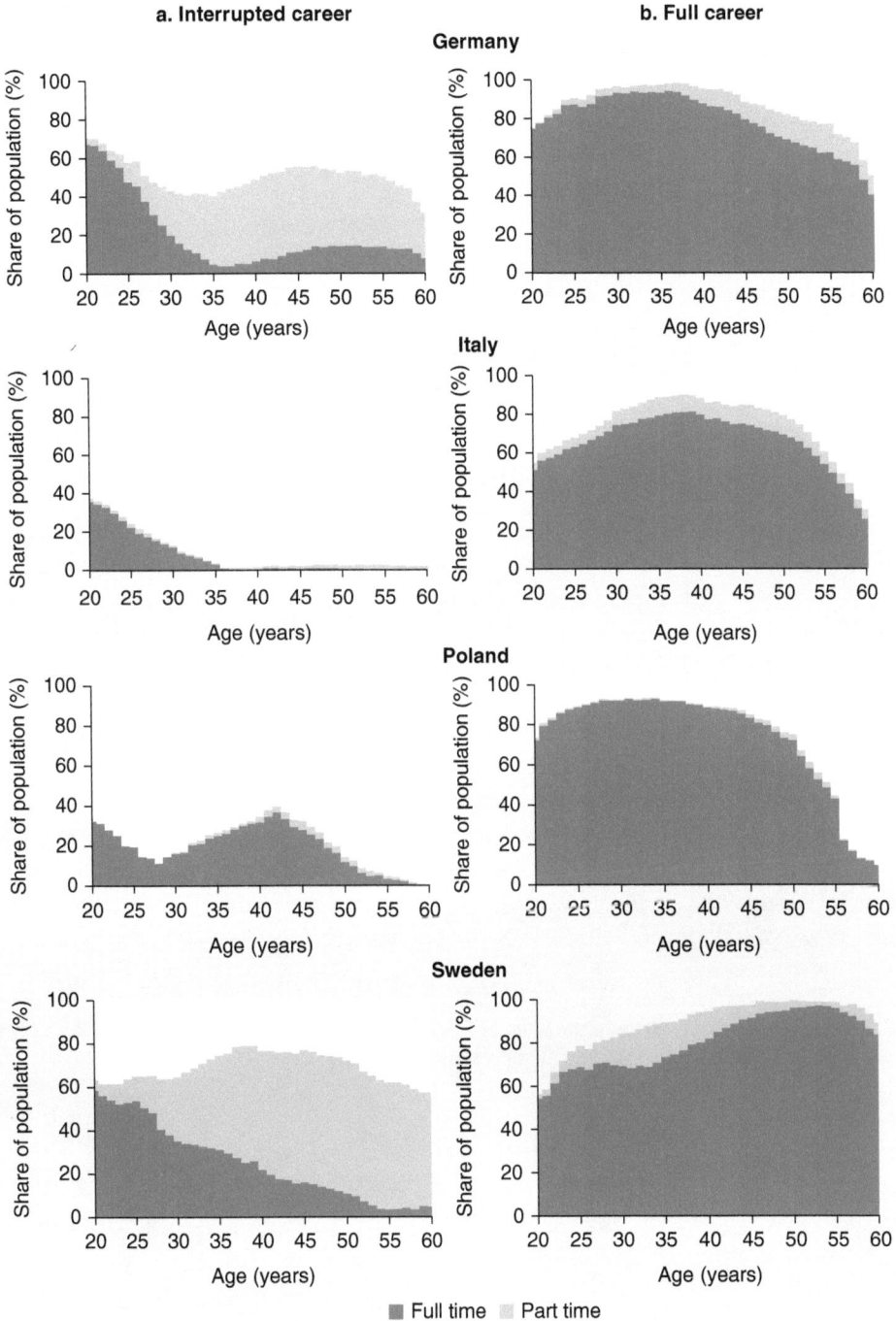

SOURCE: Original estimates based on SHARE Job Episodes Panel data.

The differences in the employment rates, combined with differences in wage levels calculated for age groups 20–29, 30–49, and 50 and older for people with full-time and part-time employment, translate into differences in the life course labor income gap. The estimated life course labor income in the four groups for all countries is compared, taking the level of labor income of men with full careers as the baseline (table 19.2). Career interruptions give the highest penalty in lifetime labor income in the case of women with interrupted work careers. In Italy, the life course income of these women consists of only 6 percent on average of men's income with a full career (100 percent). This means that the gap between the life course income of men with full careers and women with interrupted careers ranges from 94 percent in Italy to about 54 percent in Sweden. It should be noted that even if women have relatively full careers, the gap with men with full careers still remains high—between 37 percent and 17 percent. In fact, in Germany, Italy, and Poland, the lifetime income of women with full careers is relatively similar to that of men with interrupted careers. These differences have an important influence on individual pension rights in NDC schemes or point systems, as discussed in subsequent sections.

Employment Histories and Pension Levels

This section presents simulations of pension levels for men and women in the four countries. Different employment paths by country and sex are assumed. Note that the approach here differs from that used to compute hypothetical income replacement rates by the OECD (OECD 2015) and the European Commission's Pension Adequacy Reports (for example, European Commission 2018). The OECD and EC focus on comparing expected pension benefits under different pension systems for people with standard profiles of employment careers; the assumptions usually applied refer to the full (or almost full) employment length and different (but standardized) earnings levels.

The goal here is to assess the expected outcomes of pension systems considering the country-specific labor market situation regarding gender-related biographies, employment, and wages. As shown in the previous section, labor market differences among countries and between men and women within countries are significant. The adequacy of future pensions will depend on those distinct employment histories.

TABLE 19.2 **Relationship between the level of life course labor income of men and women with full and interrupted careers, compared with men with full careers**

	Men		Women		Share of persons in interrupted career cluster (%)	
	Full (%)	**Interrupted (%)**	**Full (%)**	**Interrupted (%)**	**Men**	**Women**
Germany	100	64	68	26	21.3	53.3
Italy	100	66	64	6	27.1	48.9
Poland	100	57	63	16	35.7	24.4
Sweden	100	41	83	46	4.1	37.0

SOURCE: Original table.

PENSION SIMULATIONS: ASSUMPTIONS AND THE APPROACH

To estimate the expected levels of future pensions, a microsimulation model was prepared to calculate the level of old-age pensions in the four countries. The model calculates HFPs in relation to the country average wage in the year of retirement. HFPs are calculated for individuals who start their employment at age 20 in 2017 and continue their labor market careers according to profiles specified in the respective scenario. Four different scenarios of employment paths for both men and women are applied in the simulations:

- *Average Eurostat scenario.* Probabilities of employment are set according to the average employment rates by country, sex, and age (in 5-year age groups). Levels of wages (compared with the average) are set using the average wages by country, sex, and age (in 10-year age groups).

- *NTA scenario.* The labor income that is the basis for the contribution calculation is based on the NTA age profiles of labor income by country and sex.

- *SHARELIFE scenario for workers with interrupted careers.* Probabilities of employment are set according to the first cluster identified in the sequence analysis, and levels of wages are similar to those in the Eurostat scenario.

- *SHARELIFE scenario for workers with full careers.* Probabilities of employment are set according to the second cluster identified in the sequence analysis, and levels of wages are similar to those in the Eurostat scenario.

The simulations are simplified for comparative purposes. They do not take into account country-specific regulations that result in capping the covered wage (which is the case in Sweden); nor do they include the recognition of pension rights from career interruptions, for example, in conjunction with child care.

Other assumptions in the simulations are based on the Ageing Working Group (AWG) assumptions (European Commission 2015), as listed in table 19.3. The value of life expectancy used for pension calculation presented below is based on the 2013 Eurostat population projections (EUROPOP 2013).

HYPOTHETICAL FUTURE PENSIONS

In this section, hypothetical future pensions (HFPs) are calculated separately for men and women according to the four scenarios. In the calculation model used, the amount of contributions paid at a given age depends on the age- and sex-specific employment probability and labor income, according to the applied scenario. It is assumed that both men and women retire at age 67 (the target retirement age in Germany, Italy, and Sweden). For Poland, results are also presented for lower ages: 65 for men and 60 for women, the legal retirement age as of October 2017.

Figure 19.14 shows the simulation results. Men can expect higher pensions, compared with women in all countries. The difference is largest in Italy and Germany (26.8 percentage points and 22.9 percentage points, respectively, in the Eurostat scenario). In the remaining two countries, the difference slightly exceeds 10 percentage

TABLE 19.3 **Country-specific assumptions used in pension simulations**

	Germany	Italy	Poland	Sweden
Wage, employment, and economic growth				
Average wage growth rate (%)	1.5	1.2	2.2	1.5
Employment growth rate (%)	−0.5	0.1	−0.6	0.5
Wage bill growth rate (%)	1.0	1.0	1.0	1.0
GDP growth rate (%)	1.0	1.3	1.6	2.0
Contributions				
Contribution NDC (% of wage)	n.a.	33.00	12.22	14.88
Contribution NDC-2 (% of wage)	n.a.	n.a.	4.38	n.a.
Contribution FDC (% of wage)	n.a.	n.a.	2.92	2.33
Indexation and rates of return				
Indexation of NDC account (%)	n.a.	1.3	1.0	1.5
Indexation of NDC-2 account (%)	n.a.	n.a.	1.6	n.a.
Rate of return on FDC account (%)	n.a.	n.a.	2.0	2.0
Annuity calculation				
Discount rate for annuity calculation (%)	n.a.	1.5	0.0	1.60
Adjustment of point value due to life expectancy (%)	14	n.a.	n.a.	n.a.

SOURCE: Original assessment based on AWG and OECD assumptions.

NOTE: FDC = financial defined contribution; GDP = gross domestic product; n.a. = not applicable; NDC = nonfinancial defined contribution.

points at the retirement age of 67. Under the lower retirement age in Poland, the difference increases to 12.0 percentage points. This is an outcome of accumulated differences in both labor market participation and average wages by sex.

Differences also arise between countries. The Eurostat and NTA scenario results are similar. In the Eurostat scenario with average employment rates and average wages by age, the highest level of HFPs for men is in Italy, exceeding 56 percent of average wage, followed by Germany, Sweden, and Poland. For women in the same scenario, HFPs in Sweden and Italy are close to 30 percent and are slightly lower in Germany. In Poland, assuming a retirement age of 67, women's HFPs remain below 20 percent; for the lower retirement age at age 60, they fall below 15 percent.

Last, the HFPs based on the two profiles of interrupted and full careers indicate the gaps in the HFPs generated by the accumulated impact of career breaks. For men, the largest difference is seen in Sweden (28.6 percentage points), but it should be noted that most of them (almost 96 percent) are in the full career group. In Italy and Germany, men with interrupted careers withdraw from employment earlier. As a result, they can expect their pensions to be lower by 25.8 percentage

FIGURE 19.14 **Hypothetical future pensions (HFPs) of men and women under different assumed country-specific labor force paths**

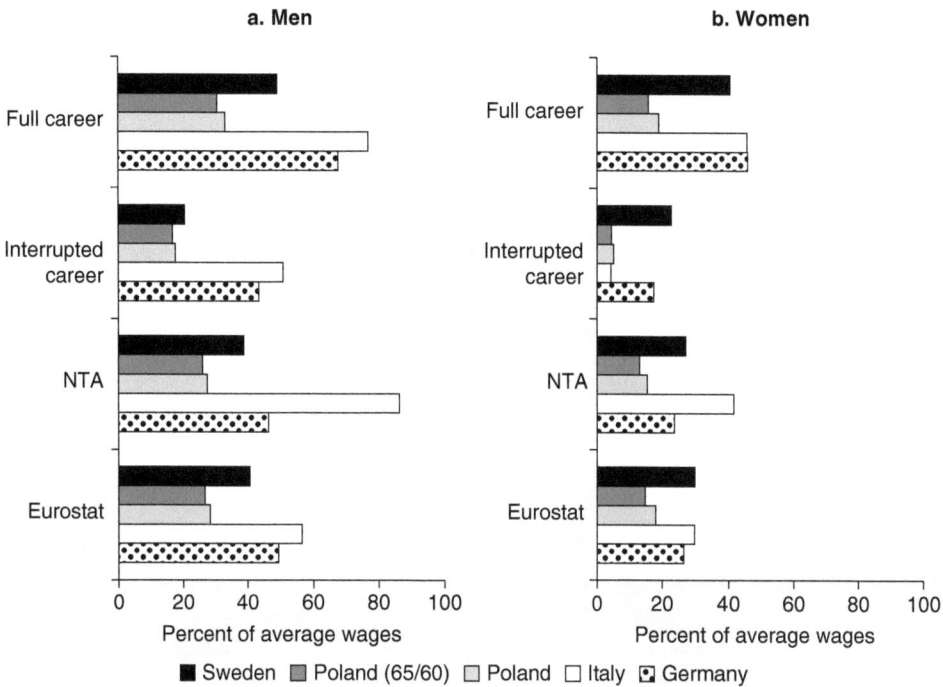

SOURCE: Original calculations.

NOTE: 65/60 for Poland means retirement at 65 for men and 60 for women. Retirement for other countries is at age 67. NTA = National Transfer Accounts.

points and 24.0 percentage points, respectively. Poland has the lowest difference, at 15.5 percentage points. The share of men with interrupted careers is also higher in the three latter countries.

The pattern of interrupted careers of women in Poland and Italy leads to the expected level of HFPs of less than 5 percent of average wage; this level is significantly below the poverty line and a minimum pension guarantee. This outcome for Italy is mainly due to the very short work careers of women, who withdraw from employment early, presumably as they establish families and have children. In Poland, higher participation rates are seen; given the design of the pension system, however, with the lower contribution rate and no discount rate used in the calculation of the annuity as in Italy and Sweden, the estimated benefits are low. The gap caused by career interruption in Italy is very high at 41.6 percentage points, whereas in Poland it is much smaller at 13.9 percentage points. In Germany and Sweden, career interruptions for women lead to gaps of 17.9 percentage points and 28.5 percentage points, respectively, although the gap is reduced to about 20 percentage points in Sweden through child-care credits following the birth of a child (Klerby, Larsson, and Palmer 2019).

FIGURE 19.15 **Pension levels using the Swedish nonfinancial defined contribution model and country-specific assumptions on wages and employment**

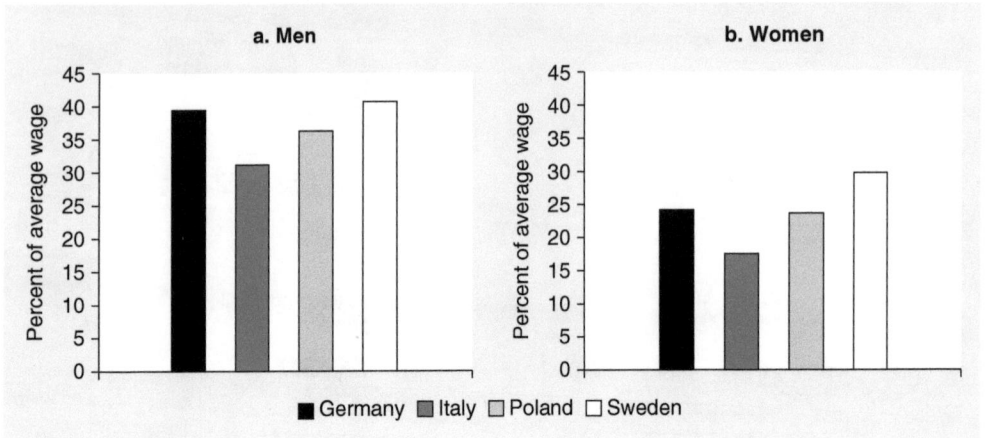

SOURCE: Original calculations.

FIGURE 19.16 **Comparison of hypothetical future pensions in Sweden with the other three countries**

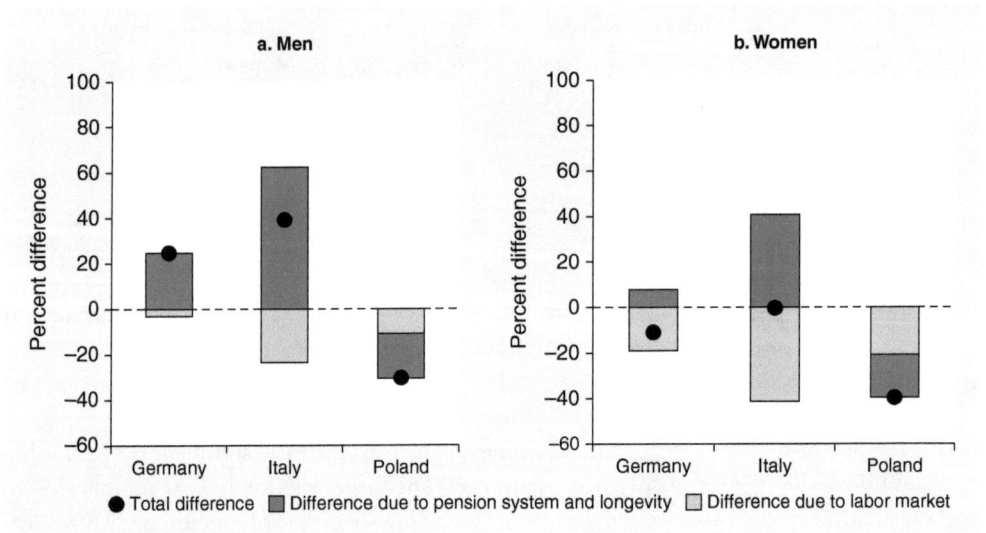

SOURCE: Original calculations.

IMPACT OF EMPLOYMENT PATHS AND PENSION SYSTEM DESIGN ON THEORETICAL FUTURE PENSIONS

To assess how differences in age and wage income profiles by sex affect the countries' pension levels, pensions were simulated using gender and age-based wage and employment rate profiles according to national statistics to retain national characteristics. In addition, as discussed earlier, the same NDC model (the Swedish model) was employed for all pension calculations. In the next step the simulated average gender-differentiated pensions for all four countries were divided by the average wage (gender neutral) to derive separate income replacement rates for men and women. The income replacement rates are reported in figure 19.15. In figure 19.16 the country-wise pension calculations are then broken down into two components and these are compared using Sweden's results as the benchmark.

The decomposition of the difference in the level of HFPs between Sweden and the other three countries has three components: the pension scheme design and longevity effects and the labor market effect are presented in figure 19.16. Note that "the pension scheme design" includes the differences in the level of contribution rates in the three NDC countries and the fact that, unlike NDC schemes, the German point scheme has no built-in "budget constraint" due to its NDB construction.

The results show that the pension schemes in Germany and Italy provide more generous benefits compared with Sweden and Poland. Labor market differences lead to lower benefits, because the labor market participation of both men and women in Sweden is higher than in the other three countries.

Summary and Conclusions

The labor market plays a crucial role in all types of pension systems. In prepaid systems, especially in NDC and FDC schemes, that role is also strong and visible at the individual level. The strong labor market link of NDC and FDC schemes has many advantages, as discussed in Góra and Palmer (2019). At the same time, this means that accumulated differences by gender in aggregated labor income over the life course translate to differences in pension levels. These differences are less pronounced in other types of pension systems that do not have a direct link between lifetime earnings and pensions, such as NDB or FDB schemes. The analysis here shows that patterns of interrupted careers mean much shorter time spent in employment compared with full careers, particularly in Italy and Poland. Career interruptions affect significant shares of both men and women. Women with interrupted careers in Poland and Italy are at risk of having extremely low old-age pensions in NDC systems (below 5 percent of the average wage). Women in Germany, if the patterns of interrupted careers remain unchanged, can expect pensions that are less than 20 percent of the average wage, while in Sweden they barely exceed one-quarter of the average wage. This means that if their old-age income relied only on their own old-age pensions linked to life course earnings, they would face a high risk of old-age poverty. The results do not tell the entire story, however. Sweden has income replacement benefits, whereby the state pays pension contributions into individual accounts when children are born or parents are home caring for sick children, in addition to the child-care credits mentioned above. Furthermore, Sweden has a pension guarantee supplement to the NDC (and FDC) benefit that over half of women receive (see Klerby, Larsson, and Palmer 2019). Germany has a similar but less generous arrangement.

This risk may be mitigated by two types of policy interventions. The first one, more difficult politically but sustainable in the long run, focuses on finding ways to improve labor market outcomes, particularly for groups at risk of interrupted careers. Longer working lives and higher wages lead to improved life course wages and higher pensions. The second type of intervention is the adjustment of pension rules, which may seem more attractive in the short term, but some of the types of such interventions merely hide problems rather than solve them. Women who interrupt their careers frequently rely on their husband's benefits or survivors' pensions as a source of income in old age. Pension systems also recognize selected periods of breaks, such as for child care, in the form of additional pension rights or dedicated mothers' pensions, as in Germany. A similar measure is being considered in Poland. As a result actual poverty among older women is significantly reduced.

Given population aging and the increasing financial strain of public pensions, it is important to consider solutions that enable women to accumulate their own pension rights. It should be stressed that solutions, such as generous survivors' benefits or lower retirement age of women, encourage career interruptions and earlier withdrawal from the labor force. An alternative within the context of an NDC scheme is to offer the option of contracting a joint annuity. The policy can go one step further and automatically grant the joint annuity upon retirement of the younger partner unless both partners agree to delay the annuity payments (see Klerby, Larsson, and Palmer 2013). This could be the default option.

A mix of policies including those aimed at reducing gender differences in the labor market and transparent compensation for selected justified career breaks, such as maternity or child care leave,[10] is a sustainable policy direction.

Two directions in labor market policy should be seen jointly. The first one is the increase in labor market participation over an entire life course. Differences at different stages of life accumulate when it comes to receiving pensions. At the beginning of employment activity, such policies need to focus on smoothing the school-to-work transition. Population aging, late parenthood, and increasing numbers of generations living in parallel, as well as more diverse life histories, challenge the traditional perception of "rush hours," which refers to coinciding life activities (education, entering the labor market and starting employment, union formation, and parenthood) at some stages of life. Therefore, reconciliation of work and family over a life course seems to better address the needs of people at different stages of their lives. The key issue is the redistribution of work and care within family networks, especially between women and men. Moreover, because family obligations related to children seem to be crucial for establishing a labor market position and career prospects of both women and men, policies supporting reconciliation of work and parenthood are highly relevant. Measures that strengthen women's role as breadwinners and foster men's involvement in family care will result in more gender equality in the labor market. To this end, Klerby, Larsson, and Palmer (2019) make the case for the sharing of pension accounts under NDC schemes. Later, policies are needed to support the return to employment after longer spells of remaining outside the labor force. Finally, policies should aim to prolong working lives and prevent early labor market withdrawal of both men and women. All of these interventions are equally important to reduce the risk of interrupted and short careers.

GPGs are substantial. They do not diminish for new cohorts of workers and will remain an important contributor to women's pension disadvantage once these women retire. These labor market inefficiencies need to be tackled—both better enforcement of equal pay policies and, again, more policies promoting equal shares of unpaid work and child care are needed. Those in place so far helped bring more women into the labor market over the past two decades. As this chapter's data and analyses show, however, they failed to improve women's pay in relation to men's.

This analysis presents the nature and approximate scale of selected (and arguably the most important) labor market problems affecting the outcome of pension systems at the micro level. Country-specific assumptions about labor market participation are combined with pension system design to compare the outcomes of the combined effect of pension system design applied in the specific labor market context of selected countries. This approach expands the up-to-date comparisons in the literature, which focuses primarily on differences in the design of pensions, ignoring the pronounced differences in the employment careers of men and women between countries. The analysis also shows that differences in the patterns of interrupted careers lead to a high risk of low and very low pensions. The chapter provides new evidence on the development of NDC pension systems under different labor market performance and institutional settings. For women, differences in expected future pensions are caused to a larger extent by differences in their employment profiles, more than by the design of pension systems and longevity.

The transparent link between contributions and benefits in NDC systems makes such systems sustainable in the long run. They also provide clear incentives for individuals for higher and longer labor market participation, which is necessary in the context of population aging and shrinking working-age populations. To fully exploit the benefits of such systems, it is important to highlight the existing risks related to the existing labor market gaps, including, in particular, interrupted careers. These risks need to be tackled through labor market policies, not by fiddling with the pension system design, which would weaken the link between contributions and benefits. Compensation for care periods, such as maternity or child-care leave, in the form of transparent contributions paid to the NDC system in an amount that compensates for the pension loss, may help reconcile work and family life without affecting pension system transparency and sustainability. Transparent pension systems are an asset of the countries discussed herein. Changing them to hide labor market problems would not help solve labor market problems and could lead to destabilization of their pension systems.

ANNEX 19A

The results of the sequence analysis and segmentation of work careers in Germany, Italy, Poland, and Sweden are shown in the figure 19A.1. Each panel presents the individual work careers (vertical axis) by age (horizontal axis), which can consist of three possible states (not working, working full time, and working part time for two clusters: 1 = interrupted careers and 2 = full careers.

FIGURE 19A.1 **Individual work careers in four countries, by age and sex**

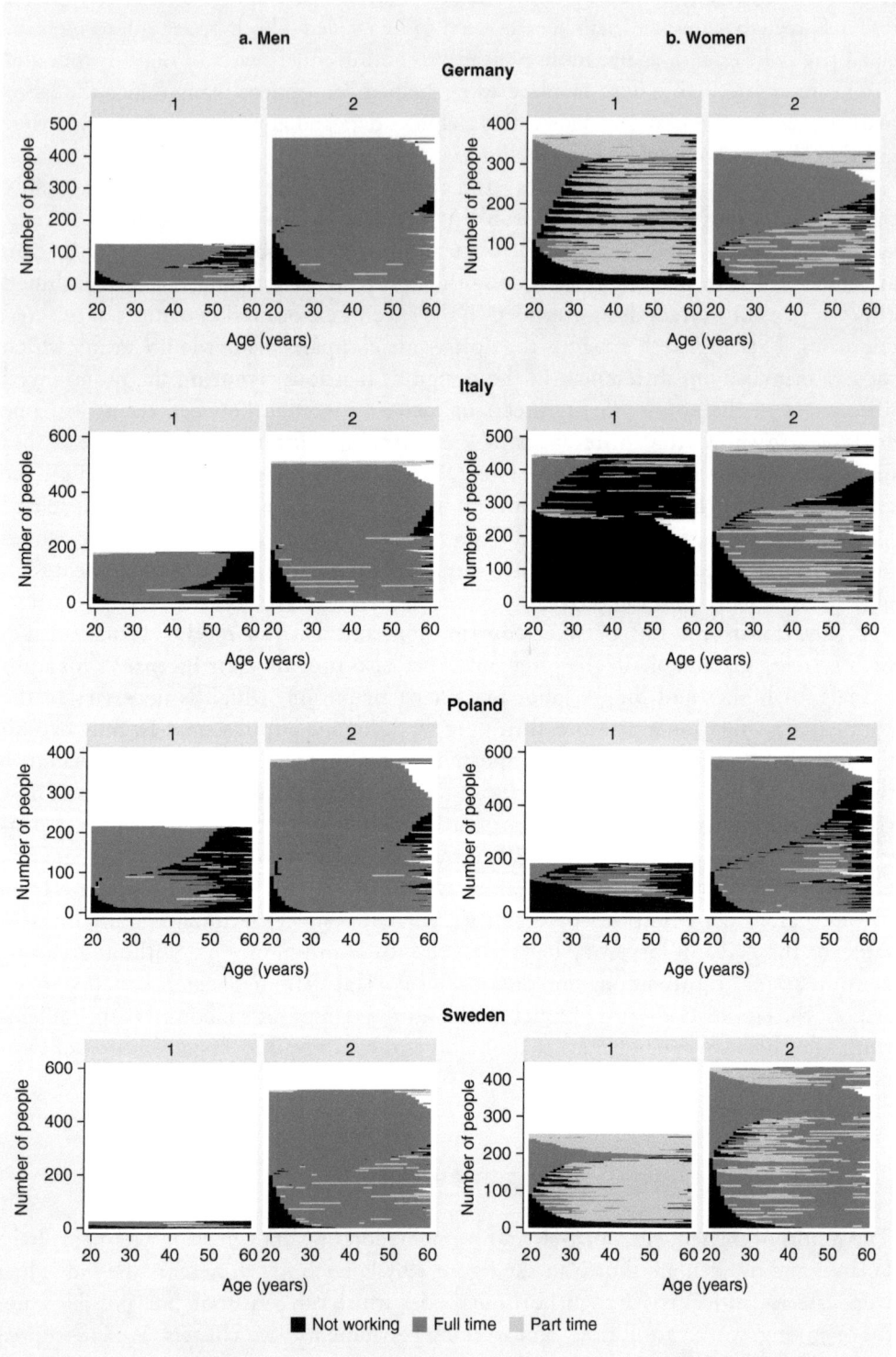

SOURCE: Estimates based on SHARE Job Episodes Panel data.

Notes

1. Prepaid means contribution-financed as opposed to tax-financed (Góra and Palmer 2019).

2. NDC/NDB and FDC/FDB understanding in the chapter follows Góra and Palmer (2004).

3. See, for example, Chłoń-Domińczak, Franco, and Palmer (2012) for a comparison of NDC pension system design in Sweden, Italy, Poland, and Latvia.

4. To some extent that can be an effect of a lower retirement age for women in Poland and Italy, who are in a worse competitive position relative to men.

5. The analyses were carried out within the framework of a "Gender Pay Gaps—A Cohort Analysis" project supported by the Polish National Science Centre (Grant No. 2013/10 / E / HS4 / 00445). The analyses are based on the European Structure of Earnings Survey (2002, 2006, 2010, and 2014 waves) provided by Eurostat. All errors are the authors'.

6. The choice of these reference points is due to data availability. In particular, 2002 data are unavailable for Germany.

7. (DOIs: 10.6103/SHARE.w1.610, 10.6103/SHARE.w2.610, 10.6103/SHARE.w3.610, 10.6103/SHARE.w4.610, 10.6103/SHARE.w5.610, 10.6103/SHARE.w6.610)

8. (DOI: 10.6103/SHARE.jep.600)

9. (DOIs: 10.6103/SHARE.w1.600, 10.6103/SHARE.w2.600, 10.6103/SHARE.w3.600). The SHARE data collection was primarily funded by the European Commission through FP5 (QLK6-CT-2001-00360), FP6 (SHARE-I3: RII-CT-2006-062193, COMPARE: CIT5-CT-2005-028857, SHARELIFE: CIT4-CT-2006-028812), and FP7 (SHARE-PREP: N°211909, SHARE-LEAP: N°227822, SHARE M4: N°261982). Additional funding from the German Ministry of Education and Research, the Max Planck Society for the Advancement of Science, the U.S. National Institute on Aging (U01_AG09740-13S2, P01_AG005842, P01_AG08291, P30_AG12815, R21_AG025169, Y1-AG-4553-01, IAG_BSR06-11, OGHA_04-064, HHSN271201300071C), and from various national funding sources is gratefully acknowledged (see www.share-project.org).

10. For a discussion of solutions applied in NDC countries, see Chłoń-Domińczak, Franco, and Palmer (2012).

References

Adeline, Amelie, and Eric Delattre. 2017. "Some Microeconometric Evidence on the Relationship between Health and Income." *Health Economics Review* 7: 27. doi: 10.1186 /s13561-017-0163-5.

Antonova, Ludmila, Luis Aranda, Giacomo Pasini, and Elisabetta Trevisan. 2014. "Migration, Family History and Pension: The Second Release of the SHARE Job Episodes Panel." SHARE Working Paper 18-2014, MEA, Max Planck Institute for Social Law and Social Policy, Munich.

Baran, Jan, Atilla Bartha, Agnieszka Chłoń-Domińczak, Olena Fedyuk, Agnieszka Kamińska, Piotr Lewandowski, Maciej Lis, Iga Magda, Monika Potoczna, and Violetta Zentai. 2014. "Women on the European Labour Market." Neujobs Policy Brief (16.5). CEPS, Brussels. http://www .neujobs.eu/publications/policy-briefs/women-european-labour-market.

Börsch-Supan, Axel, Martina Brandt, Christian Hunkler, Thorsten Kneip, Julie Korbmacher, Frederic Malter, Barbara Schaan, Stephanie Stuck, and Sabrina Zuber. 2013. "Data Resource

Profile: The Survey of Health, Ageing and Retirement in Europe (SHARE)." *International Journal of Epidemiology* 42 (4): 992–1001.

Brugiavini, Agar, Danilo Cavapozzi, Giacomo Pasini, and Elisabetta Trevisan. 2013. "Working Life Histories from SHARELIFE: A Retrospective Panel." SHARE Working Paper 11-2013, MEA, Max Planck Institute for Social Law and Social Policy, Munich.

Brzinsky-Fay, Christian, Ulrich Kohler, and Magdalena Luniak. 2006. "Sequence Analysis with Stata." *Stata Journal* 6 (4): 435–60 (26).

Chłoń-Domińczak, Agnieszka. 2017. *Gender Gap in Pensions: Looking Ahead, Study for the European Parliament.* www.europarl.europa.eu/.../IPOL_STU(2017)583150_EN.pdf.

Chłoń-Domińczak, Agnieszka, Daniele Franco, and Edward Palmer. 2012. "The First Wave of NDC Reforms: The Experiences of Italy, Latvia, Poland, and Sweden." In *Nonfinancial Defined Contribution Pension Schemes in a Changing Pension World: Volume 1 Progress, Lessons, and Implementation*, edited by Robert Holzmann and Edward Palmer, 31–84. Washington, DC: World Bank. http://dx.doi.org/10.1596/9780821388488_CH02.

Elger, Tony. 2015. "Dual Labor Market Theories." In *The Wiley Blackwell Encyclopedia of Race, Ethnicity, and Nationalism*, 2nd edition, edited by George Ritzer. Malden, MA: John Wiley & Sons, Ltd. doi:10.1002/9781118663202.wberen097.

European Commission. 2015. "The 2015 Ageing Report. Economic and Budgetary Projections for the 28 EU Member States (2013–2060)." European Economy 3, European Commission, Brussels.

———. 2018. *The 2018 Pension Adequacy Report: Current and Future Income Adequacy in Old Age in the EU Country Profiles.* Luxembourg: Publications Office of the European Union.

European Parliament. 2016. "Precarious Employment in Europe. Part 1: Patterns, Trends, and Policy Strategy." Study, European Union, Brussels.

Góra, Marek, and Edward Palmer. 2004. "Shifting Perspectives in Pensions." IZA Discussion Paper 1369, Institute of Labor Economics, Bonn.

———. 2019. "NDC: The Generic Old-Age Pension System." In *Progress and Challenges of Nonfinancial Defined Contribution Pension Schemes: Volume 1 Addressing Marginalization, Polarization, and the Labor Market*, edited by Robert Holzmann, Edward Palmer, Robert Palacios, and Stefano Sacchi, Chapter 8. Washington, DC: World Bank.

Hakim, Catherine. 2003. "A New Approach to Explaining Fertility Patterns: Preference Theory." *Population and Development Review* 29 (3): 349–74. doi: 10.1111/j.1728-4457.2003.00349.x.

Hofäcker, Dirk, and Stefanie König. 2013. "Flexibility and Work-Life Conflict in Times of Crisis: A Gender Perspective." *International Journal of Sociology and Social Policy* 33 (9/10): 613–35.

Istenic, Tania, and Joze Sambt. 2016. "NTA Age Profiles in the EU Countries Results of the WP 1." AGENTA Project Results, Vienna.

Klerby, Anna, Bo Larsson, and Edward Palmer. 2013. "To Share or Not to Share: That Is the Question." In *Nonfinancial Defined Contribution Pension Schemes in a Changing Pension World: Volume 2 Gender, Politics, and Financial Stability*, edited by Robert Holzmann, Edward Palmer, and David Robalino, 39–65. Washington, DC: World Bank.

Klerby, Anna, Bo Larsson, and Edward Palmer. 2019. "Bridging Partner Life-Cycle Earnings and Pension Gaps by Sharing NDC Accounts." In *Progress and Challenges of Nonfinancial Defined Contribution Pension Schemes: Volume 2 Addressing Gender, Administration, and Communication,* edited by Robert Holzmann, Edward Palmer, Robert Palacios, and Stefano Sacchi, Chapter 20. Washington, DC: World Bank.

Kotowska, Irena E., Joanna Stachura, and Pawel Strzelecki. 2008. "Equality of Retirement Benefits Received by Men and Women in Selected European Countries. Childbearing and Future Benefits." ENEPRI Research Report 56, CEPS, Brussels. https://www.ceps.eu/publications /equality-retirement-benefits-received-men-and-women-selected-european-countries.

Lee, Ronald D., and Andrew Mason. 2011. *Population Aging and the Generational Economy: A Global Perspective*. Cheltenham, UK: Edward Elgar Publishing.

Mason, Andrew, Ronald Lee, Gretchen Donehower, Sang-Hyop Lee, Timothy Miller, An-Chi Tung, and Amonthep Chawal. 2009. *National Transfer Accounts Manual: Overview of National Transfer Accounts*. New York: United Nations.

Matysiak, Anna, and Stephanie Steinmetz. 2008. "Finding Their Way? Female Employment Patterns in West Germany, East Germany, and Poland." *European Sociological Review* 24 (3): 331–45.

Matysiak, Anna, and Dorota Węziak-Białowolska. 2016. "Country-Specific Conditions for Work and Family Reconciliation: An Attempt at Quantification." *European Journal of Population* 32 (4): 475–510.

OECD (Organisation for Economic Co-operation and Development). 2015. *Pensions at a Glance 2015: OECD and G20 Indicators*. Paris: OECD Publishing. http://dx.doi.org/10.1787 /pension_glance-2015-en.

———. 2017. *Dare to Share: Germany's Experience Promoting Equal Partnership in Families*. Paris: OECD Publishing.

Reich, Michael, David M. Gordon, and Richard C. Edwards. 1973. "A Theory of Labor Market Segmentation." *American Economic Review* 63 (2): 359–65.

Rostgaard, Tine. 2014. *Family Policies in Scandinavia*. Berlin: Friedrich-Ebert-Stiftung.

Spasova, Slavina, Denis Bouget, Dalila Ghailani, and Bart Vanhercke. 2017. "Access to Social Protection for People Working on Non-Standard Contracts and as Self-Employed in Europe." European Social Policy Network (ESPN), European Commission, Brussels.

Vitali, Agnese, Francesco C. Billari, Alexia Prskawetz, and Maria Rita Testa. 2007. "Preference Theory and Low Fertility: A Comparative Perspective." Working Paper 001, Carlo F. Dondena Centre for Research on Social Dynamics (DONDENA), Università Commerciale Luigi Bocconi, Milan. https://ideas.repec.org/p/don/donwpa/001.html.

CHAPTER 20

Bridging Partner Life-Cycle Earnings and Pension Gaps by Sharing Nonfinancial Defined Contribution Accounts

Anna Klerby, Bo Larsson, and Edward Palmer

Introduction

Sweden can take pride in being one of the top five performers in the World Economic Forum's 2018 Gender Gap Index—a position it has held since the index was created in 2006 (World Economic Forum 2018). Sweden's very generous family policy compensates parents for lost earnings from early child care and later for absence from work to care for sick children. This policy is in addition to highly subsidized universal preschool and after-school child care. So social policy already plays—and even before the introduction of the public nonfinancial defined contribution (NDC) and financial defined contribution (FDC) schemes in 1999 had begun to play—an important role in enabling parents to combine paid work with time with their children in the early years of their children's lives. This chapter assesses what happens with the earnings and total account values of spouses after the initial years of children's lives and asks the question: Is the already generous policy sufficient, or is a piece of the puzzle still missing?

The track record of women's increased labor force participation since the introduction of the NDC reform in 1999 is impressive. What has happened since 2000? The number of years women have worked before claiming retirement benefits increased from 37 years in 2001 (shortly after the NDC was introduced) to almost 42 years in 2015, compared with an increase for men from 40 to 42 years (European Commission 2015, 2018). The gender pension gap, based on public earnings–related pensions alone, fell from 50 percent to 33 percent between 2003 and 2013 (Swedish Ministry of Social Affairs 2016). Nevertheless, no direct evidence enables one to attribute all progress since 2000 to the reform per se. Instead, it is more likely that the reform supported an already ongoing evolution, and that the remaining two-year gap reflects the fact that women are, on average, two years younger than their husbands and tend to retire at the same time.

Also taking into account the guaranteed minimum pension, means-tested housing allowance, and—for women born before 1944—the widow's pension to get the total public pension paid reduces the pension gender gap even more, from 33 percent to 17 percent. These additional, minimum-income guarantee benefits fulfill an important function, but

The authors are grateful to Sonia Buchholtz and Eduardo Fajnzylber for many helpful comments and suggestions on an earlier draft of this chapter.

they also reveal that the lifetime earnings of many women fall short of those of men. The result of the current situation is that about 80 percent of Swedes ages 65 and older who qualify for a minimum pension are women (Swedish Ministry of Social Affairs 2016, 283).[1] In other words, more is needed to close the earnings-related gender gap in pensions.

There are three explanations for the gap in earnings and, ultimately, in the resulting pensions. The first is that labor market sectors dominated by women (for example, care work) have considerably lower average pay than comparable male-dominated sectors (for example, industry, construction, and transportation). The second is the prevalence of part-time work among women. Statistics Sweden's time-use surveys show that the likely root of the gender gap in earnings is the gap between women's and men's time devoted to work in the home (60/40, respectively), with the care of younger children being the dominant component. The third explanation is the prevailing culture of male-dominated top positions—combined with the belief that women are generally more predisposed to providing care, whereas caregiving at home reduces the time left for formal supply of labor and opportunities to move up the career ladder.

By definition, defined contribution (DC) pension schemes are linked directly to lifetime earnings. Because market mechanisms seek first-best solutions, gender pension equality implies spending equal time in the labor force and equal sharing of nonmarket work at home over a whole working life. Not sharing comes at the expense of the caregivers, usually the mothers. What remains is for partners to share individual claims on future pensions. This means sharing (N)DC pension accounts, either over the life of the marriage or for a period of a specified number of years in conjunction with children born during the relationship. Presently, the result of not doing this is that more than 60 percent of married and cohabiting women ages 66–90 have a guaranteed pension (Swedish Ministry of Social Affairs 2016, 83).[2]

To understand what is happening, Sweden's individual NDC account database is used, with individual accounts covering contributions of all working cohorts 1960–2012 (including generous account "add-ons" in conjunction with childbirth), to follow earnings careers of parents from the birth of the first child. The story told by the data is that women are more dedicated to parenthood than men.[3] This is in line with Akerlof and Kranton (2000, 2010), who argue that social status and social identity are the main drivers of preferences and choices, with pure economic incentives often taking second seat. Economic incentives compete with the preferences of the social and cultural environment, and traditions and expectations reinforce this behavior.

The revealed preferences of families, as expressed through the labor supply choice of women (such as for part-time work), provide utility returns to both parents at the micro level and enhance the quality of the inputs of each generation's contribution to gross domestic product at the macro level—through higher quality of human capital. The implication is that sharing is the optimal state, which is what all married couples do anyway; not sharing brings with it the risk that the dominant caretaker is penalized economically if the couple divorces, which is the case for Sweden and other advanced economic societies since about 50 percent of marriages end in divorce—with the economically dominant partner (usually the man) in the best position.

The conclusion easily reached is that a policy is needed that encourages the sharing of pension rights between parents after the birth of the mother's first child. This is the topic explored in this chapter, relying on the research results of work on "nudging" by Thaler and Sunstein (2008). If the societal goal is to push parents in the direction of equal sharing of time at home and in market-based work, the instrument to achieve this in the context of pensions is sharing—that is, creating a nudge in the right direction. Nudging in this case means setting as the default option the sharing of pension accounts, for example, from the time of the birth of the first child forward to a designated stop time, with a formal mutual agreement required to opt out of the default.

The potential power of nudging in this situation finds support in related work of Chetty et al. (2014) that Danish pension savers who defaulted to a financially superior option for retirement saving predominantly chose not to exercise their opt-out option. In the pension account-sharing context, sharing is expected to remain the dominant option chosen (by not opting out). In addition, mandating sharing as the default can be expected to lead to a conversation at the dinner table inducing the main breadwinner to push the home partner into the formal labor market, allocating more of his or her own time to after-school care of children.

"Overview of the Swedish Pension System and Parental Rights within the Context of Family Policy" describes the Swedish pension landscape and family policy in conjunction with childbirth. Using the Swedish NDC individual account database with data for the period 1960–2012 and simulated outcomes with unchanged career behavior through 2036, "A Picture of Earnings and the Impact of Child Year Credits on Individual Accounts" examines the development of the earnings careers of couples before and after the birth of their first child, without and with the existing child-care account add-ons. In "Estimation of Future Pensions and the Income Inequality of Married Couples," future pensions are estimated and income inequality of married couples is examined. "The Risk of Receiving a Guarantee Pension" illustrates the change in the distribution of women's and men's individual accounts, before and after account sharing. "The Effects of Sharing" estimates the odds of women receiving a guarantee pension fully or as a supplement to the combined public NDC and FDC benefits and gives the key characteristics and circumstances of partners, without and with sharing of pension accounts. "Discussion and Conclusions" provides a summary and conclusions.

Overview of the Swedish Pension System and Parental Rights Within the Context of Family Policy

GENERAL OVERVIEW OF THE PUBLIC PENSION AND WELFARE SYSTEMS

Sweden's public pension system consists of a large NDC scheme (16 percent contribution rate) and a small FDC scheme (2.5 percent contribution rate) with a defined benefit minimum pension guarantee. Contributions are paid on earnings up to a ceiling, including social insurance compensation for lost earnings. The ceiling is indexed to the nominal average wage rate based on the earnings of all contributors. In addition to the minimum pension guarantee, pensioners who risk a low standard of living because of high housing costs enjoy a fully means-tested housing allowance.

The public pension system is topped up by occupational schemes that cover about 80 percent of all employees in Sweden. These schemes provide additional coverage for earnings under the ceiling with, on average, another 4.5 percent contribution rate on earnings below the ceiling. The occupational schemes also provide benefits for earnings above the ceiling. This chapter focuses solely on the public universal NDC and FDC schemes, treated in the calculations as one NDC scheme.

Contributions to the public pension schemes originate from two sources. The main source is taxable earned incomes. The other source is the pension-qualifying amounts provided by the general public welfare system, based on years of higher education, conscripted military service, and years with children up to age five. The most important of the latter is the child year credit. Taxable earned income encompasses individual earnings, compensation from social insurance that replaces earnings for workdays lost because of sickness, staying at home in conjunction with a child's sickness, unemployment, partial or full disability, and parental leave of 480 days in conjunction with childbirth. All of these sources of income give rise to actual contributions paid to the NDC and FDC schemes and ascribed to individual accounts.

The source of money for the contributions paid in addition to contributions paid on earnings is largely tax-financing via the public budget; in the case of NDC, this is noted on accounts and transferred into the NDC fund, and in the case of FDC directly to individual accounts, where it is invested in individuals' chosen financial portfolios. The data on income underlying individual accounts, which is the database used here, show that the ceiling on earnings on which contribution payments are made to the public pension scheme is within the range of the eighth income decile for men and the ninth income decile for women.

OVERVIEW OF FAMILY BENEFITS OF IMPORTANCE FOR INDIVIDUAL PENSION ACCOUNTS IN THE PUBLIC SCHEMES

For the purposes of this chapter, it is important to emphasize that Swedish family policy acknowledges the value of the care work of children by crediting the account of the parent with the lower earnings (usually the mother) with a tax-financed pension-qualifying amount—a child year credit for the first four years of a child's life. The amount is the same for one or more children but is paid as long as there is one child younger than age five in the household. The value of the child year credit is labeled the Pension Qualifying Amount for Children (PQAC) and is shown in the following empirical analysis to be of considerable importance for mothers' individual account values.

The child year credit constitutes an add-on to individual accounts with the birth of a child. In preparation for implementation of the NDC reform in 1999, NDC accounts were created using data on earnings and contributions, already computerized from 1960. The amount of the PQAC is based on the per capita earnings corresponding to at least 75 percent of the Swedish mean for the same year[4]; credits were calculated ex post for childbirths from 1969; and child-care rights were credited to the accounts of mothers (ex post) by the Swedish Social Insurance Agency to prepare individual accounts before the introduction of the NDC scheme in 1999. This chapter makes use of a statistical database of individual account data from 1960 onward—the same data used in practice to calculate NDC pensions—to analyze the role played by the child-care rights and more generally the increase in income from the add-ons to accounts of mothers, the main recipients of the child-care credits in the first four years of a child's life.

Another feature of Sweden's family policy is a child allowance that compensates for lost earnings in conjunction with childbirth. Compensation is paid for 480 days that do not have to be consecutive, of which 120 days are irreversibly devoted to each parent since 2016. In 2017, Swedish mothers claimed 72 percent and Swedish fathers 28 percent of the total available allowance days compensating for child care directly in connection with childbirth. The allowance replaces only 77 percent of lost earnings up to the contribution ceiling, in some cases filled out by occupational supplements (Statistics Sweden 2018).[5] However, the parent can choose to replace fewer days with benefits than the amount of days off from work. Data from the Swedish Social Insurance Agency show that women were away from work in conjunction with childbirth on average 15.3 full months, while replacing income with the child allowance for a number of days corresponding to 9.5 months of full-time work; men were away from work on average 3.8 full months, while replacing earnings with child allowance days corresponding to 2.2 months of full-time work (Swedish Social Insurance Agency 2013b, 5).

A Picture of Earnings and the Impact of Child Year Credits On Individual Accounts

THE SWEDISH NDC PENSION DATABASE AND THE NOMENCLATURE USED

The database made available for this chapter was provided by the Swedish Pensions Agency and covers 1960–2012.[6] The empirical analysis uses the following terms for taxable earned income (Inc), which in the present context encompasses earnings from employment or self-employment, as well as the various forms of social insurance that replace loss of earnings or income as described in the preceding section. In addition, pension qualifying amounts (PQA)—the separate rights that take the form of add-ons to the accounts for those who qualify—are granted in conjunction with completed periods of higher education and conscripted military service, as well as in conjunction with the first four years of a newly born child's life, which are the child-care rights described in the preceding section.

Together, these sources of income constitute the pension base (PB) on which contributions are paid into individual accounts. In the NDC scheme, individual accounts are credited yearly with an annual rate of return based on the increase in the average nominal taxable earned income per contributor. At retirement, the amount of yearly benefits to be paid throughout the remaining life of the retiree is calculated based on the individual's pension account at retirement and the annuity divisor, based on the average life expectancy of the retiree's birth cohort. The resultant pension is then also indexed to the rate of inflation and the rate of growth in real income, through another index encompassing a deduction of a fixed rate of 1.6 percent already included in the calculation of the annuity.

Also used in the analysis is available information on individual characteristics: birth year, country of birth, level of highest education, marriage year, number of children, and family relationships. The total number of individuals in the database is 6,781,839, from which different subsets are drawn for the different analyses. The selection criteria are: (1) married women born between 1954 and 1973 and their spouses, where (2) the mother's first child was born in the selected year—sorted with the criterion that it is the mother's first child since both spouses could have had children before the current marriage—depending on the analytical purpose.[7]

DEVELOPMENT OF PARENTS' EARNINGS IN CONJUNCTION WITH CHILDBIRTH

The empirical analysis starts with a visualization of the impact of the birth of the first child on the relative income of parents. Panel a of figure 20.1 shows the average levels of taxable earned income[8] (Inc) and the PB for mothers and fathers around the birth of the mother's first child, from T−2 to T+17. T = 0 is the birth year of the first child. In panel a of figure 20.1, the average ratio of mothers' taxable income to that of fathers is compared with the average ratio of mothers' PB to that of fathers for the same period.

Striking in panel a of figure 20.1 is the clear difference between mothers' and fathers' average earned taxable income before and after the birth of the mother's first child. Before the birth of the mother's first child, the average of mothers' income relative to that of fathers is slightly less than 80 percent. Given that the average age difference within couples is only two years, a possible difference in earnings from age cannot be an important explanation of the gap.

Panel b of figure 20.1 shows a large earnings gap during the early childhood years, when earnings also include the child allowance, of which about 80 percent is claimed by mothers. Comparison of the PBs of mothers and fathers during the initial years shows

FIGURE 20.1 **Comparing the earnings and pension bases of mothers and fathers before and after birth of the mother's first child**

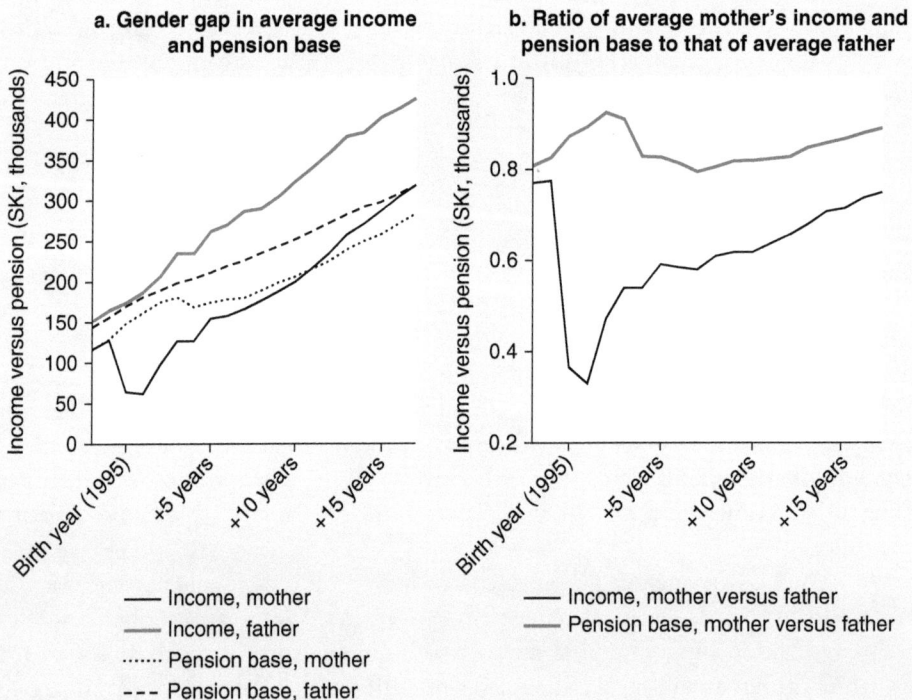

a. Gender gap in average income and pension base

b. Ratio of average mother's income and pension base to that of average father

—— Income, mother
—— Income, father
······· Pension base, mother
– – – Pension base, father

—— Income, mother versus father
—— Pension base, mother versus father

SOURCE: Swedish Pensions Agency's NDC database.

NOTE: The number of couples with a first-born child in these panels is 3,712. NDC = nonfinancial defined contribution; SKr = Swedish kronor.

that the income gender gap is small. This is largely explained by the child year credits granted to the parent with the lowest declared income each of the child's first four years; predominantly mothers. Clearly, the child year credit is fulfilling its function during the initial years following childbirth.

Most significant, however, is the gender gap that emerges around years five and six in average incomes that remains largely unchanged during the 17-year follow-up period (panel a of figure 20.1). In fact, it does not even match the gap before the birth of the mother's first child. As women tend to have higher education, the implication is that the gap mainly reflects the different circumstances men and women meet on the labor market and the consequences of women's part-time work.

Panel a of figure 20.2 shows the ratio of the average mothers' to the average fathers' total PB (the same as PB in panel b of figure 20.1) divided into those who had only one child before 2012 and those who had two or more children. In panel a of figure 20.2, the same groups are shown, but the PB is net of child year credits. The solid line denotes mothers with only one child; the dashed line denotes mothers who have two or more children. Mothers in this context are those with their first child born in 1992.

The average drop in average earnings of mothers relative to their partners is about 30 percent for women with one child and 37 percent for women with two children or more.

FIGURE 20.2 **Ratio of mothers' to fathers' pension base, by one-child-families and families with two or more children**

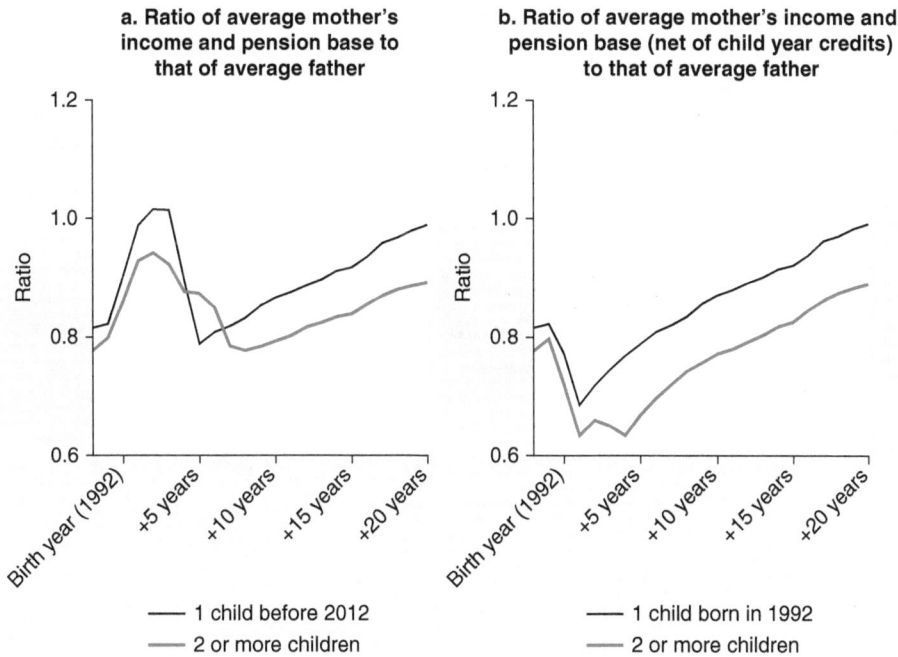

a. Ratio of average mother's income and pension base to that of average father

b. Ratio of average mother's income and pension base (net of child year credits) to that of average father

— 1 child before 2012
— 2 or more children

— 1 child born in 1992
— 2 or more children

SOURCE: Swedish Pensions Agency's NDC database.

NOTE: The number of mothers with only one child is 6,591; the number of mothers with several children is 33,934. NDC = nonfinancial defined contribution.

For women having two children or more, the gap is also prolonged relative to those having one child. This suggests that for the average two-child family, the gender gap is long-lived. Finally, the difference between the two panels in figure 20.2 supports the conclusion that the child year credits are very important in strengthening the PB of mothers relative to fathers in the initial years following the births of their children.

The majority of mothers will have a second child around the time when the first child turns three; accordingly, taxable earnings drop again after having increased gradually after year 1, illustrating the importance of the PQAC. This is apparent in panel a of figure 20.2 from the small hump reducing the drop from its bottom value. At the same time, the long-term negative effect of part-time work increases in scale for mothers of two or more children.

Panel a of figure 20.2 also reveals that the taxable earnings of mothers with one child do not drop much relative to those of their spouses, so in the initial years the child year credits (PQAC) compensate for lost earnings practically fully. Mothers' PB is, on average, even higher than the average PB of their spouse the third and fourth year after the birth, indicating mothers have also returned to work part time. Not surprisingly the PB of mothers with only one child also catches up with that of fathers faster than for those giving birth to two or more children. This finding suggests that mothers of one child have relatively high incomes, or more equal income status with respect to their partner, for example, as a result of career choice but also possibly because of higher average age.

Summing up, child year credits in the initial years are very important for continuity in the development of mothers' PB. After the initial years, women are still predominantly the ones to claim income compensation for the care of sick children up to age 12. As the years pass, however, the gender gap remains slightly less than 20 percent because of the direct effect of part-time work on earnings and the indirect effect of career choice or lack of possibilities and lower wages on average. However, the underlying issue is more complex. Several studies show that the average working woman faces a wage penalty from parenthood relative to women without children, while men are rewarded a "father bonus" (for example, higher incomes relative to men without children) (Boschini and Sundström 2018; Budig and Hodges 2010; Correll, Benard, and Paik 2007; Hodges and Budig 2010).

Estimation of Future Pensions and the Income Inequality of Married Couples

PREVIOUS STUDIES OF SHARING—THE UNITED STATES AND SWEDEN

This section begins with a short review of some earlier studies of sharing of pension rights. Klerby, Larsson, and Palmer (2013) estimate the effect of defaulting into joint annuities in NDC at retirement using Swedish national income data on earnings to estimate pension accounts. Using national income data instead of actual account data, the study also finds that the estimated account balances of Swedish men at retirement were approximately 30 percent higher than those of women.

Others have also worked with analyses relating to sharing of pension rights. For example, Burkhauser (1982) concludes that the U.S. Social Security spousal benefits were paid primarily to wives of high-earning males. Ferber, Simpson, and Rouillon (2006) suggest that U.S. Social Security retirement payments to spouses of workers should be eliminated to "cut off" the economic dependency of wives on their husbands and that this practice should be replaced with earnings sharing. Favreault and Steuerle (2007) estimate the outcome of sharing using U.S. data projected until 2049 and find that the effects were not as large as expected.

OVERVIEW OF THE INCOME STATUS OF MARRIED COUPLES AND ASSUMPTIONS UNDERLYING OUTSIDE-SAMPLE PROJECTIONS

This section uses a sample from the Swedish Pensions Agency's NDC database of married women born between 1954 and 1973 and their spouses to examine how sharing pension rights affects the pension outcome. The selected subset comprises couples who have been married once and are still married as of 2012 and whose husband's year of birth is within the range of ± 9 years of his spouse. The data for income and contributions use the entire database for 1960–2012.

In addition, individuals' PB after 2012 are projected extrapolating previous earnings careers. Moreover, the rate of return given to account balances and the pension divisor used to convert individual pension balances into yearly benefits at retirement also have to be projected. For example, for the birth cohort of 1973, taxable earned income is projected for 2013–38 for women and to 2047 for spouses who are nine years younger. Panel a of figure 20.3 displays the rate of inflation, the real rate of return on contributions paid, and the actual overall "income" index used to valorize accounts (adjusted for balancing according to a projection of the Swedish Pensions Agency, from the *Orange Report 2017*). Panel b of figure 20.3 also shows the economic divisors (based on projected life expectancy and a 1.6 percent real rate of return on savings in the pension pool) used in the Swedish pension system, supplemented with the projections through 2047.

FIGURE 20.3 **The rate of growth of income (income index), return on nonfinancial defined contribution accounts (income base), inflation, and pension divisor**

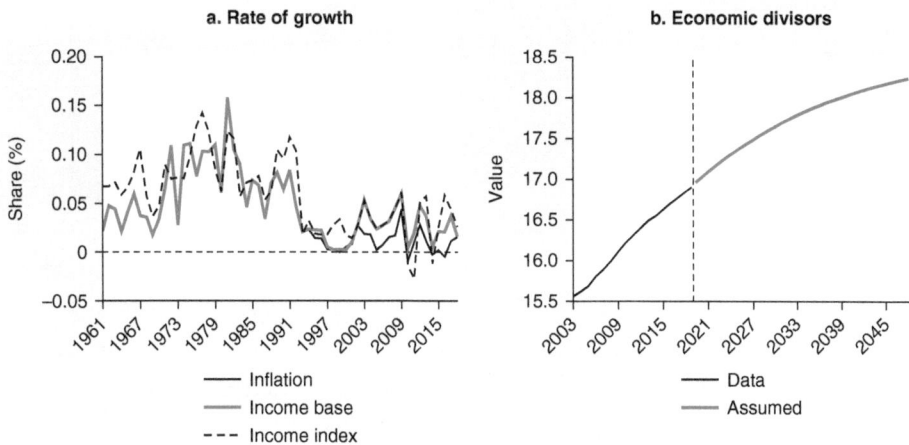

SOURCE: Swedish Pensions Agency's NDC database.

NOTE: NDC = nonfinancial defined contribution.

Average real wages grew at a rate of about 1.5 percent per year from 1960 to 2012. Nevertheless, a rate of 1.0 percent is used for the projections. A higher level would erode the guarantee pension threshold significantly because it follows the rate of inflation and not the growth of real earnings. Even with 1 percent real income growth, the PB will grow in real terms approximately 22 percent for women born in 1973 and 33 percent for their youngest husbands. Because the guarantee tapers off, increasingly fewer will have pensions of less than the threshold.

Figure 20.4 shows the taxable earned income for 2012 for the subsample of married women born in 1956, thus at age 56 with husbands younger than age 65—at that time. The information for this subsample is the basis for the continued analyses of contribution histories. The concentration of people at the top of the income scale is due to the income ceiling for contribution-based income, which was SKr 409,500 in 2012. The smaller concentration at the bottom is the group with hardly any taxable earnings. This group will qualify for only a small NDC or FDC benefit, which will be supplemented by a guarantee benefit up to the maximum guarantee pension level. The sample of 25,544 consists of women in married couples who have been married only once (at the time the database was constructed) and are still married with a husband younger than age 65.

Figure 20.5 shows a histogram of the difference in taxable earned income for married couples in 2012 (husband's taxable earned income minus wife's taxable earned income) where the woman is born in 1956 (women with retired husbands, husbands older than age 64, and spouses who could not be identified in the data set are excluded). It is noteworthy that 35 percent of the wives in the sample of 25,544 have a larger PB than their husbands in 2012.

FIGURE 20.4 **Taxable earned income for 2012 for married women born in 1956**

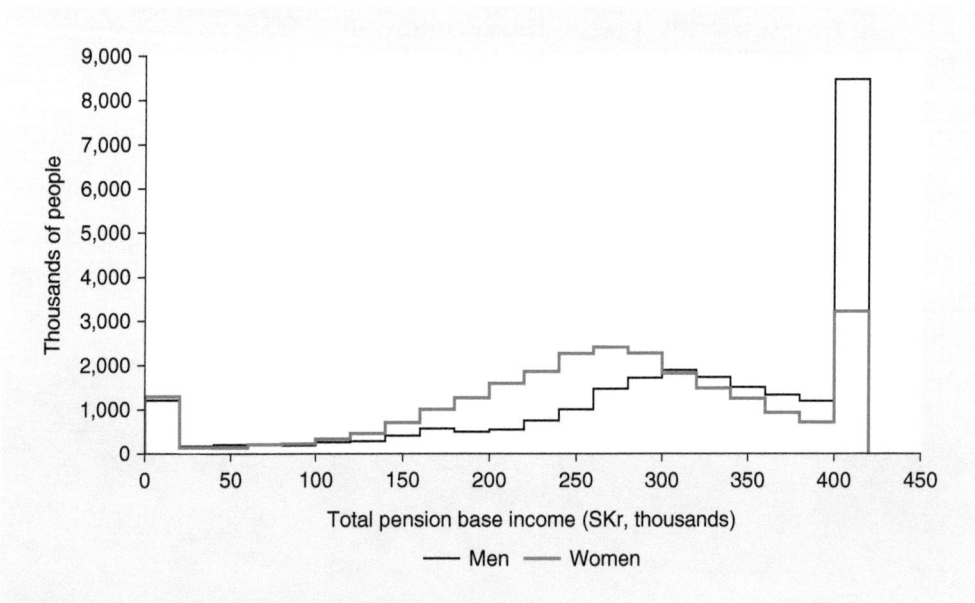

SOURCE: Swedish Pensions Agency's NDC database.

NOTE: NDC = nonfinancial defined contribution; SKr = Swedish kronor.

FIGURE 20.5 **Histogram of the difference in yearly taxable earned income for married couples, 2012**

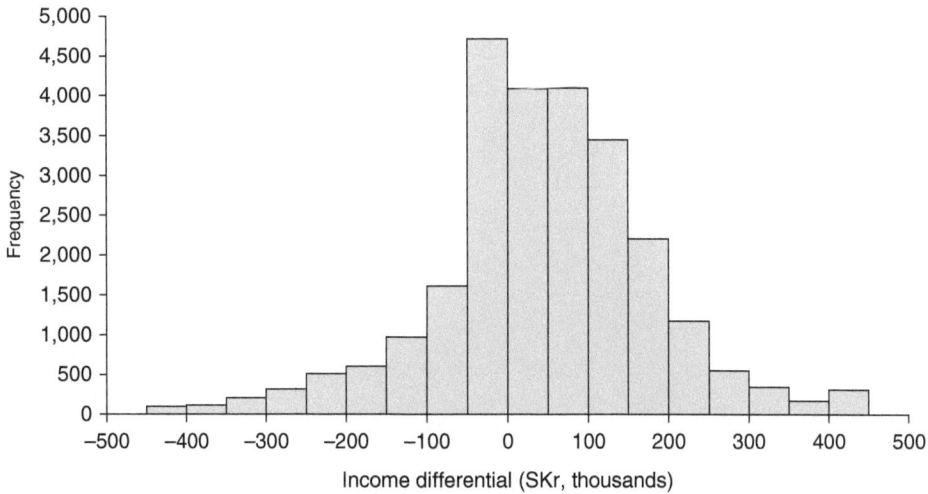

SOURCE: Swedish Pensions Agency's NDC database.

NOTE: Difference is defined as husband's income minus wife's income. NDC = nonfinancial defined contribution; SKr = Swedish kronor.

The data in figure 20.5 are representative of the overall population, looking back in time. These data patterns are used to complete earnings careers and accumulated contributions (with interest) at retirement to project the historical patterns forward.

Using the extended database with individual account information, and with projections, for the period 1960–2048, the analysis identifies the need for a guarantee benefit for women, all assumed to claim a pension at age 65. The question now asked is, What are the social circumstances and characteristics (assuming no change in their status after 2012—the last actual data point) of persons who will get a pension that is less than the guarantee pension threshold? The focus is first mainly on mothers' pensions as a proxy for the main caregivers. The second focus is on the relationship between (and "effect" of) the breadwinner's work pattern and the partner's pension. In this context, the focus is on the extent to which the guarantee pension, predominantly claimed by women (both with and without children), is correlated with marriage to a male high-income earner.

The Risk of Receiving a Guarantee Pension

PROJECTING THE RISK OF RECEIVING A GUARANTEE PENSION FOR PRESENTLY WORKING BIRTH COHORTS

Given that the youngest person in the projection of future outcomes does not turn age 65 until 2048, it is necessary to forecast a large number of account values and annuities from the last data point in the 2012 database.[9] Figure 20.6 breaks down the lowest forecasted monthly pensions decile (10 percent) of couples, presented through the projected

FIGURE 20.6 **Projections of account balances from 2013 until the pension age of 65**

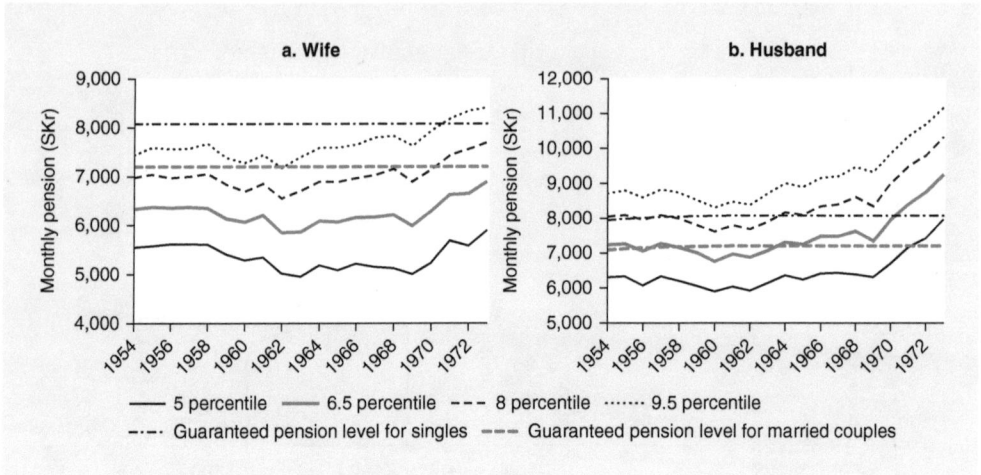

SOURCE: Swedish Pensions Agency's NDC database.

NOTE: NDC = nonfinancial defined contribution; SKr = Swedish kronor.

monthly pension for the 5th, 6.5th, 8th, and 9.5th percentile for husbands and wives separately (women born between 1954 and 1973 and their husbands). The threshold for the guarantee pension is displayed as horizontal lines for singles and married couples, respectively.

The pension needed for a single person to rise completely above the guarantee pension level in fixed prices—because the guarantee is indexed only to inflation—is slightly greater than SKr 8,100 per month, and SKr 7,200 for an individual cohabiting with another adult. It is estimated that a single household needs an income of 62.5 percent of a couple's joint incomes (rather than 50 percent) to obtain the standard of living enjoyed as a couple (Klerby, Larsson, and Palmer 2013). If a couple divorces or separates, the relevant guarantee level to focus on is that of singles; therefore, both are displayed.

The projection shows that of the cohort of women born in 1955, about 8.5 percent will qualify for a guarantee pension supplement of some size; for younger cohorts born in 1970 and later, however, this falls to about 7 percent. For their husbands, the situation is better. Among the equivalent birth cohorts, the share below the guarantee pension threshold is about 6.5 percent, decreasing to less than 5.0 percent for the youngest birth cohorts. It is clear that men have higher taxable earned income than their spouses and that this spills over to pensions and creates inequality, especially for those with extremely low pension account balances, at the bottom deciles. Finally, if these women and men were to divorce, the share of women below the guarantee pension threshold would increase to more than 10 percent for the oldest and to about 9 percent for the youngest. The corresponding shares for their husbands are from 8 percent to about 5 percent.

Because the guarantee level is a fixed level that is price indexed over time, gradually fewer and fewer persons will fall under the line because of increased real wage growth. Single persons falling below the threshold for a guarantee are definitely in relative poverty (which is based on joint household income with a spouse). Persons in this group are likely to also have the right to a means-tested (against living costs) housing assistance benefit in

FIGURE 20.7 **Predicted distribution of monthly public pension for married women and men (once and still married)**

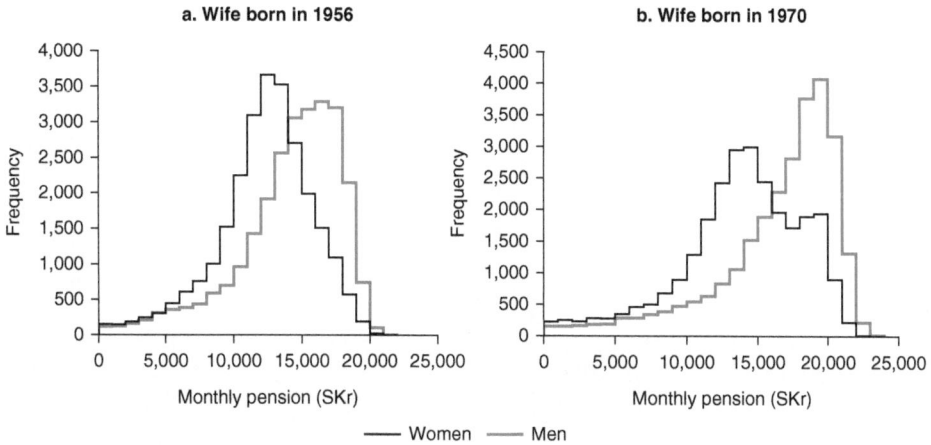

SOURCE: Swedish Pensions Agency's NDC database.

NOTE: NDC = nonfinancial defined contribution; SKr = Swedish kronor.

addition to the guarantee, which gradually fills a growing gap between the price-indexed guarantee and earnings that are continuously growing at the assumed average rate of real growth of 1 percent in addition to inflation. The reason for this is that the guarantee benefit is indexed only to inflation. In this respect, the information in figure 20.6, reflecting relative incomes of spouses or partners with children, is relevant even in the future.

Figure 20.7 shows the predicted distribution of monthly pension amounts among the group of women born in 1956 and 1970 who in 2012 and earlier were married, where the husband's birth year is in an interval of ± 9 years with respect to his wife. It is hard to predict exactly what will happen with the lower earnings and thus pensions of married women compared with their spouses; what is most likely is that men's future pensions will continue to dominate those of women's, in line with figure 20.7. Nevertheless, it is clear that the top fraction of women is expected to close the gap with the top fraction of men.

From the difference between the cumulative distributions for each of the birth cohorts, men's pensions are slightly more dominant for the later birth cohort, despite the result that there are relatively more women with higher pensions. However, this reflects the ceiling on contributions to the public pension scheme and the resultant outcome that men's earnings rise to a greater degree above the ceiling. Increasingly, more women also have earnings that surpass the ceiling, but they are likely to maintain their relative position vis-à-vis men. Finally, for the women in the example (and most of the men), the threshold for the guarantee pension is SKr 7,200 per month, as in figure 20.6.

In conclusion, figures 20.6 and 20.7 indicate that a fairly large group of women is at risk of receiving a low pension in the future because they fall below the guarantee pension threshold. The next question addressed is, What is their socioeconomic profile? To determine the circumstances and characteristics that increase the relative odds of being

TABLE 20.1 **Logit model, explanatory factors for women's guarantee pension**

	Individual		Sharing	
	1956	**1970**	**1956**	**1970**
Intercept	−2.39569	−2.62002	−3.20789	−4.28271
	(0.1597)	(−0.1895)	(0.1814)	(0.2792)
Guarantee pension (husband)	2.13472	2.36464	n.a.	n.a.
	(0.0713)	(0.0684)	n.a.	n.a.
Not born in Sweden	1.99211	1.99656	2.58950	2.50899
	(0.0713)	(0.0686)	(0.0871)	(0.1520)
Education	−0.07169	−0.04818	−0.06091	−0.02439
	(0.0049)	(0.0046)	(0.0056)	(0.0062)
Children (at least one)	−0.92079	−1.27250	−1.34130	−1.54499
	(0.0893)	(0.09079)	(0.09794)	(0.11484)
Education (husband)	0.02486	0.01827	−0.00172	−0.00036
	(0.0047)	(0.0045)	(0.0054)	(0.0062)
Husband not born in Sweden	0.30406	0.46890	1.53150	2.61670
	(0.0774)	(0.0705)	(0.0808)	(0.1483)
Age difference	0.01390	0.01008	−0.02473	0.07732
	(0.0079)	(0.0079)	(0.0090)	(0.0106)
Marriage age	0.00710	0.01147	0.01414	−0.02107
	(0.0030)	(0.0042)	(0.0034)	(0.0055)
Degrees of freedom	25,989	26,719	25,990	26,720
McFadden Pseudo R^2	0.332	0.328	0.386	0.310

SOURCE: Original table.

NOTE: n.a. = not applicable.

in this group, a logistic regression is estimated with women below the guarantee pension threshold as the dependent variable. Table 20.1 presents the results.

CIRCUMSTANCES AND CHARACTERISTICS THAT INCREASE THE RELATIVE ODDS OF BECOMING A GUARANTEE PENSIONER

In this segment of the analysis, all women are included, even those who have no children. Table 20.1 presents the results from four regressions, in which the dependent variable is a binary variable with the value of 1 for women below the guarantee pension threshold. Two regressions are without pension sharing and two are with sharing. To check whether the results are stable over time, the regressions are estimated for two birth cohorts of women—that is, those born in 1956 and in 1970.

In the logistic regressions with sharing, the indicator for "husband expected to be below the guarantee pension threshold" is dropped, given that it may be endogenous because of high correlation between the spouses' incomes. This is because imposing sharing increases the probability of pushing the spouse with the higher income down into the guarantee region, resulting in an increase in the number of couples in which both the husband and wife receive a share of the guarantee pension. Noteworthy from the underlying data is that the correlation between being below the guarantee pension threshold increases by more than 20 percentage points when sharing is imposed, from 0.46 to 0.68.

An immigrant will find it harder to land a job than a native, all else being equal, because of the need to learn Swedish. In addition, immigrants often enter the labor force when it no longer is possible for them to work a full working career in Sweden, which increases the risk of receiving at least a partial guarantee. To capture this effect, the individual's and spouse's heritage (Swedish born or non-Swedish born) are included as binary variables in the regression. Level of education can also be expected to play a role, and both (women's) own and (male) spouse's education are included (coded 0–25, representing the scale from no education up to PhD). A binary variable with the value of 1 is included for those having one or more children (where information is available up to the woman's age of 40) and a value of 0 for no children. The regression also includes the couple's age difference (the man's age minus the woman's) and the woman's age at the time of their marriage.

Table 20.2 shows the effect on the odds of receiving a guarantee benefit with the results in table 20.1 converted into odds ratios. The values shown in table 20.2 are the result of a unit change in the explanatory variable. A value of 1.0 means that changes in the variable have neither a positive nor a negative effect on the outcome; that is, the odds that they will affect the outcome of receiving a guarantee benefit are thus zero. Odds greater than 1.0 mean that the characteristic represented by the explanatory variable increases the probability of receiving a guarantee benefit and a value lower than 1.0 means the category is associated with lower odds of this outcome.

The most important variables explaining the incidence of women being entitled to a (partial or full) guarantee pension without sharing are "Guarantee (husband)" and "Not born in Sweden." Both increase the risk of having a guarantee pension, whereas

TABLE 20.2 **Odds ratios based on the estimated parameters in table 20.1**

	Individual		Sharing	
	1956	**1970**	**1956**	**1970**
Guarantee (husband)	8.455	10.640	n.a.	n.a.
Not born in Sweden	7.331	7.364	13.323	10.124
Education	0.931	0.953	0.941	0.959
Children (at least one)	0.398	0.280	0.262	0.180
Education (husband)	1.025	1.018	0.998	1.003
Husband not born in Sweden	1.355	1.598	4.625	4.223
Age difference	1.014	1.010	0.976	1.002
Marriage age	1.007	1.012	1.014	0.996

SOURCE: Original table.

NOTE: n.a. = not applicable.

the variable "Children" reduces the risk of having a guarantee pension (all three are 0–1 binary variables). Being born in 1956 and married to a man who is expected to be below the guarantee pension threshold raises the odds that the wife will also be a guarantee pension recipient, by 8.46 times the neutral outcome.[10]

The other variables are education (an ordinal scale, proportional to the length of education, with a mean of about 10 years); age difference (defined as husband's age minus the wife's age, a continuous variable with a mean of about 1 and a range from −9 to +9); and woman's age at marriage (with a mean of 31 for the still young 1970 cohort and a range of 16–42). Even if the effect from the husband's education has a low odds ratio of 1.025, completing high school (three more years of education after elementary school) compared with only finishing elementary school (nine years of education) raises the variable by a scale-factor of 6; thus, the odds of a woman being below the threshold increase with her husband's increased education.

Without sharing, having a husband who is expected to receive a guarantee pension increases the odds more than 8 and 10 times for women born in 1956 and 1970, respectively. A husband not born in Sweden gives seven times higher odds of becoming a guarantee pensioner for both birth cohorts. Another large effect is coupled to having children, which lowers the odds of ending up with a guarantee pension by at least 60 percent (the factor change is 0.4). Having a husband who was born abroad also raises the odds of receiving a guarantee pension by 36 percent and 60 percent for women born in 1956 and 1970, respectively.

The odds of being below the guarantee pension threshold are roughly 0.09 for both birth cohorts without sharing. When sharing pension contribution rights, the odds fall to 0.065 and 0.058 for the two birth cohorts, respectively. Both being born abroad and having a husband born abroad raise the odds of receiving a guarantee pension, whereas having children lowers the odds substantially.

The Effects of Sharing

This section presents the sharing model examined in the tables. It first refers back to figures 20.6 and 20.7, where the density in the lower tail of the income distribution for women is higher than that for men. "The Risk of Receiving a Guarantee Pension" provides a good picture of the characteristics underlying this outcome. Earlier sections discuss what is known about what underlies the profile of the time dimension of the factors of the gender pension gap—going back to the time of the birth of the mother's first child. Figure 20.8 shows how sharing moves the central values of pension payments closer to each other, creating a tighter distribution around the central values for both mothers and fathers. In the calculations the sharing of pension rights stops as soon as one spouse reaches age 65, regardless of whether either continues to work.

Calculating the difference between the cumulative distribution function for sharing and no sharing reveals that women's pensions are raised more than men's pensions shrink. However, most of the effect is above the threshold for the guarantee pension because of a positive correlation of spouses' income. If the woman is a low-income lifetime earner and subsequently below the guarantee pension threshold, as seen in the preceding section, it is fairly likely that her husband is below the threshold as well. The largest equalizing effect of a policy of sharing pension rights occurs if spouses' incomes are negatively correlated.

FIGURE 20.8 **Distribution of projected monthly pensions, with and without sharing, for couples in which the woman was born in 1956**

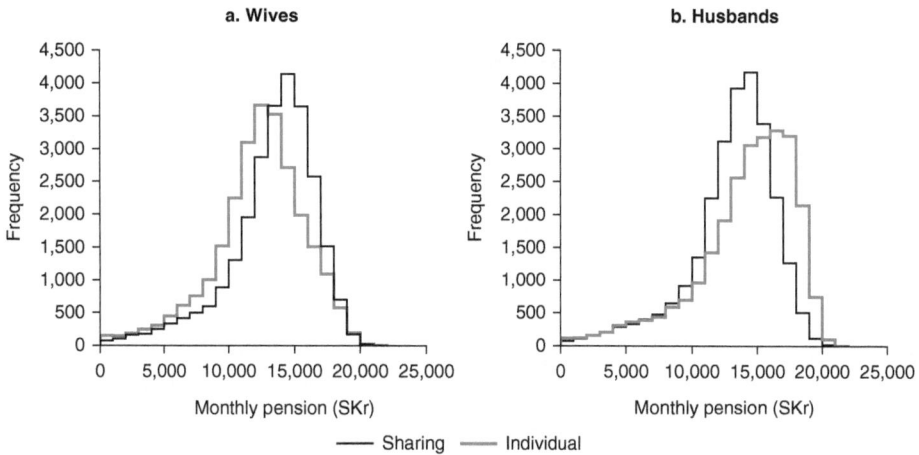

SOURCE: Swedish Pensions Agency's NDC database.

NOTE: NDC = nonfinancial defined contribution; SKr = Swedish kronor.

Figure 20.9 is similar to figure 20.8 but for couples in which the wife is born in 1970. The difference between sharing and not sharing is much larger in the lower tail for women born in 1970, suggesting an increasing gap between men with higher earnings and their female partners. The shrinkage in men's pensions versus women's is now virtually the same when calculating the difference between the cumulative distribution functions.

Figure 20.10 returns to the uptake of the guarantee pension. Panel a shows the share of husbands and wives who are projected to receive a guarantee pension if they stay married, and panel b shows projections if all of them were to divorce. Projections show both with (Sharing) and without (Individual) sharing. Some of the men in the sample already receive a guarantee pension because they are already retired. Slightly more than 8 percent of the married women born in the mid-1950s are expected to end up below the guarantee pension threshold. The shares rise with younger cohorts to a peak of 9.6 percent for those born in 1962. From 1963, the share falls to about 4 percent for married women born in 1973 (possibly as a result of the assumptions, and a resultant increasing distance down to the guarantee threshold, because the guarantee is only price indexed by assumption, whereas wages experience real growth). This same effect increases relative poverty, especially among single, elderly women, in the absence of sharing or joint annuities. Notable in panel a is that if the individual pension contribution rights were to be shared continuously, in the selected population the share of women ending up below the guarantee pension threshold would drop by 2 percentage points.

If one considers the outcome of divorce (or being widowed), as forecast in panel a of figure 20.10, the fraction of women who would be expected to be below the threshold for a guarantee pension supplement is as high as 11.5 percent for those born in the mid-1950s, peaks at roughly 12.0 percent in 1962, and then falls back to roughly 5.5–6.0 percent;

FIGURE 20.9 **Distribution of projected monthly pensions, with and without sharing, for couples in which the woman was born in 1970**

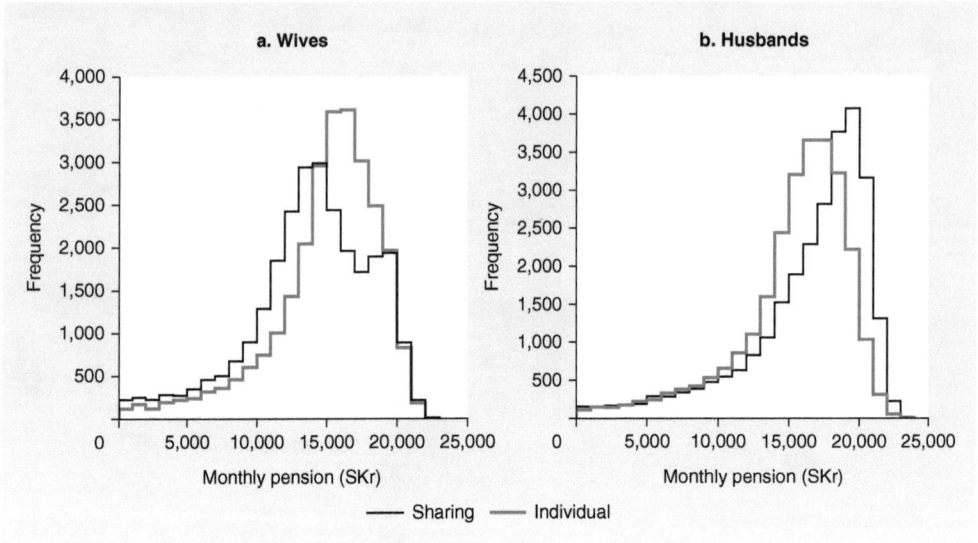

SOURCE: Swedish Pensions Agency's NDC database.

NOTE: NDC = nonfinancial defined contribution; SKr = Swedish kronor.

FIGURE 20.10 **Projections of the share of wives and husbands (for each age cohort) who will be below the guarantee pension threshold, with and without sharing, and the effect of divorce**

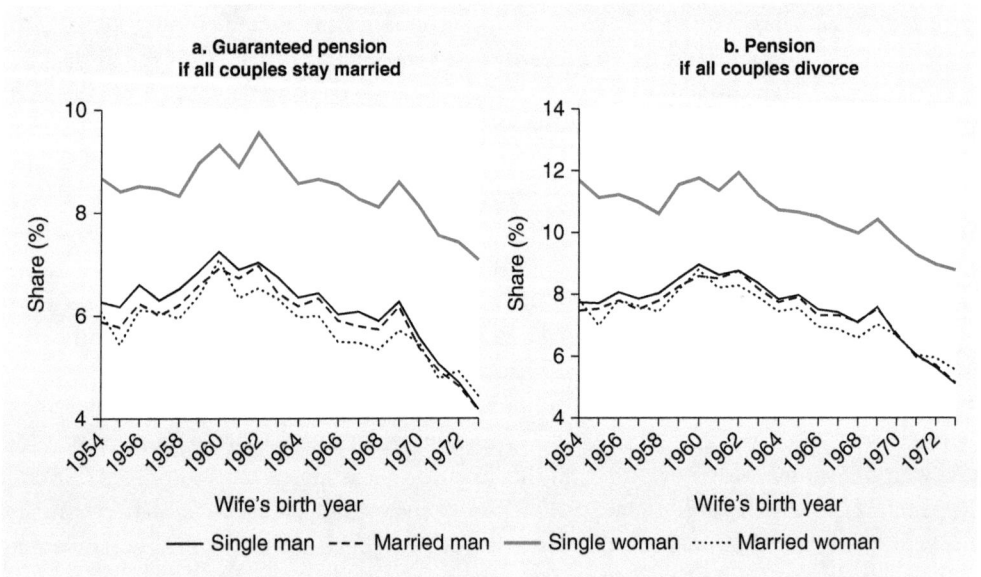

SOURCE: Swedish Pensions Agency's NDC database.

NOTE: NDC = nonfinancial defined contribution.

this is a result of not indexing the guarantee pension to real income growth. A big difference with the higher threshold for singles is that now the reduction of those expected to end up below the threshold falls by 4 percentage points with sharing.

Moreover, the risk that some married women will end up single, willingly through divorce or sadly by becoming widowed, puts a much larger fraction of the population into the group of potentially poor elderly (that is, relative poverty). In the Swedish context, this is cushioned by the means-tested housing allowance (given a static guarantee), but only if its ceiling increases commensurately with the NDC income index.

Finally, Klerby, Larsson, and Palmer (2013), who present the case for joint annuities in (N)DC schemes, suggest the use of two policy instruments with dual effects evening out the distribution of income between couples. The first is sharing of pension contribution rights within couples to counteract differences in time use, which becomes particularly relevant given the approximately 50 percent risk of becoming divorced. The second is making a joint annuity the default when the youngest spouse retires. The joint annuity would enable the widow or widower to maintain a standard of living on par with that before the death of his or her partner. In practice, both are expected to yield a transfer of pension contribution rights to the low-income spouse (usually the wife), given the difference in life expectancy of men and women and the likelihood that the female partner is two or more years younger than the male partner. Finally, unless income is perfectly correlated, sharing will also lower the take-up of guarantee pension recipients (and taxpayers and government expenditures on these).

Discussion and Conclusions

BEHAVIOR VERSUS POLICY EXPECTATIONS

With Sweden's NDC reform in the 1990s came two gender equality goals: equalization of labor force participation of men and women and the sharing of informal work in the home, especially the care of children. Using individual pension account data, this chapter digs deeper into the behavior of mothers and fathers by studying earnings careers—and hence the development of pension accounts—after the birth of the first child, typically followed by the birth of a second child two to three years later. The general conclusion from the data is that parents' behavior has not lived up to policy expectations that parents would share roughly equally into the children's teens both time at home caring for children and time in the formal labor force.

This is shown by the first important result of this chapter—the NDC account data show that the child-care rights perform their job well and fill most of the earnings gap that arises between partners up to the six-year juncture after the birth of the first child. This is in line with policy.

GENDER GAP IN TAXABLE EARNINGS

The second important result is that the gender gap in taxable earnings narrows only gradually to 25 percent on average, where it remains throughout a follow-up period of 17 years. This was not in line with the ambitions of policy makers. The conclusion from the analysis on earnings and time use data is that a large component of the gender earnings gap—and the resulting gender pension gap—reflects nonremunerated time of mothers extending into the last-born child's early teens, most likely in conjunction with after-school time. This is witnessed by the fact that the gender earnings gap has not improved much in the two decades since the NDC scheme was introduced.

With this result in hand, this chapter suggests a policy of sharing pension accounts between parents as the default option, which is the unquestioned natural behavior for the more than 50 percent of couples that do not separate after having children. Nevertheless, to date the option of sharing pension accounts—which most would agree is reasonable and fair—has been left outside the domain of options seriously discussed in public policy circles.

DISTRIBUTIONS OF MEN'S AND WOMEN'S PENSION VALUES

The consequences of sharing NDC accounts with sharing as the universal default are also examined, specifically the distribution of earnings before and after sharing. This yields the third important result: the distributions of men's and women's pension values—which are already strongly clustered around their means—move even closer to each other. Sharing of accounts as the default policy option finds support in the literature, based on a still dominant culture underlying the revealed preference of parents to delegate a portion of their total time to being at home for children, no matter which parent is the main caregiver. Sharing by default has the additional merit of putting the dominant caregiver's opportunity costs of forgone formal labor market participation on the table—making transparent the economic disadvantage of this position in the partnership.

SHARING PENSION RIGHTS

A fourth conclusion is that sharing pension rights challenges "men's economic rationality" by emphasizing that the basis for a sound partnership should not be partnership coerced by economic dependence. The absence of an agreement on sharing is obviously to the detriment of the female partner, where in the context of Sweden and many other countries a 50 percent likelihood of divorce looms somewhere down the line. In this perspective, the default option of sharing is a form of mandated insurance for the partner who fulfills the family's joint interest in caring for offspring as they become young adults.

LIKELIHOOD OF WOMEN RECEIVING A GUARANTEED BENEFIT

A fifth conclusion is empirical. It is derived from the simulated future earnings careers of the presently working NDC account holders and assuming the default of sharing of accounts applies to the whole population. Logistic regression analysis shows that sharing pension accounts reduces the likelihood of women receiving a guarantee pension from 9.0 percent to 5.8 percent. However, on the margin it also increases the probability of receiving a guaranteed benefit for some, namely, by pulling the partner who from the outset did not have a guarantee benefit below the threshold to receive at least a partial guaranteed supplement.

The analysis shows that the odds of the female spouse qualifying for a full guaranteed benefit or benefit supplement decrease with increasing education but increase with an increasing age difference between her and her spouse. The odds of receiving a guaranteed benefit are also very significantly greater for a foreign-born woman with a foreign-born husband.

CONCLUSIONS

In conclusion, assuming the overriding goal of social policy is to promote individual responsibility for both one's own lifetime economic results and the care of one's children, nudging partners into the default option of sharing moves them in the "right" direction, that is, sharing more equally both time spent on formal work outside the home and time caring for children at home. At the macroeconomic level it reduces the need to tax already sharing couples and singles to support the spouse of the dominant income earner in a nonsharing partnership in old age. Additionally, being there for adolescents produces other benefits. It allows more time for parental guidance, encouragement, and support—and for those teens who would otherwise fall by the wayside, a better chance of being integrated into society as they become young adults, which per se is an argument in favor of granting smaller child-care credits into the final years of adolescence.

A final argument for "nudging" couples into doing more sharing is the expected positive macroeconomic effect on their children—not the least because the children will be the main tax source for financing the guarantee benefits. This is squarely in line with the welfare goals of society, and, as such, is simply both good social and good economic growth policy.

Notes

1. The income gap between women and men is also reflected in individual disposable income, which by definition includes earnings below the ceiling for the public NDC and FDC schemes as well as earnings above the ceiling and other sources of taxable income, including capital income—after tax (Swedish Ministry of Social Affairs 2016, 292).

2. In 2013, 64 percent of cohabiting women ages 66–90 had guarantee pensions, whereas only 58 percent of women in single households did.

3. This is confirmed, for example, by the fact that in couples where the mother has a high salary and her earnings make up a majority of the joint income, the mother still allocates more time to being at home with children (Swedish Social Insurance Agency 2013a).

4. There are three ways of calculating the rights. The lowest contribution amount noted on an individual account corresponds to a taxable earned income of 75 percent of the mean income (Swedish Ministry of Social Affairs 2016, s. 285ff).

5. Days for care of children temporarily home from preschool or school because of sickness were distributed 62 percent for women and 38 percent for men.

6. Due to the introduction of a new data storage routine, it was not possible to extend the database beyond 2012.

7. Some couples were excluded from the database because the data for when their children were born are missing.

8. This encompasses sick leave benefits, parental benefits, and compensation for time away from work for care of sick children.

9. Pension base income consists of both regular earnings and several non-income supplements, such as child year credits (PQAC), which are named pension qualifying amounts (PQA).

10. If the independent variables are such that women have a probability of 0.51 of ending up below the guarantee pension threshold when the husband is above the guarantee pension. Changing husband to a man with a pension below the guarantee pension threshold also increases the probability of the woman ending up below the guarantee pension threshold to 0.90. Odds are calculated as $odds = p(x) / (1 - p(x))$.

References

Akerlof, George A., and Rachel E. Kranton. 2000. "Economics and Identity." *Quarterly Journal of Economics* 115 (3): 715–53.

———. 2010. *Identity Economics: How Our Identities Shape Our Work, Wages, and Well-Being.* Princeton, NJ: Princeton University Press.

Boschini, Anne, and Marianne Sundström. 2018. "Det Ojämlika Faderskapet." *Ekonomisk Debatt* 4 (46).

Budig, Michelle, and Melissa Hodges. 2010. "Differences in Disadvantage: Variation in the Motherhood Penalty across White Women's Earnings Distribution." *American Sociological Review* 75: 705–28.

Burkhauser, Richard V. 1982. "Earnings Sharing: Incremental and Fundamental Reform." In *A Challenge to Social Security,* edited by Richard V. Burkhauser and Karen C. Holden, 229–34. New York: Academic Press.

Chetty, Raj, John N. Friedman, Søren Leth-Petersen, Heien Torben Nielsen, and Tore Olsen. 2014. "Active vs. Passive Decisions and Crowd-Out in Retirement Savings Accounts: Evidence from Denmark." *Quarterly Journal of Economics* 129 (3): 1141–219.

Correll, Shelley J., Stephen Benard, and In Paik. 2007. "Getting a Job: Is There a Motherhood Penalty?" *American Journal of Sociology* 112 (5): 1297–338.

European Commission. 2015. *Pension Adequacy Report.* Brussels: European Commission.

———. 2018. *Pension Adequacy Report.* Brussels: European Commission.

Favreault, Melissa M., and C. Eugene Steuerle. 2007. "Social Security Spouse and Survivor Benefits for the Modern Family." Working Paper 2007-7, Center for Retirement Research at Boston College, Chestnut Hill, MA.

Ferber, Marianne, Patricia Simpson, and Vanessa Rouillon. 2006. "Aging and Social Security: Women as the Problem and the Solution." *Challenge* 49 (3): 105–19.

Hodges, Melissa J., and Michelle J. Budig. 2010. "Who Gets the Daddy Bonus? Organizational Hegemonic Masculinity and the Impact of Fatherhood on Earnings." *Gender and Society* 24: 717–45.

Klerby, Anna, Bo Larsson, and Edward Palmer. 2013. "To Share or Not to Share: That Is the Question." In *Nonfinancial Defined Contribution Pension Schemes in a Changing Pension World: Volume 2 Gender, Politics, and Financial Stability,* edited by Robert Holzmann, Edward Palmer, and David Robalino, 39–65. Washington, DC: World Bank.

Statistics Sweden. 2018. *Women and Men in Sweden 2018 Facts and Figures.* Stockholm.

Swedish Ministry of Social Affairs. 2016. Ds 2016:19 *Jämställda Pensioner?* The Swedish Government Offices. Stockholm: Elanders.

Swedish Pensions Agency. 2018. "Orange Report 2017—The Annual Report of the Swedish Pension System." Swedish Pensions Agency, Stockholm.

Swedish Social Insurance Agency. 2013a. *Social Insurance Report 2013:8.* Stockholm: Sweden.

———. 2013b. *Social Insurance Report 2013:9.* Stockholm: Sweden.

Thaler, Richard H., and Cass R. Sunstein. 2008. *Nudge: Improving Decisions about Health, Wealth, and Happiness.* New Haven, CT: Yale University Press.

World Economic Forum. 2018. *The Global Gender Gap Report 2017.* Geneva: World Economic Forum. (accessed November 23, 2018), https://www.weforum.org/reports /the-global-gender-gap-report-2017.

PART VII

NDC Prospects in Emerging Market Economies

Administrative Requirements and Prospects for Universal Nonfinancial Defined Contribution Schemes in Emerging Market Economies

Robert Palacios

Introduction

Many public policies—from expanding health insurance coverage to collecting taxes—are impossible to implement (or at least to implement well) without adequate administrative systems in place. This is true for modern pension schemes and for nonfinancial defined contribution (NDC) schemes in particular. Today these systems must be digital; yet most pension systems predate computerization and must find a way to bridge the past and present to implement reforms. The shift from nonfinancial defined benefit (NDB) to NDC schemes brings special challenges in recordkeeping. This chapter briefly reviews some of the administrative requirements of NDCs and offers a simple checklist for countries considering this type of reform. The last section describes a universal NDC scheme that harnesses the modern digital infrastructure, including unique identification systems and digital commerce, that may allow developing countries to overcome the limitations of traditional contributory systems and their reliance on payroll taxes.

The Evolution of Pension Policy and Pension Administration

Few pension systems that exist today were started in the digital age. Exceptions are those recent cases like the Republic of Korea in 1988 and Ethiopia in 2011.[1] The vast majority of contribution-based schemes predate computers and began with paper records. Aside from the former Yugoslavia, most of the former socialist countries relied on paper records until very recently. Although digitization was introduced in most systems in recent years, it has sometimes proven to be too difficult or costly to include historical records.

In defined benefit (DB) schemes, the reliance on paper was not a major problem because the benefit formula was applied to a final salary, which was easy to track. The first civil service pension was awarded in 1684 to Martin Horsham and was simply defined as one-half of his salary. No formula was applied. Only later did the British civil service pension formula emerge and account for years of service in the calculation.

The author is grateful to Nick Barr, Csaba Feher, and Will Price for comments and suggestions.

This noncontributory DB was later introduced in economies ranging from India and Nigeria to Hong Kong SAR, China. The calculation was relatively simple—the number of years in service multiplied by the accrual rate multiplied by the final salary.

In the past few decades, however, starting with the more advanced economies, a shift to electronic records occurred. This development is especially important to those seeking to reform pension systems. Almost all Organisation for Economic Co-operation and Development (OECD) countries now effectively use lifetime average earnings (or close to lifetime) valorized by wages or prices, instead of the final salary, to determine the pension value. They also index benefits to inflation, wages, or a combination of the two. Making such calculations for millions of people manually would result in delays, errors, and added costs. These policies became feasible only with the transition to digital systems.

At the same time, systemic reforms that introduced privately managed and financial defined contribution (FDC) schemes[2] made electronic recordkeeping for individual account tracking even more of a necessity. Chile was the first case, but by the late 1990s, more than a dozen countries had introduced this type of reform, a figure that has now more than doubled. Major hiccups arose in many of the countries; the term "rezagos" came to be used in the Latin American context to refer to funds collected that could not be matched to a worker and were placed into a suspense account, sometimes forever.

Similarly, although the first NDC schemes were introduced in the 1990s, the demands of an individual account–based system led to problems in almost every country that introduced this kind of reform. Additional requirements for good administration beyond recordkeeping also arose. Some of these are common to FDC and NDC schemes; a few were specific to NDCs.

The Demands of NDCs on Administrative Systems

One of the arguments made by proponents of defined contribution (DC) schemes generally and NDCs in particular is that they are relatively transparent. At any given moment, contributors should, in principle, be able to see how much pension wealth they have accumulated in their individual accounts. In contrast, although such a calculation is technically possible, it is not generated by DB scheme administrators. Even if it were, it would be difficult to understand, because it involves a complex calculation and relies on a number of assumptions. To achieve this level of transparency for FDC or NDC accounts, however, records must be continually updated and should be accessible to account holders.

Most legacy information systems, even when computerized, are not set up to perform these functions. Migrating from old to new systems is a major project in itself, even when the database includes all relevant information. In many cases, the database will not contain the entire history of contributions, reflecting an earlier shift from paper to electronic records. In Greece, the original NDC plan of 2013 was to convert contributions to notional capital starting in 2002. The choice of this cutoff date was due to the fact that digitized contribution records were not available before this date. In fact, electronic contribution records for both public and private sector workers were first available only in 2015 after a new centralized information system was installed.[3]

One extreme example is Mongolia.[4] Before 1994, there were no contributions in the Soviet-style DB scheme. Between 1994 and 1999, paper-based records were available and eventually digitized, and a new computer system has kept track of contributions since 2000. It is still not clear how those years of service were credited in the NDC system. A similar conversion of paper booklets to digital form had to be done in Latvia; the struggles of the Polish pension fund administration in this regard and the significant delays that they caused are well documented (Chłoń-Domińczak and Góra 2006).

Accuracy and timeliness are also required both for reporting in real or close to real time and for the purposes of accruing interest. In the case of a typical DB scheme, delays in crediting contributions, even for years, do not affect the pension value as long as they are credited before the calculation. The loss in interest, if there are reserves, is borne by the fund, not the individuals. This is not the case with DC schemes; for this reason, the time lag between when funds are collected and then reflected in the accounts must be minimized.

Even if the pension fund's information system is sound, delays and errors can start with the submission of data on individual contributions from employers. In many countries, these submissions are still made on paper. Only recently, and in most cases partially, is electronic filing possible. Among the 12 countries surveyed, only the Maldives and the United Kingdom received e-filings of contribution records from most employers (table 21.1). However, because large employers tend to participate more, the share of covered workers whose reporting is done electronically is much higher. These figures—from the mid-2000s—are certain to have improved, but in many low-income countries, the infrastructure that would allow the pension fund to mandate e-filing is unavailable to all but the largest employers.[5]

TABLE 21.1 E-filing prevalence in selected countries, mid-2000s

	Armenia	Czech Republic	Chile	Hungary	Kosovo	Maldives	Mexico	Moldova	Morocco	Philippines	St. Kitts and Nevis	United Kingdom
Mandate	—	—	Voluntary	—	100+ emp'ees	Public sector	—	—	—	—	—	Yes(a)
Participating employers (%)	0.8	15	—	2	8	100	—	—	8	23	1	98
Covered employees (%)	17	48	Around 80	71	49	100	>60	75	26	74	4	—
E-payment available	—	—	Yes	—	No(a)	No	Yes	—	Yes	—	—	—

SOURCE: Compilation based on data from national social security agencies (Sluchynsky 2015).

NOTE: — = not available.

a. In the United Kingdom, e-filing was made mandatory for large employers (250 or more employees) in 2004–05; for medium employers (50–250 employees) in 2005–06; and for small employers (fewer than 50 employees) in 2010.

In Myanmar, for example, large amounts of cash and a handwritten list of contributors and the relevant amounts are brought by someone from the employer to the social security fund branch office monthly. The paper record is brought manually to the capital, where the data are entered and, eventually, reconciliation with the cash that has been since deposited in the bank takes place. This process allows many errors and obviously cannot be quickly reflected in individual accounts.

Another key building block of the database is the identification number of each contributor. In many DC schemes, the lack of a unique identifier leads to multiple individual accounts because workers are registered each time they change employers. This leads to inconvenience and often to lower pensions because workers are unable to connect all of their work histories. Although this is also a problem for DB schemes, it may be more complicated to correctly value broken individual account histories than to credit DB accounts with past years of service once they are located because of the impact of compound interest in the DC schemes. It is also not possible to report workers' individual account balances upon request, raising again the question of transparency and trust in the system.

Indonesia provides an interesting example. After the biometrically based unique digital ID was introduced in 2010, it was incorporated into the database of the pension fund. As a result, the pension fund administration found that close to 40 percent of the accounts were actually duplicates. The actual coverage rate was only two-thirds of what had been estimated. India's Employees' Provident Fund Organization is in the process of implementing a similar exercise using the well-known Aadhaar unique ID number; it is already finding millions of multiple accounts. Another example is Uganda, which conducted a national campaign to register, update, and clean records in 2005 using biometrics; in the process, it dramatically reduced the number of duplicate accounts.

In fact, the verification of identity should take place earlier in the process, starting at registration. When an employer or a self-employed person registers, the unique ID number should be checked against the database of the agency that issues it. The more robust this ID, the fewer problems that will occur down the line (for example, uncertainties about the date of birth). Subsequently, when contributions are being collected, the records should be accepted by the pension fund only after the unique ID number is checked and found to exist in the pension fund database. Otherwise, the submission should be rejected, and the employer should be asked to correct the information. In Mexico, US$400 million had accumulated in a suspense account because the ID numbers entered were incorrect or nonexistent. Figure 21.1 shows the various stages in the pension life cycle to emphasize that any break in the chain over a 30- or 40-year period affects the final pension.

In addition to digitized inflow and management of contribution records based on robust identification, the information system may need to generate the notional interest rate. In contrast, the valuation for FDCs is the same as for other assets. It must be able to use market prices to generate a value for the individual account balance, ideally as a daily net asset value calculation. This calculation can be especially difficult in developing countries because either the data required for the notional interest rate calculation are not available or the assets in the FDC portfolio are largely illiquid.

FIGURE 21.1 **Identification throughout the pension life cycle**

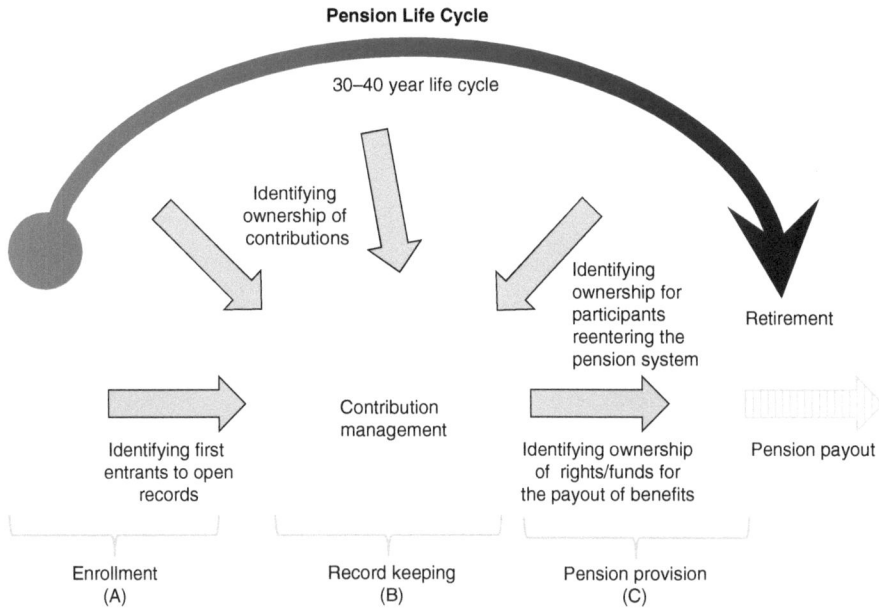

SOURCE: Ernesto Brodersohn.

Notional interest rates are mostly linked to the growth of wages or to the covered wage bill of the scheme in question. Links to the latter can be especially problematic, particularly in the case of an increase in coverage. This means that to generate a notional interest rate, the system must be able to calculate and resolve most or all contribution claims in a timely manner.[6] This essentially means that the system can aggregate the individual-level contribution histories and generate the wage bill growth figure. To the extent that it becomes difficult to finalize these figures, notional rate calculations may be delayed. The same can be said for gross domestic product (GDP) growth, which is used as an alternative indicator and is often revised substantially.

The issue is more serious for countries that are characterized by more volatile movements in these key indicators (Disney 1999). Countries such as Italy and Sweden have very stable movements in employment and average wages as well as GDP growth. In many developing countries, however, especially those that rely heavily on commodity prices and are subject to external shocks, the fluctuations can be much larger. Once again, the case of Mongolia is instructive. The country experienced large discrete changes from 2000 to 2015 in the ratio of contributors to labor force (figure 21.2).[7] The same figure for Italy or Sweden would hover close to zero throughout the period. With such volatility, the timing effects on individual cohorts can be huge in the same way that FDC schemes can be affected by sudden changes in asset prices.[8] This may argue for some mechanism to smooth notional returns, which would require even more sophisticated calculations.

FIGURE 21.2 **Yearly change in ratio of contributors to labor force in Mongolia, 2000–15**

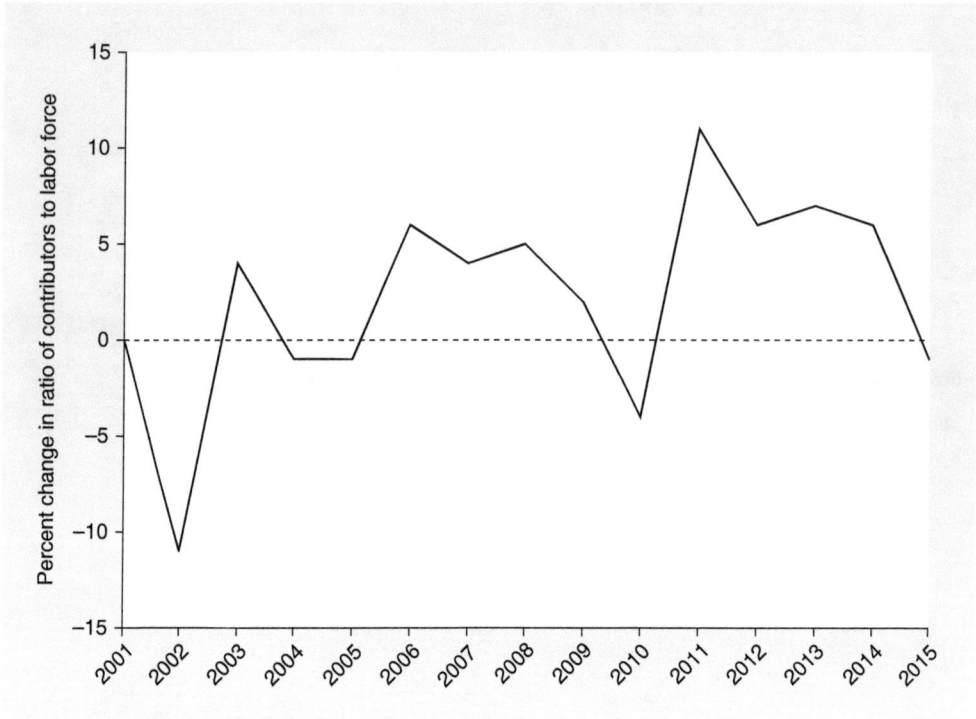

SOURCE: World Bank 2017.

The final administrative requirement applies to both NDC schemes and FDC schemes that mandate annuitization. To convert account balances of either type into annuities, cohort mortality tables must be available. In the FDC world, such tables can be prescribed by the regulator, or some flexibility can be allowed to insurers who can use different tables, subject to some limitations. In NDC schemes, this is the responsibility of the government. In both cases, the accuracy of these tables will affect the financial outcome.[9] Underestimated life expectancy will increase the NDC deficits and will reduce profits for insurance companies offering annuities to the FDC system. The converse will have the opposite effect and will shortchange pensioners.[10]

In developing countries with low or even moderate coverage, this poses a special challenge. The fact that workers contributing to pension schemes tend to have higher incomes than those in the informal sector is well documented.[11] At the same time, empirical evidence supports the intuitive relationship between mortality and income level (Ayuso, Bravo, and Holzmann 2017; Bannerjee and Duflo 2007; Pal and Palacios 2008). As a result, it is clear that using national mortality tables to convert NDC balances to flows will end up costing more than it would if the actual mortality rates were applied. Yet surprisingly few countries calculate these rates, despite the fact that they should be fairly easy to generate from individual records. Using such data from Ghana, Majoka (2014) finds significant differences in annual mortality rates, with a difference of up to 3 percentage points at age 78 (figure 21.3). Figure 21.4 shows similar magnitudes of mortality differentials for Mexico.

FIGURE 21.3 **Mortality rates of Ghanaian contributors compared with United Nations data**

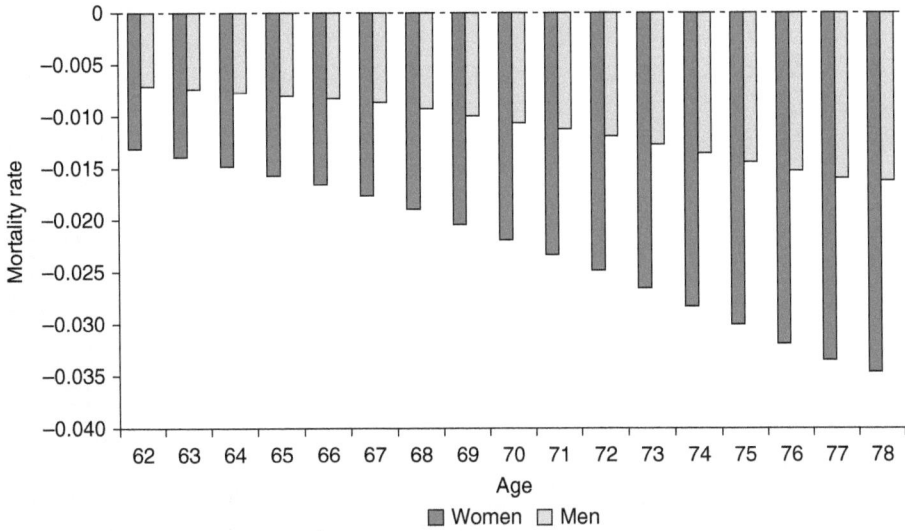

SOURCE: Majoka 2014.

FIGURE 21.4 **Mortality rate differentials in Mexico, by sex, national versus covered population**

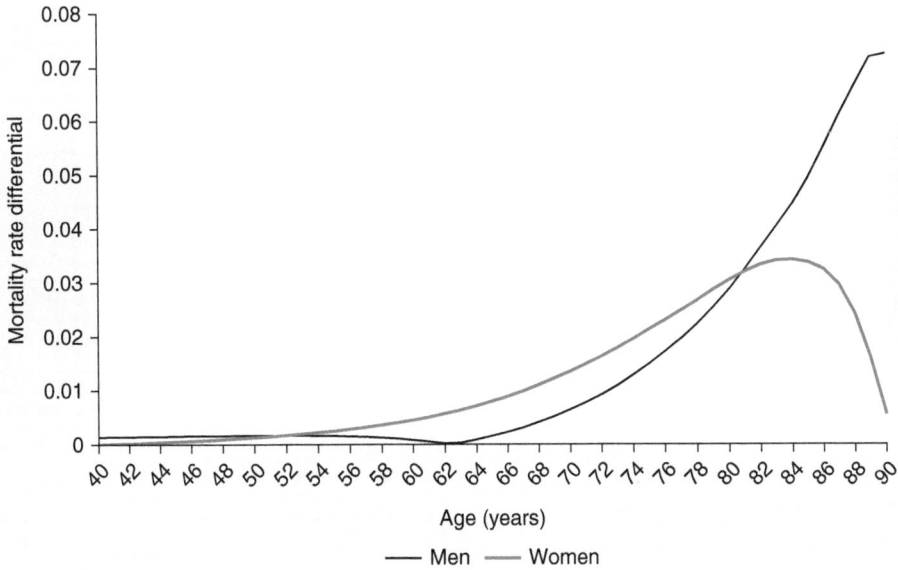

SOURCE: World Bank 2016.

NOTE: Difference between IMSS ISSSTE EMSSA-09 mortality tables and UN mortality tables. IMSS = Mexican Social Security Institute ISSSTE = Institute for Social Security and Services for State Workers.

A Checklist to Assess Readiness for NDC Reform Implementation

The administrative system must be able to perform several functions that are not necessary in a traditional DB scheme but are crucial for good implementation of an NDC scheme. Most of these functions are also needed to administer an FDC scheme, albeit with some differences that tend to affect developing countries more than developed ones. The resulting checklist includes the following:

- Digitized, complete, and accurate historical contribution records linked to unique identifiers
- Digitized contribution data that flow from employers and the self-employed using unique identifiers
- Information system configured to generate individual account balances with accuracy and timely reporting
- Information system capable of generating aggregate indicators used for notional interest rate calculations (possibly using some techniques to smooth volatility)
- Cohort life (mortality) tables by age and sex that correspond to the covered population.

Many countries would not be able to show that all or even most of the items on this list are in place. This is not to say, however, that they could not be achieved with some preparation and investment. Policy makers tend to ignore these implementation challenges until after the reform is supposed to begin. As a result, these teething problems can undermine the credibility of the scheme from the start. As one reformer put it,

> IT support for the administration was not designed sufficiently well to reconcile individual information with aggregate employer payments; in fact, it took about two years after the implementation of the reform to do this. The chaos thus created directed the public discussion away from the content of the reform and toward the perceived incompetence of the administration (Chłoń-Domińczak 2002). And once the mistake had been made, reconciliation of pension accounts in Poland was a lengthy process. (Chłoń-Domińczak, Franco, and Palmer 2012, 42)

The desired increase in transparency from an NDC reform also makes recordkeeping mistakes much more obvious than in DB schemes, where few people understand exactly how their pensions are being calculated. Most DB scheme members do not see their contribution records during their working lives, while NDC balances can be checked at any time. The credibility of the scheme depends crucially on those balances being accurate. A transition from DB to NDC that involves converting past contributions to notional capital is especially challenging, given that historical records are often in poor condition.

In addition to these items, the ability to manage liquidity reserves, which are recommended to absorb short-term volatility (Holzmann 2019), is an important element of capacity. Finally, local expertise or at least familiarity with the underlying theory behind NDCs as a model within the framework of pension economics is clearly important. The absence of such local expertise in some cases signals a lack of ownership in the reform process itself.

Feasibility of a Universal NDC

In developing countries, the debate over the appropriate contributory pension model took a back seat as the focus over the past decade or more shifted to coverage. Over the past 25 years, the ratio of contributors to the working-age population hardly changed in most countries. This situation led to the introduction of noncontributory or social pensions in many countries, especially in Asia and Latin America (Rofman, Apella, and Vezza 2014). At the same time, experiments with special schemes aimed at informal sector workers were rolled out in a wide range of countries (World Bank 2015). With the exception of China, however, with its unique social pension–linked rural pension, none of these attempts managed to scale up. At the same time, some economists have expressed concern that noncontributory schemes may discourage participation in contributory schemes by making informality more attractive. Mexico and Thailand, for example, exclude those with formal sector pension income from the social pension program.

Anton, Hernandez, and Levy (2013) propose an innovative reform plan that would result in universal coverage. Using Mexican data and parameters, the authors simulate a shift from the payroll tax–based social insurance scheme for pensions and health to a universal scheme in which an earmarked value-added tax (VAT) would be used to make deposits into individual accounts of all adults. It was similar to a proposal made by Kotlikoff, Smetters, and Walliser (1999) for the United States whereby the social security program would be ended and a national sales tax would help finance the transition to an individual account–based scheme. Both studies find that the positive general equilibrium effects of moving from a payroll to a consumption tax were likely to be significant.

Was implementation of such a plan feasible? Mexico introduced FDC plans managed by specialized pension firms (AFORES) in 1997, but at any given time, only about 40 percent of workers were contributing to the system. Nevertheless, the individual account infrastructure required for such a program was arguably in place and could be leveraged for this innovative approach. The title of the book, *The End of Informality*, suggested the objective of such a proposal (Anton, Hernandez, and Levy 2013). By delinking coverage in the pension system from formality, this plan would eliminate this distinction. Unlike the U.S. proposal, the plan was apparently seriously considered by the Mexican government but never implemented.

Had such a scheme gone forward, the implications for the fiscal situation and for the capital markets would have been profound. A massive increase in the size of pension fund assets would be matched by a huge increase in government spending financed by the increased VAT revenues. The impact of the growth of pension fund assets on the capital markets would depend on the absorption capacity of those markets and portfolio regulations (including the ability to invest abroad). In short, it would have been a complex affair.

There is no reason that the same reform could not be done using the NDC model. This approach might have certain advantages over the FDC model.[12] First, unlike Mexico, few countries have well-developed infrastructure for managing pension funds, regulatory capacity, or capital markets that could efficiently channel the massive inflows that such a scheme would imply. Conversely, the potential for these funds to increase savings and encourage capital market development would not be harnessed in an NDC approach.[13] The other advantage of an NDC scheme is that it does not require additional revenues to be raised nor does it require a well-developed capital market. However, the NDC version of the universal system creates a large unfunded liability and forgoes the potential benefits of capital market development.

What would the parameters of a universal NDC look like? First, the contribution amount would be calculated to generate an acceptable minimum benefit level under reasonable assumptions about the notional interest rate. It could, for example, be set as a percentage of median income per capita so as to accumulate enough to produce an annuity equivalent to the relative poverty line, also measured in terms of median income per capita. It could also use a notional interest rate based on a moving average of GDP growth, as is done in Italy.

The equivalent amount could then be exempt from the payroll tax so that the formal sector contribution rate would only apply to wages greater than, say, twice the minimum wage. In this way, the redistribution would be financed from taxes while the consumption-smoothing function would, by definition, be financed by contributions. This approach would encourage employment, especially for low-skilled workers affected most by automation and regulations such as the minimum wage. Mandated contributions over and above the government-financed minimum would then generate higher replacement rates for formal sector workers with higher incomes up to a ceiling, providing for further consumption smoothing and reducing the moral hazard that may result from the provision of the minimum annuity. This segment could take the form of an FDC or an NDC scheme. In either case, one pension should be paid out that is the sum of both elements of the system.

Implementation would rely crucially on the government's ability to identify every person of working age[14] in the country so that his or her individual account balance can be reported. Few countries are able to do this, but many are in the process of creating such population registers.[15] Notable examples are India, Pakistan, Peru, Rwanda, and Thailand. As is true for any pension scheme, the administrative database should be directly linked to the civil registry, in which deaths would be automatically reflected.[16] As mentioned, the ability to calculate annuities based on projected, cohort-specific mortality rates would be required.[17]

Voluntary contributions, perhaps with an incentive in the form of a flat match, would also allow informal sector workers to smooth consumption. This could be facilitated by emerging technology for payments. The explosive growth of mobile money, especially in Africa and Asia, has reduced transaction costs dramatically. Thailand and Uganda[18] recently began to allow pension contributions through mobile phones, following the lead of the Mbao Pension Plan in Kenya.

Looking forward, the shift away from cash could be a major opportunity to formalize a large portion of the economy. In a growing number of countries, the value of mobile transactions and digital commerce is already larger than the formal sector wage bill. In Kenya, for example, the value of M-Pesa transactions is four to five times higher than the wage bill covered by the pension schemes for public and private sector workers. East Africa has historically led the world in the use of mobile money, but China is the clear leader today, and the rest of developing Asia is moving very quickly in this direction (GSMA 2018).

Voluntary savings plans, including for pensions, could be devised that add a pension contribution to an individual account every time a purchase is made. Features that nudge individuals to save every time they consume could be added. Depending on the context,

the voluntary contributions could go into an NDC or an FDC scheme or some combination of the two. The government would essentially be adding to the available asset
choices by offering a GDP- or wage-indexed instrument that does not otherwise exist in
the market.[19]

A universal NDC or FDC scheme financed by the government to achieve a basic
pension level would address the intractable coverage problem that has plagued contributory pension schemes in developing countries. The NDC version would do so without
adding a significant short-term fiscal burden or testing the limits of regulatory capacity.
As it matures, it would achieve the goal of ensuring a minimum income in old age and
would preempt the need for social pensions. By doing essentially the same thing but in the
context of an individual account, mandatory and voluntary contributions over and above
this minimum NDC layer would be seamlessly integrated. These could also be set up to
be partially or fully funded. Everyone would be in the same pension scheme, one that
minimizes labor market distortions and automatically adjusts to increasing life expectancy.
As an added bonus, everyone would now have a stake in achieving higher GDP growth
so as to raise their future pensions—perhaps a new and more robust version of Drucker's
(1976) "pension fund socialism."

Notes

1. This applies to Ethiopia's new scheme for private sector workers. The public sector workers'
   scheme is 50 years old and has a backlog of 2.5 million paper records. Ethiopia intends to
   digitize them when funding is available.
2. Many former British colonies have provident funds, including India; Hong Kong SAR, China;
   and Malaysia. Their accounting was simpler in that the interest rates were administered and
   applied at the start of each year. Nevertheless, recordkeeping was onerous as were transaction
   costs for members.
3. Personal communication with George Symeonidis (2018).
4. Thanks to Mark Dorfman for this information (personal communication, 2018).
5. In Azerbaijan for example, the paper workbooks used since 1938 were moved to a consolidated online system in 2014. Now information provided by employers can be accessed by
   relevant government agencies and employees.
6. Interestingly, wage growth in the Greek NDC scheme is calculated by the statistical agency,
   which uses a sampling approach.
7. In their influential report on China, Barr and Diamond (2010) recognize the problem in the
   context of secular growth in the covered labor force and recommend using wage rather than
   wage bill growth.
8. This is one reason that many funded DC schemes now use life-cycle defaults, which shift
   workers nearing retirement to less volatile portfolios.
9. See Palmer and Zhao de Gosson de Varennes (2019) for evidence of the potential impact of
   inaccurate mortality tables.
10. It may be easier for an NDC than an FDC scheme to adjust annuity values as life expectancy
    changes because the NDC scheme does not require changes to assets.
11. For one recent example using a large cross-country sample, see Evans and Palacios (2015).
12. Either DC model would seem to be superior to an attempt to extend a DB model, with its
    reliance on regular and monitorable wages.

13. It is true, however, that an NDC scheme design can include partial funding, as in the case of "buffer" funds.

14. Countries with significant migrant worker populations would face an additional complication.

15. Interestingly, the same prerequisites apply to the implementation of a universal basic income program.

16. This raises another important constraint for many developing countries, where deaths are not systematically reported to the civil registration system. This can be partly addressed with mechanisms to authenticate the contributors or pensioners but would add to the administrative cost and complexity of the system.

17. An advantage of a universal scheme is that these population-wide forecasts are produced by the United Nations Demographic section and are available for most countries.

18. http://allafrica.com/stories/201709130154.html.

19. A similar logic could allow for a transition from a pay-as-you-go DB scheme to an individual DC arrangement, although this would involve securitizing past revenues (Valdes-Prieto 2005).

References

Anton, Arturo, Fausto Hernandez, and Santiago Levy. 2013. *The End of Informality: Fiscal Reform for Universal Social Insurance*. Washington, DC: Inter-American Development Bank.

Ayuso, Mercedes, Jorge Bravo, and Robert Holzmann. 2017. "On the Heterogeneity in Longevity among Socioeconomic Groups: Scope, Trends and Implications for Earnings-Related Pension Schemes." *Global Journal of Human Social Sciences–Economics* 17 (1): 33–58.

Bannerjee, Abhijit, and Esther Duflo. 2007. "Aging and Death under a Dollar a Day." Working Paper 13683, National Bureau of Economic Research, Cambridge, MA.

Barr, Nicholas, and Peter Diamond. 2010. "Pension Reform in China: Issues, Options and Recommendations." Report prepared as part of the China Economic Research and Advisory Programme (CERAP).

Chłoń-Domińczak, Agnieszka. 2002. "The Polish Pension Reform of 1999." In *Pension Reform in Central and Eastern Europe: Volume 1 Restructuring with Privatization, Case Studies of Hungary and Poland*, edited by Elaine Fultz, 95–205. Budapest: International Labour Office.

Chłoń-Domińczak, Agnieszka, Daniele Franco, and Edward Palmer. 2012. "The First Wave of NDC Reforms: The Experiences of Italy, Latvia, Poland, and Sweden." In *Nonfinancial Defined Contribution Pension Schemes in a Changing Pension World: Volume 1 Progress, Lessons, and Implementation*, edited by Robert Holzmann, Edward Palmer, and David Robalino, Chapter 2. Washington, DC: World Bank.

Chłoń-Domińczak, Agnieszka, and Marek Góra. 2006. "The NDC System in Poland: Assessment after Five Years. In *Pension Reform: Issues and Prospects of Non-Financial Defined Contribution (NDC) Schemes*, edited by Robert Holzmann and Edward Palmer, 425–47. Washington, DC: World Bank.

Disney, Richard. 1999. *Notional Accounts as a Pension Reform Strategy: An Evaluation*. Washington, DC: World Bank.

Drucker, Peter. 1976. *The Unseen Revolution: How Pension Fund Socialism Came to America*. London: William Heinemann Limited.

Evans, Brooks, and Robert Palacios. 2015. *An Examination of Elderly Co-Residence in the Developing World*. Washington, DC: World Bank.

GSMA (Groupe Spéciale Mobile Association). 2018. "2017 State of the Industry Report on Mobile Money." GSM Association, London.

Holzmann, Robert. 2019. "The ABCs of NDCs." In *Progress and Challenges of Nonfinancial Defined Contribution Pension Schemes: Volume 1 Addressing Marginalization, Polarization, and the Labor Market*, edited by Robert Holzmann, Edward Palmer, Robert Palacios, and Stefano Sacchi, Chapter 9. Washington, DC: World Bank.

Kotlikoff, Lawrence, Kent Smetters, and Jan Walliser. 1999. "Privatizing Social Security in the United States: Comparing the Options." *Review of Economic Dynamics* 2 (3): 532–74.

Majoka, Zaineb. 2014. "Ghana Mortality Analysis." Unpublished.

Pal, Sarmistha, and Robert Palacios. 2008. "Understanding Poverty among the Elderly in India: Implications for Social Pension Policy." Discussion Paper Series, IZA, Institute of Labor Economics, Bonn, Germany.

Palmer, Edward, and Yuwei Zhao de Gosson de Varennes. 2019. "The Importance of Unbiased Estimation of Life Expectancy for Financial Stability, Heterogeneity, and Fair Outcomes in DC Pension Schemes." In *Progress and Challenges of Nonfinancial Defined Contribution Pension Schemes: Volume 1 Addressing Marginalization, Polarization, and the Labor Market*, edited by Robert Holzmann, Edward Palmer, Robert Palacios, and Stefano Sacchi, Chapter 13. Washington, DC: World Bank.

Rofman, Rafael, Ignacio Apella, and Evelyn Vezza. 2014. *Beyond Contributory Pensions: Fourteen Experiences with Coverage Expansion in Latin America*. Washington, DC: World Bank.

Sluchynsky, Oleskiy. 2015. "Benchmarking Administrative Expenditures of Mandatory Social Security Programmes." *International Social Security Review* 68 (3): 15–41.

Valdes-Prieto, Salvador. 2005. "Market Based Social Security without Transition Costs." Working Paper, Universidad Catolica de Chile, Santiago, Chile.

World Bank. 2015. *Matching Contributions for Pensions: A Review of International Experience*. Washington, DC: World Bank.

———. 2016. *Analisis Cuantitativo del Sistema de Pensiones en Mexico*. Washington, DC: World Bank.

———. 2017. *Mongolia's Pension System*. Washington, DC: World Bank.

CHAPTER 22

The Notional and the Real in China's Pension Reforms

Bei Lu, John Piggott, and Bingwen Zheng

Introduction

This chapter discusses the potential role of the nonfinancial defined contribution (NDC) paradigm in the ongoing reforms of retirement provision in China, in the context of the continuing growth and development of one of the world's largest economies.[1] China has remarkably high nominal retirement provision coverage of its population. Four separate pension systems and a non-age-specific minimum living allowance (*Dibao*) combine to offer financial support for people in the later stages of their lives. At the same time, the issues of sustainability, equity, and governance are challenging and real. Although coverage is comprehensive, benefit levels for some major plans are very low. Furthermore, although many broad policy guidelines are set by the central government, jurisdictions at other levels—province, city, and sometimes even district—have significant control over implementation, covering administration, benefit rates, and other important features of retirement policy. Economic and social conditions vary dramatically among these administrative regions, suggesting serious limitations around the extent to which effective centralization can be achieved.

The NDC paradigm is already effectively embodied in one part of the most important contributory plan, the Urban Employee Pension Scheme (UEPS), although it is not so labeled. Currently, a mandatory 8 percent employee contribution within the UEPS is paid into an "individual account," supplementing a defined benefit (DB) supported by a 20 percent employer contribution, which is the scheme's foundation. These individual accounts were originally conceived to be prefunded; however, because of fiscal pressures in China's retirement space, they have remained "empty" almost since their inception.

The policy debate about how to improve what exists is ongoing. Retirement policy and provision, regardless of the approach adopted, are necessarily shaped by the labor market experience of fund members. In China, labor market heterogeneity is dramatic across provinces and between urban and rural settings—in development stage, cost of living, formalization level, and other characteristics. In this sense, China might be viewed as multiple countries.

The authors acknowledge the research support of the ARC Centre of Excellence in Population Ageing Research (CEPAR), ARC grant number CE11E0099 in Australia, and by a Major Project of the National Nature Science Foundation of China (grant number 71490733). The authors are grateful to Robert Holzmann, Xinmei Wang, and Edward Palmer for comments and suggestions and to Rafal Chomik for his creative work on the figures and tables.

An expanded NDC paradigm was previously recommended for China and was the centerpiece of the commissioned review by Barr and Diamond (2010). Zheng (2012) provides projections of a hybrid defined contribution (DC) model, replacing the current UEPS, that embodies many of the ideas behind the NDC paradigm, although the projections themselves, which assumed convergence to a reformed system by 2020, have been largely overtaken by events (or rather, nonevents). Oksanen (2012) provides an excellent overview of proposals up to that time.

Zheng (2015) produces a thorough NDC proposal that includes projections under a range of policy scenarios, as summarized in annex 21A. Barr and Diamond (2010) recognize that moving to a true national system involves a major power shift away from local officials and a geographic redistribution of costs and benefits, but they otherwise pay little detailed attention to the institutional constraints that China confronts. Zheng (2015) does not seriously consider complementary social support for those whose earnings capacity has been exhausted and which would need to be part of any comprehensive NDC-based reform.[2]

This chapter's contribution is therefore threefold. First, it documents the existing pension policy landscape ("China's Retirement and Pension Landscape"), and it explains the demographic and institutional constraints within which any pension plan in China must operate ("Demographic and Institutional Considerations"). Second, the chapter offers stylized projections of benefits, coverage, and liabilities of alternative policy scenarios that expand the NDC system within the UEPS ("Model Assumptions and Parameterization"). In undertaking this, attention is paid to induced or regulated increases in retirement age, which is critical in improving sustainability with an aging demographic; the "limited" heterogeneity in mature age life expectancy across pension groups is also take into account ("Individual Contributions and Benefits"). Third, the chapter examines the costs of alternative and complementary retirement-based social support mechanisms ("System Cash Flow"). It then discusses how the costs of pensions in the future might be managed under an NDC paradigm, taking into account the cost of a social pension ("The Role of the Social Pension").

The "Conclusion" states that an expansion of the NDC paradigm within the UEPS is likely to be welfare improving. Although the NDC paradigm has advantages in terms of sustainability and mature labor supply incentives, it also exposes individuals to risks that, given this paradigm, can only be covered by a social pension. The overall costs of reform are, therefore, greater than those associated with the NDC paradigm alone.

China's Retirement and Pension Landscape

Traditionally, most support in later life for most Chinese came from self-provision and family. At the beginning of this century, less than 20 percent of the urban population ages 60 and older listed "pension" as their main source of retirement income; in the rural sector, the proportion was less than 5 percent. This is changing rapidly. By 2010, more than one-half of the urban group listed "pension" as the main source of retirement income, as did nearly one-third of rural residents (figure 22.1). This provides a pension take on both the rapid growth of China, partly through formalization of its workforce, and its rapid aging. These underlying economic forces lend urgency to pension reform in China.

FIGURE 22.1 **Changes in main sources of retirement income in China, by urban and rural populations, between 2000, 2006, and 2010**

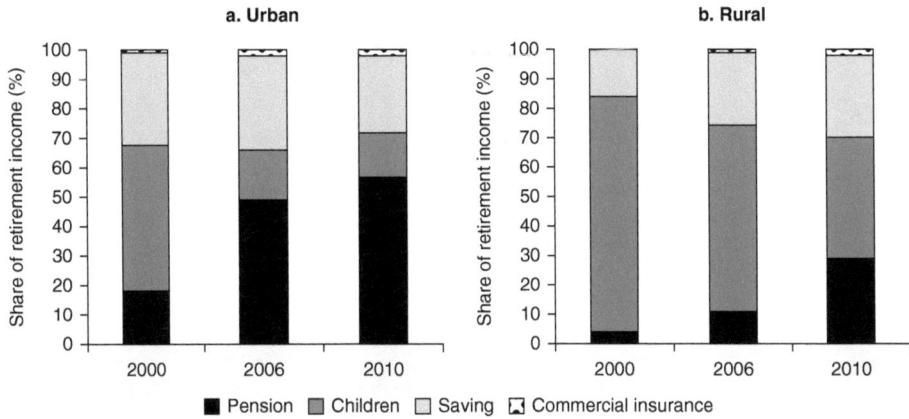

SOURCE: Original summary from three waves of the Sample Survey of the Aged Population in Urban/Rural China in 2000, 2006, and 2010, conducted by the National Ageing Committee.

The centerpiece of China's current retirement provision policy is the UEPS, established in the late 1990s, as state-owned enterprises shed their "cradle to grave" obligations. The UEPS currently has 403 million members, including both workers and retirees. In common with many emerging market economies, China also has a generous, noncontributory, and unfunded Public Sector Pension Scheme, although it has now undergone major reforms. Third comes the Enterprise Annuity scheme, essentially a DC plan for high-income individuals. Finally, over the past decade, two interrelated plans targeting those who have no other pension affiliation were established—the Rural and Urban Residents Pensions.

Table 22.1 lays out the essential characteristics of these four plans. In terms of aggregate revenue flows, the UEPS is, by far, the largest plan. The overall contribution rate of 28 percent is split between employers and employees, with the latter making an 8 percent contribution to the individual accounts. The pure pay-as-you-go DB component of the UEPS relies on a contribution of 20 percent of the scheduled wage to deliver a retirement income of about 35 percent of the scheduled wage after 35 years of contributions. The individual account is estimated to deliver a further 24.5 percent, for a total of about 60 percent of the scheduled wage.[3]

Benefits are calculated according to a benefit formula reflecting both wage level and years of contribution. Vesting requires 15 years of contributions. A crediting rate is applied to the individual notional account balance, which, until recently, was differentiated by province.[4] In 2016, this rate was set at a uniform 8.6 percent nationally, approximately reflecting member wage growth. Benefits are available at between ages 50 and 55 years for women and at age 60 for men, although various exemptions exist for specific occupations granting earlier benefit access. No earnings test applies.

TABLE 22.1 **China's existing pension schemes, as of 2015**

Schemes	Urban Employee Pension	New Rural and Urban Residents Pension	Enterprise Annuity	Public Sector Pension (reformed in 2016)
Contribution	20% of wage to social pooling; 8% to individual account (60–300% of wage base).	RMB 100–2,000 per year	12% of wage free of tax	No contribution
Benefit	Social pooling: DB formula based on covered years, contribution amount, and local average wage. Ad hoc adjustment after retirement.	RMB 70 per month plus annuitized personal contributions and government subsidies by retirement.	DC plan	82–88% of final wage
Contributors (millions)	263	357	22	8
% of population ages 15–59	28	39	2	1
Pensioners (millions)	91	148	—	9
Access age (years)	Women 50–55 Men 60	Women 60 Men 60	Women 55 Men 60	Women 55 Men 60

SOURCE: Original table.

NOTE: RMB = Chinese renminbi; — = not available.

The UEPS is coming under increasing stress as people live longer, and an important piece of the ongoing reform debate revolves around raising the access, or retirement, age. This has been under review for some time, but no final decision has been made.

The Public Sector Pension, while embracing only a small membership, is probably the next most important, if only because of its generosity. A noncontributory scheme, it pays a full career civil servant between 82 and 88 percent of final wage, typically indexed to wage growth. The scheme has been under review over the past several years, however. Various groups of public sector workers have been separated from the plan and integrated into the UEPS, and civil servants remaining in the plan who are still working have now (as of 2016) been enrolled in the UEPS, with organization of the additional benefit still to be resolved. The government set up a supplementary occupational scheme along the lines of the Enterprise Annuity plan, but it is not yet fully implemented. This course of action has the merit of making explicit the additional value of the Public Sector Pension relative to the UEPS.

Since 2009, two complementary plans have been introduced that are essentially social pensions, although they have a contributory element. The Rural Residents Pension was introduced in 2009, offering residents older than age 60 with rural Hukou[5] immediate enrollment and benefits. The scheme instantly became the world's largest pension fund based on the number of members. The basic benefit was introduced at RMB 55 per month and is now RMB 70 per month, still well under US$1 per day. More prosperous provinces offer supplements that can substantially increase this payment. In addition, those younger than age 60 are supposed to pay a minimum of RMB 100 per year in contributions, which will be converted to an additional annuity at age 60. In 2010, a matching Urban Residents Pension scheme was introduced, providing cover to people with urban Hukou who are not members of other pension schemes. These are treated here as a single policy, the Rural and Urban Residents Pension Scheme (RURPS).

To offer some sense of the structure and function of this retirement policy, figure 22.2 is a generic schema that identifies the functions of a retirement policy as comprising poverty alleviation (or adequacy), compulsory income replacement, and voluntary supplementary lifetime saving. The rural and urban residents' plans are seen as poverty alleviation instruments, tested against other pension resources. They are supplemented by the Minimum Living Allowance (*Dibao*). This is not strictly a social pension, given that it is not age dependent, although the elderly probably perceive it as a pension payment. It is available to those with no significant labor, capital, or family resources. It is much more generous than the RURPS, but only a small proportion of those in receipt of the RURPS receive the Dibao. This may be because they hold other resources, or because they enjoy family support.

The UEPS and the Public Sector Pension are both mandatory income replacement schemes. Given the current reform of the Public Sector Pension, the focus here is on the UEPS. Two important points arise. First, the benefit, although calibrated as a proportion of final salary, is thereafter not indexed. Various discretionary adjustments are made to the pension in payment, reflecting increases in cost of living and community standards. Second, although membership in the UEPS is mandatory for formal employees, these remain the minority of workers in China. The self-employed are not compelled to join; most migrants are not members; and those who are will likely not receive full benefits because of vesting rules.

FIGURE 22.2 **China's retirement income system design**

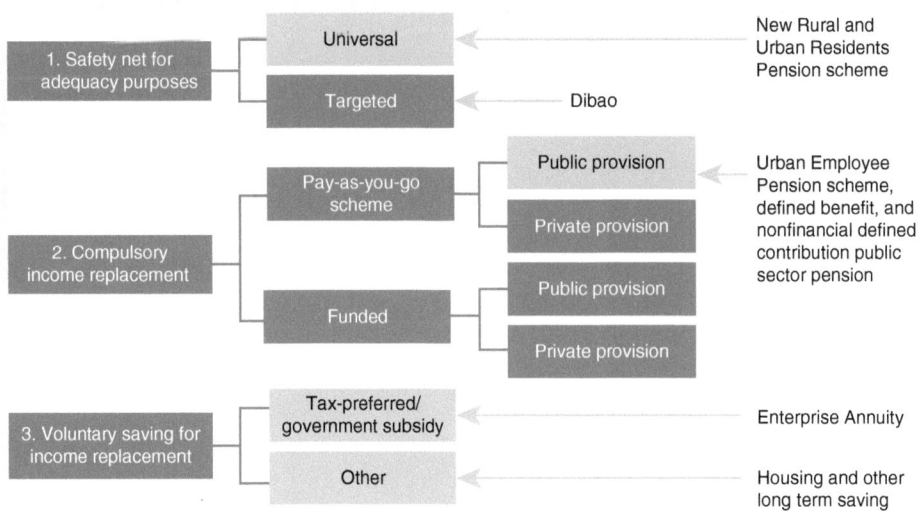

SOURCE: Original figure.

NOTE: Dibao = Minimum Living Allowance.

The Enterprise Annuity scheme is treated as a voluntary saving mechanism under the third pillar of this schema (in China, it is regarded as a second-pillar scheme). Few workers are members; benefits are mostly paid as a lump sum at retirement, rather than an annuity. It is not a major focus of this chapter.

On current settings, these plans will generate large deficits going into the future. Already, the annual balance between contributions and benefits is negative for the UEPS. The DB component is negative for women, and roughly in balance for men, the difference arising both from women's earlier retirement age and their greater life expectancy.[6] Thus far, the individual account is a minor component of retirement benefits for current retirees, but it will become more important as the system matures. Over the next period, longer lifespans and limitations to contributor growth are likely to drive ever larger shortfalls.

One longstanding policy response is to increase the overall contribution flow, sometimes by offering lower contribution rates to marginal groups such as new entrants, possibly migrants. Negotiations are often undertaken on an enterprise-by-enterprise basis to increase coverage of their employees. Compliance effort varies by jurisdiction; in general, poorer jurisdictions expend less effort on ensuring compliance, relying instead on central transfers for benefit payment. Often, additional enrollments will lead to still-higher future debt, the cost of solving an immediate financial shortfall.

In addition, the standard social pooling contribution rate of 20 percent is widely perceived as a disincentive to formal sector UEPS enrollment, and there have been periodic calls for some reduction. The national government recently moved to marginally reduce this rate (Lu 2017).

The present value of the implicit pension debt (IPD) is difficult to estimate, because DB promises are not well defined beyond the initial payout year, and discount rates are hard to agree on. The current estimates of the IPD are considerably inflated by the legacy debt of pre-1996 arrangements, when a noncontributory scheme operated. In terms of currently accruing liabilities, it is the individual account obligations that dominate.

As a result, no consensus exists yet for the calculation of IPD costs. The Ministry of Human Resources and Social Security (MOHRSS), the Ministry of Finance (MOF), and the National Development and Reform Commission have all estimated the IPD, with values between RMB 1.4 trillion and RMB 6.3 trillion (based on 1995–2005 report estimates), although these figures seem low even at the upper bound. Other estimates suggest that the IPD might be much higher. The Chinese Academy of Social Science reports that the overall IPD totaled RMB 60.6 trillion in 2014, nearly 100 percent of gross domestic product (GDP), and more than four times current total fiscal revenue (Lu 2017; Zhang 2015, 10).

The IPD estimates do point to the need for long-term pension reform, and this is acknowledged by policy makers. The NDC paradigm figures in this debate, as indicated. Thus far, however, the nature and timing of reform have not been agreed upon.

The overall structure of China's retirement policy may appear piecemeal, but it is important to appreciate that it operates in a country that is itself piecemeal. The urban-rural divide, the heterogeneity in living standards across provinces, the multiple levels of administrative jurisdiction, and the range of public financing authorities for these schemes all interact to make integration challenging. In addition, the different legal and background characteristics of the working and retired population—urban, rural, migrants—compound this issue. These institutional and social structures are discussed in the next section.

Demographic and Institutional Considerations

DEMOGRAPHY

China is one of the world's most rapidly aging economies, a phenomenon driven by both increasing lifespans and declining fertility. Both of these components are important for pension design, but here the focus is principally on life expectancy and its trends through time.

Figure 22.3 depicts changes in life expectancy over time and compares these trends with those in two other countries with high life expectancy—Australia and Japan. Japan and China both experienced very rapid increases in life expectancy, because they emerged from less developed status, followed by an impressive catching-up process with the developed world. China still falls significantly below these countries in life expectancy, probably because the forces behind declining mortality at mature age, which has driven most of the life expectancy increase in developed countries since the mid-1980s, have yet to manifest themselves in China's mortality statistics.[7] Mature age life expectancy still has some way to go in China, a point relevant to the debate about pension policy, and especially access, or retirement, age.

However, figure 22.3 masks several interacting trends germane to pension policy design. First, surprisingly wide variation exists in life expectancy at birth by province—more than 10 years (map 22.1). This immediately calls into question the idea of a uniform pension plan—there is an important sense in which China can be seen as a number of countries, at different stages of development, with associated differences in socioeconomic characteristics.

Official data from 2005 suggest that life expectancy at age 60 varies much less, however—from 18.4 to 20.2 years, according to a 2008 press release issued by the Chinese

FIGURE 22.3 **Life expectancy at birth, by gender, in Australia, China, and Japan, 1901–2050**

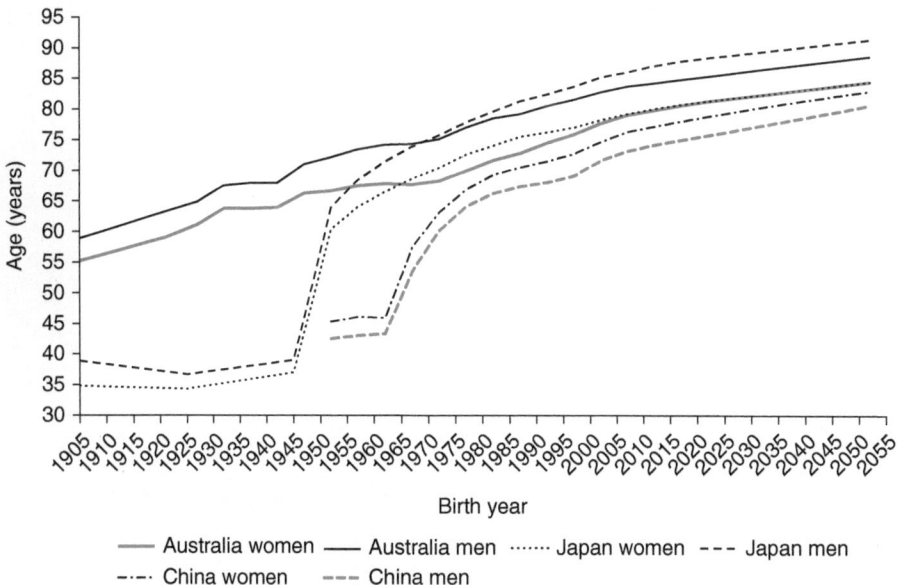

SOURCES: Human Mortality Database (www.mortality.org); ABS Cat 3302.0.55.001; ABS Cat 3105.0.65.001; UN 2011.

Ministry of Human Resources and Social Security.[8] The analysis here independently calculated provincial differences in life expectancy at age 60 using 2010 census data that also suggest much greater homogeneity—an overall range of less than three years. These estimates are preliminary, and refinements may reveal more differentiation; for now, similar lifespans after age 60, on average, might be assumed across provinces.

The current heterogeneity in remaining life expectancy at retirement age can be observed by rural and urban separations, representing different income groups and

MAP 22.1 **Life expectancy at birth, by Chinese province, 2013**

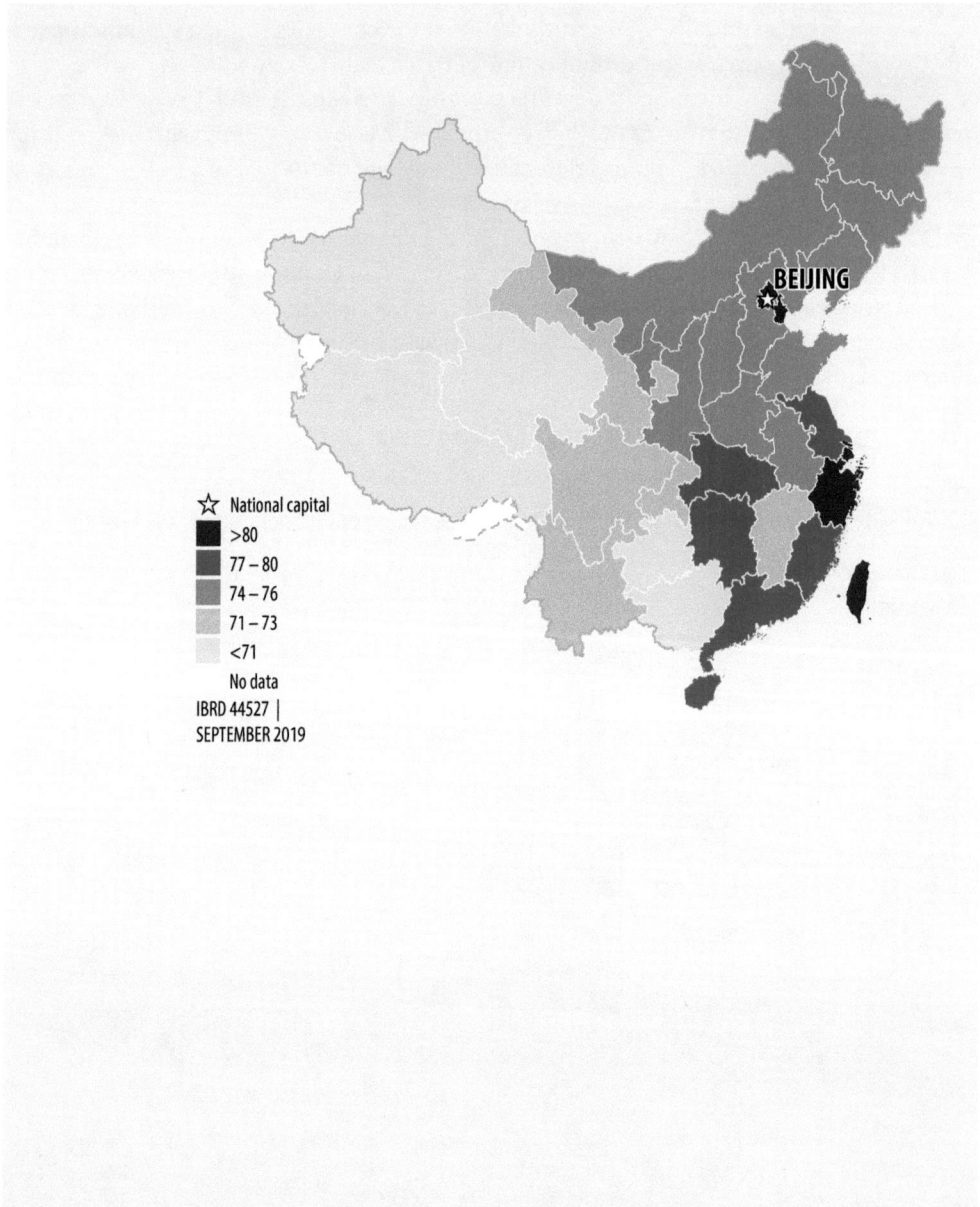

SOURCE: Developed from estimates in Zhou et al. (2016).

TABLE 22.2 **Life expectancy (years) at ages 60 and 65 for national, urban, and rural residents and the urban-rural gap**

Year	National	Urban	Rural	Urban-rural
Life expectancy at 60				
2000	18.4	19.6	17.9	1.7
2005	19.2	20.5	18.3	2.2
2010	20.0	21.5	18.9	2.6
2015	20.9	22.0	19.8	2.0
Life expectancy at 65				
2000	14.7	15.6	14.3	1.4
2005	15.4	16.6	14.7	2.0
2010	16.1	17.5	15.2	2.3
2015	16.9	17.9	16.0	2.0

SOURCE: Original table.

NOTE: Life expectancy is calculated using national census data with adjustments.

TABLE 22.3 **Average city life expectancy in high- and low-income provinces, 2010**

	High-income region		Low-income region	
	Guangdong	Zhejiang	Guizhou	Gansu
GDP per capita (RMB)	44,736	51,711	13,119	16,113
Life expectancy at birth (years)	80.0	80.4	79.7	79.7
Life expectancy at 60 (years)	22.8	23.2	22.5	22.4

SOURCE: Original calculations based on provincial data of the 6th National Census in 2010 for life expectancy and GDP per capita data from the China Bureau of Statistics website.

NOTE: GDP = gross domestic product; RMB = Chinese renminbi.

economic development stages. Table 22.2 estimates life expectancy at ages 60 and 65 based on the past four censuses.

The gap between rural and urban life expectancy stood at 1.7 and 1.4 years in 2000 at ages 60 and 65, respectively. Inequality in life expectancy increased from 2000 to 2010 but has since declined.

Importantly, when the UEPS is considered, it is predominantly urban, even city, life expectancies that matter. Table 22.3 reports city life expectancies at birth and at age 60 for three high-income regions and three low-income regions, along with associated estimates of GDP per capita.

These are remarkably uniform. The difference in life expectancy at age 60 between city residents in the richest province, Zhejiang,[9] and those in the poorest province, Guizhou, is only 0.8 years. The presumption is that city residents in low-income jurisdictions are an elite group, whereas in Zhejiang, the city catchment is much broader. What matters for UEPS pension reform, however, is that life expectancies are not as heterogeneous geographically as overall provincial estimates of life expectancy might suggest.

Finally, the rural-urban migration that took place over the past three decades and continues currently is the largest migration in human history. In 2015, about 250 million people were "floating": their Hukou was different from their place of residency and work.

Most of these are rural residents. A small proportion joined the UEPS; the others have potential rights under the RURPS. This presents enormous challenges to pension fund governance. The extraordinary difference in entitlements between these undocumented workers and their documented counterparts has not been at all adequately addressed in China's pension policy reform.

INSTITUTIONS

Institutional arrangements in China are remarkably robust. Averaging the World Bank Governance Index components, and excluding "Voice and Accountability," China places on average at nearly the halfway mark worldwide, a remarkable achievement for a country at its present stage of development. These social structures, while robust, are also inflexible, at least those embodying the administration of pensions, and must be reckoned as institutional constraints on pension reform. This section provides a brief overview of the governance of retirement policy.

It is convenient to begin with the political and administrative structures. At the immediate subnational level, China is made up of 31 jurisdictions: 22 provinces, 4 cities, and 5 autonomous regions.[10] At lower levels of administration, there are more than 300 cities and nearly 3,000 towns and villages, or counties.[11]

Pension-related administrative agencies are located in more than 3,400 offices, which by Social Security Law are the operating bodies for all contribution collection and distribution records. The fund collection channels are either through social security agencies or local tax offices, and ongoing disagreement remains as to which channel should be used. For example, although 14 provinces currently collect social insurance contributions through the Tax Agency and the MOF would like to have that practice standardized, the MOHRSS does not agree for reasons of control (Lu 2017).

The "social pooling" that constitutes the heart of the DB component of the UEPS takes place within these subjurisdictions. Although most provinces claim to have pooling at the provincial level, they mostly have an adjustment fund system instead of actual pooling at this level. Only a few provinces and cities (Beijing, Chongqing, Qinghai, Shanghai, Shanxi, and Tianjin) have achieved actual provincial pooling. Relatedly, agencies continue to move only slowly toward greater harmonization on data sharing. In mid-2015, the MOF connected to the MOHRSS *Jinbao* information system on social insurance for the first time, but the long-awaited memorandum of understanding between the two ministries to exchange more complete data in real time on social insurance contributors and contributions is still being discussed. Given this background of practice and context, what follows in the next section should be considered illustrative.

Pension Reform and the NDC

This section imagines that the three major pension systems identified in table 22.1 are converted to an NDC structure, and it explores the implications for contributions, individual benefits, and system cash flow. Because the NDC structure offers no minimum guarantee, it must be paired with an effective social pension; this section draws on Lu, He, and Piggott (2014) to present a social pension scenario.

MODEL ASSUMPTIONS AND PARAMETERIZATION

One advantage of an NDC system is that it ensures the contribution history meets longevity trends by automatically adjusting retirement age. Parameterization of the retirement age adjustment is based here on a fixed remaining life expectancy. Remaining life expectancy is fixed at the 2010–15 level (20.5 years at age 60). According to both Lu, He, and Piggott (2014) and OECD (2017), overall life expectancy at age 65 is about 20.5 years in 2060–65.[12]

This assumption of fixed remaining life expectancy is used as the anchor for the automatic retirement adjustment mechanism for the NDC approach. Assuming a linear trend increase in life expectancy, retirement age in 2035 would be 62.5, for example. Heterogeneity across pension plans is also taken into consideration.

The calculations of the operation of an NDC reform in China are embedded in some plausible assumptions about the evolution of the Chinese economy, changing life expectancy, and the evolution of the UEPS. The scenario is informed by considerations of global convergence and of likely patterns of mortality decline and pays some regard to long-term targets of Chinese policy.

Figure 22.4 plots these assumptions on the convergence of wage and GDP growth. Assumptions include linear convergence from 2017 to a steady state 3 percent nominal wage growth and 2 percent price growth by 2050.

In practice, countries adopting an NDC paradigm choose some index of growth, such as GDP per capita or nominal wage growth, as a guide to the crediting rate.[13] For present purposes, nominal wage growth is assumed as the crediting rate.

FIGURE 22.4 **Historical and projected wage and price growth in China, 2000–60**

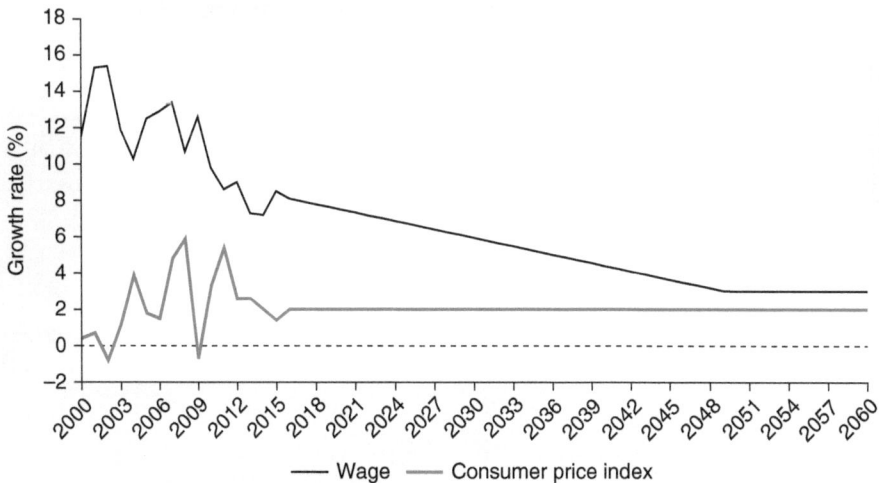

SOURCE: Historical data from the China Bureau of Statistics website.

NOTE: Projections are based on assumed convergence to productivity growth of 1 percent by 2050.

INDIVIDUAL CONTRIBUTIONS AND BENEFITS

The NDC paradigm can be applied to all three pension schemes in China, which are differentiated by contribution rate and retirement age (table 22.4). In all three systems, an 80 percent contribution density ratio is assumed.[14]

The most radical change occurs within the RURPS. Currently, the minimum contribution is 100 yuan per year. The NDC model calculations assume a 10 percent contribution, which is likely to substantially increase the annual contribution amount, although a wide range of contributions will likely exist. It is assumed that employees and employers based in small and medium enterprises pay a 20 percent contribution, the rate currently paid by the enrolled self-employed. The current formal large-scale enterprise members, as well as civil servants, are assumed to maintain the 28 percent contribution scheme. Benefits, expressed as a percentage of final wage, are wage indexed.

Consistent with results in "Demographic and Institutional Considerations," only minor differences in mature age life expectancy are assumed (table 22.4).

SYSTEM CASH FLOW

To generate estimates of system sustainability and cost, estimates of NDC membership are also needed. The assumptions made are given in table 22.5. The urbanization rate is set according to the government target, and the formal labor force participation rate is assumed to converge to current OECD levels by 2035.

With these assumptions, it is possible to generate the evolution of NDC membership through to 2060. Figure 22.5 depicts projections of both contributors and retirees, assuming that 80 percent of contributor accounts are active at any time (the current rate).

The cost of a reformed NDC system with characteristics as outlined can now be calculated. Figure 22.6 depicts cash flow projections for a reformed system, in which benefits gradually decrease from the current replacement rate to the NDC outcomes by 2060. Essentially, the net costs are the transition costs of moving from the promised UEPS benefits to those implied by an NDC paradigm—thereafter, given these assumptions, the system is self-sustaining.

The NDC plan consists of three contribution groups. For simplicity, assume that 40 percent of pension system members will belong to the 10 percent contribution group, mainly rural and urban residents with low income. The second group comprises the

TABLE 22.4 **Various contribution rates and their replacement rate scenarios, 2060**

	Contribution rate (%)	Replacement rate in 2060 (%)	Number of contribution years	Retirement age
RURPS	10	18	35	64.0
UEPS	20	35	35	65.5
Enterprise Annuity and Public Sector	28	49	35	67.0

SOURCE: Original table.

NOTE: The large-scale enterprise and civil servants' contribution plan includes the current 8 percent individual account contribution to the NDC account. RURPS = Rural and Urban Residents Pension Scheme; UEPS = Urban Employee Pension Scheme.

TABLE 22.5 **Assumptions to generate projections of Urban Employee Pension Scheme membership**

Variable	Assumed value
Urbanization ratio	From 50% currently to 75% in 2050
Pension system contributors	From current 40% of labor force population to 65% in 2035, then constant thereafter
Retirement age	Access age is adjusted to maintain remaining life expectancy constant at 20.5 years with adjustment to three different income groups
Number of pensioners	From the current 101 million to 280 million in 2050 (70% of ages 65 and older population)
Population projection	TFR set at 1.55 (Lu, He, and Piggott 2014)

SOURCE: Original table.

NOTE: TFR = total fertility rate.

FIGURE 22.5 **Projection of number of members of Urban Employee Pension Scheme, 2015–60**

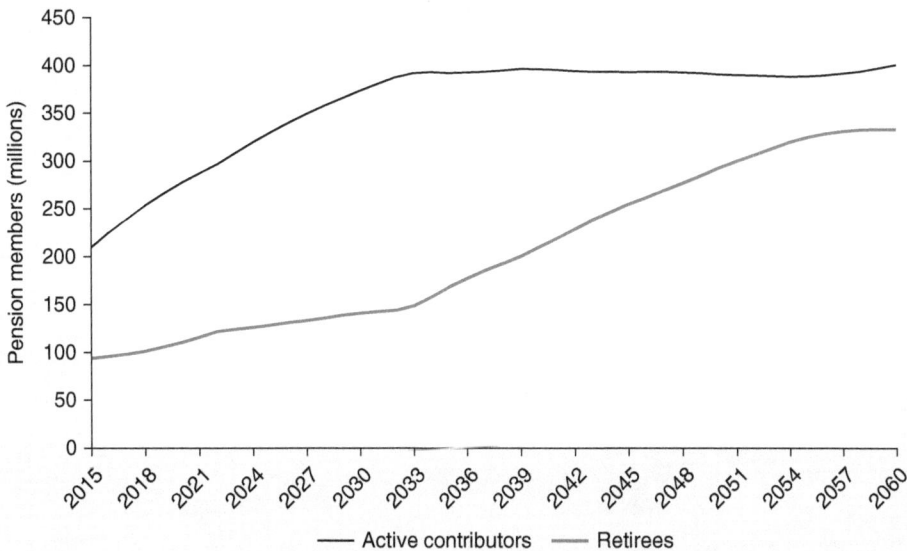

SOURCE: Original calculations.

self-employed and small enterprise employees, accounting for another 40 percent with a 20 percent contribution rate. The last 20 percent of the labor force consists of civil servants and large-scale enterprise employees, who have a 28 percent contribution rate.

The aggregated contribution rate based on this structure will be about 18 percent. The aggregate average national retirement benefit replacement rate will be 31 percent based on the calculation of each group's replacement rate. The projected aggregate cash flow is depicted in figure 22.6, including prereform entitlements.

FIGURE 22.6 **Cash flow projection with nonfinancial defined contribution plan by 2030 and onward, under three different contribution rate groups**

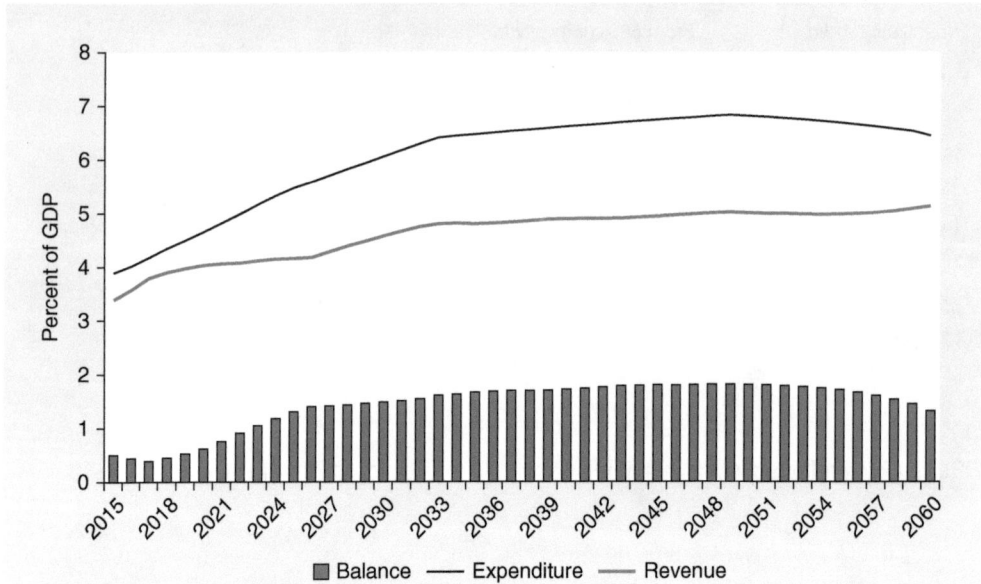

SOURCE: Original calculations.

NOTE: GDP = gross domestic product.

In practice, however, it is unlikely that all system members will contribute for 35 years. Shorter contribution histories will naturally lower the benefit and replacement rates. The experience over the past decade in Chile has shown that a social pension is necessary to support elders with inadequate pension entitlements. Because the NDC paradigm carries no minimum pension guarantee, a social pension is seen as integral to an NDC reform. Estimates of the cost of establishing such a safety net are presented in the next section.

THE ROLE OF THE SOCIAL PENSION

A central feature of the NDC paradigm is that it is not redistributive. This naturally places additional weight on the role of social pensions. Lu, He, and Piggott (2014) analyze a social pension framework in which payments are pension tested—that is, vested members of the UEPS and the Civil Service Pension System were not eligible to receive such a pension. Table 22.6 gives costs, as a percentage of GDP, for benefits set at alternative proportions of GDP per capita, for alternative ratios of the eligible elderly and for alternative fertility rates. As China develops, the target benefit rate would probably lie at the upper end of these projections.

If formal pension coverage evolves as projected, the eligible elderly will likely decline as a fraction of the elderly population. By 2050, it is likely that only 30 percent of the elderly will be eligible for a social pension, and costs will be reduced proportionately. However, NDC members with low accumulations—and current practice suggests that there may be many such members—will require social pension–type support, perhaps along the lines of the recent Chilean reform, in which a social pension supports those with funded pension accumulations that are insufficient to alleviate poverty.

TABLE 22.6 **Social pension cost as a percentage of GDP at age 65: Alternative benefit levels, fertility assumptions, and rates of eligible ratios of elderly[a] by 2050**

Eligible elderly ratio	TFR	Benefit as a % of GDP per capita		
		6.60	10.00	15.00%
75% of elderly	0.9	1.55	2.34	3.52
	1.55	1.45	2.20	3.30
	2.2	1.37	2.07	3.10
50% of elderly	0.9	1.02	1.54	2.31
	1.55	0.96	1.45	2.17
	2.2	0.90	1.36	2.04

SOURCE: Original table.

NOTE: The low and high variants converge linearly to these long-term steady states by 2050, from the current fertility rate of 1.55 (Lu, He, and Piggott 2014). GDP = gross domestic product; TFR = total fertility rate (children per woman); the TFR of 1.55 is static until 2050.

a. Administration costs are not calculated here. It is difficult to estimate the cost of a social pension system given that staff and information systems are usually shared by various programs. According to Grosh et al. (2008, 93), targeting costs average about 4 percent of total program cost.

Conclusion

This chapter reviews the possibilities that the NDC paradigm generates in thinking about pension reform in China. The analysis suggests an important role for an NDC structure, especially within the UEPS. In particular, the NDC model would provide additional leverage in changing access age with increasing mature age life expectancy. The NDC model also provides some help in moderating benefits: parameters set to encourage formal labor force participation generate quite modest benefits under the assumptions. Post-tax replacement rates can be considerably higher, however; in some circumstances, the standard 35 percent UEPS replacement rate under the NDC calculations will translate to more than 50 percent.

Much has been made of heterogeneity in life expectancy across regions in China, and it is certainly true that life expectancy at birth differs markedly, both between urban and rural sectors and across geographic regions. When considering mature age workers who are covered by the UEPS, however, differences largely disappear. This is because considering groups at age 60 removes, by definition, the differential mortality experience before that age and also because of preselection to formal pension membership. Urban workers in western provinces, for example, appear to have mature age life expectancy very close to those in urban east coast jurisdictions, and it is these groups that will dominate UEPS membership. It is, therefore, anticipated that UEPS mature age life expectancy is likely to remain quite homogeneous. Somewhat greater heterogeneity does exist when membership of the RURPS is considered, but even here, mature age life expectancy varies by only a couple of years.

To the extent that the NDC paradigm becomes more widespread in China, a well-functioning and substantial social pension plan becomes more necessary. The chapter discusses a proposal in Lu, He, and Piggott (2014) that describes the design and implementation of a social pension and offers some initial costings. This proposal uses lack of pension fund membership as a criterion for social pension receipt. Within an NDC structure, such a criterion would have to be replaced by some minimum notional accumulation threshold.

ANNEX 22A

Summary of Zheng (2015) for an NDC Proposal and Projection in China

Name	Description	Benefit	Inheritance of individual account	NDC credit rate	Fund balance implication	New retiree replacement rate
Small NDC	20% PAYG social pooling+8% NDC individual account	Current scheme	Yes	80% of average wage growth rate		
Large NDC	12% PAYG social pooling+16% NDC individual account	0.5*years of contribution*average on post-basic wage (transition: 1.7*years of before-reform contribution*salary indexation)	No	80% of average wage growth rate		
Full NDC	28% individual NDC account	Actuarially fair payment, with a 5% replacement rate of social pension	No	100% of average wage growth rate	Fund balance to 69% of GDP by 2050 then decline to 0 by 2087	69% in 2050 and 62% in 2090
	24% individual NDC account	Actuarially fair payment, with a 5% replacement rate of social pension			Fund balance to 50% of GDP by 2050 then decline to 0 by 2078	62% in 2050 and 56% in 2090

NOTE: GDP = gross domestic product; NDC = nonfinancial defined contribution; PAYG = pay-as-you-go. * = multiplication sign.

Notes

1. The NDC paradigm is explained well by Ayuso, Bravo, and Holzmann (2016); Barr and Diamond (2011); Holzmann (2017); Holzmann and Hinz (2005); Holzmann and Palmer (2012); and Lu, Mitchell, and Piggott (2008). It is not further elaborated here.

2. Zheng (2015) does suggest a minimum pension of 5 percent of the national average wage, but they do not consider those who are not eligible for the UEPS pension.

3. The term "scheduled wage" used here is the wage upon which the 28 percent contribution is calculated. In many cases, the wage used is 60 percent of the average wage, which is the minimum base for a 28 percent contribution. Many employers make additional payments to employees that are excluded from the social security calculation.

4. The Social Security Law (section 14) in 2011 authorizes that any remaining individual account balance can be inherited if the pensioner dies.

5. An official document issued by the Chinese government, certifying that the holder is a legal resident of a particular area, meaning the permanent residential place, usually the registration place when the person was born unless he or she is granted a new Hukou by another migration place.

6. World Bank calculations, available on request.

7. For example, the incidence of male adult smokers is about the same in China now as it was 40 years ago in Australia.

8. Source: http://www.chinajob.gov.cn/SocialSecurity/content/2008-11/12/content_479917.htm.

9. Excludes direct municipal cities.

10. Hong Kong SAR, China; Taiwan, China; and Macao SAR, China are excluded.

11. Data from China Statistics Year Book 2016.

12. The OECD (2017) estimates that remaining life expectancy at age 65 is 21.6 years for women and 20.1 years for men in 2060–65.

13. "Notional [nonfinancial] account systems where the interest rate is credited ex post and is the growth rate of the average covered wage, or the growth rate of the covered wage bill, or the growth rate of gross national product, do not exhibit automatic financial stability, although it is believed that the system will adjust in the right direction and will converge to an equilibrium, if and when the factors that are driving the change stabilize (Valdes-Prieto 2000, 404)." Palmer and Stabina (2019) demonstrate how this process works in practice in Latvia, a country that has experienced a strong, continuous decline in the labor force due to low fertility rates and emigration. Also, simulations in Chłoń-Domińczak, Franco, and Palmer (2012) show that the adjustment process is much faster if the NDC scheme is equipped with a (Swedish) solvency ratio and an automatic balancing index. In the projection presented here in the Chinese context, the number of contributors remains fairly constant from 2030 onward and the assumed real wage growth converges to 1 percent as well. A stylized benefit calculation can thus be used in which access age is adjusted to maintain remaining life expectancy constant at 20.5 years.

14. According to Zheng (2015), the density of contribution declined over the past decade to about 80 percent. This rate is assumed to remain the same in the rest of this analysis.

References

Ayuso, Mercedes, Jorge Bravo, and Robert Holzmann. 2016. "Addressing Longevity Heterogeneity in Pension Scheme Design and Reform." IZA Discussion Paper 10378, Institute of Labor Economics, Bonn, Germany.

Barr, Nicholas, and Peter Diamond. 2010. "Pension Reform in China: Issues, Options and Recommendations." https://econ.lse.ac.uk/staff/nb/Barr_Diamond_China_Pensions_2010.pdf.

————. 2011. "Improving Sweden's Automatic Pension Adjustment Mechanism." Issue Brief Number 11-2, Center for Retirement at Boston College, Chestnut Hill, MA. http://crr. bc.edu/wp-content/uploads/2011/01/IB_11-2-508.pdf.

Chłoń-Domińczak, Agnieszka, Daniele Franco, and Edward Palmer. 2012. "The First Wave of NDC Reforms: The Experiences of Italy, Latvia, Poland, and Sweden." In *Nonfinancial Defined Contribution Pension Schemes in a Changing Pension World: Volume 1 Progress, Lessons, and Implementation*, edited by Robert Holzmann, Edward Palmer, and David Robalino, 31–84. Washington, DC: World Bank.

Grosh, Margaret E., Carlo del Ninno, Emil Tesliuc, and Azeidine Ouerghi. 2008. *For Protection and Promotion: The Design and Implementation of Effective Safety Nets*. Washington, DC: World Bank.

Holzmann, Robert, 2017. "The ABCs of Nonfinancial Defined Contribution (NDC) Schemes." Policy Paper 130. IZA, Institute of Labor Economics, Bonn, Germany. http://ftp.iza.org/pp130.pdf.

Holzmann, Robert, and Richard Hinz. 2005. *Old-Age Income Support in the 21st Century: An International Perspective on Pension Systems and Reform*. Washington, DC: World Bank.

Holzmann, Robert, and Edward Palmer. 2012. "NDC in the Teens: Lessons and Issues." In *Nonfinancial Defined Contribution Pension Schemes in a Changing Pension World: Volume 1 Progress, Lessons, and Implementation*, edited by Robert Holzmann, Edward Palmer, and David Robalino, 3–30. Washington, DC: World Bank.

Lu, Bei. 2017. "China Strengthening Social Protection and Labor Systems—China Pension Status Update." Unpublished, World Bank, Washington, DC.

Lu, Bei, Wenjiong He, and John Piggott. 2014. "Should China Introduce a Social Pension?" *Journal of the Economics of Aging* 4 (December): 76–87.

Lu, Bei, Olivia Mitchell, and John Piggott. 2008. "Notional Defined Contribution Pension with Public Reserve Funds in Aging Economies: An Application to Japan." *International Social Security Review* 61: 4.

OECD (Organisation for Economic Co-operation and Development). 2017. *Pensions at a Glance 2017: OECD and G20 Indicators*. Paris: OECD Publishing. https://doi.org/10.1787 /pension_glance-2017-en.

Oksanen, Heikki. 2012. "China: Pension Reform for an Ageing Economy." In *Nonfinancial Defined Contribution Pension Schemes in a Changing Pension World: Volume 1 Progress, Lessons, and Implementation*, edited by Robert Holzmann, Edward Palmer, and David Robalino, 213–55. Washington, DC: World Bank.

Palmer, Edward, and Sandra Stabina. 2019. "The Latvian NDC Scheme: Success under a Decreasing Labor Force." In *Progress and Challenges of Nonfinancial Defined Contribution Pension Schemes: Volume 1 Addressing Marginalization, Polarization, and the Labor Market*, edited by Robert Holzmann, Edward Palmer, Robert Palacios, and Stefano Sacchi, Chapter 3. Washington, DC: World Bank.

UN (United Nations). 2011. "World Population Prospects: The 2010 Revision." UN, New York.

Valdes-Prieto, Salvador. 2000. "The Financial Stability of Notional Account Pensions." *Scandinavian Journal of Economics* 102 (3): 395–417.

Zhang, Yinghua. 2015. "Civil Servants and Public Sector Unit Pension Reform: Design and Sustainability of a Notional Defined Benefit Proposal." *Research on Development* 178 (3): 7–11. China Academic Journal Electronic Publishing House.

Zheng, Bingwen. 2012. "China: An Innovative Hybrid Pension Design Proposal." In *Nonfinancial Defined Contribution Pension Schemes in a Changing Pension World: Volume 1 Progress, Lessons, and Implementation*, edited by Robert Holzmann, Edward Palmer, and David Robalino, 189–209. Washington, DC: World Bank.

————. 2015. "China Pension Report 2014." CASS, Economic and Management Publishing House, Beijing.

Zhou, Maigeng, Haidong Wang, Jun Zhu, Wanqing Chen, Linhong Wang, Shiwei Liu, et al. 2016. "Cause-Specific Mortality for 240 Causes in China during 1990–2013: A Systematic Subnational Analysis for the Global Burden of Disease Study 2013." *The Lancet* 387 (10015): 251–72.

CHAPTER 23

Harnessing a Young Nation's Demographic Dividends through a Universal Nonfinancial Defined Contribution Pension Scheme: A Case Study of Tanzania

Bo Larsson, Vincent Leyaro, and Edward Palmer

Introduction

Since the mid-1990s, Africa has recorded impressive macroeconomic performance with sustained economic growth. Since 2000, 6 of the world's 10 fastest growing economies have been in Sub-Saharan Africa (SSA). Arguably, this growth trend began with the comprehensive macroeconomic reforms in 1987–91 recommended by the World Bank and the International Monetary Fund following the economic crisis of 1980–86. Tanzania, the country of focus in this chapter, is in this group: its average real growth rate was 6–7 percent from 1995–2014 (WTO 2016; World Bank 2017).[1] The benefits of growth have been slow to reach the broader Tanzanian population, however.

Of the United Nation's (UN's) projected world population growth of 2.4 billion people by 2050, about one-half will be born in SSA—and the region will account for almost 80 percent of the increase in the global population up to 2100 (Ncube 2015). According to UN projections, the growth rate of the working-age population in Tanzania will be greater than that of the age group of 65 and older throughout most of this century (figure 23.1, panel a). Fertility rates are presently high, at about 5.0 children per woman, and are projected to decline slowly, reaching 2.1 toward the end of the century (figure 23.1, panel b). At the same time, SSA will experience a continuously inflating demographic bubble, stimulating economic growth, which, in turn, will lead to an increasingly larger percentage of the increasing number of working-age persons entering into formal work. This dual process can be expected to continue throughout the current century as the countries of SSA combine demographic and economic development.

Using Tanzania as a case study, this chapter introduces a nonfinancial defined contribution (NDC)[2] life-cycle saving scheme that leads to an annuity at retirement for formal workers. Based on Tanzanian labor market data from the 2014 Integrated Labour Force Survey (ILFS) and UN demographic projections, the chapter first calculates the

The authors express thanks to Gustavo Demarco and Andrew Mason for their insightful comments provided during the course of this work.

demographic surplus in the NDC fund that Tanzania can expect if the growth of the formal labor force follows those of the projected working-age and old-age (60 and older, 65 and older) populations over the remainder of the century.

The approach is in the spirit of the work of Bloom and Williamson (1998), Mason and Lee (2006, 2010), and Mason, Lee, and Jiang (2016). This chapter focuses on how introduction of an NDC pension scheme in the context of a young emerging market economy can generate savings for NDC bond-financed investments in human and physical infrastructure capital. However, whereas the economic support ratio and transfer accounts are the focus of these earlier studies, in this chapter the old-age support ratio is implicitly a determinant of the savings outcome. Therefore, the financial surplus is available for investment, thereby promoting inclusive economic growth, with even greater dividends for future pension savers.

The public pension scheme encompasses the entire formal labor force and can be viewed as the bottom pillar in the country's overall pension system, which includes occupational and private individual schemes. As the economy grows and formalizes and as contributors reach pension age, individuals' savings in the working phase of the life cycle are gradually transformed into consumption in retirement. As figure 23.1 indicates, the process generating saving surpluses may continue up to and perhaps beyond 80 years into the future, depending on actual fertility rates. The model developed also includes a partial transfer of workers' savings to consumption for the elderly as the system matures.

For those already participating in an existing private pension scheme, the overall pension system becomes a two-pillar system, with private occupational schemes as the second pillar. The NDC scheme, covering the entire contribution-paying population, is the first (individual savings) pillar, while existing (and emerging) occupational schemes constitute an

FIGURE 23.1 **Tanzania population trends**

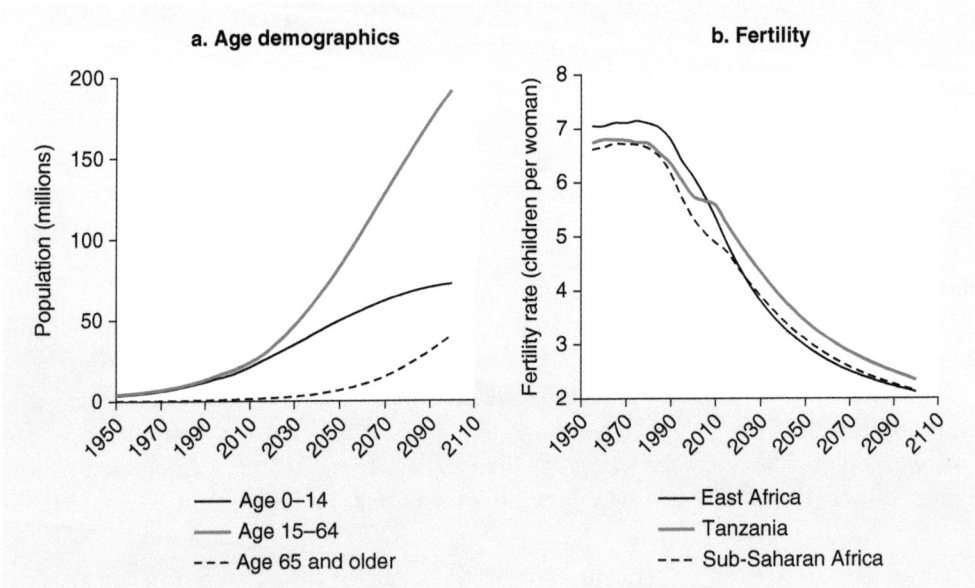

a. Age demographics
b. Fertility

— Age 0–14
— Age 15–64
--- Age 65 and older

— East Africa
— Tanzania
--- Sub-Saharan Africa

SOURCE: United Nations 2017.

occupational second pillar. At the same time, the current elderly (age 65 and older) receive a portion of the emerging NDC contributions for their current consumption. The NDC pillar increases with time as investments in human capital (for example, education, child care, and health care) and physical capital continuously fuel economic growth.

The Economic Setting

Presently, about two-thirds of Tanzania's urban working-age population is employed in the informal sector. High economic growth rates are characterized by the "growth without job creation" problem: labor is attracted to urban areas because of increasing economic activity (suggesting a vibrant informal sector) rather than because of demand for labor for formal employment. Typically, either effective unemployment rises or average earnings fall to accommodate the growing supply of labor (Leyaro et al. 2014).

Tanzania's poverty rate—based on "headcount" and minimum consumption measures—fell from 39 percent in 1991 to 28 percent in 2012, but the absolute number in poverty rose by an estimated 3.3 million persons (World Bank 2015a). At the same time, inequality remains high, with a Gini coefficient of 38 in 2011,[3] partly due to a middle class that constitutes well under 10 percent of the population (Arbache and Page 2009). These are clear symptoms of the need for fundamental structural change.

The approach presented in this chapter can help change the picture through investments in physical infrastructure and human capital (for example, education and skills development). The latter conforms with the message of modern growth theory and empirical analyses,[4] especially with respect to the economic returns to investments in the quantity and quality of education and training (Banerjee and Duflo 2005; Hanushek and Woessmann 2007; Psacharopoulos and Patriono 2002), and with a focus on an emerging market economy (Kotásková Kobzev et al. 2018) and on health care (Banerjee and Duflo 2005; Rentería et al. 2016).

The key question is how to put theory into practice, given that raising capital in a country like Tanzania is challenging if it is not designated for physical investments, such as office buildings and hotels. However, investments in human capital and physical investments that are less suitable for credit scoring are virtually impossible to finance in the emerging market economy context. It is well-recognized that an overwhelming portion of an emerging market economy's population needs physical assets at the micro level—for example, livestock, machinery for agriculture, access roads and major rail transportation lines connecting the countryside with the main urban areas, irrigation, solar power, clean water, and sewage disposal (Conceição and Levine 2015). It is important to craft an overall strategy that promotes participation in the formal workforce that, combined with large- and small-scale physical investments, yields growth in income by steadily increasing the potential productivity for an increasing number of persons in the labor force. Through implementation of an NDC system, it is possible to harvest the demographic dividend and use it for the "low-profile" investments that normally are not attractive for institutional investors, such as the country's private pension funds.

An avenue with a proven positive effect on increased labor force participation is public preschool care of children, which enables women to work in the formal labor market. Using the OECD database, Castles (2003) and Théveron (2011) evaluate the transition from home care to preschool care outside the home in a large number of

OECD countries. A general conclusion of the literature in this area is that the introduction of public preschool first and foremost is an asset in the development of preschool-age children. In macroeconomic terms, it enhances household productivity by taking advantage of economies of scale in preschool care, in addition to facilitating labor market participation of both genders. The social investments envisaged here are likely to have positive effects on local economic growth through the multiplier effects of increased formality of local labor markets, resulting in higher locally produced consumption items.

In the face of macro and micro shocks, such as loss of employment, the social engagement and cohesion that a universal pension scheme promotes can play an important role in reducing the need for negative coping strategies that can reduce growth. Examples include removing children from school to earn money for the family or selling off the only physical capital a family owns.

Finally, one outcome of health care investments is the increased survival of younger children. This is one of the driving factors behind the projected decline in the fertility rate. In addition, this is an outcome of increased economic well-being in the development context. As time progresses, the proportion of the elderly population will inevitably increase as a result of improved health care and lifestyles. This argument favors starting a demographic NDC fund now, supported by the growing numbers of small contributions.

The NDC Universal Public Pension Scheme

In the emerging market economy setting, no comprehensive, monetized, universal public pension scheme exists initially, just as there is no full-fledged formal labor force. The universal pension scheme is instead couched in intergenerational familial arrangements and informal labor markets; the challenge for social insurance is to make the transition to a formal market economy. Given this setting, the following is proposed: individual contributions are made into NDC savings accounts with the designated purpose of financing individual contributors' own future consumption in old age. This creates an NDC fund of money that is transformed into human and physical capital investments through government-issued NDC bonds intended to increase gross domestic product (GDP) growth and its quality, with an explicit goal of developing the microeconomy throughout the country.

The yield on the NDC bonds provides a return on individual contributors' accounts. With the startup of NDC, a minimum pension is created for the current elderly, who had no opportunity to participate in a monetary market-based social insurance scheme in their earlier working lives. This is the beginning of a basic pension at age 65, for example, that can increase over time. This helps reduce the elderly's reliance on money transfers from adult working-age "children." With modernization and migration of young people from rural to urban areas, the changing social landscape will require this. Moreover, during the first decades as formality increases and the contributory scheme matures, the basic pension can remain as the minimum income benefit.

The logic of saving for old age through a universal NDC pension scheme is that it provides a structured universal longevity insurance—in principle, everyone is covered by the scheme and no special financial knowledge is required—although participation is gained by paying contributions, which, given new technologies, does not require local administrative buildings (although this can be essential to spreading information and recruiting participants). The entire nation is the insurance pool, and the pension everyone receives is a life annuity based on individuals' own lifelong contributions based on the same rules. The underlying principle is that "you get what you pay for"—a principle of fairness that most can accept. The annuity is computed with respect to an individual's birth cohorts' life expectancy, maintaining macro financial sustainability over generations. The NDC rate of return is derived from the economy's growth rate (in practice, the growth of the underlying contributions per capita), where the demographically driven growth component (that is, the growth of the formal labor force underlying contributions) creates a demographic reserve fund. The principal component of the reserve fund is the demographic dividend. In addition, the indexation of accounts to economic growth (in practice, the underlying wage sum upon which contributions have been paid) maintains financial stability and intragenerational and intergenerational fairness in the NDC scheme.

In the emerging market economy context, the emphasis on the concept of fairness at the individual (micro) and societal (macro) levels is key to the success of creating universal social protection. At the individual level, one enters into a pension scheme where one's savings become one's own pension (future consumption) in old age. At the societal level, fairness means individuals continue to honor their commitment to their parents' generation, now supplemented by small monetary means. In this way, the cultural principle of intergenerational fairness is upheld.

The vehicle for intergenerational transfers generating the desired result is the NDC fund—that is, the NDC pension scheme "savings bank." The financial instrument is the NDC bond issued by the government. This bond is designed as a "consol" bond, which means that it delivers its yield to the NDC fund on a yearly basis; over time, it is gradually amortized, but the rate of amortization is not necessarily determined with the emission of the bond. The pace of amortization is determined by the fund's needs for liquidity to finance pension expenditures several decades in the future. It is important to keep in mind that it is difficult to judge the pace of economic development and its potential to reduce the fertility rate for parents focused on increasing their own economic welfare. What is certain is that as the demographic dependency profile shifts from an extremely youthful to an increasingly older society, pensioners will increasingly draw upon their savings through NDC pensions.

The advantage of an NDC scheme in the emerging market economy context is that, if properly designed and implemented in harmony with a generic set of rules, the system will be geared from the outset toward moving to financial stability, regardless of the future demography. Moreover, this process can start with less than the desired "end" rate, given a desired average replacement rate. In fact, the increasing contribution rate over time further increases liquidity; when the point is reached at which the net change in the working-age population is "constant" and the minimum pension age and calculation of pensions are determined by life expectancy, then fluctuations should only be small cycles around a long-term equilibrium. What clearly distinguishes an NDC scheme in the emerging market economy context is the flexibility it provides to use contributions either as transfers for consumption from current GDP by the current elderly, or as savings put aside and used for current investments and then converted into own consumption in old age.

DC Incentives and Coverage—Learning From Experience

The defined contribution (DC) design of a pension scheme is believed to be economically efficient; that is, it creates incentives to participate in a pension scheme at the micro level, thereby enhancing total GDP at the macro level. The coverage and density of contributions are expected to increase with the growth of the formal labor market. The counterfactual to this story is the overwhelming lack of success of financial defined contribution (FDC) schemes in Latin America in creating high coverage levels. Coverage for most Latin American countries ranges from 20 to 40 percent[5]; the exceptions are Brazil (64 percent), Chile (71 percent), and Uruguay (77 percent). Levy (2017) identifies the basic design flaw:

> In most (Latin American) countries, only workers hired by firms are enrolled. These workers, known as formal workers, are mostly urban and employed by relatively larger firms or directly by the government as public employees. The rest, known as informal workers, are employed in a variety of ways that leaves them without coverage. They can be self-employed or work in rural areas or in small firms in urban areas where it is difficult to enforce social insurance laws.

Part of the intention behind introducing NDC in Tanzania is to encourage workers in the informal economy to participate in the national pension scheme as economic transactions become formalized, but not necessarily through employment contracts, because it would not be practical to enforce compliance with a universal mandate at the country's present stage of economic development. For this reason, workers' decisions to contribute will have more to do with the fact that they can see that they are saving for themselves and that their 65-year-old and older relatives and friends are receiving small benefits that constitute a relative improvement in their living standards. In addition, people will begin to observe infrastructure investments in their geographic vicinity and will benefit from local growth.

In Latin America, FDC schemes have taken the particular form of employer contributory social insurance. In practice, this means that contributions are conditional upon contractual employment, generally with contributions from both the employer and the employee. Although the employer is a partner in the administrative process for formal contractual employees, the degrees of freedom in setting up the institutional framework must make it possible for participation through one's own initiative, especially for the self-employed and employees at smaller places of work. The only requirement is that contributions are paid, which individuals can do directly without the intervention of employers.

Employer-based FDC schemes may also needlessly emulate the classical Anglo-Saxon insurance model, whereby employers choose providers of accounts and annuities based on account values. This antiquated model is not appropriate in a country where mobility will for the majority replace contracts between the individual, through an employer, with a financial-market-based pension scheme. This sort of small-scale operation would be extremely inefficient in the emerging market economy context—and is so even in the developed economy context. Only a small proportion of the labor force will be privy to this sort of arrangement in the emerging market economy labor environment, because formal contract employment will probably be as much the exception as the rule. Instead, many will be self-employed or working for small employers.

In addition, the employer-based model implies that at the micro level there is only a weak transparent connection to the idea that people are saving individually for their own pensions. At the macro level, it is difficult for people in an employer-based model to see that their savings will contribute to the development of their own country, let alone to their own region, because institutional financial savings in the current global financial world find their way more easily into international investments and at home into traditional infrastructure investments.

The idea of introducing NDC in the emerging market economy is that all are welcome and encouraged to participate. The scheme is mandated by the government, and contributions are paid to a pension administration, perhaps through the tax authority. A formal attachment to the tax system suggests that the process must be easily adaptable to the idea of the "personal savings scheme," where the measuring rod is putting nonwithdrawable money into individual accounts in the DC insurance scheme; this is a property that both universal public NDC and FDC schemes share and that makes it possible to use NDC accounts as if they were FDC accounts for the purpose of investing NDC fund savings.

To ensure this requires an approach different from that pursued in more or less fully formalized economies, where tax collection is regulated with the help of registered employers. Thus, organizational avenues for paying contributions other than through one's own employer need to be considered, especially given the prevalence of self-employment in Tanzania. In other words, contractual employment is not a necessary point of entry; on the contrary, it would eliminate potential participants who do not have contractual employment. In Tanzania, most employees are in this category; of the working-age population of 23 million people, 17–18 million are not formally employed.

Regardless of how the NDC scheme is set up, everyone must have a unique identification (ID) number and must be connected to a means of payment, in which what is important is the payment period but not its frequency or timing. In Tanzania, all old tax identification numbers have been converted to new ones using fingerprint technology.[6] Furthermore, the government is currently giving all small businesses individual IDs to formalize the taxation process. In an NDC scheme, a government clearinghouse is part of the public NDC administration that collects and registers contributions and administers one or more funds and payment of pensions.

Tanzania's Economic Performance and Institutional Readiness for NDC

Since independence in the early 1960s, Tanzania has experimented with two major economic policy frameworks: socialist-oriented and open market–oriented development strategies. During the first six years after independence (1961–66), the economy was fairly open and market oriented, with no specific policy instruments to regulate foreign exchange or prices. There were no import duties; exports, mostly traditional agricultural crops, were taxed as a source of government revenue. The predominantly agriculture- and services-based economy performed quite well in the early years, although the manufacturing sector remained very small (table 23.1, first column).

In the late 1960s, Tanzania began a process of nationalization—African Socialism (Ujamaa)—following the Arusha Declaration of 1967. By the early 1970s, the government had control of almost all sectors; for example, the banking sector and major industries

TABLE 23.1 **Tanzania's economic performance, 1961–2015**

Period	1961–66	1967–79	1980–85	1986–95	1995	2000	2005	2010	2015
GDP growth	6.0	4.0	1.4	3.2	3.6	5.0	7.4	7.0	6.9
Agriculture	53.0	41.0	50.0	49.0	47.1	29.5	26.1	22.7	21.6
Mining	2.5	1.1	1.1	1.1	1.3	1.5	2.4	2.4	2.3
Manufactured products	5.3	10	7.0	8.7	7.2	8.8	8.9	9.6	9.9
Exports	19.3	11.4	4.0	16.2	20.5	13.4	20.8	27.8	28.2
Gross investments	18.5	24.3	19.9	24.1	21.5	17	25.2	32	34.6

SOURCES: Bank of Tanzania 1983, 2012; World Bank 2015b.

NOTE: Agriculture, Mining, and Manufactured products are expressed as "value-added" in percent of GDP; Exports and Gross investments are expressed as a percent of GDP; and GDP growth is expressed in percentage terms. GDP = gross domestic product.

were state owned. The 1970s witnessed a series of shocks that weakened the economy: the 1973–74 drought, the 1973–74 and 1979–80 oil crises, the breakup of the East African Community in 1977, the collapses of cash crop prices in the international markets, and the costly 1978–79 Kagera War with Uganda.

From 1995 onward, following a first wave of economic reforms, Tanzania's growth and macroeconomic performance improved (table 23.1). Growth is high, and investments are significant, but as noted in the introduction, growth is unequally spread within the population. According to the United Nations Development Programme's Human Development Index, Tanzania ranked 151 out of 188 countries in the world in 2015 (UNDP 2016). In addition, public services are inadequate and the perceived quality of those available has deteriorated (Leyaro et al. 2014). What is clearly wanting are micro-level investments.

What is the present potential for introducing an NDC scheme? Defining employment is tenuous in the Tanzanian context, because many participate in the labor force informally and often through agricultural work in the countryside. In addition, more than 66 percent of people in urban areas are in the informal sector. Based on the most recent Integrated Labour Force Survey (ILFS) (Tanzania National Bureau of Statistics 2014), Tanzania had a workforce of about 23 million. Of these, 17–18 million are in agriculture and the informal sector, and about 2 million can be regarded as unemployed. About 2.5–3.0 million persons are formally employed. Fewer than 2 million persons are registered members of social security schemes. This suggests tremendous potential for increasing the formal labor force.

The current pension age is 60 for everyone except medical personnel and professors in universities (where it is age 65), with a unisex life expectancy at this age of about 18 years. The contribution rate is at least 10 percent of the gross salary, with an option to contribute up to 20 percent. A sum of 180 months (the number of months totaling 15 years) is required to claim a full benefit at age 60, and it is possible to continue to work and contribute past this age. Obviously, it is not possible for 15 years of contributions to deliver a very significant benefit during an average life expectancy of 18 years—with a contribution rate of 10 percent of gross earnings.

Informal workers can already opt into Tanzania's present pension and social security system by voluntarily paying contributions, but few do so. The clear remedy is for young workers to begin to contribute with a contribution rate higher than 10 percent and to continue contributing regularly during a long working life—with a pension age around 65 for someone entering the labor force in 2020–25 and retiring around 2065–70. This is clearly not possible for today's older workers, but it can suggest a template for new labor market entrants.

The bottom line is that the young country of Tanzania may be in the "golden time" of growth for using an NDC pension system to harvest its demographic dividend—if people can be convinced of its benefits for them. Enticing informal labor into the formal labor market would enhance a substantial second dividend in addition to the pure demographic dividend. As the next section illustrates, increasing informal workers' participation in an NDC system adds to the system's liabilities but gives rise to a positive cash flow that can be invested to spur growth and reduce poverty and inequality.

One target area to channel NDC funds into is education. Public education is free in theory, but transportation, food, and books still cost money; the quality of Tanzania's public education is low, so parents with the means to do so to send their children to private schools. Education investments could focus on raising access to high-quality education across the country, especially primary and secondary public schools. The return on education in Tanzania is already high at the secondary level, and university degrees are exceptionally attractive. Running a regression of education and employment sectors on wages from the ILFS (Tanzania National Bureau of Statistics 2014) reveals that the only thing that trumps the effect of a university degree is employment through international organizations. Wages at these agencies are roughly seven times that of the overall average wage for paid employees in Tanzania (Tanzania National Bureau of Statistics 2014).

Broader access to high-quality education would bring more workers into the formal economy, inducing higher wages and ultimately higher GDP. This, in turn, would lead to higher levels of contributions and consequently higher liquidity in the initial decades of the NDC scheme. The large wage effect from education, together with the fact that the common labor of farming has by far the lowest income (Tanzania National Bureau of Statistics 2014), means that the potential gain from education for the coming younger generation is a potentially strong motor to harness for individual and aggregate economic welfare.

This chapter investigates how to use the double demographic dividend to support current pensioners, while investing the initial liquidity surplus and gradually phasing in new birth cohorts as the population ages.

The Dynamics of the Demographic Dividend

This section illustrates the possibilities of harvesting the demographic dividend more or less immediately by introducing an NDC pension scheme. The analysis has two channels: the future demographic profile of Tanzania, and the potential in the large share of informality in the Tanzanian labor market. The data used in this section are from the United Nations World Population Prospects (UN 2017) and the 2014 ILFS (Tanzania National Bureau of Statistics 2014). As noted, only about 2 million Tanzanian workers are enrolled in the present social security scheme, or about 8 percent of the working-age population. Fewer than 40 percent of all employees are enrolled, and close to none of the self-employed (1.5 percent), based on the 2014 ILFS. The analysis begins with a simple three-generation model of younger workers, older workers, and pensioners to illustrate the demographic and labor force dynamics of starting an NDC scheme.

Consider an economy with three categories of people, denoted L, all of equal size: young workers (y), old workers (o), and the retired. Workers earn average wage $\bar{W}$ and—with a contribution rate of c—they pay $c \times L(\bar{W}^o + \bar{W}^y)$ in contributions to the pension system. Retired individuals receive an average pension $\bar{P}$. In a financial steady state with stable demographics it is necessary and sufficient that $c \times L(\bar{W}^o + \bar{W}^y) = \bar{P} \times L$ in this simple framework. Assume that L are the formally employed who pay taxes and contributions to the social security scheme. For Tanzania, this is initially roughly 8 percent, based on the data presented above. N denotes current workers with informal employment who can be enticed to voluntarily participate in the social security scheme. Also, note that the number of individuals with paid employment is three times greater than the number of workers participating in the social security scheme; thus, the dividend forthcoming as informal workers gradually enter the labor force is low-hanging fruit for a pension system. Table 23.2 includes a time index on the formally employed cohorts to see how they pass through the different stages of life. The first period is $t-1$, when contributions paid in balance the pensions paid out.

In period t, N informal workers have been enticed to participate in the social security scheme, leading to a financial surplus in time t because the number of retired is unchanged. This becomes a permanent feature of the labor force so that even the young in $t+1$ increase in number by N individuals. The addition of N young workers continues, and in $t+2$ the first group of $L + N$ pensioners arrives. This returns the system to perfect balance, where contributions paid in equal pensions paid out. In addition, there is now an uncommitted fund as long as workers do not start flowing from formal into informal employment. The surpluses from time t and $t+1$ constitute a "free lunch," with many alternative uses, as described.

Consider that N in this illustration can represent either (a) the increase in the working-age population with a constant rate of formal labor force participation, or (b) an increase in the percentage of a given population that enters the formal labor force—or in a country with Tanzania's starting point, both: that is, the entire double dividend. Note also that this process continues yearly into the future ($t + 3$, $t + 4$, ..., $t + x$), as long as the labor force is growing, either through population dynamics or continued formalization of the labor force. The demographic component—with the large projected increase in the working-age population, increase in savings, and investment potential—is formidable. Given Tanzania's current formal labor market of only 5 percent, which will potentially approach 100 percent

TABLE 23.2 **Nonfinancial defined contribution balance with an increasing formal labor force**

	$t-1$	t	$t+1$	$t+2$
Pension	$\bar{P}_{t-1} \times L_{t-3}$	$\bar{P}_t \times L_{t-2}$	$\bar{P}_{t+1} \times L_{t-1}$	$\bar{P}_{t+2} \times (L_t + N)$
y contribution	$c \times \bar{W}^y_{t-1} \times L_{t-1}$	$c \times \bar{W}^y_t \times (L_t + N)$	$c \times \bar{W}^y_{t+1} \times (L_{t+1} + N)$	$c \times \bar{W}^y_{t+2} \times (L_{t+2} + N)$
o contribution	$c \times \bar{W}^o_{t-1} \times L_{t-2}$	$c \times \bar{W}^o_t \times L_{t-1}$	$c \times \bar{W}^o_{t+1} \times (L_t + N)$	$c \times \bar{W}^o_{t+2} \times (L_{t+1} + N)$
Surplus	0	$c \times \bar{W}^y_t N$	$c\left(\bar{W}^o_{t+1} + \bar{W}^y_{t+1}\right) \times N$	0

SOURCE: Original table.

in several decades, this produces an extraordinary potential source of financing in a savings- (and investment-) constrained economy, while also paying basic pensions to the elderly.

In summary, this demographic dividend can be harvested in many ways by investing in both human and physical capital. The list is comprehensive and well-known: encompassing an increasingly greater share of the growing young population in education, vocational, and skills training at all levels; investing in physical infrastructure that supports broad-based development at the local and regional level, such as investments in farm machinery, storage and transportation networks, and basic amenities (including the efficient local provision of electricity, clean drinking water, and sewage removal and treatment); and making regional and local capital investments. The accumulated return on these investments is likely to be huge, given the point of departure.

Simulations Using the United Nations Demographic Projections for Tanzania

This section's calculations illustrate the potential of introducing an NDC pension saving scheme in an emerging market economy. Tanzania was chosen for this illustration because a precondition is that the country has a solid historical growth track record and an existing institutional framework that can be readily developed to introduce what is intended to become a universal NDC public pension scheme—"intended" because a large portion of the labor force is still presently informal. This means that the scheme will have the same rules for all covered, but the process of achieving true universality (coverage of all who work and earn a formal income) may take several decades.

It is presumed that the NDC fund created by the introduction of the public NDC scheme will contribute to accelerating achievement of universal coverage by creating growth-enhancing investments. The first simulations answer the question, What if the current participation rates reign "forever," but the demographic dividend characterizing the UN demographic projections in figure 23.1 characterizes the future? The purpose of this conservative approach is to isolate the dividend created "purely" by the demographic forces at work. In this perspective, the second dividend that will inevitably arise with increased labor force participation becomes a potentially huge "bonus" to the example. The simulations thus answer the question, What would introduction of the NDC pension system bring in the form of domestic savings available for investments to create growth and more jobs?

The calculations follow the model specified in table 23.2, coupling the Tanzanian economic labor market data from the 2014 ILFS with the UN demographic projections. In the calculations of the future population, the number of births per woman declines and the longevity of each successive birth cohort increases until 2100, in accordance with the UN assumptions. The proportions of the working-age population paying contributions are shown in table 23.3, which also displays current income.

In summary, the calculations are performed for (a) persons already contributing to the present pension scheme—primarily civil servants and persons in large enterprises; (b) all paid employees; and (c) everyone with a reported income of any scale in 2014. The starting average annual income for each group is based on data from the 2014 ILFS. The third group is about 30 percent of the total working-age population (those ages 15–60).

The simulations start the NDC scheme in 2015. This implies that a two-pillar scheme moves into action. The first pillar is "universal" in that it covers all income earners

TABLE 23.3 **Average annual wage and number of individuals in the different groups selected for pension simulations**

Age	Current pension contribution		Paid employees		All with income	
	Average wage (US$)	Number of individuals	Average wage (US$)	Number of individuals	Average wage (US$)	Number of individuals
15–19	811	5,105	548	261,027	528	583,740
20–24	1,864	54,729	966	413,563	817	1,248,511
25–29	2,423	157,651	1,508	488,907	1,094	1,835,927
30–34	3,431	181,553	2,104	460,072	1532	1,949,259
35–39	2,807	148,635	2,046	305,424	1,483	1,865,568
40–44	3,571	149,817	2,599	267,841	1,421	1,508,224
45–49	3,592	131,021	2,756	205,007	1,585	1,215,050
50–54	3,474	94,726	3,166	147,714	1,431	983,235
55–59	3,989	73,746	3,043	115,268	1,317	688,921
Total	3,167	996,983	1,858	2,664,822	1,303	11,878,435

SOURCES: Original calculations based on data from Tanzania National Bureau of Statistics 2014.

NOTE: US$ = U.S. dollar.

(and regardless of density of payments, which is indirectly factored into the average wage for the group). The second pillar is for the "exclusive" group (1) contributors, or more broadly, the group (2) contributors. These two groups of income earners are also implicitly subgroups of group (3), in which all are covered by the universal NDC scheme. In this sense, group (3) is the most relevant for the NDC calculations, whereas groups (1) and (2) suggest potential for a second FDC pillar on top of a universal NDC scheme.

The NDC contribution rate in the first example is 20 percent. Contributions that do not go to current pensioners become savings in the NDC fund. The fund purchases NDC bonds that have an annual yield determined by the nominal rate of growth of the country's GDP, in the calculations assumed equal to the real wage growth rate. This enables bond-financed investments, as opposed to purchase of general government debt instruments, to ensure that the money gets an adequate rate of return and is used to generate economic growth and development for the country.

The average replacement rate is calculated using the development of the average wage for age cohorts in the 2014 ILFS report. A moderate assumption of real wage growth of 1 percent is used when "rolling" wages forward. A participant begins his or her career with the average wage from the 2014 ILFS estimated wages per age cohort. Each year, the individual moves up one year to the next age group, with the wage for this group raised assuming 1 percent real growth. This process is repeated until retirement. The final annual wage in 2014 prices under the assumption of 1 percent real wage growth is US$5,440 at age 60; the annual pension granted is US$1,820, meaning that the old-age pension would be about one-third of the final wage. Raising the retirement age to 65 would increase the replacement rate to slightly less than 50 percent.[7] Raising the retirement age in contemporary Tanzania is possible, given the improvement in health status of most families and given that longevity is steadily increasing.

Table 23.4 shows that it is possible to harvest a demographic dividend in cash, regardless of the pension policy adopted. The calculation assumes the present rate of formal labor force

TABLE 23.4 **Debt, flow, and contribution surplus from a nonfinancial defined contribution system using 2014 Tanzanian data on income and population** at a 20 percent contribution rate and a retirement age of 60

	Current pension system participants			Paid employees			All with income		
	Liability to workers	Pensions paid	Contribution surplus	Liability to workers	Pensions paid	Contribution surplus	Liability to workers	Pensions paid	Contribution surplus
2015	0	0	683,036,333	0	0	1,098,621,532	0	0	3,404,865,109
2020	651,751,849	17,833,633	840,777,220	1,075,817,246	21,263,784	1,353,224,502	3,374,649,725	54,989,355	4,208,890,381
2025	1,436,856,119	58,731,342	1,019,385,449	2,380,168,683	74,176,614	1,646,526,862	7,482,562,955	202,714,684	5,130,538,612
2030	2,334,482,220	142,592,661	1,206,882,537	3,920,710,896	179,925,364	1,968,795,156	12,297,596,640	519,975,231	6,130,917,394
2035	3,333,076,864	282,550,253	1,401,333,487	5,694,410,147	358,171,148	2,312,234,366	17,842,406,107	1,061,521,616	7,201,046,014
2040	4,460,084,258	476,619,035	1,605,468,996	7,733,303,807	612,093,710	2,672,014,899	23,997,515,940	1,900,135,013	8,290,411,487
2045	5,664,598,705	748,249,439	1,808,412,480	9,953,481,201	978,407,088	3,027,933,976	30,700,612,168	3,100,042,442	9,361,788,961
2050	7,021,867,332	1,080,852,049	2,036,452,297	12,422,595,116	1,450,052,909	3,399,714,894	38,254,610,383	4,609,702,299	10,505,837,943
2055	8,620,213,768	1,456,632,120	2,315,763,406	15,224,139,535	2,012,208,069	3,818,712,213	46,929,256,292	6,389,083,489	11,784,936,825
2060	10,519,130,404	1,873,782,112	2,653,948,779	18,470,632,007	2,653,044,823	4,299,205,333	57,038,431,068	8,347,312,047	13,314,962,937
2065	12,617,540,794	2,330,931,228	3,028,714,583	22,056,298,440	3,358,024,998	4,826,349,341	68,202,213,292	10,494,637,336	15,007,961,556
2070	14,917,829,117	2,898,030,503	3,375,222,619	25,987,182,063	4,212,443,243	5,314,582,728	80,447,237,417	13,126,050,561	16,572,531,513
2075	17,416,027,124	3,584,492,386	3,677,839,906	30,252,312,304	5,223,969,029	5,752,657,355	93,752,361,841	16,260,116,837	17,979,989,450
2080	20,219,790,666	4,373,175,516	3,972,276,599	35,008,442,152	6,372,658,166	6,183,264,022	108,619,941,672	19,831,439,784	19,343,106,806
2085	23,299,677,238	5,259,595,329	4,256,220,625	40,208,209,046	7,659,953,351	6,595,468,632	124,893,116,127	23,836,817,384	20,629,835,974
2090	26,591,245,198	6,249,777,974	4,507,744,035	45,753,717,919	9,097,432,699	6,955,560,705	142,251,349,237	28,309,403,209	21,753,558,902
2095	30,046,544,321	7,348,034,562	4,709,738,364	51,571,899,441	10,691,358,848	7,238,811,108	160,466,990,205	33,268,677,076	22,645,331,491
2100	33,660,350,046	8,557,723,112	4,858,022,616	57,651,761,263	12,446,645,965	7,436,673,809	179,514,206,020	38,729,874,239	23,274,206,399

SOURCES: Original simulations based on National Bureau of Statistics Tanzania 2014; and United Nations 2017.

participation—a level of contributions actually payable (and presently paid) into the pension system. Not until 2065 does the demographic profile start to reduce the inflow relative to the outflow to the pension system, and even then there is still a net surplus. The large pension contribution surplus probably prevails far into the next century. For capital-constrained economies such as Tanzania's, this can be a significant stepping stone to prosperity if used with caution. Combining the "harvest" of the demographic dividend with sound economic policy to foster growth can multiply economic development and significantly reduce poverty and inequality.

Investing in education and skills training could yield a high return, given that only 13 percent of ILFS respondents in 2014 stated they had a secondary school or higher level of education.[8] This implies that fewer than 6 million Tanzanians out of the more than 23 million working-age population have a secondary or higher level of education. There is a strong positive impact of education and skills training on income in Tanzania, an outcome well-grounded in the literature reviewed in the initial section. Supplying more and better education and skills training should, according to economic growth models, act as a strong multiplier, increasing both economic efficiency and real per capita income. This effect leads to larger pension contributions that can be continuously harvested for further growth-enhancing investments and social welfare.

An obvious issue in an emerging market economy is that a very large percentage of working-age cohorts have very low incomes. Thus, it may be impossible for them to participate in a "developed economy–style" pension system designed to maintain a high standard of living after retirement. Clearly, for those close to the point of starvation, very little room remains for "saving for retirement"—setting aside 20 percent in contributions for a pension. As an experiment, this chapter therefore investigates how a modification of the contribution rate affects the contribution surplus. Instead of a pension system that tries to sustain a high standard of living, it sets a low 5 percent contribution rate. The primary target is to alleviate extreme poverty in old age during the initial decades. It can be thought of as the startup of a first antipoverty pillar (minimum pension) in, for example, a three-pillar system, in which the contribution rate is gradually increased to 20 percent, as used in the preceding example. The system can then be opened up for voluntary "top-up" and occupational schemes.

Table 23.5 presents the experiment assuming only a 5 percent contribution rate. Unlike in table 23.4, the more relevant subgroup is now "all with income," with even low-wage earners paying 5 percent of earnings to the pension scheme. They would do this to secure a small pension in old age and become less dependent on their children or an extended family member.

Comparing tables 23.4 and 23.5, it is obvious that the system with the lower contribution rate yields a contribution surplus that is in between the surpluses for the group that already participates in the pension system and the larger group of paid employees. Because the informal sector comprises the majority of the working-age population, incentives—such as physical and human capital investments—must make people want to participate.

Another effect apparent in the UN life-expectancy tables is that although life expectancy at birth is considerably lower than for a high-income country (a difference of almost 20 years between Western Europe and Tanzania), life expectancy at age 60 differs by roughly only 5 years. With a life expectancy of about 18 years at age 60 in Tanzania, it may be more appropriate to have a formal pension age of 65. One advantage of an NDC system is the possibility to affect replacement rates by postponing one's retirement age, if one is in good enough health to continue to work. To investigate this avenue, the pension model is recalculated with the 5 percent contribution rate and a retirement age of 65 years (table 23.6).

TABLE 23.5 **Debt, flow, and contribution surplus from a nonfinancial defined contribution system using 2014 Tanzanian data on income and population** at a 5 percent contribution rate and a retirement age of 60

	Current pension system participants			Paid employees			All with income		
	Debt to workers	Pensions paid	Contribution surplus	Debt to workers	Pensions paid	Contribution surplus	Debt to workers	Pensions paid	Contribution surplus
2015	0	0	170,759,083	0	0	274,655,383	0	0	850,654,931
2020	162,937,962	4,458,408	210,194,305	268,954,311	53,15,946	338,306126	843,072,152	13,747,339	1,051,532,287
2025	359,214,030	14,682,835	254,846,362	595,042,171	18,544,154	411,631,716	1,869,295,448	50,678,671	1,281,772,528
2030	583,620,555	35,648,165	301,720,634	980,177,724	44,981341	492,198,789	3,072,081,969	129,993,703	1,531,664,718
2035	833,269,216	70,637,563	350,333,372	1,423,602,537	89,542,787	578,058,592	4,457,133,285	265,357,525	1,798,978,098
2040	1,115,021,064	119,154,759	401,367,249	1933,325,952	153,023,428	668,003,725	5,994,527,679	474,969,003	2,071,100,813
2045	1,416,149,676	187,062,360	452,103,120	2,488,370,300	244,601772	756,983,494	7,668,703,571	774,866,964	2,338,716,491
2050	1,755,466,833	270,213,012	509,113,074	3,105,648,779	362,513,227	849,928,724	9,555,367,411	1,152,165,179	2,624,499,310
2055	2,155,053,442	364,158,030	578,940,851	3,806,034,884	503,052,017	954,678,053	11,722,300,893	1,596,783,482	2,944,113,771
2060	2,629,782,601	468,445,528	663,487,195	4,617,658,002	663,261206	1074,801,333	14,247,600,446	2,086,064,286	3,326,482,112
2065	3,154,385,199	582,732,807	757,178,646	5,514,074,610	839,506,249	1,206,587,335	17,036,363,839	2,622,589,331	3,749,587,678
2070	3,729,457,279	724,507,626	843,805,655	6496,795,516	1053,110,811	1,328,645,682	20,095,207,589	3,280,073,214	4,140,617,479
2075	4,354,006,781	896,123,096	919,459,976	7,563,078,076	1,305,992,257	1438,164,339	23,418,888,839	4,063,241518	4,492,315,115
2080	5,054,947,667	1,093,293,879	993,069,150	8,752,110,538	1,593,164,541	1,545,816,005	27,132,931,696	4,955,687,054	4,832,934,599
2085	5,824,919,309	1,314,898,832	1,064,055,156	10,052,052,262	1,914,988,338	1,648,867,158	31,198,130,357	5,956,602,679	5,154,479,252
2090	6,647,811,299	1,562,444,493	1,126,936,009	11438,429,480	2,274,358,175	1,738,890,176	35,534,420,536	7,074,272,321	5,435,297,080
2095	7,511,636,080	1,837,008,641	1,177,434,591	12,892,974,860	2,672,839,712	1,809,702,777	40,084,904,911	8,313,549,107	5,658,175,832
2100	8,415,087,512	2,139,430,778	1,214,505,654	14,412,940,316	3,111,661,491	1,859,168,452	44,843,189,286	9,678,267,857	5,815,353,300

SOURCES: Original simulations based on Tanzania National Bureau of Statistics 2014; and United Nations 2017.

TABLE 23.6 **Debt, flow, and contribution surplus from a nonfinancial defined contribution system using 2014 Tanzanian data on income and population** at a 5 percent contribution rate and a retirement age of 65

	Current pension system participants			Paid employees			All with income		
	Liability to workers	Pensions paid	Contribution surplus	Liability to workers	Pensions paid	Contribution surplus	Liability to workers	Pensions paid	Contribution surplus
2015	0	0	172,501,396	0	0	277,440,709	0	0	881,191,446
2020	179,469,513	629,718	216,228,190	288,665,568	1,006,691	346,140,687	894,046,881	11,036,708	1,092,892,105
2025	396,851,595	7,303,754	264,976,395	643,823,935	9,295,078	425,278,563	2,005,697,211	43,370,008	1,337,295,524
2030	660,815,451	21,675,437	319,280,668	1,077,514,464	28,183,799	514,731,131	3,365,067,581	108,742,913	1,615,788,164
2035	967,969,068	49,391,763	376,344,586	1,594,758,354	63,369,499	611,850,047	4,975,205,417	222,707,959	1,925,148,349
2040	1,318,219,004	91,062,612	435,707,348	2,197,876,332	117,098,498	713,916,864	6,854,129,292	399,455,411	2,256,118,698
2045	1,718,972,206	148,149,576	498,906,623	2,894,852,794	191,716,929	822,482,734	8,976,245,421	663,379,893	2,588,499,676
2050	2,160,156,885	224,779,412	564,346,304	3,667,978,375	296,808,427	931,299,575	11,332,291,532	1,025,925,895	2,922,491,091
2055	2,664,092,833	314,829,271	640,484,830	4,538,356,754	427,067,782	1,050,189,992	14,012,097,396	1,466,459,888	3,288,526,526
2060	3,256,189,229	416,032,834	731,062,912	5,532,269,868	581,206,623	1,181,096,090	17,092,785,354	1,965,342,914	3,712,957,131
2065	3,953,600,611	526,718,244	832,714,925	6,679,926,164	753,574,969	1,323,726,756	20,663,015,581	2,518,863,743	4,195,459,204
2070	4,723,550,949	661,630,641	931,146,482	7,945,812,753	960,070,007	1,460,795,294	24,602,606,834	3,191,001,787	4,658,452,680
2075	5,568,010,102	825,403,345	1,020,256,164	9,331,447,391	1,204,933,336	1,587,304,570	28,919,498,633	3,996,973,902	5,085,715,221
2080	6,484,300,941	1,023,706,537	1,098,270,614	10,833,007,229	1,495,919,304	1,699,995,303	33,605,479,643	4,961,420,459	5,451,389,541
2085	7,505,589,312	1,247,136,014	1,173,900,792	12,497,656,237	1,821,286,361	1,809,844,294	38,804,937,595	6,042,992,182	5,805,651,229
2090	8,622,353,286	1,492,360,103	1,246,681,344	14,310,455,894	2,178,240,869	1,914,397,317	44,467,430,143	7,229,933,238	6,150,015,151
2095	9,813,482,423	1,763,965,637	1,308,607,322	16,239,868,691	2,573,468,987	2,002,001,848	50,494,735,686	8,544,497,407	6,446,034,022
2100	11,063,015,145	2,065,707,703	1,355,352,728	18,261,843,360	3,012,457,765	2,065,679,102	56,814,080,504	10,004,934,394	6,665,130,714

SOURCES: Original simulations based on Tanzania National Bureau of Statistics 2014; and United Nations World Population Prospects 2017.

The calculation shows only a small increase in revenues because all that has happened is that one more five-year cohort is paying. This is straightforward and linked to the large demographic dividend to be harvested; at this stage of the demographic development, only a relatively few more elderly workers will pay contributions as a result of the increased retirement age.

More important is the increase in the pension from a longer working life. With a pension age of 60 and a 5 percent contribution rate, the replacement rate is only slightly greater than 9 percent, or US$190. When the retirement age is raised to 65, the replacement rate increases by more than 3.5 percentage points, or to US$225. This is considerably more than the earned income of 12 million Tanzanians in 2016. Even a retirement age of 60 renders a pension larger than US$182.5 per year. Also, there are scale effects to increasing the rate of growth from the assumption of 1 percent to the more realistic assumption of continued growth of 5–7 percent tapering off in the future.

Summary and Policy Implications

The question addressed in this study is, Can a public pension scheme with an NDC design be introduced into an economy with the starting conditions of the Tanzanian economy and evolve into universal coverage? Not surprisingly, the answer is yes. In fact, a golden opportunity arises in doing so now rather than later because the present life-cycle model is still largely a three-generation family in the sense that goods and services for the younger and older generations are largely transferred informally through the working-age generation. This means that no previous pension arrangement needs to be replaced, avoiding the issue of how acquired rights are to be honored; however, it is likely that the working-age population will only be gradually relieved of both paying into their own scheme and still caring for the parents.

Through the introduction of a universal public pension scheme, the country sets out on a path to distribute pension rights for the working-age population via establishment of NDC accounts. In the absence of formal financial pension liabilities at the outset, monetary minimum income transfers can be made to the already elderly population. In addition, gearing pension expenditures to a contribution rate that is reasonable at the outset given the very large number of persons with low incomes (where the point of departure is the complete absence of such a transfer), savings will nevertheless arise through NDC pension scheme contributions. When the scheme is introduced, it should be done with the prospect of increasing the contribution rate (for example, from 5 percent to 20 percent) over a well-thought-out path over time, with check points.

The assumptions underlying the calculations in this study are conservative given that they presume a constant participation rate despite the facts that (a) the growing economy will generate considerable demand for labor in the formal labor force, and (b) the increases in the formal labor force will create a second demographic dividend (which is not fully reflected in the calculations). Put differently, this increase has the potential to create an increase as the decades pass in the savings flowing into the NDC fund, creating the opportunity to provide even more generous pensions for the current generation of pensioners at the outset, as well as an increasing pension for the older retiring working-age population.

The culmination of this process can be a full-fledged universal NDC around 2060–65, depending on the target pension age in 40–45 years. The liquidity needed to accomplish this would be invested in NDC bonds. Amortization of this debt will start about the same time the system becomes universal and the demographics begin to converge to equilibrium. The NDC scheme will earn the NDC bond rate of return, whereas indexation of accounts and pensions can be tied to the rate of growth of per capita real wages of the underlying collective of contributors. This leaves the liquidity created by the increasing formalization of the labor force in the NDC funds to be invested during the many decades covered by the underlying demographic dividend.

In summary, this chapter presents a rough sketch, with an extremely conservative set of assumptions, of the capacity of an emerging market economy such as Tanzania to support broad-based economic growth and social cohesion through the introduction of an NDC scheme. The savings in the NDC fund achieve the first goal, while payment of pensions to the elderly generation achieves the second goal. The latter allows individuals to realize their life-cycle objectives to transfer income earned from formal work to their children through investments in education and health care, for example, and to their parents and eventually themselves through their contributions to the universal NDC pension scheme. At a societal level, the whole country becomes richer through a better educated and increasingly formal labor force and accompanying continued strong economic growth.

Notes

1. http://www.worldbank.org/en/country/tanzania/overview.

2. See Palmer (2013) for a technical presentation of NDCs, including the mechanics of creating a fund. See Góra and Palmer (2019) for a conceptual presentation of individual saving, funding, and NDCs.

3. https://data.worldbank.org/indicator/SI.POV.GINI?locations=CO%29-TZ.

4. As a result of the endogenous growth theory work by Romer (1986, 1988, 1990) and Lucas (1988) and work by Levine and Renelt (1992) on a set of basic variables to model growth, there appears to be agreement that, given initial per capita GDP, the underlying growth model is a function of physical capital, human capital, and population growth. This is because the ultimate drivers of per capita growth are technological growth and growth of human and physical capital. Initial per capita GDP determines the rate at which countries converge with each other.

5. In Tanzania only about 8 percent of the working-age population is covered in a formal pension scheme.

6. This development will also take advantage of the spread of increasingly less expensive mobile phone technology and Internet access. Tanzania has already recognized the important role of communications technology as a driver supporting its path toward industrialization.

7. Income of employees ages 15 and 16 is not provided in the 2014 ILFS. Regardless, all employed workers are included in the simulation.

8. The share of inhabitants ages 20–64 with secondary education or higher is 19 percent.

References

Arbache, Jorge S., and John Page. 2009. "How Fragile Is Africa's Recent Growth?" *Journal of African Economies* 19: 1–24.

Banerjee, Abhijit V., and Esther Duflo. 2005. "Growth Theory through the Lens of Development Economics." In *Handbook of Economic Growth*, 1st ed., edited by Philippe Aghion and Steven Durlauf, Volume 1, 473–552. Amsterdam: Elsevier.

Bank of Tanzania. 1983. *Tanzania, Twenty Years of Independence (1961–1981): A Review of Political and Economic Performance.* Dar es Salaam: Bank of Tanzania.

———. 2012. *Tanzania Fifty Years of Independence (1961–2011).* Dar es Salaam: Bank of Tanzania.

Bloom, David E., and Jeffery G. Williamson. 1998. "Demographic Transitions and Economic Miracles in Emerging Asia." *World Bank Economic Review* 12 (3): 340–75.

Castles, Francis G. 2003. "The World Turned Upside Down: Below Replacement Fertility, Changing Preferences and Family Friendly Public Policy in 21 OECD Countries." *Journal of European Social Policy* 13 (3): 209.

Conceição, Pedro, and Sebastian Levine. 2015. "Long-Term Social Protection for Inclusive Growth: Can Social Protection Help Promote Inclusive Growth?" International Policy Centre for Inclusive Growth (IPC—IG) Poverty Practice, Bureau for Development Policy, UNDP, Brasilia, Brazil.

Góra, Marek, and Edward Palmer. 2019. "NDC: The Generic Old-Age Pension Scheme." In *Progress and Challenges of Nonfinancial Defined Contribution Pension Schemes: Volume 1 Addressing Marginalization, Polarization, and the Labor Market,* edited by Robert Holzmann, Edward Palmer, Robert Palacios, and Stefano Sacchi, Chapter 8. Washington, DC: World Bank.

Hanushek, Eric A., and Ludger Woessmann. 2008. "Role of Cognitive Skills in Economic Development." *Journal of Economic Literature* 46 (3): 607–68.

Kotásková Kobzev, Sylvie, Petr Procházka, Luboš Smutka, Mansoor Maitah, Elena Kuzmenko, Markéta Kopecká, and Vladimír Hönig. 2018. "The Impact of Education on Economic Growth: The Case of India." *Acta Universitatis Agriculturae et Silviculturae Mendelianae Brunensis* 66 (1): 0253–62.

Lee, Ronald, and Andrew Mason. 2010. "Fertility, Human Capital, and Economic Growth over the Demographic Transition." *European Journal of Population* 26 (2): 159–82.

Levine, Ross, and David Renelt. 1992. *Education Quality and Economic Growth.* Washington, DC: World Bank.

Levy, Santiago. 2017. "The Great Failure: Retirement Pensions in Latin America." Brookings Institution, Washington, DC.

Leyaro, Vincent, Priscilla Twumass Baffour, Oliver Morrissey, and Trudy Owens. 2014. "Determinants of Urban Labour Earnings in Tanzania, 2000–06." Centre for Research in Economic Development and International Trade Research Paper No. 3, School of Economics, University of Nottingham, Nottingham, UK.

Lucas, Robert E. Jr. 1988. "On the Mechanics of Economic Development." *Journal of Monetary Economics* 22: 3–42.

Mason, Andrew, and Ronald Lee. 2006. "Reform and Support Systems for the Elderly in Developing Countries: Capturing the Second Demographic Dividend." *GENUS* 52 (2): 11–35.

Mason, Andrew, Ronald Lee, and Jennifer X. Jiang. 2016. "Demographic Dividends, Human Capital, and Saving." *Journal of the Economics of Ageing* 7: 106–22. http://www.sciencedirect.com/science/article/pii/S2212828X16000050.

Ncube, Mthuli. 2015. *Inclusive Growth in Africa: Current Performance and Prospects.* Tunis: African Development Bank Group.

Palmer, Edward. 2013. "Generic NDC: Equilibrium, Valuation and Risk Sharing with and without NDC Bonds." In *Nonfinancial Defined Contribution Pension Schemes in a Changing Pension World: Volume 2 Gender, Politics, and Financial Stability,* edited by Robert Holzmann, Edward Palmer, and David Robalino, 309–33. Washington, DC: World Bank.

Psacharopoulos, George, and Harry Anthony Patriono. 2002. "Returns to Investment in Education: A Further Update." Working Paper 2881, World Bank, Washington, DC.

Rentería, Elisenda, Guadalupe Souto, Iván Mejía-Guevara, and Concepció Patxot. 2016. "The Effect of Education on the Demographic Dividend." *Population and Development Review* 42 (4): 651–71.

Romer, Paul. 1986. "Increasing Returns and Long-Run Growth." *Journal of Political Economy* 94 (5): 1002–37.

———. 1988. "Endogenous Technology Change." *Journal of Political Economy* 98 (5): 71–102.

———. 1990. "Human Capital Growth: Theory and Evidence." *Carnegie-Rochester Conference Series on Public Policy* 32: 251–86.

Tanzania National Bureau of Statistics. 2014. *Tanzania Integrated Labour Force Survey.* Dar es Salaam, Tanzania: TNBS.

Théveron, Oliver. 2011. "Family Policies in OECD Countries: A Comparative Analysis." *Population and Development Review* 37 (1): 57–87.

United Nations. 2017. Department of Economic and Social Affairs, Population Division. *World Population Prospects: The 2017 Revision.* DVD edn. https://population.un.org/wpp/Download/Standard/Population/.

UNDP (United Nations Development Programme). 2016. *Human Development Report 2016.* New York: United Nations. http://hdr.undp.org/en/2016-report.

World Bank. 2015a. *Tanzania Mainland Poverty Assessment.* Washington, DC: World Bank.

———. 2015b. *World Development Indicators (WDI).* Washington, DC: World Bank. http://datatopics.worldbank.org/world-development-indicators/.

———. 2017. *Tanzania Economic Update: Money Within Reach—Extending Financial Inclusion in Tanzania.* Washington, DC: World Bank.

World Trade Organization (WTO). 2016. *African Perspectives on Trade and the WTO: Domestic Reforms, Structural Transformation and Global Economic Integration,* edited by Patrick Low, Chiedu Osakwe, and Maika Oshikawa. Cambridge, UK: Cambridge University Press.

PART VIII

Communicating with Participants

CHAPTER 24

Communicating NEST Pensions for "New" DC Savers in the United Kingdom

Will Sandbrook and Ranila Ravi-Burslem

Introduction

In 2011, 69 percent of private sector employers in the United Kingdom (U.K.) did not offer a workplace pension to workers (DWP 2011b). Those offering a scheme were concentrated among larger employers; workers in smaller firms, on lower incomes, or in higher-turnover sectors were particularly poorly served. As of 2018, all U.K. employers offer a pension scheme that meets a set of legal standards, including automatic enrollment, and with a mandatory employer contribution for those employees choosing to enroll (box 24.1). More than 9 million people started saving in a workplace pension through automatic enrollment. The introduction of automatic enrollment was successful and popular—77 percent of consumers thinks it is a good idea (NEST 2015). Annual saving in workplace pensions is estimated to increase by £17 billion by 2019/20 as a consequence of these changes (DWP 2016).

This chapter briefly describes the background of the United Kingdom's reforms and the advent of the National Employment Savings Trust (NEST). It then describes the evidence base that NEST has gathered on its members and how this evidence has informed its communications approach to support members in saving for their retirement.

Background to the U.K. Reforms and NEST

Before 2006, the U.K. pension system comprised a state pension that shifted between poverty alleviation and income-replacement objectives. It was overly complicated and did not provide benefits at a sufficient level to meet most people's income needs or expectations in retirement. Second-pillar provision[1] was primarily through defined benefit (DB) workplace pension schemes; however, as in other countries, workplace schemes were in decline. The defined contribution (DC) schemes that replaced them were often less generous, and participation rates were significantly lower. By 2011, only about 32 percent of private sector workers were contributing to a pension fund (ONS 2011). Importantly, in addition to those who had been offered pension plans through their employment and had declined to participate, 41 percent of unpensioned workers had turned down the

The authors acknowledge the research support from NEST. The authors are grateful to the editors and to David Mann and Mark Rowlands for comments and suggestions.

BOX 24.1 The national employment savings trust and automatic enrollment

The United Kingdom introduced mandatory automatic enrollment for all employers, starting with the largest in 2012 and reaching all firms by early 2018. Employers must enroll all eligible workers—those between age 22 and the state pension age, and earning at least a certain level (£10,000 per year in 2018, although eligibility is calculated on the basis of pay period to pay period). Workers have the right to opt out; employers are required to make contributions for workers who opt in. Overall, contributions must be at least 8 percent of a band of earnings (currently around £6,000–£46,000 per year), of which at least 3 percent must come from employers.

Employers may comply by using any pension scheme that meets a minimum prescribed set of standards—known as a "qualifying workplace pension scheme." The National Employment Savings Trust (NEST) is one optional scheme available to employers. NEST differs from other schemes in that it has a statutory obligation to accept any firm, irrespective of its commercial profile.

NEST was set up this way to ensure that all employers had at least one high-quality, low-charge scheme available through which to meet their obligation, with a particular focus on those customers who were previously poorly served by private pension provision: those on low and moderate incomes, those in higher job-churn sectors of the labor market, or those working for smaller firms. As a consequence, NEST has grown rapidly since it launched in 2011 to more than 7 million members[a] from 650,000 firms in 2018; about 20 percent of U.K. workers have an account with NEST (NEST Insight and Vanguard Asset Management 2018). With an average income of £18,000, these members have lower incomes and are slightly younger than the average U.K. worker.

a. This includes those who enrolled and then subsequently ceased contributions, usually because they moved to a different employer offering a different scheme. The 7 million NEST members and the 9 million new savers cited are therefore not directly comparable.

---

opportunity to save through work when offered; an additional 33 percent had started saving but then stopped on one or more occasions (NEST 2013).

Attempts to reverse the decline by encouraging saving on a voluntary basis were not successful. The Welfare Reform and Pensions Act of 1999 introduced legislation that required employers with more than five employees to set up a "stakeholder" pension scheme open to all workers. The government also ran a number of pilot programs of workplace pension information and guidance under the banner of the informed choice program. The combination of simpler products and better information was intended to increase voluntary retirement saving, but it had little impact on participation levels, particularly among lower earners. The final report of the Pensions Commission (2005) recommended a new system for workplace pension saving intended to encourage retirement saving. This report set out the basis of a new pension settlement for the United Kingdom.

For second-pillar pensions, the commission was particularly attracted to the results of behavioral economics and evidence highlighting the impact of simple shifts in default options for workers, especially shifting from an opt-in system to one requiring people to actively opt out (Madrian and Shea 2001; Thaler and Benartzi 2004). Evaluation of these programs showed that they could dramatically increase participation across all social classes. Originating in individual occupational plans, this approach, known as *automatic enrollment*, was beginning to be adopted at the public policy level, either through enabling or encouraging legislation, such as in the United States, or as a mandatory requirement at the employer level, such as in New Zealand.

Based on a broad consensus across the political spectrum, consumer groups, employers, and the pensions industry, the government proposed a set of reforms (DWP 2006a, 2006b) based on the commission's recommendations. These reforms would require all U.K. employers to automatically enroll eligible workers into a scheme that meets certain qualifying standards; the reforms further require those employers to make contributions to the pensions of those workers electing to remain in their scheme. At the same time, the commission proposed changes to the state pension to make it a simpler, flat-rate benefit focused primarily on poverty alleviation. Pension saving through automatic enrollment would be the primary mechanism for earnings replacement to help workers achieve their aspirations to maintain their quality of life in retirement. The workplace provided a convenient way of reaching almost everyone who is employed and of providing them with an accessible way to save. It was easier for both employees and employers to make contributions at the source of the income.

Following extensive public consultation, the government enacted the commission's main proposals through legislation passed in 2007 and 2008. One concern was that some individuals—those on lower incomes, or in higher job-churn professions—would remain commercially unattractive to existing providers. It was generally agreed that some form of additional provision was needed to ensure that all employers had access to suitable workplace schemes at suitably low member charges. NEST was established for this purpose, as a multi-employer scheme providing all aspects of a traditional workplace pension: contribution collection and reconciliation, account administration, member and employer support, and investment of assets. NEST would be run as a "mastertrust"—a structure similar to the "profit-for-members" industry superannuation funds in Australia or to an "open multi-employer plan" in the United States—and it would be available to employers of any size to fulfill their new duties under the Pensions Act 2008. Crucially, NEST's statutory obligation to accept any employer is part of what characterizes NEST's unique role within the pension industry.

NEST is run in the interests of its members by a trustee—the NEST Corporation. It does not have shareholders and does not distribute a profit. It has a 0.3 percent annual management charge and 1.8 percent charge on contributions, roughly equivalent to a 0.5 percent annual management charge over the long term.[2]

Understanding the "At-Risk" Population—NEST's Evidence Base

As a new organization that would be managing retirement savings for millions of people, an important consideration for NEST was to understand where existing approaches to DC design could be replicated—and where the needs of a population that is largely new to pension saving might require something different. Accordingly, NEST drew heavily on research, both primary and secondary, in developing the overall proposition for members, employers, and advisers. This research program ensures that the decisions made reflect the characteristics, circumstances, and attitudes of the members and employers who use NEST's services. Over the course of developing and operating the scheme, NEST conducted research using large-scale quantitative studies (on occasion, merging the results with third-party data sets), in-depth interviews, focus groups, and behavioral experiments and trials. NEST also made extensive use of third-party data sets—such as the U.K. government's Wealth and Assets Survey and the longitudinal Understanding Society database, as well as literature reviews and direct analysis of NEST's administrative data—to inform the understanding of members' characteristics and needs.

More recently, the NEST Insight Unit was established; it works in collaboration with academics and other partners to explore mechanisms for improving the retirement income adequacy of NEST members and those like them. The Insight Unit is particularly focused on behavioral research (box 24.2) and on digging more deeply into what can be learned through NEST's administrative data.

The remainder of this chapter describes key research insights to date and sets out how these insights have been translated into NEST's communication approach.

BOX 24.2 **Support from behavioral economics**

Much of NEST's research was based on new, primary activity through surveys, focus groups, and qualitative interviews. The research also drew on the broader insights of behavioral economics, both in designing the approach and in generating hypotheses and areas of focus for further research. The major insights relating to savings behavior in NEST's target market are as follows:

- People exhibit a strong preference for the present over the future (Laibson 1997). Retirement saving represents the deferral of consumption today for a future benefit, but people tend to view the value of that benefit at a heavily discounted rate.

- This tendency can encourage procrastination and status quo bias (Samuelson and Zeckhauser 1988)—if unsure what to do or unconvinced of the value of deferred benefits, it is easier for people to take no action.

- As set out in Prospect Theory (Kahneman and Tversky 1979), losses loom much larger than gains. In the case of saving, this can mean people will focus on the "loss" of current consumption or the risk of investment loss and will place a higher "value" on those losses relative to the equivalent potential for gains.

- Paradox of choice (Iyengar, Huberman, and Jiang 2004) also comes into play—above a certain number of options, people find more choices can be paralyzing, especially if the choices are complicated or poorly understood, and this response can exacerbate the status quo bias.

- People fear taking a proactive course of action that might turn out to be wrong or might cause regret, further exacerbating the status quo bias; this is known as regret theory and omission bias (Loomes and Sugden 1988).

As well as informing research hypotheses, these themes return frequently and are reinforced in the outputs of NEST's research; accordingly, they feature heavily in the findings described in this chapter.

CHARACTERISTICS AND ATTITUDES AMONG UNPENSIONED WORKERS

Automatic enrollment was expected to bring about 10 million people into workplace pensions (DWP 2006b). Importantly, those saving in a pension before automatic enrollment were not highly representative of the population as a whole, with average incomes of about £30,000, compared with about £23,000 for the broader population (NEST 2013). Accordingly, automatic enrollment would bring a more diverse audience into the pensions market.

These previously unpensioned workers represented the 68 percent of private sector workers not paying into a workplace pension (ONS 2011). Given the size of the group, it was not surprising that unpensioned workers had characteristics similar to those of the working population generally (and dissimilar to the pensioned group).

Unpensioned workers existed across the range of gender, age, earnings, and social class. Within the eligible group, those not in a pension scheme—the target group—were more likely to have the following characteristics:

- *Male*. About two-thirds of the target group were men. The smaller proportion of women in the target group was due to the fact that a greater number of women earn less than the earnings threshold and were ineligible for automatic enrollment.

- *Younger*. Almost one-third of the target group was younger than age 30. A clear majority of this age group was unpensioned.

- *Working full-time*. Full-time workers accounted for 91 percent of the target group. The majority of part-time workers were ineligible for automatic enrollment because they were not earning in excess of the earnings threshold.

Pensioned workers tended to earn more than the working population generally. Higher earnings are linked with higher educational attainment, higher occupation levels, and higher financial literacy. Pensioned workers, then, were not the average and differed in a number of important ways from most people. Rather than being a niche minority, those coming into pensions as a result of automatic enrollment were more representative of mainstream society.

These unpensioned workers could be found in all types of employment, from small organizations to large. Approximately two-fifths of them worked for employers with no more than 49 workers. One-third worked for organizations with 1,000 or more workers. Unpensioned workers could be found across all sectors, but some sectors had a much lower proportion enrolled in pension schemes than others. For example, the hospitality sector had the lowest level of pension scheme membership as a proportion of workers (84 percent), but the sector only constituted 6 percent of the target group. About 60 percent of employees in the target group were employed in only three industries: wholesale, retail, and motor trade; real estate and business activities; and manufacturing.

Unpensioned workers displayed a mixed picture in terms of financial confidence. For example, they were often skilled domestic budgeters who creatively managed very tight budgets to cover all essentials and spending priorities (NEST 2013). Some adopted a mental accounting approach, applying different rules to different mental pots of money. In some cases, these pots might be physical, such as cash put to one side to cover an expense expected in the short term.

However, confidence was lower with respect to longer-term financial planning. Three-quarters (74 percent) said they were confident handling day-to-day financial decisions, but only 39 percent were confident handling long-term decisions. About 82 percent of pensioned workers felt confident with short-term planning; 57 percent felt confident with long-term planning—notably more than unpensioned workers (NEST 2013).

Long-term financial planning was also seen as a low priority for many. This group had far less in savings than pensioned workers; 38 percent had less than £5,000 in savings, compared with 20 percent of pensioned workers. When asked about retirement plans, 80 percent stated that they planned to work as long as they could, while 70 percent mentioned the state pension.

Many of the reasons for this lack of long-term planning are provided by the evidence from behavioral economics leading to the concepts described in box 24.2. Crucially for NEST's target group, some evidence indicates that present bias becomes stronger when people feel short of money (Carvalho, Meier, and Wang 2016). This is perhaps, in part, because of the real-world financial environments within which these groups plan. NEST research showed that many people felt that they had no option but to focus on the present because of tight budgets.

One-third of unpensioned workers said that all the money they earned was typically spent on the basics. When pressed to give a figure on what they had to spend after living costs, more than one-quarter of unpensioned workers said they had less than £50 a week, and three in five said less than £100 per week. Pensions, therefore, could be considered a luxury rather than a necessity for these people.

The economic climate also exacerbated this tendency. About 20 percent of unpensioned workers reported that their income had decreased over the previous five years.

The level of confidence in retirement plans was relatively low; nearly one-half have put off saving for fear of making the wrong decisions. However, even those who appeared to have rejected pensions in the past still generally supported the reforms. One-half of unpensioned workers claimed to have only a basic knowledge of pensions. Both those with and without previous experience shared a number of common misunderstandings, mostly related to investment and outcomes.

When asked about their retirement, most unpensioned workers pointed to some sort of retirement plan. The state pension was mentioned by 70 percent, 49 percent planned to downsize their home, and 26 percent expected an inheritance to help them. However, only 14 percent were reasonably confident that their retirement plans would be adequate. These findings may account to a large extent for the support for the reforms; two-thirds believe that automatic enrollment is a good idea (NEST 2013).

Before automatic enrollment, many had failed to take action for their retirement. Again, much of this intention-behavior gap can be explained by concepts such as procrastination and status quo bias. NEST research, however, highlighted additional attitudinal factors.

- First, while pensions were simultaneously dull and complicated, they provoked a negative emotional response from some people. The responsibility for making the right decision about something so important can be daunting, and many simply do not have the confidence to act. The concepts and language generally used in the pensions industry did not help people understand what they were getting involved with or communicate the information they needed to take control.

- Second, pensions were often simply not on people's minds most of the time, especially for younger people. People struggled to imagine themselves in the future, and this difficulty potentially deterred them from doing anything about it.

Despite pensions not being a priority for many people, 63 percent overall agreed with the idea of automatic enrollment. Of those who had been offered a pension at work before and refused it, or had started but then stopped contributions, 59 percent agreed with the principle.

One-half of unpensioned workers claimed to have only a basic knowledge of pensions. NEST research suggested that even this basic knowledge was likely to be based on misunderstandings and misconceptions. NEST's research showed that even people who have contributed to a workplace pension make fundamental errors and have gaps in their understanding (NEST 2014). Most of these concern investment and outcomes. Those experienced with pensions were more likely to be familiar with DB schemes. This means they usually think that their employer is responsible for managing the pension and will turn their pension fund into an income for them in the end.

People were eager to know more. Although they were not interested in detailed information on pensions, they wanted clear answers to two central questions: (1) What happens to their money—where does it go, and how safe is it? (2) How much will they get at the end?

UNDERSTANDING OF INVESTMENT

NEST's research on investment communications started with a foundational qualitative study in 2010 (NEST 2010). This research made it clear that not everyone understood that money contributed to a pension is invested. Many of those who did understand this were unclear about what investment actually meant. Everyone understood that the goal of a pension was to grow their contributions so that they would have more money in retirement. People were less clear about where this growth would originate. Some expected that growth would simply come from employer contributions on top of theirs plus interest. As such, they expected their pensions to grow in a uniform upward fashion.

People are used to the term "investment" and often feel they know what it means. However, they struggle to picture what happens to their money or where it actually goes. The concept was intangible, even for people who felt familiar with the term. There was reasonable awareness that investment has something to do with the stock market. Media coverage and discussion of the financial crisis and related slumps and crashes conjured up negative connotations of the financial sector. Similarly, although people were generally familiar with the phrase "the value might go down as well as up," few understood how or why this could be. Many imagined that it referred exclusively to their final outcome, rather than any fund value variance along the way, and to their contributions, rather than fluctuations in the level of growth achieved.

There was a general sense of unease around pensions. Many people—both with and without any previous experience of pensions—were concerned about how safe their money was. News stories of pensions being raided and savers losing all of their money lingered in the collective memory. It seemed to them that investment contributed to and exacerbated this.

For unpensioned workers, retirement planning was all about being prudent, sensible, and conservative. It was implicitly about safety and securing the future, and therefore at odds with chance, risk, and uncertainty. Respondents saw the decision to give up money now in order to have money in retirement as a protectionist course of action on both the emotional and practical levels. They felt better knowing that they were taking these steps and expected that they would have at least the equivalent of their contributions to spend in retirement.

For the automatically enrolled members, risk was inherently negative and had more to do with the chance of making a loss than the chance of making a gain. Similarly, uncertainty was perceived in a negative light and suggested a disappointing or worst-case scenario, rather than the possibility of getting a better outcome than expected.

Many unpensioned workers imagined an "all or nothing" scenario, largely based on their understanding of investment and as a consequence of the economic context and erosion of faith in the financial sector. The global economic events since 2008 had reaffirmed their conviction that anything can and does happen. Most people tended to focus their response to risk on the chance of losing.

EXPECTED OPT-OUT BEHAVIORS

The policy driver for introducing automatic enrollment in the United Kingdom was clear, but based on this evidence base, it was less clear how individuals might react. The experience of the United States suggested that following automatic enrollment, workplace pension participation would stabilize at about 85 percent. Department for Work and Pensions (DWP) research showed that 70 percent of those eligible for automatic enrollment would probably or definitely stay in; 15 percent were undecided; and 15 percent would definitely opt out. However, all countries differ in their policy environment and culture, and stated intentions in surveys often do not translate into actual observed behaviors. Accordingly, it was very uncertain what the overall opt-out rate might be once the reforms were implemented, or what other behaviors might be seen in terms of additional contribution levels or degrees of member engagement with their accounts.

NEST's research asked a sample of unpensioned workers to consider what would influence them to opt out of the scheme. Affordability was the top reason given, cited by 82 percent of those surveyed; 79 percent said that a lack of information at the time that they were automatically enrolled could influence their decision to opt out; and 61 percent expressed a high level of concern about automatic deductions taking place at the source (NEST 2013).

However, the triggers for opting out were more immediate and practical than the motivators for staying in. Evidence suggested that the motivators for staying in the scheme were more emotional. The knowledge that their pension was being taken care of through a low-maintenance approach driven by their employers gave savers peace of mind. Flexibility was also a strong message, considering the history among qualifying members of taking breaks in pensions and employment throughout their lives.

Perceptions of affordability remained a clear potential trigger for opting out and a front-of-mind concern for the majority. More than one-half, however, thought that not missing the money taken out before they were paid would be something that would motivate them to stay in the scheme (NEST 2013). This finding suggested that if the initial possibility of opting out was overcome, retention could be easier once the habit of saving was acquired.

SUMMARY

The overall conclusions from the program of research described here can be summarized as follows: Automatic enrollment created a new target market for retirement saving—much more representative of the general population than those previously well served by the industry. This new group was likely to exhibit many of the behavioral biases and barriers to saving well documented in the behavioral literature. They were skilled short-term money managers but much less skilled, prepared, and confident when it came to longer-term financial decisions. Many were supportive of the reforms and recognized the need to take action to prepare for retirement. However, they lacked knowledge and a sense of self-efficacy, were fearful of pensions and of the possibility of error, and were highly risk- and loss-averse. They were perhaps particularly unclear and lacking in confidence when it came to the question of how their money might be invested.

The clear expectation for the policy of automatic enrollment was that inertia would lead many more people to save for retirement, irrespective of many of the psychological, attitudinal, and knowledge barriers described in this chapter, often without much conscious thought or any direct engagement. Nevertheless, the communications approach developed by NEST was predicated on addressing many of these issues for three main reasons:

- First, NEST believed that addressing those who might be inclined to opt out would help to minimize the number of those doing so for the "wrong" reasons, for example, fear and uncertainty.
- Second, the goal over time was to build trust in NEST among members of the scheme as a necessary precondition for greater engagement in the future.
- Third, for the minority who initially seek more active engagement or who are inclined to use the choices available to them around, for example, fund choice or contribution level, addressing potential emotional issues and structural issues should enable this group to make better decisions in accord with their own needs.

The next section explains NEST's approach to communications in more detail.

Developing NEST's Communication Approach

Many of the challenges facing consumer confidence in DC schemes centered on people's understanding—or misunderstanding—of pensions and investment. A natural response, therefore, was to explore how to improve understanding. This path had been trodden by many providers before, although more to improve financial literacy or capacity than boost consumer confidence (de Meza, Irlenbusch, and Reyniers 2008). Although no one could reasonably question the good intention of improving consumer fluency with financial products, and pensions in particular, evidence from behavioral sciences and impact analyses of financial education projects suggested that gains in financial understanding did not necessarily improve financial decision making (Choi, Laibson, and Madrian 2010).

This evidence indicated that it may not be enough to simply create communications that members could easily understand. NEST also needed to be aware of the human capacity for cognitive bias and the tendency to adopt mental shortcuts (Benartzi and Thaler 2001). If one of the communication goals is to lessen the possibility of poor financial decision making—because people are not always rational decision makers—correcting their understanding will not always be sufficient to make a difference.

Furthermore, NEST research showed that learning about pensions did not necessarily give people peace of mind. Instead, in many cases, it put the spotlight on features they did not know about and would rather not see, namely, risk. Given the goals of NEST's communications approach described in the previous section, the focus was therefore on identifying the best ways to explain unfamiliar concepts and bolster confidence in the path down which savers were being defaulted.

Where members do engage, framing information carefully can make a difference to both comprehension and behavior. People tend not to proactively engage with pension communications. When they do, it is often driven by concern. Communications need to be sensitive to this. For most people, the starting point with pensions is negative; accordingly, communications need to reassure in addition to inform.

This section sets out high-level guidance on what NEST believes is effective when talking to members about investment, risk, uncertainty, and outcomes. It uses as its main evidence base two additional, more-specific NEST research projects. One sought to identify ways in which to communicate investment to members. The other explored responses to deterministic and probabilistic retirement projections.

WHAT MEMBERS NEED FROM A COMMUNICATIONS APPROACH

DWP research (2011a) identified a number of key information needs of new members. These center on workplace pension schemes and automatic enrollment generally, for example, "When can I take my money out?" "How much do I have to contribute?" "What happens to my money if I die before I retire?" NEST undertook in-depth interviews with people who matched the demographic characteristics of the unpensioned, and it asked them to imagine they had been enrolled in a workplace pension scheme and what their first questions would be (NEST 2014). Almost everyone wanted to know "What happens to my money?" "Is my money safe?" "What will I get in the end?" None of the people interviewed expressed interest in investment, but it is notable that these three questions do ultimately concern investment.

As discussed, the demographic makeup of the unpensioned population is extremely diverse. It includes different levels of education, a wide range of life stages, and varying knowledge of pensions; about two-thirds have some experience with pensions. Members start from different stages, want to know different things, and expect different levels of detail. In short, people have very different communications needs. Some common themes emerged through the in-depth interviews, enabling the following loose clustering of attitudinal groups.[3] NEST considers these themes when developing a communications approach:

- *The cynical.* This group is the most distrusting of pension providers and the financial sector generally. They are aware that risk is taken and that outcomes are not certain in DC pensions. This group's views will generally be very difficult to change. People in this group tend to have been in a pension before or have friends or family members who are disappointed with their pensions.

- *The compliant.* This group is the least likely to show any interest in the scheme or any member communications. They share the lack of understanding of the curious group but openly declare their lack of interest in finding out more. Some in this group defer to the better judgment of professionals, even if they do not trust those in the financial sector. There is an implicit notion that they do not need to concern themselves with the product and that those running the scheme will know best. Although this group appears to be fewer in number than the cynical and cautious groups, its members present an interesting challenge through their deference. As in more traditional doctor-patient relationships, these members trust that the experts will take care of everything.

- *The cautious.* People in this group are keen to engage to get answers to their questions and are the most likely to become more positive in their view of workplace pensions as they learn more. The sense here is that the pension is not as bad as they imagined based on, for example, the NEST proposition and outcome scenarios of modeled members.

- *The curious.* This group is the most likely to be shocked at what they learn from investment-related communications. They do not know how workplace schemes grow their money, they do not know about uncertainty and volatility, and they are concerned when they find out. This group tends to be younger and has the least experience with pensions, whether directly or indirectly through family members, partners, or friends.

Given the different starting positions of these groups, they each go on different communication journeys and do not necessarily end up in the same place, despite being exposed to the same material. Some people will remain unconvinced by the DC proposition, no matter how it is framed. The qualitative nature of NEST's research meant it could not be said with confidence what percentage of the unpensioned population would exhibit each of these characteristics. The view was that communication strategies should focus on reaching the compliant, the cautious, and the curious groups, while recognizing members' different journeys.

For workers, automatic enrollment was an unprecedented event. The newness and strangeness of how automatic enrollment worked presented a real opportunity to engage workers in planning and saving for their later lives. However, the newness of automatic enrollment also presented a challenge to worker engagement. DWP research (2011a) found that there was a danger that the communication of how it will happen could overwhelm the communication of its benefits. People had questions; in particular, some people were worried about the impact of automatic enrollment on their employers—"Why would they do it?" "Can they afford it?"—as well as on their jobs—"Will it mean reduced hours or pay, or will it lead to redundancies?"

DESIGNING NEST COMMUNICATIONS

If information addresses some of the questions people have in response to automatic enrollment and gives them the facts they need, they are more likely to feel confident about staying in. Information content and tone can have an important emotional, as well as rational, impact and can help address concerns. Real potential exists for information centered around automatic enrollment to have a far-reaching and positive impact on people's confidence in making plans for their own futures.

As a result, one area of focus was on the language and vocabulary traditionally used to describe pensions. Based on an extensive program of market research, NEST began replacing words such as "annuity" with phrases that people find more understandable, such as "retirement income." Over time, NEST built up a "dictionary" of approved words and phrases that it knows works with its target market (NEST 2016).

NEST also focused on developing a framework within which to think about communicating with members, described as the "Golden Rules" in the following section. For example, research revealed that people wanted to feel in control, even though the process of being enrolled would be a passive one. One application of this was in the design of the opt-out process, which had to be easy and clear in communications to new savers. Knowing they can get out when they want to may, paradoxically, make people more willing to accept automatic enrollment.

The third step was the market testing of NEST's operational communications. NEST's annual statement, for example, was designed, tested extensively with potential customers for ease of understanding, and then redesigned based on their feedback. A similar process was used for the transactional area of the website.

Finally, a brand was developed for NEST—based on evidence—with a name and logo that would resonate with a potentially large and diverse range of audiences. Specific objectives considered included the following: conveying the scheme as a vehicle for retirement savings; creating a brand that would help build trust and credibility in the scheme; representing the focus of the scheme on low-to-moderate earners; and encapsulating all of these in a clear identity that would engage a socially and culturally diverse audience.

Implementing the Approach

"GOLDEN RULES" OF COMMUNICATIONS

Talking about pensions with a new generation of savers required a different framework to guide NEST's communications. The evidence base suggested that NEST should communicate with members in a clear, meaningful, and reassuring way. Essentially, NEST members wanted to know that their money was safe and was being managed for their benefit. The challenge was how to put this into practice. In response, NEST developed key principles for communicating to members, based on qualitative research with members of the NEST target market (NEST 2012). These principles are used when NEST designs any new piece of communications and are the basis for all member communications.

Keep it real

Pensions communications should be as practical as possible and should use examples to which people can relate. Theoretical concepts are harder to grasp and should be avoided. The Golden Rules research suggested people respond well to familiar descriptions of what they need to save. This means using examples of everyday shopping items, goods, or services, and expressing values such as contribution levels in pounds and pence rather than as percentages. When using examples of individuals, selecting people with whom they can identify is more effective than anything invented or exaggerated compared with their life experiences.

Rights not responsibility

People respond more positively to language that focuses on their entitlements rather than what they ought to be doing. Messages emphasizing an "obligation" to save for the future performed poorly and were seen as threatening, whereas messages stressing an entitlement or potential benefit were received more positively.

Out with the old

Communications about the advantages of being in a pension scheme should not focus on the details of retirement. It is not an idea that people like to think about; many feel it is too far away to be relevant to them. This finding is consistent with the literature on psychological distance (Hershfield et al. 2011). Thus, it is important to engage with people in their present situation and bring messages about pensions into their current working lives. Equating the benefits of saving with positive experiences today, for example, can help overcome this distance.

One for all

Those people who are likely to be affected by pension reform and automatic enrollment take comfort in numbers. They like to know that what is happening to them is also happening to lots of other people. For communications strategies, this means reassuring people that they are part of a group of people affected by the changes. Evidence for this can be found in the literature on social norming effects (Schultz et al. 2007). DWP research also suggests that knowing automatic enrollment is happening to many people and is official helps people understand it is something their employer is required to do. NEST research shows that although people do not respond well to assumptions about their lives and circumstances, they do feel safer knowing they are part of something larger.

Tell it like it is

NEST should present the facts and let people reach their own conclusions. People want information expressed in plain language so they can form their own value judgments. This was a key driver behind NEST's phrasebook and behind its approach to naming fund choices (for example, the "higher risk" fund).

Give people control (even if they do not use it)

The people in NEST's target group like to feel in control, even if they choose not to exercise it. For example, the message that people can opt out works much better if it is delivered sooner in the enrollment process rather than later. For example, the Golden Rules research suggested people respond badly to messages suggesting everything is "taken care of for them."

Take people as you find them

Communications should be designed to fit with where people are in their understanding. New savers might have quite different levels of understanding from one another and from existing scheme members. Communications should be designed to keep up with people as they make the transition to different stages.

Be constructive

People who are likely to be affected by pension reform and automatic enrollment often want to see problems as something they can put right. Even when they have worries about how financially prepared they are for retirement, they want to focus on what can be done about it and how they can be helped. Communications should emphasize the constructive aspects of saving in a pension scheme.

NEST'S BRAND VALUES

It is important to communicate with everyone who uses NEST in a way that works for them. NEST's brand values also provide a very strong framework for its communications. The following values are based on research and insight and respond to specific customer needs.

Ease

Communications with members and employers are as jargon-free as possible so that NEST is easy to understand. Pensions have traditionally been viewed as complicated.

Transparency

NEST is open about what the scheme is, how it is run, where funds are invested, and how members will get their savings. NEST has a single charge, irrespective of members' earnings profiles. All communications are also as clear as possible. The pensions industry has traditionally been perceived as opaque.

Empowerment

NEST seeks to give its audiences all the information they need to understand NEST and make decisions about their pension saving. It is important to help members be in control of the key decisions that affect their lives.

COMMUNICATING THROUGH THEIR JOURNEY

NEST provides a range of communications, using the NEST brand, "NEST's Golden Rules of Communication," and the NEST phrasebook as guides. The phrasebook includes information on costs and charges, investment choices, and when and how members can access their retirement savings. Once enrolled, members can choose to have communications sent to them in electronic format via their secure mailbox or in paper format.

Pre-enrollment communications

NEST's research showed that providing good-quality information to workers at the pre-enrollment stage is important and may influence members' decisions to opt out or remain in an automatic enrollment scheme. NEST aims to communicate with workers at this stage to explain what automatic enrollment is, how it works, and what NEST is so that potential members can make informed decisions about how automatic enrollment will affect them personally and if saving with NEST is the right choice for them. Because NEST cannot communicate directly with prospective members, NEST provides employers with a set of communication tools designed to meet both statutory and nonstatutory communication requirements. (Although there is, in theory, some incentive for employers to encourage members to opt out, this is carefully controlled through a compliance and enforcement regime, and so, in practice, such inducement or encouragement is rare.)

Statutory communications

NEST provides guidance and letter templates for employers to meet their legal duty to inform their workforce about their new pension rights. This guidance explains the statutory information that employers will need to give their workers in straightforward terms. Letter templates can be downloaded from the NEST website; the templates can be edited by employers with their own additional content.

Nonstatutory communications

These communications can be used by employers to provide an overview of NEST and how automatic enrollment works to potential members. They contain information on workers' rights, the joining and contribution processes, how to opt out, and how and when they can take their money out of NEST. Employers can download these tools from NEST's website. Information is presented in a variety of formats to cater to different learning styles and communication preferences, including presentations, PDFs, pay slip messages, and existing member case studies.

Line manager and HR communications

NEST believes that clear and concise communications are important for all those affected by automatic enrollment, including line managers and human resources (HR) departments. These key staff members will be communicating the most with members before enrollment with NEST. NEST developed materials for these audiences to make understanding automatic enrollment and communicating information about it to their workers as simple as possible. These materials include presentations, PDF guides, videos, posters, and FAQ sheets, all available on the NEST website.

Welcome communications

Members receive a welcome packet when they enroll in NEST. The welcome packet contains information about why they were enrolled in NEST, their opt-out rights, and their member IDs to register and activate online accounts. For most members, this is the first interaction they will have with NEST.

The "Quick Guide to NEST" document included in the packet informs members how to make the most of saving for their future. The information in this document was determined from a combination of regulatory requirements, guidance from the Pensions Regulator and DWP, and NEST's own research and insight into information that members want to know. It provides an overview of how to activate accounts with NEST, how NEST works, how to make the most of saving with NEST, charges members pay, and how NEST invests their money.

Ongoing communications

Members receive an annual benefit statement from NEST. For a large majority of NEST's membership, this is the only engagement they have with NEST until retirement. The benefit statement uses plain language and graphical representations to explain important information, including the following: how much is in their retirement pot; an estimate of what their pot might be worth in the future given their current retirement date; a breakdown of contributions made by members, their employers, and tax relief collected from the government; the contribution charge applied to the pot; the annual management charge applied to the pot; what the change in pot value was because of investment returns and after all components have been taken into account; any nominated beneficiaries; and information on assumptions that NEST made when calculating retirement income. The provision of an annual benefit statement containing this information not only meets regulatory requirements; it also reassures members that their contributions are being collected and invested appropriately.

Should members make any changes to their accounts with NEST (for example, switch from the default fund or nominate a beneficiary), they receive written confirmation of this change through their preferred communication channel. These operational communications are designed to provide members with records of changes they make. NEST also communicates any system changes that might affect members' experiences on NEST's website via email or pop-up communication channels when members log in.

NEST also provides help and supports communications with members via an online member help center, designed to be self-service so that members can quickly locate information. Members not able to resolve issues or questions using the help center can communicate with NEST via the contact center, web chat, or email channels.

"AT RETIREMENT" COMMUNICATIONS

NEST communicates with members in the lead-up to their specified retirement dates. The contact strategy in this period includes packets sent six months, three months, and three weeks before the intended retirement date.

As a consequence of reforms in 2015, savers now have a greater range of choices and decisions about when and how to access their retirement savings.[4] The packet provides a clear and easy-to-understand overview of the different options that members have available. It also highlights that members who wish to continue working and contributing to NEST, may do so. Members are signposted to view the online booklet "Taking Your Money out of NEST," which contains more detailed information.

At retirement, communications encourage members to get professional independent financial advice and signposts them to free government services, including The Money Advice Service and Pension Wise. They also point out additional items that members should consider when determining what to do with their retirement pot, including tax implications and pension scams.

Further communications are sent six weeks after the retirement date to members who have taken no action on their accounts.

Summary and Conclusions

THE IMPACT OF NEST COMMUNICATIONS

At this stage, it is arguably too early to come to definitive conclusions about the impact of NEST communications. As described, the drivers behind NEST's approach to date have been to cater to—and reassure—those who seek more active engagement with NEST, either because they are considering opting out or for some other reason.

In practice, the dominant finding from NEST's experience so far is the overall strength of inertia. Only about 7 percent of people automatically enrolled into NEST have opted out, a number that has fallen to 6 percent for those now being enrolled as a result of starting a new job. This finding bears out previous evidence that default-based choice structures can be powerful in changing behavior. In NEST's case, coupled with other aspects of the evidence base presented, this is true even in the presence of, for example, relatively low levels of understanding of core aspects of pensions and investment and a relatively high risk of negative affective responses to some of that detail when presented.

At the same time, this inertia acts powerfully in other ways once members are saving. Only about 16 percent of NEST members have registered their online accounts. Fewer than 10 percent try to opt out when first enrolled, and much smaller numbers still cease contributions for a reason other than moving to different employers with different schemes in place. Fewer than 1 percent of members make an active investment choice of something other than the default fund; a similar percentage choose to make additional contributions above the default rate (NEST Insight and Vanguard Asset Management 2018; internal NEST data). This passivity on the part of members makes strong conclusions about the impact of NEST communications difficult, and any initial conclusions are only tentative.

For example, the very low opt-out and voluntary cessation rates might suggest that NEST has successfully reassured some of those who sought additional information. NEST also seeks direct feedback on its approach via surveys, drawn from a random sample of members, with results weighted back to the known age and gender profile of its membership. Previous research[5] indicated that only a minority (13 percent) of NEST members surveyed felt that its communications were unclear or unhelpful. However, this survey evidence also confirmed that overall engagement levels are very low: approximately two-thirds of recently enrolled members state they have at least skimmed their welcome pack; one-fifth do not recall receiving it; fewer than one-third of members report ever visiting the NEST website.

In truth, much of NEST's approach has not yet been tested in any depth. This is not unintentional; in the first years of its existence, NEST was focused on the massive operational challenge of onboarding nearly 700,000 employers and almost 7 million new members. At the same time, with initial contribution rates set at a low level, and increasing automatically in April 2018 and April 2019, much of NEST's focus and that of the broader policy was to allow the policy, and the act of saving regularly for retirement, to normalize. Poorly designed communications risked disrupting this process; and avoiding negative outcomes is a further modest sign of success in the approach.

The real test of the approach is yet to come. Beginning in April 2019, minimum contributions reach the full statutory rate of 8 percent of a band of earnings. For many in the lower-to-moderate-income member population, this will likely be sufficient—coupled with a relatively full savings career and their state pension entitlement—to generate a decent level of income replacement in retirement. For others, however, it will likely be within their capacity and best interests to contribute more. Even without focusing on contribution levels, there will be other benefits to greater member engagement, both in terms of helping them understand to what degree they are on track for their retirement goals and of enabling decisions they will need to make later, for example, how to convert their assets into income in retirement, something that now requires a much more active and less constrained choice since the abolition of compulsory annuitization in 2014.

In this regard, a promising difference is observed between the attitudes of NEST members surveyed who had activated their NEST accounts and logged on compared with the majority of unregistered members. Almost one-half of them (49 percent), compared with slightly fewer than one-third of all members (31 percent), gave a satisfaction rating of 8 or higher out of 10 for NEST providing clear and helpful communications. Within this group, only 6 percent felt NEST communications were unclear and not helpful. The potential impact of communications to act as a trigger for engagement can also be observed; the welcome guide all members received was cited as the most likely cause of their decision to visit the NEST website or activate their accounts. In some respects, the biggest challenge may be how to create the triggers, as well as the underlying motivation, for people to seek more information. A much greater focus on the personalization of user experiences is expected to be a key element of addressing this challenge.

The evolution of the NEST approach will enable more evaluation of its effectiveness using a number of elements. The greater use of A-B tests will allow evaluation of the effectiveness of interventions before they are rolled out.[6] NEST's ongoing program of tracking research facilitates the monitoring of overall customer satisfaction, including satisfaction with aspects of the communications approach; that program is supplemented with ad hoc quantitative research. NEST is also setting up an online community of members that will enable monitoring of attitudes toward members' experiences of NEST. Most importantly, as the scheme matures, NEST will be able to evaluate the impact of its communications on member outcomes by monitoring key behaviors such as contribution levels over time.

WHERE NEST WILL GO NEXT

As saving for retirement normalizes among the previously unpensioned population, NEST's focus will shift to supporting members through more proactive choices that they face—such as whether and how much more to contribute and how to access their savings once they reach retirement. This shift will present more rigorous opportunities to evaluate the approaches described in this chapter and to test the effectiveness of more focused interventions.

Crucially, NEST's intention is to do this through the increased use of A-B testing and randomized control trial methodologies. As outlined in this chapter, communicating with members in an automatic enrollment context carries risk as well as opportunity, for example, risk of triggering a negative affective response and prompting undesirable behavior, such as cessation of contributions. People's behavior can be hard to predict in response to communications interventions and can depend on preexisting attitudes and dispositions—rolling out large-scale interventions based on theoretical frameworks, however well researched, carries a significant downside risk. The use of appropriately developed trials with subsets of members will allow NEST to robustly test interventions and roll out only those that are effective. NEST has begun to use this approach, with the field stage of a trial testing different forms of the opt-out journey recently concluded; further trials are planned for 2019. Publishing the results of these trials will help inform the approach that others in the industry might take to improving member outcomes.

One particular area of focus may be to further investigate the interaction between overall default structures and individual barriers to saving. Automatic enrollment is sufficient to overcome otherwise significant barriers, such as low understanding of how pension savings are invested. At the same time, NEST wants to help members better understand these things—a "test and learn" approach will provide an understanding of the tipping points and tradeoffs between addressing these individual knowledge gaps and the overall effectiveness of a default.

CONCLUSIONS

The approach to developing NEST was based on a comprehensive program of primary and secondary research. NEST's communications approach led to outputs, such as its phrasebook and Golden Rules, with a major underlying focus on providing reassurance that saving is a good thing and that NEST will look after members' money. This approach was built on harnessing inertia and responding to behavioral biases in the target group, while recognizing that this same inertia means that many will, in practice, have little or no interaction with NEST in the early years of their participation.

As retirement savings become the norm, contribution rates increase through phasing, and more people actively engage with the choices they now have at retirement, NEST's approach will need to evolve. Technology is transforming the way members are consuming everyday financial services; therefore, their expectations of their pension providers are also shifting.

In this new world order, NEST's communication message will need to evolve to more actively engage members throughout their life stages to ensure members are saving adequately for retirement. It will need to use lessons learned as a foundation for future approaches. For example, the effectiveness of traditional education and capability programs might be questioned; more targeted "just in time" education approaches might be explored; and more personalized approaches that support more individualized decisions might be used, building on the foundation created by automatic enrollment. Crucially, these approaches will need to be empirically tested before they are rolled out at scale to ensure that NEST's communications with members help them achieve their goals in saving for retirement.

Notes

1. Using the World Bank classification; see Holzmann and Hinz (2005).

2. The exact "equivalent" reduction in yield depends on an individual savings history, but it averages out to about 0.5 percent annual management charge equivalence across the NEST membership.

3. Because the research was qualitative and small scale, it was not possible to validate or size these as formal "segments" in the traditional sense. Separately, NEST does use geodemographic segmentation to underpin analysis within its communications approach.

4. Whereas before 2015 most people had to buy a life annuity with their DC savings, DC assets can now be accessed in any form, including cash, from age 55.

5. NEST member surveys from 2014 onward.

6. For example, NEST has conducted A-B tests on different versions of the online opt-out process (to be published shortly) and on personalized outbound messages to encourage members to register online.

References

Benartzi, Shlomo, and Richard Thaler. 2001. "Naive Diversification Strategies in Defined Contribution Saving Plans." *American Economic Review* 91 (1): 79–98.

Carvalho, Leandro S., Stephan Meier, and Stephanie W. Wang. 2016. "Poverty and Economic Decision-Making: Evidence from Changes in Financial Resources at Payday." *American Economic Review* 106 (2): 260–84.

Choi, James, David Laibson, and Brigitte Madrian. 2010. "Why Does the Law of One Price Fail? An Experiment on Index Mutual Funds." *Review of Financial Studies* 23 (4): 1405–32.

de Meza, David, Bernd Irlenbusch, and Dianne Reyniers. 2008. *Financial Capability: A Behavioural Economics Perspective.* London: Financial Services Authority.

DWP (Department for Work and Pensions). 2006a. *Personal Accounts: A New Way to Save.* Cm6975. Norwich: The Stationery Office. https://assets.publishing.service.gov.uk/government/uploads /system/uploads/attachment_data /file/272383/6975.pdf.

———. 2006b. *Security in Retirement: Towards a New Pensions System.* Cm6841. Norwich: The Stationery Office. https://assets.publishing.service.gov.uk/government/uploads/system /uploads/attachment_data/file/272299/6841.pdf.

———. 2011a. *Automatic Enrolment—Information for Workers Qualitative Research.* London: Department for Work and Pensions. https://assets.publishing.service.gov.uk/government /uploads/system/uploads/attachment_data/file/188272/comms-res-auto-enrol-0711.pdf.

———. 2011b. *Employers' Pension Provision Survey 2011.* Research Report 802. Sheffield, UK: Central Analysis Division, Department for Work and Pensions. https://assets.publishing.service .gov.uk/government/uploads/system/uploads/attachment_data/file/193460/rrep802.pdf.

———. 2016. "Workplace Pensions: Update of Analysis on Automatic Enrolment 2016." Department for Work and Pensions, London. https://www.gov.uk/government/statistics/work place-pensions-update-of-analysis-on-automatic-enrolment.

Hershfield, Hal, Dan Goldstein, William Sharpe, Jesse Fox, Leo Yeykelis, Laura Carstensen, and Jeremy Bailenson. 2011. "Increasing Saving Behavior through Age-Progressed Renderings of the Future Self." *Journal of Marketing Research* 48 (SPL): S23–37.

Holzman, Robert, and Richard Hinz. 2005. *Old Age Income Support in the 21st Century: An International Perspective on Pension Systems and Reform.* Washington, DC: World Bank.

Iyengar, Sheena, Gur Huberman, and Wei Jiang. 2004. "How Much Choice Is Too Much? Contributions to 401(k) Retirement Plans." In *Pension Design and Structure: New Lessons from Behavioral Finance,* edited by Olivia S. Mitchell and Stephen P. Utkus, 83–95. Oxford, UK: Oxford University Press.

Kahneman, Daniel, and Amos Tversky. 2013. "Prospect Theory: An Analysis of Decision under Risk." In *Handbook of the Fundamentals of Financial Decision Making: Part I,* edited by William T. Maclean and Leonard C. Ziemba, 99–127. Singapore: World Scientific Publishing Company.

Laibson, David. 1997. "Golden Eggs and Hyperbolic Discounting." *Quarterly Journal of Economics* 112 (2): 443–78.

Loomes, Graham, and Robert Sugden. 1982. "Regret Theory: An Alternative Theory of Rational Choice under Uncertainty." *Economic Journal* 92 (368): 805–24.

Madran, Brigitte, and Dennis Shea. 2001. "The Power of Suggestion: Inertia in 401(k) Participation and Savings Behavior." *Quarterly Journal of Economics* 116 (4): 1149–87.

NEST (National Employment Savings Trust). 2010. *Understanding Reactions to Volatility and Loss.* London: NEST. https://www.nestpensions.org.uk/schemeweb/NestWeb/includes/public /docs/understanding-reactions-to-volatility-and-loss,PDF.pdf.

———. 2012. "Golden Rules of Communication: Talking about Pensions with a New Generation of Savers." NEST Corporation, London. https://www.nestpensions.org.uk/schemeweb /NestPublicWeb/faces/public/search/pages/simpleSearch.xhtml?search_text=golden+rules+of +communication.

———. 2013. *NEST Insight 2013, Taking the Temperature of Automatic Enrolment.* London: NEST. https://www.nestpensions.org.uk/schemeweb/NestWeb/includes/public/docs/nest-insight -2013,PDF.pdf.

———. 2014. *Improving Consumer Confidence in Saving for Retirement.* London: NEST. https:// www.nestpensions.org.uk/schemeweb/nest/aboutnest/investment-approach/investment -research.html.

———. 2015. *NEST Insight 2015, Taking the Temperature of Auto Enrolment.* London: NEST Corporation. https://www.nestpensions.org.uk/schemeweb/NestWeb/includes/public/docs /nest-insight-2015,pdf.pdf.

———. 2016. *The NEST Phrasebook: Clear Communication about Pensions.* London: NEST. https://www.nestpensions.org.uk/schemeweb/nest/nestcorporation/news-press-and-policy /thought-leadership-and-consultations/thought-leadership.html.

NEST Insight and Vanguard Asset Management. 2018. *How the UK Saves: Member Experience from the National Employment Savings Trust (NEST).* http://www.nestinsight.org.uk/wp-content /uploads/2018/06/How-the-UK-Saves.pdf.

ONS (Office for National Statistics). 2011. "Annual Survey of Hours and Earnings 2011." ONS, London. https://www.ons.gov.uk/employmentandlabourmarket/peopleinwork /earningsandworkinghours/bulletins/annualsurveyofhoursandearnings/2012-03-21.

Pensions Commission. 2005. "A New Pensions Settlement for the 21st Century: The Second Report of the Pensions Commission." Pensions Commission, London.

Samuelson, William, and Richard Zeckhauser. 1988. "Status Quo Bias in Decision Making." *Journal of Risk and Uncertainty* 1 (1): 7–59.

Schultz, P. Wesley, Jessica Nolan, Robert Cialdini, Noah Goldstein, and Vladas Griskevicius. 2007. "The Constructive, Destructive, and Reconstructive Power of Social Norms." *Psychological Science* 18 (5): 429–34.

Thaler, Richard, and Shlomo Benartzi. 2004. "Save More Tomorrow™: Using Behavioral Economics to Increase Employee Saving." *Journal of Political Economy* 112 (S1): S164–87.

CHAPTER 25

Information and Financial Literacy for Socially Sustainable NDC Pension Schemes

Elsa Fornero, Noemi Oggero, and Riccardo Puglisi

Introduction

The accumulation of pension wealth is a long and complex endeavor, with various circumstances in which individuals have to make consequential decisions, even in public systems with a strong compulsory component. Awareness is essential to increase welfare, given that conscious citizens are more likely to make sensible choices and avoid regrettable mistakes. Awareness requires both information and the ability to use it wisely, which in turn requires a minimum of economic and financial knowledge, typically called financial literacy. Workers should have some knowledge (conjecture) and a basic understanding of where they stand on their accumulated (prospective) pension wealth and retirement options. This knowledge was less important in the traditional world of defined benefit (DB) pension systems, because of their more "guaranteed" nature. It is definitely essential in the case of defined contribution (DC) schemes because of their results-oriented structure, which entails more risks and a higher level of individual responsibility for both the private and public components of the pension system. This chapter concentrates on the latter, and more specifically on systems that are run on a notional or pay-as-you-go (PAYG) basis and are characterized by a DC-type formula to calculate benefits (NDC systems, for brevity).[1]

This new pension landscape implies more, and more complex, personal choices, and greater risk (although one should not forget that in the "old" DB landscape, the political risk of unsustainable promises—a risk that people are more likely to ignore by appealing to the notion of "acquired rights"—was rarely taken into account in an explicit way and even less covered). This naturally raises concerns about the amount (and quality) of information provided to citizens, as well as about citizens' level of knowledge, which affects the ability to deal with crucial financial decisions, such as planning for retirement and managing savings for old age. It also raises the question of how to attain a universal minimum level of financial knowledge.

This chapter investigates the importance of both information and financial literacy, which both contribute by adding social sustainability to the inherent tendency of NDC pension systems toward financial equilibrium.[2] It provides a new dimension to this discussion by exploring the role of the media in the approval and implementation of pension reforms in general and in the specific case of NDC schemes. "Pension Information: Why? What? When? From Whom?" deals with the scope, content, and importance of information—and sometimes its lack of popularity among politicians, particularly in the case of retrenching reforms. More specifically, it distinguishes between formal and informal communication, the first officially supplied by the institutions in charge of pension provision, and the second by the media. "Pension Information in Practice" explores the supply side of information (that is, the role of the media in pension knowledge and in the reform debate) by analyzing the dissemination role by both the Internet and newspapers in selected European countries, with a focus on Italy in the critical context of its 2011 pension reform. "Financial Literacy Applied to Pensions: What Is 'Pension Literacy'? Why Is It Important?" deals with the demand (users) side: it highlights the notion of pension literacy as a specific component of financial basic knowledge and as an ingredient to "make sense" of pension information, to improve both personal decisions and the effectiveness of pension systems and reforms. "Conclusions" draws some preliminary findings as well as policy implications and outlines the main areas for future work.

Pension Information: Why? What? When? From Whom?

WHO IS AFRAID OF INFORMATION?

Information is critical for individual life-cycle decisions, in deciding, for example, whether to spend more or less, now or later (that is, to save, to dissave, or not to save); to participate in a supplementary pension plan; when to retire; and whether to leave on a gradual retirement option, when available. Knowledge should help workers to better plan their retirement, thus avoiding major mistakes and consequent disappointments, such as a shortfall of actual versus expected pension benefits, and painful lifestyle adjustments.

Information on the functioning of unfunded pension systems—and of NDC systems as a subset thereof—is also fundamental for systems' sustainability, and thus for the political consistency of reforms. In turn, reforms are required either to adapt the pension design to economic and demographic structural changes or to improve a previous poor design, which might be due to the interference of politicians, whose electoral purposes often tend to prevail over the system's main role of providing income security in old age. Differently from individual-level choices, citizens (that is, public opinion and voters) should also be properly informed about the aggregate behavior of the pension system. From this point of view, widespread misinterpretation of pension reforms will lead to attempts to prevent or reverse them after their approval. The reluctance of governments, politicians, and other political and social actors to provide information for fear of generating resentment and losing consensus (or even to exploit ignorance) has to be recognized and overcome, possibly with the aid of international institutions, which typically do not share the same fears and are not constrained by short-term electoral interests.

Concerns by politicians are well expressed by Juncker's oft-quoted aphorism: "We all know what to do, but we don't know how to get re-elected once we have done it" (*Economist* 2007; see also Buti et al. 2008). This statement implicitly stresses the importance of financial literacy: if politicians and experts are able to see the necessity, and thus the embedded social values, of reforms, why should citizens not do the same? And if they do, why should they punish the government or political parties that approved the reforms?[3] If people understand the need for a reform they will not necessarily vote out a politician who takes painful steps in the short run to consolidate the system in the medium to long run. This view thus provides another reason, on top of the effects on individual planning and decisions, to champion financial literacy—it also supports an important policy action: governments could indirectly generate long-term support for more effective citizenship and virtuous reforms by promoting, together with basic financial education in schools, good information and specific financial education programs for adults.

FORMAL INFORMATION (FROM THE PENSION AGENCY) AND INFORMAL INFORMATION (FROM THE MEDIA)

Information (online, written, and broadcast) has to be simple and trustworthy. Within a public pension system, it is obvious that it should be provided by the public pension agency, which is obliged by its mandate to provide formal, precise, and micro personalized information. This crucial informative task cannot be delegated to noninstitutional actors or private entities such as trade unions, workers' associations, and nonprofit organizations, although they can support, and typically do, the public pension institute. The importance of this kind of information, however, is not universally recognized, sometimes because of bureaucratic or political negligence, sometimes because of administrative deficiencies, and sometimes because of fear of losing electoral support, particularly in the case of reforms that try to restore the system's financial sustainability. As a consequence, not all countries have credible institutions capable and willing not only to inform members about their specific (current and prospective) personal situation, but also to produce periodic and reliable information about the financial status of the scheme.[4] When this does not happen, a negative impact on views about the retirement system and its reforms is likely to occur, in turn affecting decisions as well. Of course, the provision of reliable information does not guarantee that it will be used correctly and wisely: sometimes formal information is simply ignored either because it is too complex and thus not understood, or because people have misperceptions about the institution providing it.

One important problem is the need to distinguish, in each worker's specific position, what has already been accumulated (such as the "accrued-as-of-today" notional capital) with respect to what can reasonably be estimated for the future (and possibly for the far future) under specific hypotheses. Even if the accrued pension wealth—in the case of notional accounts, not backed by reserves—is nothing more than a "promise" that can be changed by a political decision (normally without the need for a constitutional law), simulations of future wealth and of the implied pension benefit are, of course, much more uncertain. Hence, it is important that the difference be made transparent and understandable. The first type of information is perceived as more objective; the second as more "speculative" (something like "your future pension benefit in this specific 'scenario,' including the time profile of your future contribution and a given retirement age"). Although fundamental for a proper understanding, the distinction is not easily grasped, also because the state can always "tax," either directly or indirectly through cutbacks, the accrued pension wealth or amend the rules for its future accumulation.

General information, particularly about the pension system's characteristics, problems, updates, innovations, and policy proposals, is provided by the media. Pensions and pension reforms are very popular topics, because all individuals are involved, either directly or indirectly (for example, as spouses, partners, or dependent children).

The incentives of mass media in disseminating basic pension knowledge are likely to be quite different from those of the official pension institution, which in principle should be more neutral, but in practice might be sensitive to the government's requirements. It is still unclear whether individual opinions about pensions are more influenced by the media or by the official pension provider, a question that can depend on, among other things, the institute's public reputation. One can easily argue that the latter has a comparative advantage in providing personalized information about accrued capital, returns, and the like. However, the relative novelty of NDC systems—and of regulations imposing informative tasks on them—could imply that citizens still rely more heavily on information provided by better-known media, both traditional ones (newspapers, magazines, radio, and TV, particularly talk shows) and, increasingly, new ones (social networks).

WHAT WORKERS SHOULD KNOW ABOUT THEIR OWN PENSION AND RETIREMENT OPTIONS

Precise information on future pension benefits can be given only to those somewhat close to retirement, and thus with a high degree of certainty about their pension level. For others the pension statement should clearly refer to "projections," "simulations," or "estimates," none of which are easy terms. The probabilistic nature of more distant benefits should always be emphasized, to avoid the idea that precise calculations imply the promise of a "sure amount."

On a personal level, it is therefore important that citizens be informed of the following:

- The (notional) accrued capital, that is, the present value of pension wealth.
- How much of this wealth is due to their own contributions (that is, both the employee and the employer's share), credited contributions (financed by general taxation for periods of education, unemployment, and care activities), and returns (typically calculated by using the rate of growth of the total wage bill or gross domestic product [GDP]).
- How the notional amount is transformed into a pension benefit (the conversion factor used to convert the capital into an annuity).
- Whether this transformation takes into account the cohort-averaged expected longevity at retirement.
- Possible retirement ages, together with a description of how the pension benefit will evolve in case of deferral, highlighting the incentives to the continuation of work—or at least the absence of disincentives—that are typical of the DC method; in particular, people should know that postponing retirement contributes twice to the increase of individual benefits: through higher contributions and lower expected longevity (when longevity is taken into account).
- How the pension benefit will evolve in retirement (the indexation rule).
- Supplementary benefits, such as survivors' pensions and the possibility to draw on accumulated pension wealth, particularly when they are optional and not included in the default options.[5]

- For those whose careers have developed—at least partially because of a transition toward the NDC regime—under a DB scheme, the gap between actualized pension benefits and accrued capital through paid contributions. The purpose of this is to give a measure of the "gift" implied by the DB scheme and to contrast people's perceptions of having more than what they "paid" for their own pension, even when this is largely untrue.

WHAT SHOULD BE KNOWN ABOUT NDC SYSTEMS?

An NDC pension system is a complex structure that does not lend itself to straightforward interpretation. It is not a market mechanism but a public institution, which means that even when it mimics the market—as the NDC scheme does—it necessarily performs roles that the market does not or cannot perform, the first being social cohesion. In particular—even when it is largely based on insurance principles—it cannot be exempt from performing some redistribution tasks. It is very important that people be informed, even at a very basic level, about the nature of this institution, particularly its "social compact" features, which the notional personal accounts somehow tend to conceal. More specifically, workers should be informed of the following:

- A PAYG system (whether DB or DC) is an "intergenerational contract": retirees receive their pensions because of contributions paid by current workers, who contribute under the assumption that future generations will also pay and thus, indirectly, finance their own pensions. In the contract, the state is also supposed to represent the interests of future generations, which obviously cannot participate directly in the deal.
- When combined with a DC formula, the system (NDC) can achieve both financial equilibrium (notwithstanding its implicit debt dimension, stemming from its very creation) and greater intragenerational fairness than a "pure" DB formula.[6]
- The adequacy of benefits (that is, their capability to provide financial security in old age) depends mainly on the individual's whole contributory history, thus a good working career, and on adequate tax rates.
- Contributions are credited, even if partially, for unemployment spells or work leave made necessary by care activities, to avoid gaps in the accumulation process.
- Returns are credited to contributions, which are a form of compulsory saving, not a pure tax.
- To make the social contract sustainable, and thus to protect future generations, the rate of return that is recognized must mirror the growth in the contributory base. In turn, this is typically approximated by the rate of growth of GDP (approximately n+g, the sum of population and productivity growth rates). The notion that returns are not determined by financial markets but by the rate of growth of labor income (or of the economy) should also be transparent.[7] Because people often seem to be rather impatient with a notion of financial equilibrium, the amount of intergenerational fairness that is implied by using this rate of return on contributions should help to make the system less abstract and friendlier.[8]

- The system contains "automatic stabilizers" that encourage people to work longer as longevity increases: (a) for any given pension wealth, the benefit increases with retirement age (normally up to a maximum); and (b) when longevity increases, the coefficients that transform the notional capital into a pension are normally reduced for any permissible retirement age.

All this information is not easily conveyed; even when it is, its reading is complex and certainly hardly stimulating. Nevertheless, information is essential to enhance one of the main features of the NDC system (that is, its transparency), and to help contrast privileges and other forms of perverse redistribution. To strengthen this mission, it is important that this information be officially provided by the pension institute in an independent way.

Pension Information in Practice

INFORMATION THROUGH PUBLIC PENSION STATEMENTS: A SELECTIVE SURVEY

Because public pension programs provide the foundation for retirement income for a vast majority of workers (if not all of them), it is important for governments to give individuals detailed information about their public retirement benefits. Public pension statements are one way governments can provide workers with information about their retirement duties, rights, and options. The following discussion looks especially at countries that have adopted NDC systems (without considering the entire list).

In Sweden, which launched its NDC system in 1998 and fully implemented it in early 2003, a substantial amount of pension and financial information is systematically and regularly provided to the population at large. The famous "Orange Envelope" has been a forerunner and a benchmark. It is sent by the pension institute once a year and contains individual information about previous years' contributions, personal account balances at the beginning and end of the year, annual returns, plus individual-specific projections translating the account balances into an expected monthly pension benefit calculated at three different retirement ages (Almenberg and Säve-Söderbergh 2011). It is important to note that the projections are calculated for two assumptions about the real wage growth rate: 0 percent and 2 percent. The Orange Envelope also contains information about the direct relationship between the annuity and the retirement age, consistent with the view of a pension as insurance against the risk of longevity. The widespread dissemination of information is likely to have lowered the barriers to planning for retirement.

As a supplement to the NDC pillar, which provides contributions-related benefits that represent the largest share of retirement income, the Swedish system also includes a funded part. Consequently, information about the functioning of financial markets is also provided, in particular with reference to the relative risks of equities versus bonds, and the inappropriateness of having high exposure to equities close to retirement. This can be expected to have raised awareness of basic financial concepts (Almenberg and Säve-Söderbergh 2011). For example, Swedish adults show a good understanding of the risk diversification concept: more than two-thirds (68 percent) of them correctly answered the risk question designed by Lusardi and Mitchell (2008) to test basic financial literacy. On the other hand, it can also be the case that not everybody opens the Orange Envelope; even when they do, there is no guarantee that they can adequately absorb and understand the information. Even though most recipients claim to read the information in the Orange Envelope, less than one-half of the sample population reported having a good understanding of the pension system, and many individuals reported that they lack sufficient knowledge to manage their individual accounts (Sundén 2009).

A comparison with Italy is instructive. Italy introduced its NDC system in 1996 but the phase-in process was so long and the general information to the people so limited (and not infrequently biased) that it took 20 years to introduce the Italian version of the Orange Envelope. It is thus not surprising that the new formula and even the PAYG method of financing are not yet properly understood by the population. Paradoxically, even though pensions have always occupied a wide space in the news, very little has been done to explain in an official way the advantages and limitations of the new method of calculating benefits.

Similarly to Sweden, the United States' Social Security Administration is required by law to send out the Social Security Statement, that is, the public pension statement. Even though the United States does not have an NDC pension system, legislation specifies that the statement must contain the worker's earnings history, the Social Security taxes paid by the worker, an estimate of potential retirement benefits at different retirement ages, and estimates of disability, survivors', and other auxiliary benefits. In 2000, a paragraph was added about the advantages and disadvantages of retiring early. Many studies found a significant increase in the number of respondents who knew (a) about the relationship between Social Security benefits and earnings, (b) how benefits are financed, (c) that benefits increase automatically as the cost of living rises, and (d) that the full retirement age is increasing. Moreover, respondents who reported receiving, and who had thus presumably looked at or read the statement, were more knowledgeable about the program than those who did not (Kritzer and Smith 2016). A sizable percentage of respondents also reported using the statement for financial planning, thought the information in the statement was useful for retirement planning, and expressed overall satisfaction with the information about savings and investment. However, more than one-half of workers did not believe that Social Security benefits would exist when they reach retirement age (Gallup 2015). Although Mastrobuoni (2011) finds that Social Security Statements had a significant impact on workers' knowledge about their benefits, he also suggested that workers did not change their retirement behavior. In particular, they did not change their expected age of retirement after receiving the statement, and their monthly claiming patterns did not show any change after introduction of the Social Security Statement.

Likewise, Canada has a legislative requirement to send workers statements of contributions on request. For recipients age 30 or older, the statement includes information on their contributions, pensionable earnings, retirement pension, and disability and survivors' benefits. For recipients younger than 30, the statement only includes information on their contributions and pensionable earnings, omitting information on the retirement pension and disability and survivors' benefits. Surveys found that more than two-thirds of respondents said the information was important to them, they had a better understanding of the Canadian pension plan and the services it provides, and they were more likely to plan for their retirement (Kritzer and Smith 2016).

In Poland, the launch of the NDC pension formula in 1996 altered the incentives for future pensioners, because postponing retirement now leads to significantly higher pension levels. However, incentives to work longer only function if society is provided with information about the pension system (Chłoń-Domińczak 2009). A systematic public education effort is required to improve the "pension literacy" of the population, and a step taken by Poland in this direction is the annual information on individual accounts that the social insurance institution sends to covered workers. Since 2008, this information has also included the calculation of the accrued pension based on the current account value, and the projected account value for selected potential retirement ages (Chłoń-Domińczak 2009). In Latvia as well, the State Social Insurance Agency as of 1997 took initiatives aimed at improving public understanding and promoting acceptance of the NDC pension system. Media campaigns were undertaken, and contribution statements are sent to contributors once a year, with an explanation of the system (Fox and Palmer 1999).

Even this brief analysis of these cases leads to the conclusion that pension information is critical for individual knowledge and planning in many areas, and both low literacy and lack of information affect the ability to secure a comfortable retirement.

PENSION INFORMATION IN THE MEDIA

How much information about pension systems and reforms can be found in the media, as compared with other personally or politically relevant issues? Do articles and editorials simply report the facts and the political contests surrounding pension reforms, or do they also deliver basic concepts as a precondition to understanding the mechanics and main implications of PAYG systems and DC formulae? To the authors' knowledge, these empirical research questions have not been explicitly tackled yet. The three following analyses try to answer them:

- *Attention to online media.* For a sample of European countries (France, Germany, Italy, Sweden, and the United Kingdom), Google Trends is used to measure the relative amount of online searches about pensions and compare them across countries and over time.

- *Volume of coverage by traditional media.* For the same sample of countries, the dynamics of newspaper coverage of pensions and pension reforms in the past 15 years are examined by exploiting the Dow Jones Factiva news archive.

- *Type of coverage for a specific pension reform.* To check the type of coverage devoted to pension reforms, the focus is turned on Italy, looking at the amount and type of newspaper coverage devoted to the last major pension reform (that is, the Monti-Fornero reform), introduced in December 2011 in an emergency situation, very close to a financial crisis (Fornero 2015).[9] More specifically, the analysis investigates how the treatment of pensions differed across newspapers and changed before and after the "natural experiment" of the reform itself.

Regarding the first type of analysis, figure 25.1 shows the relative importance of pension information in France, Germany, Italy, Sweden, and the United Kingdom from 2004 to 2017, as proxied by the Google Trends data on the volume of online searches. Italy and France show the highest rates of online searches about pensions, with Italy having the maximum number of searches at the beginning of 2015. On the other hand, Germany, Sweden, and the United Kingdom—countries that have already "sorted out" their reforms—showed less interest in pension themes in recent years. More frequent online searches by Italians and the French may indicate higher sensibility toward social security issues in these countries. Whereas searches in France

FIGURE 25.1 **Google Trends, online searches of pensions in France, Germany, Italy, Sweden, and the United Kingdom, 2004–17**

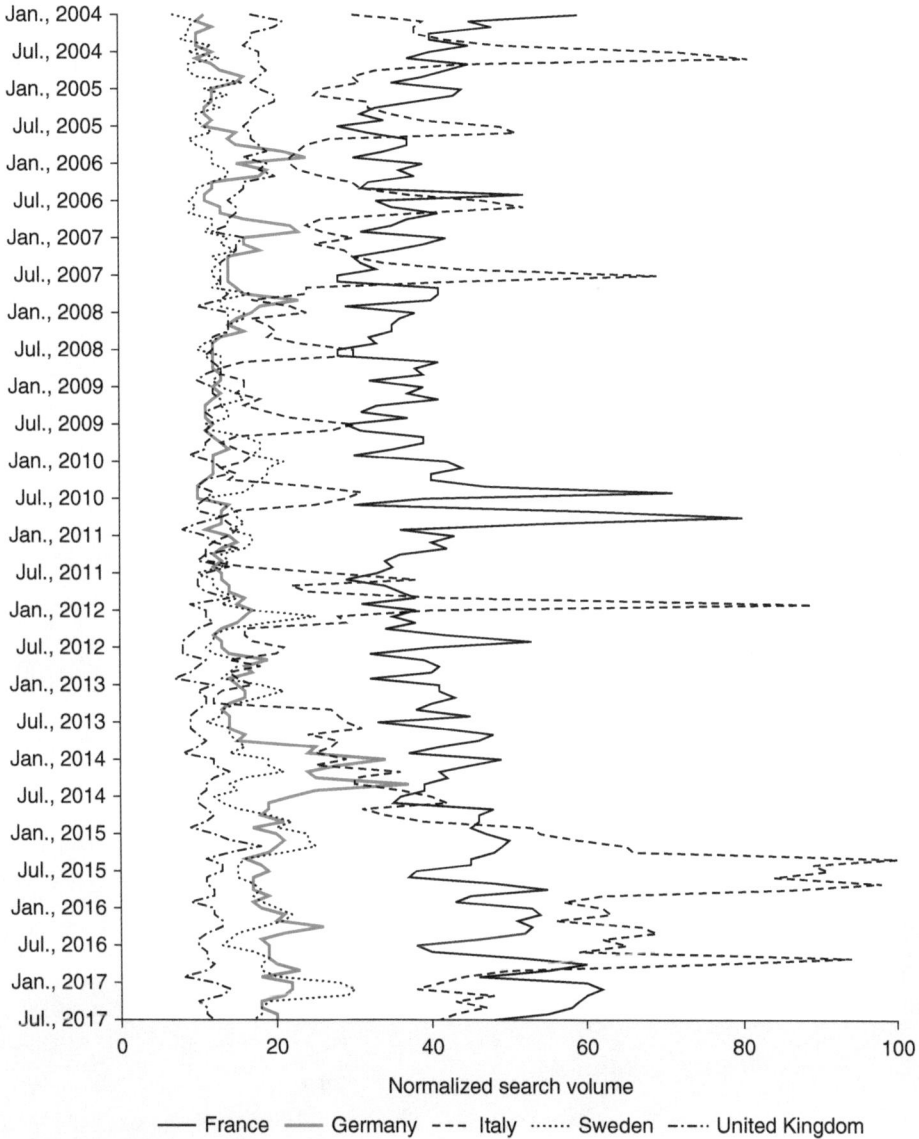

SOURCE: Original calculations.

were quite steady from 2004 to 2017, Italy shows two peaks: one at the end of 2011–beginning of 2012, when the Monti-Fornero pension reform was introduced; and the other at the beginning of 2015, when the Constitutional Court's decisions on price adjustment of pensions affected many retirees.[10] Thus, searches were especially high when changes in the retirement landscape happened, and people probably tried to gather more information on the Internet.

FIGURE 25.2 **Google Trends, searches of Daesh (ISIS), immigrants, crime, unemployment, and pensions in France, 2004–17**

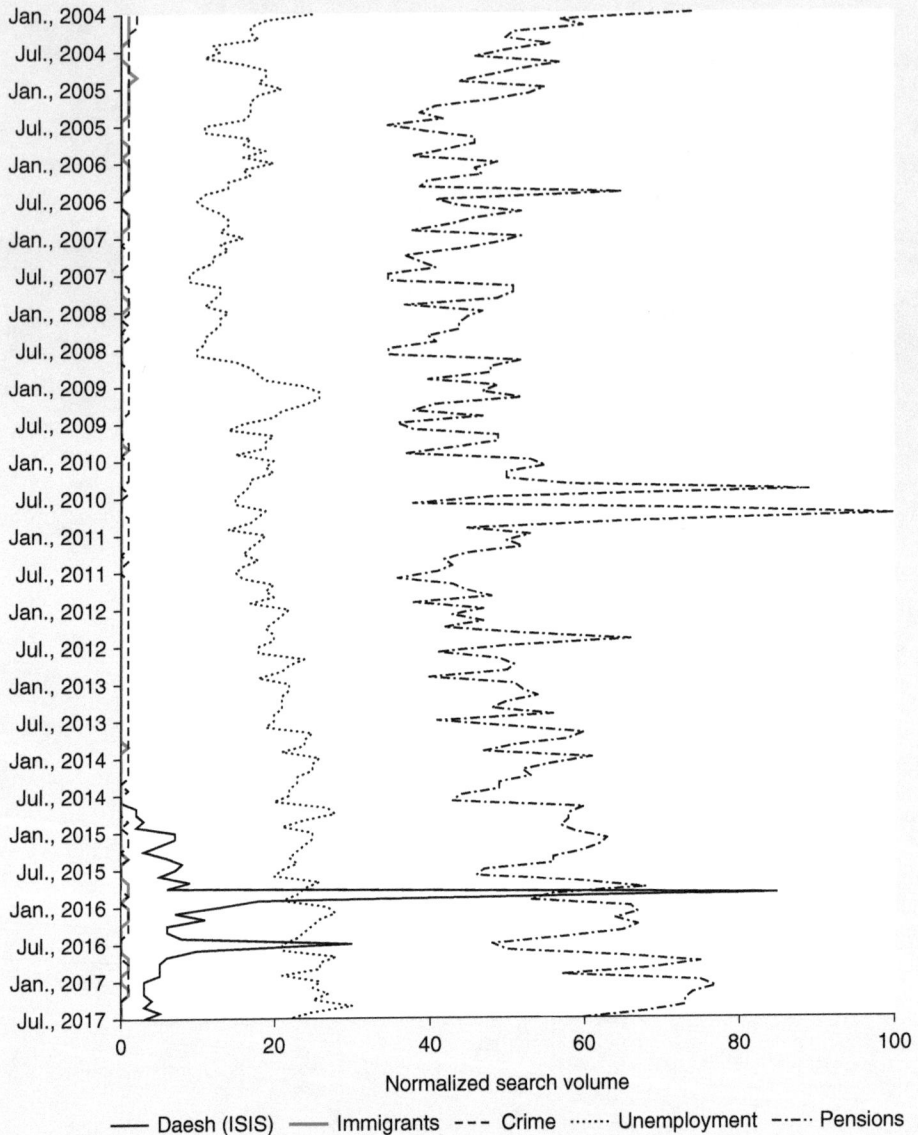

SOURCE: Original calculations.

Figures 25.2, 25.3, 25.4, 25.5, and 25.6 compare the volume of online searches on pensions with the volume of searches on other policy-relevant issues, for each sampled country. Figures 25.2 and 25.4 confirm that social security is a hot topic in both France and Italy: from 2004 to 2017, people looked for more information on pensions than on unemployment, immigrants, crime, or ISIS. In Sweden as well, where the NDC pension system was introduced in 1998, the volume of online searches over time was larger for pensions than for other relevant topics (figure 25.5).[11]

FIGURE 25.3 **Google Trends, searches of Daesh (ISIS), refugees, crime, unemployment, and pensions in Germany, 2004–17**

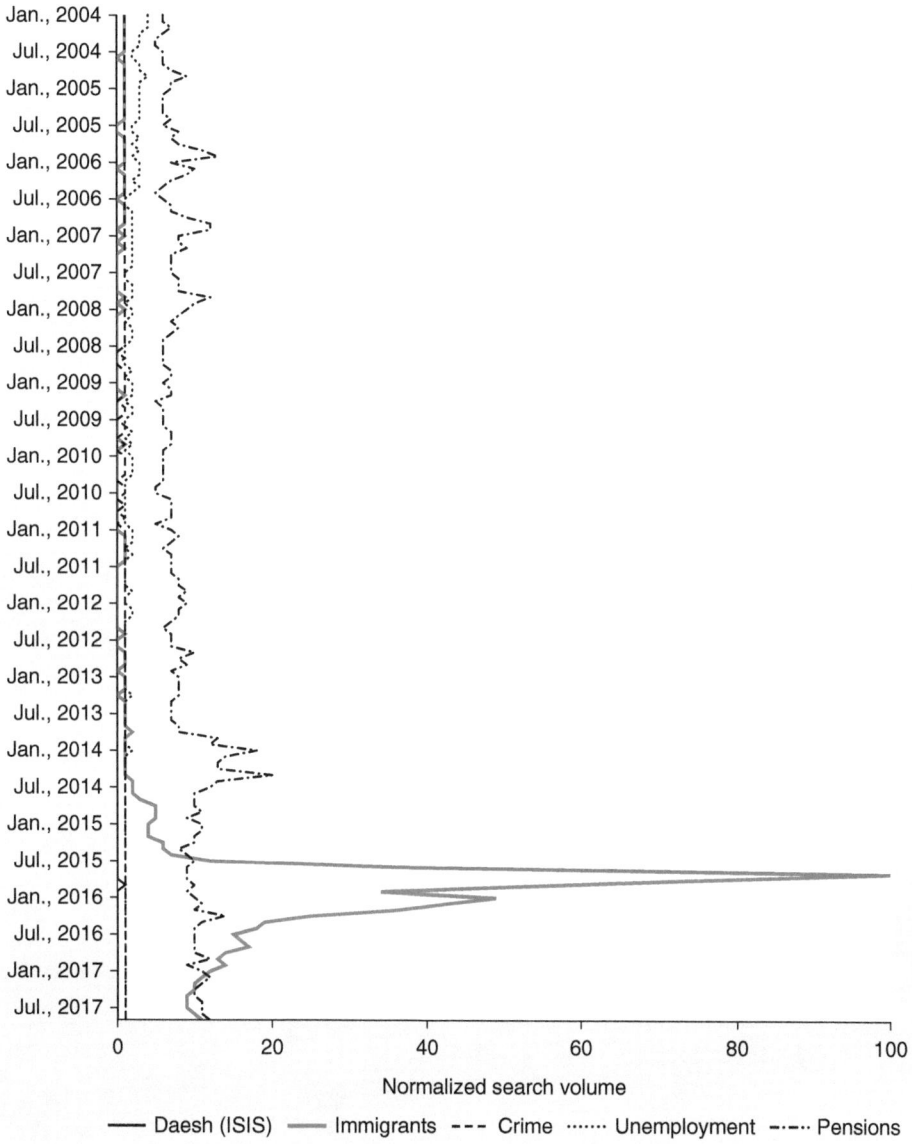

SOURCE: Original calculations.

FIGURE 25.4 **Google Trends, searches of ISIS, immigrants, crime, unemployment, and pensions in Italy, 2004–17**

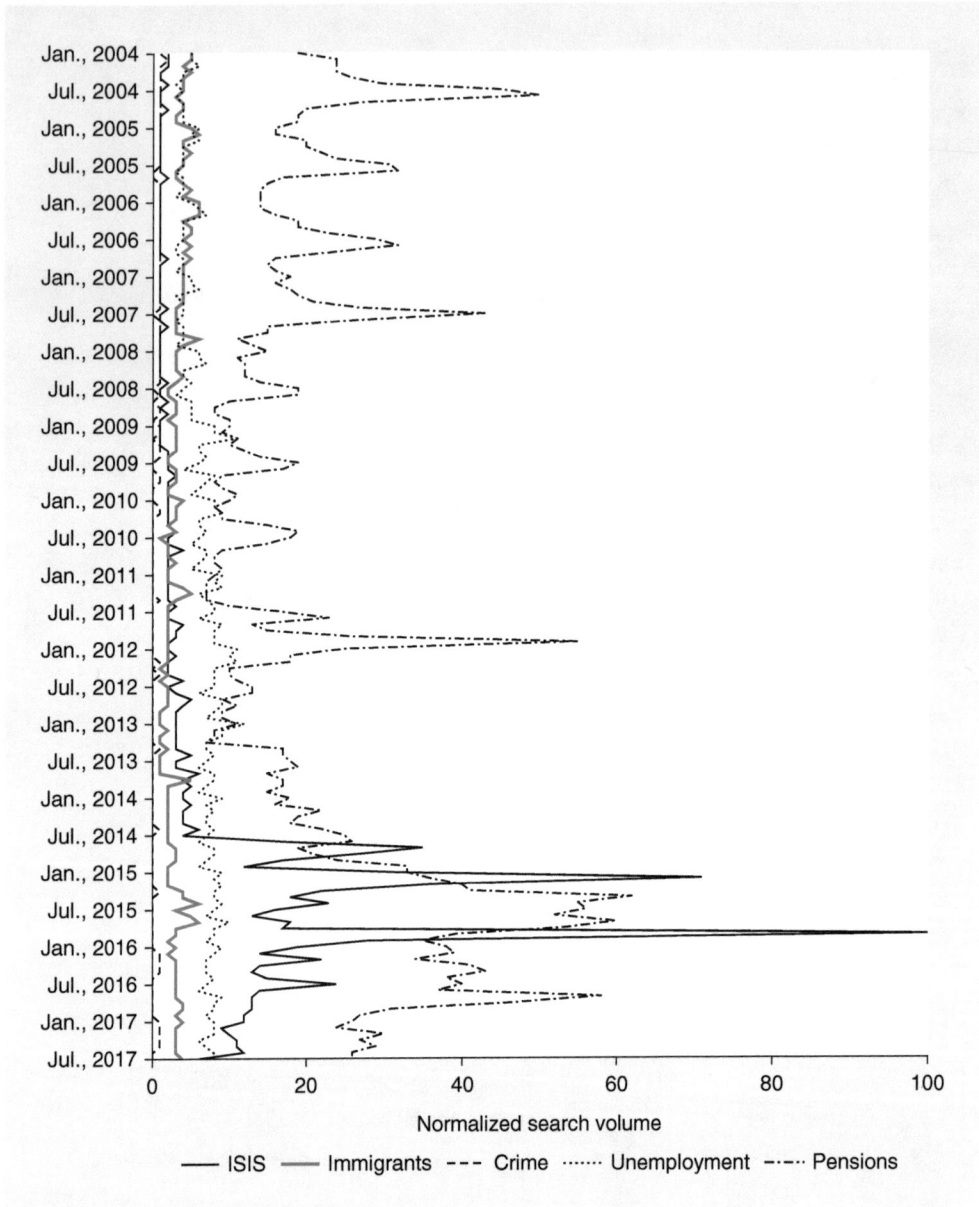

SOURCE: Original calculations.

The second research question investigates how online searches regarding pensions compare with the coverage devoted to this topic by traditional media outlets over time. The availability of easily searchable news archives allows the gathering of monthly coverage data on selected newspapers for the countries under consideration. Data were gathered for the 2004–17 period for *Le Monde* in France, *Frankfurter Allgemeine Zeitung (FAZ)* in Germany, *Corriere della Sera* in Italy, *Svenska Dagbladet*

FIGURE 25.5 **Google Trends, searches of ISIS, immigrants, crime, unemployment, and pensions in Sweden, 2004–17**

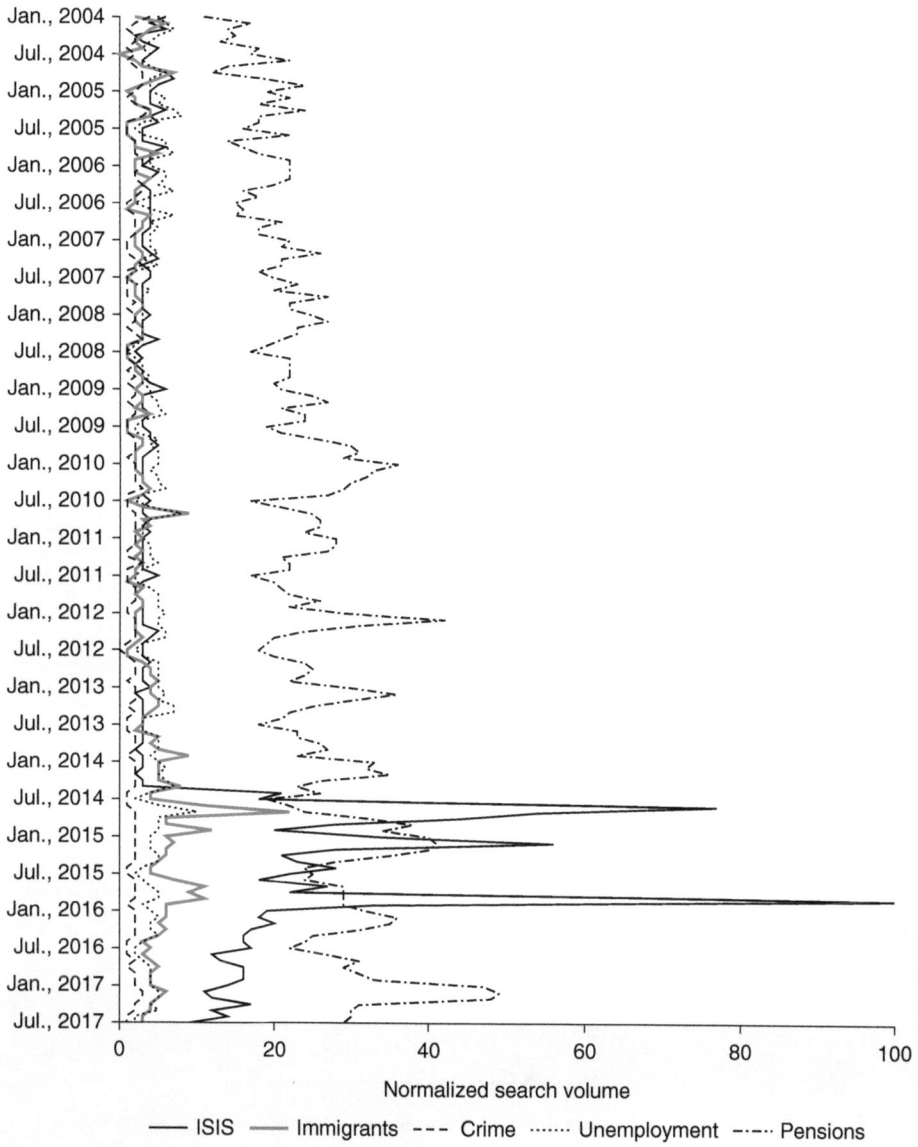

SOURCE: Original calculations.

FIGURE 25.6 **Google Trends, searches of ISIS, immigrants, crime, unemployment, and pensions in the United Kingdom, 2004–17**

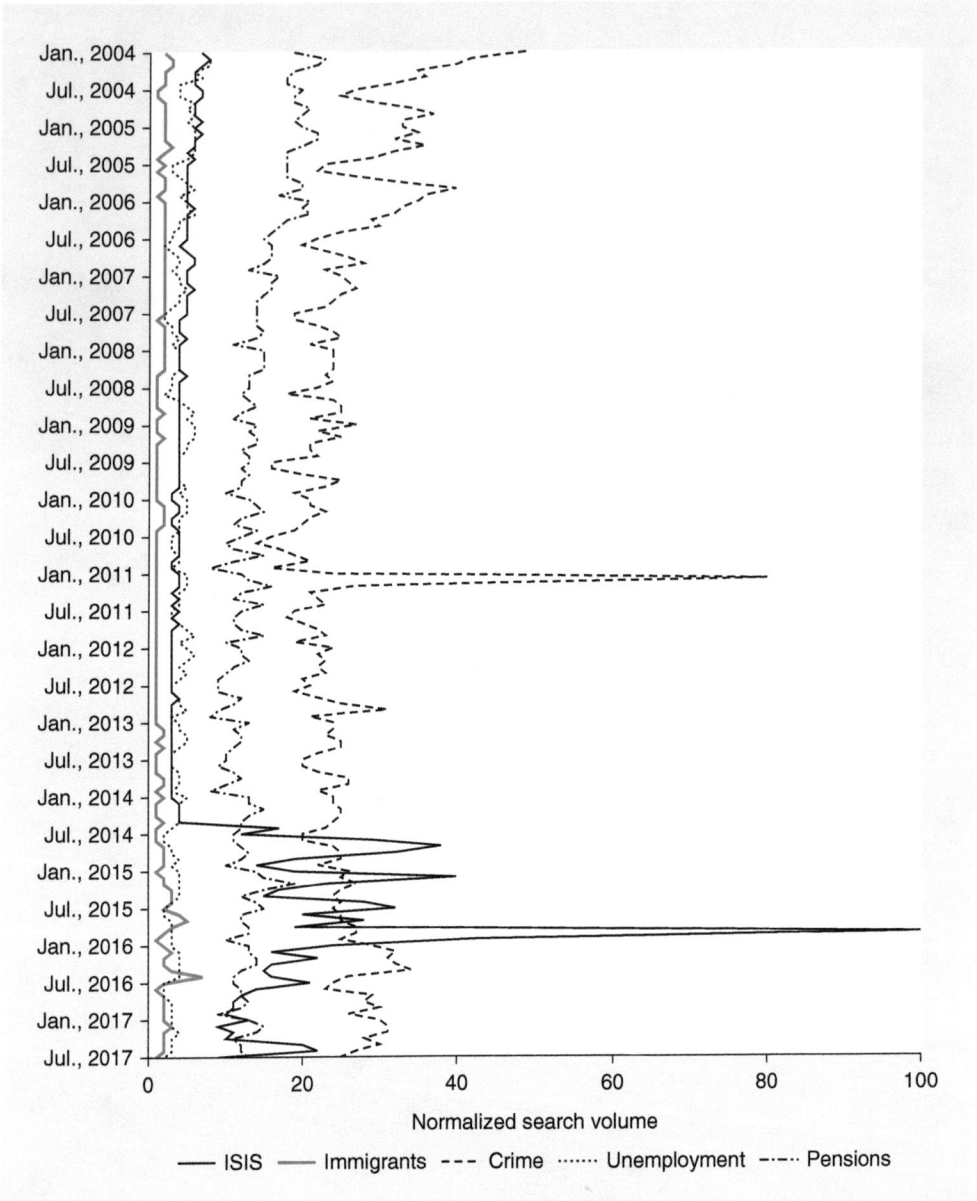

SOURCE: Original calculations.

in Sweden, and *The Times* in the United Kingdom. Figures 25.7, 25.8, 25.9, 25.10, and 25.11 show for each country the time series of online search volume on pensions together with the monthly count of stories[12] in which the word "pension" appears in the selected newspapers. The figures show a very close correlation between online searches and newspaper coverage of the pension theme. If anything, newspaper coverage appears to be generally leading online searches. A plausible rationale for this is

FIGURE 25.7 **France: Google searches on pensions versus *Le Monde* articles on pensions, 2004–17**

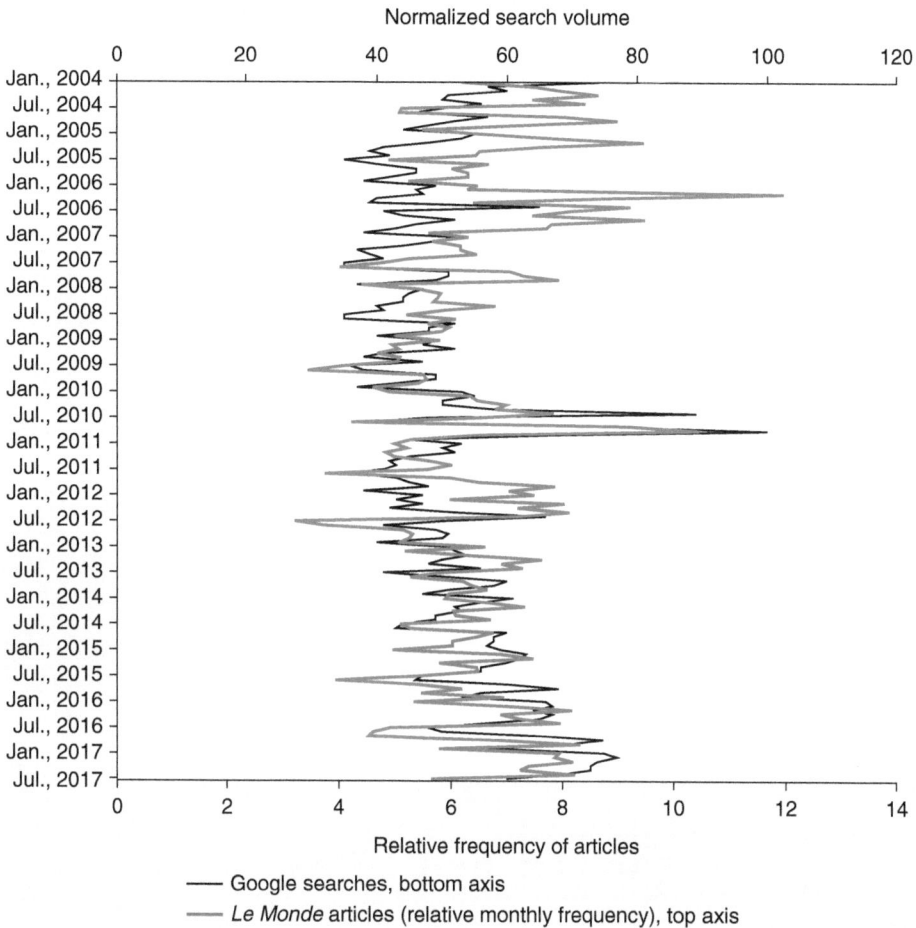

SOURCE: Original calculations.

that citizens initially get informed through traditional media outlets and then may be induced to search for additional information on the Internet. This positive correlation is confirmed by multivariate regression analysis.

The third research question on content analysis analyzes the case of Italy, with a specific focus on enactment of the Monti-Fornero reform at the end of 2011, and on its media coverage in four national newspapers. More precisely, exploiting the Dow Jones Factiva archive, the texts of all articles in four national dailies (*Corriere della Sera, Repubblica, Stampa,* and *Giornale*) that mention anywhere the word "pensioni" (pensions) were obtained for a four-month timespan starting in November 2011 and ending in February 2012. Overall, 2,045 articles were published during the period, split as follows: 621 articles in *Corriere,* 604 in *Repubblica,* 424 in *Stampa,* and 396 in *Giornale.* Figure 25.12 shows the histogram of articles on a daily basis in all

FIGURE 25.8 **Germany: Google searches on pensions versus *FAZ* articles on pensions, 2004–17**

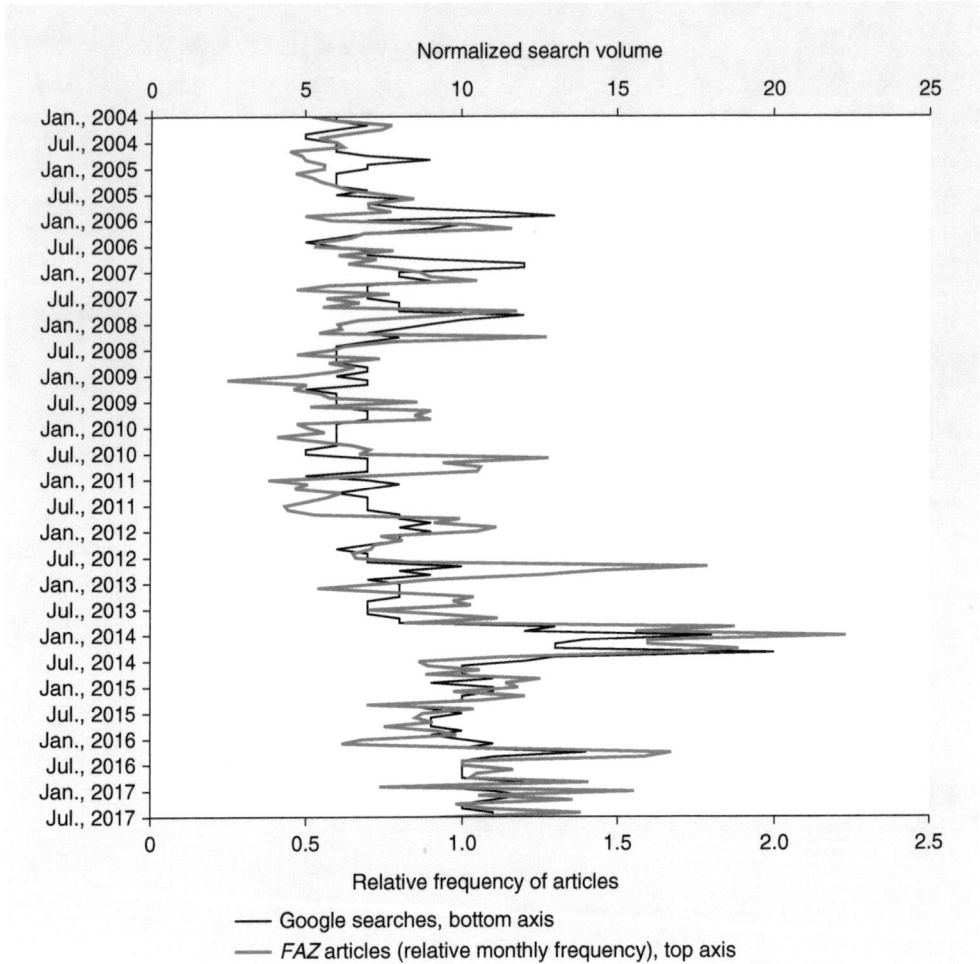

SOURCE: Original calculations.

four newspapers: there is a clear increase in coverage of pensions that rapidly reaches a maximum on December 5, that is, the day before enactment of the Decree-Law by the newly established Monti cabinet. Then coverage slowly drops in December (with a further spike on December 23, when the Decree-Law was converted into law), and more rapidly so in 2012, when the government was engaged in preparing the labor market reform (Fornero 2013). The topic, however, became a preferred subject for heated TV talk shows.

FIGURE 25.9 **Italy: Google searches on pensions versus *Corriere della Sera* articles on pensions, 2004–17**

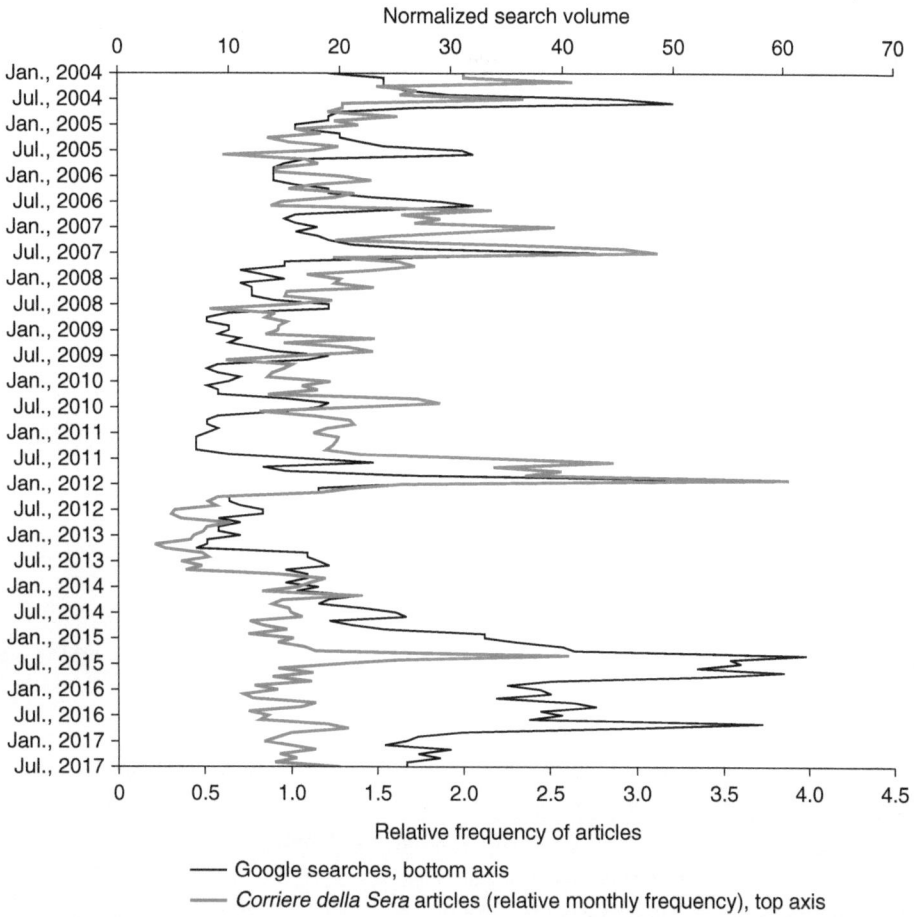

SOURCE: Original calculations.

The next step is regression analysis of daily coverage data, in which the dependent variables are the relative frequencies of pension articles that mention various concepts (table 25.1) and political figures and countries (table 25.1). The focus is on understanding how coverage varies before and after enactment of the reform (that is, the day the Decree-Law was issued) and as a function of the newspaper under consideration. Thus, each regression includes newspaper-specific fixed effects, a postreform

FIGURE 25.10 **Sweden: Google searches on pensions versus *Svenska Dagbladet* articles on pensions, 2004–17**

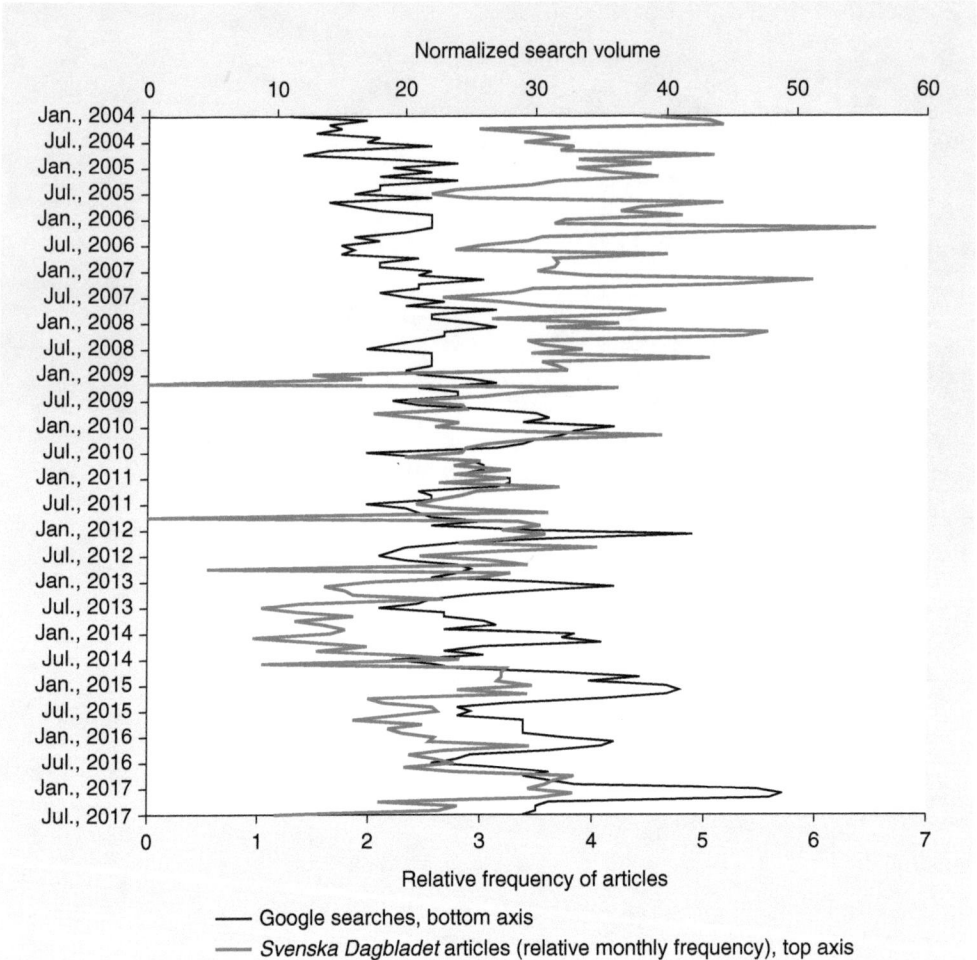

Google searches, bottom axis
Svenska Dagbladet articles (relative monthly frequency), top axis

SOURCE: Original calculations.

binary (dummy) variable, and a linear time trend. To avoid inflating the precision of the estimates, standard errors are clustered at the daily level. For each concept or figure, two different specifications are shown: the first one checks how the relative frequency of coverage changes after the reform unconditionally (that is, it does not allow for newspaper-specific differences in those potential postreform changes), whereas the second specification interacts the postreform dummy variable with the newspaper-specific dummy variables.

As shown in table 25.1, the words "reform," "spread" (between the returns of Italian and German bonds), and "austerity" are cited significantly less after the reform, while no

FIGURE 25.11 **United Kingdom: Google searches on pensions versus _The Times_ articles on pensions, 2004–17**

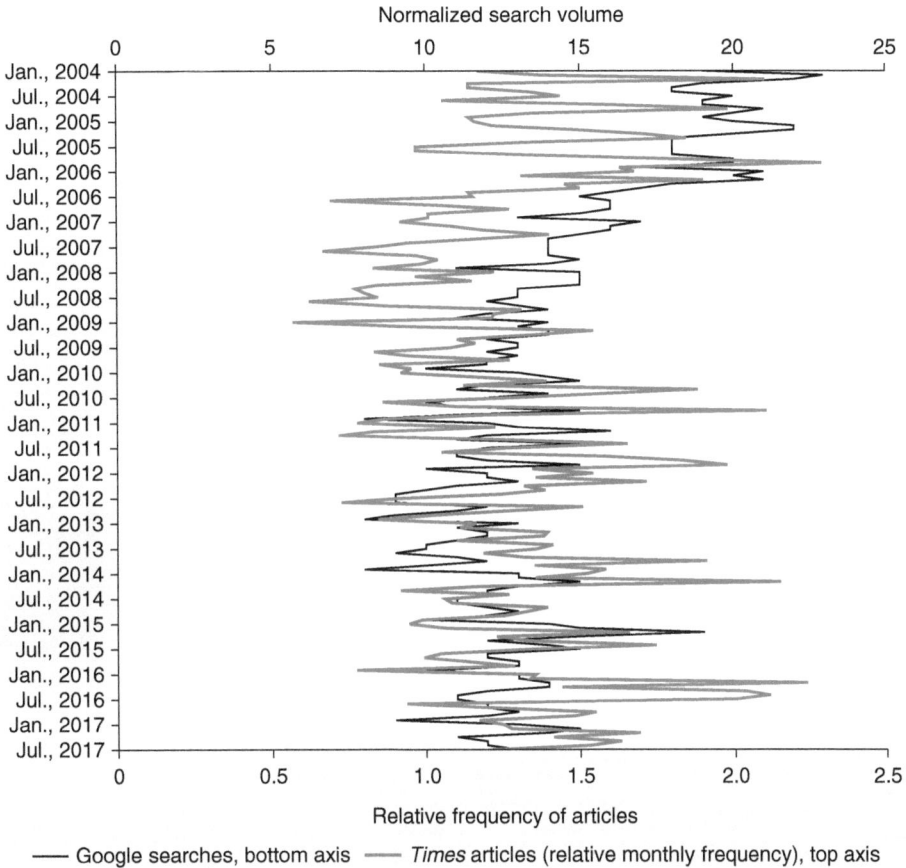

SOURCE: Original calculations.

significant change is found for "growth" and "firms." On the other hand, the mention of "trade unions" significantly increases after the reform, which appears to be driven by the increase in coverage by _Corriere_ and _Repubblica_. Comparing newspapers—taking _Corriere_ as the excluded category—_Repubblica_ and _Giornale_ give significantly more coverage to the "spread" when dealing with pensions, while _Giornale_—and less robustly so _Stampa_—devote less attention to "growth."

Table 25.1 shows that Europe is less significantly covered after the reform—albeit with an overall increasing trend. The same applies to Bersani (secretary of the Democratic Party, the main left-wing party in Italy), Berlusconi (leader of the main right-wing party and former prime minister), and German Chancellor Angela Merkel. On the other hand, no significant change occurs in the coverage of Monti, Fornero, and Germany after

FIGURE 25.12 **Histogram of articles about pensions in four Italian newspapers, November 2011 through February 2012**

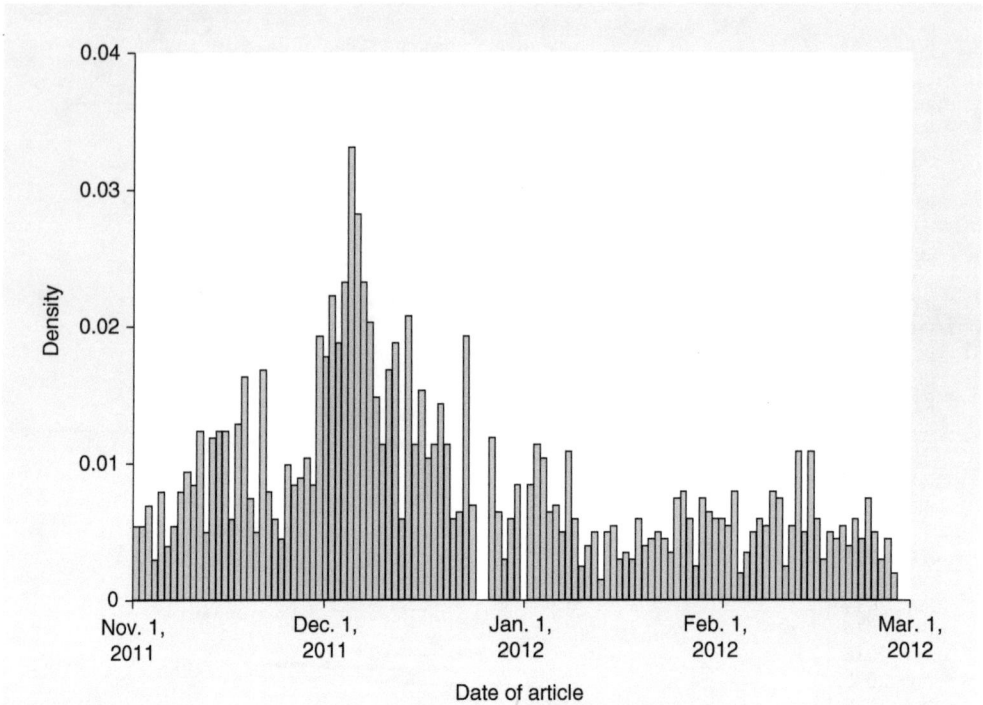

SOURCE: Original calculations.

NOTE: Sampled newspapers are *Corriere della Sera, Repubblica, Stampa,* and *Giornale.*

the reform. Interestingly, the more extreme newspapers in the sample (that is, *Repubblica* on the left and *Giornale* on the right) devote significantly more coverage to political figures compared with *Corriere*: this applies to Monti, Bersani, Berlusconi, and—to a lesser extent—Merkel.

This is just a first attempt to analyze the ways media outlets cover major pension reforms in a time of crisis, but some preliminary conclusions can be drawn. First, the media frame that is centered around the need for the reform itself appears to be replaced after its enactment by more actor-centered coverage, and trade unions and their discontent get more media attention. Second, when covering pensions, more ideologically extreme newspapers give more coverage to political actors than do more moderate outlets, but it is unclear whether this is a general pattern or is pension specific.

TABLE 25.1 Coverage of the Monti-Fornero pension reform by four national newspapers (*Corriere, Repubblica, Stampa, Giornale*), regression analysis

Dependent variable: relative frequency of pension articles that mention:	(1) Reforms	(2) Reforms	(3) Spread	(4) Spread	(5) Austerity	(6) Austerity	(7) Trade unions	(8) Trade unions	(9) Crisis	(10) Crisis	(11) Growth	(12) Growth	(13) Firms	(14) Firms
Postreform dummy	-0.144** (0.0602)		-0.137*** (0.0400)		-0.0465** (0.0215)		0.143*** (0.0524)		-0.0586 (0.0544)		0.0258 (0.0518)		-0.0533 (0.0473)	
Corriere dummy × postreform dummy		-0.0517 (0.0685)		-0.0706 (0.0493)		-0.0570** (0.0257)		0.148** (0.0642)		-0.0141 (0.0683)		-0.0379 (0.0627)		-0.0657 (0.0604)
Repubblica dummy × postreform dummy		-0.216** (0.0862)		-0.221*** (0.0666)		-0.0448 (0.0398)		0.252*** (0.0693)		-0.121 (0.0784)		0.0553 (0.0761)		-0.0958 (0.0730)
Stampa dummy × postreform dummy		-0.0424 (0.0802)		-0.143** (0.0565)		-0.0329 (0.0309)		0.132* (0.0685)		-0.0523 (0.0802)		0.109 (0.0747)		-0.0136 (0.0691)
Giornale dummy × postreform dummy		-0.266*** (0.0829)		-0.115* (0.0668)		-0.0503* (0.0302)		0.0387 (0.0689)		-0.0483 (0.0761)		-0.0184 (0.0624)		-0.0365 (0.0706)
Repubblica dummy	0.00242 (0.0427)	0.113** (0.0545)	0.0725** (0.0329)	0.173*** (0.0642)	0.0341 (0.0223)	0.0258 (0.0236)	0.0230 (0.0329)	-0.0446 (0.0383)	0.0515 (0.0371)	0.123* (0.0622)	0.0418 (0.0383)	-0.0214 (0.0545)	0.0303 (0.0394)	0.0498 (0.0585)
Stampa dummy	0.0309 (0.0365)	0.0265 (0.0564)	-0.0285 (0.0259)	0.0212 (0.0496)	0.0144 (0.0199)	-0.00186 (0.0135)	-0.0169 (0.0324)	-0.00556 (0.0439)	0.0554 (0.0397)	0.0819 (0.0621)	-0.0258 (0.0399)	-0.125* (0.0604)	-0.00480 (0.0369)	-0.0398 (0.0558)
Giornale dummy	-0.0626 (0.0389)	0.0823 (0.0565)	0.114*** (0.0359)	0.145** (0.0623)	0.0195 (0.0187)	0.0149 (0.0151)	0.0221 (0.0373)	0.0957** (0.0475)	0.0309 (0.0398)	0.0546 (0.0744)	-0.137*** (0.0284)	-0.151*** (0.0463)	-0.0178 (0.0349)	-0.0376 (0.0586)
Time trend	0.00176*** (0.000871)	0.00174*** (0.000878)	0.000912* (0.000537)	0.000912* (0.000539)	0.00157*** (0.000469)	0.00157*** (0.000471)	-0.000311 (0.000693)	-0.000326 (0.000697)	-0.000433 (0.000814)	-0.000433 (0.000817)	-0.00115* (0.000679)	-0.00115* (0.000683)	0.00118* (0.000629)	0.00118* (0.000629)
Constant	-32.74** (16.51)	-32.52* (16.63)	-17.12* (10.18)	-17.17* (10.21)	-29.82*** (8.883)	-29.82*** (8.924)	6.051 (13.13)	6.326 (13.21)	8.603 (15.42)	8.573 (15.49)	22.14* (12.86)	22.18* (12.95)	-22.06* (11.91)	-22.14* (11.93)
Observations	425	425	425	425	425	425	425	425	425	425	425	425	425	425
R-squared	0.027	0.046	0.077	0.087	0.057	0.058	0.044	0.059	0.023	0.026	0.061	0.070	0.012	0.014

SOURCE: Original table.

NOTE: The dependent variables are the relative frequencies of pension articles that also mention other keywords. The postreform dummy takes on the value of one the day after the enactment of the Decree-Law ("Decreto Salva Italia") that introduced the Monti-Fornero pension reform, that is, December 6, 2011, and zero otherwise. Standard errors are clustered at the daily level and are shown below each coefficient. *** $p < 0.01$, ** $p < 0.05$, * $p < 0.1$.

TABLE 25.1 Coverage of the Monti-Fornero pension reform by four national newspapers, regression analysis (cont.)

Dependent variable: relative frequency of pension articles that mention:	(1) Europe	(2) Europe	(3) Germany	(4) Germany	(5) Monti	(6) Monti	(7) Fornero	(8) Fornero	(9) Bersani	(10) Bersani	(11) Berlusconi	(12) Berlusconi	(13) Merkel	(14) Merkel
Postreform dummy	-0.221*** (0.0609)		0.000423 (0.0353)		0.0164 (0.0605)		0.0518 (0.0519)		0.0866** (0.0349)		-0.197*** (0.0509)		-0.0996*** (0.0333)	
Corriere dummy × postreform dummy		-0.140* (0.0739)		-0.00775 (0.0493)		0.0458 (0.0734)		0.0889 (0.0577)		-0.0352 (0.0419)		-0.0854 (0.0594)		-0.0923** (0.0451)
Repubblica dummy × postreform dummy		-0.250*** (0.0857)		0.00537 (0.0487)		0.00742 (0.0776)		0.0726 (0.0708)		-0.0453 (0.0478)		-0.361*** (0.0698)		-0.117** (0.0539)
Stampa dummy × postreform dummy		-0.209** (0.0845)		0.0346 (0.0594)		-0.0700 (0.0799)		-0.00347 (0.0683)		-0.120* (0.0620)		-0.213*** (0.0747)		-0.121** (0.0609)
Giornale dummy × postreform dummy		-0.288*** (0.0767)		-0.0293 (0.0547)		0.0788 (0.0765)		0.0462 (0.0563)		-0.150*** (0.0507)		-0.132* (0.0716)		-0.0683 (0.0419)
Republica dummy	0.146*** (0.0407)	0.221*** (0.0631)	0.00419 (0.0285)	-0.00468 (0.0389)	0.120*** (0.0386)	0.146*** (0.0450)	-0.0106 (0.0332)	0.00124 (0.0388)	0.0359* (0.0200)	0.0441 (0.0324)	0.0461 (0.0372)	0.230*** (0.0609)	0.0606** (0.0296)	0.0772 (0.0508)
Stampa dummy	0.0194 (0.0422)	0.0674 (0.0760)	0.0137 (0.0303)	-0.0147 (0.0510)	-0.00553 (0.0395)	0.0723 (0.0571)	-0.0625** (0.0310)	-0.000192 (0.0482)	0.0723** (0.0279)	0.130** (0.0589)	-0.0102 (0.0334)	0.0771 (0.0669)	0.0199 (0.0270)	0.0393 (0.0542)
Giornale dummy	0.00767 (0.0382)	0.108* (0.0585)	0.0163 (0.0321)	0.0306 (0.0539)	0.110*** (0.0411)	0.0888 (0.0618)	-0.0414 (0.0320)	-0.0122 (0.0331)	0.0535** (0.0232)	0.131*** (0.0465)	0.0942** (0.0361)	0.128* (0.0645)	0.0485* (0.0256)	0.0325 (0.0384)
Time trend	0.00214*** (0.000810)	0.00213*** (0.000813)	0.000659 (0.000496)	0.000657 (0.000498)	-0.000842 (0.000910)	-0.000839 (0.000912)	0.000134 (0.000661)	0.000130 (0.000663)	-0.000266 (0.000497)	-0.000278 (0.000501)	-0.00144* (0.000782)	-0.00143* (0.000775)	0.00143*** (0.000455)	0.00143*** (0.000459)
Constant	-40.02** (15.34)	-39.86** (15.41)	-12.37 (9.407)	-12.33 (9.439)	16.49 (17.26)	16.41 (17.30)	-2.368 (12.52)	-2.307 (12.57)	5.197 (9.426)	5.387 (9.489)	27.73 (14.82)	27.58 (14.70)	-27.00*** (8.631)	-27.06*** (8.698)
Observations	425	425	425	425	425	425	425	425	425	425	425	425	425	425
R-squared	0.066	0.073	0.011	0.013	0.034	0.039	0.022	0.026	0.073	0.085	0.214	0.240	0.031	0.033

SOURCE: Original table.

NOTE: The dependent variables are the relative frequencies of pension articles that also mention other keywords. The postreform dummy takes on the value of one one day after the enactment of the Decree-Law ("Decreto Salva Italia") that introduced the Monti-Fornero pension reform, that is, December 6, 2011, and zero otherwise. Standard errors are clustered at the daily level and are shown below each coefficient. *** $p < 0.01$, ** $p < 0.05$, * $p < 0.1$.

Financial Literacy Applied to Pensions: What Is "Pension Literacy"? Why Is It Important?

WHY FINANCIAL LITERACY IS IMPORTANT FOR RETIREMENT: A SELECTIVE REVIEW OF THE LITERATURE

Welfare gains from individual choices depend on the efficiency of those choices, which in turn require, among other things, at least a basic understanding of their main elements and likely consequences, both in the short and the medium-long run. In the case of retirement saving, for example, even when it is compulsory and disguised under the payment of payroll taxes, understanding that "each dollar or euro of contribution counts" for the future pension benefit is crucial to make wiser and more farsighted choices, such as turning away from moonlight jobs, even if they appear more convenient in terms of net pay.[13]

To grasp the basic features of pensions, good information should thus complement widespread financial literacy. Illiteracy is instead associated with inattention to information, misinterpretation of pensions, and lack of knowledge of one's rights or, at the opposite, to claims of "acquired entitlements" that are hardly justifiable according to principles of social justice. This is, for example, the case for very generous—in terms of the difference between the amount (the present value) of benefits and contributions—DB pensions awarded to high income earners.

Research has shown that widespread pension illiteracy can generate myopia, distortions, inconsistencies, and opportunistic conduct, such as a preference for early retirement not justified by hazardous working conditions or health flaws, and not supported by a parallel willingness "to pay for it" in terms of correspondingly reduced pension benefits (Calcagno, Coda Moscarola, and Fornero 2016). An excessively early retirement exposes workers to the risk of inadequate pension benefits at an older age, and the public budget to the moral pressure of adding resources so as not to abandon older people in need (the so-called Samaritan's dilemma).

As mentioned in the introduction, most advanced economies witnessed a rather radical change in the retirement landscape in the past two to three decades. DC pensions[14] have significantly expanded and are expected to expand more in the near future; thus, as already mentioned, individuals all over the world are (and will be) increasingly called to take greater responsibility to save, invest, and draw down their retirement wealth. DC pensions are normally more flexible than DB ones, implying more choices, even when—as is often the case—DCs are guided by appropriate design of default options. In addition, in most countries life expectancy is increasing, with people spending more years in retirement because minimum retirement ages have not yet increased. And a longer retirement requires greater savings and resources to pay for the extra consumption and health care costs of these additional years (Kritzer and Smith 2016).

In this new pension landscape it is important to understand the extent to which individuals are equipped to make decisions and whether they are sufficiently knowledgeable about basic economic and financial notions and principles to make wise decisions, when required, and to plan for retirement. From this point of view, research finds that those reporting that they are unable to plan for retirement or cannot carry out their retirement saving plans are also those who are least aware of fundamental economic concepts driving economic well-being over the life cycle (Lusardi and Mitchell 2011). Many people lack key knowledge of financial concepts and fail to plan for retirement even when retirement is only 5–10 years off. This has important consequences, since 30–40 percent of wealth inequality can potentially be attributed to financial knowledge (Lusardi, Michaud, and Mitchell 2017).

Numeracy and inflation are fundamental concepts required for making saving decisions, and knowledge of risk diversification could help people make decisions about participating in a pension fund, as a way to combine the different risk-return combinations of an unfunded and a funded scheme. The knowledge of these simple concepts is strongly associated with successful retirement planning: those who cannot do a simple interest calculation or do not know about inflation and risk diversification are also much less likely to calculate how much they need to save for retirement (Lusardi and Mitchell 2008). The concept of compound interest is especially important to know in the presence of NDC pension schemes: like most financial instruments, the rate of return in NDC plans works in a "compounded" way, generating returns from previous returns. Hence, in determining the final (notional) capital and thus the pension benefit, earlier contributions will have a higher weight than those paid at older ages.

Behrman et al. (2010) identify the impact of financial literacy and schooling on wealth accumulation and pension contribution patterns. Their estimates indicate that financial literacy is at least as important, if not more so, than schooling in explaining variation in household wealth and pension contributions. Van Rooij, Lusardi, and Alessie (2012) show that financial sophistication boosts households' retirement planning behavior, thereby providing an important channel for the development of savings plans and creating instruments for self control. Financially savvy employees are also most likely to participate in their DC plan (Clark, Lusardi, and Mitchell 2017). Lusardi, Mitchell, and Oggero (2017, 2018) also show that financial literacy is among the factors reducing exposure to debt when on the verge of retirement.

Although much research on this topic is focused on the United States, a positive relationship between financial literacy and planning for retirement has been found in many other countries, such as Australia, Canada, Chile, France, Germany, Japan, the Netherlands, New Zealand, and Sweden, with some country-specific peculiarities (Agnew, Bateman, and Thorp 2013; Alessie, van Rooij, and Lusardi 2011; Almenberg and Säve-Söderbergh 2011; Arrondel, Debbich, and Savignac 2013; Boisclair, Lusardi, and Michaud 2017; Bucher-Koenen and Lusardi 2011; Crossan, Feslier, and Hurnand 2011; Garabato Moure 2016; Sekita 2011). In the Italian pension landscape in which private pensions are very gradually playing a greater role in ensuring old-age income, financial literacy increases the probability of saving for retirement through a private pension plan (Fornero and Monticone 2011).

BASIC UNDERSTANDING OF NDC PENSIONS AS INSURANCE THAT CAN ACCOMMODATE REDISTRIBUTION AND MAKE IT MORE TRANSPARENT

Correct information and basic financial knowledge, at both the micro personalized and macro levels, should contribute to citizens' understanding that pensions are not (or should not be considered) the result of the generosity of politicians, but of personal savings in the working period of the life cycle, and of the sound functioning of the labor market, which is the source of income by which pensions in a PAYG system are paid. The pension system, as designed by law, can translate this saving into adequate pension benefits with efficiency, equity, and sustainability, but it does not create new wealth per se. This social compact has an inherent insurance function, made explicit by the transformation, at retirement, of individuals' notional pension wealth into an income flow to be paid conditional on workers' (or their survivor's) existence. Citizens should also understand the "unfunded" nature of notional (PAYG) systems—that is, the reliance on contributions paid by current workers to finance pensions, with additional funds possibly coming from the overall government budget, which in turn is financed by taxation, reduction of other expenditures or additional deficit. Those additional funds should finance the redistributive part of the pension expenditure; that is, the assistance component on top of the insurance one (the integration needed to reach the minimum pension level, or the contributions paid by the state in case of unemployment, maternity leave, or care activities).

The insurance feature embedded in the NDC system does allow for both solidarity and flexibility of retirement, concepts that people normally attach to a public pension system. Solidarity may come during the working life by contributions paid out of progressive general taxation for periods of unemployment, care, education, and training. Flexible retirement is a "natural" good feature of NDC systems, in that it does not come at the expense of the young and future generations (as was the case with early retirement options under the DB method). Of course, in NDC systems as well, pensions are not mechanically determined only by an objective formula taken from "actuarial mathematics." In a public system, some redistribution will always be present and thus political choices will always have a role to play. NDC systems allow workers employed in specific jobs to retire earlier on the basis of scientific knowledge about their health and mortality conditions. People should be aware that an efficient pension system is certainly not unsuited to solidarity. To the contrary, efficiency and transparency of the NDC system make it more likely that its redistributive consequences are equitable and perceived as such, while lack of transparency is usually associated with hidden privileges and mounting disapproval rates for the system itself. Exceptions to the rule of the actuarial correspondence between contributions and benefits are possible (indeed, are due in a public system), but they should favor the unlucky members of society, not the lucky ones, generating intolerable privileges. As mentioned above, people should also recognize that an expensive pension system is financed mainly from contributions by workers and employers, implying a tradeoff between "generous" pensions and high (gross) labor costs, which discourages employment and might also be associated with lower net wages. It is important to convey these essential concepts in a few simple messages. This means that both politicians and the media should have a sufficient level of economic and financial literacy.

PENSION LITERACY AND THE SUSTAINABILITY OF PENSION SYSTEMS AND REFORMS

Pension reforms affect people's lives and are often very unpopular, implying an electoral cost. Financial literacy can help improve politics by providing antidotes to populist tendencies in difficult situations. Financial knowledge is not a panacea, but can provide a firm basis for higher social payoffs.

Reforms are meant not only to change laws but, more importantly, to change people's behavior. Their effectiveness crucially depends on the ability of citizens (that is, public opinion) to recognize the importance, or in some cases the necessity, of reforms, their general design, and their "sense of direction." They have the nature of social investments, requiring sacrifices today with the expectation of benefits tomorrow. The electorate's ability to understand essential economic concepts is a relevant element for the evaluation of the electoral costs of pension reforms. Fornero and Lo Prete 2019 show that the electoral cost of a pension reform is significantly lower in countries where the level of financial literacy is higher. If entitlements are greater than contributions, and people understand that their pension entitlements are partly built on debt to be honored by future generations, they can be less hostile to pension restructuring.

Again at the macro level, the "lump of labor fallacy" is still widespread. Jobs are too often regarded to be fixed in number and early retirement is often considered, even at the government level, to be an easy way to create jobs for the young. This in turn might induce politicians to recommend generous early retirement options, to the detriment not only of the system's financial equilibrium but also of the adequacy of the benefits, with little or no gain in job creation for the young (Kalwij, Kapteyn, and de Vos 2010).

Even though information and financial literacy can intuitively be seen as complements, objections have been raised that the cost-effectiveness of educational programs aimed at universal financial literacy is low relative to, for example, nudges. The increase of financial literacy (even on a very large scale) cannot, of course, be expected to be the successful answer to all economic and financial problems (the "silver bullet"). This chapter asserts that this supposed contrast is wrong: financial literacy is not, of course, the only factor that would help devise a good pension design or increase the effectiveness of reforms. At the same time, the importance of well-designed choice options is not to be underrated. Behavioral nudges can encourage even financially literate people to make wiser choices; there is no need for one to exclude the other. Moreover, the process of trial and error as a substitute for financial knowledge might be extremely costly (more than investing in financial literacy). And a complementarity likely exists between financial literacy and reliance on experts: reliance on experts without diffusion of financial knowledge among the public might result in adverse selection and the troubling emergence of charlatans. This phenomenon might be particularly intense—and worrisome—during periods with peak demand for experts and pundits, such as during severe economic and social crises and in their long aftermath.

This is not to suggest that the combination of good information and financial literacy is a sufficient condition for the success of reforms. However, it is reasonable to argue that citizens who understand the basic principle of a reform should be less opposed to it when the reform is needed (and on the other hand, should be more opposed if the reform is meant to create differentiations and privileges). Because financial literacy can be improved by investing in education, governments may increase their citizens' awareness of what is involved in a reform by investing in specific educational programs for adults and basic financial education in school, which may in turn help change the reform's electoral cost and future viability.

Conclusions

This chapter revolves around the complementarity between information and financial literacy for an efficient and equitable functioning of NDC pension systems, and more generally of unfunded systems, at both the micro- and macroeconomic level. More specifically, it provides some new evidence—in the shape of stylized facts—about how public opinion in five European countries (France, Germany, Italy, Sweden, and the United Kingdom) is concerned with pensions, both from a cross-country perspective and in comparison with other policy issues. To do so, it exploits information on online searches, as provided by Google Trends, and matches these data with media coverage of pensions in traditional media (in this case, daily newspapers). It also looks at a specific case study—newspaper coverage of the 2011 Italian pension reform, introduced when Italy was on the verge of a financial crisis (Fornero 2013).

Much work on the topic of the complementarity between pension information and financial literacy is still to be done, both at the individual and macro levels. First—in addition to developing a theoretical model to empirically test this relationship—a strong need exists for survey data providing evidence on what kind of information is provided about pensions, where people get this formal and informal information, and how they use it. Then one could check whether and how this use is influenced by the level of financial literacy, and whether the combination of good personalized information and basic financial knowledge effectively produces better retirement choices. To the authors' knowledge, this combination of data on the provision of information, their use, and individuals' basic financial knowledge is not available yet.

Second, a more comprehensive content analysis of newspaper articles and editorials and TV news about pensions should be performed, with a specific focus on the quasi-experiment of pension reforms, to check whether and how the amount and tone of coverage change before and after reforms' actual enactment. A natural extension of this work would be to investigate how this coverage is correlated with the partisan bias of the media outlets under consideration (Gentzkow, Shapiro, and Stone 2015; Puglisi and Snyder 2015).

Finally, in the current era in which social networks are playing an exponentially increasing role in the social, political, and media sphere, one could investigate the connection between coverage of pensions and pension reforms on traditional media (TV and newspapers, together with their online counterparts) and conversations on social network on the topic. A purpose of this analysis would be to investigate whether elite discourse on traditional media still happens to lead the conversation on social networks, or whether the opposite holds; that is, online conversations take place first and influence arguments and proposals that are then featured on traditional media and possibly in the formal political arena (for example, in parliament).

Notes

1. More specifically, the word "nonfinancial" or "notional" is used to denote a pension system that does not rely on the accumulation of funds (reserves) to pay for pensions, but on current workers' contributions that are used to pay for current retirees' benefits. The term is thus a synonym for a PAYG system. Unfunded pension systems are in general public because it is harder and certainly riskier—particularly in the case of a single profession or even a firm—to maintain the capacity to "tax" future workers to finance the benefits of current ones.

2. Although the NDC system can fix the financial problems created by aging and by a structural decline in productivity growth, social sustainability relates to (a) whether pensions in the future will be sufficient to provide adequate living conditions for older people, and (b) people's understanding and involvement. This kind of sustainability depends essentially on the good performance of the labor market and on social protection to cover the unlucky by resorting

to general taxation. The majority of pensioners in rich countries today enjoy more or less the same standard of living of the average population, but the future looks bleaker for young and future generations given their greater difficulties on the labor market.

3. Fornero and Lo Prete (2019) test this hypothesis by looking at pension reforms in 21 advanced economies over 20 years, from 1990 to 2010. The study shows that although the probability of being reelected following a pension reform normally decreases, it falls less in countries with higher financial literacy scores.

4. Sweden, the United States, and Japan are generally considered good benchmarks.

5. As in the Italian case of an "Advance on Pension" (APE, *Anticipo Pensionistico,* introduced in 2015), which comes in two versions: "social," when the costs are socialized, that is, covered by general taxation, and "voluntary," when the person has to repay the debt, including the subsidized interest.

6. Provided mortality rates do not differ substantially by social class. When this is not the case, corrections to the pure DC formula should be adopted (see chapters 12, 13, and 14).

7. Interestingly, according to an Italian survey, individuals showed adequate knowledge of GDP growth in 2016 resulting in an average estimated value of 0.6 percent compared with 0.8 percent registered by Istat. On the other hand, average estimated values for unemployment and inflation rates were significantly greater than official data (Istat 2016).

8. On the other hand, long-run financial equilibrium implies that the "implicit" pension debt is matched by the system's "assets"; that is, the present value of future contributions (plus any other financial asset).

9. Decree-Law 201/2011, issued on December 6, 2011 (the so-called *Decreto Salva Italia*) and then converted into Law 214/2011.

10. In March 2015, the Italian Constitutional Court declared unconstitutional the freeze of price indexation for pension benefits higher than three times the minimum (that is, approximately higher than €1,500), which had been one measure of the 2011 pension reform. As a result, the price indexation of pensions for a large number of retirees had to be resumed.

11. Unfortunately, Google Trends does not allow checking the extent to which those searches landed Internet users on the pension organization's official website or on specific news sites.

12. Relative to the average number of monthly articles.

13. Of course, this is not always a choice for workers subject to binding financial constraints, in which case, the loss in pension wealth could be seen as the cost of overcoming the liquidity constraint.

14. Or, more generally, formulae characterized by a stronger correlation, at the individual level, between contributions paid and benefits received, and by an actuarial factor that takes into account the age of retirement and thus the different expected longevity at retirement.

References

Agnew, Julie R., Hazel Bateman, and Susan Thorp. 2013. "Financial Literacy and Retirement Planning in Australia." *Numeracy* 6 (2): Article 7.

Alessie, Rob, Maarten van Rooij, and Annamaria Lusardi. 2011. "Financial Literacy and Retirement Planning in the Netherlands." *Journal of Pension Economics and Finance* 10 (4): 527–45.

Almenberg, Johan, and Jenny Säve-Söderbergh. 2011. "Financial Literacy and Retirement Planning in Sweden." *Journal of Pension Economics and Finance* 10 (4): 585–98.

Arrondel, Luc, Majdi Debbich, and Frédérique Savignac. 2013. "Financial Literacy and Financial Planning in France." *Numeracy* 6 (2): Article 8.

Behrman, Jere, Olivia S. Mitchell, Cindy Soo, and David Bravo. 2010. "Financial Literacy, Schooling, and Wealth Accumulation." NBER Working Paper 16452, National Bureau of Economic Research, Cambridge, MA.

Boisclair, David, Annamaria Lusardi, and Pierre-Carl Michaud. 2017. "Financial Literacy and Retirement Planning in Canada." *Journal of Pension Economics and Finance* 16 (3): 277–96.

Bucher-Koenen, Tabea, and Annamaria Lusardi. 2011. "Financial Literacy and Retirement Planning in Germany." *Journal of Pension Economics and Finance* 10 (4): 565–84.

Buti, Marco, Alessandro Turrini, Paul Van den Noord, and Pietro Biroli. 2008. "Defying the 'Juncker Curse': Can Reformist Governments Be Re-elected?" European Economic Papers 3241, Directorate-General for Economic and Financial Affairs, European Commission, Brussels.

Calcagno, Riccardo, Flavia Coda Moscarola, and Elsa Fornero. 2017. "Too Busy to Stay at Work. How Willing Are Italian Workers 'To Pay' for Earlier Retirement?" *Economics Bulletin* 37 (3): 1694–707.

Chłoń-Domińczak, Agnieszka. 2009. "Retirement Behaviour in Poland and the Potential Impact of Pension System Changes." ENEPRI Research Report 61/January, Brussels.

Clark, Robert, Annamaria Lusardi, and Olivia S. Mitchell. 2017. "Employee Financial Literacy and Retirement Plan Behavior: A Case Study." *Economic Inquiry* 55 (1): 248–59.

Crossan, Diana, David Feslier, and Roger Hurnard. 2011. "Financial Literacy and Retirement Planning in New Zealand." *Journal of Pension Economics and Finance* 10 (4): 619–35.

Economist. 2007. "The Quest for Prosperity," March 15. http://www.economist.com/node/8808044.

Fornero, Elsa. 2013. "Reforming Labor Markets. Reflections of an Economist Who (Unexpectedly) Became the Italian Minister of Labor." *IZA Journal of European Labor Studies* 2: 20.

———. 2015. "Reform, Inform and Educate. The New Paradigm for Pension Systems' Sustainability." In *The Future of Welfare in a Global Europe*, edited by Bernd Marin, 297–324. Surrey, UK: Ashgate Publishing.

Fornero, Elsa, and Anna Lo Prete. 2019. "Voting in the Aftermath of a Pension Reform: The Role of Financial Literacy." *Journal of Pension Economics and Finance* 19 (1): 1–30.

Fornero, Elsa, and Chiara Monticone. 2011. "Financial Literacy and Pension Plan Participation in Italy." *Journal of Pension Economics and Finance* 10 (4): 547–64.

Fox, Louise, and Edward Palmer. 1999. "Latvian Pension Reform." Social Protection Discussion Paper 9922, World Bank, Washington, DC.

Gallup. 2015. "In Depth: Topics A to Z. Social Security." http://www.gallup.com/poll/1693/social-security.aspx.

Garabato Moure, Natalia. 2016. "Financial Literacy and Retirement Planning in Chile." *Journal of Pension Economics and Finance* 15 (2): 203–23.

Gentzkow, Matthew, Jesse M. Shapiro, and Daniel F. Stone. 2015. "Media Bias in the Marketplace: Theory." In *Handbook of Media Economics,* edited by Simon Anderson, Joel Waldfogel, and David Stromberg, Volume 1B, 623–45. Amsterdam: North Holland Publishing.

Istat. 2016. "The Knowledge of Economic Data by Italian Consumers." http://www.istat.it/en/archive/189746.

Kalwij, Adriaan, Arie Kapteyn, and Klaas de Vos. 2010. "Retirement of Older Workers and Employment of the Young." *De Economist* 158 (4): 341–59.

Kritzer, Barbara E., and Barbara A. Smith. 2016. "Public Pension Statements in Selected Countries: A Comparison." *Social Security Bulletin* 76 (1): 27–56.

Lusardi, Annamaria, Pierre-Carl Michaud, and Olivia S. Mitchell. 2017. "Optimal Financial Knowledge and Wealth Inequality." *Journal of Political Economy* 125 (2): 431–77.

Lusardi, Annamaria, and Olivia S. Mitchell. 2008. "Planning and Financial Literacy. How Do Women Fare?" *American Economic Review* 98 (2): 413–17.

———. 2011. "Financial Literacy and Planning: Implications for Retirement Wellbeing." In *Financial Literacy. Implications for Retirement Security and the Financial Marketplace,* edited by Annamaria Lusardi and Olivia S. Mitchell, 17–39. New York: Oxford University Press.

Lusardi, Annamaria, Olivia S. Mitchell, and Noemi Oggero. 2017. "Debt and Financial Vulnerability on the Verge of Retirement." NBER Working Paper 23664, National Bureau of Economic Research, Cambridge, MA.

———. 2018. "The Changing Face of Debt and Financial Fragility at Older Ages." *American Economic Association Papers and Proceedings* 108: 407–11.

Mastrobuoni, Giovanni. 2011. "The Role of Information for Retirement Behavior: Evidence Based on the Stepwise Introduction of the Social Security Statement." *Journal of Public Economics* 95 (7–8): 913–25.

Puglisi, Riccardo, and James M. Snyder, Jr. 2015. "Empirical Studies of Media Bias." In *Handbook of Media Economics,* edited by Simon Anderson, Joel Waldfogel, and David Strömberg, Volume 1B, 647–67. Amsterdam: North Holland Publishing.

Sekita, Shizuka. 2011. "Financial Literacy and Retirement Planning in Japan." *Journal of Pension Economics and Finance* 10 (4): 637–56.

Sundén, Annika. 2009. "Learning from the Experience of Sweden: The Role of Information and Education in Pension Reform." In *Overcoming the Saving Slump*, edited by Annamaria Lusardi, 324–44. Chicago: University of Chicago Press.

van Rooij, Maarten, Annamaria Lusardi, and Rob Alessie. 2012. "Financial Literacy, Retirement Planning, and Household Wealth." *Economic Journal* 122: 449–78.

CHAPTER 26

Sweden's Fifteen Years of Communication Efforts

María del Carmen Boado-Penas, Ole Settergren, Erland Ekheden, and Poontavika Naka

Introduction

Pensions are sufficiently complex to be very hard to understand. Barr and Diamond (2008) emphasize that public pension systems likely need to be adjusted because of changes in demographic and economic conditions and may also change with political circumstances, adding even more complexity. New (1999) states that the problem may not be lack of information but an information-processing problem. With an information-processing problem, the problem is too complex for many agents to make rational choices even when they have the necessary information. Specifically, for pension products, the long-time horizon between the payment of contributions and receipt of benefits produces inherent difficulties in understanding the product (Larsson, Sundén, and Settergren 2009).

According to Fornero (2015), political parties tend to look at reforms from an ideological perspective and conceal their more technical aspects. If system participants do not understand the reform and accept its basic principles, it risks underperforming relative to desired behavioral effects and even being repealed. Information is thus important not only for individual well-being but also for society. For individuals, knowledge of the system's rules is essential to avoid mistakes about the difference between expected and actual pension benefits. Information on the financial sustainability of the pension system is also fundamental in the sense that if participants misinterpret the system and the need for reform, they will try to reverse it. Lusardi and Mitchell (2007a, 2007b) and Biggs (2010) state that access to financial information and appropriate planning may have a positive impact on decision making concerning retirement. Moreover, information about pension benefits influences the age at which individuals retire (Sundén 2013). Similarly, Boeri and Tabellini (2012) point out that reforms can obtain popular support if they are well-described, explained, and understood. However, empirical evidence (Lusardi and Mitchell 2007a, 2011; Mitchell 1988) indicates that most individuals have very limited information about the core elements of social insurance systems and on the key variables that define the amount of their pensions.

In the past decades, governments in several countries have tried to facilitate contributors' decision making by regularly sending statements about their individual pension positions and estimates of expected pension benefits. For example, the Social Security

María del Carmen Boado-Penas acknowledges the research support from the Spanish Ministry of the Economy and Competitiveness (project ECO2015-65826-P). The authors are grateful to Ann-Christin Meyerhöffer for the survey data provided.

Statement in the United States, the Orange Envelope in Sweden and, since 2016, in Italy, and the Yellow Envelope in Germany all do this.[1]

Whenever pension reforms are carried out to restore financial sustainability, pension authorities in the involved countries face new trials. Sweden has spent nearly two decades grappling with the difficulties of providing mass information on something as complicated as the pension system, and several scholarly articles are already published on the subject.

With this in mind, this chapter aims to assess the Swedish pension experience with both individual information and information on financial sustainability in terms of its effectiveness toward participants' understanding of and confidence in the pension system. Special attention is given to the main changes carried out toward communication to improve individuals' pension knowledge and help them make better decisions. The chapter also examines how changes in the solvency of the system that affects (or risks affecting) the value of the pension benefit influence individuals' confidence in the system over time.

The remainder of the chapter is structured as follows. "Sweden's Public Pension System" describes the Swedish public pension system. "Channels of Communication" describes the main channels of communications—the actuarial balance together with its main financial indicators over the 2007–16 period (global information) and the so-called Orange Envelope (individual information). Main changes in the accounting information and the Orange Envelope over time are also discussed together with the role of the Swedish Pensions Agency. "Survey Results: Does the Information Work?" shows one measure of the effectiveness of the Swedish information on communication by means of survey results. The annual surveys mainly assess the level of confidence in the pension system, the main channels used by individuals to get pension information, their understanding of the pension system, and pension participants' knowledge for making retirement decisions. "Conclusions" provides the main conclusions, and annex 26A provides a sample of the Orange Envelope.

Sweden's Public Pension System

Sweden's public pension system consists of two different earnings-related benefit schemes: a nonfinancial defined contribution (NDC) scheme (called the *inkomstpension*) on a pay-as-you-go (PAYG) financing basis, and a fully funded financial defined contribution (FDC) pension (called the *premium pension*).[2] The contribution rates for the two schemes are 18.5 percent of the pension base, with a split of 16 percent for the NDC pension and 2.5 percent for the FDC scheme.[3] A tax-financed guaranteed pension, annually adjusted according to the consumer price index, also provides supplementary support for retirees with low NDC pensions.

NONFINANCIAL DEFINED CONTRIBUTION (NDC) SCHEME

NDCs, also known as defined contribution unfunded pension schemes, are ruled by a common principle: they attempt to reproduce the logic of a defined contribution pension plan within a PAYG framework. However, the PAYG financing principle has not excluded the accumulation of a substantial buffer fund. The notional account is a virtual one that records individual contributions, together with the fictitious return that they generate throughout each contributor's working life. The return that contributions earn is calculated on the basis of a macroeconomic index, not market returns. The index either tries to directly reflect the financial health of the system (that is, contribution base or gross domestic product [GDP] growth) or, as in the Swedish scheme, what is thought of as a socially and intergenerationally desirable "return," such as the change in average income, but adjusted if financial health so requires. The account balance is called notional because it is only used for revaluing past contributions (that is, the system does not invest funds given that the scheme is based on PAYG financing). When an individual retires,[4] his or her accumulated contributions (or the notional account) are converted into a life annuity according to standard actuarial practice. Therefore, the amount of the initial pension depends on the expected mortality of the retiring cohort, expected future pension indexations, and the rate used to discount the cash flows.

Under the Swedish NDC scheme, both accounts and benefits are, normally, indexed by the change in average income, as measured by the so-called income index. When the initial pension is calculated—that is, when the notional account value is converted into an annuity—the pension is increased or front-loaded on the basis of an assumed annual real growth rate of 1.6 percent for the income index. This rate of advanced interest is then deducted every year from the increase in the income index. Thus, the NDC pension is indexed annually by the change in the income index reduced by 1.6 percent.

THE AUTOMATIC BALANCING MECHANISM APPLIED TO THE NDC SCHEME

In certain situations, exceptions to the regular income indexation of accounts and benefits may apply. These exceptions are governed by the ratio of assets to liabilities (balance ratio[5]) as provided in the legislation on the automatic balancing mechanism (ABM). The balance ratio is an indicator that emerges from the actuarial balance sheet of the NDC scheme and is expressed as the ratio of assets (for example, contribution asset and fund assets) to pension liabilities. The balance ratio used in Sweden has a dual purpose—to measure whether the system can fulfill its obligations to its contributors and to decide whether the ABM should be applied.

If for some reason the balance ratio is less than 1, the ABM is triggered (Settergren 2001). This process basically consists of reducing the growth in pension liability (that is, the pensions in payment and the pension account balances of the economically active population).

FUNDED FDC SCHEME

Under the FDC scheme, participants have an individual financial account and their pension contributions are invested in funds chosen by the members themselves. A large number of funds exist from which to choose. The rate of return on the individual accounts is determined by the return on the funds chosen by the individual. The FDC pension can be drawn in either traditional insurance with profit annuity or fund insurance—also known as unit-linked insurance. In both forms of insurance, the value of the pension account is divided by an annuity divisor in the same way as with the NDC scheme. But for the premium pension, unlike the NDC, the annuity divisor is based on forecasts of future life expectancy rather than the current period life expectancy. The initial pension of both forms of insurance is credited with an interest rate of 1.75 percent and a deduction for costs of 0.1 percent (Swedish Pensions Agency 2017).

Channels of Communication

To make decisions about at which age to retire and how much to save, participants in the Swedish pension system need information about how the level of benefits is affected by their income, their number of years of contributions, and the retirement age. One challenge for the communication is to convey that the ABM is a regular component of the indexation of earned pension rights. The annual report (which includes accounting information) and the Orange Envelope provide information to participants regarding their individual pensions and the sustainability of the whole pension system.

ACCOUNTING INFORMATION: THE ACTUARIAL BALANCE SHEET

The Swedish administration produces an actuarial balance sheet and an income statement every year following the principle of double-entry bookkeeping. Since 2001, its annual report has presented an overall picture of the financial health[6] of the Swedish pension system. For those who want to delve deeper into the details, the annual report also provides a detailed description of how the national pension works, gives three scenarios (optimistic, pessimistic, and base) for the future of the pension system, and includes some special discussion features on pensions.

The balance sheet for the Swedish NDC scheme, shown in table 26.1, can be defined as a financial statement listing the pension system's obligation to contributors and pensioners (that is, liabilities to contributors and pensioners) on a particular date together with the amounts of the various assets (for example, financial assets and the value of the flow of contributions) that back up these commitments. The balance sheet also contributes to the management and disclosure of financial information because it is useful not only for the authority administering the system but also for contributors and pensioners in general and for the body that guarantees payment (that is, the state and the contributors it represents) (Boado-Penas et al. 2008; Boado-Penas, del Carmen, and Vidal-Meliá 2013).

The NDC system's assets include the estimated value of future pension contributions— referred to as the contribution asset—and the buffer fund. The contribution asset is calculated as the turnover duration multiplied by the value of the contributions made in a specific period. Its value in 2017 is 173.6 percent of GDP, as shown in table 26.1. The turnover duration is the expected average length of time between the payment of a monetary unit of contribution into the system and the disbursement of the corresponding credit in the form of a pension.[7] The turnover duration in Sweden has been roughly 31–32 years.

In the balance sheet, the pension liability includes a liability toward contributors and a liability toward pensioners. The liability to contributors is estimated as the notional accumulated capital in contributors' accounts. The liability to pensioners is estimated as the present value of the expected total of all pensions paid to current pensioners during their lifetimes, taking into account the current life expectancy and the interest rate applied (1.6 percent) when the amount of the initial pension was calculated. The pension liability varies from 212.2 percent to 197.4 percent of GDP in 2017 (table 26.1).

TABLE 26.1 **Balance sheet of the Swedish nonfinancial defined contribution pension system on December 31, 2007–17**

Item	2007	2008	2009	2010	2011	2012	2013	2014	2015	2016	2017
Assets (% of GDP)											
Fund assets	27.2	20.9	25.1	25.4	23.9	26.0	28.1	30.1	29.3	30.0	30.7
Contribution asset	185.5	191.2	193.5	186.8	186.7	187.7	188.9	187.5	177.6	175.6	173.6
Total assets	212.7	212.1	218.6	212.2	210.6	213.7	217.0	217.6	206.9	205.6	204.3
Liabilities and results brought forward (% of GDP)											
Opening results brought forward	3.0	0.5	−7.4	−9.2	2.8	4.3	−2.1	3.2	10.1	3.9	7.5
Net income or loss for the year	−2.5	−7.7	−2.4	12.1	1.5	−6.4	5.5	7.5	−6.0	3.9	−0.6
Closing results brought forward	0.5	−7.2	−9.8	2.9	4.3	−2.2	3.4	10.7	4.1	7.8	6.9
Pension liability	212.2	219.3	228.4	209.3	206.3	215.8	213.6	206.8	202.8	197.8	197.4
Total liabilities and results brought forward	212.7	212.1	218.6	212.2	210.6	213.7	217.0	217.6	206.9	205.6	204.3
Financial Indicators											
Balancing year	2009	2010	2011	2012	2013	2014	2015	2016	2017	2018	2019
Balance ratio, original definition[a]	1.0026	0.9672	0.9570	1.0138	1.0208	0.9901	1.0158	1.0521	1.0201	1.0395	1.0347
Balance ratio, modified legislation[b]	n.a.	0.9826	0.9549	1.0024	1.0198	0.9837	1.0040	1.0375	1.0067[c]	1.0132	1.0116
Turnover duration (years)	31.76	31.67	31.66	31.51	31.44	31.48	31.40	30.37	n.a	n.a	n.a
Smoothed turnover duration (years)	31.93	31.76	31.76	31.67	31.66	31.51	31.48	31.44	30.38	30.14	29.86
GDP (SKr, billions)	3,297	3,388	3,289	3,520	3,657	3,685	3,770	3,937	4,200	4,404	4,600

SOURCE: Original compilation based on data from the Swedish Pensions Agency (2008–18).

NOTE: Original information is stated in Swedish currency. GDP = gross domestic product; n.a.= not applicable; SKr = Swedish kronor.

a. The balance ratio calculated according to the previous definition (in 2007). It is calculated solely on the basis of the buffer fund's market value as of December 31 of the corresponding year, formerly called the financial position.

b. The balance ratio calculated according to the new definition (2008 onward). It is calculated on the basis of a three-year average of the buffer fund's market value.

c. The damped balance ratio is used instead of the balance ratio from 2015 onward. It is equal to 1 plus one-third of the difference between the balance ratio fixed for that year and the number 1.

Under the FDC scheme, the insurance assets are reported at their so-called true value, defined as the market value. The insurance assets have increased continuously since 2007. Specifically, the value of insurance assets increased from 10 percent of GDP in 2007 to 25 percent in 2017.[8] The main component of the insurance assets of the fully funded system is fund insurance, which amounted to almost 94 percent of total assets and is invested 90 percent in stocks and shares and 10 percent in bonds and other interest-bearing securities. The change in insurance assets chiefly refers to newly earned pension credit, positive changes in value, allocated management fees, and pension disbursements. With traditional insurance, the pension liability is the value of the remaining guaranteed disbursement.

CHANGES IN THE ACCOUNTING INFORMATION

Before 2008, the system's balance ratio was greater than 1, and total assets and the pension liability had risen, with a rather higher growth in liabilities than in total assets. In 2008, the financial position of the pension system substantially deteriorated. The balance ratio dropped below 1 for the first time, amounting to 0.9672, as shown in table 26.1, because of a large net loss of SKr 261 billion, equivalent to 7.7 percent of GDP. According to the original legislation, balancing should have been activated with a 3.28 percent reduction of the indexation of notional accounts and pensions in 2009/10. However, in 2009, the parliament changed the legislation so that rather than using the buffer fund value at December 31, a three-year average of the buffer fund should be used for calculating the balance ratio. As a result, the modified balance ratio increased to 0.9826, and the balancing effect was reduced to 1.74 percent.

In 2009, the system still faced financial deficit, but the loss (2.4 percent of GDP) was not as large as that of the previous year. The total assets were less than 4.3 percent of the pension liability, for a balance ratio of 0.9549. The pension liability was 228.4 percent of GDP, the highest value during the period. The negative indexation of notional accounts and benefits in 2009 and 2010 forced a significant drop in the value of the pension liability, and then, assets exceeded liabilities at the end of 2010. This surplus was equal to 0.0024 percent, for a balance ratio of 1.0024.

Pension system solvency was restored for a couple of years, but at the end of 2012, the pension liability exceeded total assets again, producing a balance ratio of 0.9837. Balancing was activated, and the indexation of pension balances and pension disbursements was decreased in 2013/14. Consequently, the pension system has been strengthened financially since 2013. The pension liability reached a value of 213.6 percent of GDP in 2013 and dropped to 206.8 percent of GDP in 2014, while the balance ratio increased to 1.004 in 2013 and 1.0375 in 2014. The surplus in assets over liability has been used, as is stipulated by the ABM legislation, to restore the value of benefits and accounts; as of 2018 the value of benefits and accounts are back where they would have been if no reduction of the indexing had occurred. In 2015, new rules were introduced with the aim of reducing the volatility in the balance ratio, caused mainly by the smoothing used in the income index. With this objective, smoothing of the indexation, identified to be inefficient at best and counterproductive at worse, was abolished and replaced by a smoothing of the balance ratio (referred to as the damped balance ratio). As a result, the balance ratio in 2015 amounted to 1.0067. The damped balance ratio restricts balancing to one-third, resulting in less volatility in pension benefits when balancing is activated at the cost of regaining financial solvency more slowly.

INDIVIDUAL INFORMATION TO PARTICIPANTS: THE ORANGE ENVELOPE

In 1999, as part of the reform of the Swedish pension system, a so-called Orange Envelope was introduced to provide individuals with a full picture of their up-to-date national pension accounts. Annually, the pension administration sends out the Orange Envelope to participants who have contributed to the pension system as well as to retirees receiving pension benefits. At the same time, the government launched a public information campaign to inform workers about the new system.

This personal statement includes separate account information on the NDC and premium pension accounts containing the current value of each account, changes in value since the last statement, pension contributions made during the year, administrative costs, and estimates of the future pension amount. In addition to providing information on expected benefits, the Orange Envelope summarizes how the new pension system works and highlights to insured persons that benefits are determined, through contributions, by lifetime earnings. For the funded account, a breakdown of information by fund is also provided, including the allocation of each fund that the participant chooses, and the actual distribution. The specifics are shown in annex 26A and summarized below:

The first page displays the monthly national public pension forecast that the member is expected to receive before tax under the retirement ages of 61, 65, and 70.[9] The reason for having several different retirement ages is to explain how retirement age impacts the size of monthly pension payments; that is, the longer the contributor works, the higher the pension amount. This page also illustrates the hierarchy of the pension sources that the participant would earn. The first order indicates the national public pension, both NDC and FDC, while the occupational pension is in the middle of the hierarchy, followed by the private pension, if any.

On the second page, the dynamics of the pension values of each account—income pension and premium pension account—during the year are presented (based on information from two years before). The statement consists of the account value of the previous year, the contributions assigned, the amount received for the survivors' dividend (the pension balance of contributors who die before reaching retirement age, which is distributed among surviving members of their birth cohorts) and the administrative and fund fees charged. Furthermore, this page illustrates the values of the premium pension account with the breakdown of the portfolio, the allocation of each fund that the accountholder chooses, and their actual values. Contributors will know the development of the premium pension funds in more detail, in particular where the money is invested and how much they pay in fees. The changes in value are also shown in percentage terms that can be compared with the data for the average participant.

The third page provides forecasts of the individual monthly pension amount under different retirement ages. An explanation of the alternative retirement age is also provided.

The last page gives the total pension credits, which basically means the money paid in during the year, and decomposes the contributions made for each account. The amount of pensionable income is also illustrated.

CHANGES IN THE ORANGE ENVELOPE

The contents and the number of pages of the Orange Envelope have been continuously redesigned[10] since its introduction in 1999. The aim of the changes is to make the information mailed out as simple and concise as possible. But for interested and knowledgeable individuals, other ways of finding out more are available (for example, online services), as explained next.

In 2002, the statement started to include information on the premium pension account so that individuals would have a better idea of the overall pension they could expect to receive.

In 2006, an effort was made to enhance individuals' understanding of pension issues, including an explanation of how the pension system works.

It was acknowledged that contributors (that is, pension savers, new entrants to the labor market, and old-age pensioners) had different interests regarding information provided. Therefore, since 2007, there have been three different versions of the Orange Envelope targeting these three specific population groups. The new pension savers receive almost the same version as the one for existing pension savers except that new savers receive a separate insert with general information on choosing funds, whereas existing savers receive specific information about their premium pension choices. Pensioners' statements contain the pension payments for the year, the value of the premium pension account, the pension payments made in the previous year, and tax deductions.

In 2011, the assumption of the 2 percent wage growth used to project pension benefits was removed because the surveys indicated that it was too confusing. There would be only one scenario, 0 percent average wage growth, included in the Orange Envelope. Zero growth over a long period is highly improbable, but this scenario is easier for individuals to understand because the forecasted pension amount is expressed in current price and wage levels at the time of the projection.[11]

In 2012, a graph was added to explain the relationship between increasing life expectancy and an "alternative" retirement age. The alternative retirement age is specific for each birth cohort and is defined as the age until which an individual should be working to receive the same pension amount he or she would have received at age 65 if life expectancy had remained unchanged. This graph is intended to make people aware of how improvements in life expectancy affect the amount of benefits.

In 2013, the Swedish Pensions Agency and the Premium Pension Authority, together with the insurance companies for the occupational plans, launched a website (https://secure.pensionsmyndigheten.se/B3). This website presents individual projections of both the public pension and occupational pension benefits and the total projected pensions. As a result, an insert was included on the first page of the Orange Envelope to announce that forecasts of the entire pension (that is, national, occupational, and private) were available online.

The 2014 version of the Orange Envelope was redesigned and shortened to four pages by eliminating two graphics: a pyramid to describe the three pension pillars and "piggy banks." This version also provided a personal code to access online information and stressed the importance of all three pillars of the retirement income system.

THE ROLE OF THE SWEDISH PENSIONS AGENCY

In 2010, the Swedish Pensions Agency was established, taking over administration of the national retirement pension, which was previously Försäkringskassan's responsibility, and the premium pension, which had previously been handled by the Premium Pensions Agency. The informational challenge was one of the main reasons for establishing the new Swedish Pensions Agency. Therefore, one of its important tasks is to work toward providing accessible and simple information on the total pension, including the public pension, occupational pensions, and private pensions.

To meet these information needs, the customer service operations of the agency provide face-to-face meetings, telephone customer services, e-services, and printed reports such as the Orange Envelope, the annual report, and statistics, among others.

In 2010, the Swedish Pensions Agency made the webpage www.minpension.se, containing individual information on both public and occupational schemes, available as an embedded service from its own website www.pensionmyndigheten.se.

Survey Results: Does the Information Work?

Since 1999, and about one week after individuals should have received the Orange Envelope in the mail, the Swedish Pensions Agency has conducted an annual survey about the Orange Envelope to evaluate to what extent participants open the envelope, read it, and think that they understand the content. The sample consists of 2,000 individuals interviewed by telephone and includes the three different target groups: existing pension savers (46 percent of the sample), new pension savers (27 percent), and old-age pensioners (27 percent). Currently, three-fourths of participants confirm that they open the Orange Envelope and one-half of them read some of the content.

Two other surveys are carried out annually in Sweden. The first one, called the Image Study, consists of a sample of 1,600 individuals (1,000 contributors and 600 pensioners) and assesses the confidence of pension participants in the Swedish Pensions Agency and the pension system. The Self-Confidence and Predictability Study, with a sample of 1,000 individuals, is a more recent survey that focuses on individuals' knowledge and self-confidence regarding their own upcoming pension and the pension system as a whole. Both knowledge and self-confidence are considered two relevant dimensions for estimating how efficient information is.

Reported confidence in the Swedish Pensions Agency has slowly but steadily increased over time for both retirees and workers (figure 26.1). In 2018, 61 percent of retirees and 45 percent of workers had some or great confidence in the pension system administration (including information and services), while the share of those with little or no confidence decreased slightly.

However, the share of participants with confidence in the pension system only reached 36 percent for pensioners and 25 percent for contributors in 2018 (figure 26.2). At the same time, the share of participants with no confidence decreased slightly over the period 2010–18.

Figures 26.1 and 26.2 illustrate that the confidence level in both the pension system and the pension system administration worsened in 2011, presumably because of the negative income indexation that year (and the year before) as a result of the ABM being triggered.

The level of self-reported understanding of the functioning of the Swedish pension system has improved (figure 26.3). One-half of workers and retirees (specifically, 53 percent of retirees and 49 percent of workers) find the Swedish pension system's

FIGURE 26.1 **Level of confidence in the Swedish Pensions Agency, 2010–18**

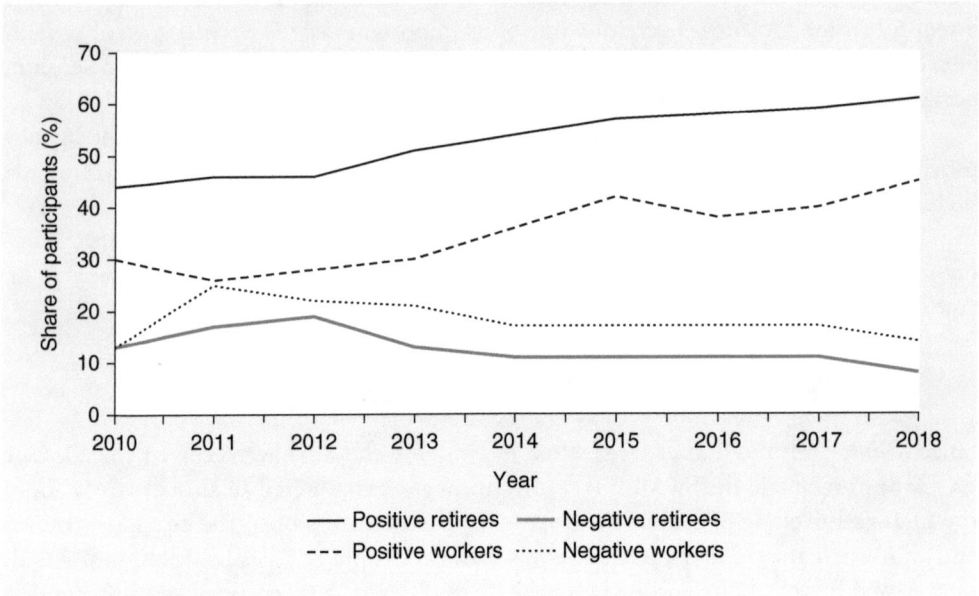

SOURCE: Annual Image Study survey.

NOTE: The grades to answer this question are 1–5. Grades 1 and 2 are grouped as negative while 4 and 5 are grouped as positive. Grade 3 is rated as neutral, and is disregarded in the figure.

FIGURE 26.2 **Level of confidence in the Swedish pension system, 2010–18**

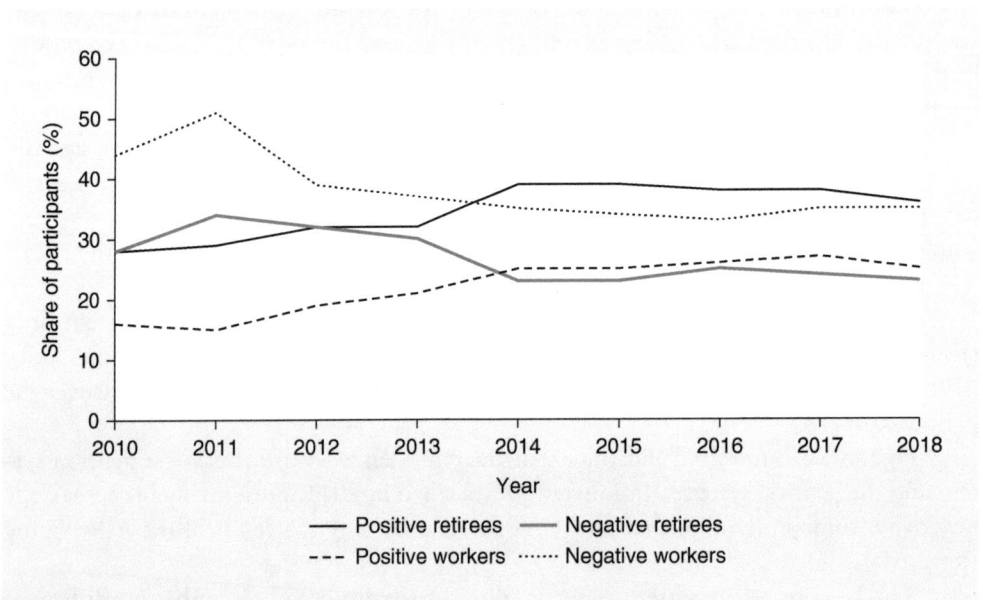

SOURCE: Annual Image Study survey.

NOTE: The grades to answer this question are 1–5. Grades 1 and 2 are grouped as negative while 4 and 5 are grouped as positive. Grade 3 is rated as neutral, and is disregarded in the figure.

operations easy to understand. The proportion of participants who respond that they find the system difficult to follow has decreased over time, from 41 percent of workers (33 percent of retirees) in 2010 to 21 percent of workers (20 percent of retirees) in 2018. Self-reported understanding of issues relating to pension savings has also increased over time; by 2018 almost everybody (97 percent) had some knowledge of pension issues (figure 26.4). The share of respondents with enough or good knowledge to make active choices is 48 percent while 49 percent of workers report having some grasp of economic and financial concepts. These questions predict the ability and probability of gathering and understanding information regarding pensions.

The share of participants who value the information and support provided has continuously increased (figure 26.5). In particular, according to the annual Self-Confidence and Predictability Survey, 62 percent of respondents in 2018 reported that the Swedish Pensions Agency provided information and support needed to make decisions on retirement.

As shown in panel a of figure 26.6, 65 percent of pension participants know where to get an estimate of the total amount of their future pension. The number of individuals getting the information from the webpage www.minpension.se has increased continuously (panel b of figure 26.6). In fact, in 2018, 50 percent of individuals used this site as their main channel for getting information and support regarding their pension. This increase in the number of individuals using www.minpension.se as their main information channel happened to the detriment of other channels, such as the Orange Envelope and the general webpage www.pensionsmyndigheten.se (although that webpage also links to www.minpension.se). Individuals older than 55, however, still prefer the material of the

FIGURE 26.3 **Self-reported understanding of the functioning of the Swedish pension system, 2010–18**

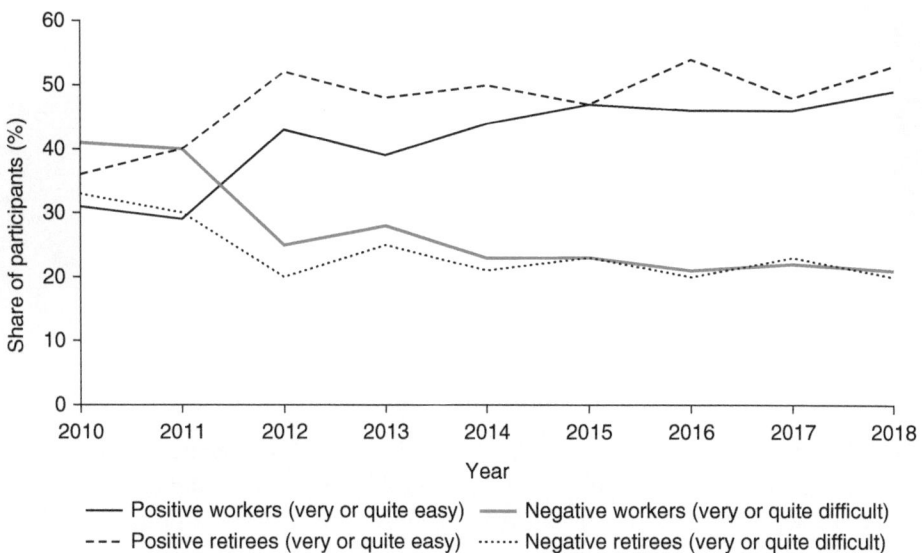

SOURCE: Annual Image Study survey.

FIGURE 26.4 **Self-reported understanding of financial and pension issues, 2010–18**

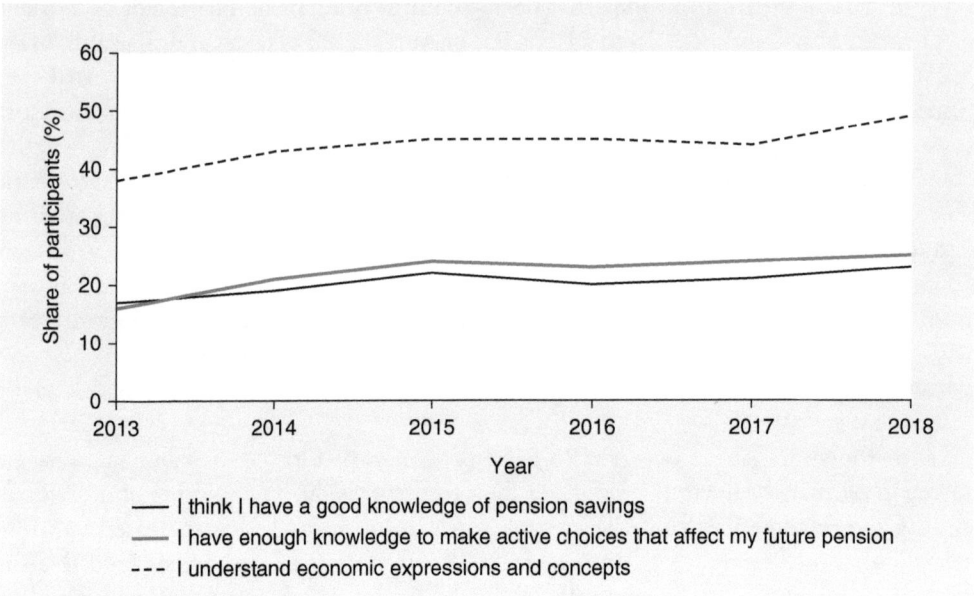

SOURCE: Annual Image Study survey.

FIGURE 26.5 **Do you think you have information and support needed to make decisions on retirement?**

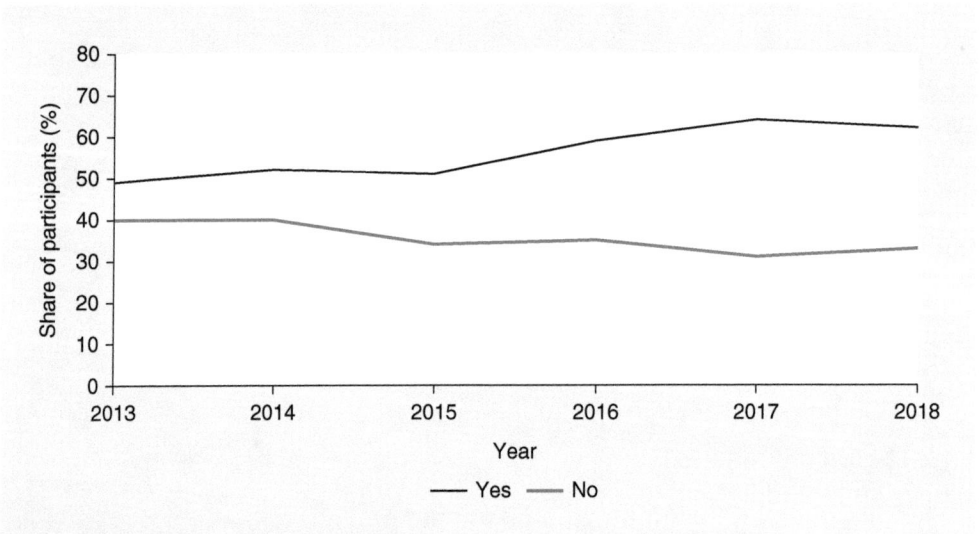

SOURCE: Annual Self-Confidence and Predictability Survey.

Orange Envelope to a larger extent than younger individuals. Specifically, 70 percent of individuals age 18–28 and 58 percent of those age 29–54 prefer the digital information as opposed to 44 percent of individuals age 55 and older. Other channels such as bank advisors or the call center of the Swedish Pensions Agency are now only used by 12 percent and 6 percent of the population, respectively.

FIGURE 26.6 **Forecast of the total pension amount**

a. Do you know how to get a forecast of the total amount of your pension?

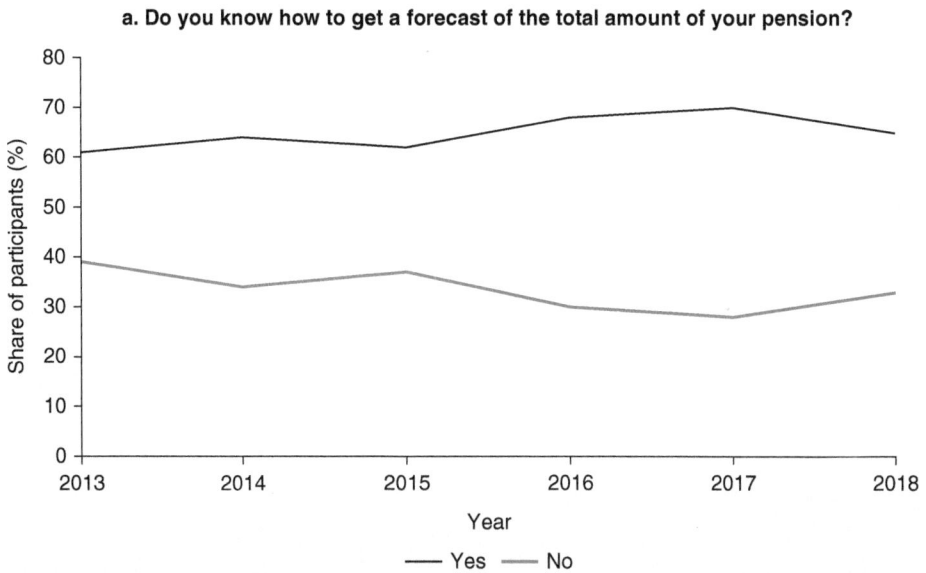

b. Knowledge about different channels to get information on your upcoming pension sum

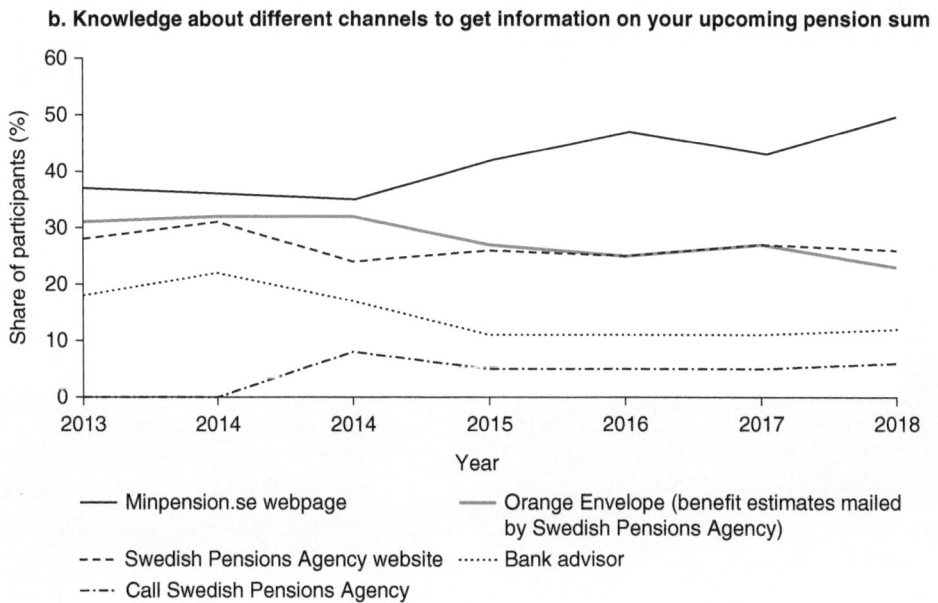

Legend:
— Minpension.se webpage
— Orange Envelope (benefit estimates mailed by Swedish Pensions Agency)
--- Swedish Pensions Agency website
······ Bank advisor
–·– Call Swedish Pensions Agency

SOURCE: Annual Self-Confidence and Predictability Survey.

Conclusions

This chapter describes the main channels of communication used by the Swedish administration, that is, the annual report on the solvency of the public system and the Orange Envelope, with information on individual accumulated capital and forecasts of expected benefits.

Both the annual report and the Orange Envelope have changed over time. The annual report's changes mainly reflected changes in the way of calculating the balance ratio—which is used to trigger the ABM—with the aim of reducing its volatility. Changes in the Orange Envelope were targeted to improve the understanding of pension participants.

Surveys carried out show that self-reported use and understanding of the information received has slowly increased. Also, the surveys show that confidence in the pension system decreased when the ABM was first triggered. It is not surprising that to most people the abstract issue of the financial situation of the public pension plan is not understood or accepted as a viable argument for reducing what for most people amounts to an important benefit. However, it seems that the communication and information to pension participants made the mechanism better understood and, as a result, the level of confidence for both workers and retirees did not decrease in successive applications of the mechanism.

Currently, participants have many channels through which they can get information on the pension system in general and individual forecasts of their own pension. The Orange Envelope provides a simple and concise explanation of the pension system and gives individual information regarding estimates of pensions under different retirement ages to help people make better retirement decisions. But the Swedish Pensions Agency provides more information for those who wish to delve deeper into the details. In recent years, according to the surveys, the main channel used by participants to get pension information is www.minpension.se. It is remarkable that one-half of the population reports finding the pension system easy to understand and 65 percent of contributors say they know where and how to get an estimate of their future pension.

The Swedish approach to pension communication has seemingly improved self-reported understanding of pension issues and confidence in the system, but room remains for improvement, given that almost one-third of individuals, according to the surveys, still state that they do not have enough support when making retirement decisions. From the Swedish experience, the projected future total pension from www.minpension.se has proven to be the most appreciated and valuable information for pension participants. Furthermore, information on future pensions likely increases confidence in the public and occupational plans as well, although no proof exists yet for this assertion.

It is worth noting that, in Sweden, the purpose of pension information is to make each insured feel well-informed about his or her projected future pension and thus increase the level of "self-control" over the future pension, and subsequently the insured's confidence in the pension plan. The surveys' questions only reveal the level of self-reported confidence in the pension plan and the Swedish Pensions Agency, however.

Because there is no control group, for obvious reasons, the effectiveness of the information in these two vital aspects cannot be measured with any degree of confidence. The possible actions of those insured with regard to the information are no action, a change in work hours, a change in planned retirement age, increased private savings, or amortization or other economic action. Because such changes cannot be observed, it is still not possible to claim that any changes are caused by the information.

ANNEX 26A

The Orange Envelope

Demo Person

SWEDISH
PENSIONS AGENCY

Annual Statement 2014

Your National Public Pension

According to our forecast, this is how much you will
receive as national public pension per month before tax. The amount
may vary depending on when you decide to retire.

age 61	age 65	age 68 and 3 month	age 70
SEK 10 300	SEK 13 100	SEK 16 000	SEK 18 500

Do you have a pension from different sources?

In addition to the national public pension, most employees also have a pension
from their employer. Some also have private pension savings.

National Public Pension
+
Occupational pension
+
Private pension
=

Your entire pension

Log in and see your entire pension

www.pensionsmyndigheten.se/B3

Use electronic identification or your personal code   27346

2014

You have earned this much towards your National Public Pension

Your Pension Credits

Changes during 2013 in SEK	Income pension	Premium pension	
Value 2012-12-31	854 596	106 942	
Pension credit for 2012	57 264	8 947	
From deceased contributors	603	560	
Administration and fund fees	-277	-985*	**Totally earned to the national public pension**
Change in value	-10 382	8 709**	
Value 2013-12-31	901 804	124 173	**SEK 1 025 977**

* Including SEK 716 discount on fund fee for 2012.
** Including SEK 135 as interest on your pension credit for 2012.

Your Premium Pension

Premium pension account 2013-12-31	Value, SEK	Change in value, per cent	Fund fee, per cent	Chosen allocation, per cent	Current allocation, per cent
Equity Fund Sverige	50 626	22	0,29	40	41
Equity Fund Global	31 156	22	0,51	25	25
Interest Fund Sverige	27 863	3	0,13	25	22
Generation Fund	14 528	13	0,20	10	12
Total	124 173	17	0,30	100	100
The average pension saver		21	0,31		

Mutual Fund Fee. Keep in mind that high fees mean worse performance for your savings.

Fund transfers. In order to increase safety, all fund transfers, from 20th February 2014, take place with electronic identification or Mobile BankID. You can also switch funds using a form that you order from the Swedish Pensions Agency and which will be sent to your registered address.

②

2014

How much will you get per month?

Forecast for your National Public Pension

Retirement age	age 61	age 65	age 68 and 3 month	age 70
Amount SEK/month	10 300	13 100	16 000	18 500

Your national public pension from age 65 (SEK 13 100 per month before tax) is estimated at SEK 9 800 in income pension and SEK 3 300 in premium pension. The pension will be paid out for the rest of your life.

We calculated as follows. The forecast is based on the SEK 1 025 977 you have earned towards your national public pension so far and your annual income until you retire. We have assumed that you will have the same pensionable income per year as in 2012, that is SEK 303 300.

The forecast is calculated in todays value. This means that you can compare the amounts in the forecast with your current earnings. The forecast is developed in accordance with the pension industry forecast standard. Read more on www.pensionsmyndigheten.se /prognosstandard.

Why 68 years and 3 months? The life expectancy in Sweden is rising. You, who were born in 1973 need to work until the age of 68 years and 3 months to receive the same pension amount you would have received at age 65 if life expectancy had remained unchanged. Your pension is calculated as your account value divided by the average remaining life expectancy of your age class.

When is the best time for you to retire? At www.pensionsmyndigheten.se/B3, you can obtain forecasts that also include your occupational pension and possible private pension. The forecasts make it easier for you to plan and make the right decisions about your future. The forecasts are generated by Minpension.se, a collaboration between the Swedish Pensions Agency and the private pension companies.

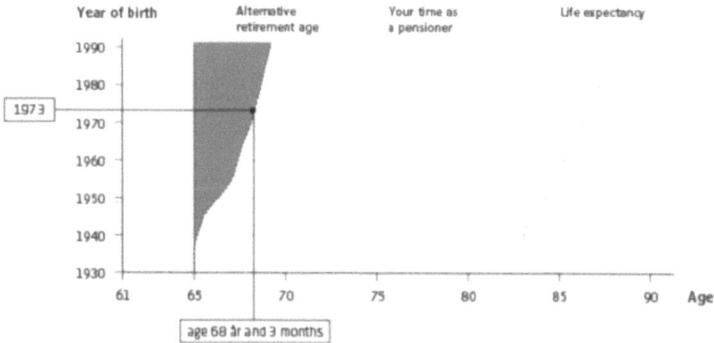

2013-12-05

Decision about your Pension Credits

The decision regarding your pension credits concerns 2012 since it is based on your latest established declared income.

Demo Person (eng)
Vägen 14
123 45 Landsorten

Pension credit for income pension		Pension credit for premium pension		Your total pension credits 2012
SEK 57 264	+	**SEK 8 947**	=	**SEK 66 211**

Basis for calculation of your pension credits

Pensionable income:	SEK 303 300
Pensionable amount:	
child years	SEK 54 600
This provides a pension basis of:	SEK 357 900

To request a reconsideration of the decision

The regulations that are the basis for the decision are to be found in chapters 59–61 of the Social Insurance Code (2010:110). If you want the decision to be reconsidered, please write to the Pensionsmyndigheten, Box 304, 301 08 Halmstad. Indicate the decision that you want reconsidered, how you want it changed and why. Write also your name, Swedish personal ID number, address and telephone number. If you engage a legal representative you must enclose an original power of attorney. Swedish Pensions Agency must receive the letter at the latest on 31st December 2014 or, if you have not been informed before 1st November 2014, within two months from the day you receive notice of the decision.

Notes

1. See Kritzer and Smith (2016) for more information. In the United States, distribution of information on paper has stopped but participants can request their Social Security Statement online.

2. For a more detailed description of the Swedish pension system, see the Swedish Pensions Agency (2008–18) and Barr (2013). Barr (2013) also evaluates the pension system in Sweden against the goals established at the time of the reforms in the late 1990s.

3. Contributions only give pension credits for incomes up to the "ceiling" in the public pension system, which is approximately 130 percent of an average income. This is low in international comparison.

4. In Sweden, retirement is flexible and pension benefits can be withdrawn beginning at age 61. When converting benefits into annuities, the life expectancy of the cohort is taken into account.

5. To indicate that the solvency ratio of a PAYG scheme is different from that of a premium reserve plan, which is a fully funded plan, the *inkomstpension* system calls this ratio the balance ratio rather than the solvency ratio.

6. Allowing for particular differences between countries, actuarial balances are compiled, on a regular basis, in countries such as the United States (OASDI 2015), Japan (Actuarial Affairs Division 2014), and Canada (Office of the Chief Actuary 2015), among others, to reveal the financial position of the pension system. When calculating the actuarial balance, these countries follow the aggregate accounting projection model (see Boado-Penas, del Carmen, and Vidal-Meliá 2013). In Sweden, an actuarial balance sheet, in the accounting sense of the term, is used in the Swedish notional pension system.

7. After 2014, the disclosure about the turnover duration has been calculated in terms of the difference between the weighted average ages of pensioners and contributors. See Swedish Pensions Agency (2016), Appendix B, Formula B.3.1.

8. For more details, see Swedish Pensions Agency (2008–18).

9. Age 61 is the earliest possible age at which old-age pension may be received. Age 65 is chosen because it was the normal retirement age, being the retirement age under the old system. Age 65 is also when certain social insurance benefits, such as sickness and disability benefits and unemployment insurance, come to an end, and others start, such as a guarantee pension and housing supplements for pensioners. Age 70 was chosen to provide a retirement age after 65.

10. For more details, see Kritzer and Smith (2016).

11. The assumed rate of return on the funded individual account is 3.5 percent. Also, only known values for the balance ratio and balance index are used in the projection for the national pension, because it is unclear how long and how fast the financial balance is recovering and when income indexation should apply again.

References

Actuarial Affairs Division. 2014. "Summaries of the 2014 Actuarial Valuation and Reform Options." Pension Bureau, Ministry of Health, Labour and Welfare, Government of Japan, Tokyo.

Barr, Nicholas. 2013. "The Pension System in Sweden." Report to the Expert Group on Public Economics 2013:7, Ministry of Finance, Government of Sweden, Stockholm.

Barr, Nicholas, and Peter Diamond. 2008. *Reforming Pensions: Principles and Policy Choices.* New York: Oxford University Press.

Biggs, Andrew G. 2010. *Improving the Social Security Statement.* Santa Monica, CA: RAND Corporation.

Boado-Penas, María del Carmen, and Carlos Vidal-Meliá. 2013. "The Actuarial Balance of the PAYG Pension System: The Swedish NDC Model Versus the DB-type Model." In *Nonfinancial Defined Contribution (NDC) Pension Systems in a Changing Pension World: Volume 2 Gender, Politics, and Financial Stability,* edited by Robert Holzmann, Edward Palmer, and David Robalino, 443–80. Washington, DC: World Bank.

Boado-Penas, María del Carmen, Salvador Valdés-Prieto, and Carlos Vidal-Meliá. 2008. "The Actuarial Balance Sheet for Pay-As-You-Go Finance: Solvency Indicators for Spain and Sweden." *Fiscal Studies* 29 (1): 89–134.

Boeri, Tito, and Guido Tabellini. 2012. "Does Information Increase Political Support for Pension Reform?" *Public Choice* 150 (1): 327–62.

Fornero, Elsa. 2015. "Reform, Inform and Educate: A New Paradigm for Pension Systems' Sustainability." In *The Future of Welfare in a Global Europe,* edited by B. Marin, 297–24. Surrey, UK: Ashgate Publishing.

Kritzer, Barbara E., and Barbara A. Smith. 2016. "Public Pension Statements in Selected Countries: A Comparison." *Social Security Bulletin* 76 (1): 27–56.

Larsson, Lena, Annika Sundén, and Ole Settergren. 2009. "Pension Information: The Annual Statement at a Glance." *OECD Journal: General Papers* 2008 (3): 131–71.

Lusardi, Annamaria, and Olivia S. Mitchell. 2007a. "Baby Boomer Retirement Security: The Roles of Planning, Financial Literacy, and Housing Wealth." *Journal of Monetary Economics* 54 (1): 205–24.

———. 2007b. "Financial Literacy and Retirement Preparedness: Evidence and Implications for Financial Education." *Business Economics* 42 (1): 35–44.

———. 2011. "Financial Literacy and Planning: Implications for Retirement Wellbeing." In *Financial Literacy: Implications for Retirement Security and the Financial Marketplace,* edited by Olivia S. Mitchell and Annamaria Lusardi, 17–39. New York: Oxford University Press.

Mitchell, Olivia S. 1988. "Worker Knowledge of Pension Provisions." *Journal of Labor Economics* 6 (1): 21–39.

New, Bill. 1999. "Paternalism and Public Policy." *Economics and Philosophy* 15 (1): 63–83.

Office of the Chief Actuary. 2015. "Actuarial Report (27th) on the Canada Pension Plan." Office of the Superintendent of Financial Institutions Canada (OSFIC), Ottawa, Ontario.

Old-Age, Survivors, and Disability Insurance (OASDI). 2015. *The 2015 Annual Report of the Board of Trustees of the Federal Old-Age and Survivors Insurance and Federal Disability Insurance Trust Funds.* Washington, DC: U.S. Government Publishing Office.

Settergren, Ole. 2001. "The Automatic Balance Mechanism of the Swedish Pension System: A Non-Technical Introduction." *Wirtschaftspolitische Blätter* 48 (4): 339–49.

Sundén, Annika. 2013. "The Challenge of Reaching Participants with the Message of NDC." In *Nonfinancial Defined Contribution Pension Schemes in a Changing Pension World: Volume 2 Gender, Politics, and Financial Stability,* edited by Robert Holzmann, Edward Palmer, and David Robalino, 257–72. Washington, DC: World Bank.

Swedish Pensions Agency. 2010. "Orange Report 2009—The Annual Report of the Swedish Pension System." Swedish Pensions Agency, Stockholm.

————. 2011. "Orange Report 2010—The Annual Report of the Swedish Pension System." Swedish Pensions Agency, Stockholm.

————. 2012. "Orange Report 2011—The Annual Report of the Swedish Pension System." Swedish Pensions Agency, Stockholm.

————. 2013. "Orange Report 2012—The Annual Report of the Swedish Pension System." Swedish Pensions Agency, Stockholm.

————. 2014. "Orange Report 2013—The Annual Report of the Swedish Pension System." Swedish Pensions Agency, Stockholm.

————. 2015. "Orange Report 2014—The Annual Report of the Swedish Pension System." Swedish Pensions Agency, Stockholm.

————. 2016. "Orange Report 2015—The Annual Report of the Swedish Pension System." Swedish Pensions Agency, Stockholm.

————. 2017. "Orange Report 2016—The Annual Report of the Swedish Pension System." Swedish Pensions Agency, Stockholm.

————. 2018. "Orange Report 2017—The Annual Report of the Swedish Pension System." Swedish Pensions Agency, Stockholm.

Swedish Social Insurance Agency. 2008. "Orange Report 2007—The Annual Report of the Swedish Pension System." Swedish Social Insurance Agency, Stockholm.

Swedish Social Insurance Agency. 2009. "Orange Report 2008—The Annual Report of the Swedish Pension System." Swedish Social Insurance Agency, Stockholm.

CHAPTER 27

Setting Up a Communication Package for the Italian NDC

Tito Boeri, Maria Cozzolino, and Edoardo Di Porto

Introduction

Since the beginning of the 1990s, the Italian pension system has been subject to several significant reforms. The Fornero reform, introduced in 2012, is merely the last of a series of measures that modified Italy's national pension system. The first reform in 1992 (the so-called Amato reform) was followed by the Dini reform in 1995 and by three minor subsequent adjustments introduced in 1997, 2005, and 2007.[1]

This process resulted in an increase in the minimum pension age, the gradual transition from a defined benefit (DB) system toward a defined contribution (DC) one, and a drop in the replacement rate. These reforms standardized the rules for the future, but also generated major differences in treatment between younger workers (those who had no contributions paid before 1995), middle-age workers (with fewer than 18 years of contributions paid in 1995), and older workers.

These are the most significant changes in the Italian pension system in the past 20 years. However, this was no smooth ride because these changes often overlapped and were incoherent with one another: periods of tightening were suddenly followed by periods of loosening and derogations, undoing some of the previous reforms. This inevitably produced anxiety and uncertainty among future retirees.

As a result, today a vast number of people tend to overestimate their future pensions, and Italy's low rate of financial literacy exacerbates the situation. Analyses, based on data by the Bank of Italy, indicate a widening of the gap between the expected and effective replacement rate, together with heterogeneity in the population's knowledge of basic social security concepts.[2]

A survey carried out by INPS (the Italian Social Security Institute) in 2016 seems to confirm these findings. The questionnaire asked respondents a few basic questions about the functioning of the pension system in a multiple-choice framework, in which only one answer was correct. The results from this survey show that people with higher education levels tend to have higher scores, probably because they are more financially literate and have a better understanding of the mechanisms that regulate the national social security system (figures 27.1 and 27.2).

The probability of receiving a wrong answer is relatively higher for questions that refer to how the contributions deposited into the system are employed. The majority of

The authors acknowledge the research support from Isabella Rota Baldini and are also grateful to Tullio Jappelli, Imma Marino, and Mario Padula and others for comments and suggestions.

FIGURE 27.1 **Knowledge of the Italian pension system financial situation by level of education**

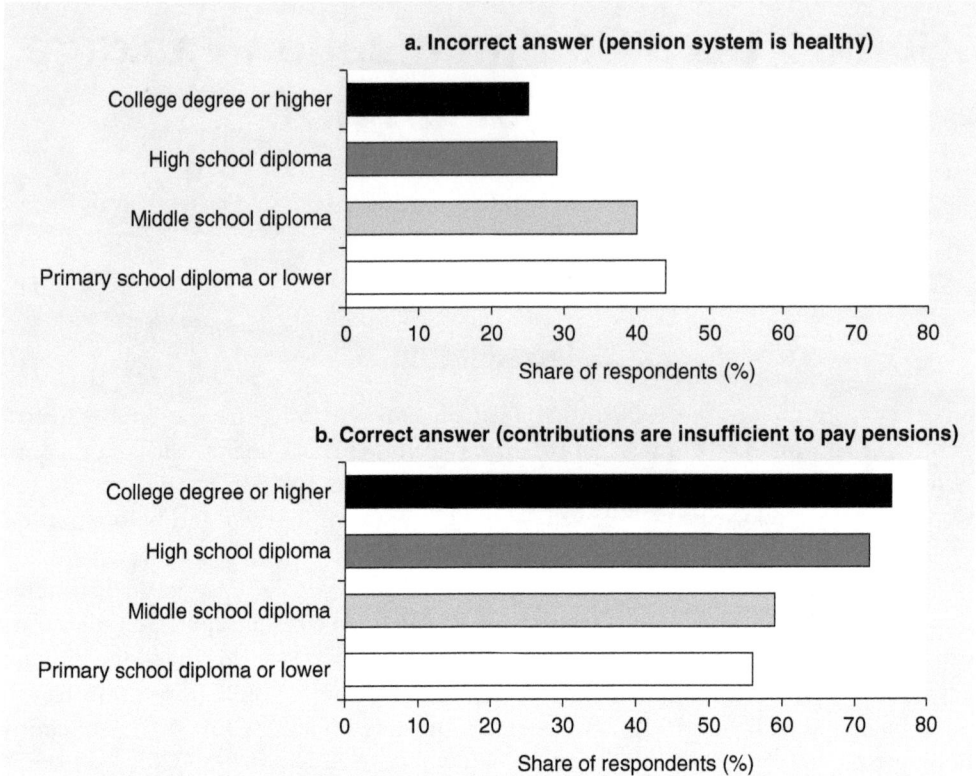

a. Incorrect answer (pension system is healthy)

b. Correct answer (contributions are insufficient to pay pensions)

SOURCE: Italian Social Security Institute (INPS) survey 2016.

respondents believe that contributions are deposited into a personal account that they will tap into when they retire. About one-third (32 percent) of university graduates (33 percent of those with a high school diploma) are aware of the fact that Italy has a pay-as-you-go system. This figure drops to 24 percent among those with only a primary school diploma.

Evidence shows that the number of correct answers (current contributions are used to pay current pensions and contributions are not enough to fund them) increases with age, as people get closer to retirement, while younger people appear to be less familiar with the functioning of the pension system. This age effect is evident in the above-mentioned analyses on the expectations regarding the replacement rate. Workers who entered the labor force more recently display a higher tendency to have naive expectations. This is true also for workers with discontinuous careers, for employees in small firms, and for the self-employed. In addition to lacking information, these groups of people do not have solid certainties about their future incomes. They also do not seem to have adequate tools enabling them to make informed choices that will allow them to reduce the risk of having low incomes after retirement.

This chapter shows the first results of a communication campaign (the so-called *La mia pensione futura*; referred to as "My future pension" hereafter) launched by INPS in 2015 to let all INPS-insured workers know when they will be able to retire and to predict their future pension level.

FIGURE 27.2 **Knowledge of the Italian pension system features by level of education**

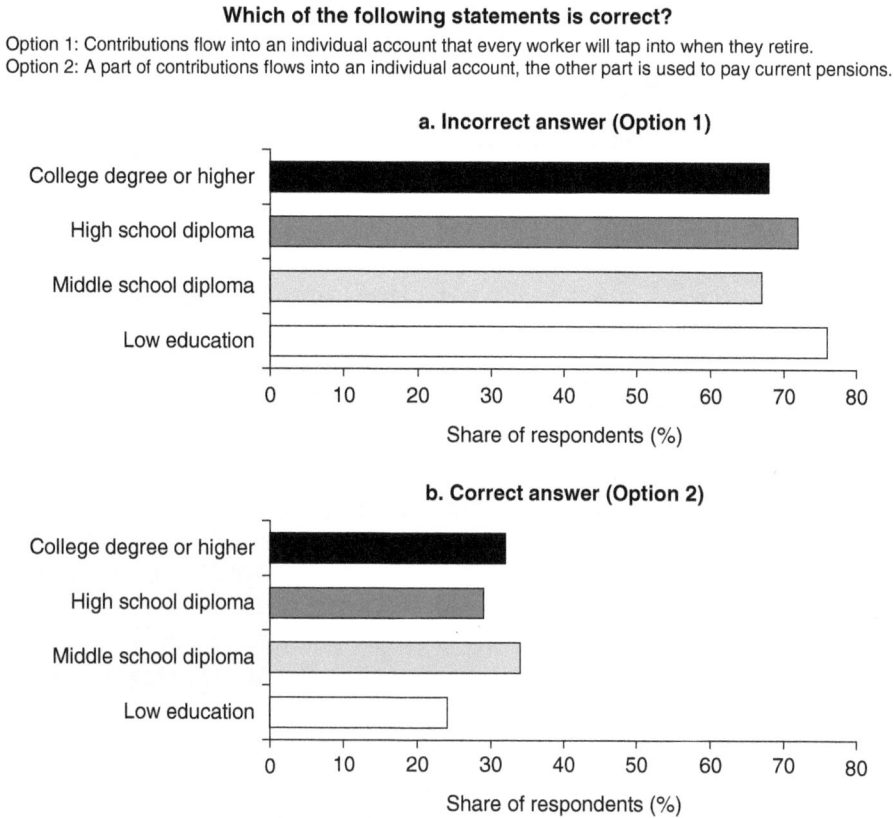

Which of the following statements is correct?

Option 1: Contributions flow into an individual account that every worker will tap into when they retire.
Option 2: A part of contributions flows into an individual account, the other part is used to pay current pensions.

a. Incorrect answer (Option 1)

b. Correct answer (Option 2)

SOURCE: Italian Social Security Institute (INPS) survey 2016.

Pension Reforms and Communication

The Italian pension system reform process, starting in 1992 with the Amato reform, put greater responsibility on all workers, who are responsible for planning their retirement. To maintain their current standard of living when they retire, workers should invest part of their savings into a complementary pension scheme along with the first-pillar public pension.[3] Moreover, the 1995 reform changed the calculation method, making the assessment of future benefits more difficult. Specifically, like Sweden, Italy opted for a DC retirement plan in which notional accumulated contributions are transformed into an annuity at retirement.[4]

Current literature clearly points out that workers' ability to carefully plan their retirement, and adjust consumption and savings over the working life, is closely related to financial literacy levels: higher literacy results in more knowledgeable behavior. Lusardi and Mitchell (2011) show that 30–40 percent of the differences in the savings rate of individuals close to retirement can be attributed to differences in their levels of financial literacy.

Italy is a country with a low level of financial literacy. Italian financial literacy lags behind other advanced economies, as highlighted by the Organisation for Economic

Co-operation and Development (OECD 2014) and by Klapper, Lusardi, and van Oudheusen (2015). The latter show that only 37 percent of Italians correctly understand basic financial concepts, much lower than the European Union (EU) average of 52 percent. In addition, di Salvatore et al. (2017), using the results of Bank of Italy surveys conducted in 2017, demonstrate that just a minor part of this gap depends on Italian sociodemographic differences compared with other countries.

This low level of financial literacy is one of the main reasons why pension reforms, especially the most disruptive ones, should be adequately communicated and explained to workers. For example, Sweden also moved to a contribution-based method for the calculation of pensions at the end of the 1990s.[5] Since 1999, just one year after the reform passed, the Swedish social security agency (Försäkringskassan) has automatically sent a statement (the Orange Envelope) to all resident citizens age 28 or older of their current personal pension position, including an estimate of their future pension benefit conditional on their planned retirement age and on different assumptions about the growth of the Swedish economy. Swedish workers can obtain a forecast that also includes their occupational pension and any private pension. In 2018 the Swedish Pensions Agency decided to exclude the projection from the statement. The aim is to move toward a digital Orange Envelope, and projections (state pension, occupational pension, private pension plans) will be made in digital interactions with contributors via MinPension.se, the agency's website.

In Italy, the law that introduced the 1995 reform, which radically changed the pension calculation method, envisaged a communication campaign to ensure that all Italian citizens would be able to fully grasp the implications of the reform for their future pensions. In contrast with Sweden, however, it took more than 20 years after the Dini reform to launch this campaign.

"INPS 'My Future Pension' Campaign" provides details on Italy's communication campaign, and "User Feedback on 'My Future Pension' and Orange Envelopes" analyzes user satisfaction with the "My future pension" program using feedback collected on a survey.

INPS "My Future Pension" Campaign

ESTABLISHMENT OF "MY FUTURE PENSION"

The expectations of Italian workers regarding their replacement rates trend downward irrespective of the categories under analysis (figure 27.3). This means that Italian workers have negative expectations regarding their future pensions, understandable given the characteristics of the new regime. However, there is a distance between expected retirement age and the legal retirement age that applies to younger workers. As for the retirement age, "during the last 15 years, expectations have been very optimistic, and young generations may have accumulated an insufficient amount of wealth" (Jappelli, Marino, and Padula 2014, 183).

In this specific setting it is always advisable to give clear financial information.

In 2015, INPS launched a project called "My future pension" to inform insured workers (at least those insured by INPS—that is, almost 90 percent of the Italian workforce) of when they will be able to retire and to give them some order of magnitude of their future pension incomes at retirement. This online service will gradually allow all

FIGURE 27.3 **Italy's expected replacement rate by employment group, 1990–2016**

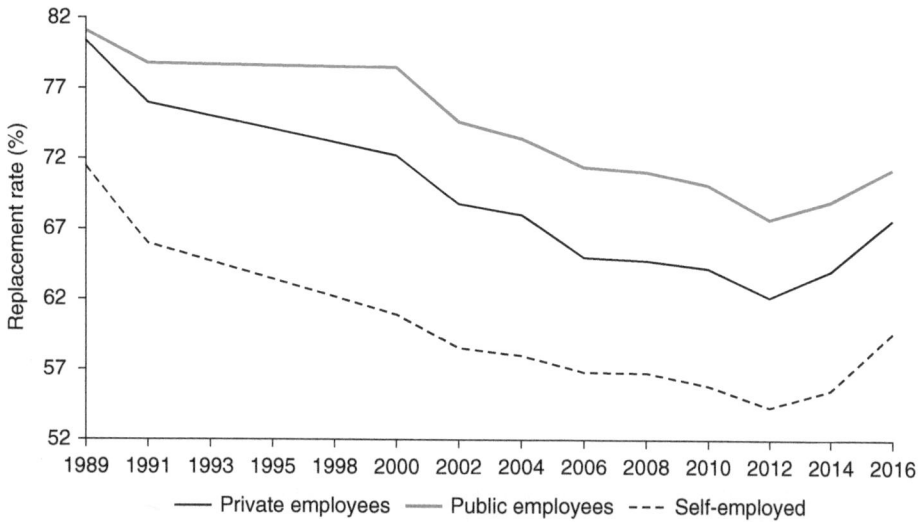

SOURCE: Jappelli, Marino, and Padula computation based on data from Bank of Italy Surveys of Household Income and Wealth (Jappelli, Marino, and Padula 2014).

workers to estimate their future pension on the basis of their past careers and on the projection of their future contributions until retirement.

To start with, the service was opened to roughly 19 million INPS-insured workers,[6] beginning with the youngest ones with at least a three-year contribution record. The service was offered to private sector employees, the self-employed, most of the workers contributing to "special" industry-level funds (a legacy of past ad hoc rules for some specific categories of workers), and workers contributing to the so-called *gestione separata*, a fund established in 1995 for those workers who did not, at that time, have a dedicated social security fund (that is, some independent workers, occasional workers, and others). Three years after the launch of the project, essentially all private sector employees and the self-employed now had the opportunity, if they register and log onto the platform, to use this tool.

In its start-up phase, an email was sent to 5.6 million INPS-insured workers (registered on the INPS website), inviting them to use the online program. This was followed by the delivery of about 4 million Orange Envelopes, starting in 2016, only to those who were not registered on the INPS website. The Orange Envelopes contain a worker's account of past contributions, date of earliest possible retirement, and a forecast of the future pension, based on expected economic scenarios and on likely future salary progression (assuming the current job is held until retirement). Furthermore, an accompanying letter invited workers to get an INPS PIN code and to use the online service.[7]

In early 2018, INPS started to open up this service to public sector employees. Their access to the program is currently limited, though, because it is difficult to map the entire working career of a number of civil servants (particularly those who are most mobile and change employers often), and especially to track their payments to their specific social security funds. However, INPS is investing time and resources to solve these difficulties and recently opened up the program to a sample of 30,000 public sector employees.

USE OF "MY FUTURE PENSION"

Over the first three years of "My future pension," more than 3 million unique users logged onto the INPS website to estimate their future pensions. Between 2015 and May 2018, users made 14.5 million simulations. This means that many users took advantage of the interactive features of the program, and used it more than one time (4.5 times on average), simulating different scenarios such as gaps in their future contributions or a less favorable growth scenario for the Italian economy.

Access to the service was highest in the first two years (figure 27.4), which suggests that people responded to the emails and Orange Envelopes sent in 2016 to reach those workers who, not being registered on the INPS portal, did not have a PIN code and thus could not access "My future pension."

The 2018 data in figure 27.4 suggest that legislative changes play a role in increasing people's propensity to gather information on their pension records. In 2018, there is, in fact, an increase in the number of users of the service. This is probably related to the new voluntary early retirement option (*Ape volontaria*) that allows individuals to retire early but with a penalty on the amount.

Ape volontaria, introduced by the 2017 Budget Law, is essentially a pension-guaranteed financial loan. This scheme allows all workers who satisfy certain conditions (among which the most important are to have fewer than three years until retirement, and to have an estimated monthly pension greater than 1.4 times the minimum) to be granted a loan from a bank during the three-year period in which they can retire early. This loan is then paid back over 20 years and the monthly payment deducted from the INPS pension.

FIGURE 27.4 **Number of users and simulations of future pensions on the Italian Social Security Institute's "My future pension" website, 2015–May 2018**

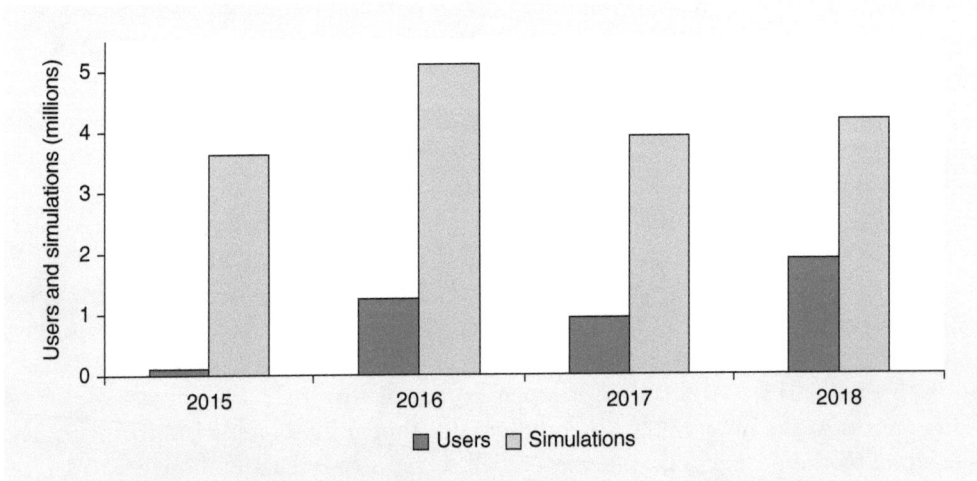

SOURCE: Italian Social Security Institute (INPS) data.

To help workers understand this sophisticated scheme, and to ensure they are informed of the fact that *ape volontaria* will have a permanent impact on their future pension, INPS created an online simulator. This tool allows users to estimate the minimum and maximum monthly loan they will be granted from the bank, the monthly payment that will be deducted from their future pension, and their retirement date.

In addition to the legislative shock, which pushes people to evaluate whether it is possible to exploit the new available option, a more direct effect may increase the number of visits to the "My future pension" service. The *ape volontaria* simulator, in fact, requires people to insert an estimated value for their future pension, an estimate that few people can make correctly without using the ""My future pension" online service.

User Feedback on "My Future Pension" and Orange Envelopes

After using the "My future pension" program, online users are asked to complete a questionnaire that allows for monitoring of user satisfaction, usability, and usefulness of the service provided. The following tables and figures show the results of almost 90,000 questionnaires (85,527 filled in by private sector employees and the self-employed, 1,831 by civil servants), accounting for almost 3 percent of users who ran a simulation.

The percentage of those who find the program extremely or very useful is high (more than 76 percent on average) (figure 27.5); the majority (59 percent on average) think the program gave them significant additional information; and 95 percent of respondents judge it to be user friendly.

Table 27.1 shows descriptive statistics for the key variables in the analysis, including a set of sociodemographic controls: *age, gender,* and a set of binary variables (dummies) indicating *level of education*. Overall, 26 percent of respondents are women; the age bracket spans from 21 to 80 years, with an average of 52; and most respondents have a high school diploma (58 percent) and about 20 percent of respondents have a bachelor's degree or higher.

A series of statistics about the difficulty of performing the simulation is also collected. *Need help* is a dummy equal to 1 if the respondent needed some help using the program, and the dummy *unfriendly* indicates that the online service was difficult to use. Overall, about 5 percent of respondents find the task difficult. A variable *night* indicates that the simulation was performed between 10 pm and 7 am, when productivity is generally lower and it is more difficult to focus on financial tasks, even the most elementary ones. Some 7 percent of respondents completed the questionnaire at night.

Another set of variables is analyzed to understand whether the simulation helped individuals improve their knowledge of their future pensions. The variable *overestimating* is a dummy equal to 1 if the simulated pension was lower than expected and 0 if the simulated pension was higher or very similar to the expected one. Notably, 42 percent of respondents overestimated their future pension (table 27.1). The variable *willing_change* describes the propensity to change expectations on the future pension. This question is asked after the results of the simulation are provided, thus when respondents should update their expectation. This variable is equal to 1 for those individuals willing to change their expectations; after using the program, 38 percent of respondents are willing to change their expectation on their future pension. After computing it for just those who overestimate, the figure increases to 47 percent.

FIGURE 27.5 **Users' satisfaction with "My future pension" service by level of education**

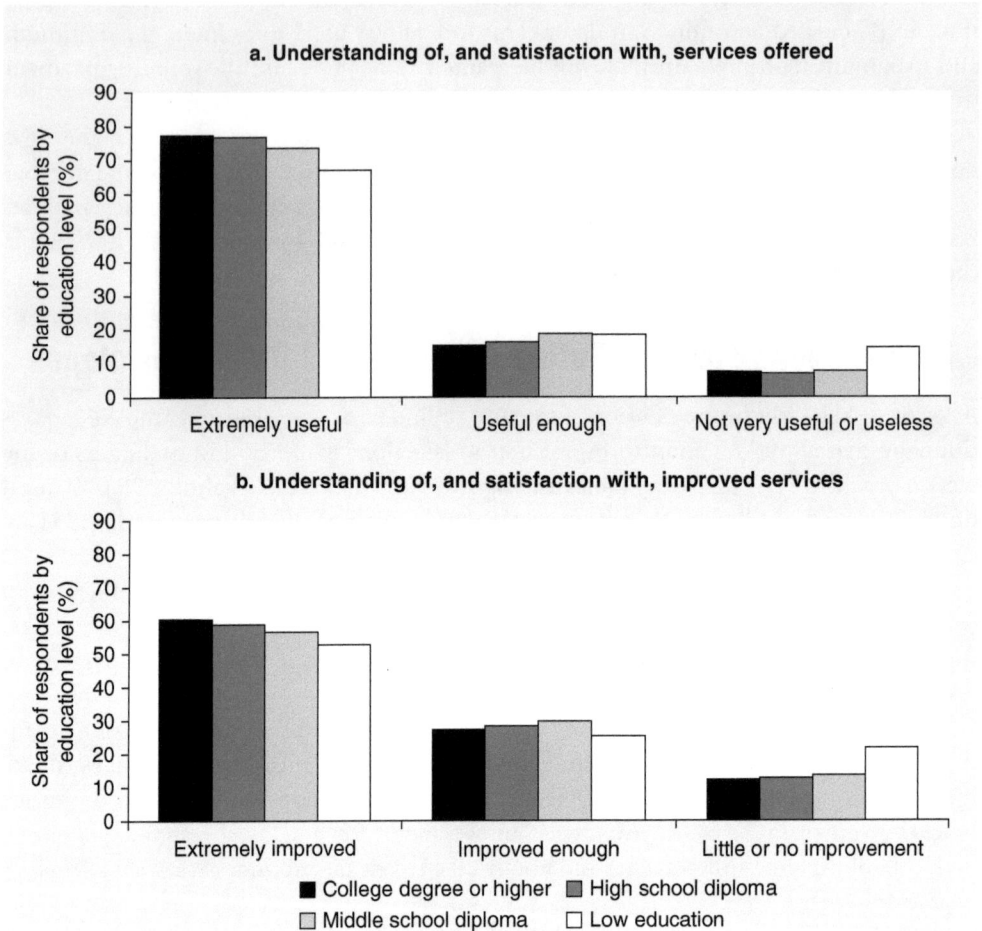

a. Understanding of, and satisfaction with, services offered

b. Understanding of, and satisfaction with, improved services

SOURCE: Italian Social Security Institute (INPS) data.

This is interpreted as "bare bones" proof that respondents might take precise actions based on new information received about their future pensions.

A series of nonparametric local polynomial regressions was also performed to show how the age profile is associated with a different probability of overestimating the future pension or of taking action after the simulation (as indicated by the *willing_change* dummy). Figure 27.6 shows much heterogeneity in the ability to estimate the future pension along different age profiles. In particular, between ages 45 and 65, where the sample is thicker and the local polynomial is estimated more precisely, the inability to estimate the pension properly has a reverse U-shaped form. This inability grows until about age 55 and then tends to decrease sharply. This demonstrates that individuals tend to gather more information on their pension only when they start to approach retirement. In line with this tendency, the willingness to take action after receiving information about the future pension also has a reverse U-shaped pattern (figure 27.7). The growth pattern is less pronounced for the age bracket 45–65 than before, but the propensity to change

TABLE 27.1 **Summary statistics from "My future pension" user satisfaction survey**

Variable	Mean	Median	Standard deviation
Willing_change	0.38	0.0	0.48
Overestimating	0.42	0.0	0.49
Female	0.26	0.0	0.44
Age	52.15	54.0	8.31
No education	0.00	0.0	0.04
Primary school	0.01	0.0	0.10
Middle school diploma	0.19	0.0	0.39
High school diploma	0.58	1.0	0.49
BA degree	0.18	0.0	0.39
Higher than BA	0.04	0.0	0.19
Very useful	0.76	1.0	0.42
Unfriendly	0.05	0.0	0.22
Need_help	0.06	0.0	0.24
Night	0.07	0.0	0.26

SOURCE: Original estimates based on Italian Social Security Institute (INPS) data.

FIGURE 27.6 **Local linear regression of *overestimating* as a function of *age***

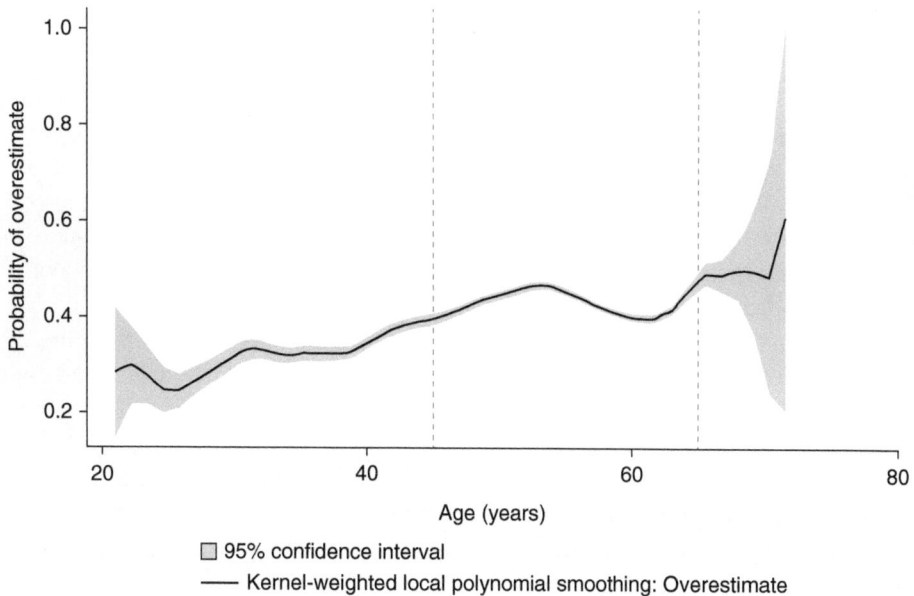

SOURCE: Original estimation based on Italian Social Security Institute (INPS) data.

NOTE: Dependent variable: *overestimating*; Regressor: *age*.

FIGURE 27.7 **Local linear regression of *willing_change* as a function of *age***
whole sample

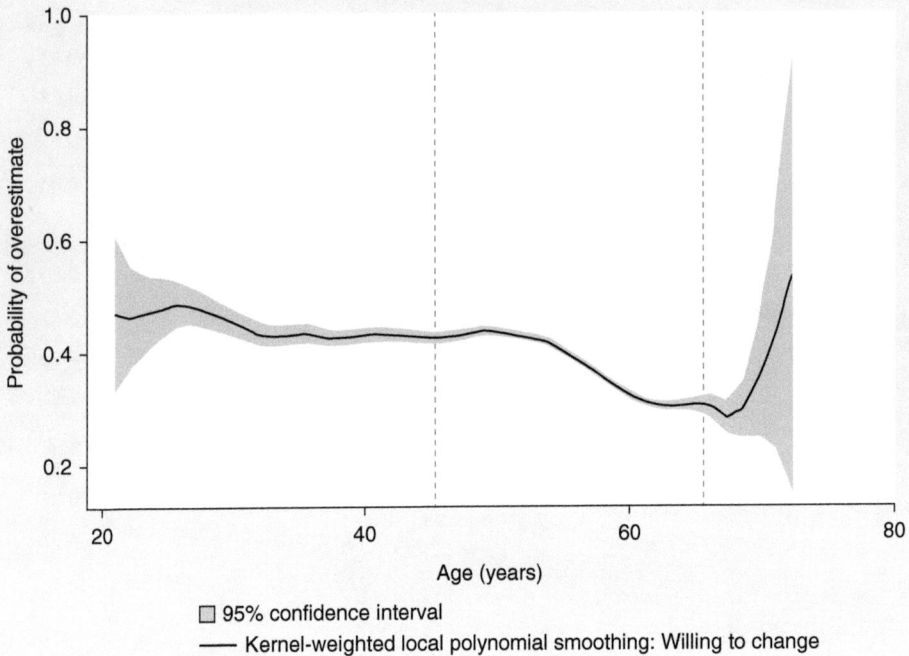

SOURCE: Original estimation based on Italian Social Security Institute (INPS) data.

NOTE: Dependent variable: *willing_change*; Regressor: *age*.

expectations is high until age 55 and decreases sharply afterward. Figure 27.8 shows a similar pattern, but the willingness to change is always higher than that shown in figure 27.7. This evidence is straightforward considering that these data include just people who overestimate their future pensions.

Taken together these two pictures suggest that those who overestimate their future pension are then more willing to change their habits after receiving information on their realistic pension check—that is, when the information gap shrinks.

Finally, individuals age 55 and older found the simulation less useful (figure 27.9), confirming that the information provided is less useful when individuals already have a decent estimate of their pensions in mind. These last results are interpreted as bare bones proof that when respondents tend to overestimate more, the information provided by the simulation is more useful and respondents are therefore more satisfied with the program. Conversely, the slight drop just after age 60 suggests that older people are less satisfied because they have less time and fewer opportunities to take action to increase their future pension.

The last set of estimates is aimed at understanding why individuals overestimate their future pensions and which characteristics induce them to revise their expectations and to subsequently take some action after receiving better information about their pensions.

FIGURE 27.8 **Local linear regression of *willing_change* as a function of *age***
sample of overestimators

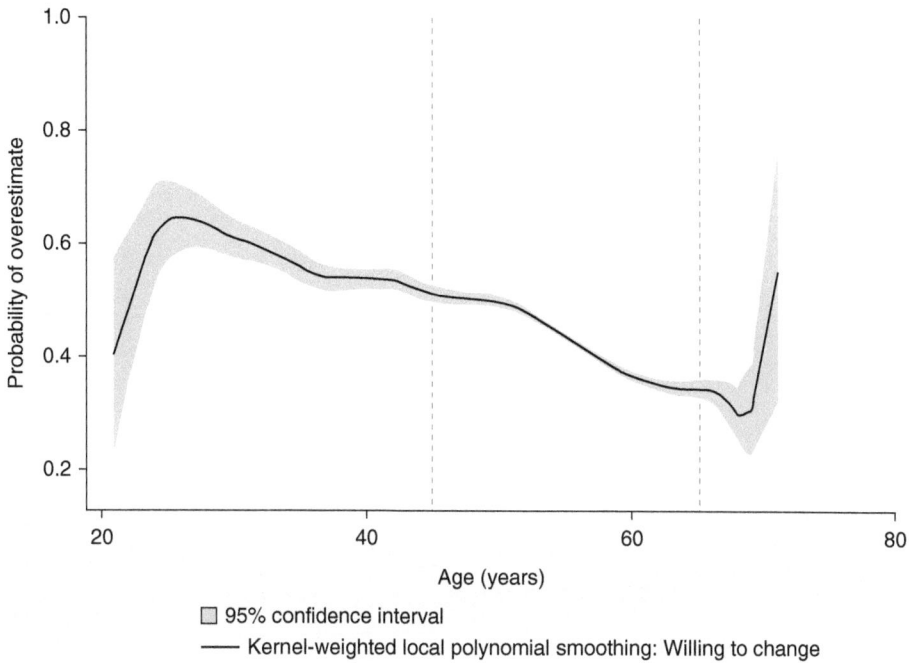

◻ 95% confidence interval
—— Kernel-weighted local polynomial smoothing: Willing to change

SOURCE: Original estimation based on Italian Social Security Institute (INPS) data.

NOTE: Dependent variable: *willing_change* conditioned; Regressor: *age*. Analytic sample restricted to those who overestimated their future pensions.

First, it is worth remembering that an empirical analysis on this sample cannot claim causal results. The online simulations were performed by individuals who self-selected into the INPS website; these individuals have a higher demand for financial information and are probably more literate on this topic. To control for this self-selection bias, information on education and on the difficulties encountered in performing the simulation is used.

The first two columns of table 27.2 show the first specification. This is an instrumental variable (IV) regression in which *willing_change* is the dependent variable. It is assumed that *willing_change* might be predicted by *overestimating,* so the analysis studies how overestimating the future pension affects willingness to take action after being given new financial information. This setup specifies *overestimating* as the endogenous variable, instrumented using the education dummies *unfriendly, need_help,* and *night.*

The rationale behind this specification is that one's precision in estimating a future pension derives from one's financial literacy and ability to perform the simulation; the instruments want to capture these skills. The model's specification implicitly assumed that education and ability to perform the simulation predict *willing_change* just through the ability to estimate. The first-stage regression on *overestimating* should resolve the selection bias due to unobserved financial literacy and produce consistent estimates on the

FIGURE 27.9 **Local linear regression of *very useful* as a function of *age***

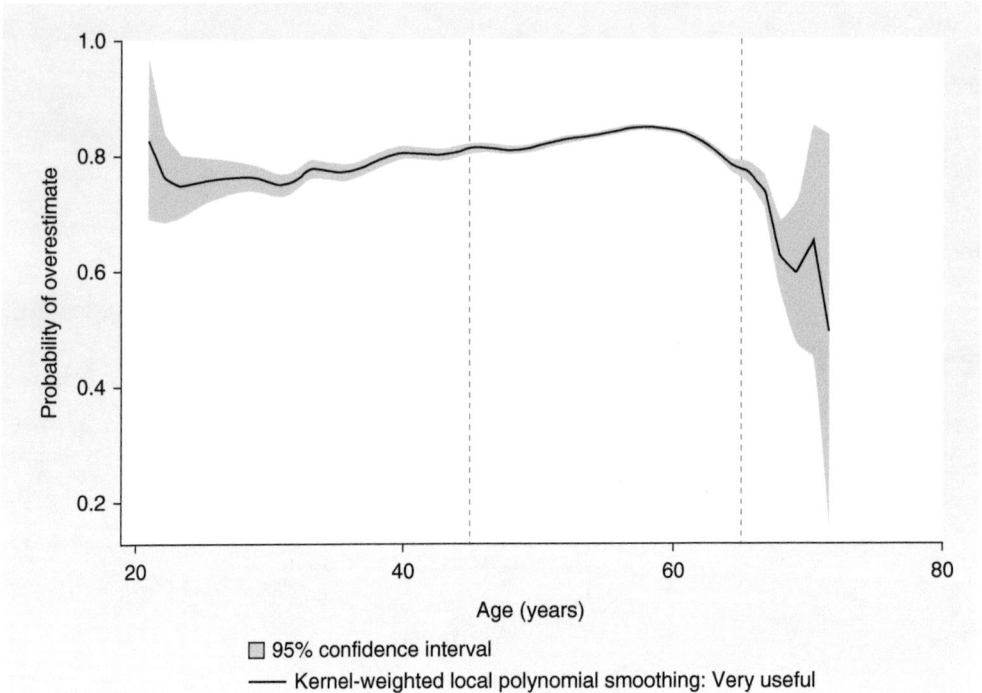

SOURCE: Original estimation based on Italian Social Security Institute (INPS) data.

NOTE: Dependent variable: *very useful*; Regressor: *age*.

correlation between *overestimating* and *willing_change* in the second stage. The model is closed by controlling for sociodemographic characteristics and a set of 20 regional and 6 education dummies. For brevity, estimates for these dummies are not reported, but they are mostly in line with theoretical expectations.[8] Even if far from being causal, some of the results are still informative.

The IV model shows that when individuals fail to accurately estimate their future pension, they tend to change their willingness to take action in the future. Individuals who overestimate have a higher propensity to declare that they will change their future decisions regarding their pension, 29 percent more on average in comparison with individuals who do not overestimate. It is also worth noticing that the constant term in this regression indicates that a benchmark individual who does not overestimate[9] declares a willingness to change his or her future actions in just 7 percent of the cases. A Kleibergen-Paap test shows that the instruments are relevant. In general, women do not tend to overestimate more than men, but they seem to be more prone to take action after an overestimation (3 percent more compared with men). Those who do not find the program user friendly, or who declared to have asked for help using the program, have a higher probability of overestimating. The age profile results confirm the reversed U-shaped relationship already shown in the local linear regression analysis. The third column of table 27.2 is the "acid" form model[10] for the IV shown in the first and second columns. The "acid" specification confirms the previous findings and reports a positive and significant relation for *overestimating*.

TABLE 27.2 **Results of instrumental variable and ordinary least squares regressions of** *willing_change* **on** *overestimating*

	Instrumental variable First stage		Instrumental variable Second stage		Ordinary least squares Willing_change		Ordinary least squares Willing_change	
	Coefficient	P value	Coefficient	P value	Coefficient	P value	Coefficient	P value
Overestimating			.297	0.000	.169	0.000	.164	0.000
Female	.001	0.735	.032	0.000	.034	0.000	.033	0.000
Age	.030	0.000	.015	0.000	.014	0.000	.014	0.000
Age squared	−.000	0.000	−.000	0.000	−.000	0.000	−.000	0.000
Unfriendly	.182	0.000			−.063	0.000	−.063	0.000
Need_help	.048	0.000			−.010	0.117	−.010	0.000
Night	−.008	0.178			− 0.15	0.010	−.015	0.010
No education							−.110	0.175
Primary school							−.079	0.018
Middle school diploma							−.043	0.000
BA degree							.064	0.000
Higher than BA							.084	0.000
Constant	−.3635082	0.000	.070	0.140	.166	.000	.173	0.000
Education level in financial education	YES		YES		YES		YES	
Regional financial education level	YES		YES		YES		YES	
Kleibergen-Paap test		863.615						
Observations		89,358						

SOURCE: Original estimation based on Italian Social Security Institute (INPS) data.

As expected by the "acid" form, the coefficient is lower in magnitude in comparison with the IV coefficient. The "acid" model confirms almost all the findings of the IV specification; notably, the reversed U-shaped pattern for the age profile is confirmed.

In the last column of table 27.2, the "acid" specification is enhanced with a series of interaction dummies created by multiplying the *overestimating* dummy and the six education dummies. The results from this specification confirm the previous findings on the relationship between the main variables of interest. Moreover, the interaction terms suggest that an "overestimating" individual with a higher education level is more willing to change his or her actions concerning future pensions than someone with a lower education level. These results lead to two interesting interpretations. First, more educated individuals exploit new financial information more easily, and are thus more prone to take action. Second, lower-educated individuals might give up after receiving negative information about their ability to estimate their future pensions because they get discouraged when they realize that they did not estimate well.

Finally, the impact of providing additional information about future pensions on workers' behavior is evaluated using a sample of 1,000 people (who completed the survey) who used the program twice: the first time between June and September 2015, the second time between June and September 2016. For this sample, the analysis looks at the amount of contributions accrued in 2015 and 2016 (based on the last salary available on users' records).

The findings suggest that those workers who had a tendency to overestimate their future pensions before using the program increased the amount of hours worked (thus increasing their yearly salary and contributions). In fact, all respondents who overestimated their future pension showed an average increase in their salaries from one year to the next of about 7.8 percent. In contrast, those people who correctly estimated (or underestimated) the amount of their future pensions displayed an average increase in their salary of about 3.5 percent.

Summary and Conclusions

In the mid-1990s Italy made the transition to a nonfinancial defined contribution pension system. However, this transition was implemented very gradually, and will be fully completed only in the 2040s. The law that introduced this radical change in the Italian pension system envisaged a communication campaign to ensure that all Italian citizens would be able to fully grasp the implications of the reform to their future pensions. Yet this campaign was not launched for 20 years. Considering that financial literacy in Italy is below the EU average (37 percent versus 52 percent), this type of communication is essential.

In May 2015 INPS developed an online program "My future pension"—followed by the dispatch of about 4 million Orange Envelopes—that allows contributors to calculate an estimated future pension on the basis of their past careers and on the projection of their future contributions until retirement.

During the first three years of the project, more than 3 million contributors logged onto INPS's website to calculate their future pensions. Taking advantage of the program's interactive features, users simulated different scenarios (more than four on average), such as simulating gaps in their future contributions or a less favorable growth scenario for the Italian economy.

The feedback received thus far on this communication campaign is encouraging. About 80 percent of all users rate this service as either "very helpful" or "extremely helpful." Roughly two-thirds of all users declare that the service significantly improved their understanding of the different factors that will determine their future pensions. Roughly one-third state that they are likely to revise their expectations regarding their future pensions. These revisions are more frequent among contributors who overestimated their future pensions, and, conditional on this overestimation, among those who are better educated.

To establish a causal effect of information on expectations, and potentially behavior, one would need to draw on random samples of treated and untreated individuals. The only available data to date are from a survey of those who used the service and completed the questionnaire attached to the simulation exercise. However, the IV estimates are consistent with a causal effect of the information provided by the survey on the revision of expectations.

These results are reassuring for the current communication campaign launched by INPS among workers planning to take the *ape volontaria*, a bank loan provided at a subsidized rate for workers close to retirement, using the future pension as collateral. Given the complexity of the measure and the quasi-permanent effects it will have on monthly pensions, INPS structured a communication package to ensure that workers who opt for this measure are fully aware of all of its implications. Working closely with trade unions, INPS developed a communication kit, published on its website, that describes the different early retirement options introduced by the 2016 Budget Law and the potential beneficiaries. It also developed a new online simulator that allows interested parties to estimate the amount of their future pensions and the amount to be repaid if they opt for *ape volontaria*.

INPS
Istituto Nazionale Previdenza Sociale

ANNEX 27A

Mario Rossi
Address

Subject: Calculate your future pension

Dear Mr Mario Rossi,

INPS has recently released on its website the pension estimator "My future pension." This useful tool can help you estimate the amount of **your future pension**.

In this letter we provide some information on the monthly allowance you will be able to count on when you retire.

The calculation is based on your contribution record and on an estimate of your future contributions. This calculation is not legally binding.

The forecast of your pension

The calculation of your future pension is based on current legislation. Its amount depends on GDP growth rate, retirement age, working career and salary profile.

You can find the retirement date, the pension amount and both gross and net replacement rate in the table below.

	Old age benefit	Early retirement benefit
Retirement date		
Forecast of pension		
Forecast of last salary before the retirement		
Gross replacement rate		
Net replacement rate		

Warning: Extra rules/conditions allowing you to anticipate the retirement are not considered

Personal contribution account

The personal contribution record used to forecast your pension consists of two components: the first includes the sum of contributions you have already paid, the second is a projection of the amount of contributions you will pay, provided that your career path will not change.

Your contribution record

Contribution source	Period		Contribution accrued (week)		Earning	INPS Code
	Since	To	Right	Measure		
Employee fund						
Deemed contribution: sickness						

Warning: You may need personal assistance from INPS to collect information on the different options available to you to value your contributions from different periods and INPS funds.

Your future contribution record—simulated

Contribution Source	Period		Contribution accrued (week)		Earning
	Since	To	Right	Measure	
Employee fund					

You can use the online pension calculator "My future pension" (www.inps.it) to assess the impact of changes in key assumptions (retirement age, total contribution accrued etc.) on your future pension and to make a tailored simulation of the future benefit. To use "My future pension" you need SPID (Public Digital Identity System), if necessary, we can provide SPID upon request.

EXAMPLE OF SWEDISH ORANGE LETTER

Annual Statement 2018

PENSIONS
MYNDIGHETEN

You have earned this much towards your National Public Pension

Your Pension Accounts

Changes during 2017 in SEK	Income pension	Premium pension	
Value 2016-12-31	1 078 853	226 710	
Pension entitlement for 2016	52 448	8 238	
Reduction of the pension entitlement due to balancing	- 552	-	
From deceased contributors	368	168	
Administration and fund fee	- 354	- 1 314*	**Total earned to the national public pension**
Change in value	29 503	16 289**	
Value 2017-12-31	1 160 266	250 091	**1 401 185 kr**

* Including SEK 1710 discount on the fee for 2016.
** Including SEK 82 as interest on your pension entitlement for 2016.

Your Premium Pension

Premium pension account 2017-12-31	Value, SEK	Change in value, per cent	Fund fee, per cent	Chosen allocation, per cent	Current allocation, per cent
Equity Fund Sverige	73 502	11	0,47	30	29
Equity Fund Global	82 510	13	0,57	25	33
Interest Fund Sverige	18 759	1	0,14	25	8
Generation Fund	49 852	10	0,21	10	20
Pharmaceutical Fund	25 468	8	0,49	10	10
Total	250 091	10	0,43	100	100
The average pension saver		*10*	*0,23*		

Notes

1. Legislative Decree n.503/1992; Law n. 335/1995; Law n. 449/1997; Law n. 243/2004; and Legislative Decree n. 252/ 2005.

2. Comparing the prereform period (1989–91) and the postreform period (2000–02), the percentage of people who overestimate or underestimate their replacement rate by 25 percent or more increased from 10 percent to 14 percent among employees, from 10 percent to 16 percent among civil servants, and from 11 percent to 29 percent among the self-employed (Bottazzi, Jappelli, and Padula 2006).

3. One year after the Amato reform, changes in complementary pension systems were approved to develop a supplementary funded pillar (D.Lgs n.124/1993).

4. Pensions are related to the contribution paid over the working life, indexed every year until retirement by a five-year moving average of gross domestic product growth. Capitalized contributions are then annualized at retirement by multiplying them by an age-related conversion coefficient.

5. The proposal for Swedish reform was drawn up between 1992 and 1994 but it was adopted in 1998. For a detailed description of the Swedish pension reform, see Pollnerová (2002).

6. Of these INPS-insured employees, about 15 million are in the private sector and almost 4 million are self-employed.

7. Examples of the personal statement sent by INPS and by the Swedish Pensions Agency are shown in annex 27A.

8. These results are available upon request from the authors.

9. The benchmark individual is a male resident in Abruzzo Region with a high school diploma.

10. In the IV setting, the "acid form" is a specification in which the dependent variable is regressed on the endogenous covariates and the instruments.

References

Botazzi, Renata, Tullio Jappelli, and Mario Padula. 2006. "Retirement Expectations, Pension Reforms and Their Impact on Private Wealth Accumulation." *Journal of Public Economics* 90 (12): 2187–212.

di Salvatore, Antonietta, Francesco Franceschi, Andrea Neri, and Francesca Zanichelli. 2017. "Measuring Financial Literacy of the Italian Adult Population." Paper presented at the 61st World Statistics Congress of the International Statistics Institute, Marrakech, Morocco, July 16–21.

Jappelli, Tullio, Immacolata Marino, and Mario Padula. 2014. "Households' Saving and Debt in Italy." *Journal of Economic Policy* 2–3: 175–202.

Klapper, Leora, Annamaria Lusardi, and Peter van Oudheusden. 2015. *Financial Literacy around the World: Insights from the Standard & Poor's Ratings Services Global Financial Literacy Survey.* https://www.finlit.mhfi.com.

Lusardi, Annamaria, and Olivia S. Mitchell. 2011. "The Outlook for Financial Literacy." In *Financial Literacy: Implications for Retirement Security and the Financial Marketplace*, edited by Olivia S. Mitchell and Annamaria Lusardi, 1–13. New York: Oxford University Press.

OECD (Organisation for Economic Co-operation and Development). 2014. *PISA 2012 Results: Students and Money. Financial Literacy Skills for the 21st CENTURY, Volume VI.* Paris: OECD Publishing.

Pollnerová, Štěpánka. 2002. "Analysis of Recently Introduced NDC Systems." Research Institute for Labour and Social Affairs, Prague, Czech Republic.

CHAPTER 28

The Politics of NDC Pension Scheme Diffusion: Constraints and Drivers

Igor Guardiancich, Kent Weaver, Gustavo Demarco, and Mark C. Dorfman

Introduction

Proponents of pension reforms based on nonfinancial defined contribution (NDC) principles argue that NDC displays a number of desirable properties in terms of efficiency, fairness, and financial sustainability. NDC schemes influence individuals' choices to work in the formal labor market and contribute to their own pensions (micro efficiency). Inclusion of life expectancy in the benefit calculation encourages participants to work longer, because postponing retirement is rewarded. If these incentives work, then the supply of a country's labor, and thereby gross domestic product (GDP), increase (macro efficiency). NDC schemes guarantee both intragenerational fairness—that is, that each monetary unit contributed yields one unit in benefits (plus imputed interest)—and intergenerational fairness by guaranteeing that each generation pays the same percentage of income in contributions. The NDC approach facilitates financial sustainability, as do financial defined contribution (FDC) schemes, but without the burden of financing the transition costs.

NDC-based reforms have, at times, enjoyed support from powerful international actors such as the World Bank. Reversals of some FDC reforms (Holzmann 2013) and growing awareness of the associated financial market challenges might also create further openings for NDC reforms. The NDC design offers potential political advantages to policy makers, notably, eliminating or lowering the need for repeated ad hoc pension retrenchment measures that may be politically costly to the officeholders who impose them (Brooks and Weaver 2006). Repeated ad hoc reforms may also have negative impacts on the legitimacy of and trust in pension systems.

Despite these potential advantages, the diffusion of NDC pensions has been limited in recent years. A first cluster of NDC pension system adoptions occurred in the 1990s in Italy, Latvia, Poland, and Sweden. Countries with successful implementation, such as Sweden, required only minor subsequent adjustments (Weaver 2016). Countries with more challenging implementation, such as Italy, needed more extensive interventions, but they seldom directly clashed with the NDC logic (Jessoula and Raitano 2017). Ultimately, Italy's NDC scheme was tightened up with the 2011–12 Fornero reform.

The authors are grateful to Bernhard Ebbinghaus, Alexi Gugushvili, and Marek Naczyk for comments and suggestions.

This relatively successful first wave was not followed by massive adoption elsewhere. Around the turn of the century, reforms followed in places such as the Kyrgyz Republic and the Russian Federation, but they were never properly implemented or, as in Russia, were reversed. In 2009, Norway introduced an NDC pillar and has retained it.

In the 21st century, especially since the global financial crisis of 2008–09, adoption of more limited automatic stabilizing mechanisms (ASMs), often accompanied by incremental retrenchment mechanisms and sometimes by the creation of small FDC tiers, largely supplanted NDC pension reforms in the policy repertoires of most advanced industrial economies. Balancing mechanisms were introduced in Germany, Lithuania, and Spain. Benefits are tied to life expectancy in Finland, France, Portugal, and Spain. The statutory retirement age is tied to life expectancy in Cyprus, Denmark, Finland, Greece, the Netherlands, Portugal, and the Slovak Republic (European Commission 2018, 36).

Hence the puzzle addressed in this chapter is as follows: Why, given that NDC appears to address many of the policy design and political problems confronted by pension planners, has it not been accepted more frequently by policy makers? Is it due to complex transitional arrangements, opposition from powerful societal actors, or perceptions that it will harm some societal groups (such as women or workers with low lifetime earnings) (Foster 2014; James 2012)? Or does it result from the technically demanding implementation that requires a trained and qualified administration, or from the shortcomings in the communication strategies of its proponents? Does the very "transparency" of NDC systems in making the redistributive elements of pensions clear and paying contributions for them out of general revenues rather than cross-subsidies from other workers heighten distributional conflicts? Or are the causes more explicitly political: the fear of reelection-oriented politicians that imposing cutbacks in pension promises, albeit unsustainable, through NDC reforms will be used against them in the next election?

A central argument of this chapter is that the causal forces are complex. Although political constraints are ubiquitous, politicians in some countries are better positioned than others to create durable cross-party cartels in favor of NDC. The weight of other factors has differed across reform "waves" and regions. In many European Union (EU) countries, adoption of limited ASMs, advocated by European institutions, serves as a substitute for NDC reforms. These boundary-straddling reforms are easier for policy makers to understand; can be tailored to path-dependent policy inheritances; send clearer signals about expectations for longer working lives; and pose a lower risk of unexpected blame-generating, year-on-year nominal cuts in benefits as a result of the triggering of ASMs. In developing and transitional economies, NDC-based reforms are often adopted with little buy-in or even understanding of NDC pensions by domestic elites, making them vulnerable to reversal when problems arise or elite preferences change.

Definitions and Patterns

BACKGROUND INFORMATION

NDC pension systems are usually defined as having four characteristics (Holzmann 2017; Holzmann and Palmer 2006b; Palmer 2006, 2012). First, they operate on a pay-as-you-go (PAYG) basis, although they may have modest buffer funds to cover the cyclical effects on liquidity. Second, benefits are based on lifetime earnings rather than earnings over a certain number of years; each additional year of contributions provides additional benefits. Third, the retirement age is flexible, and benefits are adjusted to reflect a longer or shorter duration of anticipated payment. Finally, they contain automatic mechanisms to adjust benefits for changes in life expectancy and macroeconomic and demographic (including fertility and net migration) performance. Contribution rates are fixed.

The outcomes of pension reform processes are divided into two dimensions (table 28.1). The rows contain different outcomes with respect to NDC pension reforms. Countries that adopted NDC early (Italy and Sweden) are labeled "Innovators." Countries that adopted NDC later or with external technical assistance are called "Adapters." Countries that adopted NDC reforms and then either did not implement them or dropped them are called "Dropouts." Those that adopted some form of ASMs without a full NDC reform are labeled "Boundary Straddlers." Countries where NDC was considered but rejected, or where NDC never reached the agenda and incremental reforms were adopted instead, are labeled "Incrementalists." Because NDC and FDC pillars both have the objective of tightening the link between lifetime contributions and pension benefits (Góra 2001), the columns show outcomes with respect to adoption of FDC tiers.

The patterns shown, while hardly startling, are nonetheless noteworthy: Latin American countries generally adopted FDC reforms early, before NDC reforms were on the international reform agenda. A first NDC reform wave was confined to Western Europe (Italy and Sweden) and some postsocialist countries (Latvia and

TABLE 28.1 **Nonfinancial defined contribution policy-making outcomes in selected countries**

Outcome	Countries without FDC pillars	Countries with FDC pillars
NDC innovators		Italy (1995); Sweden (1991–98)
NDC adapters	Norway (2009)	Latvia (1996); Poland (1997–98)
Boundary straddlers		
Statutory retirement age linked to life expectancy	Cyprus; Denmark (2011); Finland (2015); Greece (2010); Italy (2010); Malta; Netherlands (2012); Portugal (2013)	Slovak Republic (2012)
Benefits linked to life expectancy	Finland (2005); France (2003); Portugal (2007); Spain (2011)	
Other or multiple stabilizing mechanisms	Canada (1997) and Quebec (2011); Greece (2012); Germany (1997 and 2004); Spain (2013)	Lithuania (2016)
Dropouts	Kyrgyz Republic (1997); Mongolia (1999)	Russian Federation (2002); Egypt, Arab Rep. (2010)
Incrementalists	Austria; Brazil; Japan; Slovenia	Hungary; Estonia

SOURCE: European Commission 2018, 54.

NOTE: The year of reform adoption is in brackets. Several years apply to incrementalists. FDC = financial defined contribution; NDC = nonfinancial defined contribution.

Poland); it occurred for the most part in the late 1990s. FDC-expanding reforms were often enacted simultaneously or in close temporal proximity with NDC reforms. A second wave of NDC reforms in former Soviet bloc countries occurred at the turn of the century, but these reforms proved more fragile; most of these NDC systems were not sustained. A third wave of boundary-straddling reforms that use automatic stabilizing adjustments without full-blown adoption of NDC took place since the early 2000s, especially in EU countries. However, neither NDC nor boundary-straddling reforms have had sustained takers outside Europe and the former Soviet bloc. In Latin America, for example, where the shortcomings of privatized FDC pensions led to many policy changes in recent years, there has not been a rush to NDC as a substitute or complement. Understanding these patterns and the underlying political logic is the purpose of the rest of this chapter.

THEORETICAL PERSPECTIVES ON NDC DIFFUSION

To address the politics of diffusion of NDC, this chapter uses the analytical framework developed by Kingdon (2002). Kingdon argues that for issues to reach and remain on the policy agenda, there must be a conjunction between at least two of three (and preferably all three) policy-making streams—problems, policy, and politics. These policy streams often operate quite separately from one another, with distinctive sets of actors and dynamics.

- In the problem stream, the public and policy elites must perceive a problem to be both important and solvable; issues tend to get on the agenda after a "focusing event," such as a financial crisis.

- In the policy stream, there must be policy proposals that appear to be technically, financially, and politically feasible. Its proponents must have resources, skills, and communication strategies to connect their proposals to concrete concerns of policy makers, the public, and social actors and to address their potential shortcomings. Skilled policy entrepreneurs often play a critical role in selling policy prescriptions that they have already developed to politicians.

- Finally, in the politics stream, changes in the public's policy priorities (often as a result of focusing events), changes in policy elites (often resulting from elections), and pressure from interest groups all influence which issues and proposals make it onto the agenda and which remain on it or fall off.

Path dependence matters for both the policy and politics streams; proposals that impose substantial costs on identifiable groups relative to the status quo are unlikely to remain on the policy agenda. In moving from agenda setting to policy adoption, the structure of political institutions—the existence of multiple veto points or supermajority requirements—affects the prospects for changes from the status quo.

Applying the framework to NDC reforms, in the problem stream a fiscal or economic crisis is likely to turn policy makers' attention to festering pension financing problems. Yet this is not a sufficient condition for adoption of NDC reforms, given that they provide little immediate fiscal relief unless applied retroactively. Governments that also face substantial medium- and long-term financing problems in their public pension systems may consider structural pension reforms. However, restructuring through NDC is unlikely to make it to the agenda unless incremental refinancing and retrenchment options have been exhausted. So,

> Hypothesis 1 (H1): NDC-based reforms are most likely to make it on the agenda during a fiscal or economic crisis, when (a) a short-term budget crisis is combined with (b) medium- and long-term pension funding problems, and (c) incremental pension refinancing and retrenchment initiatives have already been exhausted.

In the policy stream, path dependence also influences the direction of pension reform (Bonoli and Palier 2007). As Pierson (1994, 1998) explains, any set of pension or other entitlements being disbursed according to some criterion generates interest groups who will fight against the elimination of such a distributive status quo. Additionally, there is negativity bias—a term borrowed from cognitive psychology—in which people (in this case, voters) are more sensitive to the imposition of losses than to the granting of benefits. The problem of path dependence worsens the larger the pension system is and the more special benefits (for example, rights to early retirement) it distributes to specific groups of beneficiaries who seek to retain those benefits.

A move to an NDC system is most likely from pension systems that are earnings-related, because it involves less redistribution (and hence, fewer perceived losses) than transitions from systems such as universal flat-rate systems (Weaver 2010). However, if the link is already fairly strong, the extra political capital needed to move to an NDC system may be perceived as wasted. Thus, intermediate cases—defined benefit (DB) systems with weak contribution-benefit links—may be the likeliest candidates for adoption. Indeed, Italy, Latvia, and Poland were all cases of unsustainable single-pillar DB systems. Groups enjoying special pension privileges can be expected to fight to continue those privileges, however. Overall,

> H2: NDC reforms are most likely to be adopted (a) in DB benefit systems, in which (b) adequate historical payroll records exist, (c) pension benefits are fragmented across multiple benefit regimes, and (d) benefit–lifetime contribution linkages exist but are relatively weak.

Also in the policy stream, multiple transnational actors have long been involved in advocating for particular approaches to public pension provision, from the International Labour Organization (ILO) and the International Social Security Association to the World Bank and the Organisation for Economic Co-operation and Development (Brooks 2005; Ervik, Kildal, and Nilssen 2009; Melo 2004; Orenstein 2008; Stepan and Anderson 2014; Teichman 2004). Policy experts from Chile were also involved in many of the Latin American privatization reforms, and Swedish experts in providing technical advice on NDC reforms. Transnational actors can participate in several stages of the pension reform process, including formulation and commitment building within the government, coalition building to promote adoption of the proposal, and policy implementation (Orenstein 2005, 2008).

The views of the international community evolved, with the World Bank moving away from a focus on FDC reforms toward giving "enhanced focus on basic income provision for all vulnerable elderly" (Holzmann and Hinz 2005, 2) and increased recognition to the importance of initial conditions for correct policy design (Gill, Packard, and Yermo 2004).

In addition to the norm-teaching potential of transnational actors, there may be coercion through conditionality: governments facing fiscal difficulties are likely to respond to the preferences of transnational actors if financial incentives are attached. Most research suggests, however, that even where international financial institutions played a strong role in advocating particular actions, the preferences of domestic elites and path dependency from previous pension policy choices were the dominant factors in individual governments' decisions.

Earlier research suggests that several mechanisms may be at work in the transnational spread of pension reform models. Weyland's research on the pattern of FDC pension diffusion in Latin America emphasizes the cognitive limitations of domestic policy makers that restrict "policy makers' range of attention and restricts the options they consider" (Weyland 2005, 290). For example, the widespread knowledge of the Chilean model and its perceived successes help explain the extensive adoption of FDC on the continent. By contrast, NDC reforms were "for most of the 1990s not cognitively available in Latin America" (Weyland 2005, 289–90). Moreover, lower-income countries adopting FDC reforms expected rewards in international status and investment associated with the privatization of their pension system (Brooks 2007). Thus, for a number of mutually nonexclusive reasons, NDC failed to become the dominant pension reform option in any region. This may have inhibited its adoption because it lowered both its cognitive availability and perceived plausibility. The concept underscoring NDC is as understandable, if not easier, to comprehend than that of some competing options on offer, but its implementation is technically demanding. This challenge may inhibit its salability to domestic ministries, especially where the potential "buyer" sees its country's situation and capacity as very different from that of earlier European adopters of NDC-based pension reforms.

EU policy recommendations and direct legislative intervention are another potential institutional influence on the design of EU member states' pension systems, despite the absence of the EU's competences in the field. As a consequence of the sovereign debt crisis, the EU's involvement in pension policy making has been stepped up through the European Semester, a tool for macroeconomic coordination (Guardiancich and Natali 2017), and tougher conditionality mechanisms, such as the financial assistance programs provided to several Southern and Eastern European member states.

The single firm recommendation of the European Commission was the adoption of a specific ASM—that is, linking retirement age to life expectancy (European Commission 2011). In addition, the Council of the EU added the possibility of linking life expectancy to either retirement age or pension benefits, thereby increasing the palette of available options and, hence, of political room for maneuver for individual member states (Guidi and Guardiancich 2018).

In practical terms, ASMs were adopted in a dozen EU countries (table 28.1). Such adoptions, of course, do not solve the underlying financial problems of individual pension systems generated, for example, by excessively generous benefits. At most, they may help avoid a further decline in sustainability. Accordingly, the advantages of defined contributions have not been seized, as European reforms have fallen short of a full transition to NDC and long-term financial sustainability.

In contrast to the EU, the World Bank has strongly advocated NDC pension reform, publishing several volumes on the subject (Holzmann and Palmer 2006a; Holzmann, Palmer, and Robalino 2012, 2013) and including NDC reforms in advice to a number of countries. NDC-based reforms, however, never have enjoyed the hegemonic position within World Bank advice-giving that FDC reforms did in the 1990s.

The OECD and the ILO have not been strong advocates for NDC-based pension reforms. Neither organization recommends a particular type of pension system for adoption by its members, and both often discuss one or another pension system characteristic. For example, the ILO (2017) engaged in the promotion of noncontributory basic pension schemes, and the OECD (2017) suggested how to implement flexible retirement effectively. Yet both organizations have openly shown some aversion to NDC schemes. The ILO has been skeptical about defined contributions because they shift the responsibility on to the future beneficiary in the absence of explicit redistribution. Whitehouse (2010, 2012) claims that few benefits are to be reaped by implementing complex NDC reforms. Similarly, Cichon (1999, 87) argues that "most of [NDC's] potential financial and distributive effects could also be achieved by a classical, linear defined-benefit formula." NDC proponents disagree with both analyses, which focus only on the benefit calculation formula and do not address the other advantages of NDC regarding fairness, efficiency, and fiscal sustainability.

Considering both the norm-teaching potential and the coercive potential of transnational actors and the "availability heuristic,"

> H3: NDC reforms are most likely to be adopted when (a) there are close linkages between host country elites and policy experts advocating for NDC reforms, and (b) conditionality and/or promises of financial assistance make adoption of NDC reforms financially attractive. (c) Adoption of NDC reforms by other countries in the same region perceived as "peers" also increases the probability of their adoption. Adoption of NDC is less likely (d) when EU bodies are the primary providers of advice and financing to their own member states in the wake of the global financial crisis.

Most of the cross-national research on pension reform suggests that even countries under economic duress are not pure "policy takers"; the nature of the interaction between transnational and domestic actors is critical. In the politics stream, NDC proposals are unlikely to make it to the policy agenda unless they have at least one powerful domestic institutional advocate. In a survey-based study of pension reform processes, Chłoń and Góra (2003) find that ministries of labor generally played the most important role, followed by ministries of finance and international institutions, but substantial variation arose across countries and regions. Given the key roles of ministries of finance in most countries, their support is likely to be especially important. Hence,

> H4: NDC-based reform is more likely to be adopted (a) if at least one prominent domestic agency in the host country supports it, especially (b) the ministry of finance.

In the politics stream, even if NDC pension proposals make it to the agenda, they are unlikely to be adopted in political systems featuring multiple veto points (for example, separation of powers, bicameral legislatures, and powerful courts that can overturn reform legislation) unless all veto points are controlled by actors with similar policy preferences. Thus,

> H5: NDC-based reforms are most likely to be adopted in political systems with fewer veto points.

Another set of potential hypotheses focuses on the specific nature of the pension reform process when NDC was considered. Because pension policy making has high conflict potential, there are certainly risks that it will become bogged down in group conflict and end up in stalemate or incremental reform. In comparing the Estonian and Latvian pension reforms, for example, Tavits (2003) argues that a perceived need for a quick solution to a pressing problem, in combination with lack of experience in policy reform, is likely to lead to the wholesale adoption of a foreign model. Overall, then,

> H6: NDC pension reforms are likely to be adopted (a) when a specially tailored process rather than the normal legislative process is used to develop the proposal, (b) when that process is closed rather than open in terms of the number and preferences of participants, and (c) when its development is done through a fast single-round process rather than an extended, multiround one.

The positions of social and political actors are an additional set of factors that are likely to influence the possibility for shifts away from the policy status quo. FDC reforms are more likely to appeal to conservatives because of their potential to lower government's role in pension provision and strengthen financial markets and hence economic growth, but the members of this group are still likely to prefer NDC over incremental adjustments to DB schemes. A shift toward NDC may split social democratic parties if it ends special privileges enjoyed by some of their members. Parties of all political persuasions may fear that current or future cutbacks triggered by NDC reforms will be used against them in future elections. Thus,

> H7: In democratic systems, NDC pension reforms are (a) most likely to be adopted by governments dominated by technocrats or where broad cross-party "cartels" in favor of NDC are established before the reform is adopted, and (b) most likely to be sustained where a durable cross-party consensus can be maintained.

Civil society actors may also influence the prospects for adoption of NDC reforms. The role of labor is likely to be especially important. Myles and Pierson (2001, 332) argue that "almost everywhere, [pension] reform has been backed either by the active or passive consent of organized labor." However, labor confederations are very diverse with respect to who is included and how they are structured. Some labor confederations may oppose NDC pensions if they believe that they disadvantage their members relative to other plausible alternatives (such as increased injection of general revenues), but they may acquiesce in an NDC reform if they get sufficient assurances for the long-term pension prospects for their members. High government transfers to the current pension scheme are likely to lower trade union support for a shift to NDC, because this shift may eventually lead to the elimination of the transfer. If NDC reforms are perceived to reduce disparities that disadvantage long-career union workers vis-à-vis other workers (for example, in highly fragmented pension systems), they may win labor confederation support or at least acquiescence. Blue-collar unions may prefer NDC to some alternatives, notably, linking the statutory retirement age to life expectancy, because of the traditional labor aversion to elimination of seniority pensions and, in general, to the compulsory extension of working lives. Overall, a plausible starting hypothesis is that

> H8: NDC-based reforms are unlikely to be adopted unless labor confederations are either politically marginal actors or support or acquiesce in their adoption.

These hypotheses, it should be noted, are complementary rather than mutually exclusive. They represent starting points for organizing expectations rather than arguments where there is a strong a priori sense that the hypotheses will be confirmed.

Innovators

SWEDEN

Sweden not only has the oldest NDC system, it also has the one whose origins are best documented (Anderson 2001; Loxbo 2007; Lundberg 2009; Marier 2008). By the late 1960s, Sweden had developed a three-tier pension system composed of a flat-rate universal tier financed by a combination of payroll contributions and general revenues, a contributory earnings-related tier, and an income-tested tier financed by general revenues. A long-term decline in the financial sustainability of the flat-rate and contributory pension tiers buffeted the system after the 1960s. Other design flaws meant that many blue-collar workers made contributions for which they received no credits. An economic and financial crisis that hit in 1991 led to lower indexation and cuts in early pensions. The 1991 election brought a minority coalition government of center-right parties to power. The new Minister of Health and Social Affairs, Bo Könberg, sought the collaboration of the then-dominant Social Democratic Party, both to win broad support in the Riksdag for the adoption of a long-term solution and to prevent it from becoming politicized in the next election, thereby increasing its sustainability.

A multiparty group representing the four coalition partners and the Social Democrats (but not the far right and left) negotiated the agreement. Business, labor, and pensioners were excluded from direct participation in negotiations out of fear that compromise would become more difficult (Lundberg 2009). The working group developed the broad outlines of an agreement by early 1994, which included a shift to a dominant NDC tier, an expanded income-tested tier to protect workers with low earnings histories, and a modest mandatory FDC tier. The 1994 election brought the Social Democrats back into power in a minority government, and negotiations on the details of the new system continued until 1998. Some renegotiation was made necessary by strong grassroots opposition in the blue-collar labor union confederation (Landsorganisationen, or LO) and in the Social Democratic Party (Loxbo 2007).

The reform has undergone only modest modifications since that time, such as measures to reduce the automatic balancing mechanism's volatility and changes in tax policy to minimize nominal benefit cuts (Weaver 2016). In recent years, concern has arisen over a number of issues, including increased rates of poverty among Swedish seniors.

The working group that negotiated the reform has also been continued. Indeed, commentators have focused on the five-party "cartel" that crossed ideological bloc boundaries as a critical factor in its success both in negotiating the Swedish reform and in sustaining it (Lundberg 2009; Weaver 2016). A number of commissions were established in the past half-decade, investigating, for example, the possibility of increasing the minimum eligibility age for receipt of the income (NDC) and guarantee (income-tested) pension. However, the need to develop a consensus within the working group to keep pensions out of partisan competition has meant that little change was made in the core NDC tier.

The Swedish case provides mixed support for this chapter's hypotheses. Despite experiencing both a short-term crisis and longer-term funding problems (H1), the Swedish reform was a continuation of a long process that started in the mid-1980s, rather than a crisis decision (Marier 2008). Sweden had adequate payroll records, an unfragmented system, and strong linkages to lifetime contributions (H2). As an NDC "Innovator," Sweden had high domestic capacity, so no external help was needed (H3).

The Swedish political system has few veto points (H5) and relied on a specially tailored, relatively insulated process (H6). This process was extended as a result of opposition within LO and the Social Democratic Parties. The reform straddled periods of center-right and Social Democratic governments, with cross-bloc support both in initiation and implementation (H7). The leadership of Sweden's blue-collar labor confederation endorsed the new system, while grassroots opposition to the reform was defeated in motions at LO Congresses (H8).

Italy

Italy is the archetypical example of the Southern European welfare state model (Ferrera 1996). It developed a segmented, inequitable, and wasteful single-pillar DB pension system, in dire need of reform. However, because of the divided nature of the government coalitions with the Democrazia Cristiana acting as pivot, change proved impossible to achieve until the early 1990s.

Two factors contributed to this turn of events: (a) the downsizing of the public pillar followed the sudden change of political actors in the early 1990s and the tightening of external constraints; and (b) the newly formed technocratic governments started inclusive concertation, while being less exposed to parliamentary control and electoral punishment (Ferrera and Jessoula 2007). Four reform rounds followed in the 1990s in Italy, named after Prime Ministers Amato (1992), Berlusconi (1994), Dini (1995), and Prodi (1997).

The common denominator of the reforms was that they were shaped by changes in internal and external conditions. Internally, corruption scandals engulfed the Italian Parliament in the early 1990s, leading to the demise of most of the First Republic's parties. Externally, compliance with the euro area convergence criteria set by the Maastricht Treaty represented the strongest external constraint on Italian runaway public spending.

After the demise of the Berlusconi government (primarily caused by protests against its pension reform initiative), his former Labor Minister Lamberto Dini became Prime Minister of a largely independent government. Given the spiraling debt of more than 125 percent of GDP and ongoing speculative attacks, pension reforms were central to the program of this technocratic executive (Ferrera and Gualmini 2004).

Dini launched institutionalized tripartite concertation rounds on a new social pact that included changes in the pension system (Jessoula 2009). Three main issues were discussed: the separation of social insurance from social assistance, the introduction of a new calculation formula, and the revision of seniority pensions. The main employers' association, Confindustria, condemned the timid approach toward seniority pensions and did not sign the new pact. The unions proved to be more cooperative, because of the maturation of reform-minded fringes within the labor movement, the collaborative style of the Dini government, and concessions, including an extremely slow phasing in of the NDC formula, which de facto excluded older workers, the unions' main constituency (Ferrera and Jessoula 2007). On their behalf, the unions surveyed their members to secure grassroots acceptance and supplied the government with information on their preferences, thereby allowing a balancing of technical soundness with political feasibility (Baccaro 2002; Ferrera and Jessoula 2007).

The government signed a formal pact with the unions leading to the new pension law in August 1995. The NDC formula substantially increased the pension system's fiscal sustainability. However, excessive haste generated several technical errors (Schøyen and Stamati 2013). The link between annuity divisors and life expectancy was to be updated by decree every 10 years instead of automatically. The divisors related to age groups rather than birth cohorts, reducing the incentives to remain active. The rate of return on contributions was linked to GDP growth, whereas benefits were indexed to prices, hence, a non-NDC feature.

After the global financial crisis, the problem of financial unsustainability resurfaced. The imperfect NDC design attracted widespread criticism, including from its main authors (Gronchi and Nisticò 2006). The Fornero-Monti reform of 2011, which directly hit the interests of older workers, had the political advantages of external conditionality, imposed by the European Central Bank, and of being legislated by Mario Monti's technocratic government. In particular, the phasing-in period was radically shortened, and most coefficients were tied to life expectancy (Jessoula and Raitano 2017; Natali and Stamati 2014).

In sum, the inequitable prereform Italian pension system (H2) faced short-term emergencies mixed with longer-term financial unsustainability (H1), thereby bringing to the fore more audacious policy solutions. The external constraints were so formidable that the unions accepted collaboration with a technocratic government (H8). Despite enjoying room for maneuver (H5), the cabinet supported concertation, which resulted in a quick special legislative procedure (H6). However, precisely because of the excessive haste, further adjustments to the NDC system were required.

Adapters: Poland

Poland inherited from socialism an inequitable and expensive DB pension system that entered a deep crisis during the transformational recession (Guardiancich 2013). To make things worse, the newly democratized polity had an unstable party system and highly politicized trade unions (the conservative Solidarność pitched against the socialist successor All-Poland Alliance of Trade Unions, OPZZ), which made traditional policy making almost impracticable (Ost 2000; Rae 2008). The powerful public administration had a say in all matters related to social policy reform. Moreover, the Ministry of Finance and the Ministry of Labor were at loggerheads, with the former favoring radical restructuring and the latter preferring incremental adjustments.

The pension reforms in the mid-1990s were simply emergency policy making to rein in runaway spending. After the Constitutional Tribunal demanded proper restructuring (Hausner 2001), Poland embarked on the lengthiest legislative process in the region under a government led by the Democratic Left Alliance (SLD) in coalition with the Polish Peasants Party (PSL) (Guardiancich 2013; Müller 1999; Orenstein 2000, 2008).

Three peculiarities characterized the reform: the establishment of a Government Plenipotentiary for Pension Reform with a markedly technocratic policy-making approach, the active position of the government at the center of political and social dialogue, and the unbundling of reforms into two phases under two different executives.

Selling a partisan reform to the public was impossible because of intense left-right animosity. World Bank official Michał Rutkowski appealed for the creation of an independent team of experts to end an impasse between the finance and labor ministers. Consequently, the Office of the Government Plenipotentiary for Social Security Reform was created and was chaired by Rutkowski. Most of its members were politically unaffiliated to more easily carry out the complex negotiations. Its three plenipotentiaries (Andrzej Bączkowski, Jerzy Hausner, and Ewa Lewicka) were highly respected figures with ties to both center-left and center-right political camps.

With assistance from international organizations, the office produced the reform package "Security through Diversity," which espoused a multipillar NDC-cum-FDC design. The United States Agency for International Development (USAID) financed the improvement of regulatory capacity. The Swedish International Development Agency supported the NDC pillar. The Phare Consensus program funded the reorganization of the Social Insurance Institute; and ILO experts offered technical advice.

As a result of unbundling, the "easier," new second-pillar laws were legislated during the SLD-PSL government in 1996–97, and the "difficult" ones (those regulating the public pillar and the Social Insurance Institution, ZUS) by the center-right coalition between Solidarity Electoral Action and the Freedom Union in 1997–98. The role of the plenipotentiary in selling the reforms was crucial and required multiple concessions. Disability pensions and the heavily subsidized farmers' pension system were excluded from reforms to appease the rural electorate of PSL and SLD (Armeanu 2011). Tax-financed security provisions for uniformed services, prosecutors, and judges were maintained. Granting bridging pensions (early exits financed by employers) was crucial to convincing the miners. The retirement ages of women and men were not equalized to get the conservative Solidarity Electoral Action on board. Workers older than age 50 were excluded from the NDC (and FDC) system, a necessary concession to the unions.

Most importantly, the office skillfully used the credit-claiming potential of systemic reforms and convinced the public that multiple objectives were obtainable at once (Office of the Plenipotentiary 1997, ii–iv). The reform's four policy aims were to institute a defined contribution, partially funded, multipillar pension system that guaranteed high replacement rates (Golinowska and Żukowski 2007).

In reality, Polish reformers and interest groups faced significant tradeoffs. Financial viability and economic competitiveness were key political objectives. The public was more interested in increased equity, conceived of as the elimination of unfair redistribution (through the NDC pillar), and improved effectiveness (through the FDC pillar).

The public shared a negative consensus against the old DB schemes (Perek Bialas, Chłoń-Domińczak, and Ruzik 2002). By April 1997, clear majorities approved of the main elements of "Security through Diversity": accumulation in individual accounts, a tightened contribution-benefit link, and funding (Chłoń 2000). The updated concept of equity, encapsulated in the NDC design, gained acceptance. The replacement of the state by private funds increased public support, and the use of multipillar terminology served as successful propaganda, thereby partly concealing the aim of lowering benefits through defined contributions (Chłoń 2000; Golinowska and Żukowski 2007).

Implementation of the reforms was far from flawless: the ZUS was ill-prepared for the new tasks; some minor technical difficulties arose with the NDC system; and the insufficiently precise older employment records led to recounts. None of these put into question the essence of the NDC pillar. Instead, the hot topics on the agenda became (a) the low retirement age, which was equalized at age 67 under the center-right Civic Platform government in 2012 (later reversed by the ultraconservative Law and Justice); and (b) the budget deficits created by the FDC pillar and its underwhelming performance, which led to partial dismantlement under the premiership of Donald Tusk.

Most of this chapter's hypotheses hold for Poland. In the problem and policy streams, adherence is almost total: the short- and long-term fiscal prospects and the Constitutional Tribunal's stop to incremental reforms show that in the mid-1990s the problem topped the political agenda (H1). The Polish DB pension system was fragmented and inequitable, and by excluding elderly workers, most problems with patchy past employment records could be resolved (H2). The World Bank seconded a Pole as head of the well-endowed Office of the Plenipotentiary, which boosted the reform's credibility (H3). In the political stream, all major political players supported a thorough restructuring of the system (H4). (The actual legislation of the NDC pillar was dominated by parties on the right [H7].) Thus, the reform was able to proceed despite the veto-rich political environment (H5). The special consultative procedure and the prestige and independence of the plenipotentiaries (H6) compensated for the relative openness of the process. Finally, the unions never questioned the NDC design (H8), in part as the result of several generous quid pro quos.

Boundary Straddlers: Germany

The German pension system is a classic one-tier social insurance system with a strong link between contributions and benefits. State subsidies played an important role in funding the German pension system in recent years, however. Germany's steep demographic decline put a strong strain on its pension system financing as contribution rates approached 20 percent, with projections in the late 1980s that they could reach 36 percent by 2030 (Schmähl 2007, 323).

Incremental refinancing and retrenchment preceded serious debate on restructuring. A relatively closed and depoliticized process of pension policy making involving employers and unions broke down in the mid-1990s. In 1997, the Christian Democratic Union–led coalition under Helmut Kohl enacted a pension reform that included a "demographic factor" stabilizing mechanism. This was suspended and cancelled after the Social Democrats (SPD) and Greens came to power following the 1998 election (Schulze and Jochem 2007). By 2003, Chancellor Schröder admitted that eliminating the demographic factor had been a mistake.

Following the recommendation of a new government-appointed commission, a new "sustainability factor" was enacted in 2004. Unlike the demographic factor, the new ASM is based on the ratio of pension beneficiaries to contributors; it includes changes in fertility rates, net migration, and labor force participation. It is not designed to adjust for all demographic change but rather to hold contribution rates to 20 percent in 2020 and 22 percent in 2030, much less than would be required for full long-term balance (Rüb and Lamping 2010, 159). Moreover, in response to opposition from trade unions and the left wing of the Social Democrats, the impact of the sustainability factor was capped: it could not cause pensions for workers with a full earnings history to fall to less than a 46 percent replacement rate. Since 2008, the German government has intervened several times on the ASM to prevent cuts from going into effect (Weaver 2016). Despite the reputation of the German point system, further reforms are probably needed. In May 2018, pursuant to the coalition agreement between Christian and Social Democrats, the German government established a commission to consider further reforms to enhance the system's long-term sustainability.

In the German case, both long-term demographic pressures (H1b) and short-term pension funding crises (H1a) were critical drivers of pension reform initiatives, and adoption of ASMs occurred after a long sequence of refinancing and retrenchment interventions (H1c). A transition to NDC was certainly technically feasible, given the DB structure (H2a) and the availability of payroll records (H2b), but the consolidated structure of the German pension system, with the exception of civil servants (H2c), and the relatively strong linkage to lifetime earnings (H2d) meant that relatively few gains in equality would occur from a shift to NDC. German domestic actors were aware of the NDC reform option, and the reform process was driven by domestic actors and interests rather than transnational ones (H3). NDC, however, lacked a powerful institutional champion within the government (H4a). Within the commission developing the 2004 reform proposals (H6), its trade union members opposed ASMs (H8). Hence, the commission endorsed only the more limited sustainability factor rather than a full NDC approach. Governments of both the right (first) and the left (later) came to see some form of ASM as essential to increasing the affordability of the pension system (H7a), but there was only agreement on restraining the increase in contribution rates rather than freezing them.

Incrementalists: Slovenia

As in most postsocialist countries, pension reforms have dominated the Slovenian political agenda for the past 25 years. The single-pillar nonfinancial defined benefit (NDB) system underwent two parametric reforms in 1992 and in 1999 that never really solved its fiscal sustainability problems (Stanovnik 2002). This failure was the result of a political system rife with veto points and powerful trade unions, especially the successor Association of Free Trade Unions of Slovenia, that have a quasi-pivotal role within the Economic and Social Council (Guardiancich 2012, 2013).

The center-left coalition between Borut Pahor's Social Democrats, the Democratic Party of Pensioners of Slovenia (DeSUS), and two other leftist parties elected in September 2008 had little appetite for reforms. The financial crisis changed all this. In December 2009, the EU started an excessive deficit procedure against Slovenia and urged Pahor's government to lower the budget deficit by 2013. Under increasing pressure from the financial markets, European institutions, and the OECD, Labor Minister Ivan Svetlik tabled several retrenchment measures and started preparing the continuation of the 1999 parametric reform.

For the first time, the NDC concept landed on the Slovenian political agenda. In March 2009, Svetlik nominated the head of a steering committee of experts on pensions. The ensuing document, "Modernization of the Pension System in the Republic of Slovenia," envisioned a radical two-step restructuring of the Slovenian pension system.

The first step (2011–15) would introduce drastic parametric changes, such as higher retirement age (age 65 for all), Swiss indexation (half wages, half prices), elongation of the calculation period for the assessment base, and fewer credited periods for such activities as military service, parenthood, and university studies. Even more dramatic was the second step, applicable to all workers born after 1960. It envisioned a new multipillar design that included a zero pillar partly financed by the state budget; a first NDC pillar; a second, occupational supplementary pillar; and individual savings accounts. The proposal had several problems, including a failure to provide microeconomic simulations showing who would lose or gain from the new system. Hence, negotiations with the unions and employers were inconclusive.

Pahor was initially committed to achieving broad consensus: the government organized more than 50 meetings with the social partners and produced about 300 documents between March 2009 and September 2010. The government conceded a number of points: most important, the 2010 Pension and Disability Insurance Act eliminated the second phase—that is, the introduction of an NDC pillar—and settled for a nonnegligible parametric reform.

Nevertheless, the negotiations irremediably broke down because the social partners felt that their alternative proposals were not taken into account. Consequently, in September 2010, the government submitted the text to the National Assembly without either the consent of the unions or the support of DeSUS. After collecting enough signatures for a referendum, the Association of Free Trade Unions of Slovenia, various opposition conservative parties, DeSUS, and others constituted an "unholy alliance" to bring the pension reform down. After a faulty campaign, the government's defeat was memorable: 72.2 percent voted against (Stanovnik and Turk 2011, 16). Ultimately, Pahor suffered a vote of no confidence in September of the same year.

Slovenia shows that even if the problem and policy streams are aligned, political settings with many veto points (H5) and militant trade unions (H8) need skilled negotiators and overall awareness that reforms are necessary. It took a far worse deepening of the crisis during the following center-right government to pass a parametric reform, paradoxically similar to the one rejected a year earlier. It is possible that Pahor's government used the NDC proposal as a Trojan horse to push for a substantial parametric reform and never intended to enact it.

Dropouts

FORMER SOVIET UNION AND CENTRAL ASIA

Most, if not all, former Soviet Union countries inherited inequitable and unsustainable single-pillar NDB pension systems. The NDC concept was thus contemplated in a number of cases (Georgia, the Kyrgyz Republic, Russia, and Mongolia) to better align contributions and benefits and bring fiscal costs under control. Additional common elements included the involvement of external experts, especially from the World Bank. Despite the at least formal adoption of NDC, none of those reforms survived intact.

How did NDC reforms get on the agenda in places such as Mongolia? Three factors appear to have been important. First, in the late 1990s, FDC reforms were still the dominant model for transnational actors such as the World Bank and USAID. Concerns were raised in these organizations about the applicability of FDC reforms in countries that lacked basic financial market infrastructure and strong rule of law. As one person involved in the Mongolian reform initiatives put it, however, "There was a persistent belief among many in the development community that somehow 'demand would generate supply' and that a captive pool of investment capital would somehow magically promote capital market development without putting future pensions at risk" (confidential personal communication). In Mongolia, NDC reforms emerged in part as a compromise between parametric reforms, perceived as insufficiently transformative, and FDC reform, which was seen as not immediately practical. Because NDC created notional accounts, it could be portrayed as paving the way for funded accounts later. Second, the experiences of Latvia, Poland, and Sweden meant that NDC was perceived as a plausible alternative, as had happened earlier with FDC reforms in Latin America. NDC models also enjoyed growing support from staff in the World Bank. Finally, "border-straddling" ASMs, such as linkages of retirement age to longevity, were beginning to emerge and may not have been well known among the consultants advising the authorities.

The Mongolian reform was enacted by a Democratic Union Coalition government composed of the Mongolian National Democratic Party and the Mongolian Social Democratic Party elected in 1996. However, the former communist Mongolian People's Revolutionary Party, which returned to power in 2000, lacked commitment to the new system. Also, according to international observers, policy, political economy, and institutional weaknesses were present (Bogomolova 2014; World Bank 2012).

Policy shortcomings were substantial. The reforms went ahead despite the absence of the key precondition of having proper employment histories for post-1960 cohorts. Most important, the abrupt transition between pre- and post-1960 cohorts would have excessively penalized the latter, thereby forcing the authorities to prevent the scheme from being applied until 2033. Among political economy concerns, no "white paper" explained the rationale behind the NDC design choice, nor was there an independent research and vetting office to guide legislators on the technical aspects of any of the legislation. The reform was prepared by an external consulting team funded by USAID. Although some technical staff understood the reform at the time, it was never explained to senior policy makers. According to those involved, the consultants worked closely with members of parliament sympathetic to the Democratic Union Coalition government, but little effort was put into building a broader consensus for reform. Operational challenges and confusion over the concept of NDC contributed to public skepticism.

Hence, the lessons from Mongolia are that both careful thinking about smooth transitions between cohorts and public information to ensure the reform's credibility are needed.

The Russian reform reversal was born out of different causes, given that serious design flaws were absent. Russia inherited from Soviet times an NDB system that by 1989 counted 44 million retirees and granted replacement rates between 60 and 100 percent of the average wage. Its positive attributes were that it awarded generous credits to women and early retirement provisions in cases of sickness, injury, and child-care leave. The negative attributes included the system's complexity—more than 250 categories existed for privileged eligibility (Cook 2007).

Population aging and the transition to a market economy, characterized by a sharp drop in contributors because of evasion and unemployment, rendered the system unsustainable. Until 1999, arrears of three to six months built up and replacement rates collapsed to 30–40 percent of average wages (Williamson, Howling, and Maroto 2006).

The policy responses were piecemeal and inconclusive, such as periodically raising minimum pensions while simultaneously limiting their maximum level. The 1998 financial crisis precipitated the situation.

The arrival of Vladimir Putin in 1999 broke many of the stalemates that characterized Boris Yeltsin's weakened presidency (Cook 2007). Putin unified the government around a liberalized welfare state model, and the Duma passed several social security reforms, including reforms of pensions. In this liberalizing vein, a multipillar NDC-cum-FDC pension system design, advocated and supported by the World Bank, was chosen.

Putin appointed the National Soviet for Pension Reform, headed by Prime Minister Michael Kasiyanov, which included actors with diverse views. The World Bank stepped in by offering a Social Protection Adjustment Loan worth some US$800 million. Although the World Bank was not directly involved in the negotiations, the National Soviet opted for the multipillar model presented by the Ministry of the Economy.

In the aftermath of the crisis, which witnessed growing deficits in the Pension Fund of Russia, some reform of the pension system was required (Eich, Gust, and Soto 2012). Yet in 2013, instead of intervening on the very low statutory and effective retirement ages, the authorities replaced the NDC scheme with a point system.

The precise motives for replacing the NDC with a points formula in Russia are unknown. One potential motive, compatible with this chapter's framework, may have been to generate fiscal savings by squeezing the pension replacement rates more than under the NDC scheme and using less transparent tools under the point system. With a points formula based on discretionary indexation patterns, the government can modify the expenditures according to fiscal constraints, regardless of their impacts on beneficiaries. The points formula does not automatically adjust for changes in the contribution rate or lengthening life expectancy. For a government that plans to reduce the contribution rate and hesitates to raise the retirement age, points may provide useful room to maneuver. Similarly, exceptionally high late retirement bonuses, granted through additional points, would have to be explicitly contributed in the NDC system. Finally, points may have been a more attractive framework in 2016, when second-pillar members were allowed to opt back in to the PAYG system, with bonuses awarded for such a decision.

In sum, the political economy of the adoption of NDC in Russia neatly fits within this chapter's theoretical framework. Russia inherited a fragmented, unsustainable PAYG-DB system (H2) that could not survive the 1998 financial crisis (H1). The insulated reform process (H5 and H6), supported by the World Bank (H3), within a political environment that wanted to show its commitment to world society (H4), was conducive to the conversion to NDC-cum-FDC. The political situation, however, changed dramatically in a matter of years. The very effects of the NDC reform clashed with the Putin regime's immediate needs. In fact, all the arguments in favor of the introduction of NDC schemes in 2006—transparency, automatic adjustment, and insulation from political discretion—may have been critical political liabilities in 2013.

THE ARAB REPUBLIC OF EGYPT

The single-pillar Egyptian PAYG-DB pension system had obvious shortcomings, including undercoverage, high rates of evasion, unfairness, fiscal unsustainability, and poor management. Treasury subsidies amounted to 35 percent of total pensions paid in

2009 (Maait and Demarco 2012, 161). In 2004, a window of opportunity opened when a cabinet reshuffle brought in a group of ministers with strong credentials as reputed entrepreneurs. Egypt embarked on an ambitious wave of reforms, including of the pension system.

Between 2005 and 2010, the Ministry of Finance, with the World Bank's technical assistance, prepared a comprehensive pension system overhaul, whose multipillar architecture included an NDC-cum-FDC pillar. The team operated within a rather closed environment, thereby excluding a wider spectrum of actors, most notably, the National Social Insurance Authority. The phase-in was expected to be very slow, since participants in the current DB system could not constitutionally be compelled to switch to the new system (Maait and Demarco 2012). The new 135/2010 pension law, passed in May 2010, was a paramount achievement and sign of strength of the Ministry of Finance's team, which took part in multiple public debates, including with members of parliament. However, implementation of the new pension system required executive regulations, which had not been passed at the time of the Arab Spring (or Egyptian Revolution) of January 2011, and which resulted in the resignation of former president Hosni Mubarak and his cabinet.

A political impasse followed the first months of the revolution, and most economic transformational projects were called to a long halt, including the pension reform. The election of Mohamed Morsi and the Muslim Brotherhood in June 2012 reversed several of these projects, and during the short life of this government, pension law 135/2010 was cancelled. Several reasons may be credited for this decision. Although the Ministry of Finance steered the reform process, the World Bank's strong involvement led to a public perception that the process was being driven by an international financial institution long viewed with suspicion in Egypt (Hanieh 2015). In 2011, key decision makers shared the view that the reform was insufficiently domestically owned. If the exclusion from discussions of the technical staff of the National Social Insurance Authority was instrumental to push for more radical solutions, it was detrimental in the long term. Soon after the revolution, pension policy was shifted to the Ministry of Social Solidarity, whose views were aligned with those of the National Social Insurance Authority. Despite communication efforts, the reform did not achieve wide understanding among the population, thereby undermining government efforts to gain strong public support. Most crucial, the delay in issuing executive regulations was a factor that enabled the decision to be reversed: as a result of low implementation capacity, the new pension system was only a law and was not yet operational at the time of the revolution.

After President Morsi was deposed, the current government was left with the legacy of a necessary but postponed reform. As of early 2018, the executive was considering a parametric reform, without endorsing the previous NDC design. It is also very unlikely that FDC schemes will be part of this reform, except on a voluntary basis and as a small complementary tier.

Conclusions and Prospects for NDC Systems

This chapter begins with the puzzle of why NDC-based pension reforms were not broadly adopted after a promising start in the 1990s. The analysis herein suggests a number of conclusions about (a) the patterns of diffusion of NDC pension reforms, (b) the conditions that facilitate or impede their adoption, (c) the prospects for further diffusion, and (d) issues of sustainability of NDC-based reforms already in place.

PATTERNS OF DIFFUSION

The diffusion of NDC schemes is notable for both its limited geographic scope and timing. Three distinct waves of NDC and boundary-straddling pension reforms can be seen over time. The first wave was confined to Western and Central Europe in the mid-to-late 1990s. "Innovator" countries (Sweden and Italy) developed the NDC reform concept and were quickly followed by "Adapters" (Poland and Latvia). A second wave in former Soviet bloc countries occurred around the turn of the century, but these proved fragile. A third wave of stabilizing, boundary-straddling reforms in the EU countries occurred mostly during and after the financial crisis, but they all fell short of full NDC adoption. A few other countries, notably Egypt and Norway, adopted NDC reforms, but they do not fit neatly into these waves.

FACILITATING AND IMPEDING CONDITIONS FOR NDC-BASED REFORMS

The multicase analysis in this chapter suggests no clear set of necessary and sufficient conditions that are likely to lead either to the adoption and sustaining of an NDC pension system or to its rejection, abandonment, or weakening. The forces shaping pension reform politics, variations in existing pension systems, and institutional rules governing pension reform are simply too complex to be governed by a few propositions. The cases do suggest, however, that a number of probabilistic relationships affect pension reforms. More important, the cases suggest, consistent with Kingdon's (2002) analysis of multiple policy streams, that it is not individual causal relationships that matter, but rather connections among causal forces across the problem, policy, and political streams that open windows for NDC reforms or other types of pension reforms, including ASMs.

In the problem stream, long-term pension funding problems get pension reform issues onto the broad discussion agenda among policy experts and government ministries (H1b). Given the political sensitivity of pension reform, it is generally a short-term fiscal crisis that moves pension reform near the top of politicians' priorities (H1a). Although a shift to restructuring is generally associated with the exhaustion of refinancing and retrenchment reforms (H1c), the cases of Southern European countries under pressure from the Troika, the decision group formed by the European Commission, the European Central Bank, and the International Monetary Fund, suggest that "exhausted" is an elastic concept: reforms that might not have been politically acceptable in the absence of that pressure become viable. Dependence on external financing to resolve a fiscal crisis can add pressure (H3b), but such pressure was absent in several cases, notably, Norway and Sweden. Even where that pressure exists, it only pushes countries in a particular reform direction if the external funder is strongly supportive of NDC. Moreover, the "third wave" of cases in Europe suggests that when short- and medium-term fiscal concerns are dominant, parametric reforms and ASMs that fall short of full NDC are likely to be more attractive than NDC to policy makers and the funders on whom they depend.

In the policy stream, NDC schemes are most likely to emerge to replace DB schemes (H2a), but adequate payroll records are not a necessary condition for their adoption (H2b), as the experience of the former socialist countries demonstrates. Similarly, NDC has emerged in both unified (Sweden) and highly fragmented (Italy) pension regimes (H2c), as well as in those systems in which the linkage to lifetime benefits was both moderate and weak (H2d).

Transnational policy entrepreneurs and external financing are important in determining whether NDC reforms emerge as options to be seriously considered in some countries (H3a).

- In the first wave, NDC emerged domestically among policy expert communities in Italy and Sweden. In Poland—where national experts played a role—and Latvia, but less so in Norway, experts associated with Sweden and the World Bank helped in not simply convincing domestic elites to seriously consider NDC, but also in designing, financing, and implementing the reforms.

- In the second wave of reforms, former Soviet bloc countries with limited domestic expertise drew on expertise from the World Bank and national and international aid agencies. With insufficient political stability, weak domestic buy-in, and limited understanding of NDC, these experiments proved fragile.

- In the third round of boundary-straddling reforms, it was largely European actors plus the International Monetary Fund that were responsible for setting financial conditions; organizations such as the OECD also provided advice. These organizations generally favored tailored incremental reforms with immediate impact coupled with boundary-straddling ASMs rather than adoption of NDC (H3d). Dissemination of the NDC paradigm was weak, in part because no international organization has to date taken it on as a core and consistent policy recommendation.

Another potential influence on reform choice within the policy stream is whether a particular reform becomes a dominant reform among peer countries in a region, triggering the "availability heuristic" (H3c). Although definitive evidence is lacking, the cases here suggest that an "endorsement heuristic" may also be at work, that is, whether a policy option has been widely adopted in the region (and thus won implicit endorsement from others) and is widely perceived to produce desirable results. As noted, NDC reforms never became the dominant reform paradigm in any region. Thus, NDC reforms incurred multiple disadvantages from their perceived rigidity, the availability of plausible alternatives to achieve fiscal objectives in developed countries, their virtual absence in most regions of the world (Africa, East and Southeast Asia, and Latin America), and their record of fragility in several former socialist countries.

Until a more fine-grained analysis of cases of adoption and nonadoption can be conducted, only provisional conclusions for the political stream are possible from the cases. NDC pension schemes have been adopted in countries with both high (Sweden) and low (Latvia) domestic institutional expertise in pension policy, but the latter cases were accompanied by strong external support. It has generally occurred in relatively closed planning processes, but those were quite lengthy in some cases (both Sweden and Norway). Rather than reflecting the preferences of right party governments, they have generally been enacted by technocratic governments (Italy) or with multiparty consensus (Poland, Norway, and Sweden) (H7). Although organized labor has usually not been an enthusiastic proponent of NDC reforms, it has mostly acquiesced when offered sufficient side payments (Italy and Poland). In other cases, unions have been too weak to resist (H8).

Overall, a key lesson about the politics stream is that actively selling of NDC reforms to the public is less important to their successful enactment than achieving a durable near-consensus among political and economic elites (H6 and H7). The reason for this almost certainly lies in the loss aversion and differential attention to negative information of voters (Eckles and Schaffner 2010) and the blame-avoiding and blame-generating instincts of politicians. Elements of NDC, such as "quasi-ownership of NDC balances," flexible retirement ages, and fiscal sustainability of the pension system in the long run may be attractive to voters (Bodor and Rutkowski 2012), but their under-standing of and attentiveness to these factors is likely to be low. Moreover, framings of NDC by opponents that emphasize potential losses to voters, such as "brakes" and automatic balancing mechanisms, are likely to be more powerful. NDC schemes often achieve financial sustainability in large part through reductions in replacement rates. Although policy makers try to avoid this politically toxic narrative, opposition parties, unions, and representatives of the elderly often seize upon the adequacy of benefits. There is no way to square this circle; reforms that seek to achieve financial sustainability will come at the expense of some combination of lower benefits, longer work lives, and more costly contributions (Barr 2012).

The political problem, in short, is not just that politicians are myopic (though they often are, as the case of Russia neatly shows), but that it is difficult to create a single reform option that all groups in society will see as preferable to the status quo and to all plausible alternatives. Thus, in democratic countries, keeping NDC reform proposals away from electoral competition and from the temptation of opposition parties to generate blame against potential losses through a cartel of major parties has been critical to their adoption and maintenance (Weaver 2018).

PROSPECTS FOR FURTHER DIFFUSION OF NDC REFORMS

Several issues concerning policy considerations and political dynamics emerge as central to the prospects for additional diffusion of NDC pension systems.

A first issue is whether NDC systems are perceived to produce the benefits their advocates claim, without offsetting costs and risks. Here, as von Nordheim (2012, 122) noted, "The devil is in the details"—and not only the details of the NDC scheme but other pension and social assistance tiers serving the elderly. If workers are to lengthen their working lives, both the expectation of longer work and the costs of not working longer on retirement incomes must be communicated effectively to the public (Sundén 2012), as was attempted, for example, in Sweden and Italy through so-called Orange Envelopes. Given the public's willful inattentiveness to retirement issues, notions of a flexible retire-ment age embedded in NDC are less likely to be effective in changing retirement behavior than signals sent by boundary-straddling mechanisms, such as linking retirement age to life expectancy.

A second issue concerns whether the advantages of a well-designed NDC system can be produced through alternative designs or incremental reform measures. Although few countries have adopted full-blown NDC systems, core principles of NDC have entered into recent pension policy discourse. Several countries have moved toward increasing the number of years of earnings that are included in calculating pension benefits and other-wise increasing incentives for extending working lives. ASMs have been incorporated in national policy in countries such as Germany, without moving fully to NDC. Only the notion of imputed interest on previous contributions among core NDC principles seems to have been largely bypassed. Many of these reforms straddle the boundaries between "retrenchment" and "restructuring" reforms, as outlined.

Proponents of NDC systems argue that incremental and boundary-straddling reforms inadequately address both the microeconomic issues confronting DB pension systems and their long-term financial sustainability. At the macro level, financial sustainability of a pension system is not solved by simply introducing an ASM that links either benefits or the retirement age to life expectancy: these expedients are likely only to limit the damage. As for the micro advantages of efficiency, adequacy, and fairness, NDC is not without problems of its own. The lifetime contribution focus of the NDC approach to pension reform fits reasonably well in a system such as Sweden's, where something close to full working careers for both men and women are facilitated by social supports, such as generous child care, and credits are given for some noncontributory periods (for example, parental leave). However, benefit adequacy requires that NDC designs must be complemented with a zero pillar to alleviate poverty and explicit social policy components to cover those earnings gaps that apply to people with interrupted working careers. The Norwegians and Swedes in their guarantee pension programs have recognized that mandatory credit splitting between married couples under NDC is insufficient to tackle the difficulties arising from inadequate lifetime earnings, primarily of women. In countries where social supports are lacking, a robust zero pillar will be even more necessary. The fact that the problem of incomplete contributory histories is very visible in NDC systems does not mean that the alternatives do not have similar shortcomings.

A third issue in the policy stream affecting further diffusion concerns the "availability and endorsement heuristics." As noted, NDC never became the dominant reform option in any region, and it is unlikely that this will occur in the near future, as expert opinion has shifted away from one-size-fits-all pension reforms. Indeed, the dominant notion today, as Börsch-Supan (2012, 9) expressed it, is that "There is no such thing as an 'optimal pension reform,' since current systems vary significantly in terms of the causes of future problems, and no single reform element suffices quantitatively to offset population aging. Country-specific policy mixes are the appropriate solution under these circumstances." In this context, the more prominent role that NDC design might play in national pension policy discussions is that of a yardstick against which to measure the available solutions.

A fourth policy issue concerning further diffusion of NDC reforms is whether most of the potential adopters of NDC-based reforms in middle- and lower-income countries have the information and technical expertise needed to successfully design and operate an NDC pension scheme. In countries with limited technical capacity, it cannot be assumed that data on GDP or employment growth, let alone projections of life expectancy, will be free from contestation when public benefits and scarce budget dollars are at stake. Any attempt at implementing NDC pension schemes should be accompanied by an adequate training plan for policy makers and administrators, as well as by widespread public information campaigns.

Political constraints are also likely to limit the further diffusion of NDC reforms. A pension reform that will last to the "next Ice Age" may not have a strong intrinsic attraction for pragmatic politicians and those occasionally profiting from benefit clientelism.

Reforms that do not provide immediate budgetary relief will not either when there is immediate pressure from creditors and international financial institutions to reduce spending. The scant opportunities for program control, and the potential that NDC schemes could produce "blind-siding" blame from triggering of an ASM that could be avoided with an alternative scheme that allows for more discretion, may lead politicians to believe that these risks outweigh any benefits of being "lashed to the mast" of automatic adjustments. The sensitivity of German and Swedish politicians to the potential political fallout from stabilizing mechanisms when they were triggered suggests that such triggers need to be designed so as to minimize backlash.

The record so far suggests, in short, that NDC-based reforms are likely to remain an important option—perhaps even a key benchmark—for pension reformers in the near future, but NDC is unlikely to become the dominant reform option in the near or medium term as long as it lacks strong and consistent backing from a powerful international actor like the World Bank or the OECD and is not the dominant reform in any region. Rather, what is witnessed is a piecemeal and incremental adoption of core NDC principles that are gradually bringing many PAYG-DB schemes closer to this benchmark.

SUSTAINABILITY OF NDC REFORMS

A final question is whether NDC schemes are durable and resilient to social and political challenges once they are adopted. Here the picture is decidedly mixed. In the European Economic Area, NDC reforms have been sustained with modest revisions, especially when political elites are able to keep them out of electoral contestation (H7b). Although only limited changes have been made in Sweden under electoral pressure, countries such as Italy considered intrusive re-reforms, such as the reintroduction of seniority pensions.

Outside of Western Europe, the picture for resilience is less clear. NDC-based reforms in Poland and Latvia have survived basically intact, but Egypt and former Soviet bloc countries have either never had or just claimed they had introduced NDC reforms, only to backtrack at the most convenient occasion. Outside of Europe, the inconsistency in implementation of NDC can be attributed to political instability (both political unrest and governing party turnover) and to low public and elite understanding of, and even lower political commitment to, the reforms. The bottom line on NDC mechanisms appears to be that they have the potential to add significantly to the resilience of government efforts to improve pension system sustainability, but they are only as strong as the broader political system's capacity to resist popular pressures and politicians' short-term electoral fears.

References

Anderson, Karen M. 2001. "The Politics of Retrenchment in a Social Democratic Welfare State: Reform of Swedish Pensions and Unemployment Insurance." *Comparative Political Studies* 34 (9): 1063–91.

Armeanu, Oana I. 2011. *The Politics of Pension Reform in Central and Eastern Europe—Political Parties, Coalitions and Policies.* New York: Palgrave Macmillan.

Baccaro, Lucio. 2002. "Negotiating the Italian Pension Reform with the Unions: Lessons for Corporatist Theory." *ILR Review* 55 (3): 413–31.

Barr, Nicholas. 2012. *Economics of the Welfare State.* 5th ed. Oxford: Oxford University Press.

Bodor, András, and Michal Rutkowski. 2012. "NDC Schemes as a Pathway toward Politically Feasible Pension Reform." In *Nonfinancial Defined Contribution Pension Schemes in a Changing Pension World: Volume 2 Gender, Politics, and Financial Stability,* edited by Robert Holzmann, Edward Palmer, and David Robalino, 215–31. Washington, DC: World Bank.

Bogomolova, Tatyana. 2014. "Kyrgyz Republic: Public Expenditure Review Policy Notes: Pensions." World Bank, Washington, DC.

Bonoli, Giuliano, and Bruno Palier. 2007. "When Past Reforms Open New Opportunities: Comparing Old-Age Insurance Reforms in Bismarckian Welfare Systems." *Social Policy and Administration* 41 (6): 555–73.

Börsch-Supan, Axel. 2012. "Policy Mixes in the Current European Reform Process." *DICE Report* 10 (4): 9–15.

Brooks, Sarah M. 2005. "Interdependent and Domestic Foundations of Policy Change: The Diffusion of Pension Privatization around the World." *International Studies Quarterly* 49 (2): 273–94.

———. 2007. "When Does Diffusion Matter? Explaining the Spread of Structural Pension Reforms across Nations." *Journal of Politics* 69 (3): 701–15.

Brooks, Sarah M., and Kent Weaver. 2006. "Lashed to the Mast?: The Politics of NDC Pension Reform." In *Pension Reform: Issues and Prospects for Non-Defined Contribution (NDC) Pension Schemes,* edited by Robert Holzmann and Edward Palmer, 345–85. Washington, DC: World Bank.

Chłoń, Agnieszka. 2000. "Pension Reform and Public Information in Poland." Pension Reform Primer, World Bank, Washington, DC.

Chłoń, Agnieszka, and Marek Góra. 2003. "Commitment and Consensus in Pension Reform." In *Pension Reform in Europe: Process and Progress,* edited by Robert Holzmann, Mitchell A. Orenstein, and Michal Rutkowski, 131–55. Washington, DC: World Bank.

Cichon, M. 1999. "Notional Defined-Contribution Schemes: Old Wine in New Bottles?" *International Social Security Review* 52 (4): 87–105.

Cook, Linda J. 2007. *Postcommunist Welfare States: Reform Politics in Russia and Eastern Europe.* Ithaca, NY: Cornell University Press.

Eckles, David L., and Brian F. Schaffner. 2010. "Loss Aversion and the Framing of the Health Care Reform Debate." *Forum* 8 (1), Article 7.

Eich, Frank, Charleen Gust, and Mauricio Soto. 2012. "Reforming the Public Pension System in the Russian Federation." IMF Working Paper 12/201, International Monetary Fund, Washington, DC.

Ervik, Rune, Nanna Kildal, and Even Nilssen. 2009. *The Role of International Organizations in Social Policy: Idea, Actors and Impact.* Cheltenham, UK: Edward Elgar.

European Commission. 2011. "Annual Growth Survey: Advancing the EU's Comprehensive Response to the Crisis." Communication (2011) 11 final. European Commission, Brussels.

———. 2018. *The 2018 Ageing Report. Economic and Budgetary Projections for the 28 EU Member States (2016–2070).* Luxembourg: Publications Office of the European Union.

Ferrera, Maurizio. 1996. "The 'Southern Model' of Welfare in Social Europe." *Journal of European Social Policy* 6 (1): 17–37.

Ferrera, Maurizio, and Elisabetta Gualmini. 2004. *Rescued by Europe? Social and Labour Market Reforms in Italy from the First Republic to Berlusconi.* Amsterdam: Amsterdam University Press.

Ferrera, Maurizio, and Matteo Jessoula. 2007. "Italy: A Narrow Gate for Path-Shift." In *Handbook of West European Pension Politics*, edited by Ellen M. Immergut, Karen M. Anderson, and Isabelle Schulze, 396–453. Oxford: Oxford University Press.

Foster, Liam. 2014. "Women's Pensions in the European Union and the Current Economic Crisis." *Policy and Politics* 42 (4): 565–80.

Gill, Indermit S., Truman G. Packard, and Juan Yermo. 2004. *Keeping the Promise of Social Security in Latin America*. Washington, DC: World Bank.

Golinowska, Stanisława, and Maciej Żukowski. 2007. "Polish Pension System and Its Reform." Unpublished, Warsaw.

Góra, Marek. 2001. "Polish Approach to Pension Reform." *OECD Private Pensions Conference 2000*. http://financedocbox.com/Retirement_Planning/65589148-Polish-approach-to -pension-reform-1.html.

Gronchi, Sandro, and Sergio Nisticò. 2006. "Implementing the NDC Theoretical Model: A Comparison of Italy and Sweden." In *Pension Reform: Issues and Prospects for Non-Financial Defined Contribution (NDC) Schemes*, edited by Robert Holzmann and Edward Palmer, 493–515. Washington, DC: World Bank.

Guardiancich, Igor. 2012. "The Uncertain Future of Slovenian Exceptionalism." *East European Politics and Societies* 26 (2): 378–97.

———. 2013. *Pension Reforms in Central, Eastern, and Southeastern Europe: From Post-Socialist Transition to the Global Financial Crisis*. New York: Routledge.

Guardiancich, Igor, and David Natali. 2017. "The Changing EU 'Pension Programme': Policy Tools and Ideas in the Shadow of the Crisis." In *The New Pension Mix: Recent Reforms, Their Distributional Effects and Political Dynamics,* edited by David Natali, 239–65. Brussels: PIE Peter Lang.

Guidi, Mattia, and Igor Guardiancich. 2018. "Intergovernmental or Supranational Integration? A Quantitative Analysis of Pension Recommendations in the European Semester." *European Union Politics* 19 (4): 684–706.

Hanieh, Adam. 2015. "Shifting Priorities or Business as Usual? Continuity and Change in the post-2011 IMF and World Bank Engagement with Tunisia, Morocco and Egypt." *British Journal of Middle Eastern Studies* 42 (1): 119–34.

Hausner, Jerzy. 2001. "Security through Diversity: Conditions for Successful Reform of the Pension System in Poland." In *Reforming the State: Fiscal and Welfare Reform in Post-Socialist Countries*, edited by János Kornai, Stephan Haggard, and Robert R. Kaufman, 210–34. Cambridge, UK: Cambridge University Press.

Holzmann, Robert. 2013. "Global Pension Systems and Their Reform: Worldwide Drivers, Trends and Challenges." *International Social Security Review* 66 (2): 1–29.

———. 2017. "The ABCs of Nonfinancial Defined Contribution (NDC) Schemes." *International Social Security Review* 70 (3): 53–77.

Holzmann, Robert, and Richard Hinz. 2005. *Old-Age Income Support in the 21st Century: An International Perspective on Pension Systems and Reform*. Washington, DC: World Bank.

Holzmann, Robert, and Edward Palmer. 2006a. *Pension Reform: Issues and Prospects for Non-Defined Contribution (NDC) Pension Schemes*. Washington, DC: World Bank.

———. 2006b. "The Status of the NDC Discussion: Introduction and Overview." In *Pension Reform: Issues and Prospects for Non-Defined Contribution (NDC) Pension Schemes*, edited by Robert Holzmann and Edward Palmer, 1–15. Washington, DC: World Bank.

Holzmann, Robert, Edward Palmer, and David Robalino, eds. 2012. *NDC Pension Schemes in a Changing Pension World: Volume 1 Progress, Issues, and Implementation*. Washington, DC: World Bank.

———. 2013. *NDC Pension Schemes in a Changing Pension World: Volume 2 Gender, Politics, and Financial Stability*. Washington, DC: World Bank.

ILO (International Labour Organization). 2017. *World Social Protection Report 2017–19: Universal Social Protection to Achieve the Sustainable Development Goals (Report)*. Geneva: International Labour Organization.

James, Estelle. 2012. "Gender in the (Nonfinancial) Defined Contribution World: Issues and Options." In *Nonfinancial Defined Contribution Pension Schemes in a Changing Pension World: Volume 2 Gender, Politics, and Financial Stability*, edited by Robert Holzmann, Edward Palmer, and David Robalino, 3–33. Washington, DC: World Bank.

Jessoula, Matteo. 2009. *La Politica Pensionistica*. Bologna: Il mulino.

Jessoula, Matteo, and Michele Raitano. 2017. "Italian Pensions from 'Vices' to Challenges: Assessing Actuarial Multi-Pillarization Twenty Years On." In *The New Pension Mix in Europe*, edited by David Natali, 39–66. Brussels: PIE Peter Lang.

Kingdon, John. 2002. *Agendas, Alternatives and the Policies of Governments*. 2nd ed. New York: Pearson.

Loxbo, Karl. 2007. "Bakom Socialdemokraternas Beslut:—Från 1950-Talets ATP-Strid Till 1990-Talets Pensionsuppgörelse." Doctoral thesis. Växjö, Sweden: Växjö University Press.

Lundberg, Urban. 2009. "The Democratic Deficit of Pension Reform: The Case of Sweden." In *The Politics of Age: Basic Pension Systems in a Comparative and Historical Perspective*, edited by Klaus Petersen and Jørn Henrik Petersen, 179–201. Frankfurt, Brussels, and Oxford: PIE Peter Lang.

Maait, Mohamed, and Gustavo Demarco. 2012. "Egypt's New Social Insurance System: An NDC Reform in an Emerging Economy." In *Nonfinancial Defined Contribution Pension Schemes in a Changing Pension World: Volume 1 Progress, Lessons, and Implementation*, edited by Robert Holzmann, Edward Palmer, and David Robalino, 159–85. Washington, DC: World Bank.

Marier, Patrik. 2008. *Pension Politics: Consensus and Social Conflict in Ageing Societies*. London and New York: Routledge.

Melo, Marcus A. 2004. "Institutional Choice and the Diffusion of Policy Paradigms: Brazil and the Second Wave of Pension Reform." *International Political Science Review* 25 (3): 320–41.

Müller, Katarina. 1999. *The Political Economy of Pension Reform in Central-Eastern Europe*. Cheltenham, UK: Edward Elgar.

Myles, John, and Paul Pierson. 2001. "The Comparative Political Economy of Pension Reform." In *The New Politics of the Welfare State*, edited by Paul Pierson, 305–33. Oxford: Oxford University Press.

Natali, David, and Furio Stamati. 2014. "Reassessing South European Pensions after the Crisis: Evidence from Two Decades of Reforms." *South European Society and Politics* 19 (3): 309–30.

OECD (Organisation for Economic Co-operation and Development). 2017. *Pensions at a Glance 2017*. Paris: OECD Publishing.

Office of the Plenipotentiary. 1997. *Security through Diversity—Reform of the Pension System in Poland*. Warsaw: Office of the Government Plenipotentiary for Social Security Reform.

Orenstein, Mitchell A. 2000. "How Politics and Institutions Affect Pension Reform in Three Postcommunist Countries." Policy Research Working Paper, World Bank, Washington, DC.

———. 2005. "The New Pension Reform as Global Policy." *Global Social Policy* 5 (2): 175–202.

———. 2008. *Privatizing Pensions: The Transnational Campaign for Social Security Reform.* Princeton, NJ: Princeton University Press.

Ost, David. 2000. "Illusory Corporatism in Eastern Europe: Neoliberal Tripartism and Postcommunist Class Identities." *Politics and Society* 28 (4): 503–30.

Palmer, Edward. 2006. "What Is NDC?" In *Pension Reform: Issues and Prospects for Non-Defined Contribution (NDC) Pension Schemes,* edited by Robert Holzmann and Edward Palmer, 17–33. Washington, DC: World Bank.

———. 2012. "Generic NDC: Equilibrium, Valuation, and Risk Sharing with and without NDC Bonds." In *Nonfinancial Defined Contribution Pension Schemes in a Changing Pension World,* edited by Robert Holzmann, Edward Palmer, and David Robalino, 309–33. Washington, DC: World Bank.

Perek Bialas, Jolanta, Agnieszka Chłoń-Domińczak, and Anna Ruzik. 2002. "Public Participation and the Pension System: The Case of Poland, Public Participation and the Pension Policy Process." The Citizen and Pension Reform (PEN-REF Project). PONT Info, Warsaw.

Pierson, Paul. 1994. *Dismantling the Welfare State? Reagan, Thatcher, and the Politics of Retrenchment.* New York: Cambridge University Press.

———. 1998. "Irresistible Forces, Immovable Objects: Post-Industrial Welfare States Confront Permanent Austerity." *Journal of European Public Policy* 5 (4): 539–60.

Rae, Garvin. 2008. *Poland's Return to Capitalism: From the Socialist Block to the European Union.* London: Taurus Academic Studies.

Rüb, Friedbert W., and Wolfram Lamping. 2010. "German Pension Policies: The Transformation of a Defined Benefit System Into... What?" *German Policy Studies* 6 (1): 143–85.

Schmähl, Winfried. 2007. "Dismantling an Earnings-Related Social Pension Scheme: Germany's New Pension Policy." *Journal of Social Policy* 36 (2): 319–40.

Schøyen, Mi Ah, and Furio Stamati. 2013. "The Political Sustainability of the NDC Pension Model: The Cases of Sweden and Italy." *European Journal of Social Security* 15 (1): 79–101.

Schulze, Isabelle, and Sven Jochem. 2007. "Germany: Beyond Policy Gridlock." In *The Handbook of West European Pension Politics*, edited by Ellen M. Immergut, Karen M. Anderson, and Isabelle Schulze, 660–710. Oxford and New York: Oxford University Press.

Stanovnik, Tine. 2002. "The Political Economy of Pension Reform in Slovenia." In *Pension Reform in Central and Eastern Europe Volume 2, Restructuring of Public Pension Schemes: Case Studies of the Czech Republic and Slovenia,* edited by Elaine Fultz, 19–73. Budapest: International Labour Office.

Stanovnik, Tine, and Nataša Turk. 2011. *ASISP Annual National Report 2009. Pensions, Health and Long-Term Care.* Slovenia, Brussels: European Commission DG Employment, Social Affairs and Equal Opportunities.

Stepan, Matthias, and Karen M. Anderson. 2014. "Pension Reform in the European Periphery: The Role of EU Reform Advocacy." *Public Administration and Development* 34: 320–31.

Sundén, Annika. 2012. "The Challenge of Reaching Participants with the Message of NDC." In *Nonfinancial Defined Contribution Pension Schemes in a Changing Pension World*: *Volume 2 Gender, Politics, and Financial Stability,* edited by Robert Holzmann, Edward Palmer, and David Robalino, 257–72. Washington, DC: World Bank.

Tavits, Margit. 2003. "Policy Learning and Uncertainty: The Case of Pension Reform in Estonia and Latvia." *Policy Studies Journal* 31 (4): 643–60.

Teichman, Judith. 2004. "The World Bank and Policy Reform in Mexico and Argentina." *Latin American Politics and Society* 46 (1): 39–74.

von Nordheim, Fritz. 2012. "On the First Wave of NDC Schemes." In *Nonfinancial Defined Contribution Pension Schemes in a Changing Pension World: Volume 1 Progress, Lessons, and Implementation,* edited by Robert Holzmann, Edward Palmer, and David Robalino, 122–25. Washington, DC: World Bank.

Weaver, Kent. 2010. "Paths and Forks or Chutes and Ladders? Negative Feedbacks and Policy Regime Change." *Journal of Public Policy* 30 (2): 137–62.

———. 2016. "Privileging Policy Change? Sustaining Automatic Stabilizing Mechanisms in Public Pensions." *Social Policy and Administration* 50 (2): 148–64.

———. 2018. "The Nays Have It: How Rampant Blame Generating Distorts American Policy and Politics." *Political Science Quarterly* 133 (2: Summer): 259–89.

Weyland, Kurt. 2005. "Theories of Policy Diffusion: Lessons from Latin American Pension Reform." *World Politics* 57 (2): 262–95.

Whitehouse, Edward. 2010. "Decomposing Notional Defined-Contribution Pensions: Experience of OECD Countries' Reforms." Social, Employment and Migration Working Paper 109, Organisation for Economic Co-operation and Development, Paris.

———. 2012. "Parallel Lines: NDC Pensions and the Direction of Pension Reform in Developed Countries." In *Nonfinancial Defined Contribution Pension Schemes in a Changing Pension World: Volume 1 Progress, Lessons, and Implementation,* edited by Robert Holzmann, Edward Palmer, and David Robalino, 86–105. Washington, DC: World Bank.

Williamson, John B., Stephanie A. Howling, and Michelle L. Maroto. 2006. "The Political Economy of Pension Reform in Russia: Why Partial Privatization?" *Journal of Aging Studies* 20 (2): 165–75.

World Bank. 2012. *Mongolia: Policy Options for Pension Reform.* Washington, DC: World Bank.

PART IX

Globalization: Portability, Taxes, and Private DC Supplements

Pensions in a Globalizing World: How Do (N)DC and (N)DB Schemes Fare and Compare on Portability and Taxation?

Bernd Genser and Robert Holzmann

Introduction

Pensions and broader forms of retirement income do not stop at national borders. As part of globalization and the increasing mobility of labor and capital, an increasing number of individuals spend at least part of their working lives abroad and acquire benefit rights that they want to take home or on to a new country of work or residence. Some individuals want to spend part or all of their retirement life in places with a better climate, a lower cost of living, or more benign taxation of their retirement income. However, the increasing mobility of individuals before and after retirement creates issues of the portability and taxation of cross-border pensions in accumulation and disbursement. Both topics—portability and taxation—have found limited attention in pension economics so far.

Simply put, full portability of pensions allows labor migrants to accumulate, keep, and transfer pension rights and to receive benefits in disbursement anywhere in the world. Without that ability, potential migrants may decide not to migrate, or to migrate although they risk losing their acquired rights. In the first case, international labor mobility is impeded; in the second, risk management is constrained and reduces the welfare of the migrant over his or her life cycle. Such obstacles may also arise even if pension benefits are portable but other benefits are not, particularly health care benefits during retirement.

The income taxation of cross-border pensions may increase or reduce individuals' migration incentives, because the tax burden of the retired migrant abroad may rise or fall depending on the total tax burden in working and residence countries. For the relevant tax burden of the migrant's pension, the tax treatment across the whole life cycle matters because taxes may be levied at the time of contribution or premium payment, return receipt, and disbursement.

Differences in the portability of social benefits and in the taxation of cross-border pensions raise issues of individual fairness (that is, do I get out what I paid in, and is my tax treatment equivalent to that of a nonmobile individual?). Portability also raises issues of fiscal fairness at the country level (that is, does the portability arrangement favor one country through tax arrangements under double taxation treaties?). A final issue concerns

The authors are grateful to Csaba Feher and Will Price for very helpful comments and suggestions.

the bureaucratic efficiency by which individual and fiscal fairness can be achieved (that is, how burdensome and time-consuming is tax compliance for all involved?).

This chapter addresses both portability and taxation issues from the angle of which type of pension scheme is more aligned with globalization by better establishing individual fairness, fiscal fairness, and bureaucratic efficiency. The focus is mostly on the benefit type—defined benefit (DB) versus defined contribution (DC)—with funding and administrative issues given secondary importance. The relevant literature on both topics is briefly summarized or referenced.

"The Rise of International Labor and Benefit Mobility" briefly establishes the facts of rising labor and benefit mobility across the world. "Portability Issues: Objectives, Instruments, and DB–DC Comparison" presents portability issues (absent taxation), how portability can be achieved, and the role of benefit types. "The Taxation of Cross-Border Pensions: Facts, Issues, and Suggested Solutions" presents cross-border issues regarding income taxation of benefits, current international disarray, and how it can be addressed. "Front-Loaded Taxation, Payment Options, and DB and DC in Comparison" extends the analysis and asks whether the type of scheme matters for the possible solutions. "Conclusions" summarizes and concludes on the ease of pension scheme alignment in a globalized world.

The Rise of International Labor and Benefit Mobility

The share of individuals living outside their home countries is increasing again after a temporary low in the 1970s, reaching 3.4 percent of the world population in 2017 (up from 2.3 percent in 1980), or an estimated 258 million people (UNDESA 2017). Figure 29.1 presents the dynamics of the number of migrants and their share in the world population since 1960. On January 1, 2016, the number of people living in the European Union-28 (EU-28) who were citizens of nonmember countries was 20.7 million, representing 4.1 percent of the EU-28 population, while the number of people living in the EU-28 who were born outside of the European Union was 35.1 million. In addition, 16.0 million persons were living in one of the EU member states on January 1, 2016, with the citizenship of another EU member state (Eurostat 2017).

These migrant stock numbers—impressive as they are—underestimate the underlying labor mobility dynamics, because the numbers in figure 29.1 only capture individuals who have lived outside their traditional country of residence in the observation year. Given that individuals may take multiple migration spells of varying length, sometimes in different countries, the relevant number of individuals with past migration spells is significantly higher. Evidence from across the world is strong that the number of spells spent abroad is increasing. The EU figures for individuals who spend at least some of their adult lives living outside their home country (as a student, intern, intra- or interfirm mobile employee, labor migrant, or "snowbird" retiree) are definitely rising and may soon be as high as one out of every five individuals (Holzmann 2015). Past labor market spells abroad translate into rising numbers of pension payments to and from abroad. For example, such payments amounted to about 11.1 percent of the total number of pensions paid in Germany in 2013, up from 9.8 percent in 2005. Table 29.1 details the composition and trends in former labor and more recent retirement mobility to and from Germany.

FIGURE 29.1 **Number and share of migrants in world population, 1960–2017**

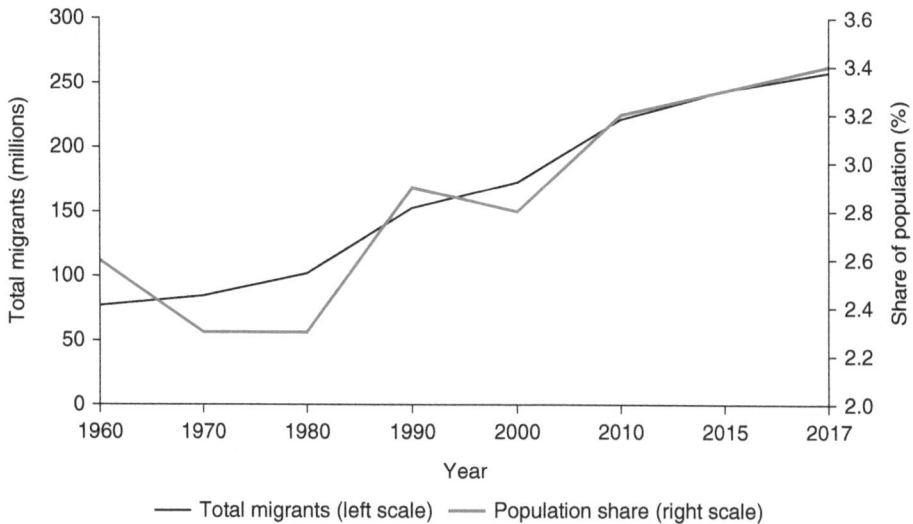

SOURCES: UNDESA 2017; Migration Policy Institute, Data Hub; original compilation.

TABLE 29.1 **Recipients of statutory German pensions—in Germany and abroad**

	Number of pensioners in thousands (% of total pensioners)		
	2013	**2010**	**2005**
Pensioners with non-German citizenship	2,562 (100)	2,367 (100)	2,032 (100)
• Living in Germany	1,059 (41.3)	944 (39.9)	774 (38.1)
• Living outside Germany	1,503 (58.7)	1,423 (60.1)	1,258 (61.9)
Pensioners with German citizenship	22,602 (100)	22,646 (100)	22,452 (100)
• Living outside Germany	222 (0.98)	206 (0.91)	170 (0.76)
Total number of pensioners	25,164 (100)	25,013 (100)	22,484 (100)
• Living outside Germany	1,725 (6.85)	1,629 (6.51)	1,427 (5.83)
• Non-German citizens living in Germany	1,059 (4.21)	944 (3.77)	774 (3.44)
• Potential recipients of cross-border pensions	2,784 (11.1)	2,573 (10.3)	2,201 (9.8)

SOURCE: Genser and Holzmann 2018, based on Eurostat online database (June 2015).

Warnes (2009) presents data for Germany, the United Kingdom, and the United States on the popularity and dynamics of their respective retirement destinations for the period mid-1990s to 2005. His data show a dynamic similar to that presented in table 29.1.

Portability Issues: Objectives, Instruments, and DB-DC Comparison

The topic of cross-border portability of pensions (and other social benefits) is a relatively new area in pension economics. Although the portability of pension benefits within countries and between occupational plans has been explored for quite some time (for example, Foster 1994), portability between countries has received little attention by economists. This field was generally left to social policy and social law experts.

This chapter focuses on the economic issues of portability, which might be captured by the following working definition[1]:

> Cross-border portability of pension benefits is the ability of labor migrants to preserve, maintain, and transfer both acquired pension rights and rights in the process of being acquired from one private, occupational, or statutory pension scheme, to another independent of nationality and aligned with the country of residence. Pension rights refer, in principle, to all rights stemming from contributory payments or residence criteria in a country. Not portable typically are benefit components that are not based on contributions such as benefit top-ups for low-income individuals or minimum income guarantees.[2]

This section presents the economic foundation of portability based on three elements: a brief discussion of the economic objectives of international portability of pensions and more broadly of social security benefits; a brief presentation of the key instruments used to establish pension benefit portability; and an assessment of the implications for the DB-DC selection.

OBJECTIVES OF PORTABILITY

Establishing portability of social benefits should be straightforward, given that three key considerations—economic, social, and human rights—favor it (Holzmann and Koettl 2015).

From a first-best economic point of view, individuals' labor mobility decisions should not be hampered by the lack of portability of social benefits for which they have acquired rights. Global efficiency and global growth are increased if distortionary obstacles toward portability are absent. To ensure that international labor mobility profits the home as well as the host country, select and appropriate bilateral interventions may be necessary.

The lack of benefit portability can influence labor migrants' international mobility decisions. Workers may decide not to take jobs abroad if they have to pay social security contributions in the host country but cannot profit from its benefit coverage or cannot take their acquired rights home. Nonportability is particularly relevant for the long-term benefits of pensions and health care. For pensions, nonportability may exist because of long vesting periods of 10, 15, or more years or to restrictions on cross-border benefit payments. Access to health care services in retirement is typically linked to the eligibility of pension benefits and residence in the host country, unless cross-country legal arrangements exist.

From a social policy point of view, such acquired rights are a critical element of individuals' (or families') life-cycle planning and social risk management. Denying portability—particularly once the mobility decision has been made and cannot be reversed—increases the risk of life-cycle planning for individuals and their families and creates substantial welfare losses.

For emigrants a lack of portability of acquired rights means that they can establish pension rights only in their host country. Although a higher (comparable) wage level in the host country may provide some compensation, labor emigrants will face a lower replacement rate after retirement. This situation typically happens for mid-career labor migrants. A migrant who plans to return home but cannot transfer pension rights acquired abroad or receive cross-border benefits will need to increase private saving or continue working. These adjustments in life-cycle planning are beneficial, but they do not avoid welfare losses compared with the portability case.

From a human rights point of view, migrants have the right to enjoy social protection according to national legislation and international conventions. These rights should carry over when individuals leave the country or change profession. A key question is whether these human rights apply only to acquired (contributory or residential) pension rights or to all social rights. Because they are resource-consuming, economic and human rights tradeoffs will emerge.

INSTRUMENTS OF PORTABILITY

Essentially three approaches are available to establish cross-border portability of pension benefits between countries:

- Enacting binding portability arrangements between countries
- Using multinational private pension providers
- Changing the pension benefit design to make benefits portable without further government action

Portability arrangements between countries

Most portability analyses and discussions focus on bilateral agreements (BAs), but the scope is much larger and includes unilateral and multilateral arrangements (MAs).

Unilateral actions can be taken by the country where migrants earn labor income and are able to acquire pension rights. Examples of unilateral actions include the following:

- If migrants are denied access to the national social security scheme,[3] they can be given the option to contribute to pension schemes in their home countries, as is feasible in Mexico, the Philippines, and Sri Lanka.

- If migrants are denied access to the national social security scheme, they can be given voluntary access to either the host or the home country pension system. Enrollment in a scheme in the home country pension system avoids host country constraints on cross-border benefit payments.[4]

- Granting migrants full access to the statutory national pension scheme as well as full exportability of eligible pension rights may establish full portability. Hence all pensioners with a contribution length beyond the vesting period keep their acquired pension rights and receive pension benefits after the minimum retirement age is reached and other eligibility conditions are fulfilled. Ineligibility typically emerges because of a contribution record that falls short of the vesting period.

BAs are the centerpiece of current portability arrangements between countries. Although they can, in principle, cover the whole range of exportable social benefits, they typically focus on long-term benefits such as old-age, survivors', and disability pensions, and to a much lesser extent on health care benefits, if at all.[5,6]

With regard to pensions, BAs can do the following:

- Focus on temporary migrants only (for example, waiving the contribution requirement to the pension scheme in the host country while making contributions mandatory in the home country).

- Establish mutual exportability of pension claims between the two countries.

- Allow migrants to continue paying their social security contribution to their home country for an extended period.

- Establish "totalization" (that is, summing up) of the insurance periods across both countries, thus eliminating or at least reducing the binding effects of vesting periods in individual countries.

- Cover all migrants (legal or even illegal) who have established acquired rights.

- Establish full eligibility across the two agreement countries.

- Establish benefits for migrants in the case of different benefit types between countries, such as the complex case between a residence-based basic benefit country (such as Australia) and an earnings-related, contribution-based benefit country (such as Germany).

MAs represent a general framework for portability for a group of countries for all or a subset of social benefits. These general rules are in most cases supported by more detailed BAs. Traditional MAs have been established in Latin America (MERCOSUR) and the Caribbean (CARICOM) and in 15 French-speaking countries in Africa (CIPRES); one was recently established between Latin America and Spain and Portugal (Ibero-American Social Security Convention); and one is under development for the Association of Southeast Asian Nations (ASEAN) countries.

The most developed MA is the one among EU member states (plus Norway, Liechtenstein, and Switzerland). Strictly speaking the EU arrangement is not an MA but an EU directive that obliges EU member countries to adjust their existing regulations accordingly (that is, to revise their existing BAs). The main objective of the directive is essentially to make all social benefit claims portable among EU member states, including unemployment and family benefits, to avoid discrimination and to establish full labor mobility, one of four core freedoms of the EU treaties.[7]

For portability of statutory pension benefits, exportability works well; for private sector schemes exportability works well in principle, but is not frictionless. Hence, benefit losses are possible for those moving between countries' public and private sector schemes.[8] Issues emerge with the portability of occupational and personal pension schemes—as within countries—when individuals leave a DB scheme that is, for example, linked to their final salary. This also happens with DC schemes, which are essentially individual savings plans. Here the tax privileges granted at the level of contribution or premium payments and rates of return received render their simple export difficult and the EU has not yet found an effective way to establish comprehensive portability (see

"The Taxation of Cross-Border Pensions: Facts, Issues, and Suggested Solutions" and "Front-Loaded Taxation, Payment Options, and DB and DC in Comparison"). Even when transfers can be made, they may inhibit the original intention of the pension policy, for example, when a pension plan offers a lump sum in cash to workers when they leave the country. If there is no requirement to invest the money into another pension plan, then the likelihood is higher that the money will be partly spent on short-term consumption rather than contributing to retirement saving. So portability should ideally be portability of assets from one pension vehicle to another.

Multinational private sector providers

A promising approach, at least for supplementary benefits, is to use the services of privately organized multinational providers, which function well for health care benefits. For example, Cigna, a Belgium-based service provider, services World Bank staff and retirees residing in Europe, as well as staff of the European University Institute. Multinational provider arrangements have been discussed, and sometimes implemented, for supplementary pensions of international workers in multinational enterprises so that these insured persons are tied to a single pension vehicle even if they work in various countries. Multinational providers may prove superior to national providers with respect to interjurisdictional risk sharing, because of risk pooling, transmission of best practices and innovations across countries, and better information on the state of the world.

Changes in benefit design

The key idea behind changing benefit design is to transparently disentangle the components that are lumped together in the pseudo-actuarial benefit design of social security schemes. For all social benefits, these components are the period insurance element, the presaving element, and the redistributive element (Holzmann and Koettl 2015, 378–80).

The period insurance component is only valid for one period, that in which it is consumed; hence, it does not require portability. This element is relevant in health insurance, does not exist in old-age pension schemes, but does exist in the form of survivors' or disability claims if all are lumped together under one contribution rate.

The presaving (or asset accumulation) component exists in all social benefit systems in one form or another. It is huge in health care and old-age benefit schemes, amounting to a high multiple of annual contributions. In a health care scheme without age-related contribution rates, this component serves to accumulate reserves for health care costs that rise with age and for catastrophic health care. In old-age pension schemes, the financial or nonfinancial presaving is the constituent component. Conceptually, a pure accumulation phase is followed by a decumulation phase in which annuities or phased withdrawals are paid out.

The redistributive component can be thought of as the deviation between accumulated individual contributions (including returns) and individual pension wealth (that is, the present value of expected future pension benefit payments) at the end of each period. The redistributive component is the consequence of a nonactuarial benefit design required by explicit or implicit redistributive considerations within the pension scheme.

For individuals the redistributive component may be positive or negative. A dominantly positive redistributive component typically emerges when a pension scheme is not only fed by contributions but also receives transfers from the general budget.

If the three components can be separated conceptually and technically, then benefit portability between countries is substantially facilitated:

- In the most drastic separation, there is no period insurance component, because disability and survivors' pensions are separately organized; there is no redistributive component, because all redistribution is done outside the pension scheme; and the remaining presaving component is purely actuarial and can be transferred across borders upon migration.

- In a less complete separation, there is again no period insurance component, and no redistributive component from interpersonal transfers, but the presaving component is not actuarially fair because of government transfers. Although this component is ready for portability, the question that emerges is, To what extent should the transferred amount be corrected to account fairly for the presaving increment, which is financed through the budget of the source country?

NDB AND NDC SCHEMES COMPARED

Against the background of the objectives, instruments, and evaluation criteria discussed so far, how do DB and DC schemes compare on portability? To simplify and shorten the comparison, the focus is only on nonfinancial DB and DC schemes (NDBs and NDCs), but most results are believed to also hold for financial DBs and DCs (FDBs and FDCs).[9]

The following properties of NDC and NDB schemes are relevant for cross-border portability:

- Ideally, an NDC scheme has no period insurance component because disability insurance is separately financed and organized (but coordinated with the NDC scheme); long-term survivors' benefits are financed by own accounts and shared accumulations of spouses; and short-term transitional benefits during child-rearing periods are financed by other structures and resources (Holzmann 2017).

- The "textbook" NDC scheme has no redistributive component within the insurance pool, and no redistributive component of budget subsidies to support financial sustainability.[10] The existing redistributive components are explicit and financed through earmarked government transfers and reflect purposeful social policy objectives. These social policy objectives emerge if individuals cannot make own contributions because of disability, unemployment, maternity leave, family leave, and so on, and are financed by the respective programs (typically by earmarked contributions). Beyond that one can also imagine selective matching or lump-sum contributions to individual accounts to encourage formal labor market contributions or to render the NDC scheme explicitly redistributive (Holzmann, Robalino, and Winkler 2018).

- Because of the above-mentioned characteristic features of an NDC scheme, the accumulated individual account values reflect own contributions, rates of return that are consistent with financial sustainability, and an external contribution earmarked for individual circumstances. Thus, these accounts are fully portable as NDC annuities or as accumulated pension wealth amounts before eligibility.

- In a traditional NDB scheme, disability and survivors' pensions are typically part of the old-age benefits scheme design. Survivors' pensions lose importance under reformed NDB schemes as receipt of an own pension above a certain amount increasingly disqualifies one from receiving a widow or widower's pension, and one's children receive flat-rate amounts. Again, these reforms reduce the contemporaneous insurance component but do not eliminate it. No good answers arise regarding which acquired rights for these risks should be portable.

- Traditional NDB schemes have a few explicit and many implicit redistributive components because of their design. Most countries also have a variable redistributive component to keep these schemes afloat. Making explicit redistributive components portable raises little objection from the perspective of family or other social policy considerations (often expressed by assimilated insurance periods or earlier retirement age); the problem is their costing. The implicit and often unknown redistributive components should, in principle, not become portable. But serious problems arise in establishing appropriate adjustment mechanisms to account for characteristic NDB features like last salary assessment period, variable annual accrual rate, or nonactuarial decrements for earlier or later retirement. Some of these components could be mitigated, for example, by basing the pension benefit on lifetime income or introducing actuarial increments or decrements for early retirement.

- As a result of the difficulties of eliminating the contemporaneous component and of reducing the redistributive component to meaningful, measurable components, the presaving component cannot be well defined; it also requires cumbersome actuarial calculations for which objective estimates are difficult if not impossible to establish. Consequently, the amount of pension benefit to be sent abroad may still require a BA to establish portability, for example, if the vesting period cannot be reduced to a few months. Making the acquired rights portable before retirement will not work unless the sustainability transfers are eliminated. This is possible with the introduction of an automatic balancing mechanism but is technically much more challenging in an NDB scheme compared with an NDC scheme.

Summarizing the comparison of NDB and NDC schemes to establish cross-border portability, the following conclusions emerge:

- Textbook NDC schemes promise full portability even in the absence of BAs and MAs. Full exportability of benefits in disbursement and preservation of the acquired rights are required. Full exportability can be established unilaterally; full preservation until eligibility is a design component of an NDC scheme given that the account values are annually indexed with the notional (sustainable) rate of return.

- Whether acquired rights in an NDC scheme before eligibility should become portable and transferred in real cash is a question of convenience and reciprocity with another NDC country, because only the annual balance of notional inflows and outflows needs to be settled in cash. However, because the annuity at retirement is determined by country-specific cohort life expectancy, such portability before retirement may invite benefit arbitrage. It would not affect the source country but would affect the receiving country if its cohort life expectancy was well below that of the sending country, while it offers access to groups with a higher life expectancy.

- NDB schemes will always need BAs or MAs to achieve portability. But the closer NDBs are to NDCs, the simpler are cross-border portability arrangements. BAs or full-fledged MAs will still exist for NDC corridor countries for purely administrative reasons as well as to establish portability for other benefits, such as health care.

- Whereas BAs exist between most industrial countries, they are the exception, not the rule, between industrial and emerging market or developing economies. As a result, in 2013 only 23.3 percent of worldwide migrants lived in countries with BAs between home and host countries, and more than 80 percent of these migrants were from high-income countries (table 29.2). Global progress since 2000—the other year for which comparable data estimates are available—has been moderate and amounts to 1.4 percentage points (table 29.3). Further progress on BAs is likely to be slow too, because their establishment depends on demanding conditions in lower-income countries (Holzmann 2016).

TABLE 29.2 **Global migrant stock estimates by origin country income group and portability regime, 2013**

Origin country income group	Regime I (%) (Portability)	Regime II[a] (%) (Exportability)	Regime III[b] (%) (No access)	Regime IV[c] (%) (Informality)	Total (millions)
High-income non-OECD	50.7	40.2	4.3	4.8	5.1
High-income OECD	76.3	19.0	0.4	4.3	33.0
Upper-middle income	23.3	54.4	0.5	21.8	33.6
Lower-middle income	20.2	58.5	8.7	12.6	104.8
Low income	2.7	61.2	18.7	17.3	75.9
Total	23.3	53.2	9.4	14.0	252.3

SOURCE: Holzmann and Jacques 2018.

NOTE: Percentage per regional income group. OECD = Organisation for Economic Co-operation and Development.

a. Legal migrants with access to social security in the host country in the absence of a bilateral or multilateral arrangement.

b. Legal migrants without access to social security in the host country.

c. Undocumented immigrants.

TABLE 29.3 **Global migrant stock estimates by origin country income group and portability regime, change between 2000 and 2013**

percentage point change per regional income group, except as noted

Origin country income group	Regime I (Portability)	Regime II[a] (Exportability)	Regime III[b] (No access)	Regime IV[c] (Informality)	Total (millions)
High-income non-OECD	10.3	−14.1	0.8	3.0	−0.4
High-income OECD	−8.4	5.9	−0.6	3.0	4.1
Upper-middle income	9.6	−4.4	−0.2	−5.0	8.2
Lower-middle income	6.1	−4.2	4.2	−6.1	26.9
Low income	1.2	−7.9	8.9	−2.2	21.8
Total (%)	1.4	−3.0	4.5	−2.9	60.6

SOURCES: Holzmann and Jacques 2018; Holzmann, Koettl, and Chernetsky 2005.

NOTE: OECD = Organisation for Economic Co-operation and Development.

a. Legal migrants with access to social security in the host country in the absence of a bilateral or multilateral arrangement.

b. Legal migrants without access to social security in the host country.

c. Undocumented immigrants.

The Taxation of Cross-Border Pensions: Facts, Issues, and Suggested Solutions

The topic of taxing cross-border pensions is terra incognita in economics. No single recognized or competing paradigms explain how internationally portable pensions should be taxed. Yet countries typically have many bilateral double taxation agreements (DTAs) that include rules on how the rights are assigned to tax income from pensions and other retirement saving instruments. But this agreed-upon tax treatment of pensions in a DTA for one migration corridor is not necessarily the same for another corridor, even if the corridor partners are neighbors. Furthermore, tax treatment typically differs substantially across pension pillars (statutory, occupational, and personal). The guidance that exists on pensions is established in the Organisation for Economic Co-operation and Development (OECD) model tax convention on income and capital. Its relevant articles 18 and 19 suggest different tax treatment of cross-border pensions for private and public sector pensions—namely residence- versus sourced-based (see annex 29A). Furthermore, they are also highly incomplete because they deal only with the disbursement phase of pension taxation, leaving out the contribution payment and saving and return receipt phases. Hardly any other area in economics has such a conceptual void, which has led to operational complexity and inconsistency in the taxation of cross-border pensions (Genser and Holzmann 2016, 2018).

This section summarizes recent attempts to highlight issues and offers a new proposal on how pensions should be taxed to address the double fairness dilemma of current pension taxation (Genser 2015; Genser and Holzmann 2016, 2018; Holzmann 2015): individuals risk unfair treatment because of the differences between and within countries, with some individuals paying the income tax on pension benefits twice—once during accumulation in the source country and again during decumulation in the residence country; others may benefit from tax exemption of pension wealth accumulation and disbursement in two countries. Of course, the latter case gives rise to tax arbitrage by strategic migration. Countries risk substantial fiscal unfairness given that the current rules propose the taxation of cross-border pension benefits in the residence country, while income tax losses emerge in the source country, if income spent on contributions and income from pension wealth returns are tax exempt. In view of the rising share of international mobility and benefit eligibility abroad (recall "The Rise of International Labor and Benefit Mobility"), such a situation is unfair and unsustainable.

To substantiate this proposal, this section highlights three areas: the state of taxation of cross-border pensions; the incompatibility of deferred income taxation and the OECD model tax convention; and a new framework for pretaxed pension and retirement income.

THE STATE OF TAXATION OF CROSS-BORDER PENSIONS

Income taxation in most OECD countries is codified according to the Schanz-Haig-Simons principle of comprehensive income taxation, which regards any annual increase in personal wealth as taxable income. This is not controversial for individual pension wealth accumulated in financial institutions such as pension funds, insurance companies, or banks, because wealth accruals increase individuals' ability to pay and should therefore be taxed as a component of comprehensive income. Economically this is also true for notional pension wealth accruals within a statutory or mandatory occupational pension scheme, because individual pension claims under these schemes increase ability to pay, although pension benefits are not capital-funded but financed on a pay-as-you-go (PAYG) basis. In fact, this difference between funded and unfunded pensions has led to different tax treatment of these pensions.

To compare national pension tax practices, three phases of capital accumulation are distinguished in which income taxes can or should be levied: pension wealth accumulation through contributions or savings, returns on accumulations, and dissaving or withdrawal of pension wealth. Technically, comprehensive income taxation of savings can be characterized by a T-T-E income tax, in which each T indicates that the respective income flow is taxed at the going tax rate and E indicates that it is tax exempt. With respect to old-age pensions' comprehensive income taxation, T-T-E requires that income used to contribute to a pension system should be taxed; growing pension claims as returns to pension wealth should be taxed as well; but withdrawals of pension wealth are tax exempt. In contrast to the comprehensive income principle, most national income tax codes tax PAYG financed pensions as E-E-T, which implies exempting income spent on pension contributions and income from accruals in pension claims and taxing withdrawals of pension benefits. Although a long-lasting dispute persists among public economists about whether to tax capital income according to either T-T-E (Schanz-Haig-Simons) or E-E-T (Fisher-Kaldor), tax lawyers argue that the difference in taxing pensions is nondiscriminatory if statutory pensions are preferentially taxed as deferred labor income and funded pensions are double taxed as capital income.

A survey of pension taxation in OECD countries shows a much broader variety of tax rules for different forms of pensions (table 29.4). To capture the different tax rules, "t" and "s" are introduced to indicate that in a certain phase of the pension cycle a lower tax rate, t<T, or even a subsidy rate s, is applied. In this sample a majority of countries

TABLE 29.4 Income taxation of pensions in Organisation for Economic Co-operation and Development member countries

Tax regime	Statutory pension	Occupational pension[a]	Personal pension[a]
T-T-E		NZL, TUR	NZL, TUR
T-t-E		AUS, DNK	AUS
T-E-t			DEU
t-T-E			SVK
t-E-T	CAN, FRA, GBR, MLT, NLD	BEL, HRV, NOR	AUT, FIN, HRV, NOR
t-t-t		FRA	
E-t-T		DNK, LVA, SWE	DNK
T-E-E		LVA, POL	AUT, HUN, USA
t-t-E		AUS	AUS
t-E-t	CHE, DEU, EST, LIE, NOR,	AUT, BEL, FRA, LUX, MLT, PRT	AUT, BEL, FRA, MLT, PRT
E-E-T	AUT, BEL, CHE, CYP, DEU, DNK, ESP, FIN, GRC, HRV, IRL, ISL, ITA, LUX, MKD, POL, ROM, SVN, SVK	CAN, CHE, ESP, FIN, DEU, GRC, HRV, ISL, NLD, SVN, USA	CAN, CHE, ESP, GRC, HRV, ISL, NLD, POL, SWE, SVN, USA
E-t-t	CZE	ITA	ITA, LVA
s-E-T	SWE		
t-E-E	AL, HUN, LT, MNE	CZE, HUN	CZE, EST,
E-t-E	MNE	CYP	CYP
E-E-t	LIE, LVA, PRT; TUR, USA	EST, GBR, IRL, ISL, ROM	GBR, IRL, LUX, POL, ROM
E-E-E	ARM, AZE, BGR, BLR, GEO, MCO, MDA, SRB, RUS, UKR	BGR, SVK	BGR, LTU

SOURCES: Genser and Holzmann 2016, 2018; International Bureau of Fiscal Documentation 2017; OECD 2015.

NOTE: Country abbreviations follow the International Organization for Standardization three-letter codes listed in annex 29B.

a. OECD (2015) does not cover Albania, Armenia, Azerbaijan, Belarus, Georgia, Liechtenstein, Moldova, Monaco, Montenegro, the Russian Federation, Serbia, or Ukraine.

apply expenditure taxation (E-E-T) and none of them apply comprehensive income taxation (T-T-E) to statutory pensions. A few of them impose a slightly higher income tax burden, but many offer additional tax preferences to statutory pensions, down to a complete tax exemption through all three phases of the pension cycle. Sweden is the only country that grants pension tax relief by not only deducting social security contributions from the personal income tax base but by granting a full tax credit for these contributions. The taxation of occupational and personal pensions reveals a similar pattern, with a less dominant cluster of countries using E-E-T. But the "Occupational pension" and "Personal pension" columns also exhibit a significantly broader scope of complexity, reaching from comprehensive income taxation down to full exemption of occupational as well as personal pensions over all three phases of the pension cycle. In addition to the different forms of tax treatment represented in table 29.4, country-specific personal pension schemes are often connected with direct subsidy payments[11] that are granted to encourage voluntary enrollment in supplementary pension saving by further reducing the individual pension tax burden.

The complexity of the tax treatment of pensions increases when pensions accrue across borders. The avoidance of international double taxation of cross-border pensions is codified in bilateral DTAs. Although these treaties usually follow the recommendations of the OECD model tax convention, room for variation arises in income tax assignments for different forms of foreign income. Table 29.5 reveals the tax assignment of cross-border pension flows in treaties signed by Germany. The residence principle shows a marked dominance, but statutory pensions are frequently assigned exclusively to the source country. Shared tax assignments allowing for limited source country tax credited in the residence country are rare.

A closer look at the bilateral network of DTAs for a richer set of countries reveals three fundamental complexities of cross-border pension taxation (Genser and Holzmann 2016, 2018). First, countries tax cross-border pension benefits differently for different forms of retirement income. Second, countries tax inbound cross-border pension benefits differently depending on the source country. Third, outbound pension benefits paid by Germany are taxed differently depending on the residence country of the pensioner.

Based on tables 29.4 and 29.5, application of different tax rules within and between countries for different forms of pensions risks violating horizontal fairness, motivates strategic pension planning, and is a source of interpersonal fiscal unfairness. In addition, inconsistent and uncoordinated assignments for income taxes on retirement income create fiscal unfairness between countries and induce strategic migration of pensioners and international competition in pension taxation.

TABLE 29.5 **Tax assignment of cross-border pensions in German double taxation treaties**

Tax assignment	Statutory	Occupational	Personal
Exclusive residence taxation	CAN, CHE, CZE, EST, ESP, FIN, GRC, HUN, IRL, ITA, LUX, PRT, SWE, SVN, GBR, USA	AUT, BEL, CHE, CZE, EST, ESP, FIN, FRA, GRC, HUN, IRL, ITA, LUX, MLT, NLD, POL, SWE, SVN, GBE, USA	AUT, BEL, CHE, CZE, DNK, EST, ESP, FIN, FRA, GRC, HUN, IRL, ITA, LUX, MT, NLD, POL, PRT, SWE, SVN, GBR, USA
Exclusive source taxation, progression proviso in residence country	AUT, BEL, DNK, FRA, ITA (citizens), MLT, NLD, POL, SWE	FRA (mandatory)	
Nonexclusive source taxation, residence taxation with tax credit		CAN, DNK	CAN, DNK (rents)

SOURCES: Genser and Holzmann 2018; Wellisch et al. 2008; and tax treaties.

NOTE: The country abbreviations follow the International Organization for Standardization three-letter codes listed in annex 29B.

THE INCOMPATIBILITY OF DEFERRED INCOME TAXATION AND THE OECD MODEL TAX CONVENTION

The OECD model tax convention addresses pensions explicitly in Article 18 (see annex 29A). According to this article, pensions disbursed across-borders "in consideration of past employment" are taxable only in the residence country of the recipient. However, the article contains a provision clause for pension benefits paid out to a recipient in the residence country who had been employed in the source country by a public body. In this case the pension is taxable in the source state unless the recipient is also a national of the resident state.

The dominance of the residence principle is motivated by administrative arguments. First, the residence state of the recipient of a foreign pension is "in a better position than the source state to take into account the recipient's overall ability to pay, which depends on the worldwide income and the personal circumstances" (OECD 2014). Second, residence taxation eases tax compliance of the recipient of foreign pension benefits because tax obligations are concentrated in the residence country only. Source taxation on public pensions according to Article 19 was originally a byproduct of income taxation of public employees "inherited from traditional rules of international courtesy." However, the scope and fiscal importance of Article 19 increased with the growth of the public sector in many countries and with the extension of public activities abroad. The OECD model tax convention thus changed the assignment of taxes on public salaries and wages (and subsequent pensions) from a potential to an exclusive right of the source state.

From an economic perspective, it is important to recognize that the assignment of tax competences in the OECD model tax convention is restricted to the third phase of the pension cycle, when pension benefits are paid out across the border. The possibility of taxing pensions while pension wealth is accumulated is addressed neither in the model tax convention nor in the elaborate commentaries on the particular articles. An immediate consequence of this gap is that pensions that were pretaxed in the source country during the accumulation period will be double taxed if the residence country taxes pension benefits.

This undesirable result can be avoided if the source country's tax code determines deferred income taxation on pensions, as proposed by the European Commission. Under an E-E-T regime no income tax is levied when contributions are paid and pension wealth earns returns, and income tax only becomes due when pension benefits are paid out. For a pensioner who emigrates after retirement, and for whom pension benefits are taxed exclusively in the immigration country, double taxation cannot occur.

Table 29.6 presents a set of simplified treaty examples that illustrate the constrained capability of the model tax convention to solve the double equity dilemma. For a given set of parameters, the table illustrates the interaction of three different tax regimes in country A and two assignments of income taxation for a pensioner who migrates to country B after retirement. To interpret the numbers, keep in mind that income taxation subject to the source principle replicates the tax situation in the no-migration case. The pensioner's tax burden differs under the three tax regimes, depending on the tax policy: expenditure taxation (E-E-T); prepaid expenditure taxation with exempt returns (T-E-E); or comprehensive income taxation (T-T-E).

TABLE 29.6 **Income tax on pensioners migrating from country A to country B under different tax assignments and tax regimes**

	Parameter selection:					
Labor income 120	Contribution rate 0.2			Income tax rate 0.3		Return rate 0.5
	Residence principle			Source principle		
	E-E-T	T-E-E	T-T-E	E-E-T	T-E-E	T-T-E
A1 income	120	120	120	120	120	120
A1 pension contributions	24	24	24	24	24	24
A1 income tax base	96	120	156	96	120	156
A1 income tax	28.8	36	46.8	28.8	36	46.8
A2 pension benefit	36	36	36	36	36	36
A2 income tax base	0	0	0	36	0	0
A2 income tax	0	0	0	10.8	0	0
B2 tax base	36	36	36	0	0	0
B2 income tax	10.8	10.8	10.8	0	0	0
Total income[a]	132	132	132	132	132	132
Total tax[a]	39.6	46.8	57.6	39.6	36	46.8

SOURCE: Original table.

NOTE: A1 = working period in country A; A2 = retirement period in country A; B2 = retirement period in country B.

a. Net present value, normal return rate zero.

Three results reveal the problems of the OECD model tax convention with respect to pension taxation:

- The last row shows that application of the residence principle avoids international double taxation only in the case of expenditure taxation, whereas the treaty rules do not eliminate double taxation if pensions are pretaxed, because tax credits only account for source country taxes on pension benefits.
- For the source country, deferred income taxation under the residence principle implies that the deferred income tax revenue on cross-border pension benefits is zero.
- For the residence country, income taxation under the source principle implies that the income tax revenue on cross-border pension benefits is zero.

A NEW FRAMEWORK FOR PRETAXED PENSION INCOME

To address the incompatibility outlined in the previous section, a new framework is proposed here. The starting position is the weakness of the prevailing taxation architecture. The framework then proposes to move toward front-loaded taxation of pensions and to codify source taxation in DTAs. In addition, three pension tax payment options are suggested to implement the framework.

The starting position

The starting point for a new framework for pension taxation is the existence of two unsolved problems in the prevailing architecture of existing pension tax systems. First, there is the simultaneous orientation of tax equity along two mutually exclusive equity standards: comprehensive income taxation and expenditure taxation.[12] These standards imply different time patterns of capital income taxation over the accumulation and use of capital. The Schanz-Haig-Simons principle requires taxation while capital wealth accrues (in other words, T-T-E), whereas the Fisher-Kaldor principle defers taxation until capital wealth is used for consumption (in other words, E-E-T). The Fisher-Kaldor approach forgoes the double taxation of savings and establishes intertemporal neutrality on consumer spending decisions. Countries typically apply comprehensive income taxation for capital income not related to retirement and apply various forms of Fisher-Kaldor-type taxes on different forms of retirement income. Pure expenditure taxation is frequently applied for statutory pensions, and less frequently for occupational pensions. Highly differentiated and country-specific forms of taxation are applied to personal pensions (table 29.4).

Second, tax assignment and balancing methods in DTAs that try to avoid double taxation of pensions are codified only for cross-border pension benefit flows. These tax regulations ignore the fact that pensions might have already been pretaxed when pension wealth was accumulated.

The proposal

Double taxation of pensions can be avoided by requiring the following:

- Pensions are taxed according to the Fisher-Kaldor principle.
- Fair taxation of pensions has to account for pension taxes over the whole pension cycle.

To satisfy the first requirement the proposal makes use of a fundamental equivalence property of the Fisher-Kaldor approach. The nonneutrality of comprehensive income taxation can be avoided not only by expenditure taxation (E-E-T), but also by a corresponding front-loaded income tax regime (T-t-E), which shares the intertemporal neutrality property of the back-loaded Fisher-Kaldor-type expenditure tax and is economically equivalent under a set of simplifying assumptions.[13] Under a T-t-E regime, income spent on pension savings is taxed when contributions are made and exempted when pension benefits are withdrawn from accumulated pension wealth. Moreover, returns on pension wealth are only liable to tax if they exceed normal returns that are tax exempt. This partial income tax exemption of returns is indicated by t. t<T also reveals that the tax liability under the two equivalent forms of Fisher-Kaldor taxation is smaller than under comprehensive income taxation.

The second requirement makes use of the time pattern of T-t-E taxation. Pensions are pretaxed in the source country, whereas pension benefits are exempt. To avoid double taxation of cross-border benefits, it is necessary to exempt pension benefits in the residence country as well. Compared with deferred income taxation, under T-t-E, the source country does not suffer from income tax revenue losses on exempt contributions when individuals migrate as retirees nor when they emigrate before retirement, because their pension wealth has been appropriately taxed upon accrual.

Pretaxing pensions following the Fisher-Kaldor principle should facilitate the achievement of a consensual solution between treaty partners on the assignment of the taxing right on cross-border pension benefits:

- Pretaxation of pension implies that the recouping pressure of deferred income taxation is absent upon migration.

- No income tax is due for pension benefits paid out to migrants and nonmigrants.

- Pretaxation of pension income accounts for the personal circumstances of the income earner and his ability to pay under unlimited tax liability as a resident of the source country.

- Two key arguments that gave reason to assign the competence of taxing cross-border pension benefits in the residence country no longer apply: the recipient is not taxed under limited tax liability on pension benefits in the source country after migration, because his or her pension benefits were already pretaxed under unlimited tax liability when a resident of the emigration country; and the recipient would only have to comply with the tax authority in the residence country after migration, because the pension benefits are tax exempt in the source country.

- If pensions are pretaxed and pension benefits are not taxed in both treaty countries, the likelihood of agreeing on exclusive source taxation to avoid double taxation should be much higher than under deferred income taxation.

The solution to the double taxation problem of cross-border pensions is simple if countries are willing to switch from deferred income taxation to front-loaded expenditure taxation. The revision to the OECD model tax convention would then only need to codify exclusive source taxation on pension benefits, replacing the present mixture of residence and source taxation depending on the type of pension.

Three tax payment options

The front-loaded pension tax approach suggests that tax liabilities must be cleared immediately upon income tax assessment. But this is not a necessary consequence. The tax authority may be ready to accept deferred payment of the assessed tax liability in the same fiscal way as expenditure taxation defers taxation of saved income. Deferred down payment of tax debt is neutral for the intertemporal government budget constraint as long as the present value of deferred tax payments is equal to the present value of the assessed tax liability. For this reason, three proposals are presented that complement the T-t-E front-loaded pension tax regime by decoupling the tax statement of the tax authority and the prescription of the tax payment.

  a. *The front-loaded tax payment option* requires that tax liabilities be immediately settled when they occur. This does not (and in this proposal should not) imply a higher tax payment by the pension saver. Taxes can be settled when an appropriate share of the individual contribution to the pension system is used to pay the tax bill, which implies that individual pension wealth accumulation is reduced by the tax factor (1-T). The same procedure can be applied to settle the income tax liability on excess returns. Pension funds are obliged to pay income tax to the tax authority and pension wealth returns are reduced by the tax factor (1-t). No income tax is due when pension benefits are disbursed after retirement. Because all income tax liabilities on pension wealth are settled immediately, no revenue loss arises if the pension saver emigrates as a worker or a pensioner.

b. Under the *deferred tax payment option*, the tax liabilities are assessed according to the T-t-E regime, accumulated until retirement, and then turned into a tax annuity that must be paid to the tax administration in line with the disbursement of the monthly pension benefit (Holzmann 2015). The approach combines the formal front-loading of tax assessment (T-t-E) with a material back-loading (E-E-T) of tax payment and defers the net income loss by paying out pension benefits net of the tax annuity. If a pension saver emigrates before retirement and the gross pension assets remain in the source country, the tax annuity is withheld when pension benefits are paid out and transferred to the treasury in the same way as for a resident retiree. If the pension wealth is transferred abroad upon migration, then the accumulated tax liability becomes due as a form of exit tax that is also paid by the pension fund, and the migrant's transferrable pension wealth is reduced accordingly. If a pensioner dies before the accumulated tax liability is redeemed, the pension fund is again required to settle the open tax debt.[14]

c. Under the *distributed tax payment option*, the payments of the accumulated tax liability are spread evenly across the whole pension cycle by charging a constant rate t^* on contributions, pension wealth returns, and pension benefit payouts. The rate t^* should be chosen to balance the expected aggregate present value of tax payments and the expected present value of the front-loaded pension tax liability. The balancing of the tax liability with the tax payment at the individual level may be left to a recalculation of the monthly payment upon retirement by means of a supplemental tax annuity, which could either be an individual surtax or a tax decrement on t^*. Emigration or death of the pensioner should be settled by the pension fund as outlined above. A constant tax payment rate t^*, which should be between one-third and one-half the average income tax rate, may increase political support because the advanced tax revenue inflows and later tax revenue losses level out over the lifespans of individuals. Moreover, t^* increases the toolbox of national tax policy and mitigates the fiscal transition effects that accompany the switch from the traditional deferred to a new pretaxed pension taxation.

Decoupling tax assessment and tax payment has no direct effect on migration and tax assignment in DTAs. The exclusive right to tax pension benefits in the source county and to exempt them when pensions are pretaxed precludes international double taxation. An unlimited income tax liability in the source country where income is earned and where pension wealth is accumulated as a resident, and an unlimited tax liability in the new residence country after migration, are in full accordance with objectives of equitable ability to pay and low costs of tax compliance and tax administration. Individual fairness with respect to residence taxation after migration can be achieved by applying the progressivity proviso in DTAs, ensuring that tax-exempt cross-border pension benefits increase the income tax rate on other taxable income in the residence country.

Front-Loaded Taxation, Payment Options, and DB and DC in Comparison

The proposed front-loaded taxation of cross-border pensions and the three payment options naturally raise the question of whether a DB or a DC scheme is better able to address the challenges that may emerge.

THE FRONT-LOADED TAX ASSESSMENT AND IMMEDIATE PAYMENT OPTION

The option for front-loaded tax assessment and immediate payment seems possible in both DB and DC schemes. No difference should arise in the taxation of contributions and savings efforts, as in both cases traditional exemptions are simply not applied.

Differences will emerge in the contribution taxation, however, if a DB scheme is redistributive and offers a higher benefit level compared with an actuarial calculation. This redistributive effect would be captured in a back-loaded scheme at the level of benefit disbursement, even under a linear income tax. For lower-income groups with relatively high pensions, the tax payment would be higher under deferred income taxation; for higher-income groups with relatively lower pensions, the tax burden would be lower under deferred income taxation. This is not the case under a front-loaded tax system, which, compared with a back-loaded system, makes a redistributive DB scheme even more redistributive. Under the front-loaded approach, both lower- and higher-income groups escape higher tax payment when government transfers keep the system afloat. For a pseudo-actuarial NDC scheme without redistribution those considerations will not matter. However, if redistribution is introduced with transfer payments to the individual accounts (as discussed in "Portability Issues: Objectives, Instruments, and DB-DC Comparison") and treated as returns to individual pension wealth, then the front-loaded tax captures these higher pension benefits in a similar way as the back-loaded taxation. If, however, these redistributive transfers are not recognized as returns to pension wealth and are only taxed under the back-loaded tax system, then this tax escape for lower-income groups makes the front-loaded approach under an NDC scheme more progressive than the back-loaded approach.

No difference should emerge in the taxation of the excess returns on pension wealth if both DB and DC schemes are funded, because the financial returns can be easily assessed at the individual fund level and taxed. Of course, this would amount to taxing the excess returns at equal rates across individuals, in line with dual income taxation but at odds with differentiated rates under a progressive income tax schedule. Progressive taxation is possible but complicated and never really considered. In unfunded schemes a difference may emerge because the rate of return in an NDC scheme is the notional interest rate, equal for all and well known. But this is not likely to matter because only the excess returns should be taxed, which are likely to be zero because the notional, or nonfinancial, rate of return should be equal or close to the riskless rate of return.[15] This may not be the case for NDB schemes, in which the rate is typically unknown and likely to differ across individuals. The individual rates of return under an NDB scheme are likely to differ by pensioners' socioeconomic characteristics and the difference may be substantial. Ignoring such differences would make a progressive scheme that offers high rates of return for lower-income groups less progressive.

Under the immediate payment option, differences between DC and DB schemes are likely to emerge with regard to their redistributive effects (that may also differ by their funding approach), but these effects may be mostly moderate. Avoiding such effects may, in some cases, be easier handled by a DC scheme, yet this does not result in strong dominance over DB schemes under this payment option.

THE FRONT-LOADED TAX ASSESSMENT AND DEFERRED PAYMENT OPTION

The option for front-loaded tax assessment and deferred payment also seems possible in DB and DC schemes but is not as easily implemented. The distributive issues outlined above remain valid under the deferred payment option but are not addressed here. In addition, differences between DB and DC schemes emerge because the taxes due are accumulated with interest until retirement and then translated into a tax annuity that is subtracted from the gross benefit as calculated.

Under both DB and DC schemes, the taxes due on contributions and the rates of return can be easily calculated, and with a selected interest rate accumulated until retirement. For unfunded DB and DC schemes, the rate of return proposes itself: in NDC schemes, the notional interest rate keeps the scheme sustainable—its calculation is part of the scheme design and is well known; in NDB schemes, the rate is normally unknown and requires a complex estimation for which the data may not be fully available. If traditionally estimated, should this (likely unsustainable) rate be used, or a hypothetical sustainable rate as for NDC schemes (which may be even more difficult to estimate for NDB schemes)? Good arguments exist to use the higher, unsustainable internal rate of return for indexing, because this would also increase the taxes due at retirement. The approach may thus overcome the distributive issues under the direct payment and proxy the T-t-E = E-E-T condition. For funded pensions, similar considerations are valid but a bit more complex.[16]

At retirement the accumulated tax liability due needs to be translated into the tax annuity. This is straightforward in an NDC scheme, because all the information for calculating the benefit annuity can be used for the tax annuity, most importantly the remaining cohort life expectancy. This is no minor issue, given that few countries have official cohort (and not only period) life-expectancy tables estimated and published. The difference between cohort and period life expectancy at age 65 can be sizable, and currently reaches up to nine years for both genders in some countries (Ayusa, Bravo, and Holzmann 2018). Applying a too-low period life expectancy would result in a too-high tax annuity and, compared with an annuity calculated with cohort life expectancy, an incorrect, too-high tax payment. However, a typical NDB scheme uses period life expectancy to estimate its financial solvency, which implies too-high pension annuities but also too-high tax annuities if the available period life expectancy were to be used. But if individuals actually live according to the survival probability of the cohort life expectancy, they have higher pension wealth and a higher tax liability at retirement. With high differences between cohort and period life expectancies, as in Australia, this may amount to an increase of pension wealth of up to 50 percent at retirement, of which only a share is recovered by future higher taxes (for example, 20 percent).

To summarize, the deferred tax payment option is potentially possible under an NDB scheme but requires more technical effort and faces more estimation and implementation challenges than under an NDC scheme, the implementation of which should be quite straightforward. This assessment also holds for the comparison between funded provisions if both were to be centralized. Under a decentralized FDC implementation the differences in achieved rates of return and applied life expectancies across pension funds and annuity providers may not ensure comparability and fairness.

THE FRONT-LOADED TAX ASSESSMENT AND DISTRIBUTED PAYMENT OPTION

The option for front-loaded tax assessment and distributed payment needs no tax annuities, in principle. The identical lower tax rate t* is applied for each payment phase—contribution, return receipt, and benefit disbursement—and should ex ante be fully aligned with front-loaded tax equivalence; that is, t^*-t^*-t^*= T-t-E = E-E-T. Hence, a perfectly chosen tax rate t* can be applied to both DB and DC schemes without any differences or technical complications.

However, in an imperfect world of information constraints and unexpected economic and demographic changes, periodic adjustment in the tax rate t* may be needed to ensure that front-loaded and back-loaded taxation benchmarks for individuals broadly match, ensuring that fiscal fairness across individuals and countries holds. Doing so requires shadow tax accumulation accounts and a correction at retirement: either of the tax rate t* or of the tax annuities applied. Under such conditions, DB schemes run into the same technical problems outlined above. During the contribution phase a substantial part of the lifetime income tax burden due has already been paid. At retirement the open tax liability can comprise between one-third and one-half of this tax burden. Consequently, the pension benefit annuity under the distributed payment option is higher than under the immediate payment option but lower than under the deferred payment option. In contrast, the tax annuity under the deferred payment option is higher than under the immediate payment option (where it is nil) but lower than under the deferred payment option.

Such adjustment considerations for t* would render the level of implementation ease of the distributed payment option difficult under both DC and DB schemes, but relatively less difficult under a DC scheme because the key measurement instruments (such as tax and benefit annuities) are easier to develop and are part of the overall design.

Table 29.7 compares DC and DB schemes under the three payment options.

TABLE 29.7 **Comparison of defined benefit and defined contribution schemes under front-loaded tax assignment and three payment options with regard to ease of implementation and equivalence with back-loaded taxation**

Payment option	DB scheme	DC scheme	Comments
Immediate	Relatively easy	Very easy	The more the DB scheme is redistributive and unsustainable, the higher the difficulty
Deferred	May be quite cumbersome	Very easy	Same as above, but in addition requires technical effort to determine tax annuities for DB schemes
Distributed	Very, very easy or very difficult	Very, very easy or moderately difficult	For both schemes, very easy if tax rate t* can be left fixed; else technically very difficult for DB, but less difficult for DC schemes

SOURCE: Original table.

NOTE: DB = defined benefit; DC = defined contribution.

Conclusions

A feature of globalization is the increasing international mobility of individuals during their working lives and after retirement. This trend has existed since the 1960s and does not seem to be easing. For mobile individuals as well as for home and host countries, this raises the issue of portability of acquired pension rights as well as the taxation of pensions. If the design and arrangements for these issues between source and destination countries are not done well, the result will be less fairness for individuals, less fiscal fairness for countries, and lower administrative efficiency. The effects on these three outcome criteria also depend on the type of pension benefit scheme in place—DB or DC.

Portability of pension benefits and related retirement income savings can be established through three types of instruments: unilateral, bilateral, or multilateral legal arrangements; multinational providers from the private sector; and benefit redesign. These three instruments are both substitutes and complements. Thus a pension benefit redesign toward DC schemes simplifies the portability of pensions because accumulated resources can be easily transferred; likewise, benefits in payment can be easily granted because they do not contain redistributive components. This feature makes BAs—the workhorse of portability—either unnecessary or easier to establish. The DC approach also makes multinational schemes easier to operate. However, portability of both DB and DC benefits may be impeded by tax considerations, particularly if tax concessions granted during accumulation must be repaid when migrating.

The current taxation of cross-border pensions across all migration corridors is highly complex and inconsistent, violating the condition of fairness to individuals and countries, and of bureaucratic efficiency. This outcome is not sustainable in a world of labor and retirement mobility. The key reasons are the mix and heterogeneity of taxation principles in countries and the economically unsound international guidance in the OECD model tax convention. This may result in no taxation of pension benefits or their double taxation in source and residence countries as often happens when tax preferences for contributions and returns on assets are granted in the source country while benefits are fully taxed in the residence country.

No conceptual guidance currently exists in the economic literature on how cross-border pensions should be best taxed to achieve the three outcome criteria. This chapter proposes moving toward a front-loaded expenditure tax treatment of pensions. In addition, it suggests three economically equivalent payment options—immediate, deferred until retirement, or distributed across the whole pension cycle of contribution payment, pension wealth return, and benefit disbursement. The chapter compares and assesses the capacity to, and ease with which DB and DC schemes can, achieve the three outcome criteria under front-loading and the three proposed payment options. DC schemes dominate DB schemes in all payment options except the distributed one. If the reduced tax rate across all three phases remains fixed, then DB and DC schemes are equally easy to operate under the distributed payment option. The results are suggested to apply for both financial and nonfinancial schemes but seem more easily achievable under NDCs, an assessment that may not be universally shared.

ANNEX 29A

OECD Model Tax Convention on Income and on Capital

Article 18 PENSIONS

Subject to the provisions of paragraph 2 of Article 19, pensions and other similar remuneration paid to a resident of a Contracting State in consideration of past employment shall be taxable only in that State.

Article 19 GOVERNMENT SERVICE

1. a) Salaries, wages and other similar remuneration paid by a Contracting State or a political subdivision or a local authority thereof to an individual in respect of services rendered to that State or subdivision or authority shall be taxable only in that State.
   b) However, such salaries, wages and other similar remuneration shall be taxable only in the other Contracting State if the services are rendered in that State and the individual is a resident of that State who: (i) is a national of that State; or (ii) did not become a resident of that State solely for the purpose of rendering the services.

2. a) Notwithstanding the provisions of paragraph 1, pensions and other similar remuneration paid by, or out of funds created by, a Contracting State or a political subdivision or a local authority thereof to an individual in respect of services rendered to that State or subdivision or authority shall be taxable only in that State.
   b) However, such pensions and other similar remuneration shall be taxable only in the other Contracting State if the individual is a resident of, and a national of, that State.

3. The provisions of Articles 15, 16, 17, and 18 shall apply to salaries, wages, pensions, and other similar remuneration in respect of services rendered in connection with a business carried on by a Contracting State or a political subdivision or a local authority thereof.

Article 21 OTHER INCOME

1. Items of income of a resident of a Contracting State, wherever arising, not dealt with in the foregoing Articles of this Convention shall be taxable only in that State.
2. The provisions of paragraph 1 shall not apply to income, other than income from immovable property as defined in paragraph 2 of Article 6, if the recipient of such income, being a resident of a Contracting State, carries on business in the other Contracting State through a permanent establishment situated therein and the right or property in respect of which the income is paid is effectively connected with such permanent establishment. In such case the provisions of Article 7 shall apply.

ANNEX 29B

International Organization for Standardization three-letter country codes

ALB Albania	CYP Cyprus	GRC Greece	MCO Monaco	ROM Romania
ARM Armenia	CZE Czech Republic	HRV Croatia	MDA Moldova	SRB Serbia
AUT Austria	DEU Germany	HUN Hungary	MNE Montenegro	RUS Russian Federation
AUS Australia	DNK Denmark	IRL Ireland	MKD North Macedonia	SWE Sweden
AZE Azerbaijan	EST Estonia	ISL Iceland	MLT Malta	SVN Slovenia
BEL Belgium	ESP Spain	ITA Italy	NLD Netherlands	SVK Slovak Republic
BGR Bulgaria	FIN Finland	LIE Liechtenstein	NOR Norway	TUR Turkey
BLR Belarus	FRA France	LTU Lithuania	NZL New Zealand	UKR Ukraine
CAN Canada	GBR United Kingdom	LUX Luxembourg	POL Poland	USA United States
CHE Switzerland	GEO Georgia	LVA Latvia	PRT Portugal	

Notes

1. For early economic research on the topic see Holzmann, Koettle, and Chernetsky (2005). Later work includes Holzmann and Koettl (2015), Jousten (2015), and Holzmann (2016).

2. This definition draws on the general definition of the portability of social security benefits developed by Cruz (2004) and Holzmann, Koettle, and Chernetsky (2005).

3. As occurs in the Gulf Cooperation Council countries for essentially all expatriates, and for some categories of foreign workers in Hong Kong SAR, China; Malaysia; and Singapore.

4. The Philippines and Mexico fall somewhere between the first and second examples. The Philippines allows workers to contribute to national pension schemes but independent of access in the host country. Similarly, Mexican migrants can get access to health care benefits for a flat-rate premium (for their families left behind or themselves when they return) independent of their insurance in the host country (that is, the United States).

5. For a historical and legal background on BAs, see Strban (2009).

6. No single study (inventory) captures the content of BAs across the world or even of subregions such as Europe; to the authors' knowledge, no single evaluation has been undertaken to assess the effectiveness of BAs and MAs.

7. The four freedoms were set out in the Treaty of Rome (1958), extended by the Single European Act (1987), and strengthened in the Lisbon Treaty (2009).

8. Both authors experienced this when leaving their former civil servants scheme as Austrian academics to join a similar scheme in Germany; in Austria, their acquired rights in the civil servants scheme were transferred to private sector schemes with substantial reductions in pension wealth. For one author this happened again when he left German academia to move to the World Bank in the United States.

9. A main difference may emerge between funded and unfunded provisions with regard to the actual portability of financial assets when changing residence versus the mere recognition of rights while the assets remain in the source country. The latter is always the case in unfunded provisions because the pay-as-you-go (PAYG) asset remains in the source country. In funded provisions the assets can remain in the source country (as is typically the case under FDBs) but may also be transferred to the new residence country under FDC schemes, but there is no obligation and possibly no incentives to do so.

10. Abstracting from heterogeneity in longevity, which can be corrected for (see Holzmann et al. 2019).

11. For more remarks on these direct financial incentives, see OECD (2015, section 7).

12. The inconsistencies in cross-border taxation of pensions are grounded in theoretical ambiguities of taxation of pensions and their implementation in the national context. For the state of the theory of pension taxation and the implementation of pension taxation in key industrial countries, consult Holzmann and Piggott (2018). Mirrlees et al. (2010) offer broader perspectives on the taxation of labor and capital and call for an integrated approach for the design of pensions and their taxation.

13. Standard assumptions are that the tax schedule remains unchanged over the pension cycle, the tax schedule is perfectly adjusted to inflation, and the tax regime treats positive and negative incomes symmetrically. Another crucial issue is the implicit assumption of progressive tax systems of what is considered tolerable and not regarded as violating tax equity under fluctuating period incomes over the life cycle, which affects the lifetime tax burden of individuals with exactly the same present value of lifetime income. Perfect lifetime tax equity would require applying the progressive tax schedule to a notional average gross period income over the life cycle. The same implicit assumption is necessary for lifetime pensions, although the tax burden differences are salient: In contrast to T-t-E

taxation, deferred income taxation E-E-T implies that low pension benefits after retirement may go untaxed if they fall below the general income tax allowance. Perfect equivalence is attained under the implicit assumption that taxable lifetime earnings including taxable pension benefits are taxed by calculating the notional gross period income over the pension cycle.

14. Note that the progressivity erosion effect of deferred income taxation does not occur in the deferred tax payment option (or in the distributed tax payment option) because the tax liability under front-loading is fixed in present value terms and only the income tax payment is deferred.

15. The excess rate of return is conceptually the difference between the rate of return of an asset minus the risk-free rate of return, typically proxied by the long-term government bond rate. Under steady-state conditions and other reasonable assumptions, the long-term government bond rate and the notional rate of return should not be different and should be equal to the gross domestic product growth rate.

16. Because this chapter deals primarily with NDC versus NDB schemes, FDB and FDC schemes are discussed only briefly here. The FDC rate of return suggests itself to be used to accumulate the taxes due as it also indexes the funds from which the benefits can be paid. Again, this proxies the T-t-E = E-E-T condition. Good arguments exist to use the annual internal rate of return for FDB schemes, as for NDB schemes. But the balancing of FDB schemes (which do not exist at a national level and have mostly been closed at the occupational level for new entrants, or transferred to FDCs) can have many forms, including partial or full default. Calculating the resulting (negative) internal rate of return and translating this into reduced and zero tax accumulations due would be very complex.

References

Ayusa, Mercedes, Jorge Bravo, and Robert Holzmann. 2018. "Getting Life Expectancy Estimates Right for Pension Policy: Period vs Cohort Approach." IZA Discussion Paper 11512, IZA Institute of Labor Economics, Bonn, Germany.

Cruz, Armando. 2004. "Portability of Benefit Rights in Response to External and Internal Labor Mobility: The Philippine Experience." Paper presented at the International Social Security Association (ISSA) 13th Regional Conference for Asia and the Pacific, Kuwait, March 8–10. http://www.issa.int/pdf/kuwait04/2cruz.pdf.

Eurostat. 2017. *Migration and Migrant Population Statistics*. Eurostat Database. http://ec.europa .eu/eurostat/statisticsexplained/Migration_and_migrant_population_statistics.

Foster, Ann C. 1994. "The Portability of Pension Benefits among Jobs." *Monthly Labor Review* July: 45–50.

Genser, Bernd. 2015. "Towards an International Tax Order for the Taxation of Retirement Income." CEPAR Working Paper 2015/25, ARC Centre of Excellence in Population Ageing Research, University of New South Wales, Sydney.

Genser, Bernd, and Robert Holzmann. 2016. "The Taxation of Internationally Portable Pensions: An Introduction to Fiscal Issues and Policy Options." *ifo DICE Report* 14 (1): 24–29.

———. 2018. "The Taxation of Internationally Portable Pensions: Fiscal Issues and Policy Options." In *The Taxation of Pensions*, edited by Robert Holzmann and John Piggott, 443–79. Cambridge, MA: MIT Press.

Holzmann, Robert. 2015. "Taxing Pensions of an Internationally Mobile Labor Force: Portability Issues and Taxation Options." CEPAR Working Paper 2015/27, ARC Centre of Excellence in Population Ageing Research, University of New South Wales, Sydney.

———. 2016. "Bilateral Social Security Agreements and Pensions Portability: A Study of Four Migrant Corridors between EU and Non-EU Countries." *International Social Security Review* 69 (3–4): 109–30.

————. 2017. "The ABCs of Nonfinancial Defined Contribution (NDC) Schemes." *International Social Security Review* 70 (3): 53–77.

Holzmann, Robert, Jennifer Alonso-García, Héloïse Labit-Hardy, and Andrés M. Villegas. 2019. "NDC Schemes and Heterogeneity in Longevity: Proposals for Redesign." In *Progress and Challenges of Nonfinancial Defined Contribution Pension Schemes: Volume 1 Addressing Marginalization, Polarization, and the Labor Market*, edited by Robert Holzmann, Edward Palmer, Robert Palacios, and Stefano Sacchi, Chapter 14. Washington, DC: World Bank.

Holzmann, Robert, and Wels Jacques. 2018. "Status and Progress in Cross-Border Portability of Social Security Benefits." IZA Discussion Paper 11481, IZA Institute of Labor Economics, Bonn, Germany.

Holzmann, Robert, and Johannes Koettl. 2015."The Portability of Pensions, Health, and Other Social Benefits: Concepts and Issues." *CESifo Economic Studies* 61 (2): 377–415.

Holzmann, Robert, Johannes Koettl, and Taras Chernetsky. 2005. "Portability Regimes of Pension and Health Care Benefits for International Migrants: An Analysis of Issues and Good Practices." Social Protection Discussion Paper 0519, World Bank, Washington, DC.

Holzmann, Robert, and John Piggott. 2018. *The Taxation of Pensions*. CESifo Seminar Series. Cambridge, MA: MIT Press.

Holzmann, Robert, David Robalino, and Hernan Winkler. 2018. "NDC Schemes and the Labor Market: The Challenges of Formal Employment and Delayed Retirement." Revised version of paper presented at the NDC III conference, "Non-Financial Defined Contribution Schemes (NDC): Facing the Challenges of Marginalization and Polarization in Economy and Society," Rome, October 5–6, 2017.

IBFD (International Bureau of Fiscal Documentation). 2017. *European Tax Handbook 2017*. Global Tax Series. Amsterdam: IBFD.

Jousten, Alain. 2015. "The Retirement of the Migrant Labor Force: Pension Portability and Beyond." *CESifo Economic Studies* 61 (2): 416–37.

Mirrlees, James A., Stuart Adam, Timothy Besley, Richard Blundell, Stephen Bond, Robert Chote, Malcolm Gammie, Paul Johnson, Gareth Myles, and James Poterba, eds. 2010. *Dimensions of Tax Design: The Mirrlees Review—Volume 1*. Oxford: Oxford University Press.

OECD (Organisation for Economic Co-operation and Development). 2014. *Developing a Multilateral Instrument to Modify Bilateral Tax Treaties*. Paris: OECD Publishing.

————. 2015. *Stocktaking of the Tax Treatment of Funded Private Pension Plans in OECD and EU Countries*. Paris: OECD Publishing.

————. 2017. *Model Tax Convention on Income and on Capital: Condensed Version 2017*. Paris: OECD Publishing.

Strban, Grega. 2009. "The Existing Bi-and Multilateral Social Security Instruments Binding EU States and Non-EU States." In *The Social Security Co-Ordination between the EU and Non-EU Countries*, edited by Danny Pieters and Paul Schoukens, 85–113. Antwerp, Oxford: Intersentia.

UNDESA (United Nations Department of Economic and Social Affairs). 2017. "Trends in International Migration, 2017." Population Facts 2017/5, United Nations, New York.

Warnes, Tony A. M. 2009. "International Retirement Migration." In *International Handbook of Population Aging*, edited by Peter Uhlenberg, 341–63. New York: Springer.

Wellisch, Diemar, Sven-Oliver Lenz, Kerstin Tiele, and Rasmus Gahl. 2008. *Besteuerung der Altersvorsorge: Ein internationaler Vergleich*. Baden-Baden: Nomos.

CHAPTER 30

Developing Coherent Pension Systems: Design Issues for Private Pension Supplements to NDC Schemes

William Price

Introduction

This chapter reviews the factors that should guide the design of private funded pensions to create a complete pension system alongside a nonfinancial defined contribution (NDC) component. It argues that a mix of public and private pensions can most effectively deliver the best combination of pension outcomes. Corner solutions that rely solely on public pensions (whether NDC or not) or just private pensions (whether defined benefit [DB], financial defined contribution [FDC], or a hybrid) have no obvious examples of sustainable success in either developed or developing countries. The design principles set out below are well-known in theory but are often not followed in practice. So, the chapter aims to restate them succinctly to reestablish some simple but powerful principles for use by NDC (and other) policy makers when designing private pensions to help complete the pension system.

The chapter defines the different pension pillars and then sets out the criteria by which to judge success or failure of a pension system: coverage, adequacy, and sustainability alongside its efficiency and security. Evaluating the success of a system is difficult if no metrics of success exist against which to judge it (including the distribution of outcomes by income and gender). It then highlights the wide range of overlapping risks to which pension pillars are subject and different ways in which the "right" mix has been investigated. The next section considers the design of a private pension pillar across two dimensions. The first design question looks at the way in which private pensions will need to be delivered—using the concept of the pension value chain and market structure to highlight the key issues and options. A key part of the value chain is who provides recordkeeping and account administration. A well-functioning NDC pillar may already deliver administrative capacity that could be leveraged to improve recordkeeping and account administration in private pensions—particularly where it is based on a well-functioning tax collection system. Thus, creating an NDC pillar may give scope for economies of scale across pension pillars.

The work on this chapter was predominantly completed when the author was a global pension expert at the World Bank. The author is grateful to Professor Barr, the editors, and the referees for comments and suggestions. An earlier version of this chapter was published as World Bank Policy Research Working Paper 8420.

The second set of design questions looks at the more "traditional" elements of benefit design, contribution levels, eligibility, and payout phase. In an ideal world, the future income to be delivered by a pension system would look at the joint distribution from the combined NDC and private pillars. NDC schemes allow clearer identification of potential outcomes in that they are (in theory) less prone to ad hoc adjustments and pre-election changes than traditional DB public pension pillars. The precise NDC rule may have important implications for optimal investment strategies in private pensions—something that governing bodies of pension funds and pension regulators should consider. For example, in many countries real per capita gross domestic product (GDP) growth (which can feature in NDC rules) is negatively correlated with the real growth of equity markets. So, an NDC rule linked to per capita GDP, sitting alongside a private pension pillar in which there are equity investments, may combine uncorrelated forms of risk. NDC payout formulas have potential use to provide an income until death in countries that will struggle to have deep and efficient traditional annuity markets. It is then important that design coherence flows to the regulatory and supervisory approach so that these can also focus on how best to achieve the long-run outcomes. Finally, a robust program management or "mission office" greatly assists the delivery of the reforms, so that great designs are not lost by poor implementation.

Using Long-Run Pension Outcomes to Guide Decision Making on Private Pensions

DEFINING THE DIFFERENT PARTS OF A PENSION SYSTEM

Before introducing the key outcomes, it is necessary to identify how NDC and private pensions can make up an overall pension system and highlight the risks to which different pension pillars are exposed. Public pension provision comes broadly in the form of "zero pillars"—poverty-alleviating payments paid out of government revenues that do not require contributions—and "first" pillars that are typically mandatory and can have the full range of benefit options, but are often DB. Many first pillars are pay-as-you-go (PAYG), whereby current contributions fund current pensions, but a number are at least partially funded. Examples range from the CCSS in Costa Rica,[1] the Social Security and National Insurance Trust in Ghana, and Vietnam Social Security (VSS). Such arrangements are very rare in Europe, where many countries are very reliant on large PAYG public pillars with systems that are in great need of diversification (European Commission 2012). The NDC debate focuses on this "first pillar." It introduces a mechanism that does not fund the benefits in advance but aims to avoid the buildup of unsustainable DB promises by altering pensions in payment with changes in factors such as longevity (if politics do not intervene). Table 30.1 describes the basic pillars and their associated risks.

Decisions on private pensions typically focus on the second and third pillars. Terminology varies globally; many European countries characterize the second pillar as employer provided, and the third pillar as individual pensions. In the World Bank framework, the key dividing line is whether pensions are mandatory (second pillar) or voluntary (third pillar). In this framework, an employer could be involved in the second or third pillar, or both. The line between mandatory and voluntary pensions is blurring with the use of autoenrollment—as introduced in New Zealand, Turkey, and the United Kingdom and under development in Ireland. A common feature across all private pensions is that

TABLE 30.1 **Different pension pillars have different functions and face common and unique risks**

Sources of retirement consumption	Risks affecting payout size
Zero pillar: poverty prevention	Fiscal, intergenerational, longevity
First pillar: public contributory—consumption-smoothing	Fiscal, intergenerational/political, longevity, labor market, GDP
Second pillar: mandatory private contributory DB, FDC, or a hybrid	Capital market (investment returns/costs), labor participation, longevity
Third pillar: private contributory DB, FDC, or a hybrid	Capital market (investment/costs), labor market, individual myopia
Fourth pillar: financial assets	Economic growth, instability
Fourth pillar: family transfers	Family size, wealth, culture, location
Fourth pillar: housing/physical	Housing market, labor income
Labor income and own consumption	Labor market, agricultural market
Longevity and inflation risk are pervasive	

SOURCE: Original table.

NOTE: DB = defined benefit; FDC = financial defined contribution; GDP = gross domestic product.

they involve the investment of assets (abstracting from the case of book reserves, which are more of an anomaly than a practical choice for modern pension design). "The First Design Question: How to Deliver Private Pensions" outlines the pros and cons of how to design these arrangements and provides some guidance for making the best choice in different contexts.[2]

COMBINING PUBLIC AND PRIVATE PENSIONS

Deciding on the "best" or "optimal" makeup of private pensions in combination with a given NDC (or other form) of public pension provision requires criteria against which to judge various options. A large literature exists on optimal pension design in terms of mixing PAYG or unfunded pension provision with a funded pension component (first pillar versus second and third pillars in the terminology above). A critical early paper (Aaron 1966) focuses on how to decide whether to choose PAYG exclusively (when the natural rate of growth is greater than the rate of return on capital) or to choose funded pensions (when the natural rate of growth is less than the rate of return on capital). Merton (1983) shows that a mix could be preferable because it allows wealth-constrained young workers with lots of human capital to share risks with higher-wealth older workers with little remaining human capital. Numerous studies since have explored different reasons why a combination of PAYG and funded pensions would be optimal, but the weight for each might vary systematically between countries or vary for different reasons. These include relaxing assumptions about certainty of knowledge about key parameters; investigating intergenerational risks; the availability of insurance for different risks; or refinements in modeling of the intergenerational welfare maximization problem being investigated (Beetsma, Romp, and Vos 2013; Bohn 2009; De Menil et al. 2016; De Menil, Murtin, and Sheshinski 2006; Devolder and Melis 2015; Gordon and Varian 1988; Knell 2010; Miles 2001).

A perhaps more intuitive way to make the case for public and private pensions is to review the experience of countries that have a single, or a very dominant, pillar. Overreliance on a public pillar will create issues with sustainability, particularly in the case of DB plans, as seen in many (but not all) European countries. Overreliance on private pensions funded with contributions will fail to deliver good coverage of retirement income across the whole population. Chile in 1981 and Mexico in 1997 both shifted from effectively wholly public to wholly private systems of pension provision. For both it was necessary to recreate core elements of public pensions to ensure sufficiently broad coverage of income in old age and to alleviate old-age poverty (Chile in reforms starting in 2008 and Mexico in a series of reforms starting with the "70 y Mas" reforms).[3]

As a practical guide to developing private pension pillars to accompany NDC (or indeed other public pension pillars), this chapter uses five key outcomes—as set out in work on outcomes based assessments (Price, Ashcroft, and Hafeman 2016) that builds on earlier work such as "International Patterns of Pension Provision II" (Pallares-Miralles, Romero, and Whitehouse 2012) and Holzmann and Hinz (2005). The five outcomes are as follows[4]:

- *Efficiency*—relating to costs, investment returns, and labor market impact of pension design. Pension provision faces numerous market failures. This means the "competitive" market can deliver suboptimal outcomes (Impávido, Lasagabaster, and García-Huitron 2010). Failures relate to the ability of consumers to understand the products and make informed decisions (Benartzi and Thaler 2007; Harrison 2012), to the quasi-utility nature of pension delivery given the huge economies of scale in administration and investment management, through to the well-documented examples of mis-selling scandals in multiple jurisdictions (United Kingdom Financial Services Authority and Financial Conduct Authority, India [Government of India 2015], Mexico, Chile). Transparency is an important element of any good system, but a simple focus on disclosure will not be sufficient to ensure members get the best outcomes. Good governance is profoundly important to ensure members get the best net-of-fee returns they can—and indeed good governance is relevant to all the outcomes in one form or another (Franzen and Ashcroft 2017).

  A critical feature for effective pension systems that is often ignored is including a clear target for (low) total costs. In a world in which real returns are likely to be only 3–4 percent in the long run, having a fee level of 1 percent means that total fees are taking 25–33 percent of returns. The objective is not low fees on their own, but to minimize costs and fees that do not increase coverage, contributions, or investment returns.

- *Sustainability*—relating to the funding of public or private DB promises, but also the affordability of given contributions by employer and employees. Private pensions that involve DB promises underwritten by employers clearly add another dimension to sustainability. Payout phases delivered by insurance companies mean that a pension policy maker needs to have confidence in the sustainability of the insurance regime. Where this confidence is lacking, or annuity markets are not well developed, other pension payouts can help deliver income. Political sustainability should also be a central focus since pension systems need to be maintained across multiple electoral cycles, which places a premium on using pension commissions to build consensus. Clarity on what each pillar of the system can and cannot deliver is critical to anchor expectations and help avoid unrealistic expectations—supported by simple clear messages, rather than attempting to turn people into pension experts.

- *Adequacy*—relating to the level of pension income, at both the point of retirement (or drawdown) and at later ages. A pension pillar should deliver in its own right, but ultimately it operates in combination with other sources of retirement income. Governments directly affect the level of income either through direct contributions or by providing incentives such as tax relief or matching. The distribution by income and by gender is especially important for assessing outcomes— particularly if scarce tax resources are used to provide incentives, which can often benefit higher-income workers if not well targeted. The rules for a "zero" pillar, if it exists, or any base level of income guaranteed to all in old age by virtue of citizenship are also clearly important in considering the size and shape of a private pension pillar.

- *Coverage*—relating to the percentage of the relevant populations contributing and receiving pensions, with coverage of informal workers possibly the single biggest challenge in global pensions (Bosch, Melguizo, and Pagés 2013). Again, the distribution by income and gender is important to understand so that projections for the "average" worker do not mask large inequalities in future outcomes that will call into question the success and legitimacy of the pension system. In the past, many countries with occupational DB pensions had long "vesting" rules whereby workers had to work for 5 or even 10 years to receive pension rights. This leads to lower pensions for women, who tend to have shorter and more broken career histories. Hence an ambition for broad coverage with gender equality would lead to a need for low or no vesting periods—which is a natural feature of most FDC pension arrangements. Likewise, rules on annuitization of income, or the sharing of pension rights on death or divorce, will also affect gender equality—because again in most countries women's labor market participation tends to be lower than that of men and pension contributions reflect this labor market experience. This gender inequality is particularly stark in some regions, for example, the Middle East and North Africa (Price et al. 2017).

- *Security*—relating to the security of assets, the reliability of promised pensions, and the central role of a regulator and supervisor. Security is critical for all private pensions, but consideration should be given to whether an NDC system should be subject to external scrutiny as well. It is essential that public confidence be created and maintained for the robustness of the formula for the notional returns, and for assurance that the inputs (such as changes in mortality or wage rates) are accurate; and that management of other issues, such as cost control, is effective. It is important in the sequencing of private pension reforms that sufficient time be given to create or improve the regulator and supervisor and ensure it is effective before the first contributions are made. Failure to allow enough time to get the regulator up and running can lead to significant problems for new pension pillars, for example, as seen in the reforms in Ghana from 2008, which have taken years to correct. It can also contribute to the implosion of reforms, as in Mexico's 1992 "SAR" reforms, which failed initially and then had to be revisited in 1997. "The Second Set of Design Questions: Product Features" includes a discussion of some key supervisory issues.

The five outcomes presented above clearly interact. A country could aim for a higher level of adequacy simply by increasing contribution rates to DC private pensions. But in combination with contributions to public sector pensions, this could make the labor market inefficient as employers and workers try to avoid contributions. It can make the system unsustainable because contributions take too large a share of employer profits or of government revenue. A country may aim to rapidly expand coverage of private pensions but will need to target incentives more effectively. It could use matching or a tax credit rather than simple tax relief but with a cap on total incentives so that broad coverage is not unaffordable. This effect was seen, for example, in the United Kingdom, where tax relief for private pensions was available for up to £1.8 million before the global financial crisis of 2008–09 but was progressively scaled back as successive governments made decisions about the best use of scarce public resources.

The First Design Question: How to Deliver Private Pensions

Before getting to questions of contribution rates, accruals, investment strategy, and payout phases and how private pension investment strategies could interact with NDC accumulation rules, it is important to have a rigorous focus on each part of the pension value chain (figure 30.1). How will individuals and employers be identified and enrolled, make contributions, have their accounts created and managed, have their investment strategies developed and executed, and finally have their pension income distributed?

Individual voluntary pension provision—or the "third pillar"—is very often structured as a product purchased by individuals from a private provider as a "normal" financial product. Providers are often insurance companies, or dedicated pension fund management companies—and are often themselves part of larger financial services groups. This can be a sensible and important first step in a journey to building all the necessary pillars of pension provision. Albania, for example, founded its third pillar in 2009 at a time when there were certainly not the preconditions for a move to a mass market second pillar,

FIGURE 30.1 **Stages of the pension value chain**

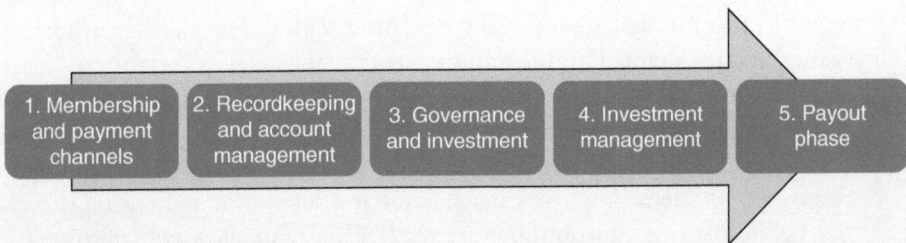

1. Membership and payment channels
2. Recordkeeping and account management
3. Governance and investment
4. Investment management
5. Payout phase

SOURCE: Original figure.

whether via compulsion or autoenrollment. Turkey in 2003 is a similar example, with its autoenrollment reforms following only in 2016–17.

This third-pillar model certainly allows pension products to be rapidly and freely available. However, translating availability into coverage can be very tough. These third-pillar pensions have a value chain that is more akin to the sales of insurance products—relying on a network of sales agents and competition between many vertically integrated providers.[5]

Moreover, when a country wants to expand coverage, policy makers face the problem of politically influential incumbent providers who may well resist the development of a different approach that is better suited to expand coverage and improve efficiency. The experience of the United Kingdom in developing autoenrollment reforms shows that even well-developed proposals by an effective pension commission that generated broad political consensus faced very strong resistance from many incumbents. This led to two separate reviews into the proposals made for autoenrollment in 2007 and 2010, both of which had the potential to derail or significantly undermine the reforms that have now added more than 9 million savers to occupational pension schemes (out of some 30 million workers) and significantly cut costs for the median saver.

MEMBERSHIP AND PAYMENT CHANNELS

A central question is how members will join a pension plan and how they will make their payments. The key message here is to make it as simple as possible for members to join a pension plan and to make their payments, and to ensure that there is a segmented strategy that matches the enrollment channel to the nature of the labor market. If the labor market is highly formal, then using the employer as an administrative channel to enroll members and make payments is a natural (and efficient) initial option. If a functional mechanism already exists whereby employers pay social security contributions for workers and deduct tax and social security contributions from workers' gross wages, then adding an extra requirement to channel a flow of income to a pension provider can be effective. An NDC pillar would clearly need high-functioning public pension administration systems to operate effectively. Informal labor markets are typically viewed as a feature of developing economies—where a lot of innovation is taking place as outlined below—but the development of the "gig economy" or the "uberization" of the labor market means that many developed country policy makers would be well advised to study how to maintain coverage in the face of these challenges (Secunda 2017)—or indeed how to use new approaches to extend coverage to the self-employed, who are often excluded.

RECORDKEEPING AND ACCOUNT MANAGEMENT

Once people are enrolled into a pension system and making payments, there is a need to keep records for all payments and to maintain their account balance (Barr and Diamond 2008). In DB schemes, the recordkeeping can be simpler than in DC schemes because a DB scheme is organized around a benefit formula focused on wages and years of service. Finally, FDC schemes need to keep track of each contribution, the assets into which they were invested, and the returns to be allocated to the individual. When contributions are made is vital in DC schemes because this determines when assets are invested. In some cases, in DB schemes it does not matter when workers contributed—only their years of service and final salary. NDCs require very strong administrative systems to support them, but because there are no assets, they do not need to have custodians or to conduct daily, market-based valuations.

The ability to manage records and accounts for 40 years (or 60 if the payout phase is included) is very unlikely to be widely distributed in an economy. Many employers, particularly those that are small and medium sized, do not have the time or expertise to deliver the added value of well-run occupational pension schemes. Running a pension administration operation has many logistical and technical challenges. Moreover, there are profound economies of scale that are critical to delivering the most efficient operations (Bikker 2013). The notion of a single administrative clearinghouse has gained popularity—particularly since the successful reforms in Sweden since 1992 (Palmer 2000). Many ways exist to deliver such a system. Some countries, including Sweden and New Zealand, use their tax authorities to act as the collection and administration agency. Others, such as India, run a competitive tender for a private company to deliver the services of a central record agency. In Mexico, the different pension fund management companies established a clearinghouse between themselves known as PROCESAR. But this does not translate automatically to lower prices because the companies control the entity. A critical feature of this option is that the public sector tax provider is able to operate at low cost (for example, about 10 basis points per year for administration in Sweden). In very many countries, this is not the case. Sluchynsky (2015) shows that some public sector providers deliver good value but many do not.

The clearinghouse model may not be preferred in a situation with concerns about governance because it presents a single point of failure in the pension regime. It may also not be preferred if the government and regulator have doubts about the ability to deliver a major information technology reform. However, in either of these scenarios one might question whether the country has achieved the preconditions necessary for the launch of a major new pension reform (Holzmann 2009).

GOVERNANCE AND INVESTMENT STRATEGY

Governance and organizational design are some of the most important elements in delivering good pensions (Ambachtsheer 2016; Clark and Urwin 2008). The key issues relate to the legal structure of the pension fund, including issues such as the separation between a governing body that focuses on long-run strategy (including investment strategy) and an expert management team that has the freedom to make decisions to implement the strategy. In relation to investment, the full board would be involved in agreeing to the long-run investment strategy as set out in the Statement of Investment Principles (along with a Statement of Investment beliefs). This will include issues such as the long-run objective for the strategy and strategic asset allocation. Clear differences will arise between a DB and a DC pension fund—but perhaps not as much as in the past, given that techniques such as asset-liability management used in DB funds are seen to help create a more disciplined approach in DC funds so that they focus on their long-run retirement income function rather than shorter-term investment returns.

A very wide range of institutional designs have been used internationally, particularly in relation to the investment strategy for member contributions. Options range from control by a public sector body (Norway's Government Pension Fund Global, for example, which is a department of the Ministry of Finance); an arms-length institution such as a Social Security Agency, provident fund, or a specific pension delivery body (for example, the Kosovo Pension Savings Trust [KPST], Malaysia's Employees Provident Fund, and the United Kingdom's National Employment Savings Trust or NEST); private fund managers and employer-sponsored pension funds with very strict investment regulations (for example, India's National Pension System particularly for public sector workers in the early years of the system, Mexico's AFORE[6] in the early years when there were very restrictive investment limits and almost 100 percent allocation to government bonds, and Turkey's Pension Foundations); and finally private fund managers and employer-sponsored funds with either no quantitative limits or much looser ones (for example, Chile, Mexico's AFORE now with greater latitude in the investment regulations, India's National Pension System now with similarly greater latitude after successive relaxation of the investment limits, and most U.K. and U.S. private providers). The latter category includes countries with "prudent person"–style investment regulations that give the governing body broad authority to make decisions on investment allocations.[7]

Individual choice of asset allocation

Some countries have a single strategy for all members (in the same way the NDC formula offers only one option). Other countries have a choice for additional voluntary contributions. In the individual pension market, a process often exists whereby potential clients are taken through options by an adviser who recommends an asset allocation that matches members' attitudes to risk. However, there is not much evidence to support the view that the typical member can really understand the options or that levels of financial education are sufficient to give confidence that members can navigate the choices in relation to pensions (Lusardi and Mitchell 2011, 2014). This is an area in which the sales agent can have a great influence—and can make members "choose" the product that benefits the agent, not the member (Halan and Sane 2016). Some countries have effectively removed sales agents from the process or banned the payment of commissions to agents because it skews their recommendations and behavior (for example, the United Kingdom following the Retail Distribution Review).

Modern pension policy is very focused on developing good default options for members. Sweden invested heavily in the early years of the Premium Pension System to encourage members to make individual decisions about their preferred pension provider and strategy. Ultimately these efforts were not judged to be effective and the quasi-government, not-for-profit default fund known originally as AP7 gained greater prominence. More than 90 percent of new entrants "choose" the default fund. In the United Kingdom, the default fund offered by NEST (the not-for-profit provider created as part of the autoenrollment reforms) has seen more than 99 percent of members move into the default fund. Enrollment of greater than 90 percent is common in many different types of pension funds. NDCs could provide transparency and clarity gains given that they make it much easier to show combined pension accounts and forecasts of combined retirement income. However, transparency for members may be more theoretical given that many will find it very difficult to really understand issues such as indexing and longevity factors—and may not even appreciate there are genuinely no assets backing their accounts.

The literature on pension performance highlights that governance of the fund is often a highly significant factor in determining performance—along with the scale and cost-effectiveness of the institution (World Bank 2017). Perhaps uniquely in global markets, it is the not-for-profit providers who tend to come out as the most effective in rigorous comparisons of different providers (Australian Treasury Department 2014; Heale and Martiniello 2017; Impávido, Lasagabaster, and García-Huitron 2010). It is important to be sure that a country has enough independence from political interference to allow independent governance to sustain the benefits of the model. Politics may always have some influence on institutions, but the key is whether there is sufficient independence to allow a focus on the best long-run interests of members to be the main driver of the pension fund. Reversals in pension reforms seen after the global financial crisis highlight that the most efficient approach can fail to create the most secure option because quasi-government structures may be more easily unwound or even nationalized (Hungary, Poland) than those that are more separated. As far as is known, no employer-sponsored pensions run as separate entities were "reversed" in the crisis.

Investment strategy in private pensions and the potential impact of the NDC rule

The NDC formula creates a return on notional capita. There are many options—and this section highlights the importance of modeling the likely joint distribution of outcomes between the NDC and funded pillars. If the NDC system is based on a GDP growth rate, or has a wage indexation or price indexation formula, how is that correlated with likely returns from different investment strategies? Are asset prices positively or negatively correlated with the formula driving the NDC payout? This is relevant to the accumulation phase of private pensions but also to the decumulation phase. How do the payout rules for private pensions (annuity, repricing or variable annuity, phased withdrawal or lump sum) interact with the NDC formula—and other pension pillars—such as "social pensions" providing minimum income for all?

Real equity market returns tend to be negatively correlated with real per capita GDP growth. The result was established in Dimson, Marsh, and Staunton's 2002 *Triumph of the Optimists*, using data from 1900 to 2000 and subsequent updates of their *Global Investment Returns Year Book* (Dimson, Marsh, and Staunton 2012). This result goes against simple intuition for many people, but as explored in detail in Ritter (2005, 2012), there are in fact sound reasons for the result. They help shed light on the nature of equity market returns—and the importance of good corporate governance in helping ensure that companies return cash flows to shareholders if they do not have rigorously evaluated investment projects that will yield a positive net present value.

The result for 19 developed countries between 1900 and 2011 is a correlation between real returns on equities and growth of real per capita GDP of minus 0.39. That is, if someone was seeking the highest real returns on equities when choosing between a sample of countries in 1900 they would have done best if they had chosen the countries that subsequently had the lowest growth in per capita GDP rather than those that had the highest growth (figure 30.2). The –0.39 correlation is for real equity returns in local prices. If U.S. dollars are used, then the correlation is still negative at –0.32 (Ritter 2012).

An obvious question is whether this is just a feature of developed countries. Using the same data set but for a shorter run of years given the later emergence of equity markets in developing countries, the same negative correlation exists. Analysis of 15 large emerging markets between 1988 and 2011 found a correlation of –0.41 (figure 30.3).

FIGURE 30.2 **Developed country correlations for real per capita GDP growth rates and real equity prices, 1900–2017**

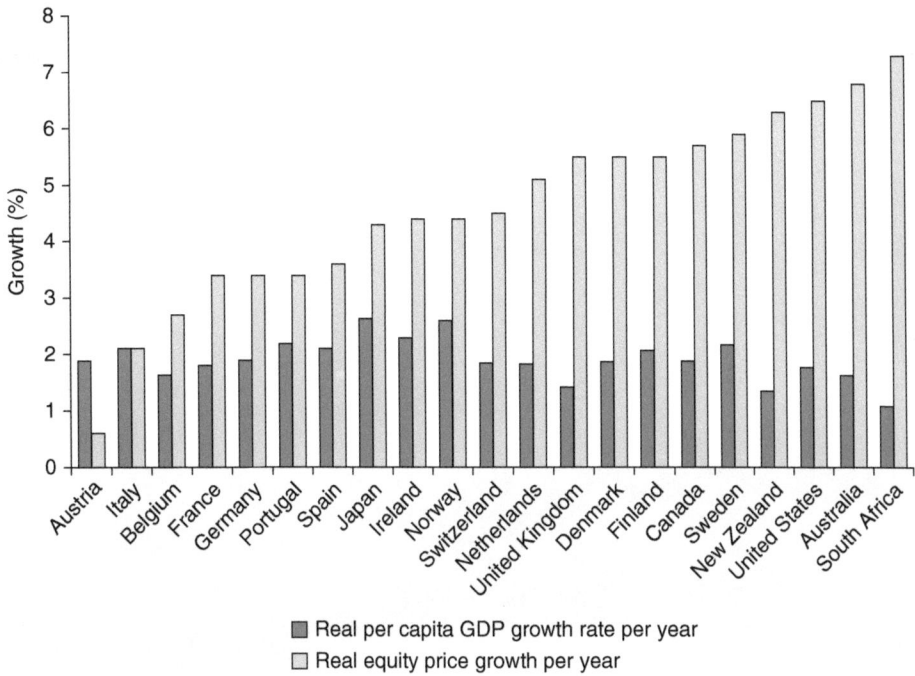

SOURCE: Credit Suisse Research Institute.

NOTE: GDP = gross domestic product.

However, if one takes aggregate GDP growth rather than per capita GDP growth, the correlation is positive. Aggregate GDP growth, however, does not abstract from the impact of population growth, with the intuition for the positive correlation being that the growth of population is akin to existing owners of capital getting extra customers. Per capita GDP growth, by adjusting for population growth, focuses on growth driven by productivity. The development of new and better ways to produce goods and services is as likely to come from new entrants, which may even harm the profits of existing owners of capital. In addition, over time in a broadly competitive market, the gains from productivity are competed away (Ritter 2012). In countries where pension funds can invest freely in any market and are not restricted to their home market, the correlations could change significantly. The picture will depend on the country and the pension funds—but the message is to investigate the correlations.

Thus, determining the "right" investment strategy for the private pension pillar in an NDC "system" should take into account whether there was a per capita GDP term or just an aggregate GDP term in the NDC formula. Likewise, but not shown here for space, where there are NDC formulas that use the growth of wages, it is important to investigate the correlations between the growth of notional assets and real assets in the funded pillars to determine likely future retirement income. A key takeaway is that these issues should

FIGURE 30.3 **Developing country correlation of real GDP growth rates and real equity prices, 1988–2011**

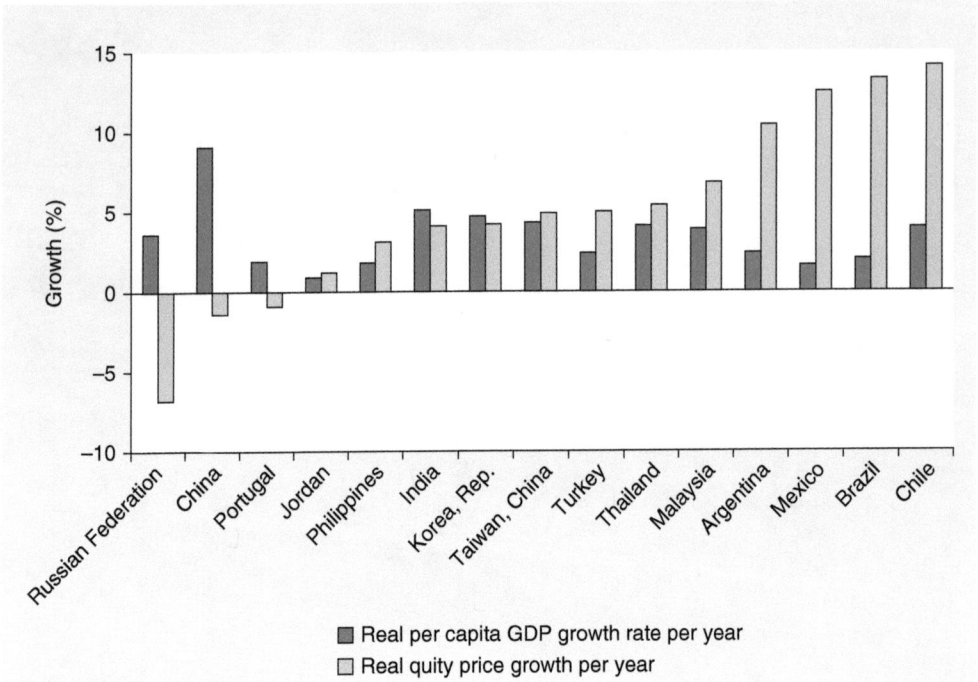

SOURCE: Ritter 2019.

NOTE: GDP = gross domestic product.

be investigated during the design phase of an NDC pillar. But even for countries where the NDC formula is already set, the regulator of private pension funds and the governing bodies of those funds should both take an interest in how the precise NDC formula might affect the optimal investment strategy for their members. It would be interesting to examine whether current NDC countries see any systematic differences in the investment allocations of their private pension pillars, to the extent that the issue has been internalized by any major fund.

INVESTMENT EXECUTION

Once an investment strategy has been determined, the issue is then to execute it. The range of options here mirror those for the investment strategy—from wholly in-house public sector or not-for-profit options to fully outsourced private fund managers. The governance of the overall process and the monitoring of implementation remain critical to deliver good value for money for members. Moreover, the political environment can play a key role in determining the "right" approach.

The United States's Thrift Savings Plan delivers DC pension benefits for federal government workers. It is probably the world's most efficient system, with total costs to members for administration and investment of less than 5 basis points per year. This is partly driven by huge economies of scale in administration. But it is also driven by the entirely passive investment execution that is a requirement of its legal provisions. This requirement was imposed by the U.S. Congress as a way of preventing any form of political control over the direction of its investments (Long, forthcoming). A very different country and context identified a similar type of mechanism: the KPST was established as a funded DC pillar to provide the major source of retirement income for future Kosovan pensioners. It was founded in a postconflict environment, with no domestic capital market to speak of. The governing board of the KPST includes three foreign members as a way of bringing international expertise and reducing domestic political interference. The board of the KPST determines the investment strategy, which it is then required to execute via external fund managers selected at scale by competitive tender. The KPST has a requirement to keep costs to a minimum and a target to progressively reach 50 basis points per year as a share of assets under management (Zalli, forthcoming). These options are useful examples for countries that may have fears that in-house investment management by public sector or arms-length bodies such as provident funds may be susceptible to political control.

However, the most robust internationally benchmarked evidence tends to suggest that the best net-of-fee returns come from the in-house management and execution of investment by very large not-for-profit funds of the type found in Canada and the Netherlands, and in some of Australia's superannuation funds (Heale and Martiniello 2017). As highlighted previously, these structures cannot be replicated in all places. But they do appear to be able to deliver an enhanced alignment of interests between the pension fund and the investment managers and can save significant costs. The longer the investment chain, the higher the costs and the higher the potential for weaker alignment.

PAYOUT PHASE—ADMINISTRATIVE ARRANGEMENTS

A pension system is only complete when it has started to pay out an income in retirement.[8] To do this requires good-quality account administration (see above) so that accumulated balances can be returned to members. It also requires the basic administrative capability to ensure proof of continuing life and the minimization of fraud and error. Perhaps too little attention is paid to the administrative requirements of the payout phase compared with the accumulation phase. An NDC pillar by design integrates the two phases and can provide useful insights for private pensions. When administrative systems are not well-developed, the process for choosing and receiving a pension can take many months and even longer. In many countries it will be simple to make payments directly into bank accounts electronically and automatically. There is substantial merit to using the most effective payments channel so that it is simple and low cost for a person to receive pension payments in old age. Issues relating to the type of payout product are covered below in "The Second Set of Design Questions: Product Features."

The Second Set of Design Questions: Product Features

Once a country is clear about what it wants private pensions to achieve in terms of additional outcomes to public pensions and has thought through the most effective market structure and governance to deliver pensions, it also needs to consider "traditional" issues of benefit design, eligibility, and payout rules. These areas are clearly not all mutually exclusive. A good policy design and public consultation process will allow iteration and adaptation in design. But a central message of this chapter is that the process should be coherent and logically consistent. A country should not promise its people no risk, certain outcomes, and high benefits and then choose an FDC private pension pillar with limited expertise and weak governance over investments. Equally, a country should not follow a global trend—for example, choosing "pure DC" private pensions with all the risk taken by individual members—if viable risk-sharing options might have been discarded in the rush to avoid the implications of final salary DB plans with fully guaranteed benefits. In terms of benefit structure, the best way to think about the suitability for the private pension pillar is to include the existing provision on the public sector side. Countries described as having "moved from DB to DC" in truth have only seen this for private pensions.

Another element in determining the "right" benefit structure is to be very precise about the actual terms of the pension. A DB pension can mean a formula based on total years of work, with a long vesting period, calculated on final salary and guaranteed against wage inflation for deferred members and then against price inflation for pensions in payment. This is very expensive to deliver, has negative impacts on gender equality through the vesting rules, and greatly enhances the impact of wage inequality. Moreover, anchoring to inflation and wages makes it very difficult to adjust to shocks in the return on investments. However, a DB formula can be much more flexible—it can focus on career average salary to deal with inequality, have low or no vesting rules to aid gender equality, and only allow indexation of benefits if funds are sufficient to pay for it. Likewise, a pure DC formula that places all the risk on the member can lead to very large differences in retirement income purely by virtue of the start and end year of a person's contributions (Cannon and Tonks 2004). This system can easily be modified to improve its risk-sharing properties. As above, nominal or real capital guarantees can be considered—with best practice being to use a backstop fund for the guaranteed elements (Antolin et al. 2011).

Contribution levels are of course central to the final pension outcome, as is the "density of contribution"; for example, the total number of payments made over a working life and when they are made. Contributing for 10 years may provide rights to some form of public pension, independently of when the contributions were made. But for private pensions it makes a very big difference if the 10 years were spent at the start of the working life and the money had 40 years to grow, or in the final 10 years of working life. In developed economies with formal labor markets, the density of contributions tends to be likely to be 100 percent for each year of employment for formal sector workers. In countries with greater informality, many workers may find it very difficult to contribute 12 months per year (Rofman, Apella, and Vezza 2013). Hence, modeling the likely payout from a 5 percent contribution as a share of wages should build in scenarios for likely payouts for those with less than a 100 percent contribution record. The current debates about the performance of the Chilean system are partly driven by the realization that many workers have far less than "official" projections—because many simple projections assume a worker will contribute the whole time. Even if many other variants are presented, the full implications may be lost on workers—even if the implications of a failure to contribute should be obvious. Working out the "right" level of contributions can be greatly assisted by models that project pension payouts from private pensions (Dowd and Blake 2013; IOPS 2014; OECD 2012; Sane and Price 2018).

The final issue in this brief overview of the nature of the pension product relates to the payout phase.[9] Without specifying the payout phase it is not possible to state clearly the outcomes that the pension system is seeking to achieve. Many private pension schemes are better described as asset accumulation systems rather than retirement income systems because they allow members to withdraw money from the pension pot for other purposes such as health, education, and housing, and then withdraw the full amount of money at retirement in a lump sum. A multipurpose accumulation vehicle can be well-designed—as in the Malaysian and Singaporean examples—with some assets permanently identified for retirement and some proportion allocated for access if needed. But early access is often not well-designed and can lead to significant leakage. The Society of Actuaries in the United States, for example, estimated that some 40 percent of U.S. retirement assets leak before retirement—principally because workers can take the full accumulated pot when they change employer.

ADAPTING THE NDC PAYOUT FORMULA FOR USE IN THE FUNDED PILLARS

The NDC formula used to generate retirement income in Sweden provides an attractive way for countries to deliver income guaranteed until death for their citizens without the need for well-functioning annuity markets (Price and Inglis 2017). The periodic repricing of income from the accumulated assets removes the need for the regulatory capital to back the promised income in a traditional single premium annuity. It also overcomes the psychological barrier people face when spending 40 years building their assets and then having to pass them all to an insurance company in one block to gain an annuity. This issue is compounded by the insurance companies often not exploiting the illiquidity premium that comes from having access to a source of capital that cannot be withdrawn (Rocha and Thorburn 2007). Another innovative example in the payout space was suggested by the United Kingdom's NEST, which would combine a phased withdrawal with a deferred annuity.

An NDC pillar, by providing an income until death (along with any basic minimum pension), may mean that the absence of annuity-like options in the private pillar is less serious for old-age poverty. It may also allow simplification of the task for private pensions by focusing on the first 10 or 15 years of retirement, which gives a fixed, and potentially manageable, target for many people. The NDC pillar could increasingly take over as people age. One way to increase the coherence of this type of arrangement is for public pensions to start at a relatively low level in the early years of retirement as people rely more on private savings, but for the public component to ramp up in the latter stages of old age when private assets have been drawn down and there are fewer people to cover and hence potentially lower costs. Because the wealthy are more likely to reach old age, the higher public pension would need to be taxed to ensure equity. This would further enhance the cost savings relative to the standard model of a payout that is anchored by the income paid at retirement (see Price and Inglis [2017] for a more detailed investigation of this idea).

Other forms of payout outside a traditional annuity include phased or systematic withdrawal options, which do not provide the guarantee of income until death but can be a simple and effective way to move beyond a "lump-sum" pension system to one that focuses on delivering income. Moreover, in systems that deliver a relatively high level of income from the public pillar, such as Australia's, one argument is that there is less of a need for an additional source of income until death, particularly if a public health provision exists.

However, even in Australia the government itself believes that the current arrangements do not maximize potential outcomes and is developing a comprehensive retirement income product (Australian Treasury Department 2014; Productivity Commission 2018).

REGULATION AND SUPERVISION

A final area of design relates to regulatory and supervisory arrangements. Many regulators have adopted risk-based supervision (IOPS 2014). But before starting to use the techniques of risk-based supervision, it is vital to set out the long-run aim or objective for the regulator. The choices between inherently different activities within a regulator, from on-site supervision through to communication and education, can be more coherently determined within a framework that considers their contribution to the long-run outcomes—even if the measures of success are sometimes focused on intermediate indicators. Price, Ashcroft, and Hafeman (2016) develop a methodology that unites the outcomes with risk-based supervision, known as Outcomes and Risk Based Supervision. The revised OECD Core Principles of Private Pension Regulation (OECD 2016) now include a clear statement that the focus of regulation should be on achieving the five long-run outcomes highlighted previously.

The best approach is one in which the regulator and supervisor choose the instruments that will best reduce the risks. For the risk of fraud that will reduce assets and hence reduce adequacy, few measures are as important as mandating the use of custodians—as well as a focus on the overall governance of an organization. In other areas, greater flexibility can be given so that the regulator can focus on the weakest institutions. NDC arrangements could be included in supervisory scope to enhance accountability, transparency, and trust.

These issues are far more important than a focus on structures—whether a supervisor is specialized or integrated with other sectors such as insurance and securities—where there is no clear pattern globally in terms of integrated, hybrid, specialized, or functional regulators (Masciandaro and Quintyn 2009). The global financial crisis highlighted that structure did not dominate outcomes. All models had examples of successes and failures. The key to dealing successfully with the challenges of regulation had more to do with the "ability to act" (having the legal powers and resources) and the "willingness to act" (having the independence, quality of staff, and behavioral characteristics for tough but proportionate decisions needed for effective regulation) (Viñals et al. 2010).

A final note is the importance of getting the implementation of policy right. Policy makers should ensure their teams have sufficient understanding of operational issues, including on identification and information technology, and the program management skills to implement major policy and operational change. The role of the program or mission office in pension reforms in the United Kingdom, in New Zealand's autoenrollment reforms, and in India's world-record-setting financial inclusion initiatives is instructive for potential reformers (Pande and Ryder 2017).

Conclusions

This chapter reviews the factors that should guide the design of private funded pensions to create a complete pension system alongside an NDC component. It argues that a mix of public and private pensions is most effective for delivering the best combination of pension outcomes.

Corner solutions that rely solely on public pensions (whether NDC or not) or just private pensions (whether DB, FDC, or a hybrid) have no obvious examples of sustainable success in either developed or developing countries.

The chapter sets out the criteria by which reformers can judge success or failure of adding a private pension pillar to the NDC pillar. Pension system outcomes cover coverage, adequacy, and sustainability alongside efficiency and security. Achieving these outcomes requires a mix of designing a value chain to deliver private pensions and what type of product will be delivered. A key part of the value chain is who provides recordkeeping and account administration. A well-functioning NDC pillar may already embody the administrative capacity that could be leveraged to improve recordkeeping and account administration in private pensions—particularly where it is based on a well-functioning tax collection system. Thus, creating an NDC pillar may give scope for economies of scale across pension pillars.

The second set of design questions looks at the more "traditional" elements of benefit design, contribution levels, eligibility, and payout phase. In an ideal world, the future income to be delivered by a pension system would look at the joint distribution from the combined NDC and private pillar. The chapter argues that NDC schemes potentially allow clearer identification of potential outcomes in that they are (in theory) less prone to ad hoc adjustments and pre-election changes than traditional DB public pension pillars. In addition, the NDC rule may have important implications for optimal investment strategies in private pensions—something that governing bodies of pension funds and pension regulators should consider. For example, in many countries real per capita GDP growth (which can feature in NDC rules) is negatively correlated with the real growth of equity markets. Also, importantly, NDC payout formulas can potentially be used to provide an income until death in countries that will struggle to have deep and efficient traditional annuity markets. It is important that design coherence flows to the regulatory and supervisory approach so that these can also focus on how best to achieve the long-run outcomes. Finally, a robust program management or mission office greatly assists delivery of the reforms, so that great designs are not lost to poor implementation.

Notes

1. CCSS = Caja Costarricense de Seguro Social.

2. However, the terminology can sometimes get in the way. Many of the issues identified in this chapter in terms of good design for "private" pensions would apply equally to a "public" pension fund that was investing assets to meet either a DB liability or with an FDC structure. A country that had an NDC pillar plus a funded "public" pension plan such as a provident fund is still effectively bringing together notional and real assets to jointly provide retirement income. The only real difference is the institutional setup, in which the choice of "public" or "private" should depend on which arrangements are likely to provide secure strong governance, scale, and expertise.

3. A good global survey of the choices of different countries is provided by "International Patterns of Pension Provision II" (Pallares-Miralles, Romero, and Whitehouse 2012), and, for a smaller set of countries, by the OECD's *Pensions at a Glance*. International comparisons of saving for old age were developed recently by the "FINDEX" index and can be found in work by Demirgüç-Kunt et al. (2015) and Demirgüç-Kunt, Klapper, and Panos (2016). Recent in-depth regional reviews of history and current practice include *The Inverting Pyramid: Pension*

Systems Facing Demographic Challenges in Europe and Central Asia (Schwarz et al. 2014); "Live Long and Prosper: Aging in East Asia and Pacific" (World Bank 2016); *Pension Systems in East and Southeast Asia: Promoting Fairness and Sustainability* (Park 2012); Pensions at a Glance Latin America and Caribbean (OECD 2013); "Pension Patterns and Challenges in Sub Saharan Africa" (Dorfman 2015); and for the 22 members of the Arab League "Arab Pension Systems: Trends, Challenges and Options for Reforms" (Price et al. 2017). For longevity comparisons, see the UN's World Population Prospects (UNDESA 2015), and for longrun international comparisons of asset returns in 22 countries since 1900, see the London Business School, Credit Suisse Global Investment Year Book (Dimson, Marsh, and Staunton 2016).

4. There are other ways to break down the outcomes; for example, see the work of the Melbourne-Mercer Global Index, whose "Integrity" category includes many of the areas in "Security" in the outcomes based assessment framework; previous work (ACFS and Mercer 2013); the Global Aging Institute (Jackson, Peter, and Howe 2013); and work by the American Academy of Actuaries (ForwardThinking Task Force 2014).

5. Insurance provision is almost never compulsory in the way that pension contributions are often mandated or quasi-mandated—except for car insurance, some forms of personal liability insurance, and in the case of Turkey, mandatory earthquake insurance. Rules set by mortgage lenders can sometimes make home insurance effectively compulsory as well as some form of life cover, but this is not universally the case, and there is typically no check once a mortgage is provided that the cover remains in place.

6. AFORE = Administradora de Fondos para el Retiro.

7. The OECD conducts a useful annual survey of global investment regulations for pension funds.

8. The term "annuity" is not used in the same way in every country. Note that the terminology around payouts and annuities can be very confusing. In some countries, products marketed as annuities provide a way to accumulate assets to be taken as a lump sum when the person retires. In other countries a lump-sum payout would indicate the opposite of an annuity, which is thought of as a stream of income payments. This chapter aims to link the payout category to the income stream it creates—hence an annuity pays an income until death in the standard form and a phased or systematic withdrawal allows periodic payments but no guarantee of income until death.

9. This section does not go into great detail on all the different annuity options found in a range of publications—for example, Rocha, Vittas, and Rudolph (2011) and Brown et al. (2001).

References

Aaron, Henry. 1966. "The Social Insurance Paradox." *Canadian Journal of Economics and Political Science* 32 (3): 371–74.

ACFS (Australian Center for Financial Studies) and Mercer. 2013. "Melbourne-Mercer Global Pension Index." Mercer, London.

Ambachtsheer, Keith. 2016. *The Future of Pension Management: Integrating Design, Governance, and Investing.* Hoboken, NJ: Wiley and Sons.

Antolín, Pablo, Stéphanie Payet, Edward Whitehouse, and Juan Yermo. 2011. "The Role of Guarantees in Defined-Contribution Pensions." OECD Working Paper on Finance, Insurance, and Private Pensions 11, OECD Publishing, Paris.

Australian Treasury Department. 2014. *Financial System Inquiry Final Report.* Canberra: Commonwealth of Australia.

Barr, Nicholas, and Peter Diamond. 2008. *Reforming Pensions*. New York: Oxford University Press.

Beetsma, Roel, Ward Romp, and Siert Vos. 2013. "Intergenerational Risk Sharing, Pensions, and Endogenous Labour Supply in General Equilibrium." *Scandinavian Journal of Economics* 115 (1): 141–54.

Bernartzi, Shlomo, and Richard Thaler. 2007. "Heuristics and Biases in Retirement Savings Behavior." *Journal of Economic Perspectives* 21 (3): 81–104.

Bikker, Jacob. 2013. "Is There an Optimal Pension Fund Size? A Scale-Economy Analysis of Administrative and Investment Costs." De Nederlandsche Bank Working Paper 376, De Nederlandsche Bank, Amsterdam.

Bohn, Henning. 2009. "Intergenerational Risk Sharing and Fiscal Policy." *Journal of Monetary Economics* 56 (6): 805–16.

Bosch, Mariano, Angel Melguizo, and Carmen Pagés. 2013. "Better Pensions, Better Jobs: Towards Universal Coverage in Latin America and the Caribbean." Inter-American Development Bank, Washington, DC.

Brown, Jeffrey, Olivia Mitchell, James Poterba, and Mark Warshawsky. 2001. *The Role of Annuity Markets in Financing Retirement*. Cambridge, MA: MIT Press.

Cannon, Edmund, and Ian Tonks. 2004. "U.K. Annuity Rates, Money's Worth and Pension Replacement Ratios 1957–2002." *Geneva Papers on Risk and Insurance* 29 (3): 394–416.

Clark, Gordon, and Roger Urwin. 2008. "Making Pension Boards Work: The Critical Role of Leadership." *Rotman Journal of International Pension Management* 1 (1): 38–45.

De Menil, Georges, Fabrice Murtin, and Eytan Sheshinski. 2006. "Planning for the Optimal Mix of Paygo Tax and Funded Savings." *Journal of Pension Economics and Finance* 5 (1): 1–25.

De Menil, Georges, Fabrice Murtin, Eytan Sheshinski, and Tite Yokossi. 2016. "A Rational, Economic Model of Paygo Tax Rates." *European Economic Review* 89: 55–72.

Demirgüç-Kunt, Asli, Leora Klapper, and Georgios Panos. 2016. "Saving for Old Age." Working Paper 7693, World Bank, Washington, DC.

Demirgüç-Kunt, Asli, Leora Klapper, Dorothe Singer, and Peter Van Oudheusden. 2015. "The Global Findex Database 2014: Measuring Financial Inclusion around the World." World Bank Policy Research Working Paper 7255, World Bank, Washington, DC.

Devolder, Pierre; and Roberta Melis. 2015. "Optimal Mix between Pay As You Go and Funding for Pension Liabilities in a Stochastic Framework." *ASTIN Bulletin* 45 (3): 551–75.

Dimson, Elroy, Paul Marsh, and Mike Staunton. 2002. *Triumph of the Optimists: 101 Years of Global Investment Returns*. Princeton, NJ: Princeton University Press.

———. 2012. *The Global Investment Returns Yearbook*. London: London Business School and Credit Suisse.

———. 2016. *Credit Suisse Global Investment Returns Yearbook*. Zurich: Credit Suisse AG.

Dorfman, Mark. 2015. "Pension Patterns and Challenges in Sub Saharan Africa." Social Protection and Labor Discussion Paper 1503, World Bank, Washington, DC.

Dowd, Kevin, and David Blake. 2013. "Good Practice Principles in Modelling Defined Contribution Pension Plans." Discussion Paper PI-1302, The Pensions Institute Cass Business School.

European Commission. 2012. "An Agenda for Adequate, Safe and Sustainable Pensions." White Paper COM (2012) 55 final, European Commission, Brussels.

Franzen, Dorothee, and John Ashcroft. 2017. "Pension Investment Governance." In *Saving the Next Billion from Old Age Poverty: Global Lessons for Local Action*, edited by Parul Khanna, William Price, and Gautam Bhardwaj, Chapter 17. Delhi: Narosa Publishing.

ForwardThinking Task Force. 2014. "Retirement for the AGES: Building Enduring Retirement Income Systems." American Academy of Actuaries, Washington, DC.

Gordon, Roger, and Hal Varian. 1988. "Intergenerational Risk Sharing." *Journal of Public Economics* 37 (2): 185–202.

Government of India. 2015. "Report of the Committee to Recommend Measures for Curbing Mis-Selling and Rationalising Distribution Incentives in Financial Products." Ministry of Finance, Government of India, Delhi.

Halan, Monica, and Renuka Sane. 2016. "Misled and Mis-sold: Financial Misbehavior in Retail Banks?" NSE-IFMR Finance Foundation Financial Deepening and Household Finance Research Initiative, India.

Harrison, Debbie. 2012. "Treating DC Scheme Members Fairly in Retirement?" Pension Institute and National Association of Pension Funds, London and Somerset.

Heale, Mike, and Paul Martiniello. 2017. "Managing Costs and Optimizing Outcomes." In *Saving the Next Billion from Old Age Poverty: Global Lessons for Local Action*, edited by Parul Khanna, William Price, and Gautam Bhardwaj, Chapter 18. Delhi: Narosa Publishing.

Holzmann, Robert. 2009. *Aging Populations, Pension Funds, and Financial Markets: Regional Perspectives and Global Challenges for Central, Eastern, and Southern Europe.* Washington, DC: World Bank.

Holzmann, Robert, and Richard Hinz. 2005. *Old-Age Income Support in the 21st Century: An International Perspective on Pension Systems and Reform.* Washington, DC: World Bank.

Impávido, Gregorio, Esperanza Lasagabaster, and Manuel Garcia-Huitron. 2010. "New Policies for Mandatory Defined Contribution Pensions: Industrial Organization Models and Investment Products." World Bank, Washington, DC.

IOPS Toolkit for Risk-based Pensions Supervision. 2014. International Organisation of Pension Supervisors. https://www.iopsweb.org/toolkit/ Modules: 0 – Introduction; 1 – Preparation; 2 – Quantitative Risk Assessment Tools; 3 – Identifying Risks; 4 – Risk Mitigants and Risk Scoring; and 5 – Supervisory Response.

Jackson, Richard, Tobias Peter, and Nick Howe. 2013. "The Global Aging Preparedness Index: Second Edition." CSIS/Jackson National Life Insurance Company/Rowman & Littlefield, Washington, DC.

Knell, Markus. 2010. "The Optimal Mix between Funded and Unfunded Pension Systems When People Care about Relative Consumption." *Economica* 77 (308): 710–33.

Long, Greg. Forthcoming. "Crisis, Pension Reform, and the Thrift Savings Plan." World Bank, Washington, DC.

Lusardi, Annamaria, and Olivia Mitchell. 2011. "Financial Literacy around the World: An Overview." NBER Working Paper 17107, National Bureau of Economic Research, Cambridge, MA.

———. 2014. "The Economic Importance of Financial Literacy: Theory and Evidence." *Journal of Economic Literature* 52 (1): 5–44.

Masciandaro, Donata, and Marc Quintyn. 2009. "Reforming Financial Supervision and the Role of Central Banks: A Review of Global Trends, Causes and Effects (1998–2008)." CEPR Policy Insights 30, Centre for Economic Policy Research, London.

Merton, Robert. 1983. "On the Role of Social Security as a Means for Efficient Risk Sharing in an Economy Where Human Capital Is Not Tradeable." In *Financial Aspects of the United States Pensions System*, edited by Zvi Bodie and John Shoven, 325–58. Chicago: University of Chicago Press.

Miles, David. 2001. "Funded and Unfunded Pension Schemes: Risk, Return and Welfare." CESifo Working Paper Series 239, CESifo Group, Munich.

OECD (Organisation for Economic Co-operation and Development). 2012. *OECD Pension Outlook*. Paris: OECD Publishing.

———. 2013. *Pensions at a Glance: Latin America and the Caribbean*. Paris: OECD Publishing.

———. 2016. *OECD Core Principles of Private Pension Regulation*. Paris: OECD Publishing.

Pallares-Mirralles, Montserrat, Carolina Romero, and Edward Whitehouse. 2012. "International Patterns of Pension Provision II: A Worldwide Overview of Facts and Figures." World Bank, Washington, DC.

Palmer, Edward. 2000. "The Swedish Pension Reform Model: Framework and Issues." Social Protection Discussion Paper 23086, World Bank, Washington, DC.

Pande, Alok, and Darren Ryder. 2017. "Delivering the Reform: The Central Role for a Mission Office." In *Saving the Next Billion from Old Age Poverty: Global Lessons for Local Action*, edited by Parul Khanna, William Price, and Gautam Bhardwaj, Chapter 23. Delhi: Narosa Publishing.

Park, Donghyun. 2012. *Pension Systems in East and Southeast Asia: Promoting Fairness and Sustainability*. Manila: Asian Development Bank.

Price, William, John Ashcroft, and Michael Hafeman. 2016. *Outcomes-Based Diagnosis and Assessments for Private Pensions: A Handbook*. Washington, DC: World Bank.

Price, William, and Evan Inglis. 2017. "Paying the Pension: Markets, Products and Choices." In *Saving the Next Billion from Old Age Poverty: Global Lessons for Local Action*, edited by Parul Khanna, William Price, and Gautam Bhardwaj, Chapter 20. Delhi: Narosa Publishing.

Price, William, Montserrat Pallares-Miralles, Gustavo Demarco, and Habib Attia. 2017. "Arab Pension Systems: Trends, Challenges and Options for Reforms." World Bank, Washington, DC.

Productivity Commission. 2018. "Competition in the Australian Financial System, Inquiry Report." Report No. 89, Commonwealth of Australia, Canberra.

Ritter, Jay. 2005. "Economic Growth and Equity Returns." *Pacific-Basin Finance Journal* 13 (2005): 489–503.

———. 2012. "Is Economic Growth Good for Investors?" *Journal of Applied Corporate Finance* 24 (3): 8–18.

———. 2019. "Financing a Business: Venture Capital, Initial Public Offerings, and the Required Return on Investment." PowerPoint presentation.

Rocha, Roberto, and Craig Thorburn. 2007. *Developing Annuities Markets: The Experience of Chile*. Washington, DC: World Bank.

Rocha, Roberto, Dmitri Vittas, and Heinz Rudolph. 2011. *Annuities and Other Retirement Products: Designing the Payout Phase*. Washington, DC: World Bank.

Rofman, Rafael, Ignacio Apella, and Evelyn Vezza. 2015. *Beyond Contributory Pensions: Fourteen Experiences with Coverage Expansion in Latin America*. Directions in Development—Human Development. Washington, DC: World Bank.

Sane, Renuka, and William Price. 2018. "Simulating Pension Income Scenarios with penCalc: An Illustration for India's National Pension System." Policy Research Working Paper 8304, World Bank, Washington, DC.

Schwarz, Anita, Omar Arias, Asta Zviniene, Heinz Rudolph, Sebastian Eckardt, Johannes Koettl, Herwig Immervoll, and Miglena Abels. 2014. *The Inverting Pyramid: Pension Systems Facing Demographic Challenges in Europe and Central Asia*. Washington, DC: World Bank.

Secunda, Paul. 2017."Uber Retirement." University of Chicago Legal Forum, Vol. 2017, No. 1, 2017; Marquette Law School Legal Studies Paper No. 17-1, Chicago.

Sluchynsky, Oleksiy. 2015. "Defining, Measuring, and Benchmarking Administrative Expenditures of Mandatory Social Security Programs." Social Protection and Labor Policy and Technical Notes 95198, World Bank, Washington, DC.

UNDESA (United Nations, Department of Economic and Social Affairs, Population Division). 2015. "World Population Prospects: The 2015 Revision, Key Findings and Advance Tables." Working Paper ESA/P/WP.241, United Nations, New York.

Viñals, Jose, Jonathan Fiechter, Aditya Narain, Jennifer Elliott, Ian Tower, Pierluigi Bologna, and Michael Hsu. 2010. "The Making of Good Supervision: Learning to Say No." IMF Staff Position Paper 10/08, International Monetary Fund, Washington, DC.

World Bank. 2016. "Live Long and Prosper: Aging in East Asia and Pacific." World Bank East Asia and Pacific Regional Report, World Bank, Washington, DC.

World Bank. 2017. "The Evolution of the Canadian Pension Model: Practical Lessons for Building World-Class Pension Organizations." World Bank, Washington, DC.

Zalli, Adrian. Forthcoming. "The Kosovo Pension Saving Trust." Kosovo Pension Savings Trust, Pristina.

CHAPTER 31

Closing Policy Panel: Observations and Reflections

Bo Könberg, Marcelo Abi-Ramia Caetano, Monika Queisser, Per Eckefeldt, and Michal Rutkowski

Introduction

Since the pioneering reforms of nonfinancial defined contribution (NDC) public pension schemes in Italy, Latvia, Poland, and Sweden in the 1990s, the debate about adoption of this reform approach has accelerated, influencing pension policy measures introduced in various countries across the world. The NDC conference held in Rome in 2017 and its papers, which now constitute the chapters in this book, offer important policy analyses and lessons on the working of NDC schemes and areas for further fine-tuning. This latest publication complements the previous NDC anthologies (Holzmann and Palmer 2006; Holzmann, Palmer, and Robalino 2012) and offers crucial guidance for countries thinking about systemic pension reform and about NDC as a crucial contender.

The 2017 Rome conference on NDC pension schemes was the official beginning of the present anthology. It concluded with a panel discussion, which focused on current topics in pension reform. The editors have given panelists the opportunity to further develop the thoughts they put forward at the conference. This chapter presents the results of their deliberations. Two of the speakers, Bo Könberg and Marcelo Abi-Ramia Caetano, both former policy makers, focused on the evolution of pension reform policy discussions in their respective countries, Sweden and Brazil, and thoughts going forward. The remaining three speakers, Monika Queisser of the OECD (Organisation for Economic Co-operation and Development), Per Eckefeldt of the European Commission, and Michal Rutkowski of the World Bank, framed the discussion in terms of future challenges facing policy makers regarding pension reform.

Reflections on Sweden's Pension Reform Process and Issues Going Forward

Bo Könberg

More than 25 years have passed since the Swedish Working Group on Pensions published its 1992 sketch, "A Reformed Pension System—Background, Principles, and Sketch," in English (Swedish Ministry of Health and Social Affairs 2017). The reform created Sweden's present universal, mandatory two-pillar public pension scheme with a nonfinancial defined contribution scheme (NDC) and a smaller financial defined contribution (FDC), the Premium Pension. The first individual contributions were paid into the Premium Pension Scheme in 1995.

Ideas similar to those that constitute an NDC pension scheme (for example, a public pension scheme based on lifetime earnings) were actually proposed by a Swedish parliamentary committee in the beginning of the 1950s (Åkesson 1950). The very general ideas expressed by Buchanan (1968) could perhaps also be relevant. But, as Swedes we are pleased to have put all the "nuts and bolts" together and implemented NDC as a coherent package from design, beginning in 1992, to implementation in January 1999.

The Swedish pension reform with NDC as the flagship was a result of five of the seven political parties working together in the Working Group on Pensions, renamed the Pensions Group after the reform. Beginning with the 1992 sketch, the NDC reform structure was developed in detail in 1992–94 and passed by an overwhelming 85 percent vote in parliament in June 1994, supported by the five parties in the working group. The same five parties, with the recent addition of the Green Party, continue to constitute the Pensions Group.

The framework for the overall reformed pension system was in place from the outset, but the details of each component—the NDC scheme, the FDC scheme, the minimum pension guarantee, and the means-tested housing allowance for pensioners—were thought through individually, each requiring its own political discussion and legislation. In the interim from 1994, the Social Insurance Agency's information technology system underwent a complete facelift and individual accounts were created from 1960 before the overall system was introduced in 1999.

About 10 countries have since introduced an NDC or modified variants thereof, with Italy, Latvia, Norway, Poland, and Sweden adopting "pure" NDCs. Like Sweden, some countries added an FDC second pillar. In addition, another 10 countries modified their public pension schemes in the direction of an NDC (Wang, Williamson, and Cansoy 2016), although some of these countries have since retracted these reforms.

Before 1960 Sweden had a universal Folkpension. This was supplemented by the earnings-related *Allmän tilläggspension* (ATP) scheme in 1960. The ATP scheme required only 30 years for a "full" pension, with the pension calculated on the basis of the 15 best years of earnings (contributions). The most important reason for the 1994 reform was the projection by the Swedish National Social Insurance Board, published in 1987, that the ATP scheme would become financially unaffordable beginning about 2010—despite already large reserve funds—when the "baby boomers" would begin to retire. This projection was reinforced by the publication of the sitting Pension Commission's report in 1991.

Affordability and financial unsustainability were not the only problems confronting the ATP scheme. On top of this came the obvious unfairness of the ATP 30/15 rule. All workers paid contributions during their entire working careers, which were well over 40 years for most blue-collar workers, whereas others could get the same benefit with 30 years. In addition, there was the obvious criticism that the 30/15 rule essentially transferred income from those who had long careers and small annual wage increases to those who had short careers but large annual increases.

In 1999 the Swedish NDC scheme inherited the large ATP reserve fund, created in the early 1960s with the explicit intention of providing "self-financing" for the baby boomers who would begin to enter the labor force in the mid-1960s. As discussed in chapter 2, since 2010 the returns on the funds have been an important component of baby boomers' financing in their initial pension years.

LESSONS LEARNED FROM SWEDEN'S EXPERIENCE

The lessons of the Swedish experience that can be of value for other countries venturing into multipillar reforms with an NDC pension scheme are as follows.

Contribution rates and overall design

The contribution rates to the public NDC and FDC schemes were—up to a ceiling—meant to be 16 percent and 2.5 percent (that is, 18.5 percent), but when the government implemented the contribution rates they became, de facto, 17.2 percent. This suggests that another 1.3 percent is available, which could be shared between the schemes or added to one of them. At the same time, the introduction of the new public scheme stimulated the conversion of largely unfunded, defined benefit (DB) occupational pension schemes to FDC schemes with for most participants a contribution rate of some 4.5 percent up to the ceiling on the contribution-based earnings for the public schemes. The combined pension rate today is thus about 22 percent. In addition to their coverage in the public schemes, about 90 percent of employees are also covered by occupational schemes, providing an additional supplement both below the ceiling on earnings for coverage in the public NDC and FDC schemes and above the ceiling. The lessons here are that (a) the move to DC for the public pension commitment was emulated by the already important occupational schemes, and (b) the occupational schemes took on the "responsibility" for supplementing the foundation set by the public scheme.

Another important lesson is the relative ease with which a traditional nonfinancial DB scheme can be transformed into an NDC scheme. Sweden's NDC accounts were created from 1960 using historical information on earnings underlying contributions before the change to an NDC pension scheme in 1999. The contribution rate was set at a rate similar to the ATP conribution rate (18 percent) retroactively for the creation of these accounts.

The guaranteed minimum standard of living for old-age pensioners

Sweden has a guarantee pension for those with low pension rights and a means-tested housing allowance that can be claimed as a supplement, among other things owing to regional differences in the cost of housing. The guarantee pension and housing allowance are price indexed yearly. What is important is that the ceiling should be raised as needed for both the guarantee benefit and the means-tested housing allowance. Sweden fell behind on this—no adjustment was made in the level of the ceiling over the period 2003–17, which became a political issue in 2017. In response, adjustments were made to the ceiling of both, raising the upper limit in 2018–19, however, still retaining price indexation.

Increasing the retirement age

In the year that elapsed between the Rome NDC Conference and February 2019, the six parties in the Swedish Pensions Group agreed on some changes in the overall Swedish public pension system. The most important is an increase in the minimum pension age from 61 to 64, in steps from 2020 to 2026. In addition, the age at which employers have the right to lay off workers only because of age will be raised from 67 to 69 (starting with

68 in 2020). The age at which a guarantee benefit can be claimed will be raised from 65 to 66 (beginning in 2023). These ages will then be indexed to changes in life expectancy.

The automatic balancing mechanism

The NDC scheme has an automatic balancing mechanism that augments indexation when current assets are projected to be lower than current liabilities—and then raises the (income) index to its original trajectory after the solvency ratio once again becomes positive. Although balancing has occurred on a couple of occasions, in 2018 pensions returned to levels that were the same as if the balancing had never occurred. The present projections of the Swedish Pensions Agency's Orange Report (Swedish Pensions Agency 2018; Palmer and Könberg 2019) are that the likelihood is low that solvency will once again fall into the negative zone. Although the Swedish construction of the balancing mechanism is still unique, other countries have taken the idea to heart and introduced other rules to the same end.

The funds in the FDC scheme

Individual accounts in the Premium Pension (FDC) scheme are invested in the Swedish and international financial markets through a clearinghouse—operated by the Swedish Pensions Agency. Individual participants order (from the clearinghouse) purchases and sales of "units"—a maximum of five funds at one time per participant—with transactions possible on all working days of the year. Participants can currently choose between about 830 national and international funds (with about 90 fund managers) registered with the clearinghouse. This mechanism enables the clearinghouse to execute at most one net buy-sell transaction per day and fund, because individual orders are aggregated into a single order vis à vis a specific fund. From the very outset registered funds have agreed to a fee schedule that requires fund owners to decrease fees as their volume of business grows. When it was introduced in 2000, the clearinghouse was a novelty on the world stage, and was generally of great interest to countries moving in the direction of mandatory FDC pension schemes.

The default fund in the public FDC scheme (the AP7 Såfa) stands out because of its glide path starting at age 55, which moves from a riskier asset-holding strategy for individuals younger than age 55 to a less risky strategy gradually thereafter. The default fund public FDC scheme can be chosen directly and is now the largest fund, with assets valued at about US$120 billion.

Significant fraud uncovered recently in a couple of funds suggests that supervision of the 830 funds has not been entirely successful. The parliamentary Pensions Group has decided that criteria for participation and supervision need to be strengthened, which will probably result in fewer funds in the future.

The "strength" of the NDC fund

The NDC reserve fund consists of five separate funds that invest the NDC reserves in the domestic and international financial markets. An important metric in this connection is the fund "strength," defined by how many months or years of the current year's pension payments the assets in the reserve funds could cover altogether.

The 1994 bill presenting the NDC reform stated that a goal should be that the fund strength should never be shorter than the finances needed to make six months worth of payments. At the end of 2017 the reserves were sufficient to cover four years and nine months of NDC benefit payments. According to the most recent of the yearly analyses performed by the Swedish Pensions Agency (2017), fund strength is estimated to be at its lowest future level in 2025, at more than four years (figure 2.4 in chapter 2), which is eight times more than the lowest level mentioned in the parliamentary bill initiating the NDC reform in 1994. The first issue going forward is to determine how the funds can be used to buffer strong recessions or depressions of the type witnessed in 2009–11, with the aim of avoiding balancing when it is clear that the economy and the stock market are following a severe downturn. A second, more general issue confronting Sweden is what to do if or when the scale of the funds starts on an upward trajectory creating reserves much beyond the presently projected low of four years' strength.

Better coordination of the rules of the occupational and public schemes

Summing up, the performance record of the public component of Sweden's overall pension system is good. The completely new NDC scheme has worked well. The FDC component has delivered higher yields than predicted and has weathered the ups and downs of the world stock market. In my opinion, the biggest overall system-related issues have to do with incongruencies in the intersection of the public and the occupational pension schemes.

PROPOSED CHANGES TO PUBLIC AND OCCUPATIONAL SCHEMES

Some changes in the public pension systems to consider are as follows:

- Improve the guarantee pension for those with the lowest pensions and raise the ceiling for the means-tested housing allowance.

- Introduce joint annuities as the default for married couples who do not have a signed agreement opting out of this default.

- Abandon the present method of calculating life-expectancy projections and adopt a more evidence-based method that does not consistently underestimate life expectancy, as is the case with the presently legislated model (Palmer and Zhao de Gosson de Varennes 2019).

- Given that the projections point toward increases in fund strength after 2025, develop new rules for the NDC buffer fund(s) more or less immediately. This would address the two issues noted above: rules regarding the use of the funds as temporary buffers in recessions when needed, and rules for what can be designated excess funds and for how excess funds should be distributed to participants.

- Given that the present de facto contribution rate of 17.2 percent for the combined public NDC and FDC schemes is not what was originally decided (18.5 percent), discuss whether it should be increased back to the legislated level, and, if so, whether it should augment the public NDC or the FDC scheme.

Some important changes to consider for occupational pensions are as follows:

- Because today's occupational pension schemes already include some 90 percent of employees, make it compulsory for employers to pay contributions for groups of employees presently not covered. Norway introduced such a change in 2005. The method would be that those employers who do not pay occupational pensions for their employees will instead have to pay contributions—for example, to be distributed between NDC or FDC accounts through the Swedish Pensions Agency.

- Require the same contribution rates paid on earnings below and above the earnings ceiling for the public system. At present, the four occupational schemes pay a much higher percentage for earnings of employees who are above the ceiling on earnings covered by the public schemes.

- Require contributions on earnings above the ceiling for the occupational pension schemes for those who continue to work beyond age 64—thereby creating better pension rights—and align the entrance age for the occupational schemes with that of the public schemes (age 16).

With these proposed changes, what is currently a good overall pension system could become even better.

Reflections on the Course of the Brazilian Pension Reform Process

Marcelo Abi-Ramia Caetano, Rogério Nagamine Costanzi, and Otávio José Guerci Sidone

The basic promises of an NDC reform—fairness for individuals and financial sustainability for countries—attracted Brazilian pension scheme thinkers and reformers early on. A group of them attended the Harvard University–World Bank pension course in summer 1998, were exposed to NDC schemes well before the NDC anthologies were published, and returned to Brazil to design and implement the "pension factor" that came into operation in 2000. The pension factor is important for the Brazilian reform experience because it represents an automatic mechanism for demography adjustment, a key trend in the international arena of pension reform. This section discusses the concept and applications of the pension factor in Brazil as an example of the expectations and limits of selective application of the NDC concept in a country.

Brazil has two public compulsory pension schemes: the General Pension Scheme and the Civil Service Pension Scheme. The former serves private sector workers as well as almost two-thirds of the Brazilian municipalities that do not have their own regimes for their employees. It thus has more contributors and beneficiaries than the Civil Service Pension Scheme, but the value of its benefits is lower. The General Pension Scheme is a pay-as-you-go (PAYG) system with expenditures currently at 8.5 percent of gross domestic product (GDP). Its spending grew at an unsustainable rate of almost 0.2 percent of GDP per year over the past three decades, and it is now under pressure given Brazil's rapid and intense population aging.

Public pension expenditure in Brazil under both schemes reached 13 percent of GDP in 2017, well above what would be expected from the country's demographic structure and development level. This high level of expenditure undoubtedly has to do with important distortions such as benefit eligibility without a minimum retirement age, only a minimum length of contribution years. To ensure sustainability in the medium and long term, Brazil attempted to end eligibility based on length of contributions and to institute a minimum retirement age in 1998. After this reform attempt failed, the government legislated the so-called pension factor in 1999.

The intent of the pension factor, similar to that of sustainability factors created in other countries, was to balance the flow of contributions paid with the expected value of benefit payments through postponement of retirement, reduction in the initial benefit value at retirement, or both. Importantly, the pension factor also represents an automatic mechanism for demography adjustment. Every year the pension factor calculation table changes according to variation in estimated life expectancy.

The formula for the pension factor (*FP*) follows the logic that the higher the age of retirement and the longer the contribution period, the greater the initial benefit value of retirement:

$$FP = \left(\frac{Tc \times a}{ES} \right) \times \left(1 + \frac{(Id + Tc \times a)}{100} \right)$$

in which *Tc* is the length of the contribution period; *a* is the contribution rate; *ES* is the expectation of survival at retirement age; and *Id* is the age at retirement.

The pension factor is applied to the average of the 80 percent highest contribution wages and usually represents a significant discount on the initial benefit value of the pension. The expectation of survival at the time of retirement is reviewed annually, which implies an annual change in the value of the pension factor. In 2017, the average retirement age was 55 for men and 52 for women for length-of-contribution pensions. Using these retirement ages and a length of contribution of 35 years for men and 30 years for women, the reduction in the initial retirement value would be, respectively, 31.3 percent and 38.4 percent.[1] Women are doubly advantaged, because the calculation is made using the sum of five years of length of contribution and using the average survival expectation for both sexes.

For urban workers who do not have 35 or 30 years of contributions, the option is retirement by a minimum age, which is 65 for men and 60 for women with at least 15 years of contributions. For those who do not have even 15 years of contributions, a noncontributory means-tested benefit exists for those age 65 or older. Special rules also exist for rural workers, teachers, military personnel, and people with disabilities. Male public servants can retire at age 60 if they have 35 years of pension contributions. And female public servants can retire at age 55 if they have 30 years of pension contributions. Because of these rules, urban workers with better qualifications and greater stability in the formal labor market end up retiring earlier, with a higher benefit value, and—probably because they have higher life expectancies—enjoy retirement for longer. In this context, the application of the pension factor is very important (figure 31.1).

Given the pension factor's intent, increases in life expectancy represent a reduction in the initial value of retirement benefits. Therefore, its logic is similar to the actuarial balance that is essential for NDC-type schemes. It was also hoped that the pension factor would stimulate postponement of length-of-contribution pensions. In practice, the pension factor was more effective in reducing the initial value of benefits than in raising the average retirement age by length of contribution. In other words, the incentive to

FIGURE 31.1 **Value of pension factor used to calculate the benefit level for people of different ages based on contribution history**

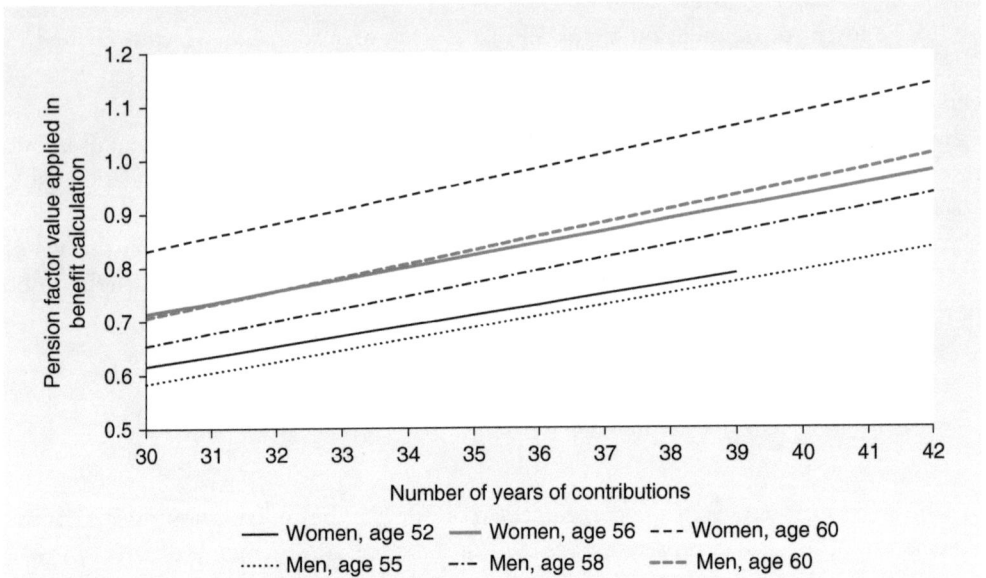

SOURCE: Brazilian Ministry of Finance using estimated life expectancy in December 2017.

postpone retirement and obtain a higher pension did not seem to affect the behavior of Brazilian workers. In any case, it represented relevant savings or reduction of expenditures.

The pension factor has some desirable characteristics that affect the economic efficiency and equity of the pension system: (a) each extra year of contribution should give rise to an additional benefit; (b) benefits should be reduced for people who retire early in their careers, to reflect the longer expected duration of payment, and should be increased for people who postpone retirement; and (c) benefits should be reduced as life expectancy increases, again to reflect the longer duration for which benefits would be paid (Whitehouse 2012b).

However, the factor was not as effective in increasing the retirement age (figure 31.2), among other reasons, because Brazil has no restriction on the accumulation of pension and labor income. Often, there is accumulation of income from work for people with high labor income by Brazilian standards, distorting the role of social security, which should guarantee income for those who have lost work capacity because of old age or other causes. The situation is similar to an insurer paying out a claim when the claim is contradicted by factual evidence (there was no loss of work capacity). Length of contribution is not a social risk. The average retirement age in 2017, in the case of length-of-contribution pensions, was 54. This level represented a slight increase compared with 1999, but it should be noted that the reform implemented in 1998 made room for the pension factor by deconstitutionalizing calculation of the value of the benefit and made other changes such as ending the proportional retirement by length of contribution, with 30 or 25 years of contribution for men and women, respectively.

FIGURE 31.2 **Average retirement age in length-of-contribution pensions by gender, 1999–2017**

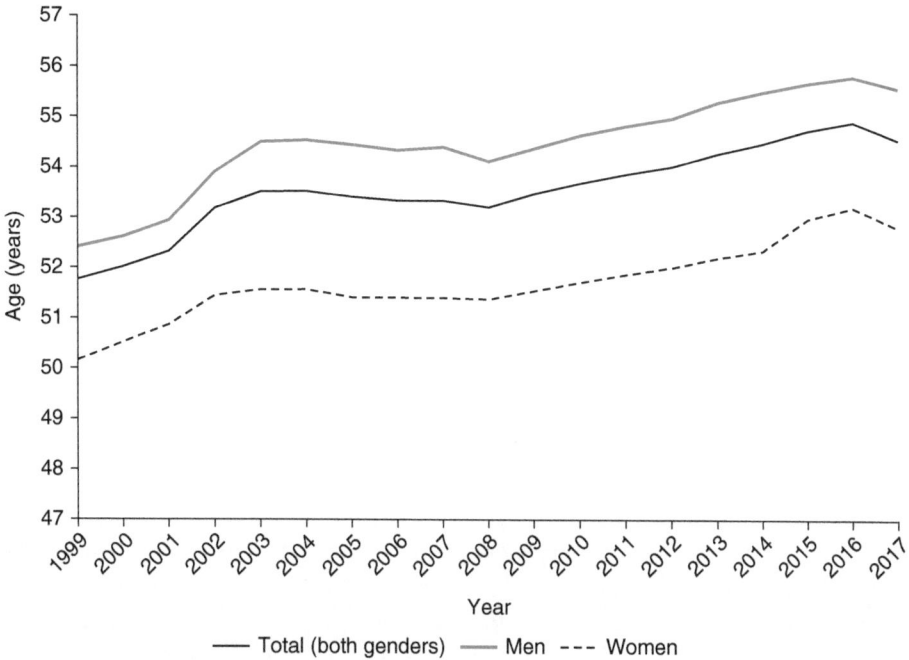

SOURCE: Brazilian Ministry of Finance.

With the relative stability of the mean age of retirement, in the case of length-of-contribution pensions, and an increase in life expectancy, the average duration of benefits terminated by death increased significantly, from 14.7 years for men and 15.2 years for women in 2001 to, respectively, 20.9 years (+ 42.2 percent) and 21.2 years (+ 39.5 percent) in 2017. The share of people's life in retirement also increased between 2001 and 2017: from 21.1 percent to 27.8 percent for men and from 22.1 percent to 28.5 percent for women.

Another limitation of the pension factor is that postponement of retirement, when it occurred, was compensated for by an increase in the replacement rate, despite cases in which the pension factor was greater than one—that is, the initial value of the benefit was higher than the average of the 80 percent highest contribution wages. For these reasons, even recognizing the importance of the pension factor in the sustainability of Brazil's general pension regime, the first-best solution is clearly the gradual end of length-of-contribution pensions by establishment of a minimum retirement age, as well as adoption of replacement rates that are compatible with fiscal sustainability in the medium and long terms.

Migration from PAYG to a funded pension system is normally associated with a high transition cost. For example, this high cost of transition has already led to the partial or even total reversal of reforms in Europe and in Latin America, such as the total reversals in Hungary and Argentina (Whitehouse 2012a). The reduced level or absence of legacy costs is an important advantage of NDC schemes. Use of the pension factor also incurred no transition cost, thus the reduction of expenditures began to benefit the sustainability of Brazil's pension regime as early as 2000, when the new inflow of benefits felt the incidence of the factor.

One potential limitation of an NDC-type scheme is, in its pure state, the explicit lack of any income redistribution mechanism. However, this redistributive function can be added with a minimum income guarantee to avoid poverty for workers with lower income and savings or those with a more precarious work path, marked by high informality with low and unstable labor income. These individuals will not have had sufficient earnings before retirement to provide an adequate benefit in old age. The pension formula in an NDC scheme contains no built-in redistribution of the scheme's revenues. As various chapters in this anthology discuss, a minimum income guarantee is now considered part-and-parcel of an (N)DC design. And social policy interventions to address contribution gaps caused by unemployment and disability can and should also be part of NDC design. In both cases it is important that these interventions remain financed from outside the scheme by budget transfers from general revenues.

One aspect that is perhaps similar to both NDC-type schemes and the experience of the pension factor in Brazil is the possibility that society does not fully understand the effective impacts of these changes on the value of benefits. This can facilitate political approval of this type of reform, but it can subsequently generate attempts to reverse the changes made, as happened in Brazil in 2015. Unfortunately, the pension factor's application was made flexible by the so-called progressive rule 85/95, which allows nonapplication of the pension factor depending on the sum of age and total years of contribution. This rule, created by Law 13.183, represented a major setback for fiscal sustainability in the medium and long terms and is contrary to the principle of financial and actuarial equilibrium. It should also have a negative effect on the distribution of income, because the affected beneficiaries are among those who receive the highest retirement value under the General Pension Scheme (Caetano et al. 2016; Costanzi, Fernandes, and Ansiliero 2018).

In general, the Brazilian experience, which was influenced by the NDC approach, reinforces the idea that NDC logic is crucial to the creation of sustainable pension schemes in an aging world. Furthermore, the largely unfunded design of NDC schemes avoids the high transition costs associated with moving from an unfunded to a funded design, especially in developing countries with their mostly delicate fiscal situations of high public debt and a high tax burden. Yet as various chapters in the anthology demonstrate, NDC (and nonfinancial defined benefit [NDB]) schemes also need some parametric adjustments. Even though NDC-type schemes may be more flexible vis-à-vis retirement age, a minimum age seems desirable to generate more adequate retirement values and avoid the risk of early retirement with lower benefits, which increases the risk of poverty for the elderly population.

Finally, NDC-type schemes may be important in overcoming deficiencies of unfunded defined benefit schemes, which tend to be quite generous for the early generations who benefit from such an approach, but which risk generating very high costs for future generations given the rapid population aging witnessed globally.

Accommodating the Need for Increased Leisure and Continued Work with Rising Pension Ages

Monika Queisser

In my commentary, I would like to focus on the wider picture.[2] As we assess the practical experience with the various nonfinancial defined contribution (NDC) models that countries have adopted, it is important to keep an eye on the context in which NDC pension schemes are functioning and how the bigger picture influences the political debate around pension reforms involving NDC elements. We have focused very often on whether NDC pension systems are perfectly balanced and self-regulating mechanisms, but I think it is also very important to recognize that they do not function in a vacuum. How NDC schemes are considered by people depends strongly on a range of factors, including those that determine people's retirement behavior and a societal notion of what is deemed fair.

In my view, three points are essential to the public debate about NDC pension schemes and need deeper consideration: retirement timing preferences, inequalities over the life cycle, and differentials in life expectancy.

One main objective of all pension reforms introducing closer links between contributions and benefits, whether they involve financial defined contribution (FDC) or NDC schemes, has been to provide incentives for people to work longer. Every additional period worked and thus every additional contribution made increases the individual worker's account balance, resulting in a higher pension at retirement. As life expectancy is also factored into the formula, thus lowering the benefit as each cohort's life expectancy increases, the assumption is that individuals would want to work longer to make sure that they receive higher pensions. In this way, financial sustainability of the pension system would be achieved simultaneously with social adequacy of pension levels.

The reality shows, however, that this assumption may be too optimistic. Although the labor force participation of older workers has indeed increased in most Organisation for Economic Co-operation and Development (OECD) countries over the past decades, often the result of higher labor force participation of women feeding through to older ages, too many people still retire comparatively early, including in countries with defined contribution (DC) pension schemes. And many of these retirees risk living for a long period in retirement on too little money.

Why is this the case? Are people not aware of what they can expect in retirement despite the many extensive public information and awareness campaigns that countries launched when they adopted NDC pension reforms? Are increases of minimum retirement ages redundant given the monetary incentives built into financial or nonfinancial DC schemes (Polakowski and Hagemejer 2018)? Certainly some cases arise of people not being fully informed about their future standards of living, which may lead them to decide to retire early, only to find out that their pension is very low. But overall, people in many countries still tend to draw pensions as soon as they become available, even if there are financial incentives to work longer. For example, in Italy the effective age of labor market exit is about 62 while the statutory retirement age is approaching 67 (OECD 2017a). In Latvia in 2016, about one-fifth of people retired through the early retirement scheme despite substantial benefit reduction (OECD 2018). In Poland, the number of newly granted old-age pensions increased by almost 60 percent in 2017 compared with 2016 following the reduction of the retirement age in 2017 (ZUS 2018).

Therefore, we should ask ourselves whether our focus has not been too narrowly concentrated on pension levels. We know that monetary incentives are in general a powerful tool in guiding people's decisions; this has been shown many times in a wide range of areas. But people's life designs are not only motivated by income. They also want to have more time to spend as they please, for family, for hobbies, or for paid work, but on their own terms and conditions. We may have underestimated the strength of this preference for leisure and lost sight of the fact that pension systems not only serve to defer income into the future but also leisure.

In trying to understand this observed strong desire for early retirement, we also need to take a closer and more honest look at the quality of work. If the economic incentives are set in a way that people should be working longer but they do not do so, there must be other powerful drivers. Is it that retirement is such an attractive proposition or is it that carrying on working is so unattractive? How does this vary across the different countries that have adopted NDC systems? And to what extent are people pushed into retirement, meaning that the retirement decision was not actually made by them on the basis of incentives, but triggered by their employers' decisions?

Looking at the numbers reveals that in Sweden, the age at which men and women first draw their pension benefit has remained fairly stable since the introduction of the NDC pension scheme: it fluctuated between 64.5 and 64.8 for both men and women between 2005 and 2017. Additionally, the share of people retiring before reaching age 64 increased from 8 percent to 24 percent across cohorts born in 1938 and 1954.[3] In Italy and Poland, the transitional provisions will enable the impact of NDC design on timing of retirement to be assessed only in the future.

The timing of and the preference for time spent in retirement varies across income groups, education levels, and occupations. In most countries, people with higher education levels are more likely to stay in the labor market longer. Recent OECD analysis of the accumulation of disadvantage over the life course shows that inequalities in education, health, employment, and income start building up from early ages and reinforce each other as a person ages. A 25-year-old university-educated man can expect to live almost 8 years longer than his lower-educated peer, on average across countries; for women the difference is 4.6 years. At all ages, people in bad health work less and earn less. Over a career, bad health reduces lifetime earnings of low-educated men by 33 percent, while the loss is only 17 percent for highly educated men (OECD 2017b).

These large differences introduce an additional dimension to the pension reform debate and pose new challenges to the discussion about what can be considered fair retirement rules. Increasingly, socioeconomic life expectancy gaps are being cited as an obstacle to raising pension ages. In the past, many OECD countries had special defined benefit pension systems for specific groups in which working conditions were particularly difficult and carried health or security risks. Many of these special schemes were closed down and their members integrated into the broader pension systems. But with increasing hard data and evidence on socioeconomic differences in life expectancy, and a general trend toward higher normal pension ages, several countries are now again debating whether there should be special retirement rules, in particular lower pension ages, for people who were exposed to higher occupational risks in their careers that could have damaged their health.

Ideally, socioeconomic differences should be addressed when they start building up; that is, over the life course and long before retirement. There is a parallel with other forms of inequality during working life, such as gender inequalities in careers and pay, that also result in large pension gaps between men and women; but at the same time, women's life expectancy is higher than that of men, which partly compensates for some inequalities. Again, despite the fact that work and pay inequalities need to be fixed in the labor market, which would result in smaller pension gaps, most countries still have some redistribution in their pension systems to benefit women.

Socioeconomic differences also affect people's retirement behavior and drive societal views on what is considered fair for whom. In this sense, the objective of pension systems goes beyond providing income in old age for those who are no longer working; it also includes an expectation that a pension system should provide a "fair" amount of leisure time so that everybody can enjoy the period in retirement they deserve.

If we accept that leisure is a good in high demand, the question of how to address inequalities is not only about redistributing income between different groups but also about redistributing leisure time.

With more data available on life expectancy for specific groups, NDC pension schemes could theoretically become more individualized and offer tailored conditions for retirement ages and benefit levels for specific socioeconomic groups and, in the future, given the advances of medical research, perhaps even on an individual level. But it seems difficult to imagine that such an approach could be desirable for public pension systems that, even in NDC shape, still have considerable elements of solidarity and redistribution. Some DC schemes, however, do pay higher pensions to retirees with lower life expectancy—for example, the enhanced annuity products in the United Kingdom and the United States. Gender-specific life expectancy, which has been available for a long time, is not applied in most countries when calculating pension benefits and even prohibited by law in European countries—though it is used in the Chilean and Mexican FDC systems.

By way of conclusion, NDC pension schemes are faced with new challenges around the timing of the retirement moment, raising the question of how much flexibility there should be for people to choose this moment while still ensuring that all retirees leave the labor market with an adequate retirement benefit. Pensioner poverty, especially among older women living alone, might increase and dependence on last-resort benefits may grow; even if the pension system itself is balanced, the broader social welfare system will experience financial pressures.

This challenge is compounded by the fact that we now have far more data and evidence on socioeconomic differences in life expectancy, which are modifying the way retirement age increases are seen and discussed. Giving groups who can expect to live shorter periods in retirement the option to leave earlier is often put forward as a solution. In an NDC pension scheme, both the earlier departure and the shorter life expectancy for each socioeconomic group could be fully factored into the calculation of the benefit, thus making the pension scheme far more individualized and moving it closer to the principles of private insurance. Whether this would be technically feasible and socially desirable, however, is a political question and for societies to decide.

Conditions for Introducing an NDC Pension Scheme as the Reform Option

Per Eckefeldt

In theory, nonfinancial defined contribution (NDC) pension systems appear to be very well suited for a viable public pension system. A strong and explicit (transparent) link exists between contributions paid and benefits received, providing for income smoothing over time and intergenerational fairness. Because of its transparency, the NDC pension scheme provides incentives for the work-leisure choice, given that people are in a position to choose the level of the pension benefit at the time of retirement (when the pension is calculated). The system also provides for pooling of risks for each cohort. Given the so far persistent increase in life expectancy seen globally, this entails an important contribution to the system's financial sustainability. These aspects are also present for financial (funded) defined contribution (FDC) pension schemes. However, a key practical advantage of an NDC system compared with an FDC one is that the double payment problem is avoided. If a country has pension liabilities at the outset, this will clearly be an issue.

Yet NDC schemes have not become the norm for pension reforms since they were introduced in a few pioneer countries in the 1990s. What is "wrong" with NDC schemes and how can they be made more attractive? This is the theme of the third NDC conference held in Rome in 2017, which points to the key challenges that need to be addressed to demonstrate the advantages of an NDC pension scheme.

It would not be fair to say that NDC systems do not work. In the countries where they were introduced more than two decades ago (Italy, Latvia, Poland, and Sweden), they are still running, suggesting that they are very successful in those cases. Rather, pension reforms carried out since then in essentially all countries in Europe have not introduced NDC systems. The exceptions are Norway (in 2011) and Greece (in part, in 2015). The key motivation for almost all pension reforms has been that the financial stability of existing pension systems (old defined benefit [DB] systems) were at risk, and this risk was broadly recognized in the policy debate. However, in most countries, the parametric reforms chosen contain aspects that are included in NDC pension schemes. This suggests that much of the emphasis is given to the transition phase, because most countries, at least in Europe, already have considerable pension liabilities. There is also an element of short-sightedness of policy makers, given that the cost of changing policies, which is often very high politically (until the next elections), can be perceived as outweighing the gains of a sustainable system that will only materialize over the longer term.

Indeed, pension reforms are not popular in general because they are motivated by fiscal sustainability risks and are thus perceived as entailing benefit cuts. Still, many reforms have been implemented, but NDC reforms are rare. What can we learn from the experience now gained by countries that implemented NDC systems and what issues need to be clarified to increase interest in them?

The overall conclusion from the pioneer NDC countries (Italy, Latvia, Poland, and Sweden) is that they have worked well, as evidenced by the fact they are still in place (as demonstrated by chapters 2 through 6). The NDC pension scheme improved financial sustainability in these cases. The reforms also contributed to the awareness that pension contributions are crucial for eventual pension benefits.

Nonetheless, scope remains for improvement, for which there is ample evidence in this book. Key issues are as follows: (a) possible poverty risks due to low (insufficient) contributions; (b) heterogeneity in longevity among different socioeconomic groups; (c) the role of NDC schemes in the context of other pension-related programs, and more broadly of government-sponsored programs for older people, such as long-term care; (d) the extent to which financial incentives work when workers are myopic; (e) safeguarding a fiscally sustainable system; and (f) ensuring a stable pension system so as to provide clear rules over the long term and avoid reform reversals. Each is discussed briefly next.

Possible poverty risks. A key strength of an NDC system is the explicit link between contributions and benefits for participants. However, for some people or groups of people with low wages or broken careers, contributions are likely to be small and therefore the pension entitlement under the NDC scheme is correspondingly low. To avoid possible poverty risks in old age, policy makers need to either provide separate minimum pension support for people in these risk groups or make an explicit commitment to "top up" their contributions, and importantly to decide on how that top-up is financed. Inevitably, this anticipated top-up reduces incentives to contribute to the NDC scheme for low-income groups. There is also a need to ensure that people with "nonstandard" salaries (for example, the self-employed) are given appropriate opportunities to participate in the system. A comprehensive approach must cater to the possible poverty risks, and an NDC scheme must be designed within an overall package for pension provision. In this context, second- and third-pillar schemes can be used to improve retirement incomes, though coverage of low-income groups is a particular issue for such schemes.

Heterogeneity in longevity among different socioeconomic groups. Life expectancy has increased significantly over the past decades but differs among different socioeconomic groups. A positive relationship between lifetime income and life expectancy has been observed. A priori, an NDC pension scheme typically uses a common assumption about life expectancy when determining the annuity (pension benefit). This entails a tax on low-life expectancy and low-income groups and a subsidy to high-life expectancy and high-income groups. Moreover, women's life expectancy is higher than that of men, with a similar effect. This can be addressed by correcting, to some degree, the annuity to better reflect life expectancy for different groups of people. This differentiation can be challenging politically, however.

The role of NDC in the context of other public (pension-related) programs. This is in part linked to the issue of possible poverty risks. An NDC pension scheme is fully contributory based for participants. However, other public programs supporting income in old age—for instance, disability and survivors' pensions—are not necessarily contributor based. In almost all countries, specific provisions exist for disability and survivors' pensions that are different from the provisions for common earnings-related old-age pensions. Moreover, long-term care is increasingly being provided by the public sector in European countries, which adds to the pension-related costs and therefore prompts a discussion on the financing of these programs. When a reform of the main pension scheme is under consideration—for example, introducing an NDC pension scheme—a comprehensive approach is needed to align all government spending programs. In this sense, reforming the main earnings-related old-age pension system provides an opportunity to review the complete package of retirement income in old age.

Incentives to work with myopic workers. A key determinant for all pension systems in terms of adequacy and sustainability is the age at which people start drawing a pension. An advantage of NDC schemes is that when calculating the annuity, life expectancy is taken into account, providing "soft" incentives to prolong working life and enhancing transparency of the pension package. This makes the system financially robust to changes in life expectancy over time. However, participants need to factor in the increase in life expectancy during both the accumulation phase (working life) and when they start drawing a pension (retired life). Unless they do so, the risk is that the pension benefit is smaller than they (myopically) had foreseen. It is also possible that current workers' perceptions of pension levels and replacement rates are influenced by concurrent pension levels (for example, those of their parents). Eligibility restrictions such as the earliest or the statutory pensionable age are a crucial policy lever for ensuring that myopic behavior is avoided (that is, "hard" incentives). Indeed, many countries initiated a link between retirement age and life expectancy to introduce an automatic adjustment with respect to gains in life expectancy. Experience in most countries has shown that introducing changes to the retirement age is very challenging in parliament and in society at large. Automatic adjustment may alleviate this challenge (though may not make it disappear). In all cases, to help people make an informed decision, it is essential for authorities to provide sufficient information and education to participants to avoid any surprises with respect to their eventual pensions.

Safeguarding a fiscally sustainable system. NDC systems are financially robust to changes in life expectancy, through the calculation of the annuity (as explained previously). However, other macroeconomic shocks can have an impact on the system's financial sustainability, for instance, lower contributions due to lower wage growth or lower returns on a reserve fund stemming from a temporary shock. Moreover, negative labor force growth (for example, stemming from a falling working-age population) would destabilize system solvency. To secure a sustainable system, a reserve fund to take account of short-term shocks can be introduced. In addition, automatic balancing mechanisms can safeguard the system's financial stability without having recourse to ad hoc political decisions over time. One way to design an automatic balancing mechanism is to estimate the system's solvency (contributions, assets [reserve fund], and liabilities), and to reduce indexation of pensions temporarily when solvency falls below a certain threshold, as is done in Sweden.

Ensuring a stable pension system to provide clear rules over the long term and avoiding reform reversals. In European countries and elsewhere, public pensions are a large part of government expenditure. Equally, public pensions in general constitute the largest part of retirement income. It is therefore essential that the rules for public pension provision be stable so that people can plan, adjust, and adapt their working careers and their retirement. Looking at the experience of the pioneer NDC countries, it appears as if the best chance of successfully implementing reforms hinges upon (a) broad political anchoring of the pension reform; (b) a fast transition period to the new scheme; and (c) ensuring full coverage in the reformed system and limiting the running of parallel pension schemes (that is, a comprehensive approach to pension policies). In fact, these factors are important for all types of pension reforms, including introduction of an NDC system.

In conclusion, NDC systems have several strong points, including a strong and explicit link between contributions and benefits (actuarial fairness) that supports work incentives and adjustment of the pension benefit (annuity) to life expectancy. NDC schemes began briskly when they were conceptualized in the 1990s, and several countries introduced them at that time (Italy, Latvia, Poland, and Sweden). These systems are still in place after about 25 years, confirming that they work well. However, very few countries have introduced NDC systems since then. Rather, most countries have introduced parametric changes to their existing pension systems, prompted by sustainability concerns. These changes in general include strengthening the link between contribution and benefits and taking account of changes in life expectancy over time.

To strengthen the case for NDC schemes, several issues must be addressed upfront, including (a) possible poverty risks caused by low contributions, (b) heterogeneity in life expectancy among participants, (c) tackling the role of NDC in the context of other public (pension-related) programs, (d) incentives to work with myopic workers, (e) safeguarding a fiscally sustainable system, and (f) ensuring a stable pension system and avoiding possible reform reversals. NDC pension schemes are particularly well suited for public pension provision both if a country is introducing a public pension system for the first time, and if it entails reforming an existing pension arrangement. But a comprehensive approach is necessary to ensure the lasting success of NDC pension schemes.

The Importance of Flexibility in Adapting Reform Models to Countries' Specific Economic, Cultural, and Technical Landscapes

Michal Rutkowski

I think that all of us who believe in nonfinancial defined contribution (NDC) pension schemes have a lot in common. We are aware that most DB schemes require nontransparent, non-rules-based, and ad hoc adjustments toward ensuring fiscal sustainability, and that in many cases they fail to provide the promised benefits. The liabilities of DB schemes can be estimated by actuarial analysis, but the results depend on the assumptions made, and the liabilities are not clearly defined and are not earmarked to individual participants. The absence of individual accounts easily leads to an uncertain commitment. Because of all these shortcomings, many countries moved to DC schemes, starting with Chile in the 1980s. Fifteen years after introduction of the public universal financial defined contribution (FDC) scheme in Chile, NDC schemes emerged in Europe as a strong option.

We would all agree that FDCs and NDCs have many characteristics that are superior to those of DB schemes. The strong link between contributions and benefits in FDC and NDC schemes as well as the predictability and transparency of both pension schemes provide incentives for people to participate in the formal labor force and to postpone retirement to receive a more adequate pension. Also, in DB schemes people feel that they are "paying taxes" because of the absence of built-in transfers and a clear link between current contributions and future pensions, whereas in FDC and NDC schemes contributions are perceived as money put into their own savings accounts. We would also agree that NDC schemes allow for automatic adjustments to economic and demographic changes without political intervention.

When we argue our NDC case, however, we need to avoid going too far in our advocacy. It is especially important to remember that we will never have a perfect NDC scheme, and if a consensus forms around the universal applicability of a specific model, the critical assumptions may nevertheless be violated in almost all national settings. Therefore, our endorsement of NDC needs to be adorned with caveats.

What is important is not to leave out important questions when advocating for NDCs. The key questions are as follows:

- What is the desired and expected scale of an NDC scheme? Should a national universal NDC scheme be chosen as the only pension vehicle or should room be left, for example, for a financial pillar, with perhaps both topped off by various (possibly DB) occupational benefits and individual pension savings arrangements?

- Must NDC schemes cover everyone, that is, the entire working-age population in a country? In principle yes, but in practice the answer depends on the culture and politics of the country.

- In which countries would an NDC scheme be feasible from a fiscal perspective? Many countries do not have the resources to afford a differentiated old-age pension, and in many countries a large segment of the population would not save or contribute to an NDC scheme if they knew that they would receive a guaranteed minimum income in old age.

- Can less economically developed countries start up an NDC scheme when a large portion of the labor force is informal at the outset? One of the chapters in the anthology addresses this question. Generally speaking this depends on the demographic profile of the country, what point it is at in the process of economic development, and the level of development of the country's administrative technology. A full-scale NDC scheme, possibly integrated with an FDC scheme, would be the end goal, and it would take several decades to transition from an informal to a formal economy.

Also, it is important to adopt a balanced approach in the discussion of advantages and disadvantages of DB and DC schemes. Clearly, all approaches have their advantages and disadvantages. Some of the results that can be achieved by FDC and NDC schemes can also be achieved by DB schemes and in some contexts a DB scheme may be sufficient and even preferable.

We also need to be very serious about implementation, especially when comparing an actual DB implementation with an ideal NDC implementation. We often downplay the benefits of good NDB schemes by arguing that the benefits do not materialize in implementation. For example, an NDC scheme takes into consideration increasing life expectancy because the pension is calculated by dividing individual account balances at retirement by average life expectancy for a specific cohort; then we should acknowledge that NDB schemes can also take changing life expectancy into consideration in the calculation of the benefit although to date this is the exception rather than the rule.

It is easy to underestimate the cultural, institutional, and political prerequisites of running NDC schemes. NDC schemes are also prone to manipulation, as evidenced by real-life cases. A discussion of the required capacity for implementation of NDC schemes is always a must, given that running them requires advanced administrative capacity, which even many developed countries do not have. The main message is that NDC schemes are working in Italy, Latvia, Norway, Poland, and Sweden, but it is important to note that, as this anthology documents, adjustments have been made and, overall, there is still room for improvement. It is also important to also discuss what went wrong and why the NDC scheme eventually was abandoned in the Russian Federation, or why Azerbaijan, the Kyrgyz Republic, and Mongolia misinterpreted and misimplemented NDC schemes.

We also have to ask why the numerous DC schemes starting in Latin America and then spreading to Europe—in many cases have not led to increased formal employment and with this increased coverage. The first twenty plus years of FDC and NDC pension schemes in Latvia led to both a strong increase in the number of formal contributors and the density of contributions as documented in Palmer and Stabina (2019) in this anthology. Many FDC schemes in Latin America have, however, not yet achieved this result. This was in part predictable because myopia means that system participants underestimate the value of future returns. And, NDC schemes are living up to the architects' expectations in Norway, Poland, and Sweden. On the other hand, Italy had to introduce a second start with the Fornero reform in 2011 owing to poor implementation.

In the world of pensions we have a great variety of situations regarding coverage, adequacy, affordability, the role of the private sector, administrative and regulatory capacity, and political context. When we add imperfect information, we get even more possibilities. The best we can do is to understand the model that best fits the cultural and political prerequisites of the country case at hand. In summary, we have "one pension economics, many recipes," to paraphrase Dani Rodrik. So, when we propose reforms let us always situate them in the context of alternative models and approaches given the particular circumstances under which the model will have to become operational.

Finally, it is my belief that we need to proceed consistently but consciously in weighing the relative merits of NDC pension schemes against those of NDB schemes. The welfare of current and future pensioners must always be our compass.

Notes

1. Using the pension factor calculation table that prevailed between December 2017 and November 2018.

2. The opinions and arguments expressed herein are those of the author and do not necessarily reflect the official views of the OECD or its member countries.

3. https://www.pensionsmyndigheten.se/nyheter-och-press/pressrum/vi-jobbar-allt-langre -men-pensionsaldern-ligger-still.

References

Åkesson, Olov A. 1950. "Allmän Pensionsförsäkring. Förslag Angivet av Pensionsutredningen." (Available only in Swedish) SOU 1950:33, Government of Sweden, Stockholm.

Buchanan, James. 1968. "Social Insurance in a Growing Economy: A Proposal for Radical Reform." *National Tax Journal* 21: 386–95.

Caetano, Marcelo A., Rogério N. Costanzi, Graziela Ansiliero, Eduardo Pereira, Leonardo Alves Rangel, and Luis Paiva. 2016. "O Fim do Fator Previdenciário e a Introdução da Idade Mínima: Questões para a Previdência Social no Brasil." Texto para Discussão Setembro de 2016,Instituto de Pesquisa Econômica Aplicada, Governo do Brasil, Brasília.

Costanzi, Rogério N., Alexandre Zioli Fernandes, and Graziela Ansiliero. 2018. "O Princípio Constitucional de Equilíbrio Financeiro e Atuarial no Regime Geral de Previdência Social: Tendências Recentes e o Caso da Regra 85/95 Progressiva." Texto para Discussão 2395, Instituto de Pesquisa Econômica Aplicada, Governo do Brasil, Brasília.

Holzmann, Robert, and Edward Palmer. 2006. *Pension Reform: Issues and Prospects for Non-financial Defined Contribution (NDC) Schemes*. Washington, DC: World Bank.

Holzmann, Robert, Edward Palmer, and David Robalino, eds. 2012. *Nonfinancial Defined Contribution Pension Schemes in a Changing Pension World: Volume1 Progress, Lessons, and Implementation.* Washington, DC: World Bank.

OECD (Organisation for Economic Co-operation and Development). 2017a. *Pensions at a Glance.* Paris: OECD Publishing. https://doi.org/10.1787/pension_glance-2017-en.

———. 2017b. *Preventing Ageing Unequally.* Paris: OECD Publishing. https://doi.org /10.1787/9789264279087-en.

———. 2018. *Reviews of Pension Systems: Latvia.* Paris: OECD Publishing. https://doi.org /10.1787/9789264289390-en.

Palmer, Edward, and Bo Könberg. 2019. "The Swedish NDC Scheme: Success on Track with Room for Reflection." In *Progress and Challenges of Nonfinancial Defined Contribution Pension Schemes: Volume 1 Addressing Marginalization, Polarization, and the Labor Market,* edited by Robert Holzmann, Edward Palmer, Robert Palacios, and Stefano Sacchi, Chapter 2. Washington, DC: World Bank.

Palmer, Edward, and Sandra Stabina. 2019. "The Latvian NDC Scheme: Success under a Decreasing Labor Force." In *Progress and Challenges of Nonfinancial Defined Contribution Pension Schemes: Volume 1 Addressing Marginalization, Polarization, and the Labor Market,* edited by Robert Holzmann, Edward Palmer, Robert Palacios, and Stefano Sacchi, Chapter 3. Washington, DC: World Bank.

Palmer, Edward, and Yuwei Zhao de Gosson de Varennes. 2019. "Annuities in (N)DC Pension Schemes: Design, Heterogeneity, and Estimation Issues." In *Progress and Challenges of Nonfinancial Defined Contribution Pension Schemes: Volume 1 Addressing Marginalization, Polarization, and the Labor Market,* edited by Robert Holzmann, Edward Palmer, Robert Palacios, and Stefano Sacchi, Chapter 13. Washington, DC: World Bank.

Polakowski, Michał, and Krzysztof Hagemejer. 2018. "Reversing Pension Privatization: The Case of Polish Pension Reform and Re-Reforms." ESS Working Paper 68, International Labour Organization, Geneva.

Swedish Ministry of Health and Social Affairs. 2017. "A Reformed Pension System—Background, Principles, and Sketch." Translation to English of Memorandum of the Pension Working Group. Ministry of Health and Social Affairs, Government of Sweden, Stockholm.

Swedish Pensions Agency. 2017. "Orange Report 2016—The Annual Report of the Swedish Pension System." Swedish Pensions Agency, Stockholm.

———. 2018. "Orange Report 2017—The Annual Report of the Swedish Pension System." Swedish Pensions Agency, Stockholm.

Wang, Xinmie, John B. Williamson, and Mehmet Cansoy. 2016. "Developing Countries and Systemic Pension Reforms: Reflections on Some Emerging Problems." *International Social Security Review* 69 (2): 85–106.

Whitehouse, Edward. 2012a. "Parallel Lines: NDC Pensions and the Direction of Pension Reform in Developed Countries." In *Nonfinancial Defined Contribution Pension Schemes in a Changing Pension World: Volume 1 Progress, Lessons, and Implementation,* edited by Robert Holzmann, Edward Palmer, and David Robalino, 85–105. Washington, DC: World Bank.

———. 2012b. "Reversals of Systemic Pension Reforms in Central and Eastern Europe: Implications." In *OECD Pension Outlook 2012,* 77–98. Paris: OECD Publishing.

ZUS (Zakład Ubezpieczeń Społecznych). 2018. "Newly-granted Old-age and Disability Pensions (Emerytury i renty nowo przyznane)." ZUS, Warsaw. http://www.zus.pl/baza-wiedzy /statystyka/opracowania-tematyczne/emerytury-i-renty-nowo-przyznaneh.

www.ingramcontent.com/pod-product-compliance
Lightning Source LLC
Chambersburg PA
CBHW050800220326
41598CB00006B/80

* 9 7 8 1 4 6 4 8 1 4 5 5 6 *